EUROPEAN COMMUNITY LAW
SELECTED DOCUMENTS

By

George A. Bermann
Professor of Law, University of Columbia
School of Law

Roger J. Goebel
Professor of Law, Fordham University
School of Law

William J. Davey
Professor of Law, University of Illinois
College of Law

Eleanor M. Fox
Professor of Law, New York University
School of Law

AMERICAN CASEBOOK SERIES®

WEST PUBLISHING CO.
ST. PAUL, MINN., 1993

American Casebook Series and the WP symbol are registered trademarks of West Publishing Co. Registered in the U.S. Patent and Trademark Office.

COPYRIGHT © 1993 By WEST PUBLISHING CO.
610 Opperman Drive
P.O. Box 64526
St. Paul, MN 55164–0526

All rights reserved
Printed in the United States of America

ISBN 0–314–01529–9

(B., G., D. & F.) EEC
Doc.Supp.

Preface

This Documents Supplement is designed to accompany European Community Law: Cases and Materials (West Publishing Co. 1993). Use of the Supplement is essential for a full understanding of the materials in the casebook.

Because European Community law is founded upon application and interpretation of the Treaty establishing the European Economic Community (EEC Treaty), as amended by the Single European Act, the Treaty is the first document in the Supplement. In view of its pending ratification, the Maastricht Treaty of European Union is provided separately, but cross-references to it are made through notes to the EEC Treaty.

The remainder of the Supplement includes the more important Community legislative measures in the form of regulations and directives that are discussed in the casebook. Certain other relevant Community documents and excerpts from the Convention for the Protection of Human Rights and Fundamental Freedoms are also included. The legislative and other documents are either fully reproduced or lightly excerpted to facilitate understanding.

The Supplement is organized in five parts, corresponding to the topic coverage of the casebook. Each part has an introduction briefly describing the documents which follow.

Reference should be made to the note on Legal Sources and Citation Forms contained in the casebook for indications of the source of these and other Community documents, modes of research and citation style.

Helpful recommendations for the inclusion of certain documents were made by many of the persons thanked in the casebook Acknowledgment. We invite the suggestions of professors and other users of the Documents Supplement to assist us in deciding what additional documents might be included in future editions.

Finally we thank the staff of the information service and library of the European Community Delegations in Washington, D.C. and New York City for their assistance in obtaining recent documentation.

*

Table of Contents

PART I. THE LEGAL AND INSTITUTIONAL FRAMEWORK OF THE EUROPEAN COMMUNITY

	Page
Introduction	1
1. Treaty Establishing the European Economic Community	4
2. Single European Act	98
3. The Treaty on European Union	104
4. Convention for the Protection of Human Rights and Fudamental Freedoms	204
5. Joint Declaration by the European Parliament, the Council and the Commission	214
6. Protocol on the Statute of the Court of Justice	215
7. Rules of Procedure of the Court of Justice of the European Communities	226
8. Convention on Jurisdiction and the Enforcement of Judgments in Civil and Commercial Matters	241

PART II. THE FOUR FREEDOMS AND THE INTERNAL MARKET

1. Commission Directive 70/50 on the abolition of measures which have an effect equivalent to quantitative restrictions on imports	264
2. Commission Communication concerning the consequences of the judgment in Case 120/78 ("Cassis de Dijon")	268
3. First Council Directive 89/104 to approximate the laws of the Member States relating to trade marks	271
4. Council Directive 79/831 on the approximation of the laws relating to the classification, packaging and labelling of dangerous substances	283
5. Council Directive 83/189 laying down a procedure for the provision of information in the field of technical standards and regulations	296
6. Council Directive 89/392 on the approximation of the laws of Member States relating to machinery	302
7. Council Regulation 1612/68 on freedom of movement for workers within the Community	309
8. Council Directive 68/360 on the abolition of restrictions on movement and residence within the Community for workers of Member States and their families	315

		Page
9.	Council Directive 64/221 on the coordination of special measures concerning the movement and residence of foreign nationals which are justified on grounds of public policy, public security or public health	319
10.	Council Directive 90/365 on the right of residence for employees and self-employed persons who have ceased their occupational activity	323
11.	Council Directive 90/364 on the right of residence	326
12.	Council Directive 90/366 on the right of residence for students	329
13.	General Programme for the abolition of restrictions on freedom of establishment	332
14.	Council Directive 86/653 on the coordination of the laws of the Member States relating to self-employed commercial agents	336
15.	Council Directive 89/552 on the coordination of certain provisions laid down by law, regulation or administrative action in Member States concerning the pursuit of television broadcasting activities	344
16.	First Council Directive 68/151 on coordination of safeguards which are required by Member States of companies with a view to making such safeguards equivalent throughout the Community	354
17.	Second Council Directive 77/91 on coordination of safeguards which are required by Member States in respect of the formation of public limited liability companies and the maintenance and alteration of their capital	359
18.	Third Council Directive 78/855 concerning mergers of public limited liability companies	368
19.	Fourth Council Directive 78/660 on the annual accounts of certain types of companies	378
20.	Council Regulation 2137/85 on the European Economic Interest Grouping	387
21.	Council Directive 89/48 on a general system for the recognition of higher-education diplomas awarded on completion of profession education and training	397
22.	Council Recommendation 89/49 concerning nationals of Member States who hold a diploma conferred in a third State	406
23.	Council Directive 77/249 to facilitate the effective exercise by lawyers of freedom to provide services	407
24.	Council Directive 88/361 for the implementation of Article 67 [free movement of capital]	410
25.	Council Directive 79/279 coordinating the conditions for the admission of securities to official stock exchange listing	414
26.	Council Directive 80/390 coordinating the requirements for the drawing-up, scrutiny and distribution of the listing particulars to be published for the admission of securities to official stock exchange listing	427
27.	Council Directive 87/345 amending Directive 80/390	445

	Page
28. Council Directive 82/121 on information to be published by companies to shares of which have been admitted to official stock-exchange listing	448
29. Council Directive 89/298 coordinating the requirements for the prospectus to be published when transferable securities are offered to the public	452
30. Council Directive 89/592 coordinating regulations on insider dealing	463
31. Council Directive 88/627 on the information to be published when a major holding in a listed company is acquired or disposed of	468
32. First Council Directive 77/780 on the coordination of laws, regulations and administrative provisions relating to the taking up and pursuit of the business of credit institutions	474
33. Second Council Directive 89/646 on the coordination of laws relating to the business of credit institutions	480

PART III. COMPETITION POLICY

1. Council Regulation 17 implementing Articles 85 and 86	502
2. Commission Notice on exclusive agency contracts made with commercial agents	514
3. Commission Notice concerning agreements, decisions and concerted practices in the field of cooperation between enterprises	516
4. Commission Notice on agreements of minor importance which do not fall under Article 85(1)	522
5. Commission Regulation 1983/83 on the application of Article 85(3) to categories of exclusive distribution agreements	526
6. Commission Regulation 1984/83 on the application of Article 85(3) to categories of exclusive purchasing agreements	532
7. Commission Regulation 417/85 on the application of Article 85(3) to categories of specialization agreements	543
8. Commission Regulation 418/85 on the application of Article 85(3) to categories of research and development agreements	549
9. Commission Regulation 4087/88 on the application of Article 85(3) to categories of franchise agreements	560
10. Council Regulation 4064/89 on the control of concentrations between undertakings [Merger Regulation]	570

PART IV. EXTERNAL RELATIONS AND COMMERCIAL POLICY

1. Council Regulation 1224/80 on the valuation of goods for customs purposes	592
2. Council Regulation 802/68 on the common definition of the concept of the origin of goods	603

	Page
3. Council Regulation 2423/88 on protection against dumped or subsidized imports from countries not members of the European Economic Community	607
4. Council Regulation 2641/84 on the strengthening of the common commercial policy with regard to protection against illicit commercial practices	631

PART V. SPECIFIC COMMUNITY POLICIES

1. Council Directive 85/374 on the approximation of the law concerning liability for defective products 642
2. Council Directive 75/129 on the approximation of the laws relating to collective redundancies 649
3. Council Directive 77/187 on the approximation of the laws relating to the safeguarding of employees' rights in the event of transfers of undertakings, businesses or parts of businesses 653
4. Council Directive 80/987 on the approximation of the laws relating to the protection of employees in the event of the insolvency of their employer 657
5. Community Charter of the Fundamental Social Rights of Workers 661
6. Council Directive 91/533 on an employer's obligation to inform employees of the conditions applicable to the contract or employment relationship 668
7. Council Directive 75/117 on the approximation of the laws relating to the principle of equal pay for men and women ... 673
8. Council Directive 76/207 on the implementation of the principle of equal treatment for men and women as regards access to employment, vocational training and promotion, and working conditions 676
9. Council Directive 79/7 on the progressive implementation of the principle of equal treatment for men and women in matters of social security 680
10. Council Directive 86/378 on the implementation of the principle of equal treatment for men and women in occupational social security schemes 683

EUROPEAN COMMUNITY LAW
SELECTED DOCUMENTS

*

Part I

THE LEGAL AND INSTITUTIONAL FRAMEWORK OF THE EUROPEAN COMMUNITY

INTRODUCTION

The fundamental European Community charter is the Treaty Establishing the European Economic Community (the "EEC" or "Rome Treaty"), signed March 25, 1957, 298 UNTS 11. The EEC Treaty, as amended as of July 1, 1992, appears as the first document in this supplement. The other two constitutive treaties (the Treaty Establishing the European Coal and Steel Community (ECSC), April 18, 1951, 261 UNTS 140, and the Treaty Establishing the European Atomic Energy Community (Euratom), March 25, 1957, 298 UNTS 167) are not reproduced. For their texts, see Treaties Establishing the European Communities (EC Off'l Pub. Office, 1987).

Chapter 1 of the casebook describes the events leading up to the conclusion of the EEC Treaty and the principal developments that followed. The Treaty of course set in motion important changes in the European economies and, through the institutions it created, produced the various legislative measures referred to throughout the book.

As a text, however, the EEC Treaty was most significantly affected by a series of subsequent agreements of a structural nature. These include: (1) the Convention on Certain Institutions Common to the European Communities, March 25, 1957 (casebook page 23), (2) the Treaty Establishing a Single Council and a Single Commission of the European Communities, April 8, 1965 ("the Merger Treaty") (casebook page 12), (3) Treaties of Accession (of new Member States) of 1972, 1979 and 1985 (casebook page 11), each with an annexed Act of Accession, and (4) Budgetary Treaties of 1970 and 1975 (casebook page 12). To the extent that these different agreements significantly modify the text of the EEC Treaty, the modifications are reflected in the Treaty text presented here, with appropriate footnote references.

It is, of course, the 1987 Single European Act (SEA) and, if ratified, the 1992 Treaty on European Union (TEU) that most directly and substantially amend the EEC Treaty. The changes brought about by the SEA, discussed throughout the casebook, but mostly in Chapter 1, 2 and 12, pertain chiefly to the internal market goal, changes in legislative process to achieve that goal (e.g., greater use of qualified majority voting, introduction of a parliamentary cooperation procedure) and introduction of certain new EC competences (e.g., environmental protection, worker health and safety, regional development). Rather than set out these SEA provisions separately, the Documents Supplement incorporates them directly into the body of the EEC Treaty wherever relevant, with appropriate SEA references in the footnotes.

As indicated in Chapters 1 and 2, however, the SEA also contained provisions of great importance to the Community that did not amend the EEC Treaty as such. These SEA provisions (the Preamble, Title I, and notably Title III on European Political Cooperation) are therefore set out separately as the second document in this Part.

The TEU, agreed upon in Maastricht, the Netherlands, in December 1991 and signed in the same city the following February, remains to be ratified by all the Member States before it can come into force. As noted in Chapters 1 and 2, the TEU deals extensively with Economic and Monetary Union (EMU) and with a range of institutional and jurisdictional issues debated under the rubric of Political Union. A first set of TEU provisions thus covers substantive and institutional aspects of the various stages involved in creating the EMU, including a system of central banks and a single currency. A second set of provisions modifies institutional aspects of the Community (e.g., further extension of qualified majority voting, a new co-decision legislative procedure) and once again enlarges the sphere of Community competence (e.g., consumer protection, culture, education). Many of these provisions would of course amend or directly supplement the EEC Treaty as we now know it, and references to them are therefore made directly in the EEC Treaty in this Supplement, through editors' notes to that document.

In view of the fact that the TEU still remains to be ratified, the editors prefer to reproduce the TEU in integral form as a separate (third) document, rather than incorporate it into the EEC Treaty text. Although the reader will find appropriate references to the TEU in editors' notes to the EEC Treaty, he or she will in most cases have to turn to the relevant provision of the TEU document itself for the precise language of those changes.

A further benefit of presenting the TEU in this fashion is that (like the SEA, but even to a greater extent) the TEU contains important provisions that are not to be incorporated in the EEC Treaty as such. These titles (notably on the European Union, Common Foreign and Security Policy, and Cooperation in the Fields of Justice and Home Affairs) are set out in full in the TEU document, as are selected protocols to the TEU, notably on the UK's entitlement to "opt out" of the third stage of EMU (casebook page 17) and on Social Policy, as well as a few selected declarations. (The texts of the remaining protocols and declarations are omitted, but a full listing of them follows the TEU document.)

Although the Community remains technically without a formal written Bill of Rights, the Court of Justice has made it clear that the principles of the European Human Rights Convention, together with constitutional provisions and traditions among the Member States, are the sources of fundamental rights principles that the institutions must respect and that the Court itself will enforce. (See Chapter 4.) Moreover, the 1977 Joint Declaration of the Parliament, Council and Commission (referred to in the casebook at page 12 and reproduced as a separate document in this Supplement) committed those institutions to respect the Convention's principles, and the Preamble to the SEA gave the institutions' adherence to Convention principles a still firmer basis. Selected provisions of the Convention and several of its protocols are thus appropriately set out as a separate document in this part of the Supplement.

The importance of the Court of Justice in establishing and enforcing basic Community law principles leads the editors to include as documents the Protocol on the Statute of the Court of Justice and the Court's Rules of Procedure. Unfortunately, space limitations do not allow inclusion of the Rules in their entirety, or the inclusion of any parallel procedural materials concerning the Council and Commission.

This Part of the Documents Supplement contains, finally, the (Brussels) Convention on Jurisdiction and the Enforcement of Judgments in Civil and Commercial Matters, referred to in Chapter 2 of the casebook as the prime example of a Member State convention specifically contemplated by the EEC Treaty. The Convention's special status, its great practical importance, and the fact that the Court of Justice has preliminary reference jurisdiction to interpret its terms justify the Convention's inclusion in this Supplement. It is followed directly by the Protocol conferring jurisdiction on the Court of Justice.

1. TREATY ESTABLISHING THE EUROPEAN ECONOMIC COMMUNITY

[*Eds. Note*: The text of the Treaty Establishing the European Economic Community (EEC) is reproduced as in effect on July 1, 1992.

Provisions amended by the Single European Act (SEA) and the so-called Merger Treaty are indicated by footnotes. Amendments by other treaties and acts, including those dealing with the accession of new Member States and financial and budget provisions, are included, but not specifically indicated.

If ratified, the Treaty on European Union, signed by the Member States at Maastricht on February 7, 1992, would make substantial changes in the EEC Treaty (even changing its name to the European Community Treaty).

When the TEU would make relative by brief alterations in the text, any language in the present EEC Treaty that would be omitted has been placed in brackets. A footnote then indicates the TEU amendment.

When the TEU would either revise the text of a present article extensively or introduce an entirely new article, a cross-reference is made to the TEU amendment. All amended or new EEC Treaty articles are set forth in consecutive order in Article G of the TEU, beginning at page 107 infra. Note that when EEC Treaty articles are amended or replaced by the TEU, they retain the same number, except in the few cases which are indicated.]

Table of Contents

Preamble
Part One: Principles
Part Two: Foundations of the Community
    Title I. Free Movement of Goods
        Chapter 1. The Customs Union
            Section 1. Elimination of Customs Duties between Member States
            Section 2. Setting up of the Common Customs Tariff
        Chapter 2. Elimination of Quantitative Restrictions between Member States
    Title II. Agriculture
    Title III. Free Movement of Persons, Services and Capital
        Chapter 1. Workers
        Chapter 2. Right of Establishment
        Chapter 3. Services
        Chapter 4. Capital
    Title IV. Transport
Part Three: Policy of the Community
    Title I. Common Rules
        Chapter 1. Rules on Competition

Section 1. Rules Applying to Undertakings
Section 2. Dumping
Section 3. Aids Granted by States
    Chapter 2. Tax Provisions
    Chapter 3. Approximation of Laws
  Title II. Economic Policy
    Chapter 1. Cooperation in Economic and Monetary Policy
    Chapter 2. Conjunctural Policy
    Chapter 3. Balance of Payments
    Chapter 4. Commercial Policy
  Title III. Social Policy
    Chapter 1. Social Provisions
    Chapter 2. The European Social Fund
  Title IV. The European Investment Bank
  Title V. Economic and Social Cohesion
  Title VI. Research and Technological Development
  Title VII. Environment
Part Four: Association of the Overseas Countries and Territories
Part Five: Institutions of the Community
  Title I. Provisions Governing the Institutions
    Chapter 1. The Institutions
      Section 1. The European Parliament
      Section 2. The Council
      Section 3. The Commission
      Section 4. The Court of Justice
    Chapter 2. Provisions Common to Several Institutions
    Chapter 3. The Economic and Social Committee
  Title II. Financial Provisions
Part Six: General and Final Provisions
  Setting up of the Institutions
  Final Provisions

PREAMBLE

HIS MAJESTY THE KING OF THE BELGIANS, THE PRESIDENT OF THE FEDERAL REPUBLIC OF GERMANY, THE PRESIDENT OF THE FRENCH REPUBLIC, THE PRESIDENT OF THE ITALIAN REPUBLIC, HER ROYAL HIGHNESS THE GRAND DUCHESS OF LUXEMBOURG, HER MAJESTY THE QUEEN OF THE NETHERLANDS.

Determined to lay the foundations of an even closer union among the peoples of Europe,

Resolved to ensure the economic and social progress of their countries by common action to eliminate the barriers which divide Europe,

Affirming as the essential objective of their efforts the constant improvement of the living and working conditions of their peoples,

Recognizing that the removal of existing obstacles calls for concerted action in order to guarantee steady expansion, balanced trade and fair competition,

Anxious to strengthen the unity of their economies and to ensure their harmonious development by reducing the differences existing between the various regions and the backwardness of the less favoured regions,

Desiring to contribute, by means of a common commercial policy, to the progressive abolition of restrictions on international trade,

Intending to confirm the solidarity which binds Europe and the overseas countries and desiring to ensure the development of their prosperity, in accordance with the principles of the Charter of the United Nations,

Resolved by thus pooling their resources to preserve and strengthen peace and liberty, and calling upon the other peoples of Europe who share their ideal to join in their efforts,

Have decided to create a European [Economic][1] Community * * *. [List of Plenipotentiaries omitted.]

PART ONE
PRINCIPLES

Article 1

By this Treaty, the HIGH CONTRACTING PARTIES establish among themselves a EUROPEAN [ECONOMIC][2] COMMUNITY.

Article 2[3]

The Community shall have as its task, by establishing a common market and progressively approximating the economic policies of Member States, to promote throughout the Community a harmonious development of economic activities, a continuous and balanced expansion, an increase in stability, an accelerated raising of the standard of living and closer relations between the States belonging to it.

Article 3[4]

For the purposes set out in Article 2, the activities of the Community shall include, as provided in this Treaty and in accordance with the timetable set out therein

(a) the elimination, as between Member States, of customs duties and of quantitative restrictions on the import and export of goods, and of all other measures having equivalent effect;

(b) the establishment of a common customs tariff and of a common commercial policy towards third countries;

(c) the abolition, as between Member States, of obstacles to freedom of movement for persons, services and capital;

(d) the adoption of a common policy in the sphere of agriculture;

---

1. TEU Article G(A) would delete "Economic".

2. TEU Article G(A) would delete "ECONOMIC".

3. Substantially amended by the TEU, notably to refer to establishment of an economic and monetary union.

4. Amended by the TEU to add new common policies and activities.

(e) the adoption of a common policy in the sphere of transport;

(f) the institution of a system ensuring that competition in the common market is not distorted;

(g) the application of procedures by which the economic policies of Member States can be coordinated and disequilibria in their balances of payments remedied;

(h) the approximation of the laws of Member States to the extent required for the proper functioning of the common market;

(i) the creation of a European Social Fund in order to improve employment opportunities for workers and to contribute to the raising of their standard of living;

(j) the establishment of a European Investment Bank to facilitate the economic expansion of the Community by opening up fresh resources;

(k) the association of the overseas countries and territories in order to increase trade and to promote jointly economic and social development.

[*Eds. Note*: The TEU would introduce a new Article 3a on activities connected with an economic and monetary union, and a new Article 3b dealing with the principle of subsidiarity.]

Article 4

1. The tasks entrusted to the Community shall be carried out by the following institutions:

a European Parliament,

a Council,

a Commission,

a Court of Justice.[5]

Each institution shall act within the limits of the powers conferred upon it by this Treaty.

2. The Council and the Commission shall be assisted by an Economic and Social Committee [6] acting in an advisory capacity.

[3. The audit shall be carried out by a Court of Auditors acting within the limits of the powers conferred upon it by this Treaty.][7]

[*Eds. Note*: The TEU would introduce new Articles 4a and 4b on a European System of Central Banks, a European Central Bank, and a European Investment Bank.]

Article 5

Member States shall take all appropriate measures, whether general or particular, to ensure fulfillment of the obligations arising out of this

---

5. The TEU would add "a Court of Auditors" to the list of institutions.

6. The TEU would add "and a Committee of Regions".

7. The TEU would delete paragraph 3, describing the Court of Auditors at new arts. 188a–188c.

Treaty or resulting from action taken by the institutions of the Community. They shall facilitate the achievement of the Community's tasks.

They shall abstain from any measure which could jeopardize the attainment of the objectives of this Treaty.

Article 6 [8]

1. Member States shall, in close cooperation with the institutions of the Community, coordinate their respective economic policies to the extent necessary to attain the objectives of this Treaty.

2. The institutions of the Community shall take care not to prejudice the internal and external financial stability of the Member States.

Article 7 [9]

Within the scope of application of this Treaty, and without prejudice to any special provisions contained therein, any discrimination on grounds of nationality shall be prohibited.

[The Council may, on a proposal from the Commission and in cooperation with the European Parliament, adopt, by a qualified majority, rules designed to prohibit such discrimination.] [10]

Article 8 [11]

1. The common market shall be progressively established during a transitional period of twelve years.

This transitional period shall be divided into three stages of four years each; the length of each stage may be altered in accordance with the provisions set out below.

2. To each stage there shall be assigned a set of actions to be initiated and carried through concurrently.

3. Transition from the first to the second stage shall be conditional upon a finding that the objectives specifically laid down in this Treaty for the first stage have in fact been attained in substance and that, subject to the exceptions and procedures provided for in this Treaty, the obligations have been fulfilled.

This finding shall be made at the end of the fourth year by the Council, acting unanimously on a report from the Commission. A Member State may not, however, prevent unanimity by relying upon the non-fulfillment of its own obligations. Failing unanimity, the first stage shall automatically be extended for one year.

At the end of the fifth year, the Council shall make its finding under the same conditions. Failing unanimity, the first stage shall automatically be extended for a further year.

---

8. The TEU would delete Article 6.

9. The TEU would renumber Article 7 as Article 6.

10. The SEA (art. 6(2)) amended the second paragraph to require use of the parliamentary cooperation procedure. The TEU would amend this paragraph to refer to this procedure as described in a new Article 189c.

11. The TEU would renumber Article 8 as Article 7.

At the end of the sixth year, the Council shall make its finding, acting by a qualified majority on a report from the Commission.

4. Within one month of the last-mentioned vote any Member State which voted with the minority or, if the required majority was not obtained, any Member State shall be entitled to call upon the Council to appoint an arbitration board whose decision shall be binding upon all Member States and upon the institutions of the Community. The arbitration board shall consist of three members appointed by the Council acting unanimously on a proposal from the Commission.

If the Council has not appointed the members of the arbitration board within one month of being called upon to do so, they shall be appointed by the Court of Justice within a further period of one month.

The arbitration board shall elect its own Chairman.

The board shall make its award within six months of the date of the Council vote referred to in the last sub-paragraph of paragraph 3.

5. The second and third stages may not be extended or curtailed except by a decision of the Council, acting unanimously on a proposal from the Commission.

6. Nothing in the preceding paragraphs shall cause the transitional period to last more than 15 years after the entry into force of this Treaty.

7. Save for the exceptions or derogations provided for in this Treaty, the expiry of the transitional period shall constitute the latest date by which all the rules laid down must enter into force and all the measures required for establishing the common market must be implemented.

Article 8a [12]

The Community shall adopt measures with the aim of progressively establishing the internal market over a period expiring on 31 December 1992, in accordance with the provisions of this article and of Articles 8b, 8c, 28, 57(2), 59, 70(1), 84, 99, 100a and 100b and without prejudice to the other provisions of this Treaty.

The internal market shall comprise an area without internal frontiers in which the free movement of goods, persons, services and capital is ensured in accordance with the provisions of this Treaty.

Article 8b [13]

The Commission shall report to the Council before 31 December 1988 and again before 31 December 1990 on the progress made towards achieving the internal market within the time limit fixed in Article 8a.

The Council, acting by a qualified majority on a proposal from the Commission, shall determine the guidelines and conditions necessary to ensure balanced progress in all the sectors concerned.

---

12. The SEA (art. 13) added Article 8a. The TEU would renumber it as Article 7a.

13. The SEA (art. 14) added Article 8b. The TEU would renumber it as Article 7b.

Article 8c [14]

When drawing up its proposals with a view to achieving the objectives set out in Article 8a, the Commission shall take into account the extent of the effort that certain economies showing differences in development will have to sustain during the period of establishment of the internal market and it may propose appropriate provisions.

If these provisions take the form of derogations, they must be of a temporary nature and must cause the least possible disturbance to the functioning of the common market.

[*Eds. Note*: The TEU would insert a new "Part Two—Citizenship of the Union," comprised of new Articles 8, 8a–8e. These articles define citizenship of the Union and identify certain rights of citizens.]

PART TWO [15]
FOUNDATIONS OF THE COMMUNITY
Title I. Free Movement of Goods

Article 9

1. The Community shall be based upon a customs union which shall cover all trade in goods and which shall involve the prohibition between Member States of customs duties on imports and exports and of all charges having equivalent effect, and the adoption of a common customs tariff in their relations with third countries.

2. The provisions of Chapter 1, Section 1, and of Chapter 2 of this Title shall apply to products originating in Member States and to products coming from third countries which are in free circulation in Member States.

Article 10

1. Products coming from a third country shall be considered to be in free circulation in a Member State if the import formalities have been complied with and any customs duties or charges having equivalent effect which are payable have been levied in that Member State, and if they have not benefitted from a total or partial drawback of such duties or charges.

2. The Commission shall, before the end of the first year after the entry into force of this Treaty, determine the methods of administrative cooperation to be adopted for the purpose of applying Article 9(2), taking into account the need to reduce as much as possible formalities imposed on trade.

Before the end of the first year after the entry into force of this Treaty, the Commission shall lay down the provisions applicable, as regards trade between Member States, to goods originating in another Member State in whose manufacture products have been used on which

---

14. The SEA (art. 15) added Article 8c. The TEU would renumber it as Article 7c.

15. The TEU (art. G(D)) would replace the present caption for Part Two with a new "Part Three—Community Policies." The new Part Three would be composed of the present Parts Two and Three.

the exporting Member State has not levied the appropriate customs duties or charges having equivalent effect, or which have benefitted from a total or partial drawback of such duties or charges.

In adopting these provisions, the Commission shall take into account the rules for the elimination of customs duties within the Community and for the progressive application of the common customs tariff.

Article 11

Member States shall take all appropriate measures to enable Governments to carry out, within the periods of time laid down, the obligations with regard to customs duties which devolve upon them pursuant to this Treaty.

Chapter 1. The Customs Union

Section 1. Elimination of Customs Duties between Member States

Article 12

Member States shall refrain from introducing between themselves any new customs duties on imports or exports or any charges having equivalent effect, and from increasing those which they already apply in their trade with each other.

Article 13

1. Customs duties on imports in force between Member States shall be progressively abolished by them during the transitional period in accordance with Articles 14 and 15.

2. Charges having an effect equivalent to customs duties on imports, in force between Member States, shall be progressively abolished by them during the transitional period. The Commission shall determine by means of directives the timetable for such abolition. It shall be guided by the rules contained in Article 14(2) and (3) and by the directives issued by the Council pursuant to Article 14(2).

Article 14

1. For each product, the basic duty to which the successive reductions shall be applied shall be the duty applied on 1 January 1957.

2. The timetable for the reductions shall be determined as follows:

(a) during the first stage, the first reduction shall be made one year after the date when this Treaty enters into force; the second reduction, 18 months later; the third reduction, at the end of the fourth year after the date when this Treaty enters into force;

(b) during the second stage, a reduction shall be made 18 months after that stage begins; a second reduction, 18 months after the preceding one; a third reduction, one year later;

(c) any remaining reductions shall be made during the third stage; the Council shall, acting by a qualified majority on a proposal from the Commission, determine the timetable therefor by means of directives.

3. At the time of the first reduction, Member States shall introduce between themselves a duty on each product equal to the basic duty minus 10 per cent.

At the time of each subsequent reduction, each Member State shall reduce its customs duties as a whole in such manner as to lower by 10 per cent its total customs receipts as defined in paragraph 4 and to reduce the duty on each product by at least five per cent of the basic duty.

In the case, however, of products on which the duty is still in excess of 30 per cent, each reduction must be at least 10 per cent of the basic duty.

4. The total customs receipts of each Member State, as referred to in paragraph 3, shall be calculated by multiplying the value of its imports from other Member States during 1956 by the basic duties.

5. Any special problems raised in applying paragraphs 1 to 4 shall be settled by directives issued by the Council acting by a qualified majority on a proposal from the Commission.

6. Member States shall report to the Commission on the manner in which effect has been given to the preceding rules for the reduction of duties. They shall endeavour to ensure that the reduction made in the duties on each product shall amount:

—at the end of the first stage, to at least 25 per cent of the basic duty;

—at the end of the second stage, to at least 50 per cent of the basic duty.

If the Commission finds that there is a risk that the objectives laid down in Article 13, and the percentages laid down in this paragraph, cannot be attained, it shall make all appropriate recommendations to Member States.

7. The provisions of this article may be amended by the Council, acting unanimously on a proposal from the Commission and after consulting the European Parliament.

Article 15

1. Irrespective of the provisions of Article 14, any Member State may, in the course of the transitional period, suspend in whole or in part the collection of duties applied by it to products imported from other Member States. It shall inform the other Member States and the Commission thereof.

2. The Member States declare their readiness to reduce customs duties against the other Member States more rapidly than is provided for in Article 14 if their general economic situation and the situation of the economic sector concerned so permit.

To this end, the Commission shall make recommendations to the Member States concerned.

Article 16

Member States shall abolish between themselves customs duties on exports and charges having equivalent effect by the end of the first stage at the latest.

Article 17

1. The provisions of Articles 9 to 15(1) shall also apply to customs duties of a fiscal nature. Such duties shall not, however, be taken into consideration for the purpose of calculating either total customs receipts or the reduction of customs duties as a whole as referred to in Article 14(3) and (4).

Such duties shall, at each reduction, be lowered by not less than 10 per cent of the basic duty. Member States may reduce such duties more rapidly than is provided for in Article 14.

2. Member States shall, before the end of the first year after the entry into force of this Treaty, inform the Commission of their customs duties of a fiscal nature.

3. Member States shall retain the right to substitute for these duties an internal tax which complies with the provisions of Article 95.

4. If the Commission finds that substitution for any customs duty of a fiscal nature meets with serious difficulties in a Member State, it shall authorize that State to retain the duty on condition that it shall abolish it not later than six years after the entry into force of this Treaty. Such authorization must be applied for before the end of the first year after the entry into force of this Treaty.

Section 2. Setting up of the Common Customs Tariff

Article 18

The Member States declare their readiness to contribute to the development of international trade and the lowering of barriers to trade by entering into agreements designed, on a basis of reciprocity and mutual advantage, to reduce customs duties below the general level of which they could avail themselves as a result of the establishment of a customs union between them.

Article 19

1. Subject to the conditions and within the limits provided for hereinafter, duties in the common customs tariff shall be at the level of the arithmetical average of the duties applied in the four customs territories comprised in the Community.

2. The duties taken as the basis for calculating this average shall be those applied by Member States on 1 January 1957.

In the case of the Italian tariff, however, the duty applied shall be that without the temporary 10 per cent reduction. Furthermore, with respect to items on which the Italian tariff contains a conventional duty, this duty shall be substituted for the duty applied as defined above, provided that it does not exceed the latter by more than 10 per cent. Where the conventional duty exceeds the duty applied as defined above by more than 10 per cent, the latter duty plus 10 per cent shall be taken as the basis for calculating the arithmetical average.

With regard to the tariff headings in List A, the duties shown in that List shall, for the purpose of calculating the arithmetical average, be substituted for the duties applied.

3. The duties in the common customs tariff shall not exceed:

(a) three per cent for products within the tariff headings in List B;

(b) 10 per cent for products within the tariff headings in List C;

(c) 15 per cent for products within the tariff headings in List D;

(d) 25 per cent for products within the tariff headings in List E;

where in respect of such products, the tariff of the Benelux countries contains a duty not exceeding three per cent, such duty shall, for the purpose of calculating the arithmetical average, be raised to 12 per cent.

4. List F prescribes the duties applicable to the products listed therein.

5. The Lists of tariff headings referred to in this Article and in Article 20 are set out in Annex I to this Treaty.

Article 20

The duties applicable to the products in List G shall be determined by negotiation between the Member States. Each Member State may add further products to this List to a value not exceeding two per cent of the total value of its imports from third countries in the course of the year 1956.

The Commission shall take all appropriate steps to ensure that such negotiations shall be undertaken before the end of the second year after the entry into force of this Treaty and be concluded before the end of the first stage.

If, for certain products, no agreement can be reached within these periods, the Council shall, on a proposal from the Commission, acting unanimously until the end of the second stage and by a qualified majority thereafter, determine the duties in the common customs tariff.

Article 21

1. Technical difficulties which may arise in applying Articles 19 and 20 shall be resolved, within two years of the entry into force of this Treaty, by directives issued by the Council acting by a qualified majority on a proposal from the Commission.

2. Before the end of the first stage, or at latest when the duties are determined, the Council shall, acting by a qualified majority on a proposal from the Commission, decide on any adjustments required in the interests of the internal consistency of the common customs tariff as a result of applying the rules set out in Articles 19 and 20, taking account in particular of the degree of processing undergone by the various goods to which the common tariff applies.

Article 22

The Commission shall, within two years of the entry into force of this Treaty, determine the extent to which the customs duties of a fiscal nature referred to in Article 17(2) shall be taken into account in calculating the arithmetical average provided for in Article 19(1). The Commission shall take account of any protective character which such duties may have.

Within six months of such determination, any Member State may request that the procedure provided for in Article 20 should be applied to the product in question, but in this event the percentage limit provided in that Article shall not be applicable to that State.

Article 23

1. For the purpose of the progressive introduction of the common customs tariff, Member States shall amend their tariffs applicable to third countries as follows:

(a) in the case of tariff headings on which the duties applied in practice on 1 January 1957 do not differ by more than 15 per cent in either direction from the duties in the common customs tariff, the latter duties shall be applied at the end of the fourth year after the entry into force of this Treaty;

(b) in any other case, each Member State shall, as from the same date, apply a duty reducing by 30 per cent the difference between the duty applied in practice on 1 January 1957 and the duty in the common customs tariff;

(c) at the end of the second stage this difference shall again be reduced by 30 per cent;

(d) in the case of tariff headings for which the duties in the common customs tariff are not yet available at the end of the first stage, each Member State shall, within six months of the Council's action in accordance with Article 20, apply such duties as would result from application of the rules contained in this paragraph.

2. Where a Member State has been granted an authorization under Article 17(4), it need not, for as long as that authorization remains valid, apply the preceding provisions to the tariff headings to which the authorization applies. When such authorization expires, the Member State concerned shall apply such duty as would have resulted from application of the rules contained in paragraph 1.

3. The common customs tariff shall be applied in its entirety by the end of the transitional period at the latest.

Article 24

Member States shall remain free to change their duties more rapidly than is provided for in Article 23 in order to bring them into line with the common customs tariff.

Article 25

1. If the Commission finds that the production in Member States of particular products contained in Lists B, C and D is insufficient to supply the demands of one of the Member States, and that such supply traditionally depends to a considerable extent on imports from third countries, the Council shall, acting by a qualified majority on a proposal from the Commission, grant the Member State concerned tariff quotas at a reduced rate of duty or duty free.

Such quotas may not exceed the limits beyond which the risk might arise of activities being transferred to the detriment of other Member States.

2. In the case of the products in List E, and of those in List G for which the rates of duty have been determined in accordance with the procedure provided for in the third paragraph of Article 20, the Commission shall, where a change in sources of supply or shortage of supplies within the Community is such as to entail harmful consequences for the processing industries of a Member State, at the request of that Member State, grant it tariff quotas at a reduced rate of duty or duty free.

Such quotas may not exceed the limits beyond which the risk might arise of activities being transferred to the detriment of other Member States.

3. In the case of the products listed in Annex II to this Treaty, the Commission may authorize any Member State to suspend, in whole or in part, collection of the duties applicable or may grant such Member State tariff quotas at a reduced rate of duty or duty free, provided that no serious disturbance of the market of the products concerned results therefrom.

4. The Commission shall periodically examine tariff quotas granted pursuant to this article.

Article 26

The Commission may authorize any Member State encountering special difficulties to postpone the lowering or raising of duties provided for in Article 23 in respect of particular headings in its tariff.

Such authorization may only be granted for a limited period and in respect of tariff headings which, taken together, represent for such State not more than 5 per cent of the value of its imports from third countries in the course of the latest year for which statistical data are available.

Article 27

Before the end of the first stage, Member States shall, insofar as may be necessary, take steps to approximate their provisions laid down by law, regulation or administrative action in respect of customs matters. To this end, the Commission shall make all appropriate recommendations to Member States.

Article 28

Any autonomous alteration or suspension of duties in the common customs tariff shall be decided by the Council acting by a qualified majority on a proposal from the Commission.[16]

Article 29

In carrying out the tasks entrusted to it under this Section the Commission shall be guided by:

(a) the need to promote trade between Member States and third countries;

(b) developments in conditions of competition within the Community insofar as they lead to an improvement in the competitive capacity of undertakings;

(c) the requirements of the Community as regards the supply of raw materials and semi-finished goods; in this connection the Commission shall take care to avoid distorting conditions of competition between Member States in respect of finished goods;

(d) the need to avoid serious disturbances in the economies of Member States and to ensure rational development of production and an expansion of consumption within the Community.

Chapter 2. Elimination of Quantitative Restrictions Between Member States

Article 30

Quantitative restrictions on imports and all measures having equivalent effect shall, without prejudice to the following provisions, be prohibited between Member States.

Article 31

Member States shall refrain from introducing between themselves any new quantitative restrictions or measures having equivalent effect.

This obligation shall, however, relate only to the degree of liberalization attained in pursuance of the decisions of the Council of the Organization for European Economic Cooperation of 14 January 1955. Member States shall supply the Commission, not later than six months after the entry into force of this Treaty, with lists of the products liberalized by them in pursuance of these decisions. These lists shall be consolidated between Member States.

Article 32

In their trade with one another Member States shall refrain from making more restrictive the quotas and measures having equivalent effect existing at the date of the entry into force of this Treaty.

---

16. The SEA (art. 16(1)) amended Article 28 to permit the Council to act by qualified majority.

These quotas shall be abolished by the end of the transitional period at the latest. During that period, they shall be progressively abolished in accordance with the following provisions.

Article 33

1. One year after the entry into force of this Treaty, each Member State shall convert any bilateral quotas open to any other Member States into global quotas open without discrimination to all other Member States.

On the same date, Member States shall increase the aggregate of the global quotas so established in such a manner as to bring about an increase of not less than 20 per cent in their total value as compared with the preceding year. The global quota for each product, however, shall be increased by not less than 10 per cent.

The quotas shall be increased annually in accordance with the same rules and in the same proportions in relation to the preceding year.

The fourth increase shall take place at the end of the fourth year after the entry into force of this Treaty; the fifth, one year after the beginning of the second stage.

2. Where, in the case of a product which has not been liberalized, the global quota does not amount to three per cent of the national production of the State concerned, a quota equal to not less than three per cent of such national production shall be introduced not later than one year after the entry into force of this Treaty. This quota shall be raised to four per cent at the end of the second year, and to five per cent at the end of the third. Thereafter, the Member State concerned shall increase the quota by not less than 15 per cent annually.

Where there is no such national production, the Commission shall take a decision establishing an appropriate quota.

3. At the end of the tenth year, each quota shall be equal to not less than 20 per cent of the national production.

4. If the Commission finds by means of a decision that during two successive years the imports of any product have been below the level of the quota opened, this global quota shall not be taken into account in calculating the total value of the global quotas. In such case, the Member State shall abolish quota restrictions on the product concerned.

5. In the case of quotas representing more than 20 per cent of the national production of the product concerned, the Council may, acting by a qualified majority on a proposal from the Commission, reduce the minimum percentage of 10 per cent laid down in paragraph 1. This alteration shall not, however, affect the obligation to increase the total value of global quotas by 20 per cent annually.

6. Member States which have exceeded their obligations as regards the degree of liberalization attained in pursuance of the decisions of the Council of the Organization for European Economic Cooperation of 14 January 1955 shall be entitled, when calculating the annual total increase

of 20 per cent provided for in paragraph 1, to take into account the amount of imports liberalized by autonomous action. Such calculation shall be submitted to the Commission for its prior approval.

7. The Commission shall issue directives establishing the procedure and timetable in accordance with which Member States shall abolish, as between themselves, any measures in existence when this Treaty enters into force which have an effect equivalent to quotas.

8. If the Commission finds that the application of the provisions of this article, and in particular of the provisions concerning percentages, makes it impossible to ensure that the abolition of quotas provided for in the second paragraph of Article 32 is carried out progressively, the Council may, on a proposal from the Commission, acting unanimously during the first stage and by a qualified majority thereafter, amend the procedure laid down in this Article and may, in particular, increase the percentages fixed.

Article 34

1. Quantitative restrictions on exports, and all measures having equivalent effect, shall be prohibited between Member States.

2. Member States shall, by the end of the first stage at the latest, abolish all quantitative restrictions on exports and any measures having equivalent effect which are in existence when this Treaty enters into force.

Article 35

The Member States declare their readiness to abolish quantitative restrictions on imports from and exports to other Member States more rapidly than is provided for in the preceding Articles, if their general economic situation and the situation of the economic sector concerned so permit.

To this end, the Commission shall make recommendations to the Member States concerned.

Article 36

The provisions of Articles 30 to 34 shall not preclude prohibitions or restrictions on imports, exports or goods in transit justified on grounds of public morality, public policy or public security; the protection of health and life of humans, animals or plants; the protection of national treasures possessing artistic, historic or archaeological value; or the protection of industrial and commercial property. Such prohibitions or restrictions shall not, however, constitute a means of arbitrary discrimination or a disguised restriction on trade between Member States.

Article 37

1. Member States shall progressively adjust any State monopolies of a commercial character so as to ensure that when the transitional period has ended no discrimination regarding the conditions under which goods are procured and marketed exists between nationals of Member States.

The provisions of the Article shall apply to any body through which a Member State, in law or in fact, either directly or indirectly supervises, determines or appreciably influences imports or exports between Member States. These provisions shall likewise apply to monopolies delegated by the State to others.

2. Member States shall refrain from introducing any new measure which is contrary to the principles laid down in paragraph 1 or which restricts the scope of the Articles dealing with the abolition of customs duties and quantitative restrictions between Member States.

3. The timetable for the measures referred to in paragraph 1 shall be harmonized with the abolition of quantitative restrictions on the same products provided for in Articles 30 to 34.

If a product is subject to a State monopoly of a commercial character in only one or some Member States, the Commission may authorize the other Member States to apply protective measures until the adjustment provided for in paragraph 1 has been effected; the Commission shall determine the conditions and details of such measures.

4. If a State monopoly of a commercial character has rules which are designed to make it easier to dispose of agricultural products or obtain for them the best return, steps should be taken in applying the rules contained in this Article to ensure equivalent safeguards for the employment and standard of living of the producers concerned, account being taken of the adjustments that will be possible and the specialization that will be needed with the passage of time.

5. The obligations on Member States shall be binding only insofar as they are compatible with existing international agreements.

6. With effect from the first stage the Commission shall make recommendations as to the manner in which and the timetable according to which the adjustment provided for in this Article shall be carried out.

Title II. Agriculture

Article 38

1. The common market shall extend to agriculture and trade in agricultural products. "Agricultural products" means the products of the soil, of stockfarming and of fisheries and products of first-stage processing directly related to these products.

2. Save as otherwise provided in Articles 39 to 46, the rules laid down for the establishment of the common market shall apply to agricultural products.

3. The products subject to the provisions of Articles 39 to 46 are listed in Annex II to this Treaty. Within two years of the entry into force of this Treaty, however, the Council shall, acting by a qualified majority on a proposal from the Commission, decide what products are to be added to this list.

4. The operation and development of the common market for agricultural products must be accompanied by the establishment of a common agricultural policy among the Member States.

Article 39

1. The objectives of the common agricultural policy shall be:

(a) to increase agricultural productivity by promoting technical progress and by ensuring the rational development of agricultural production and the optimum utilization of the factors of production, in particular labour;

(b) thus to ensure a fair standard of living for the agricultural community, in particular by increasing the individual earnings of persons engaged in agriculture;

(c) to stabilize markets;

(d) to assure the availability of supplies;

(e) to ensure that supplies reach consumers at reasonable prices.

2. In working out the common agricultural policy and the special methods for its application, account shall be taken of:

(a) the particular nature of agricultural activity, which results from the social structure of agriculture and from structural and natural disparities between the various agricultural regions;

(b) the need to effect the appropriate adjustments by degrees;

(c) the fact that in the Member States agriculture constitutes a sector closely linked with the economy as a whole.

Article 40

1. Member States shall develop the common agricultural policy by degrees during the transitional period and shall bring it into force by the end of that period at the latest.

2. In order to attain the objectives set out in Article 39 a common organization of agricultural markets shall be established.

This organization shall take one of the following forms, depending on the product concerned:

(a) common rules on competition;

(b) compulsory coordination of the various national market organizations;

(c) a European market organization.

3. The common organization established in accordance with paragraph 2 may include all measures required to attain the objectives set out in Article 39, in particular regulation of prices, aids for the production and marketing of the various products, storage and carryover arrangements and common machinery for stabilizing imports or exports.

The common organization shall be limited to pursuit of the objectives set out in Article 39 and shall exclude any discrimination between producers or consumers within the Community.

Any common price policy shall be based on common criteria and uniform methods of calculation.

4. In order to enable the common organization referred to in paragraph 2 to attain its objectives, one or more agricultural guidance and guarantee funds may be set up.

Article 41

To enable the objectives set out in Article 39 to be attained, provision may be made within the framework of the common agricultural policy for measures such as:

(a) an effective coordination of efforts in the spheres of vocational training, of research and of the dissemination of agricultural knowledge; this may include joint financing of projects or institutions;

(b) joint measures to promote consumption of certain products.

Article 42

The provisions of the Chapter relating to rules on competition shall apply to production of and trade in agricultural products only to the extent determined by the Council within the framework of Article 43(2) and (3) and in accordance with the procedure laid down therein, account being taken of the objectives set out in Article 39.

The Council may, in particular, authorize the granting of aid:

(a) for the protection of enterprises handicapped by structural or natural conditions;

(b) within the framework of economic development programmes.

Article 43

1. In order to evolve the broad lines of a common agricultural policy, the Commission shall, immediately this Treaty enters into force, convene a conference of the Member States with a view to making a comparison of their agricultural policies, in particular by producing a statement of their resources and needs.

2. Having taken into account the work of the conference provided for in paragraph 1, after consulting the Economic and Social Committee and within two years of the entry into force of this Treaty, the Commission shall submit proposals for working out and implementing the common agricultural policy, including the replacement of the national organizations by one of the forms of common organization provided for in Article 40(2), and for implementing the measures specified in this Title.

These proposals shall take account of the interdependence of the agricultural matters mentioned in this Title.

The Council shall, on a proposal from the Commission and after consulting the European Parliament, acting unanimously during the first two stages and by a qualified majority thereafter, make regulations, issue directives, or take decisions, without prejudice to any recommendations it may also make.

3. The Council may, acting by a qualified majority and in accordance with paragraph 2, replace the national market organizations by the common organization provided for in Article 40(2) if:

(a) the common organization offers Member States which are opposed to this measure and which have an organization of their own for the production in question equivalent safeguards for the employment and standard of living of the producers concerned, account being taken of the adjustments that will be possible and the specialization that will be needed with the passage of time;

(b) such an organization ensures conditions for trade within the Community similar to those existing in a national market.

4. If a common organization for certain raw materials is established before a common organization exists for the corresponding processed products, such raw materials as are used for processed products intended for export to third countries may be imported from outside the Community.

Article 44

1. Insofar as progressive abolition of customs duties and quantitative restrictions between Member States may result in prices likely to jeopardize the attainment of the objectives set out in Article 39, each Member State shall, during the transitional period, be entitled to apply to particular products, in a non-discriminatory manner and in substitution for quotas and to such an extent as shall not impede the expansion of the volume of trade provided for in Article 45(2), a system of minimum prices below which imports may be either:

—temporarily suspended or reduced; or

—allowed, but subjected to the condition that they are made at a price higher than the minimum price for the product concerned.

In the latter case the minimum prices shall not include customs duties.

2. Minimum prices shall neither cause a reduction of the trade existing between Member States when this Treaty enters into force nor form an obstacle to progressive expansion of this trade. Minimum prices shall not be applied so as to form an obstacle to the development of a natural preference between Member States.

3. As soon as this Treaty enters into force the Council shall, on a proposal from the Commission, determine objective criteria for the establishment of minimum price systems and for the fixing of such prices.

These criteria shall in particular take account of the average national production costs in the Member State applying the minimum price, of the position of the various undertakings concerned in relation to such average production costs, and of the need to promote both the progressive improvement of agricultural practice and the adjustments and specialization needed within the common market.

The Commission shall further propose a procedure for revising these criteria in order to allow for and speed up technical progress and to approximate prices progressively within the common market.

These criteria and the procedure for revising them shall be determined by the Council acting unanimously within three years of the entry into force of this Treaty.

4. Until the decision of the Council takes effect, Member States may fix minimum prices on condition that these are communicated beforehand to the Commission and to the other Member States so that they may submit their comments.

Once the Council has taken its decision, Member States shall fix minimum prices on the basis of the criteria determined as above.

The Council may, acting by a qualified majority on a proposal from the Commission, rectify any decisions taken by Member States which do not conform to the criteria defined above.

5. If it does not prove possible to determine the said objective criteria for certain products by the beginning of the third stage, the Council may, acting by a qualified majority on a proposal from the Commission, vary the minimum prices applied to these products.

6. At the end of the transitional period, a table of minimum prices still in force shall be drawn up. The Council shall, acting on a proposal from the Commission and by a majority of nine votes in accordance with the weighting laid down in the first sub-paragraph of Article 148(2), determine the system to be applied within the framework of the common agricultural policy.

Article 45

1. Until national market organizations have been replaced by one of the forms of common organization referred to in Article 40(2), trade in products in respect of which certain Member States:

—have arrangements designed to guarantee national producers a market for their products; and

—are in need of imports,

shall be developed by the conclusion of long-term agreements or contracts between importing and exporting Member States.

These agreements or contracts shall be directed towards the progressive abolition of any discrimination in the application of these arrangements to the various producers within the Community.

Such agreements or contracts shall be concluded during the first stage; account shall be taken of the principle of reciprocity.

2. As regards quantities, these agreements or contracts shall be based on the average volume of trade between Member States in the products concerned during the three years before the entry into force of

this Treaty and shall provide for an increase in the volume of trade within the limits of existing requirements, account being taken of traditional patterns of trade.

As regards prices, these agreements or contracts shall enable producers to dispose of the agreed quantities at prices which shall be progressively approximated to those paid to national producers on the domestic market of the purchasing country.

This approximation shall proceed as steadily as possible and shall be completed by the end of the transitional period at the latest.

Prices shall be negotiated between the parties concerned within the framework of directives issued by the Commission for the purpose of implementing the two preceding sub-paragraphs.

If the first stage is extended, these agreements or contracts shall continue to be carried out in accordance with the conditions applicable at the end of the fourth year after the entry into force of this Treaty, the obligation to increase quantities and to approximate prices being suspended until the transition to the second stage.

Member States shall avail themselves of any opportunity open to them under their legislation, particularly in respect of import policy, to ensure the conclusion and carrying out of these agreements or contracts.

3. To the extent that Member States require raw materials for the manufacture of products to be exported outside the Community in competition with products of third countries, the above agreements or contracts shall not form an obstacle to the importation of raw materials for this purpose from third countries. This provision shall not, however, apply if the Council unanimously decides to make provision for payments required to compensate for the higher price paid on goods imported for this purpose on the basis of these agreements or contracts in relation to the delivered price of the same goods purchased on the world market.

Article 46

Where in a Member State a product is subject to a national market organization or to internal rules having equivalent effect which affect the competitive position of similar production in another Member State, a countervailing charge shall be applied by Member States to imports of this product coming from the Member State where such organization or rules exist, unless that State applies a countervailing charge on export.

The Commission shall fix the amount of these charges at the level required to redress the balance; it may also authorize other measures, the conditions and details of which it shall determine.

Article 47

As to the functions to be performed by the Economic and Social Committee in pursuance of this Title, its agricultural section shall hold itself at the disposal of the Commission to prepare, in accordance with the provisions of Articles 197 and 198, the deliberations of the Committee.

Title III. Free Movement of Persons, Services and Capital
Chapter 1. Workers

Article 48

1. Freedom of movement for workers shall be secured within the Community by the end of the transitional period at the latest.

2. Such freedom of movement shall entail the abolition of any discrimination based on nationality between workers of the Member States as regards employment, remuneration and other conditions of work and employment.

3. It shall entail the right, subject to limitations justified on grounds of public policy, public security or public health:

(a) to accept offers of employment actually made;

(b) to move freely within the territory of Member States for this purpose;

(c) to stay in a Member State for the purpose of employment in accordance with the provisions governing the employment of nationals of that State laid down by law, regulation or administrative action;

(d) to remain in the territory of a Member State after having been employed in that State, subject to conditions which shall be embodied in implementing regulations to be drawn up by the Commission.

4. The provisions of this Article shall not apply to employment in the public service.

Article 49

As soon as this Treaty enters into force, the Council shall, acting by a qualified majority on a proposal from the Commission, in cooperation with the European Parliament and after consulting the Economic and Social Committee, issue directives or make regulations setting out the measures required to bring about, by progressive stages, freedom of movement for workers, as defined in Article 48, in particular: [17]

(a) by ensuring close cooperation between national employment services;

(b) by systematically and progressively abolishing those administrative procedures and practices and those qualifying periods in respect of eligibility for available employment, whether resulting from national legislation or from agreements previously concluded between Member States, the maintenance of which would form an obstacle to liberalization of the movement of workers;

(c) by systematically and progressively abolishing all such qualifying periods and other restrictions provided for either under national legislation or under agreements previously concluded between Member States as

---

17. The SEA (art. 6(3)) amended the first paragraph to require the adoption of legislation by a qualified majority vote of the Council, making use of the parliamentary cooperation procedure. The TEU would require instead the parliamentary co-decision procedure of new Article 189b.

Doc. 1   LEGAL & INSTITUTIONAL FRAMEWORK

imposed on workers of other Member States conditions regarding the free choice of employment other than those imposed on workers of the State concerned;

(d) by setting up appropriate machinery to bring offers of employment into touch with applications for employment and to facilitate the achievement of a balance between supply and demand in the employment market in such a way as to avoid serious threats to the standard of living and level of employment in the various regions and industries.

Article 50

Member States shall, within the framework of a joint programme, encourage the exchange of young workers.

Article 51

The Council shall, acting unanimously on a proposal from the Commission, adopt such measures in the field of social security as are necessary to provide freedom of movement for workers; to this end, it shall make arrangements to secure for migrant workers and their dependents:

(a) aggregation, for the purpose of acquiring and retaining the right to benefit and of calculating the amount of benefit, of all periods taken into account under the laws of the several countries;

(b) payment of benefits to persons resident in the territories of Member States.

Chapter 2. Right of Establishment
Article 52

Within the framework of the provisions set out below, restrictions on the freedom of establishment of nationals of a Member State in the territory of another Member State shall be abolished by progressive stages in the course of the transitional period. Such progressive abolition shall also apply to restrictions on the setting up of agencies, branches or subsidiaries by nationals of any Member State established in the territory of any Member State.

Freedom of establishment shall include the right to take up and pursue activities as self-employed persons and to set up and manage undertakings, in particular companies or firms within the meaning of the second paragraph of Article 58, under the conditions laid down for its own nationals by the law of the country where such establishment is effected, subject to the provisions of the Chapter relating to capital.

Article 53

Member States shall not introduce any new restrictions on the right of establishment in their territories of nationals of other Member States, save as otherwise provided in this Treaty.

Article 54

1. Before the end of the first stage, the Council shall, acting unanimously from the Commission and after consulting the Economic and Social Committee and the European Parliament, draw up a general

programme for the abolition of existing restrictions on freedom of establishment within the Community. The Commission shall submit its proposal to the Council during the first two years of the first stage.

The programme shall set out the general conditions under which freedom of establishment is to be attained in the case of each type of activity and in particular the stages by which it is to be attained.

2. In order to implement this general programme or, in the absence of such programme, in order to achieve a stage in attaining freedom of establishment as regards a particular activity, the Council shall, acting on a proposal from the Commission, in cooperation with the European Parliament and after consulting the Economic and Social Committee, issue directives, acting unanimously until the end of the first stage and by a qualified majority thereafter.[18]

3. The Council and the Commission shall carry out the duties devolving upon them under the preceding provisions, in particular:

(a) by according, as a general rule, priority treatment to activities where freedom of establishment makes a particularly valuable contribution to the development of production and trade;

(b) by ensuring close cooperation between the competent authorities in the Member States in order to ascertain the particular situation within the Community of the various activities concerned;

(c) by abolishing those administrative procedures and practices, whether resulting from national legislation or from agreements previously concluded between Member States, the maintenance of which would form an obstacle to freedom of establishment;

(d) by ensuring that workers of one Member State employed in the territory of another Member State may remain in that territory for the purpose of taking up activities therein as self-employed persons, where they satisfy the conditions which they would be required to satisfy if they were entering that State at the time when they intended to take up such activities;

(e) by enabling a national of one Member State to acquire and use land and buildings situated in the territory of another Member State, insofar as this does not conflict with the principles laid down in Article 39(2);

(f) by effecting the progressive abolition of restrictions on freedom of establishment in every branch of activity under consideration, both as regards the conditions for setting up agencies, branches or subsidiaries in the territory of a Member State and as regards the conditions governing the entry of personnel belonging to the main establishment into managerial or supervisory posts in such agencies, branches or subsidiaries;

---

18. The SEA (art. 6(4)) amended paragraph 2 to require the parliamentary cooperation procedure to adopt these directives. The TEU would require instead the parliamentary co-decision procedure of new Article 189b.

(g) by coordinating to the necessary extent the safeguards which, for the protection of the interests of members and others, are required by Member States of companies or firms within the meaning of the second paragraph of Article 58 with a view to making such safeguards equivalent throughout the Community;

(h) by satisfying themselves that the conditions of establishment are not distorted by aids granted by Member States.

Article 55

The provisions of this Chapter shall not apply, so far as any given Member State is concerned, to activities which in that State are connected, even occasionally, with the exercise of official authority.

The Council may, acting by a qualified majority on a proposal from the Commission, rule that the provisions of this Chapter shall not apply to certain activities.

Article 56

1. The provisions of this Chapter and measures taken in pursuance thereof shall not prejudice the applicability of provisions laid down by law, regulation or administrative action providing for special treatment for foreign nationals on grounds of public policy, public security or public health.

2. Before the end of the transitional period, the Council shall, acting unanimously on a proposal from the Commission and after consulting the European Parliament, issue directives for the coordination of the aforementioned provisions laid down by law, regulation or administrative action. After the end of the second stage, however, the Council shall, acting by a qualified majority on a proposal from the Commission and in cooperation with the European Parliament, issue directives for the coordination of such provisions as, in each Member State, are a matter for regulation or administrative action.[19]

Article 57[20]

1. In order to make it easier for persons to take up and pursue activities as self-employed persons, the Council shall, on a proposal from the Commission and in cooperation with the European Parliament, acting unanimously during the first stage and by a qualified majority thereafter, issue directives for the mutual recognition of diplomas, certificates and other evidence of formal qualifications.

2. For the same purpose, the Council shall, before the end of the transitional period, acting on a proposal from the Commission and after

---

19. The SEA (art. 6(5)) amended the second paragraph to require the parliamentary cooperation procedure in adopting these directives. The TEU would instead require the parliamentary co-decision procedure of new Article 189b.

20. The SEA (arts. 6(6) and 6(7)) amended the first paragraph and the last sentence of the second paragraph to require the parliamentary cooperation procedure in adopting the directives referred to here. The TEU in both cases would instead require the parliamentary co-decision procedure of new Article 189b. The SEA (art. 16(2)) also inserted the second-last sentence in the second paragraph.

consulting the European Parliament, issue directives for the coordination of the provisions laid down by law, regulation or administrative action in Member States concerning the taking up and pursuit of activities as self-employed persons. Unanimity shall be required for directives the implementation of which involves in at least one Member State amendment of the existing principles laid down by law governing the professions with respect to training and conditions of access for natural persons. In other cases the Council shall act by a qualified majority, in cooperation with the European Parliament.

3. In the case of the medical and allied pharmaceutical professions, the progressive abolition of restrictions shall be dependent upon coordination of the conditions for their exercise in the various Member States.

Article 58

Companies or firms formed in accordance with the law of a Member State and having their registered office, central administration or principal place of business within the Community shall, for the purposes of this chapter, be treated in the same way as natural persons who are nationals of Member States.

"Companies or firms" means companies or firms constituted under civil or commercial law, including cooperative societies, and other legal persons governed by public or private law, save for those which are non-profitmaking.

Chapter 3. Services
Article 59

Within the framework of the provisions set out below, restrictions on freedom to provide services within the Community shall be progressively abolished during the transitional period in respect of nationals of Member States who are established in a State of the Community other than that of the person for whom the services are intended.

The Council may, acting by a qualified majority on a proposal from the Commission, extend the provisions of the chapter to nationals of a third country who provide services and who are established within the Community.[21]

Article 60

Services shall be considered to be "services" within the meaning of this Treaty where they are normally provided for remuneration, insofar as they are not governed by the provisions relating to freedom of movement for goods, capital and persons. "Services" shall in particular include:

(a) activities of an industrial character;

(b) activities of a commercial character;

---

21. The SEA (art. 16(3)) amended the second paragraph to permit the Council to act by qualified majority instead of unanimity.

(c) activities of craftsmen;

(d) activities of the professions.

Without prejudice to the provisions of the Chapter relating to the right of establishment, the person providing a service may, in order to do so, temporarily pursue his activity in the State where the service is provided, under the same conditions as are imposed by that State on its own nationals.

Article 61

1. Freedom to provide services in the field of transport shall be governed by the provisions of the Title relating to transport.

2. The liberalization of banking and insurance services connected with movements of capital shall be effected in step with the progressive liberalization of movement of capital.

Article 62

Save as otherwise provided in this Treaty, Member States shall not introduce any new restrictions on the freedom to provide services which have in fact been attained at the date of the entry into force of this Treaty.

Article 63

1. Before the end of the first stage, the Council shall, acting unanimously on a proposal from the Commission and after consulting the Economic and Social Committee and the European Parliament, draw up a general programme for the abolition of existing restrictions on freedom to provide services within the Community. The Commission shall submit its proposal to the Council during the first two years of the first stage.

The programme shall set out the general conditions under which and the stages by which each type of service is to be liberalized.

2. In order to implement this general programme or, in the absence of such programme, in order to achieve a stage in the liberalization of a specific service, the Council shall, on a proposal from the Commission and after consulting the Economic and Social Committee and the European Parliament, issue directives acting unanimously until the end of the first stage and by a qualified majority thereafter.

3. As regards the proposals and decisions referred to in paragraphs 1 and 2, priority shall as a general rule be given to those services which directly affect production costs or the liberalization of which helps to promote trade in goods.

Article 64

The Member States declare their readiness to undertake the liberalization of services beyond the extent required by the directives issued pursuant to Article 63(2), if their general economic situation and the situation of the economic sector concerned so permit.

To this end, the Commission shall make recommendations to the Member States concerned.

Article 65

As long as restrictions on freedom to provide services have not been abolished, each Member State shall apply such restrictions without distinction on grounds of nationality or residence to all persons providing services within the meaning of the first paragraph of Article 59.

Article 66

The provisions of Articles 55 to 58 shall apply to the matters covered by this Chapter.

Chapter 4. Capital [22]

[*Eds. Note*: The TEU would introduce new Articles 73a–73h. As from January 1, 1994, these would replace Articles 67–73. The new Articles would generally prohibit restrictions on movements of capital and on payments between Member States.]

Article 67

1. During the transitional period and to the extent necessary to ensure the proper functioning of the common market, Member States shall progressively abolish between themselves all restrictions on the movement of capital belonging to persons resident in Member States and any discrimination based on the nationality or on the place of residence of the parties or on the place where such capital is invested.

2. Current payments connected with the movement of capital between Member States shall be freed from all restrictions by the end of the first stage at the latest.

Article 68

1. Member States shall, as regards the matters dealt with in this Chapter, be as liberal as possible in granting such exchange authorizations as are still necessary after the entry into force of this Treaty.

2. Where a Member State applies to the movements of capital liberalized in accordance with the provisions of this Chapter the domestic rules governing the capital market and the credit system, it shall do so in a non-discriminatory manner.

3. Loans for the direct or indirect financing of a Member State or its regional or local authorities shall not be issued or placed in other Member States unless the States concerned have reached agreement thereon. This provision shall not preclude the application of Article 22 of the Protocol on the Statute of the European Investment Bank.

Article 69

The Council shall, on a proposal from the Commission, which for this purpose shall consult the Monetary Committee provided for in Article 105, issue the necessary directives for the progressive implementation of the provisions of Article 67, acting unanimously during the first two stages and by a qualified majority thereafter.

22. The TEU would rename Chapter 4 as "Capital and Payments".

Article 70

1. The Commission shall propose to the Council measures for the progressive coordination of the exchange policies of Member States in respect of the movement of capital between those States and third countries. For this purpose the Council shall issue directives, acting by a qualified majority. It shall endeavour to attain the highest possible degree of liberalization. Unanimity shall be required for measures which constitute a step back as regards the liberalization of capital movements.[23]

2. Where the measures taken in accordance with paragraph 1 do not permit the elimination of differences between the exchange rules of Member States and where such differences could lead persons resident in one of the Member States to use the freer transfer facilities within the Community which are provided for in Article 67 in order to evade the rules of one of the Member States concerning the movement of capital to or from third countries, that State may, after consulting the other Member States and the Commission, take appropriate measures to overcome these difficulties.

Should the Council find that these measures are restricting the free movement of capital within the Community to a greater extent than is required for the purpose of overcoming the difficulties, it may, acting by a qualified majority on a proposal from the Commission, decide that the State concerned shall amend or abolish these measures.

Article 71

Member States shall endeavour to avoid introducing within the Community any new exchange restrictions on the movement of capital and current payments connected with such movements, and shall endeavour not to make existing rules more restrictive.

They declare their readiness to go beyond the degree of liberalization of capital movements provided for in the preceding Articles insofar as their economic situation, in particular the situation of their balance of payments, so permits.

The Commission may, after consulting the Monetary Committee, make recommendations to Member States on this subject.

Article 72

Member States shall keep the Commission informed of any movements of capital to and from third countries which come to their knowledge. The Commission may deliver to Member States any opinions which it considers appropriate on this subject.

Article 73

1. If movements of capital lead to disturbances in the functioning of the capital market in any Member State, the Commission shall, after consulting the Monetary Committee, authorize that State to take protec-

---

23. The SEA (art. 16(4)) amended paragraph 1 to permit the Council to issue liberalizing directives by qualified majority, instead of unanimity.

tive measures in the field of capital movements, the conditions and details of which the Commission shall determine.

The Council may, acting by a qualified majority, revoke this authorization or amend the conditions or details thereof.

2. A Member State which is in difficulties may, however, on grounds of secrecy or urgency, take the measures mentioned above, where this proves necessary, on its own initiative. The Commission and the other Member States shall be informed of such measures by the date of their entry into force at the latest. In this event the Commission may, after consulting the Monetary Committee, decide that the State concerned shall amend or abolish the measures.

Title IV. Transport

Article 74

The objectives of this Treaty shall, in matters governed by this Title, be pursued by Member States within the framework of a common transport policy.

Article 75

1. For the purpose of implementing Article 74, and taking into account the distinctive features of transport, the Council shall, acting unanimously until the end of the second stage and by a qualified majority thereafter, lay down, on a proposal from the Commission and after consulting the Economic and Social Committee and the European Parliament: [24]

(a) common rules applicable to international transport to or from the territory of a Member State or passing across the territory of one or more Member States;

(b) the conditions under which non-resident carriers may operate transport services within a Member State;

(c) any other appropriate provisions.[25]

2. The provisions referred to in (a) and (b) of paragraph 1 shall be laid down during the transitional period.

3. By way of derogation from the procedure provided for in paragraph 1, where the application of provisions concerning the principles of the regulatory system for transport would be liable to have a serious effect on the standard of living and on employment in certain areas and on the operation of transport facilities, they shall be laid down by the Council acting unanimously.[26] In so doing, the Council shall take into account the

---

24. The TEU would amend paragraph 1 to require use of the parliamentary cooperation procedure of new Article 189c instead of consultation of the Parliament.

25. The TEU would redesignate (c) as (d) and add: "(c) measures to improve transport safety".

26. The TEU would add at the end of this sentence: ", on a proposal from the Commission, after consulting the European Parliament and the Economic and Social Committee".

need for adaptation to the economic development which will result from establishing the common market.

Article 76

Until the provisions referred to in Article 75(1) have been laid down, no Member State may, without the unanimous approval of the Council, make the various provisions governing the subject when this Treaty enters into force less favourable in their direct or indirect effect on carriers of other Member States as compared with carriers who are nationals of that State.

Article 77

Aids shall be compatible with this Treaty if they meet the needs of coordination of transport or if they represent reimbursement for the discharge of certain obligations inherent in the concept of a public service.

Article 78

Any measures taken within the framework of this Treaty in respect of transport rates and conditions shall take account of the economic circumstances of carriers.

Article 79

1. In the case of transport within the Community, discrimination which takes the form of carriers charging different rates and imposing different conditions for the carriage of the same goods over the same transport links on grounds of the country of origin or of destination of the goods in question, shall be abolished, at the latest, before the end of the second stage.

2. Paragraph 1 shall not prevent the Council from adopting other measures in pursuance of Article 75(1).

3. Within two years of the entry into force of this Treaty, the Council shall, acting by a qualified majority on a proposal from the Commission and after consulting the Economic and Social Committee, lay down rules for implementing the provisions of paragraph 1.

The Council may in particular lay down the provisions needed to enable the institutions of the Community to secure compliance with the rule laid down in paragraph 1 and to ensure that users benefit from it to the full.

4. The Commission shall, acting on its own initiative or on application by a Member State, investigate any cases of discrimination falling within paragraph 1 and, after consulting any Member State concerned, shall take the necessary decisions within the framework of the rules laid down in accordance with the provisions of paragraph 3.

Article 80

1. The imposition by a Member State, in respect of transport operations carried out within the Community, of rates and conditions involving any element of support or protection in the interest of one or more

particular undertakings or industries shall be prohibited as from the beginning of the second stage, unless authorized by the Commission.

2. The Commission shall, acting on its own initiative or on application by a Member State, examine the rates and conditions referred to in paragraph 1, taking account in particular of the requirements of an appropriate regional economic policy, the needs of underdeveloped areas and the problems of areas seriously affected by political circumstances on the one hand, and of the effects of such rates and conditions on competition between the different modes of transport on the other.

After consulting each Member State concerned, the Commission shall take the necessary decisions.

3. The prohibition provided for in paragraph 1 shall not apply to tariffs fixed to meet competition.

Article 81

Charges or dues in respect of the crossing of frontiers which are charged by a carrier in addition to the transport rates shall not exceed a reasonable level after taking the costs actually incurred thereby into account.

Member States shall endeavour to reduce these costs progressively.

The Commission may make recommendations to Member States for the application of this Article.

Article 82

The provisions of this Title shall not form an obstacle to the application of measures taken in the Federal Republic of Germany to the extent that such measures are required in order to compensate for the economic disadvantages caused by the division of Germany to the economy of certain areas of the Federal Republic affected by that division.

Article 83

An Advisory Committee consisting of experts designated by the Governments of Member States, shall be attached to the Commission. The Commission, whenever it considers it desirable, shall consult the Committee on transport matters without prejudice to the powers of the transport section of the Economic and Social Committee.

Article 84

1. The provisions of this Title shall apply to transport by rail, road and inland waterway.

2. The Council may, acting by qualified majority, decide whether, to what extent and by what procedure appropriate provisions may be laid down for sea and air transport.

The procedural provisions of Article 75(1) and (3) shall apply.[27]

---

27. The SEA (arts. 16(5) and (6)) amended paragraph 2 to permit Council action by qualified majority, instead of unanimity, and to add the last sentence.

PART THREE [28]
POLICY OF THE COMMUNITY
Title I.[29] Common Rules
Chapter 1. Rules on Competition
Section 1. Rules Applying to Undertakings

Article 85

1. The following shall be prohibited as incompatible with the common market: all agreements between undertakings, decisions by associations of undertakings and concerted practices which may affect trade between Member States and which have as their object or effect the prevention, restriction or distortion of competition within the common market, and in particular those which:

    (a) directly or indirectly fix purchase or selling prices or any other trading conditions;

    (b) limit or control production, markets, technical development, or investment;

    (c) share markets or sources of supply;

    (d) apply dissimilar conditions to equivalent transactions with other trading parties, thereby placing them at a competitive disadvantage;

    (e) make the conclusion of contracts subject to acceptance by the other parties of supplementary obligations which, by their nature or according to commercial usage, have no connection with the subject of such contracts.

2. Any agreements or decisions prohibited pursuant to this Article shall be automatically void.

3. The provisions of paragraph 1 may, however, be declared inapplicable in the case of:

    —any agreement or category of agreements between undertakings;

    —any decision or category of decisions by associations of undertakings;

    —any concerted practice or category of concerted practices;

which contributes to improving the production or distribution of goods or to promoting technical or economic progress, while allowing consumers a fair share of the resulting benefit, and which does not:

    (a) impose on the undertakings concerned restrictions which are not indispensable to the attainment of these objectives;

    (b) afford such undertakings the possibility of eliminating competition in respect of a substantial part of the products in question.

---

28. As indicated at page 10 above, the TEU would combine the present Parts Two and Three into a new "Part Three—Community Policies."

29. Because the TEU would combine the present Parts Two and Three, the present Title I would become Title V, with a new name: "Common rules on competition, taxation and approximation of laws."

Article 86

Any abuse by one or more undertakings of a dominant position within the common market or in a substantial part of it shall be prohibited as incompatible with the common market insofar as it may affect trade between Member States.

Such abuse may, in particular, consist in:

(a) directly or indirectly imposing unfair purchase or selling prices or other unfair trading conditions;

(b) limiting production, markets or technical development to the prejudice of consumers;

(c) applying dissimilar conditions to equivalent transactions with other trading parties, thereby placing them at a competitive disadvantage;

(d) making the conclusion of contracts subject to acceptance by the other parties of supplementary obligations which, by their nature or according to commercial usage, have no connection with the subject of such contracts.

Article 87

1. Within three years of the entry into force of this Treaty the Council shall, acting unanimously on a proposal from the Commission and after consulting the European Parliament, adopt any appropriate regulations or directives to give effect to the principles set out in Articles 85 and 86.

If such provisions have not been adopted within the period mentioned, they shall be laid down by the Council, acting by a qualified majority on a proposal from the Commission and after consulting the European Parliament.

2. The regulations or directives referred to in paragraph 1 shall be designed in particular:

(a) to ensure compliance with the prohibitions laid down in Article 85(1) and in Article 86 by making provision for fines and periodic penalty payments;

(b) to lay down detailed rules for the application of Article 85(3), taking into account the need to ensure effective supervision on the one hand, and to simplify administration to the greatest possible extent on the other;

(c) to define, if need be, in the various branches of the economy, the scope of the provisions of Articles 85 and 86;

(d) to define the respective functions of the Commission and of the Court of Justice in applying the provisions laid down in this paragraph;

(e) to determine the relationship between national laws and the provisions contained in this Section or adopted pursuant to this Article.

Article 88

Until the entry into force of the provisions adopted in pursuance of Article 87, the authorities in Member States shall rule on the admissibility of agreements, decisions and concerted practices and on abuse of a dominant position in the common market in accordance with the law of their country and with the provisions of Article 85, in particular paragraph 3, and of Article 86.

Article 89

1. Without prejudice to Article 88, the Commission shall, as soon as it takes up its duties, ensure the application of the principles laid down in Articles 85 and 86. On application by a Member State or on its own initiative, and in cooperation with the competent authorities in the Member States, who shall give it their assistance, the Commission shall investigate cases of suspected infringement of these principles. If it finds that there has been an infringement, it shall propose appropriate measures to bring it to an end.

2. If the infringement is not brought to an end, the Commission shall record such infringement of the principles in a reasoned decision. The Commission may publish its decision and authorize Member States to take the measures, the conditions and details of which it shall determine, needed to remedy the situation.

Article 90

1. In the case of public undertakings and undertakings to which Member States grant special or exclusive rights, Member States shall neither enact nor maintain in force any measure contrary to the rules contained in this Treaty, in particular to those rules provided for in Article 7 and Articles 85 to 94.

2. Undertakings entrusted with the operation of services of general economic interest or having the character of a revenue-producing monopoly shall be subject to the rules contained in this Treaty, in particular to the rules on competition, insofar as the application of such rules does not obstruct the performance, in law or in fact, of the particular tasks assigned to them. The development of trade must not be affected to such an extent as would be contrary to the interests of the Community.

3. The Commission shall ensure the application of the provisions of this Article and shall, where necessary, address appropriate directives or decisions to Member States.

Section 2. Dumping

Article 91

1. If during the transitional period, the Commission, on application by a Member State or by any other interested party, finds that dumping is being practised within the common market, it shall address recommendations to the person or persons with whom such practices originate for the purpose of putting an end to them.

Should the practices continue, the Commission shall authorize the injured Member State to take protective measures, the conditions and details of which the Commission shall determine.

2. As soon as this Treaty enters into force, products which originate in or are in free circulation in one Member State and which have been exported to another Member State shall, on reimportation, be admitted into the territory of the first-mentioned State free of all customs duties, quantitative restrictions or measures having equivalent effect. The Commission shall lay down appropriate rules for the application of this paragraph.

Section 3. Aids Granted by States

Article 92

1. Save as otherwise provided in this Treaty, any aid granted by a Member State or through State resources in any form whatsoever which distorts or threatens to distort competition by favouring certain undertakings or the production of certain goods shall, insofar as it affects trade between Member States, be incompatible with the common market.

2. The following shall be compatible with the common market:

(a) aid having a social character, granted to individual consumers, provided that such aid is granted without discrimination related to the origin of the products concerned;

(b) aid to make good the damage caused by natural disasters or exceptional occurrences;

(c) aid granted to the economy of certain areas of the Federal Republic of Germany affected by the division of Germany, insofar as such aid is required in order to compensate for the economic disadvantages caused by that division.

3. The following may be considered to be compatible with the common market:

(a) aid to promote the economic development of areas where the standard of living is abnormally low or where there is serious underemployment;

(b) aid to promote the execution of an important project of common European interest or to remedy a serious disturbance in the economy of a Member State;

(c) aid to facilitate the development of certain economic activities or of certain economic areas, where such aid does not adversely affect trading conditions to an extent contrary to the common interest. However, the aids granted to shipbuilding as of 1 January 1957 shall, insofar as they serve only to compensate for the absence of customs protection, be progressively reduced under the same conditions as apply to the elimination of customs duties, subject to the provisions of this Treaty concerning common commercial policy towards third countries;

(d) such other categories of aid as may be specified by decision of the Council acting by a qualified majority on a proposal from the Commission.[30]

Article 93

1. The Commission shall, in cooperation with Member States, keep under constant review all systems of aid existing in those States. It shall propose to the latter any appropriate measures required by the progressive development or by the functioning of the common market.

2. If, after giving notice to the parties concerned to submit their comments, the Commission finds that aid granted by a State or through State resources is not compatible with the common market having regard to Article 92, or that such aid is being misused, it shall decide that the State concerned shall abolish or alter such aid within a period of time to be determined by the Commission.

If the State concerned does not comply with this decision within the prescribed time, the Commission or any other interested State may, in derogation from the provisions of Articles 169 and 170, refer the matter to the Court of Justice direct.

On application by a Member State, the Council, may, acting unanimously, decide that aid which that State is granting or intends to grant shall be considered to be compatible with the common market, in derogation from the provisions of Article 92 or from the regulations provided for in Article 94, if such a decision is justified by exceptional circumstances. If, as regards the aid in question, the Commission has already initiated the procedure provided for in the first sub-paragraph of this paragraph, the fact that the State concerned has made its application to the Council shall have the effect of suspending that procedure until the Council has made its attitude known.

If, however, the Council has not made its attitude known within three months of the said application being made, the Commission shall give its decision on the case.

3. The Commission shall be informed, in sufficient time to enable it to submit its comments, of any plans to grant or alter aid. If it considers that any such plan is not compatible with the common market having regard to Article 92, it shall without delay initiate the procedure provided for in paragraph 2. The Member State concerned shall not put its proposed measures into effect until this procedure has resulted in a final decision.

Article 94

The Council may, acting by a qualified majority on a proposal from the Commission, make any appropriate regulations for the application of Articles 92 and 93 and may in particular determine the conditions in

---

30. The TEU would redesignate (d) as (e) and add: "(d) aid to promote culture and heritage conservation where such aid does not affect trading conditions and competition in the Community to an extent that is contrary to the common interest;".

which Article 93(3) shall apply and the categories of aid exempted from this procedure.[31]

Chapter 2. Tax Provisions

Article 95

No Member State shall impose, directly or indirectly, on the products of other Member States any internal taxation of any kind in excess of that imposed directly or indirectly on similar domestic products.

Furthermore, no Member State shall impose on the products of other Member States any internal taxation of such a nature as to afford indirect protection to other products.

Member States shall, not later than at the beginning of the second stage, repeal or amend any provisions existing when this Treaty enters into force which conflict with the preceding rules.

Article 96

Where products are exported to the territory of any Member State, any repayment of internal taxation shall not exceed the internal taxation imposed on them whether directly or indirectly.

Article 97

Member States which levy a turnover tax calculated on a cumulative multi-stage tax system may, in the case of internal taxation imposed by them on imported products or of repayments allowed by them on exported products, establish average rates for products or groups of products, provided that there is no infringement of the principles laid down in Articles 95 and 96.

Where the average rates established by a Member State do not conform to these principles, the Commission shall address appropriate directives or decisions to the State concerned.

Article 98

In the case of charges other than turnover taxes, excise duties and other forms of indirect taxation, remissions and repayments in respect of exports to other Member States may not be granted and countervailing charges in respect of imports from Member States may not be imposed unless the measures contemplated have been previously approved for a limited period by the Council acting by a qualified majority on a proposal from the Commission.

Article 99 [32]

The Council shall, acting unanimously on a proposal from the Commission and after consulting the European Parliament,[33] adopt provisions for the harmonization of legislation concerning turnover taxes, excise

---

31. The TEU would require that Parliament be consulted before the Council may adopt these regulations.

32. The SEA (art. 17) required that Parliament be consulted before the adoption of the legislation referred to and added the reference to the internal market.

33. The TEU would add "and the Economic and Social Committee".

duties and other forms of indirect taxation to the extent that such harmonization is necessary to ensure the establishment and the functioning of the internal market within the time-limit laid down in [Article 8a.] [34]

Chapter 3. Approximation of Laws

Article 100

The Council shall, acting unanimously on a proposal from the Commission,[35] issue directives for the approximation of such [provisions laid down by law, regulation or administrative action in] [36] Member States as directly affect the establishment or functioning of the common market.

The European Parliament and the Economic and Social Committee shall be consulted in the case of directives whose implementation would, in one or more Member States, involve the amendment of legislation.

Article 100a [37]

1. By way of derogation from Article 100 and save where otherwise provided in this Treaty, the following provisions shall apply for the achievement of the objectives set out in [Article 8a.] [38] The Council shall, acting by a qualified majority on a proposal from the Commission in cooperation with the European Parliament and after consulting the Economic and Social Committee, adopt the measures for the approximation of the provisions laid down by law, regulation or administrative action in Member States which have as their object the establishment and functioning of the internal market.[39]

2. Paragraph 1 shall not apply to fiscal provisions, to those relating to the free movement of persons nor to those relating to the rights and interests of employed persons.

3. The Commission, in its proposals envisaged in paragraph 1 concerning health, safety, environmental protection and consumer protection, will take as a base a high level of protection.

4. If, after the adoption of a harmonization measure by the Council acting by a qualified majority, a Member State deems it necessary to apply national provisions on grounds of major needs referred to in Article 36, or relating to protection of the environment or the working environment, it shall notify the Commission of these provisions.

The Commission shall confirm the provisions involved after having verified that they are not a means of arbitrary discrimination or a disguised restriction on trade between Member States.

---

34. The TEU would renumber Article 8a as Article 7a.

35. The TEU would add: "and after consulting the European Parliament and the Economic and Social Committee".

36. The TEU would replace the bracketed language with "laws, regulations or administrative provisions of the".

37. The SEA (art. 18) added Article 100a.

38. The TEU would renumber Article 8a as Article 7a.

39. The TEU would require use of the co-decision procedure of new Article 189b instead of the parliamentary cooperation procedure.

By way of derogation from the procedure laid down in Articles 169 and 170, the Commission or any Member State may bring the matter directly before the Court of Justice if it considers that another Member State is making improper use of the powers provided for in this Article.

5. The harmonization measures referred to above shall, in appropriate cases, include a safeguard clause authorizing the Member States to take, for one or more of the non-economic reasons referred to in Article 36, provisional measures subject to a Community control procedure.

Article 100b [40]

1. During 1992, the Commission shall, together with each Member State, draw up an inventory of national laws, regulations and administrative provisions which fall under Article 100a and which have not been harmonized pursuant to that Article.

The Council, acting in accordance with the provisions of Article 100a, may decide that the provisions in force in a Member State must be recognized as being equivalent to those applied by another Member State.

2. The provisions of Article 100a(4) shall apply by analogy.

3. The Commission shall draw up the inventory referred to in the first sub-paragraph of paragraph 1 and shall submit appropriate proposals in good time to allow the Council to act before the end of 1992.

[*Eds. Note*: The TEU would introduce new Articles 100c and 100d, which provide for legislation on a common visa policy.]

Article 101

Where the Commission finds that a difference between the provisions laid down by law, regulation or administrative action in Member States is distorting the conditions of competition in the common market and that the resultant distortion needs to be eliminated, it shall consult the Member States concerned.

If such consultation does not result in an agreement eliminating the distortion in question, the Council shall, on a proposal from the Commission, acting unanimously during the first stage and by a qualified majority thereafter, issue the necessary directives. The Commission and the Council may take any other appropriate measures provided for in this Treaty.

Article 102

1. Where there is reason to fear that the adoption or amendment of a provision laid down by law, regulation or administrative action may cause distortion within the meaning of Article 101, a Member State desiring to proceed therewith shall consult the Commission. After consulting the Member States, the Commission shall recommend to the States concerned such measures as may be appropriate to avoid the distortion in question.

2. If a State desiring to introduce or amend its own provisions does not comply with the recommendation addressed to it by the Commission,

---

40. The SEA (art. 19) added Article 100b.

other Member States shall not be required, in pursuance of Article 101, to amend their own provisions in order to eliminate such distortion. If the Member State which has ignored the recommendation of the Commission causes distortion detrimental only to itself, the provisions of Article 101 shall not apply.

Title II.[41] Economic Policy

[*Eds. Note*: The TEU would replace Articles 102a–109 with new Articles 102a–109m, which provide for the structure and stages of development of an economic and monetary union.]

Chapter 1.[42] Cooperation in Economic and Monetary Policy (Economic and Monetary Union)

Article 102a [43]

1. In order to ensure the convergence of economic and monetary policies which is necessary for the further development of the Community, Member States shall cooperate in accordance with the objectives of Article 104. In so doing, they shall take account of the experience acquired in cooperation within the framework of the European Monetary System (EMS) and in developing the ECU, and shall respect existing powers in this field.

2. Insofar as further development in the field of economic and monetary policy necessitates institutional changes, the provisions of Article 236 shall be applicable. The Monetary Committee and the Committee of Governors of the Central Banks shall also be consulted regarding institutional changes in the monetary area.

Chapter 2.[44] Conjunctural Policy

Article 103 [45]

1. Member States shall regard their conjunctural policies as a matter of common concern. They shall consult each other and the Commission on the measures to be taken in the light of the prevailing circumstances.

2. Without prejudice to any other procedures provided for in this Treaty, the Council may, acting unanimously on a proposal from the Commission, decide upon the measures appropriate to the situation.

3. Acting by a qualified majority on a proposal from the Commission, the Council shall, where required, issue any directives needed to give effect to the measures decided upon under paragraph 2.

4. The procedures provided for in this Article shall also apply if any difficulty should arise in the supply of certain products.

---

41. The TEU would rename Title II as "Title VI—Economic and Monetary Policy".

42. The SEA (art. 20) added Chapter 1 and Article 102a.

43. The TEU would delete this article. See new Articles 102a–109m.

44. Renumbered by SEA article 20(2).

45. The TEU would delete this article. See new Articles 102a–109m.

Chapter 3.[46] Balance of Payments

Article 104 [47]

Each Member State shall pursue the economic policy needed to ensure the equilibrium of its overall balance of payments and to maintain confidence in its currency, while taking care to ensure a high level of employment and a stable level of prices.

Article 105 [48]

1. In order to facilitate attainment of the objectives set out in Article 104, Member States shall coordinate their economic policies. They shall for this purpose provide for cooperation between their appropriate administrative departments and between their central banks.

The Commission shall submit to the Council recommendations on how to achieve such cooperation.

2. In order to promote coordination of the policies of Member States in the monetary field to the full extent needed for the functioning of the common market, a Monetary Committee with advisory status is hereby set up. It shall have the following tasks:

—to keep under review the monetary and financial situation of the Member States and of the Community and the general payments system of the Member States and to report regularly thereon to the Council and to the Commission;

—to deliver opinions at the request of the Council or of the Commission or on its own initiative, for submission to these institutions.

The Member States and the Commission shall each appoint two members of the Monetary Committee.

Article 106 [49]

1. Each Member State undertakes to authorize, in the currency of the Member State in which the creditor or the beneficiary resides, any payments connected with the movement of goods, services or capital, and any transfers of capital and earnings, to the extent that the movement of goods, services, capital and persons between Member States has been liberalized pursuant to this Treaty.

The Member States declare their readiness to undertake the liberalization of payments beyond the extent provided in the preceding subparagraph, insofar as their economic situation in general and the state of their balance of payments in particular so permit.

2. Insofar as movements of goods, services, and capital are limited only by restrictions on payments connected therewith, these restrictions shall be progressively abolished by applying, mutatis mutandis, the provisions of the Chapters relating to the abolition of quantitative restrictions, to the liberalization of services and to the free movement of capital.

---

46. Renumbered by SEA article 20.
47. The TEU would delete this article. See new Articles 102a–109m.
48. Id.
49. Id.

3. Member States undertake not to introduce between themselves any new restrictions on transfers connected with the invisible transactions listed in Annex III to this Treaty.

The progressive abolition of existing restrictions shall be effected in accordance with the provisions of Articles 63 to 65, insofar as such abolition is not governed by the provisions contained in paragraphs 1 and 2 or by the Chapter relating to the free movement of capital.

4. If need be, Member States shall consult each other on the measures to be taken to enable the payments and transfers mentioned in this Article to be effected; such measures shall not prejudice the attainment of the objectives set out in this Chapter.

Article 107 [50]

1. Each Member State shall treat its policy with regard to rates of exchange as a matter of common concern.

2. If a Member State makes an alteration in its rate of exchange which is inconsistent with the objectives set out in Article 104 and which seriously distorts conditions of competition, the Commission may, after consulting the Monetary Committee, authorize other Member States to take for a strictly limited period the necessary measures, the conditions and details of which it shall determine, in order to counter the consequences of such alteration.

Article 108 [51]

1. Where a Member State is in difficulties or is seriously threatened with difficulties as regards its balance of payments either as a result of an overall disequilibrium in its balance of payments, or as a result of the type of currency at its disposal, and where such difficulties are liable in particular to jeopardize the functioning of the common market or the progressive implementation of the common commercial policy, the Commission shall immediately investigate the position of the State in question and the action which, making use of all the means at its disposal, that State has taken or may take in accordance with the provisions of Article 104. The Commission shall state what measures it recommends the State concerned to take.

If the action taken by a Member State and the measures suggested by the Commission do not prove sufficient to overcome the difficulties which have arisen or which threaten, the Commission shall, after consulting the Monetary Committee, recommend to the Council the granting of mutual assistance and appropriate methods therefor.

The Commission shall keep the Council regularly informed of the situation and of how it is developing.

2. The Council, acting by a qualified majority, shall grant such mutual assistance; it shall adopt directives or decisions laying down the conditions and details of such assistance, which may take such forms as:

50. Id. 51. Id.

(a) a concerted approach to or within any other international organizations to which Member States may have recourse;

(b) measures needed to avoid deflection of trade where the State which is in difficulties maintains or reintroduces quantitative restrictions against third countries;

(c) the granting of limited credits by other Member States, subject to their agreement.

During the transitional period, mutual assistance may also take the form of special reductions in customs duties or enlargements of quotas in order to facilitate an increase in imports from the State which is in difficulties, subject to the agreement of the States by which such measures would have to be taken.

3. If the mutual assistance recommended by the Commission is not granted by the Council or if the mutual assistance granted and the measures taken are insufficient, the Commission shall authorize the State which is in difficulties to take protective measures, the conditions and details of which the Commission shall determine.

Such authorization may be revoked and such conditions and details may be changed by the Council acting by a qualified majority.

Article 109 [52]

1. Where a sudden crisis in the balance of payments occurs and a decision within the meaning of Article 108(2) is not immediately taken, the Member State concerned may, as a precaution, take the necessary protective measures. Such measures must cause the least possible disturbance in the functioning of the common market and must not be wider in scope than is strictly necessary to remedy the sudden difficulties which have arisen.

2. The Commission and the other Member States shall be informed of such protective measures not later than when they enter into force. The Commission may recommend to the Council the granting of mutual assistance under Article 108.

3. After the Commission has delivered an opinion and the Monetary Committee has been consulted, the Council may, acting by a qualified majority, decide that the State concerned shall amend, suspend or abolish the protective measures referred to above.

Chapter 4.[53] Commercial Policy

Article 110

By establishing a customs union between themselves Member States aim to contribute, in the common interest, to the harmonious development of world trade, the progressive abolition of restrictions on international trade and the lowering of customs barriers.

---

52. Id.

53. Renumbered by SEA article 20. The TEU would replace Chapter 4 with a new title, "Title VII—Common Commercial Policy".

The common commercial policy shall take into account the favourable effect which the abolition of customs duties between Member States may have on the increase in the competitive strength of undertakings in those States.

Article 111 [54]

The following provisions shall, without prejudice to Articles 115 and 116, apply during the transitional period:

1. Member States shall coordinate their trade relations with third countries so as to bring about, by the end of the transitional period, the conditions needed for implementing a common policy in the field of external trade.

The Commission shall submit to the Council proposals regarding the procedure for common action to be followed during the transitional period and regarding the achievement of uniformity in their commercial policies.

2. The Commission shall submit to the Council recommendations for tariff negotiations with third countries in respect of the common customs tariff.

The Council shall authorize the Commission to open such negotiations.

The Commission shall conduct these negotiations in consultation with a special committee appointed by the Council to assist the Commission in this task and within the framework of such directives as the Council may issue to it.

3. In exercising the powers conferred upon it by this Article, the Council shall act unanimously during the first two stages and by a qualified majority thereafter.

4. Member States shall, in consultation with the Commission, take all necessary measures, particularly those designed to bring about an adjustment of tariff agreements in force with third countries, in order that the entry into force of the common customs tariff shall not be delayed.

5. Member States shall aim at securing as high a level of uniformity as possible between themselves as regards their liberalization lists in relation to third countries or groups of third countries. To this end, the Commission shall make all appropriate recommendations to Member States.

If Member States abolish or reduce quantitative restrictions in relation to third countries, they shall inform the Commission beforehand and shall accord the same treatment to other Member States.

Article 112

1. Without prejudice to obligations undertaken by them within the framework of other international organizations, Member States shall, before the end of the transitional period, progressively harmonize the

---

54. The TEU would repeal Article 111.

systems whereby they grant aid for exports to third countries, to the extent necessary to ensure that competition between undertakings of the Community is not distorted.

On a proposal from the Commission, the Council, shall, acting unanimously until the end of the second stage and by a qualified majority thereafter, issue any directives needed for this purpose.

2. The preceding provisions shall not apply to such drawback of customs duties or charges having equivalent effect nor to such repayment of indirect taxation including turnover taxes, excise duties and other indirect taxes as is allowed when goods are exported from a Member State to a third country, insofar as such drawback or repayment does not exceed the amount imposed, directly or indirectly, on the products exported.

Article 113

1. [After the transitional period has ended,][55] the common commercial policy shall be based on uniform principles, particularly in regard to changes in tariff rates, the conclusion of tariff and trade agreements, the achievement of uniformity in measures of liberalization, export policy and measures to protect trade such as those to be taken in [case][56] of dumping or subsidies.

2. The Commission shall submit proposals to the Council for implementing the common commercial policy.

3. Where agreements with [third countries][57] need to be negotiated, the Commission shall make recommendations to the Council, which shall authorize the Commission to open the necessary negotiations.

The Commission shall conduct these negotiations in consultation with a special committee appointed by the Council to assist the Commission in this task and within the framework of such directives as the Council may issue to it.[58]

4. In exercising the powers conferred upon it by this Article, the Council shall act by a qualified majority.

Article 114 [59]

The agreements referred to in Article 111(2) and in Article 113 shall be concluded by the Council on behalf of the Community, acting unanimously during the first two stages and by a qualified majority thereafter.

Article 115

In order to ensure that the execution of measures of commercial policy taken in accordance with this Treaty by any Member State is not obstructed by deflection of trade, or where differences between such

---

55. The TEU would delete the bracketed language.

56. The TEU would replace "case" with "the event".

57. The TEU would replace "third countries" with "one or more states or international organizations".

58. The TEU would add a new paragraph as follows: "The relevant provisions of Article 228 shall apply."

59. The TEU would repeal Article 114.

measures lead to economic difficulties in one or more of the Member States, the Commission shall recommend the methods for the requisite cooperation between Member States. Failing this, the Commission [shall][60] authorize Member States to take the necessary protective measures, the conditions and details of which it shall determine.

In case of urgency during the transitional period, Member States may themselves take the necessary measures and shall notify them to the other Member States and to the Commission, which may decide that the States concerned shall amend or abolish such measures.[61]

In the selection of such measures, priority shall be given to those which cause the least disturbance to the functioning of the common market [and which take into account the need to expedite, as far as possible, the introduction of the common customs tariff].[62]

Article 116[63]

From the end of the transitional period onward, Member States shall, in respect of all matters of particular interest to the common market, proceed within the framework of international organizations of an economic character only by common action. To this end, the Commission shall submit to the Council, which shall act by a qualified majority, proposals concerning the scope and implementation of such common action.

During the transitional period, Member States shall consult each other for the purpose of concerting the action they take and adopting as far as possible a uniform attitude.

Title III.[64] Social Policy
Chapter 1. Social Provisions
Article 117

Member States agree upon the need to promote improved working conditions and an improved standard of living for workers, so as to make possible their harmonization while the improvement is being maintained.

They believe that such a development will ensue not only from the functioning of the common market, which will favour the harmonization of social systems, but also from the procedures provided for in this Treaty and from the approximation of provisions laid down by law, regulation or administrative action.

Article 118

Without prejudice to the other provisions of this Treaty and in conformity with its general objectives, the Commission shall have the task

---

60. The TEU would replace "shall" with "may".

61. The TEU would amend the second paragraph to delete the reference to the transitional period and to require Member States to obtain the Commission's authorization for any necessary measures.

62. The TEU would delete the bracketed language.

63. The TEU would repeal Article 116.

64. The TEU would rename Title III as "Title VIII—Social Policy, Education, Vocational Training and Youth".

of promoting close cooperation between Member States in the social field, particularly in matters relating to:

— employment;

— labour law and working conditions;

— basic and advanced vocational training;

— social security;

— prevention of occupational accidents and diseases;

— occupational hygiene;

— the right of association, and collective bargaining between employers and workers.

To this end, the Commission shall act in close contact with Member States by making studies, delivering opinions and arranging consultations both on problems arising at national level and on those of concern to international organizations.

Before delivering the opinions provided for in this Article, the Commission shall consult the Economic and Social Committee.

Article 118a [65]

1. Member States shall pay particular attention to encouraging improvements, especially in the working environment, as regards the health and safety of workers, and shall set as their objective the harmonization of conditions in this area, while maintaining the improvements made.

2. In order to help achieve the objective laid down in the first paragraph, the Council, acting by a qualified majority on a proposal from the Commission, in cooperation with the European Parliament and after consulting the Economic and Social Committee, shall adopt, by means of directives, minimum requirements for gradual implementation, having regard to the conditions and technical rules obtaining in each of the Member States.[66]

Such directives shall avoid imposing administrative, financial and legal constraints in a way which would hold back the creation and development of small and medium-sized undertakings.

3. The provisions adopted pursuant to this article shall not prevent any Member State from maintaining or introducing more stringent measures for the protection of working conditions compatible with this Treaty.

Article 118b [67]

The Commission shall endeavour to develop the dialogue between management and labour at European level which could, if the two sides consider it desirable, lead to relations based on agreement.

---

65. The SEA (art. 21) added Article 118a.

66. The TEU would require use of the parliamentary cooperation procedure of new Article 189c.

67. The SEA (art. 22) added Article 118b.

Article 119

Each Member State shall during the first stage ensure and subsequently maintain the application of the principle that men and women should receive equal pay for equal work.

For the purpose of this Article, "pay" means the ordinary basic or minimum wage or salary and any other consideration, whether in cash or in kind, which the worker receives, directly or indirectly, in respect of his employment from his employer.

Equal pay without discrimination based on sex means:

(a) that pay for the same work at piece rates shall be calculated on the basis of the same unit of measurement;

(b) that pay for work at time rates shall be the same for the same job.

Article 120

Member States shall endeavour to maintain the existing equivalence between paid holiday schemes.

Article 121

The Council may, acting unanimously and after consulting the Economic and Social Committee, assign to the Commission tasks in connection with the implementation of common measures, particularly as regards social security for the migrant workers referred to in Articles 48 to 51.

Article 122

The Commission shall include a separate chapter on social developments within the Community in its annual report to the European Parliament.

The European Parliament may invite the Commission to draw up reports on any particular problems concerning social conditions.

Chapter 2. The European Social Fund

Article 123 [68]

In order to improve employment opportunities for workers in the common market and to contribute thereby to raising the standard of living, a European Social Fund is hereby established in accordance with the provisions set out below; it shall have the task of rendering the employment of workers easier and of increasing their geographical and occupational mobility within the Community.

Article 124

The Fund shall be administered by the Commission.

The Commission shall be assisted in this task by a Committee presided over by a member of the Commission and composed of representatives of Governments, trade unions and employers' organizations.

---

68. The TEU would amend the description of the role of the Social Fund to include adaptation to industrial changes.

Article 125 [69]

1. On application by a Member State the Fund shall, within the framework of the rules provided for in Article 127, meet 50 per cent of the expenditure incurred after the entry into force of this Treaty by that State or by a body governed by public law for the purposes of:

(a) ensuring productive re-employment of workers by means of:

—vocational retraining;

—resettlement allowances;

(b) granting aid for the benefit of workers whose employment is reduced or temporarily suspended, in whole or in part, as a result of the conversion of an undertaking to other production, in order that they may retain the same wage level pending their full re-employment.

2. Assistance granted by the Fund towards the cost of vocational retraining shall be granted only if the unemployed workers could not be found employment except in a new occupation and only if they have been in productive employment for at least six months in the occupation for which they have been retrained.

Assistance towards resettlement allowances shall be granted only if the unemployed workers have been caused to change their home within the Community and have been in productive employment for at least six months in their new place of residence.

Assistance for workers in the case of the conversion of an undertaking shall be granted only if:

(a) the workers concerned have again been fully employed in that undertaking for at least six months;

(b) the Government concerned has submitted a plan beforehand, drawn up by the undertaking in question, for that particular conversion and for financing it;

(c) the Commission has given its prior approval to the conversion plan.

Article 126 [70]

When the transitional period has ended, the Council, after receiving the opinion of the Commission and after consulting the Economic and Social Committee and the European Parliament, may:

(a) rule, by a qualified majority, that all or part of the assistance referred to in Article 125 shall no longer be granted; or

(b) unanimously determine what new tasks may be entrusted to the Fund within the framework of its terms of reference as laid down in Article 123.

69. The TEU would repeal the present text and replace it with a general authorization to take decisions relating to the Social Fund by the parliamentary cooperation procedure of new Article 189c.

70. The TEU would repeal Articles 126–128.

Article 127 [71]

The Council shall, acting by a qualified majority on a proposal from the Commission and after consulting the Economic and Social Committee and the European Parliament, lay down the provisions required to implement Articles 124 to 126; in particular it shall determine in detail the conditions under which assistance shall be granted by the Fund in accordance with Article 125 and the classes of undertakings whose workers shall benefit from the assistance provided for in Article 125(1)(b).

Article 128 [72]

The Council shall, acting on a proposal from the Commission and after consulting the Economic and Social Committee, lay down general principles for implementing a common vocational training policy capable of contributing to the harmonious development both of the national economies and of the common market.

[*Eds. Note:* The TEU would introduce a new "Chapter 3—Education, Vocational Training and Youth", comprised of Articles 126 and 127, which provide for common educational and vocational training policies and authorize legislation for each. The TEU would also introduce a new "Title IX—Culture", consisting of Article 128, which provides for action to enhance the common cultural heritage.]

Title IV.[73]   The European Investment Bank

Article 129 [74]

A European Investment Bank is hereby established; it shall have legal personality.

The members of the European Investment Bank shall be the Member States.

The Statute of the European Investment Bank is laid down in a Protocol annexed to this Treaty.

Article 130 [75]

The task of the European Investment Bank shall be to contribute, by having recourse to the capital market and utilizing its own resources, to the balanced and steady development of the common market in the interest of the Community. For this purpose the Bank shall, operating on a non-profitmaking basis, grant loans and give guarantees which facilitate the financing of the following projects in all sectors of the economy:

(a) projects for developing less-developed regions;

(b) projects for modernizing or converting undertakings or for developing fresh activities called for by the progressive establishment of the

---

71. Id.
72. Id.
73. The TEU would repeal Title IV and replace it with provisions on the European Investment Bank in new Articles 198d and e.
74. The TEU would repeal Article 129. See new Articles 198d and e.
75. Id.

common market, where these projects are of such a size or nature that they cannot be entirely financed by the various means available in the individual Member States;

(c) projects of common interest to several Member States which are of such a size or nature that they cannot be entirely financed by the various means available in the individual Member States.

[*Eds. Note:* The TEU would introduce several new titles at this point. "Title X—Public Health" would consist of new Article 129, authorizing Community action and legislation in this field. "Title XI—Consumer Protection" would consist of new Article 129a authorizing legislation for this purpose. "Title XII—Trans–European Networks" would comprise new Articles 129b–129d, which authorize guidelines and action to create and support such networks in the areas of transport, telecommunications and energy infra structures. "Title XIII—Industry" would consist of new Article 130, authorizing action to develop and support a Community industrial policy.]

Title V.[76] Economic and Social Cohesion
Article 130a [77]

In order to promote its overall harmonious development, the Community shall develop and pursue its actions leading to the strengthening of its economic and social cohesion.

In particular the Community shall aim at reducing disparities between the various regions and the backwardness of the least-favoured regions.

Article 130b [78]

Member States shall conduct their economic policies, and shall coordinate them, in such a way as, in addition, to attain the objectives set out in Article 130a. The implementation of the common policies and of the internal market shall take into account the objectives set out in Article 130a and in Article 130c and shall contribute to their achievement. The Community shall support the achievement of these objectives by the action it takes through the structural Funds (European Agricultural Guidance and Guarantee Fund, Guidance Section, European Social Fund, European Regional Development Fund), the European Investment Bank and the other existing financial instruments.

Article 130c [79]

The European Regional Development Fund is intended to help redress the principal regional imbalances in the Community through participating in the development and structural adjustment of regions whose

---

76. Title V was added by SEA Article 23. The TEU would renumber it as Title XIV.

77. The SEA (art. 23) added Article 130a. The TEU would amend the second paragraph slightly, and add "including rural areas" at the end.

78. The SEA (art. 23) added Article 130b. The TEU would amend the text and add two new paragraphs requiring regular Commission reports and authorizing certain Council action.

79. The SEA (art. 23) added Article 130c. The TEU would amend the text slightly.

development is lagging behind and in the conversion of declining industrial regions.

Article 130d [80]

Once the Single European Act enters into force the Commission shall submit a comprehensive proposal to the Council, the purpose of which will be to make such amendments to the structure and operational rules of the existing structural Funds (European Agricultural Guidance and Guarantee Fund, Guidance Section, European Social Fund, European Regional Development Fund) as are necessary to clarify and rationalize their tasks in order to contribute to the achievement of the objectives set out in Article 130a and Article 130c, to increase their efficiency and to coordinate their activities between themselves and with the operations of the existing financial instruments. The Council shall act unanimously on this proposal within a period of one year, after consulting the European Parliament and the Economic and Social Committee.

Article 130e [81]

After adoption of the decision referred to in Article 130d, implementing decisions relating to the European Regional Development Fund shall be taken by the Council, acting by a qualified majority on a proposal from the Commission and in cooperation with the European Parliament.

With regard to the European Agricultural Guidance and Guarantee Fund, Guidance Section and the European Social Fund, Articles 43, 126 and 127 remain applicable respectively.

Title VI.[82] Research and Technological Development

Article 130f [83]

1. The Community's aim shall be to strengthen the scientific and technological basis of European industry and to encourage it to become more competitive at international level.

2. In order to achieve this, it shall encourage undertakings including small and medium-sized undertakings, research centres and universities in their research and technological development activities; it shall support their efforts to cooperate with one another, aiming, notably, at enabling undertakings to exploit the Community's internal market potential to the full, in particular through the opening up of national public contracts, the definition of common standards and the removal of legal and fiscal barriers to that cooperation.

3. In the achievement of these aims, special account shall be taken of the connection between the common research and technological development effort, the establishment of the internal market and the imple-

---

80. The SEA (art. 23) added Article 130d. The TEU would amend the text, notably to create a new Cohesion Fund to help finance environmental and transport projects.

81. The SEA (art. 23) added Article 130e. The TEU would amend the text slightly.

82. The SEA (art. 24) added Title VI. The TEU would renumber it as Title XV.

83. The SEA (art. 24) added this article. The TEU would amend the text slightly.

mentation of common policies, particularly as regards competition and trade.

Article 130g [84]

In pursuing these objectives the Community shall carry out the following activities, complementing the activities carried out in the Member States:

(a) implementation of research, technological development and demonstration programmes, by promoting cooperation with undertakings, research centres and universities;

(b) promotion of cooperation in the field of Community research, technological development, and demonstration with third countries and international organizations;

(c) dissemination and optimization of the results of activities in Community research, technological development, and demonstration;

(d) stimulation of the training and mobility of researchers in the Community.

Article 130h [85]

Member States shall, in liaison with the Commission, coordinate among themselves the policies and programmes carried out at national level. In close contact with the Member States, the Commission may take any useful initiative to promote such coordination.

Article 130i [86]

1. The Community shall adopt a multiannual framework programme setting out all its activities. The framework programme shall lay down the scientific and technical objectives, define their respective priorities, set out the main lines of the activities envisaged and fix the amount deemed necessary, the detailed rules for financial participation by the Community in the programme as a whole and the breakdown of this amount between the various activities envisaged.

2. The framework programme may be adapted or supplemented, as the situation changes.

Article 130k [87]

The framework programme shall be implemented through specific programmes developed within each activity. Each specific programme shall define the detailed rules for implementing it, fix its duration and provide for the means deemed necessary.

The Council shall define the detailed arrangements for the dissemination of knowledge resulting from the specific programmes.

---

84. Id.
85. Id.
86. The SEA (art. 24) added this article. The TEU would amend it slightly and incorporate in it the present Article 130k.
87. The SEA (art. 24) added this article. The TEU would incorporate it into Article 130i and add a new Article 130j.

Article 130l [88]

In implementing the multiannual framework programme, supplementary programmes may be decided on involving the participation of certain Member States only, which shall finance them subject to possible Community participation.

The Council shall adopt the rules applicable to supplementary programmes, particularly as regards the dissemination of knowledge and the access of other Member States.

Article 130m [89]

In implementing the multiannual framework programme, the Community may make provision, with the agreement of the Member States concerned, for participation in research and development programmes undertaken by several Member States, including participation in the structures created for the execution of those programmes.

Article 130n [90]

In implementing the multiannual framework programme, the Community may make provision for cooperation in Community research, technological development and demonstration with third countries or international organizations.

The detailed arrangements for such cooperation may be the subject of international agreements between the Community and the third parties concerned which shall be negotiated and concluded in accordance with Article 228.

Article 130o [91]

The Community may set up joint undertakings or any other structure necessary for the efficient execution of programmes of Community research, technological development and demonstration.

Article 130p [92]

1. The detailed arrangements for financing each programme, including any Community contribution, shall be established at the time of the adoption of the programme.

2. The amount of the Community's annual contribution shall be laid down under the budgetary procedure, without prejudice to other possible methods of Community financing. The estimated cost of the specific programmes must not in aggregate exceed the financial provision in the framework programme.

---

88. The SEA (art. 24) added Article 130 *l*. The TEU would renumber it as Article 130k and amend it slightly.

89. The SEA (art. 24) added Article 130m. The TEU would renumber it as Article 130 *l* and amend it slightly.

90. The SEA (art. 24) added Article 130n. The TEU would renumber it as Article 130m and amend it slightly.

91. The SEA (art. 24) added Article 130 *o*. The TEU would renumber it as Article 130n and amend it slightly.

92. The SEA (art. 24) added Article 130p. The TEU would repeal it.

Article 130q [93]

1. The Council shall, acting unanimously on a proposal from the Commission and after consulting the European Parliament and the Economic and Social Committee, adopt the provisions referred to in Articles 130i and 130 o.

2. The Council shall, acting by a qualified majority on a proposal from the Commission, after consulting the Economic and Social Committee, and in cooperation with the European Parliament, adopt the provisions referred to in Articles 130k, 130 *l*, 130m, 130n and 130p(1). The adoption of these supplementary programmes shall also require the agreement of the Member States concerned.

[*Eds. Note:* The TEU would add a new Article 130p requiring the Commission to make annual reports to the Parliament and the Council.]

Title VII.[94] Environment

Article 130r [95]

1. Action by the Community relating to the environment shall have the following objectives:

(i) to preserve, protect and improve the quality of the environment;

(ii) to contribute towards protecting human health;

(iii) to ensure a prudent and rational utilization of natural resources.

2. Action by the Community relating to the environment shall be based on the principles that preventive action should be taken, that environmental damage should as a priority be rectified at source, and that the polluter should pay. Environmental protection requirements shall be a component of the Community's other policies.

3. In preparing its action relating to the environment, the Community shall take account of:

(i) available scientific and technical data;

(ii) environmental conditions in the various regions of the Community;

(iii) the potential benefits and costs of action or of lack of action;

(iv) the economic and social development of the Community as a whole and the balanced development of its regions.

4. The Community shall take action relating to the environment to the extent to which the objectives referred to in paragraph 1 can be attained better at Community level than at the level of the individual Member States. Without prejudice to certain measures of a Community

---

93. The SEA (art. 24) added Article 130q. The TEU would renumber it as Article 130 *o* and amend it slightly.

94. The SEA (art. 25) added Title VII. The TEU would renumber it as Title XVI.

95. The SEA (art. 25) added Article 130r. The TEU would substantially amend the text, notably in paragraphs 1 and 2.

nature, the Member States shall finance and implement the other measures.

5. Within their respective spheres of competence, the Community and the Member States shall cooperate with third countries and with the relevant international organizations. The arrangements for Community cooperation may be the subject of agreements between the Community and the third parties concerned, which shall be negotiated and concluded in accordance with Article 228.

The previous paragraph shall be without prejudice to Member States' competence to negotiate in international bodies and to conclude international agreements.

Article 130s [96]

The Council, acting unanimously on a proposal from the Commission and after consulting the European Parliament and the Economic and Social Committee, shall decide what action is to be taken by the Community.

The Council shall, under the conditions laid down in the preceding sub-paragraph, define those matters on which decisions are to be taken by a qualified majority.

Article 130t [97]

The protective measures adopted in common pursuant to Article 130s shall not prevent any Member State from maintaining or introducing more stringent protective measures compatible with this Treaty.

[*Eds. Note*: The TEU would add a new "Title XVII—Development Cooperation", comprised of Articles 130u–130y, which would define Community policy toward developing states and authorize aid and other measures.]

PART FOUR
ASSOCIATION OF THE OVERSEAS COUNTRIES AND TERRITORIES

Article 131

The Member States agree to associate with the Community the non-European countries and territories which have special relations with Belgium, Denmark, France, Italy, the Netherlands and the United Kingdom. These countries and territories (hereinafter called the "countries and territories") are listed in Annex IV to this Treaty.

The purpose of association shall be to promote the economic and social development of the countries and territories and to establish close economic relations between them and the Community as a whole.

---

96. The SEA (art. 25) added this article. The TEU would substantially amend it, providing for the parliamentary cooperation procedure for most legislative action in the first paragraph, but indicating in the second paragraph that certain types of legislation must be adopted by unanimous vote of the Council after consulting the Parliament.

97. The SEA (art. 25) added this article. The TEU would amend it slightly.

In accordance with the principles set out in the Preamble to this Treaty, association shall serve primarily to further the interests and prosperity of the inhabitants of these countries and territories in order to lead them to the economic, social and cultural development to which they aspire.

Article 132

Association shall have the following objectives:

1. Member States shall apply to their trade with the countries and territories the same treatment as they accord each other pursuant to this Treaty.

2. Each country or territory shall apply to its trade with Member States and with the other countries and territories the same treatment as that which it applies to the European State with which it has special relations.

3. The Member States shall contribute to the investments required for the progressive development of these countries and territories.

4. For investments financed by the Community, participation in tenders and supplies shall be open on equal terms to all natural and legal persons who are nationals of a Member State or of one of the countries and territories.

5. In relations between Member States and the countries and territories the right of establishment of nationals and companies or firms shall be regulated in accordance with the provisions and procedures laid down in the chapter relating to the right of establishment and on a non-discriminatory basis, subject to any special provisions laid down pursuant to Article 136.

Article 133

1. Customs duties on imports into the Member States of goods originating in the countries and territories shall be completely abolished in conformity with the progressive abolition of customs duties between Member States in accordance with the provisions of this Treaty.

2. Customs duties on imports into each country or territory from Member States or from the other countries or territories shall be progressively abolished in accordance with the provisions of Articles 12, 13, 14, 15 and 17.

3. The countries and territories may, however, levy customs duties which meet the needs of their development and industrialization or produce revenue for their budgets.

The duties referred to in the preceding sub-paragraph shall nevertheless be progressively reduced to the level of those imposed on imports of products from the Member State with which each country or territory has special relations. The percentages and the timetable of the reductions provided for under this Treaty shall apply to the difference between the duty imposed on a product coming from the Member State which has special relations with the country or territory concerned and the duty imposed on the same product coming from within the Community on entry into the importing country or territory.

4. Paragraph 2 shall not apply to countries and territories which, by reason of the particular international obligations by which they are bound, already apply a non-discriminatory customs tariff when this Treaty enters into force.

5. The introduction of or any change in customs duties imposed on goods imported into the countries and territories shall not, either in law or in fact, give rise to any direct or indirect discrimination between imports from the various Member States.

Article 134

If the level of the duties applicable to goods from a third country on entry into a country or territory is liable, when the provisions of Article 133(1) have been applied, to cause deflections of trade to the detriment of any Member State, the latter may request the Commission to propose to the other Member States the measures needed to remedy the situation.

Article 135

Subject to the provisions relating to public health, public security or public policy, freedom of movement within Member States for workers from the countries and territories, and within the countries and territories for workers from Member States, shall be governed by agreements to be concluded subsequently with the unanimous approval of Member States.

Article 136

For an initial period of five years after the entry into force of this Treaty, the details of and procedure for the association of the countries and territories with the Community shall be determined by an Implementing Convention annexed to this Treaty.

Before the Convention referred to in the preceding paragraph expires, the Council shall, acting unanimously, lay down provisions for a further period, on the basis of the experience acquired and of the principles set out in this Treaty.

Article 136a

The provisions of Articles 131 to 136 shall apply to Greenland, subject to the specific provisions for Greenland set out in the Protocol on special arrangements for Greenland, annexed to this Treaty.

PART FIVE
INSTITUTIONS OF THE COMMUNITY
Title I. Provisions Governing the Institutions
Chapter 1. The Institutions
Section 1. The European Parliament

Article 137

The European Parliament, which shall consist of representatives of the peoples of the States brought together in the Community, shall exercise the [advisory and supervisory] powers [which are] conferred upon it by this Treaty.[98]

Article 138 [99]

1. The representatives in the European Parliament of the peoples of the States brought together in the Community shall be elected by direct universal suffrage.

2. The number of representatives elected in each Member State is as follows:

Belgium	24
Denmark	16
Germany	81
Greece	24
Spain	60
France	81
Ireland	15
Italy	81
Luxembourg	6
Netherlands	25
Portugal	24
United Kingdom	81

3. The European Parliament shall draw up proposals for elections by direct universal suffrage in accordance with a uniform procedure in all Member States.

The Council shall, acting unanimously,[100] lay down the appropriate provisions, which it shall recommend to Member States for adoption in accordance with their respective constitutional requirements.

[*Eds. Note*: The TEU would add new Articles 138a–138e, which, among other things, authorize the Parliament to request the Commission to submit a proposal for Community action, permit citizens of the Union to petition Parliament, and create the office of Ombudsman.]

Article 139

The European Parliament shall hold an annual session. It shall meet, without requiring to be convened, on the second Tuesday in March.

The European Parliament may meet in extraordinary session at the request of a majority of its members or at the request of the Council or of the Commission.

Article 140

The European Parliament shall elect its President and its officers from among its members.

---

98. The TEU would delete the bracketed language.

99. Paragraphs 1 and 2 of this Article were replaced by Articles 1 and 2 of the Act concerning the election of the representatives of the European Parliament, as amended by later accession treaties.

100. The TEU would add: "after obtaining the assent of the European Parliament, which shall act by a majority of its component members".

Members of the Commission may attend all meetings and shall, at their request, be heard on behalf of the Commission.

The Commission shall reply orally or in writing to questions put to it by the European Parliament or by its members.

The Council shall be heard by the European Parliament in accordance with the conditions laid down by the Council in its rules of procedure.

Article 141

Save as otherwise provided in this Treaty, the European Parliament shall act by an absolute majority of the votes cast.

The rules of procedure shall determine the quorum.

Article 142

The European Parliament shall adopt its rules of procedure, acting by a majority of its members.

The proceedings of the European Parliament shall be published in the manner laid down in its rules of procedure.

Article 143

The European Parliament shall discuss in open session the annual general report submitted to it by the Commission.

Article 144

If a motion of censure on the activities of the Commission is tabled before it, the European Parliament shall not vote thereon until at least three days after the motion has been tabled and only by open vote.

If the motion of censure is carried by a two-third majority of the votes cast, representing a majority of the members of the European Parliament, the members of the Commission shall resign as a body. They shall continue to deal with current business until they are replaced in accordance with Article 158.[101]

Section 2. The Council

Article 145

To ensure that the objectives set out in this Treaty are attained, the Council shall, in accordance with the provisions of this Treaty:

— ensure coordination of the general economic policies of the Member States;

— have power to take decisions;

— confer on the Commission, in the acts which the Council adopts, powers for the implementation of the rules which the Council lays down. The Council may impose certain requirements in respect of the exercise of these powers. The Council may also reserve the right, in specific cases, to exercise directly implementing powers itself. The procedures referred to above must be consonant with principles and rules to be laid down in

---

101. The TEU would slightly amend the second paragraph.

advance by the Council, acting unanimously on a proposal from the Commission and after obtaining the Opinion of the European Parliament.[102]

Article 146 [103]

The Council shall consist of [representatives of the Member States. Each Government shall delegate to it one of its members.]

The office of President shall be held for a term of six months by each member of the Council in turn, in the following order of Member States:

— for a first cycle of six years: Belgium, Denmark, Germany, Greece, Spain, France, Ireland, Italy, Luxembourg, Netherlands, Portugal, United Kingdom,

— for the following cycle of six years: Denmark, Belgium, Greece, Germany, France, Spain, Italy, Ireland, Netherlands, Luxembourg, United Kingdom, Portugal.

Article 147 [104]

The Council shall meet when convened by its President on his own initiative or at the request of one of its members or of the Commission.

Article 148

1. Save as otherwise provided in this Treaty, the Council shall act by a majority of its members.

2. Where the Council is required to act by a qualified majority, the votes of its members shall be weighted as follows:

Belgium	5
Denmark	3
Germany	10
Greece	5
Spain	8
France	10
Ireland	3
Italy	10
Luxembourg	2
Netherlands	5
Portugal	5
United Kingdom	10

For their adoption, acts of the Council shall require at least:

— 54 votes in favour where this Treaty requires them to be adopted on a proposal from the Commission,

---

102. The SEA (art. 10) added the last indent.

103. This article was repealed by the Merger Treaty. The text quoted is the Merger Treaty provision that effectively replaced it. The TEU would add a new Article 146 that is essentially the same as the quoted text, except that the bracketed language would be replaced by: "a representative of each Member State at ministerial level, authorized to commit the government of that Member State."

104. This article was repealed by the Merger Treaty. The text quoted is the Merger Treaty provision that effectively replaced it. The TEU would add a new Article 147 that is identical to the quoted text.

— 54 votes in favour, cast by at least eight members, in other cases.

3. Abstentions by members present in person or represented shall not prevent the adoption by the Council of acts which require unanimity.

Article 149 [105]

1. Where, in pursuance of this Treaty, the Council acts on a proposal from the Commission, unanimity shall be required for an act constituting an amendment to that proposal.

2. Where, in pursuance of this Treaty, the Council acts in cooperation with the European Parliament, the following procedure shall apply:

(a) The Council, acting by a qualified majority under the conditions of paragraph 1, on a proposal from the Commission and after obtaining the Opinion of the European Parliament, shall adopt a common position.

(b) The Council's common position shall be communicated to the European Parliament. The Council and the Commission shall inform the European Parliament fully of the reasons which led the Council to adopt its common position and also of the Commission's position.

If, within three months of such communication, the European Parliament approves this common position or has not taken a decision within that period, the Council shall definitively adopt the act in question in accordance with the common position.

(c) The European Parliament may within the period of three months referred to in point (b), by an absolute majority of its component members, propose amendments to the Council's common position. The European Parliament may also, by the same majority, reject the Council's common position. The result of the proceedings shall be transmitted to the Council and the Commission.

If the European Parliament has rejected the Council's common position, unanimity shall be required for the Council to act on a second reading.

(d) The Commission shall, within a period of one month, re-examine the proposal on the basis of which the Council adopted its common position, by taking into account the amendments proposed by the European Parliament.

The Commission shall forward to the Council, at the same time as its re-examined proposal, the amendments of the European Parliament which it has not accepted, and shall express its opinion on them. The Council may adopt these amendments unanimously.

(e) The Council, acting by a qualified majority, shall adopt the proposal as re-examined by the Commission.

Unanimity shall be required for the Council to amend the proposal as re-examined by the Commission.

105. The SEA (art. 7) amended the text to provide for the parliamentary cooperation procedure. The TEU would repeal this article. The text on modes of legislation, expanded to include the co-decision procedure, would be placed in new Articles 189a–189c.

(f) In the cases referred to in points (c), (d) and (e), the Council shall be required to act within a period of three months. If no decision is taken within this period, the Commission proposal shall be deemed not to have been adopted.

(g) The periods referred to in points (b) and (f) may be extended by a maximum of one month by common accord between the Council and the European Parliament.

3. As long as the Council has not acted, the Commission may alter its proposal at any time during the procedures mentioned in paragraphs 1 and 2.

Article 150

Where a vote is taken, any member of the Council may also act on behalf of not more than one other member.

Article 151 [106]

The Council shall adopt its rules of procedure.

A committee consisting of the Permanent Representatives of the Member States shall be responsible for preparing the work of the Council and for carrying out the tasks assigned to it by the Council.

Article 152

The Council may request the Commission to undertake any studies the Council considers desirable for the attainment of the common objectives, and to submit to it any appropriate proposals.

Article 153

The Council shall, after receiving an opinion from the Commission, determine the rules governing the committees provided for in this Treaty.

Article 154 [107]

The Council shall, acting by a qualified majority, determine the salaries, allowances and pensions of the President and members of the Commission, and of the President, Judges, Advocates–General and Registrar of the Court of Justice. It shall also, again by a qualified majority, determine any payment to be made instead of remuneration.

Section 3. The Commission

Article 155

In order to ensure the proper functioning and development of the common market, the Commission shall:

— ensure that the provisions of this Treaty and the measures taken by the institutions pursuant thereto are applied;

---

106. This article was repealed by the Merger Treaty. The text quoted is the Merger Treaty provision that effectively replaced it. The TEU would add a new Article 151 that is essentially the same as the quoted text, but adds a reference to the General Secretariat.

107. This article was repealed by the Merger Treaty. The text quoted is the Merger Treaty provision that effectively replaced it. The TEU would add a new Article 154 that is identical to the quoted text.

— formulate recommendations or deliver opinions on matters dealt with in this Treaty, if it expressly so provides or if the Commission considers it necessary;

— have its own power of decision and participate in the shaping of measures taken by the Council and by the European Parliament in the manner provided for in this Treaty;

— exercise the powers conferred on it by the Council for the implementation of the rules laid down by the latter.

Article 156 [108]

The Commission shall publish annually, not later than one month before the opening of the session of the European Parliament, a general report on the activities of the Communities.

Article 157 [109]

1. The Commission shall consist of 17 members, who shall be chosen on the grounds of their general competence and whose independence is beyond doubt.

The number of members of the Commission may be altered by the Council, acting unanimously.

Only nationals of Member States may be members of the Commission.

The Commission must include at least one national of each of the Member States, but may not include more than two members having the nationality of the same State.

2. The members of the Commission shall, in the general interest of the Communities, be completely independent in the performance of their duties.

In the performance of these duties, they shall neither seek nor take instructions from any Government or from any other body.

They shall refrain from any action incompatible with their duties. Each Member State undertakes to respect this principle and not to seek to influence the members of the Commission in the performance of their tasks.

The members of the Commission may not, during their term of office, engage in any other occupation, whether gainful or not. When entering upon their duties they shall give a solemn undertaking that, both during and after their term of office, they will respect the obligations arising therefrom and in particular their duty to behave with integrity and discretion as regards the acceptance, after they have ceased to hold office, of certain appointments or benefits. In the event of any breach of these obligations, the Court of Justice may, on application by the Council or the Commission, rule that the member concerned be, according to the circumstances, either compulsorily retired in accordance with the provisions of

---

108. This article was repealed by the Merger Treaty. The text quoted is the Merger Treaty provision that effectively replaced it. The TEU adds a new article that is virtually identical to the quoted text.

109. Id.

Article [160] or deprived of his right to a pension or other benefits in its stead.

Article 158 [110]

The members of the Commission shall be appointed by common accord of the Governments of the Member States.

Their term of office shall be four years. It shall be renewable.

Article 159 [111]

Apart from normal replacement, or death, the duties of a member of the Commission shall end when he resigns or is compulsorily retired.

The vacancy thus caused shall be filled for the remainder of the member's term of office. The Council may, acting unanimously, decide that such a vacancy need not be filled.

Save in the case of compulsory retirement under the provisions of Article [160], members of the Commission shall remain in office until they have been replaced.

Article 160 [112]

If any member of the Commission no longer fulfils the conditions required for the performance of his duties or if he has been guilty of serious misconduct, the Court of Justice may, on application by the Council or the Commission, compulsorily retire him.

Article 161 [113]

The President and the six Vice-Presidents of the Commission shall be appointed from among its members for a term of two years in accordance with the same procedure as that laid down for the appointment of members of the Commission. Their appointments may be renewed.

The Council, acting unanimously, may amend the provisions concerning Vice-Presidents.

Save where the entire Commission is replaced, such appointments shall be made after the Commission has been consulted.

In the event of retirement or death, the President and the Vice-Presidents shall be replaced for the remainder of their term of office in accordance with the preceding provisions.

---

110. This article was repealed by the Merger Treaty. The text quoted is the Merger Treaty provision that effectively replaced it. The TEU would add a new Article 158 that would change the term of the Commission members from four to five years and provide a new procedure for the appointment of the President and other members of the Commission.

111. This article was repealed by the Merger Treaty. The text quoted is the Merger Treaty provision that effectively replaced it. The TEU would add a new Article 159 that is similar, but parallels the appointment procedure of new Article 158.

112. This article was repealed by the Merger Treaty. The text quoted is the Merger Treaty provision that effectively replaced it. The TEU would add a new Article 160 that is identical to the quoted text.

113. This article was repealed by the Merger Treaty. The text quoted is the Merger Treaty provision that effectively replaced it. The TEU would add a new Article 161 that substantially revises the quoted text, authorizing only one or two Vice-Presidents, to be appointed by the Commission.

Article 162 [114]

The Council and the Commission shall consult each other and shall settle by common accord their methods of cooperation.

The Commission shall adopt its rules of procedure so as to ensure that both it and its departments operate in accordance with the provisions of the Treaties establishing the European Coal and Steel Community, the European Economic Community and the European Atomic Energy Community, and of this Treaty. It shall ensure that these rules are published.

Article 163 [115]

The Commission shall act by a majority of the number of members provided for in Article [157].

A meeting of the Commission shall be valid only if the number of members laid down in its rules of procedure is present.

Section 4. The Court of Justice

Article 164

The Court of Justice shall ensure that in the interpretation and application of this Treaty the law is observed.

Article 165

The Court of Justice shall consist of thirteen Judges.

The Court of Justice shall sit in plenary session. It may, however, form Chambers, each consisting of three or five Judges, either to undertake certain preparatory inquiries or to adjudicate on particular categories of cases in accordance with rules laid down for these purposes.

Whenever the Court of Justice hears cases brought before it by a Member State or by one of the institutions of the Community or, to the extent that the Chambers of the Court do not have the requisite jurisdiction under the Rules of Procedure, has to give preliminary rulings on questions submitted to it pursuant to Article 177, it shall sit in plenary session.[116]

Should the Court of Justice so request, the Council may, acting unanimously, increase the number of Judges and make the necessary adjustments to the second and third paragraphs of this Article and to the second paragraph of Article 167.

Article 166

The Court of Justice shall be assisted by six Advocates–General.

---

114. This article was repealed by the Merger Treaty. The text quoted is the Merger Treaty provision that effectively replaced it. The TEU would add a new Article 162 that is virtually identical to the quoted text.

115. This article was repealed by the Merger Treaty. The text quoted is the Merger Treaty provision that effectively replaced it. The TEU would add a new Article 163 that is identical to the quoted text.

116. The TEU would replace this paragraph with: "The Court of Justice shall sit in plenary session when a Member State or a Community institution that is a party to the proceeding so requests."

It shall be the duty of the Advocate–General, acting with complete impartiality and independence, to make, in open court, reasoned submissions on cases brought before the Court of Justice, in order to assist the Court in the performance of the task assigned to it in Article 164.

Should the Court of Justice so request, the Council may, acting unanimously, increase the number of Advocates–General and make the necessary adjustments to the third paragraph of Article 167.

Article 167

The Judges and Advocates–General shall be chosen from persons whose independence is beyond doubt and who possess the qualifications required for appointment to the highest judicial offices in their respective countries or who are jurisconsults of recognized competence; they shall be appointed by common accord of the Governments of the Member States for a term of six years.

Every three years there shall be a partial replacement of the Judges. Seven and six Judges shall be replaced alternately.

Every three years there shall be a partial replacement of the Advocates–General. Three Advocates–General shall be replaced on each occasion.

Retiring Judges and Advocates–General shall be eligible for reappointment.

The Judges shall elect the President of the Court of Justice from among their number for a term of three years. He may be re-elected.

Article 168

The Court of Justice shall appoint its Registrar and lay down the rules governing his service.

Article 168a [117]

1. At the request of the Court of Justice and after consulting the Commission and the European Parliament, the Council may, acting unanimously, attach to the Court of Justice a court with jurisdiction to hear and determine at first instance, subject to a right of appeal to the Court of Justice on points of law only and in accordance with the conditions laid down by the Statute, certain classes of action or proceeding brought by natural or legal persons. That court shall not be competent to hear and determine actions brought by Member States or by Community institutions or questions referred for a preliminary ruling under Article 177.

2. The Council, following the procedure laid down in paragraph 1, shall determine the composition of that court and adopt the necessary adjustments and additional provisions to the Statute of the Court of Justice. Unless the Council decides otherwise, the provisions of this Treaty relating to the Court of Justice, in particular the provisions of the Protocol on the Statute of the Court of Justice, shall apply to that court.

---

117. The SEA (art. 11) added Article 168a. The TEU would modify the text to refer expressly to the Court of First Instance and to augment its possible jurisdiction.

3. The members of that court shall be chosen from persons whose independence is beyond doubt and who possess the ability required for appointment to judicial office; they shall be appointed by common accord of the Governments of the Member States for a term of six years. The membership shall be partially renewed every three years. Retiring members shall be eligible for reappointment.

4. That court shall establish its rules of procedure in agreement with the Court of Justice. Those rules shall require the unanimous approval of the Council.

Article 169

If the Commission considers that a Member State has failed to fulfil an obligation under this Treaty, it shall deliver a reasoned opinion on the matter after giving the State concerned the opportunity to submit its observations.

If the State concerned does not comply with the opinion within the period laid down by the Commission, the latter may bring the matter before the Court of Justice.

Article 170

A Member State which considers that another Member State has failed to fulfil an obligation under this Treaty may bring the matter before the Court of Justice.

Before a Member State brings an action against another Member State for an alleged infringement of an obligation under this Treaty, it shall bring the matter before the Commission.

The Commission shall deliver a reasoned opinion after each of the States concerned has been given the opportunity to submit its own case and its observations on the other party's case both orally and in writing.

If the Commission has not delivered an opinion within three months of the date on which the matter was brought before it, the absence of such opinion shall not prevent the matter from being brought before the Court of Justice.

Article 171 [118]

If the Court of Justice finds that a Member State has failed to fulfil an obligation under this Treaty, the State shall be required to take the necessary measures to comply with the judgment of the Court of Justice.

Article 172

Regulations [made][119] by the Council pursuant to the provisions of this Treaty may give the Court of Justice unlimited jurisdiction in regard to the penalties provided for in such regulations.

---

118. The TEU would substantially amend Article 171 to provide for a proceeding in which penalties can be imposed upon delinquent Member States.

119. The TEU would replace "made" with "adopted jointly by the European Parliament and the Council and".

Article 173 [120]

The Court of Justice shall review the legality of acts of the Council and the Commission other than recommendations or opinions. It shall for this purpose have jurisdiction in actions brought by a Member State, the Council or the Commission on grounds of lack of competence, infringement of an essential procedural requirement, infringement of this Treaty or of any rule of law relating to its application, or misuse of powers.

Any natural or legal person may, under the same conditions, institute proceedings against a decision addressed to that person or against a decision which, although in the form of a regulation or a decision addressed to another person, is of direct and individual concern to the former.

The proceedings provided for in this Article shall be instituted within two months of the publication of the measure, or of its notification to the plaintiff, or, in the absence thereof, of the day on which it came to the knowledge of the latter, as the case may be.

Article 174

If the action is well founded, the Court of Justice shall declare the act concerned to be void.

In the case of a regulation, however, the Court of Justice shall, if it considers this necessary, state which of the effects of the regulation which it has declared void shall be considered as definitive.

Article 175 [121]

Should the Council or the Commission, in infringement of this Treaty, fail to act, the Member States and the other institutions of the Community may bring an action before the Court of Justice to have the infringement established.

The action shall be admissible only if the institution concerned has first been called upon to act. If, within two months of being so called upon, the institution concerned has not defined its position, the action may be brought within a further period of two months.

Any natural or legal person may, under the conditions laid down in the preceding paragraphs, complain to the Court of Justice that an institution of the Community has failed to address to that person any act other than a recommendation or an opinion.

Article 176

The institution [122] whose act has been declared void or whose failure to act has been declared contrary to this Treaty shall be required to take

---

120. The TEU would substantially amend Article 173 to augment the list of reviewable acts, notably to include legislation adopted jointly by the Parliament and the Council, and acts of the European Central Bank.

121. The TEU would substantially amend Article 175 to include jurisdiction over the Parliament or the European Central Bank for a failure to act on their part.

122. The TEU would add "or institutions".

the necessary measures to comply with the judgment of the Court of Justice.

This obligation shall not affect any obligation which may result from the application of the second paragraph of Article 215.[123]

Article 177

The Court of Justice shall have jurisdiction to give preliminary rulings concerning:

(a) the interpretation of this Treaty;

(b) the validity and interpretation of acts of the institutions of the Community [124];

(c) the interpretation of the statutes of bodies established by an act of the Council, where those statutes so provide.

Where such a question is raised before any court or tribunal of a Member State, that court or tribunal may, if it considers that a decision on the question is necessary to enable it to give judgement, request the Court of Justice to give a ruling thereon.

Where any such question is raised in a case pending before a court or tribunal of a Member State, against whose decisions there is no judicial remedy under national law, that court or tribunal shall bring the matter before the Court of Justice.

Article 178

The Court of Justice shall have jurisdiction in disputes relating to compensation for damage provided for in the second paragraph of Article 215.

Article 179

The Court of Justice shall have jurisdiction in any dispute between the Community and its servants within the limits and under the conditions laid down in the Staff Regulations or the Conditions of Employment.

Article 180 [125]

The Court of Justice shall, within the limits hereinafter laid down, have jurisdiction in disputes concerning:

(a) the fulfillment by Member States of obligations under the Statute of the European Investment Bank. In this connection, the Board of Directors of the Bank shall enjoy the powers conferred upon by the Commission by Article 169;

(b) measures adopted by the Board of Governors of the Bank. In this connection, any Member State, the Commission or the Board of Directors

---

123. The TEU would add a new paragraph: "This Article shall also apply to the ECB."

124. The TEU would add "and of the ECB".

125. The TEU would revise slightly paragraphs (b) and (c) and add a new paragraph (d) on jurisdiction over disputes concerning national central banks' failure to fulfill their obligations under the Treaty.

of the Bank may institute proceedings under the conditions laid down in Article 173;

(c) measures adopted by the Board of Directors of the Bank. Proceedings against such measures may be instituted only by Member States or by the Commission, under the conditions laid down in Article 173, and solely on the grounds of non-compliance with the procedure provided for in Article 21(2), (5), (6) and (7) of the Statute of the Bank.

Article 181

The Court of Justice shall have jurisdiction to give judgment pursuant to any arbitration clause contained in a contract concluded by or on behalf of the Community, whether that contract be governed by public or private law.

Article 182

The Court of Justice shall have jurisdiction in any dispute between Member States which relates to the subject matter of this Treaty if the dispute is submitted to it under a special agreement between the parties.

Article 183

Save where jurisdiction is conferred on the Court of Justice by this Treaty, disputes to which the Community is a party shall not on that ground be excluded from the jurisdiction of the courts or tribunals of the Member States.

Article 184

Notwithstanding the expiry of the period laid down in the third paragraph of Article 173, any party may, in proceedings in which a regulation [of the Council or of the Commission is in][126] issue, plead the grounds specified in the first paragraph of Article 173, in order to invoke before the Court of Justice the inapplicability of that regulation.

Article 185

Actions brought before the Court of Justice shall not have suspensory effect. The Court of Justice may, however, if it considers that circumstances so require, order that application of the contested act be suspended.

Article 186

The Court of Justice may in any cases before it prescribe any necessary interim measures.

Article 187

The judgments of the Court of Justice shall be enforceable under the conditions laid down in Article 192.

Article 188

The Statute of the Court of Justice is laid down in a separate Protocol.

---

126. The TEU would replace the bracketed language with "adopted jointly by the European Parliament and the Council, or a regulation of the Council, of the Commission, or of the ECB is at".

The Council may, acting unanimously at the request of the Court of Justice and after consulting the Commission and the European Parliament, amend the provisions of Title III of the Statute.[127]

The Court of Justice shall adopt its rules of procedure. These shall require the unanimous approval of the Council.

[*Eds. Note:* The TEU would insert a new "Section 5—The Court of Auditors", comprised of Articles 188a–188c, describing this body and its role, effectively replacing Articles 206–206a.]

Chapter 2. Provisions Common to Several Institutions

Article 189

In order to carry out their task [128] the Council and the Commission shall[, in accordance with the provisions of this Treaty,] [129] make regulations, issue directives, take decisions, make recommendations or deliver opinions.

A regulation shall have general application. It shall be binding in its entirety and directly applicable in all Member States.

A directive shall be binding, as to the result to be achieved, upon each Member State to which it is addressed, but shall leave to the national authorities the choice of form and methods.

A decision shall be binding in its entirety upon those to whom it is addressed.

Recommendations and opinions shall have no binding force.

[*Eds. Note:* The TEU would insert new Articles 189a to 189c, describing the types of legislative procedures, including the new co-decision procedure. These effectively replace Article 149.]

Article 190

Regulations, directives and decisions [of the Council and of the Commission] [130] shall state the reasons on which they are based and shall refer to any proposals or opinions which were required to be obtained pursuant to this Treaty.

Article 191 [131]

Regulations shall be published in the Official Journal of the Community. They shall enter into force on the date specified in them or, in the absence thereof, on the 20th day following their publication.

---

127. The SEA (art. 12) added this paragraph.
128. The TEU would add: "and in accordance with the provisions of this Treaty, the European Parliament acting jointly with the Council,".
129. The TEU would delete the bracketed language.
130. The TEU would replace the bracketed language with "adopted jointly by the European Parliament and the Council, and such acts adopted by the Council or the Commission,".
131. The TEU would substantially amend Article 191, requiring that directives addressed to all Member States be published in the Official Journal and prescribing other formalities.

Directives and decisions shall be notified to those to whom they are addressed and shall take effect upon such notification.

Article 192

Decisions of the Council or of the Commission which impose a pecuniary obligation on persons other than States, shall be enforceable.

Enforcement shall be governed by the rules of civil procedure in force in the State in the territory of which it is carried out. The order for its enforcement shall be appended to the decision, without other formality than verification of the authenticity of the decision, by the national authority which the Government of each Member State shall designate for this purpose and shall make known to the Commission and to the Court of Justice.

When these formalities have been completed on application by the party concerned, the latter may proceed to enforcement in accordance with the national law, by bringing the matter directly before the competent authority.

Enforcement may be suspended only by a decision of the Court of Justice. However, the courts of the country concerned shall have jurisdiction over complaints that enforcement is being carried out in an irregular manner.

Chapter 3. The Economic and Social Committee

Article 193

An Economic and Social Committee is hereby established. It shall have advisory status.

The Committee shall consist of representatives of the various categories of economic and social activity, in particular, representatives of producers, farmers, carriers, workers, dealers, craftsmen, professional occupations and representatives of the general public.

Article 194

The number of members of the Committee shall be as follows:

Belgium	12
Denmark	9
Germany	24
Greece	12
Spain	21
France	24
Ireland	9
Italy	24
Luxembourg	6
Netherlands	12
Portugal	12
United Kingdom	24

The members of the Committee shall be appointed by the Council, acting unanimously, for four years. Their appointments shall be renewable.

The members of the Committee shall be appointed in their personal capacity and may not be bound by any mandatory instructions.[132]

Article 195

1. For the appointment of the members of the Committee, each Member State shall provide the Council with a list containing twice as many candidates as there are seats allotted to its nationals.

The composition of the Committee shall take account of the need to ensure adequate representation of the various categories of economic and social activity.

2. The Council shall consult the Commission. It may obtain the opinion of European bodies which are representative of the various economic and social sectors to which the activities of the Community are of concern.

Article 196

The Committee shall elect its chairman and officers from among its members for a term of two years.

It shall adopt its rules of procedure [and shall submit them to the Council for its approval, which must be unanimous].[133]

The Committee shall be convened by its chairman at the request of the Council or of the Commission.[134]

Article 197

The Committee shall include specialized sections for the principal fields covered by this Treaty.

In particular, it shall contain an agricultural section and a transport section, which are the subject of special provisions in the Titles relating to agriculture and transport.

These specialized sections shall operate within the general terms of reference of the Committee. They may not be consulted independently of the Committee.

Sub-committees may also be established within the Committee to prepare on specific questions or in specific fields, draft opinions to be submitted to the Committee for its consideration.

The rules of procedure shall lay down the methods of composition and the terms of reference of the specialized sections and of the sub-committees.

132. The TEU would amend this paragraph and add a new paragraph on allowances for Committee members.

133. The TEU would delete the bracketed language.

134. The TEU would add: "It may also

Article 198 [135]

The Committee must be consulted by the Council or by the Commission where this Treaty so provides. The Committee may be consulted by these institutions in all cases in which they consider it appropriate.

The Council or the Commission shall, if it considers it necessary, set the Committee, for the submission of its opinion, a time limit which may not be less than ten days from the date on which the chairman receives notification to this effect. Upon expiry of the time limit, the absence of an opinion shall not prevent further action.

The opinion of the Committee and that of the specialized section, together with a record of the proceedings, shall be forwarded to the Council and to the Commission.

[*Eds. Note:* The TEU would introduce two new chapters. "Chapter 4—The Committee of the Regions", comprised of Articles 198a–198c, would create this body, fix its membership by states, and describe its consultative role. "Chapter 5—European Investment Bank", comprised of Articles 198d and 198e, would replace Articles 129 and 130.]

Title II. Financial Provisions

Article 199

All items of revenue and expenditure of the Community, including those relating to the European Social Fund, shall be included in estimates to be drawn up for each financial year and shall be shown in the budget.[136]

The revenue and expenditure shown in the budget shall be in balance.

Article 200 [137]

1. The budget revenue shall include, irrespective of any other revenue, financial contributions of Member States on the following scale:

Belgium	7.9
Germany	28
France	28
Italy	28
Luxembourg	0.2
Netherlands	7.9

2. The financial contributions of Member States to cover the expenditure of the European Social Fund, however, shall be determined on the following scale:

Belgium	8.8
Germany	32
France	32

meet on its own initiative."

135. The TEU would amend the text slightly.

136. The TEU would add a new paragraph, authorizing the inclusion in the budget of Union expenses for the common foreign and security policy and cooperation in justice and home affairs.

137. The TEU would repeal Article 200.

Italy	20
Luxembourg	0.2
Netherlands	7

3. The scales may be modified by the Council, acting unanimously.

Article 201 [138]

The Commission shall examine the conditions under which the financial contributions of Member States provided for in Article 200 could be replaced by the Community's own resources, in particular by revenue accruing from the common customs tariff when it has been finally introduced.

To this end, the Commission shall submit proposals to the Council.

After consulting the European Parliament on these proposals the Council may, acting unanimously, lay down the appropriate provisions, which it shall recommend to the Member States for adoption in accordance with their respective constitutional requirements.

Article 202

The expenditure shown in the budget shall be authorized for one financial year, unless the regulations made pursuant to Article 209 provide otherwise.

In accordance with conditions to be laid down pursuant to Article 209, any appropriations, other than those relating to staff expenditure, that are unexpended at the end of the financial year may be carried forward to the next financial year only.

Appropriations shall be classified under different chapters grouping items of expenditures according to their nature or purpose and subdivided, as far as may be necessary, in accordance with the regulations made pursuant to Article 209.

The expenditure of the European Parliament, the Council, the Commission and the Court of Justice shall be set out in separate parts of the budget, without prejudice to special arrangements for certain common items of expenditure.

Article 203

1. The financial year shall run from 1 January to 31 December.

2. Each institution of the Community shall, before 1 July, draw up estimates of its expenditure. The Commission shall consolidate these estimates in a preliminary draft budget. It shall attach thereto an opinion which may contain different estimates.

The preliminary draft budget shall contain an estimate of revenue and an estimate of expenditure.

---

138. The TEU would replace the text with a requirement that the budget be financed from the Community's own resources and with a description of the legislative process to set the system of own resources. A new Article 201a would require the Commission to respect budgetary discipline in making budget proposals.

3. The Commission shall place the preliminary draft budget before the Council not later than 1 September of the year preceding that in which the budget is to be implemented.

The Council shall consult the Commission and, where appropriate, the other institutions concerned whenever it intends to depart from the preliminary draft budget.

The Council, acting by a qualified majority, shall establish the draft budget and forward it to the European Parliament.

4. The draft budget shall be placed before the European Parliament not later than 5 October of the year preceding that in which the budget is to be implemented.

The European Parliament shall have the right to amend the draft budget, acting by a majority of its members, and to propose to the Council, acting by an absolute majority of the votes cast, modifications to the draft budget relating to expenditure necessarily resulting from this Treaty or from acts adopted in accordance therewith.

If, within 45 days of the draft budget being placed before it, the European Parliament has given its approval, the budget shall stand as finally adopted. If within this period the European Parliament has not amended the draft budget nor proposed any modifications thereto, the budget shall be deemed to be finally adopted.

If within this period the European Parliament has adopted amendments or proposed modifications, the draft budget together with the amendments or proposed modifications shall be forwarded to the Council.

5. After discussing the draft budget with the Commission and, where appropriate, with the other institutions concerned, the Council shall act under the following conditions:

(a) The Council may, acting by a qualified majority, modify any of the amendments adopted by the European Parliament;

(b) With regard to the proposed modifications:

— where a modification proposed by the European Parliament does not have the effect of increasing the total amount of the expenditure of an institution, owing in particular to the fact that the increase in expenditure which it would involve would be expressly compensated by one or more proposed modifications correspondingly reducing expenditure, the Council may, acting by a qualified majority, reject the proposed modification. In the absence of a decision to reject it, the proposed modification shall stand as accepted;

— where a modification proposed by the European Parliament has the effect of increasing the total amount of the expenditure of an institution, the Council may, acting by a qualified majority, accept this proposed modification. In the absence of a decision to accept it, the proposed modification shall stand as rejected;

— where, in pursuance of one of the two preceding sub-paragraphs, the Council has rejected a proposed modification, it may, acting by a qualified majority, either retain the amount shown in the draft budget or fix another amount.

The draft budget shall be modified on the basis of the proposed modifications accepted by the Council.

If, within 15 days of the draft being placed before it, the Council has not modified any of the amendments adopted by the European Parliament and if the modifications proposed by the latter have been accepted, the budget shall be deemed to be finally adopted. The Council shall inform the European Parliament that it has not modified any of the amendments and that the proposed modifications have been accepted.

If within this period the Council has modified one or more of the amendments adopted by the European Parliament or if the modifications proposed by the latter have been rejected or modified, the modified draft budget shall again be forwarded to the European Parliament. The Council shall inform the European Parliament of the results of its deliberations.

6. Within 15 days of the draft budget being placed before it, the European Parliament, which shall have been notified of the action taken on its proposed modifications, may, acting by a majority of its members and three-fifths of the votes cast, amend or reject the modifications to its amendments made by the Council and shall adopt the budget accordingly. If within this period the European Parliament has not acted, the budget shall be deemed to be finally adopted.

7. When the procedure provided for in this Article has been completed, the President of the European Parliament shall declare that the budget has been finally adopted.

8. However, the European Parliament, acting by a majority of its members and two-thirds of the votes cast, may, if there are important reasons, reject the draft budget and ask for a new draft to be submitted to it.

9. A maximum rate of increase in relation to the expenditure of the same type to be incurred during the current year shall be fixed annually for the total expenditure other than that necessarily resulting from this Treaty or from acts adopted in accordance therewith.

The Commission shall, after consulting the Economic Policy Committee, declare what this maximum rate is as it results from:

— the trend, in terms of volume, of the gross national product within the Community;

— the average variation in the budgets of the Member States; and

— the trend of the cost of living during the preceding financial year.

The maximum rate shall be communicated, before 1 May, to all the institutions of the Community. The latter shall be required to conform to this during the budgetary procedure, subject to the provisions of the fourth and fifth sub-paragraphs of this paragraph.

If, in respect of expenditure other than that necessarily resulting from this Treaty or from acts adopted in accordance therewith, the actual rate of increase in the draft budget established by the Council is over half the maximum rate, the European Parliament may, exercising its right of amendment, further increase the total amount of that expenditure to a limit not exceeding half the maximum rate.

Where the European Parliament, the Council or the Commission consider that the activities of the Communities require that the rate determined according to the procedure laid down in this paragraph should be exceeded, another rate may be fixed by agreement between the Council, acting by a qualified majority, and the European Parliament, acting by a majority of its members and three-fifths of the votes cast.

10. Each institution shall exercise the powers conferred upon it by this Article, with due regard for the provisions of the Treaty and for acts adopted in accordance therewith, in particular those relating to the Communities' own resources and to the balance between revenue and expenditure.

Article 204

If at the beginning of a financial year, the budget has not yet been voted, a sum equivalent to not more than one-twelfth of the budget appropriations for the preceding financial year may be spent each month in respect of any chapter or other subdivision of the budget in accordance with the provisions of the Regulations made pursuant to Article 209; this arrangement shall not, however, have the effect of placing at the disposal of the Commission appropriations in excess of one-twelfth of those provided for in the draft budget in course of preparation.

The Council may, acting by a qualified majority, provided that the other conditions laid down in the first sub-paragraph are observed, authorize expenditure in excess of one-twelfth.

If the decision relates to expenditure which does not necessarily result from this Treaty or from acts adopted in accordance therewith, the Council shall forward it immediately to the European Parliament; within 30 days the European Parliament, acting by a majority of its members and three-fifths of the votes cast, may adopt a different decision on the expenditure in excess of the one-twelfth referred to in the first sub-paragraph. This part of the decision of the Council shall be suspended until the European Parliament has taken its decision. If within the said period the European Parliament has not taken a decision which differs from the decision of the Council, the latter shall be deemed to be finally adopted.

The decisions referred to in the second and third sub-paragraphs shall lay down the necessary measures relating to resources to ensure application of this Article.

Article 205

The Commission shall implement the budget, in accordance with provisions of the regulations made pursuant to Article 209, on its own responsibility and within the limits of the appropriations.[139]

The regulations shall lay down detailed rules for each institution concerning its part in effecting its own expenditure.

Within the budget, the Commission may, subject to the limits and conditions laid down in the regulations made pursuant to Article 209, transfer appropriations from one chapter to another or from one subdivision to another.

Article 205a

The Commission shall submit annually to the Council and to the European Parliament the accounts of the preceding financial year relating to the implementation of the budget. The Commission shall also forward to them a financial statement of the assets and liabilities of the Community.

Article 206 [140]

1. A Court of Auditors is hereby established.

2. The Court of Auditors shall consist of twelve members.

3. The members of the Court of Auditors shall be chosen from among persons who belong or have belonged in their respective countries to external audit bodies or who are especially qualified for this office. Their independence must be beyond doubt.

4. The members of the Court of Auditors shall be appointed for a term of six years by the Council, acting unanimously after consulting the European Parliament.

However, when the first appointments are made, four members of the Court of Auditors, chosen by lot, shall be appointed for a term of office of four years only.

The members of the Court of Auditors shall be eligible for reappointment.

They shall elect the President of the Court of Auditors from among their number for a term of three years. The President may be re-elected.

5. The members of the Court of Auditors shall, in the general interest of the Community, be completely independent in the performance of their duties.

In the performance of these duties, they shall neither seek nor take instructions from any government or from any other body. They shall refrain from any action incompatible with their duties.

6. The members of the Court of Auditors may not, during their term of office, engage in any other occupation, whether gainful or not. When entering upon their duties they shall give a solemn undertaking that, both during and after their term of office, they will respect the obligations

---

139. The TEU would add: ", having regard to the principles of sound financial management."

140. The TEU would replace Articles 206–206a with new Articles 188a–188c.

arising therefrom and in particular their duty to behave with integrity and discretion as regards the acceptance, after they have ceased to hold office, of certain appointments or benefits.

7. Apart from normal replacement, or death, the duties of a member of the Court of Auditors shall end when he resigns, or is compulsorily retired by a ruling of the Court of Justice pursuant to paragraph 8.

The vacancy thus caused shall be filled for the remainder of the member's term of office.

Save in the case of compulsory retirement, members of the Court of Auditors shall remain in office until they have been replaced.

8. A member of the Court of Auditors may be deprived of his office or of his right to a pension or other benefits in its stead only if the Court of Justice, at the request of the Court of Auditors, finds that he no longer fulfils the requisite conditions or meets the obligations arising from his office.

9. The Council, acting by a qualified majority, shall determine the conditions of employment of the President and the members of the Court of Auditors and in particular their salaries, allowances and pensions. It shall also, by the same majority, determine any payment to be made instead of remuneration.

10. The provisions of the Protocol on the Privileges and Immunities of the European Communities applicable to the Judges of the Court of Justice shall also apply to the members of the Court of Auditors.

Article 206a [141]

1. The Court of Auditors shall examine the accounts of all revenue and expenditure of the Community. It shall also examine the accounts of all revenue and expenditure of all bodies set up by the Community insofar as the relevant constituent instrument does not preclude such examination.

2. The Court of Auditors shall examine whether all revenue has been received and all expenditure incurred in a lawful and regular manner and whether the financial management has been sound.

The audit of revenue shall be carried out on the basis both of the amounts established as due and the amounts actually paid to the Community.

The audit of expenditure shall be carried out on the basis both of commitments undertaken and payments made.

These audits may be carried out before the closure of accounts for the financial year in question.

3. The audit shall be based on records and, if necessary, performed on the spot in the institutions of the Community and in the Member States. In the Member States the audit shall be carried out in liaison with the national audit bodies or, if these do not have the necessary

---

141. Id.

powers, with the competent national departments. These bodies or departments shall inform the Court of Auditors whether they intend to take part in the audit.

The institutions of the Community and the national audit bodies or, if these do not have the necessary powers, the competent national departments, shall forward to the Court of Auditors, at its request, any document or information necessary to carry out its task.

4. The Court of Auditors shall draw up an annual report after the close of each financial year. It shall be forwarded to the institutions of the Community and shall be published, together with the replies of these institutions to the observations of the Court of Auditors, in the Official Journal of the European Communities.

The Court of Auditors may also, at any time, submit observations on specific questions and deliver opinions at the request of one of the institutions of the Community.

It shall adopt its annual reports or opinions by a majority of its members.

It shall assist the European Parliament and the Council in exercising their powers of control over the implementation of the budget.

Article 206b [142]

The European Parliament, acting on a recommendation from the Council which shall act by a qualified majority, shall give a discharge to the Commission in respect of the implementation of the budget. To this end, the Council and the European Parliament in turn shall examine the accounts and the financial statement referred to in Article 205a and the annual report by the Court of Auditors together with the replies of the institutions under audit to the observations of the Court of Auditors.

Article 207

The budget shall be drawn up in the unit of account determined in accordance with the provisions of the regulations made pursuant to Article 209.

The financial contributions provided for in Article 200(1) shall be placed at the disposal of the Community by the Member States in their national currencies.

The available balances of these contributions shall be deposited with the Treasuries of Member States or with bodies designated by them. While on deposit, such funds shall retain the value corresponding to the parity, at the date of deposit, in relation to the unit of account referred to in the first paragraph.

The balances may be invested on terms to be agreed between the Commission and the Member State concerned.

142. The TEU would replace this text with a new Article 206 which expands the degree of Parliament's supervision of expenditures.

The regulations made pursuant to Article 209 shall lay down the technical conditions under which financial operations relating to the European Social Fund shall be carried out.

Article 208

The Commission may, provided it notifies the competent authorities of the Member States concerned, transfer into the currency of one of the Member States its holdings in the currency of another Member State, to the extent necessary to enable them to be used for purposes which come within the scope of this Treaty. The Commission shall as far as possible avoid making such transfers if it possesses cash or liquid assets in the currencies which it needs.

The Commission shall deal with each Member State through the authority designated by the State concerned. In carrying out financial operations the Commission shall employ the services of the bank of issue of the Member State concerned or of any other financial institution approved by that State.

Article 209

The Council, acting unanimously on a proposal from the Commission and after consulting the European Parliament and obtaining the opinion of the Court of Auditors, shall:

(a) make Financial Regulations specifying in particular the procedure to be adopted for establishing and implementing the budget and for presenting and auditing accounts;

(b) determine the methods and procedure whereby the budget revenue provided under the arrangements relating to the Communities' own resources shall be made available to the Commission, and determine the measures to be applied, if need be, to meet cash requirements;

(c) lay down rules concerning the responsibility of [143] authorizing officers and accounting officers and concerning appropriate arrangements for inspection.

[*Eds. Note*: The TEU would add a new Article 209a on the obligation of Member States to combat fraud affecting Community financial interests.]

PART SIX
GENERAL AND FINAL PROVISIONS

Article 210

The Community shall have legal personality.

Article 211

In each of the Member States, the Community shall enjoy the most extensive legal capacity accorded to legal persons under their laws; it may, in particular, acquire or dispose of movable and immovable property

---

143. The TEU would add "financial controllers,".

and may be a party to legal proceedings. To this end, the Community shall be represented by the Commission.

Article 212 [144]

1. The officials and other servants of the European Coal and Steel Community, the European Economic Community and the European Atomic Energy Community shall, at the date of entry into force of this Treaty, become officials and other servants of the European Communities and form part of the single administration of those Communities.

The Council shall, acting by a qualified majority on a proposal from the Commission and after consulting the other institutions concerned, lay down the Staff Regulations of officials of the European Communities and the Conditions of Employment of other servants of those Communities.

Article 213

The Commission may, within the limits and under conditions laid down by the Council in accordance with the provisions of this Treaty, collect any information and carry out any checks required for the performance of the tasks entrusted to it.

Article 214

The members of the institutions of the Community, the members of committees, and the officials and other servants of the Community shall be required, even after their duties have ceased, not to disclose information of the kind covered by the obligation of professional secrecy, in particular information about undertakings, their business relations or their cost components.

Article 215

The contractual liability of the Community shall be governed by the law applicable to the contract in question.

In the case of non-contractual liability, the Community shall, in accordance with the general principles common to the laws of the Member States, make good any damage caused by its institutions or by its servants in the performance of their duties.[145]

The personal liability of its servants towards the Community shall be governed by the provisions laid down in their Staff Regulations or in the Conditions of Employment applicable to them.

Article 216

The seat of the institutions of the Community shall be determined by common accord of the Governments of the Member States.

---

144. This article was repealed by the Merger Treaty. The text quoted is the Merger Treaty provision that effectively replaced it.

145. The TEU inserts a new paragraph: "The preceding paragraph shall apply under the same conditions to damage caused by the ECB or by its servants in the performance of their duties."

Article 217

The rules governing the languages of the institutions of the Community shall, without prejudice to the provisions contained in the rules of procedure of the Court of Justice, be determined by the Council, acting unanimously.

Article 218 [146]

The European Communities shall enjoy in the territories of the Member States such privileges and immunities as are necessary for the performance of their tasks, under the conditions laid down in the Protocol annexed to this Treaty. The same shall apply to the European Investment Bank.

Article 219

Member States undertake not to submit a dispute concerning the interpretation or application of this Treaty to any method of settlement other than those provided for therein.

Article 220

Member States shall, so far as is necessary, enter into negotiations with each other with a view to securing for the benefit of their nationals:

—the protection of persons and the enjoyment and protection of rights under the same conditions as those accorded by each State to its own nationals;

—the abolition of double taxation within the Community;

—the mutual recognition of companies or firms within the meaning of the second paragraph of Article 58, the retention of legal personality in the event of transfer of their seat from one country to another, and the possibility of mergers between companies or firms governed by the laws of different countries;

—the simplification of formalities governing the reciprocal recognition and enforcement of judgements of courts or tribunals and of arbitration awards.

Article 221

Within three years of the entry into force of this Treaty, Member States shall accord nationals of the other Member States the same treatment as their own nationals as regards participation in the capital of companies or firms within the meaning of Article 58, without prejudice to the application of the other provisions of this Treaty.

Article 222

This Treaty shall in no way prejudice the rules in Member States governing the system of property ownership.

---

146. This article was repealed by the Merger Treaty. The text quoted is the Merger Treaty provision that effectively replaced it.

Article 223

1. The provisions of this Treaty shall not preclude the application of the following rules:

(a) No Member State shall be obliged to supply information the disclosure of which it considers contrary to the essential interests of its security;

(b) Any Member State may take such measures as it considers necessary for the protection of the essential interests of its security which are connected with the production of or trade in arms, munitions and war material; such measures shall not adversely affect the conditions of competition in the common market regarding products which are not intended for specifically military purposes.

2. During the first year after the entry into force of this Treaty, the Council shall, acting unanimously, draw up a list of products to which the provisions of paragraph 1(b) shall apply.

3. The Council may, acting unanimously on a proposal from the Commission, make changes in this list.

Article 224

Member States shall consult each other with a view to taking together the steps needed to prevent the functioning of the common market being affected by measures which a Member State may be called upon to take in the event of serious internal disturbances affecting the maintenance of law and order, in the event of war, serious international tension constituting a threat of war, or in order to carry out obligations it has accepted for the purpose of maintaining peace and international security.

Article 225

If measures taken in the circumstances referred to in Articles 223 and 224 have the effect of distorting the conditions of competition in the common market, the Commission shall, together with the State concerned, examine how these measures can be adjusted to the rules laid down in this Treaty.

By way of derogation from the procedure laid down in Articles 169 and 170, the Commission or any Member State may bring the matter directly before the Court of Justice if it considers that another Member State is making improper use of the powers provided for in Articles 223 and 224. The Court of Justice shall give its ruling *in camera.*

Article 226

1. If, during the transitional period, difficulties arise which are serious and liable to persist in any sector of the economy or which could bring about serious deterioration in the economic situation of a given area, a Member State may apply for authorization to take protective measures in order to rectify the situation and adjust the sector concerned to the economy of the common market.

2. On application by the State concerned, the Commission shall, by emergency procedure, determine without delay the protective measures which it considers necessary, specifying the circumstances and the manner in which they are to be put into effect.

3. The measures authorized under paragraph 2 may involve derogations from the rules of this Treaty, to such an extent and for such periods as are strictly necessary in order to attain the objectives referred to in paragraph 1. Priority shall be given to such measures as will least disturb the functioning of the common market.

Article 227

1. This Treaty shall apply to the Kingdom of Belgium, the Kingdom of Denmark, the Federal Republic of Germany, the Hellenic Republic, the Kingdom of Spain, the French Republic, Ireland, the Italian Republic, the Grand Duchy of Luxembourg, the Kingdom of the Netherlands, the Portuguese Republic and the United Kingdom of Great Britain and Northern Ireland.

2. With regard to [Algeria and] the French overseas departments, the general and particular provisions of this Treaty relating to:

—the free movement of goods;

—agriculture, save for Article 40(4);

—the liberalization of services;

—the rules on competition;

—the protective measures provided for in Articles [108, 109] and 226;

—the institutions,

shall apply as soon as this Treaty enters into force.[147]

The conditions under which the other provisions of this Treaty are to apply shall be determined, within two years of the entry into force of this Treaty, by decisions of the Council, acting unanimously on a proposal from the Commission.

The institutions of the Community will, within the framework of the procedures provided for in this Treaty, in particular Article 226, take care that the economic and social development of these areas is made possible.

3. The special arrangements for association set out in Part Four of this Treaty shall apply to the overseas countries and territories listed in Annex IV to this Treaty.

This Treaty shall not apply to those overseas countries and territories having special relations with the United Kingdom of Great Britain and Northern Ireland which are not included in the aforementioned list.

4. The provisions of this Treaty shall apply to the European territories for whose external relations a Member State is responsible.

147. In paragraph 2, the TEU would delete "Algeria and", and replace "108, 109" with "109h, 109i".

5. Notwithstanding the preceding paragraphs:

(a) This Treaty shall not apply to the Faeroe Islands. [The Government of the Kingdom of Denmark may, however, give notice, by a declaration deposited by 31 December 1975 at the latest with the Government of the Italian Republic, which shall transmit a certified copy thereof to each of the Governments of the other Member States, that this Treaty shall apply to those Islands. In that event, this Treaty shall apply to those Islands from the first day of the second month following the deposit of the declaration.] [148]

(b) This Treaty shall not apply to the Sovereign Base Areas of the United Kingdom of Great Britain and Northern Ireland in Cyprus.

(c) This Treaty shall apply to the Channel Islands and the Isle of Man only to the extent necessary to ensure the implementation of the arrangements for those islands set out in the Treaty concerning the accession of new Member States to the European Economic Community and to the European Atomic Energy Community signed on 22 January 1972.

Article 228 [149]

1. Where this Treaty provides for the conclusion of agreements between the Community and one or more States or an international organization, such agreements shall be negotiated by the Commission. Subject to the powers vested in the Commission in this field, such agreements shall be concluded by the Council, after consulting the European Parliament where required by this Treaty.

The Council, the Commission or a Member State may obtain beforehand the opinion of the Court of Justice as to whether an agreement envisaged is compatible with the provisions of this Treaty. Where the opinion of the Court of Justice is adverse, the agreement may enter into force only in accordance with Article 236.

2. Agreements concluded under these conditions shall be binding on the institutions of the Community and on Member States.

[*Eds. Note:* The TEU would introduce a new Article 228a, authorizing the Council to adopt economic sanctions against third countries in pursuance of the common foreign and security policy.]

Article 229

It shall be for the Commission to ensure the maintenance of all appropriate relations with the organs of the United Nations, of its specialized agencies and of the General Agreement on Tariffs and Trade.

The Commission shall also maintain such relations as are appropriate with all international organizations.

---

148. The TEU would delete the bracketed language.

149. The TEU would amend Article 228, significantly modifying the respective roles of the Commission, the Council and the Parliament in the process of negotiating and concluding international agreements.

Article 230

The Community shall establish all appropriate forms of cooperation with the Council of Europe.

Article 231

The Community shall establish close cooperation with the Organization for [European Economic Cooperation],[150] the details to be determined by common accord.

Article 232

1. The provisions of this Treaty shall not affect the provisions of the Treaty establishing the European Coal and Steel Community, in particular as regards the rights and obligations of Member States, the powers of the institutions of that Community and the rules laid down by that Treaty for the functioning of the common market in coal and steel.

2. The provisions of this Treaty shall not derogate from those of the Treaty establishing the European Atomic Energy Community.

Article 233

The provisions of this Treaty shall not preclude the existence or completion of regional unions between Belgium and Luxembourg, or between Belgium, Luxembourg and the Netherlands, to the extent that the objectives of these regional unions are not attained by application of this Treaty.

Article 234

The rights and obligations arising from agreements concluded before the entry into force of this Treaty between one or more Member States on the one hand, and one or more third countries on the other, shall not be affected by the provisions of this Treaty.

To the extent that such agreements are not compatible with this Treaty, the Member State or States concerned shall take all appropriate steps to eliminate the incompatibilities established. Member States shall, where necessary, assist each other to this end and shall, where appropriate, adopt a common attitude.

In applying the agreements referred to in the first paragraph, Member States shall take into account the fact that the advantages accorded under this Treaty by each Member State form an integral part of the establishment of the Community and are thereby inseparably linked with the creation of common institutions, the conferring of powers upon them and the granting of the same advantages by all the other Member States.

Article 235

If action by the Community should prove necessary to attain, in the course of the operation of the common market, one of the objectives of the Community and this Treaty has not provided the necessary powers, the

---

150. The TEU replaces the bracketed language with "Economic Cooperation and Development".

Council shall, acting unanimously on a proposal from the Commission and after consulting the European Parliament, take the appropriate measures.

Article 236 [151]

The Government of any Member State or the Commission may submit to the Council proposals for the amendment of this Treaty.

If the Council, after consulting the European Parliament and, where appropriate, the Commission, delivers an opinion in favour of calling a conference of representatives of the Governments of the Member States, the conference shall be convened by the President of the Council for the purpose of determining by common accord the amendments to be made to this Treaty.

The amendments shall enter into force after being ratified by all the Member States in accordance with their respective constitutional requirements.

Article 237 [152]

Any European State may apply to become a member of the Community. It shall address its application to the Council, which shall act unanimously after consulting the Commission and after receiving the assent of the European Parliament which shall act by an absolute majority of its component members.[153]

The conditions of admission and the adjustments to this Treaty necessitated thereby shall be the subject of an agreement between the Member States and the applicant State. This agreement shall be submitted for ratification by all the Contracting States in accordance with their respective constitutional requirements.

Article 238

The Community may conclude with [a third State, a union of States or an international organization][154] agreements establishing an association involving reciprocal rights and obligations, common action and special procedures.

These agreements shall be concluded by the Council, acting unanimously and after receiving the assent of the European Parliament which shall act by an absolute majority of its component members.[155]

Where such agreements call for amendments to this Treaty, these amendments shall first be adopted in accordance with the procedure laid down in Article 236.

---

151. The TEU would delete Article 236, which would be effectively replaced by Article N.

152. The TEU would delete Article 237, which would be effectively replaced by Article O.

153. The SEA (art. 8) amended this paragraph to require the assent of Parliament.

154. The TEU would replace the bracketed language with "one or more States or international organizations".

155. The SEA (art. 9) amended this paragraph to require the assent of Parliament.

Article 239

The Protocols annexed to this Treaty by common accord of the Member States shall form an integral part thereof.

Article 240

This Treaty is concluded for an unlimited period.

Setting up of the Institutions

Article 241

The Council shall meet within one month of the entry into force of this Treaty.

Article 242

The Council shall, within three months of its first meeting, take all appropriate measures to constitute the Economic and Social Committee.

Article 243

The European Parliament shall meet within two months of the first meeting of the Council, having been convened by the President of the Council, in order to elect its officers and draw up its rules of procedure. Pending the election of its officers, the oldest member shall take the chair.

Article 244

The Court of Justice shall take up its duties as soon as its members have been appointed. Its first President shall be appointed for three years in the same manner as its members.

The Court of Justice shall adopt its rules of procedure within three months of taking up its duties.

No matter may be brought before the Court of Justice until its rules of procedure have been published. The time within which an action must be brought shall run only from the date of this publication.

Upon his appointment, the President of the Court of Justice shall exercise the powers conferred upon him by this Treaty.

Article 245

The Commission shall take up its duties and assume the responsibilities conferred upon it by this Treaty as soon as its members have been appointed.

Upon taking up its duties, the Commission shall undertake the studies and arrange the contacts needed for making an overall survey of the economic situation of the Community.

Article 246

1. The first financial year shall run from the date on which this Treaty enters into force until 31 December following. Should this Treaty, however, enter into force during the second half of the year, the first financial year shall run until 31 December of the following year.

2. Until the budget for the first financial year has been established, Member States shall make the Community interest-free advances which

shall be deducted from their financial contributions to the implementation of the budget.

3. Until the Staff Regulations of officials and the Conditions of Employment of other servants of the Community provided for in Article 212 have been laid down, each institution shall recruit the Staff it needs and to this end conclude contracts of limited duration.

Each institution shall examine together with the Council any question concerning the number, remuneration and distribution of posts.

Final Provisions

Article 247

This Treaty shall be ratified by the High Contracting Parties in accordance with their respective constitutional requirements. The instruments of ratification shall be deposited with the Government of the Italian Republic.

This Treaty shall enter into force on the first day of the month following the deposit of the instrument of ratification by the last signatory State to take this step. If, however, such deposit is made less than 15 days before the beginning of the following month, this Treaty shall not enter into force until the first day of the second month after the date of such deposit.

Article 248

This Treaty, drawn up in a single original in the Dutch, French, German and Italian languages, all four texts being equally authentic, shall be deposited in the archives of the Government of the Italian Republic, which shall transmit a certified copy to each of the Governments of the other signatory States.

IN WITNESS WHEREOF, the undersigned Plenipotentiaries have signed this Treaty.

[Rome, March 25, 1957. List of signing Plenipotentiaries has been omitted.]

2. SINGLE EUROPEAN ACT

[*Eds. Note:* The following text reproduces the Preamble, Title I and Title III of the Single European Act (SEA), in effect since July 1, 1987.

Title II is omitted because it comprises the amendments made to the EEC, ECSC and Euratom Treaties. All amendments made by the SEA are reflected in the text of the EEC Treaty, page 4 supra. Footnote references show where these occur and briefly describe them.

The SEA amended or added the following EEC Treaty articles: 7, 8a to 8c, 28, 49, 54(2), 56(2), 57, 70(1), 84(2), 99, 100a and b, 102a, 118a and b, 130a to 130t, 145, 149, 168a, 188, 237 and 238.

Following Title III is a list of Declarations annexed to the SEA. These Declarations relect the views and intentions on certain issues expressed by representatives of various Member States or Institutions at the Luxembourg Intergovernmental Conference which prepared the SEA. The only Declaration reproduced below is that on Article 8a.]

HIS MAJESTY THE KING OF THE BELGIANS, HER MAJESTY THE QUEEN OF DENMARK, THE PRESIDENT OF THE FEDERAL REPUBLIC OF GERMANY, THE PRESIDENT OF THE HELLENIC REPUBLIC, HIS MAJESTY THE KING OF SPAIN, THE PRESIDENT OF THE FRENCH REPUBLIC, THE PRESIDENT OF IRELAND, THE PRESIDENT OF THE ITALIAN REPUBLIC, HIS ROYAL HIGHNESS THE GRAND DUKE OF LUXEMBOURG, HER MAJESTY THE QUEEN OF THE NETHERLANDS, THE PRESIDENT OF THE PORTUGUESE REPUBLIC, HER MAJESTY THE QUEEN OF THE UNITED KINGDOM OF GREAT BRITAIN AND NORTHERN IRELAND,

MOVED by the will to continue the work undertaken on the basis of the Treaties establishing the European Communities and to transform relations as a whole among their States into a European Union, in accordance with the Solemn Declaration of Stuttgart of 19 June 1983,

RESOLVED to implement this European Union on the basis, firstly, of the Communities operating in accordance with their own rules and, secondly, of European Cooperation among the Signatory States in the sphere of foreign policy and to invest this union with the necessary means of action,

DETERMINED to work together to promote democracy on the basis of the fundamental rights recognized in the constitutions and laws of the Member States, in the Convention for the Protection of Human Rights and Fundamental Freedoms and the European Social Charter, notably freedom, equality and social justice,

CONVINCED that the European idea, the results achieved in the fields of economic integration and political cooperation, and the need for new developments correspond to the wishes of the democratic peoples of Europe, for whom the European Parliament, elected by universal suffrage, is an indispensable means of expression,

AWARE of the responsibility incumbent upon Europe to aim at speaking ever increasingly with one voice and to act with consistency and solidarity in order more effectively to protect its common interests and independence, in particular to display the principles of democracy and compliance with the law and with human rights to which they are attached, so that together they may make their own contribution to the preservation of international peace and security in accordance with the undertaking entered into by them within the framework of the United Nations Charter,

DETERMINED to improve the economic and social situation by extending common policies and pursuing new objectives, and to ensure a smoother functioning of the Communities by enabling the institutions to exercise their powers under conditions most in keeping with Community interests,

WHEREAS at their Conference in Paris from 19 to 21 October 1972 the Heads of State or of Government approved the objective of the progressive realization of Economic and Monetary Union,

HAVING REGARD to the Annex to the conclusions of the Presidency of the European Council in Bremen on 6 and 7 July 1978 and the Resolution of the European Council in Brussels on 5 December 1978 on the introduction of the European Monetary System (EMS) and related questions, and noting that in accordance with that Resolution, the Community and the Central Banks of the Member States have taken a number of measures intended to implement monetary cooperation,

HAVE DECIDED to adopt this Act and to this end have designated as their plenipotentiaries:

[List of signatories omitted]

TITLE I

COMMON PROVISIONS

Article 1

The European Communities and European Political Cooperation shall have as their objective to contribute together to making concrete progress towards European unity.

The European Communities shall be founded on the Treaties establishing the European Coal and Steel Community, the European Economic Community, the European Atomic Energy Community and on the subsequent Treaties and Acts modifying or supplementing them.

Political Cooperation shall be governed by Title III. The provisions of the Title shall confirm and supplement the procedures agreed in the reports of Luxembourg (1970), Copenhagen (1973), London (1981), the Solemn Declaration on European Union (1983) and the practices gradually established among the Member States.

Article 2

The European Council shall bring together the Heads of State or of Government of the Member States and the President of the Commission of the European Communities. They shall be assisted by the Ministers for Foreign Affairs and by a Member of the Commission.

The European Council shall meet at least twice a year.

Article 3

1. The institutions of the European Communities, henceforth designated as referred to hereafter, shall exercise their powers and jurisdiction under the conditions and for the purposes provided for by the Treaties establishing the Communities and by the subsequent Treaties and Acts modifying or supplementing them and by the provisions of Title II.

2. The institutions and bodies responsible for European Political Cooperation shall exercise their powers and jurisdiction under the conditions and for the purposes laid down in Title III and in the documents referred to in the third paragraph of Article 1.

* * *

TITLE III

PROVISIONS ON EUROPEAN COOPERATION IN THE SPHERE OF FOREIGN POLICY

Article 30

European Cooperation in the sphere of foreign policy shall be governed by the following provisions:

1. The High Contracting Parties, being members of the European Communities, shall endeavour jointly to formulate and implement a European foreign policy.

2. (a) The High Contracting Parties undertake to inform and consult each other on any foreign policy matters of general interest so as to ensure that their combined influence is exercised as effectively as possible through coordination, the convergence of their positions and the implementation of joint action.

(b) Consultations shall take place before the High Contracting Parties decide on their final position.

(c) In adopting its positions and in its national measures each High Contracting Party shall take full account of the positions of the other partners and shall give due consideration to the desirability of adopting and implementing common European positions.

In order to increase their capacity for joint action in the foreign policy field, the High Contracting Parties shall ensure that common principles and objectives are gradually developed and defined.

The determination of common positions shall constitute a point of reference for the policies of the High Contracting Parties.

(d) The High Contracting Parties shall endeavour to avoid any action or position which impairs their effectiveness as a cohesive force in international relations or within international organizations.

3. (a) The Ministers for Foreign Affairs and a member of the Commission shall meet at least four times a year within the framework of European Political Cooperation. They may also discuss foreign policy matters within the framework of Political Cooperation on the occasion of meetings of the Council of the European Communities.

(b) The Commission shall be fully associated with the proceedings of Political Cooperation.

(c) In order to ensure the swift adoption of common positions and the implementation of joint action, the High Contracting Parties shall, as far as possible, refrain from impeding the formation of a consensus and the joint action which this could produce.

4. The High Contracting Parties shall ensure that the European Parliament is closely associated with European Political Cooperation. To that end the Presidency shall regularly inform the European Parliament of the foreign policy issues which are being examined within the framework of Political Cooperation and shall ensure that the views of the European Parliament are duly taken into consideration.

5. The external policies of the European Community and the policies agreed in European Political Cooperation must be consistent.

The Presidency and the Commission, each within its own sphere of competence, shall have special responsibility for ensuring that such consistency is sought and maintained.

6. (a) The High Contracting Parties consider that closer cooperation on questions of European security would contribute in an essential way to the development of a European identity in external policy matters. They are ready to coordinate their positions more closely on the political and economic aspects of security.

(b) The High Contracting Parties are determined to maintain the technological and industrial conditions necessary for their security. They shall work to that end both at national level and, where appropriate, within the framework of the competent institutions and bodies.

(c) Nothing in this Title shall impede closer cooperation in the field of security between certain of the High Contracting Parties within the framework of the Western European Union or the Atlantic Alliance.

7. (a) In international institutions and at international conferences which they attend, the High Contracting Parties shall endeavour to adopt common positions on the subjects covered by this Title.

(b) In international institutions and at international conferences in which not all the High Contracting Parties participate, those who do participate shall take full account of positions agreed in European Political Cooperation.

8. The High Contracting Parties shall organize a political dialogue with third countries and regional groupings whenever they deem it necessary.

9. The High Contracting Parties and the Commission, through mutual assistance and information, shall intensify cooperation between their representati[ves] accredited to third countries and to international organizations.

10. (a) The Presidency of European Political Cooperation shall be held by the High Contracting Party which holds the Presidency of the Council of the European Communities.

(b) The Presidency shall be responsible for initiating action and coordinating and representing the positions of the Member States in relations with third countries in respect of European Political Cooperation activities. It shall also be responsible for the management of Political Cooperation and in particular for drawing up the timetable of meetings and for convening and organizing meetings.

(c) The Political Directors shall meet regularly in the Political Committee in order to give the necessary impetus, maintain the continuity of European Political Cooperation and prepare Ministers' discussions.

(d) The Political Committee or, if necessary, a ministerial meeting shall convene within forty-eight hours at the request of at least three Member States.

(e) The European Correspondents' Group shall be responsible, under the direction of the Political Committee, for monitoring the implementation of European Political Cooperation and for studying general organizational problems.

(f) Working groups shall meet as directed by the Political Committee.

(g) A Secretariat based in Brussels shall assist the Presidency in preparing and implementing the activities of European Political Cooperation and in administrative matters. It shall carry out its duties under the authority of the Presidency.

11. As regards privileges and immunities, the members of the European Political Cooperation Secretariat shall be treated in the same way as members of the diplomatic missions of the High Contracting Parties based in the same place as the Secretariat.

12. Five years after the entry into force of this Act the High Contracting Parties shall examine whether any revision of Title III is required.

Declarations

At the time of signing this text, the Conference adopted the declarations listed hereinafter and annexed to this Final Act:

1. Declaration on the powers of implementation of the Commission,
2. Declaration on the Court of Justice,
3. Declaration on Article 8a of the EEC Treaty [reproduced at page 103],
4. Declaration on Article 100a of the EEC Treaty,

5. Declaration on Article 100b of the EEC Treaty,
6. General Declaration on Articles 13 to 19 of the Single European Act,
7. Declaration on Article 118a(2) of the EEC Treaty,
8. Declaration on Article 130d of the EEC Treaty,
9. Declaration on Article 130r of the EEC Treaty,
10. Declaration by the High Contracting Parties on Title III of the Single European Act,
11. Declaration on Article 30(10)(g) of the Single European Act.

The Conference also notes the declarations listed hereinafter and annexed to this Final Act:

1. Declaration by the Presidency on the time limit within which the Council will give its opinion following a first reading (Article 149(2) of the EEC Treaty),
2. Political Declaration by the Governments of the Member States on the free movement of persons,
3. Declaration by the Government of the Hellenic Republic on Article 8a of the EEC Treaty,
4. Declaration by the Commission on Article 28 of the EEC Treaty,
5. Declaration by the Government of Ireland on Article 57(2) of the EEC Treaty,
6. Declaration by the Government of the Portuguese Republic on Articles 59, second paragraph, and 84 of the EEC Treaty,
7. Declaration by the Government of the Kingdom of Denmark on Article 100a of the EEC Treaty,
8. Declaration by the Presidency and the Commission on the monetary capacity of the Community,
9. Declaration by the Government of the Kingdom of Denmark on European Political Cooperation.

DECLARATION

ON ARTICLE 8a OF THE EEC TREATY

The Conference wishes by means of the provisions in Article 8a to express its firm political will to take before 1 January 1993 the decisions necessary to complete the internal market defined in those provisions, and more particularly the decisions necessary to implement the Commission's programme described in the White Paper on the Internal Market.

Setting the date of 31 December 1992 does not create an automatic legal effect.

3. THE TREATY ON EUROPEAN UNION

[*Eds. Note:* The following text reproduces most of the Treaty on European Union (TEU), as signed at Maastricht on February 7, 1992.

All of the articles relating to the European Union as such, namely the Preamble and Articles A to F and J to S, have been reproduced. All amendments to the EEC Treaty are contained in Article G, beginning at page 107. Articles H and I, which constitute the amendments to the ECSC and Euratom Treaties, have been omitted.

A list of the Protocols and Declarations is at page 186. Selected Protocols and Declarations, indicated on the list, complete the reproduced text.

The Treaty on European Union has been published, under that title, by the EC Office for Official Publications. Commerce Clearing House's Common Market Reporter reproduced the Treaty on European Union, with Protocols and Declarations, in its Pending Legislation section. The Common Market Law Reports reproduced most of the Treaty on European Union in [1992] 1 CMLR 719. The EEC Treaty as modified by Article G of the TEU is set forth at [1992] 1 CMLR 573.]

HIS MAJESTY THE KING OF THE BELGIANS, HER MAJESTY THE QUEEN OF DENMARK, THE PRESIDENT OF THE FEDERAL REPUBLIC OF GERMANY, THE PRESIDENT OF THE HELLENIC REPUBLIC, HIS MAJESTY THE KING OF SPAIN, THE PRESIDENT OF THE FRENCH REPUBLIC, THE PRESIDENT OF IRELAND, THE PRESIDENT OF THE ITALIAN REPUBLIC, HIS ROYAL HIGHNESS THE GRAND DUKE OF LUXEMBOURG, HER MAJESTY THE QUEEN OF THE NETHERLANDS, THE PRESIDENT OF THE PORTUGUESE REPUBLIC, HER MAJESTY THE QUEEN OF THE UNITED KINGDOM OF GREAT BRITAIN AND NORTHERN IRELAND,

RESOLVED to mark a new stage in the process of European integration undertaken with the establishment of the European Communities,

RECALLING the historic importance of the ending of the division of the European continent and the need to create firm bases for the construction of the future Europe,

CONFIRMING their attachment to the principles of liberty, democracy and respect for human rights and fundamental freedoms and of the rule of law,

DESIRING to deepen the solidarity between their peoples while respecting their history, their culture and their traditions,

DESIRING to enhance further the democratic and efficient functioning of the institutions so as to enable them better to carry out, within a single institutional framework, the tasks entrusted to them,

RESOLVED to achieve the strengthening and the convergence of their economies and to establish an economic and monetary union including, in accordance with the provisions of this Treaty, a single and stable currency,

DETERMINED to promote economic and social progress for their peoples, within the context of the accomplishment of the internal market and of reinforced cohesion and environmental protection, and to implement policies ensuring that advances in economic integration are accompanied by parallel progress in other fields,

RESOLVED to establish a citizenship common to nationals of their countries,

RESOLVED to implement a common foreign and security policy including the eventual framing of a common defence policy, which might in time lead to a common defence, thereby reinforcing the European identity and its independence in order to promote peace, security and progress in Europe and in the world,

REAFFIRMING their objective to facilitate the free movement of persons, while ensuring the safety and security of their peoples, by including provisions on justice and home affairs in this Treaty,

RESOLVED to continue the process of creating an ever closer union among the peoples of Europe, in which decisions are taken as closely as possible to the citizen in accordance with the principle of subsidiarity,

IN VIEW of further steps to be taken in order to advance European integration,

HAVE DECIDED to establish a European Union.

[List of signatories omitted]

TITLE I
COMMON PROVISIONS
Article A

By this Treaty, the High Contracting Parties establish among themselves a European Union, hereinafter called 'the Union'.

This Treaty marks a new stage in the process of creating an ever closer union among the peoples of Europe, in which decisions are taken as closely as possible to the citizen.

The Union shall be founded on the European Communities, supplemented by the policies and forms of cooperation established by this Treaty. Its task shall be to organize, in a manner demonstrating consistency and solidarity, relations between the Member States and between their peoples.

Article B

The Union shall set itself the following objectives:

— to promote economic and social progress which is balanced and sustainable, in particular through the creation of an area without internal frontiers, through the strengthening of economic and social cohesion and through the establishment of economic and monetary union, ultimately including a single currency in accordance with the provisions of this Treaty;

— to assert its identity on the international scene, in particular through the implementation of a common foreign and security policy including the eventual framing of a common defence policy, which might in time lead to a common defence;

— to strengthen the protection of the rights and interests of the nationals of its Member States through the introduction of a citizenship of the Union;

— to develop close cooperation on justice and home affairs;

— to maintain in full the *acquis communautaire* and build on it with a view to considering, through the procedure referred to in Article N (2), to what extent the policies and forms of cooperation introduced by this Treaty may need to be revised with the aim of ensuring the effectiveness of the mechanisms and the institutions of the Community.

The objectives of the Union shall be achieved as provided in this Treaty and in accordance with the conditions and the timetable set out therein while respecting the principle of subsidiarity as defined in Article 3b of the Treaty establishing the European Community.

Article C

The Union shall be served by a single institutional framework which shall ensure the consistency and the continuity of the activities carried out in order to attain its objectives while respecting and building upon the *acquis communautaire*.

The Union shall in particular ensure the consistency of its external activities as a whole in the context of its external relations, security, economic and development policies. The Council and the Commission shall be responsible for ensuring such consistency. They shall ensure the implementation of these policies, each in accordance with its respective powers.

Article D

The European Council shall provide the Union with the necessary impetus for its development and shall define the general political guidelines thereof.

The European Council shall bring together the Heads of State or Government of the Member States and the President of the Commission. They shall be assisted by the Ministers for Foreign Affairs of the Member States and by a Member of the Commission. The European Council shall meet at least twice a year, under the chairmanship of the Head of State or Government of the Member State which holds the Presidency of the Council.

The European Council shall submit to the European Parliament a report after each of its meetings and a yearly written report on the progress achieved by the Union.

Article E

The European Parliament, the Council, the Commission and the Court of Justice shall exercise their powers under the conditions and for the purposes provided for, on the one hand, by the provisions of the Treaties establishing the European Communities and of the subsequent Treaties and Acts modifying and supplementing them and, on the other hand, by the other provisions of this Treaty.

Article F

1. The Union shall respect the national identities of its Member States, whose systems of government are founded on the principles of democracy.

2. The Union shall respect fundamental rights, as guaranteed by the European Convention for the Protection of Human Rights and Fundamental Freedoms signed in Rome on 4 November 1950 and as they result from the constitutional traditions common to the Member States, as general principles of Community law.

3. The Union shall provide itself with the means necessary to attain its objectives and carry through its policies.

TITLE II

PROVISIONS AMENDING THE TREATY ESTABLISHING THE EUROPEAN ECONOMIC COMMUNITY WITH A VIEW TO ESTABLISHING THE EUROPEAN COMMUNITY

[*Eds. Note*: In Article G, the amendments to the EEC Treaty are set forth in numerical order. In most cases, these articles would replace the correspondingly numbered EEC Treaty articles.

An explanatory note is provided for all other changes: the introduction of entirely new titles, chapters and articles; the amendment of only part of a present article; the repeal of a present article which is not replaced by a new one; and the renumbering or renaming of present titles, chapters and articles.]

Article G

The Treaty establishing the European Economic Community shall be amended in accordance with the provisions of this Article, in order to establish a European Community.

A. Throughout the Treaty:

(1) The term 'European Economic Community' shall be replaced by the term 'European Community'.

B. In Part One 'Principles':

(2) Article 2 shall be replaced by the following:

Article 2

The Community shall have as its task, by establishing a common market and an economic and monetary union and by implement-

ing the common policies or activities referred to in Articles 3 and 3a, to promote throughout the Community a harmonious and balanced development of economic activities, sustainable and non-inflationary growth respecting the environment, a high degree of convergence of economic performance, a high level of employment and of social protection, the raising of the standard of living and quality of life, and economic and social cohesion and solidarity among Member States.'

(3) Article 3 shall be replaced by the following:

Article 3

For the purposes set out in Article 2, the activities of the Community shall include, as provided in this Treaty and in accordance with the timetable set out therein:

(a) the elimination, as between Member States, of customs duties and quantitative restrictions on the import and export of goods, and of all other measures having equivalent effect;

(b) a common commercial policy;

(c) an internal market characterized by the abolition, as between Member States, of obstacles to the free movement of goods, persons, services and capital;

(d) measures concerning the entry and movement of persons in the internal market as provided for in Article 100c;

(e) a common policy in the sphere of agriculture and fisheries;

(f) a common policy in the sphere of transport;

(g) a system ensuring that competition in the internal market is not distorted;

(h) the approximation of the laws of Member States to the extent required for the functioning of the common market;

(i) a policy in the social sphere comprising a European Social Fund;

(j) the strengthening of economic and social cohesion;

(k) a policy in the sphere of the environment;

(l) the strengthening of the competitiveness of Community industry;

(m) the promotion of research and technological development;

(n) encouragement for the establishment and development of trans-European networks;

(o) a contribution to the attainment of a high level of health protection;

(p) a contribution to education and training of quality and to the flowering of the cultures of the Member States;

(q) a policy in the sphere of development cooperation;

(r) the association of the overseas countries and territories in order to increase trade and promote jointly economic and social development;

(s) a contribution to the strengthening of consumer protection;

(t) measures in the spheres of energy, civil protection and tourism.'

(4) The following Article shall be inserted:

'Article 3a

1. For the purposes set out in Article 2, the activities of the Member States and the Community shall include, as provided in this Treaty and in accordance with the timetable set out therein, the adoption of an economic policy which is based on the close coordination of Member States' economic policies, on the internal market and on the definition of common objectives, and conducted in accordance with the principle of an open market economy with free competition.

2. Concurrently with the foregoing, and as provided in this Treaty and in accordance with the timetable and the procedures set out therein, these activities shall include the irrevocable fixing of exchange rates leading to the introduction of a single currency, the ecu, and the definition and conduct of a single monetary policy and exchange-rate policy the primary objective of both of which shall be to maintain price stability and, without prejudice to this objective, to support the general economic policies in the Community, in accordance with the principle of an open market economy with free competition.

3. These activities of the Member States and the Community shall entail compliance with the following guiding principles: stable prices, sound public finances and monetary conditions and a sustainable balance of payments.'

(5) The following Article shall be inserted:

'Article 3b

The Community shall act within the limits of the powers conferred upon it by this Treaty and of the objectives assigned to it therein.

In areas which do not fall within its exclusive competence, the Community shall take action, in accordance with the principle of subsidiarity, only if and in so far as the objectives of the proposed action cannot be sufficiently achieved by the Member States and can therefore, by reason of the scale or effects of the proposed action, be better achieved by the Community.

Any action by the Community shall not go beyond what is necessary to achieve the objectives of this Treaty.'

(6) Article 4 shall be replaced by the following:

'Article 4

1. The tasks entrusted to the Community shall be carried out by the following institutions:

— a EUROPEAN PARLIAMENT,
— a COUNCIL,
— a COMMISSION,
— a COURT OF JUSTICE,
— a COURT OF AUDITORS.

Each institution shall act within the limits of the powers conferred upon it by this Treaty.

2. The Council and the Commission shall be assisted by an Economic and Social Committee and a Committee of the Regions acting in an advisory capacity.'

(7) The following Articles shall be inserted:

'Article 4a

A European System of Central Banks (hereinafter referred to as "ESCB") and a European Central Bank (hereinafter referred to as "ECB") shall be established in accordance with the procedures laid down in this Treaty; they shall act within the limits of the powers conferred upon them by this Treaty and by the Statute of the ESCB and of the ECB (hereinafter referred to as "Statute of the ESCB") annexed thereto.

Article 4b

A European Investment Bank is hereby established, which shall act within the limits of the powers conferred upon it by this Treaty and the Statute annexed thereto.'

(8) Article 6 shall be deleted and Article 7 shall become Article 6. Its second paragraph shall be replaced by the following:

'The Council, acting in accordance with the procedure referred to in Article 189c, may adopt rules designed to prohibit such discrimination.'

(9) Articles 8, 8a, 8b and 8c shall become respectively Articles 7, 7a, 7b and 7c.

C. The following Part shall be inserted:

'PART TWO. CITIZENSHIP OF THE UNION

Article 8

1. Citizenship of the Union is hereby established.

Every person holding the nationality of a Member State shall be a citizen of the Union.

2. Citizens of the Union shall enjoy the rights conferred by this Treaty and shall be subject to the duties imposed thereby.

Article 8a

1. Every citizen of the Union shall have the right to move and reside freely within the territory of the Member States, subject to the limitations and conditions laid down in this Treaty and by the measures adopted to give it effect.

2. The Council may adopt provisions with a view to facilitating the exercise of the rights referred to in paragraph 1; save as otherwise provided in this Treaty, the Council shall act unanimously on a proposal from the Commission and after obtaining the assent of the European Parliament.

Article 8b

1. Every citizen of the Union residing in a Member State of which he is not a national shall have the right to vote and to stand as a candidate at municipal elections in the Member State in which he resides, under the same conditions as nationals of that State. This right shall be exercised subject to detailed arrangements to be adopted before 31 December 1994 by the Council, acting unanimously on a proposal from the Commission and after consulting the European Parliament; these arrangements may provide for derogations where warranted by problems specific to a Member State.

2. Without prejudice to Article 138(3) and to the provisions adopted for its implementation, every citizen of the Union residing in a Member State of which he is not a national shall have the right to vote and to stand as a candidate in elections to the European Parliament in the Member State in which he resides, under the same conditions as nationals of that State. This right shall be exercised subject to detailed arrangements to be adopted before 31 December 1993 by the Council, acting unanimously on a proposal from the Commission and after consulting the European Parliament; these arrangements may provide for derogations where warranted by problems specific to a Member State.

Article 8c

Every citizen of the Union shall, in the territory of a third country in which the Member State of which he is a national is not represented, be entitled to protection by the diplomatic or consular authorities of any Member State, on the same conditions as the nationals of that State. Before 31 December 1993, Member States shall establish the necessary rules among themselves and start the international negotiations required to secure this protection.

Article 8d

Every citizen of the Union shall have the right to petition the European Parliament in accordance with Article 138d.

Every citizen of the Union may apply to the Ombudsman established in accordance with Article 138e.

Article 8e

The Commission shall report to the European Parliament, to the Council and to the Economic and Social Committee before 31 December 1993 and then every three years on the application of the provisions of this Part. This report shall take account of the development of the Union.

On this basis, and without prejudice to the other provisions of this Treaty, the Council, acting unanimously on a proposal from the Commission and after consulting the European Parliament, may adopt provisions to strengthen or to add to the rights laid down in this Part, which it shall recommend to the Member States for adoption in accordance with their respective constitutional requirements.'

D. Parts Two and Three shall be grouped under the following Title:

'PART THREE. COMMUNITY POLICIES'

and in this Part:

(10) The first sentence of Article 49 shall be replaced by the following:

'As soon as this Treaty enters into force, the Council shall, acting in accordance with the procedure referred to in Article 189b and after consulting the Economic and Social Committee, issue directives or make regulations setting out the measures required to bring about, by progressive stages, freedom of movement for workers, as defined in Article 48, in particular:'

(11) Article 54(2) shall be replaced by the following:

'2. In order to implement this general programme or, in the absence of such programme, in order to achieve a stage in attaining freedom of establishment as regards a particular activity, the Council, acting in accordance with the procedure referred to in Article 189b and after consulting the Economic and Social Committee, shall act by means of directives.'

(12) Article 56(2) shall be replaced by the following:

'2. Before the end of the transitional period, the Council shall, acting unanimously on a proposal from the Commission and after consulting the European Parliament, issue directives for the coordination of the abovementioned provisions laid down by law, regulation or administrative action. After the end of the second stage, however, the Council shall, acting in accordance with the procedure referred to in Article 189b, issue directives for the coordination of such provisions as, in each Member State, are a matter for regulation or administrative action.'

(13) Article 57 shall be replaced by the following:

'Article 57

1. In order to make it easier for persons to take up and pursue activities as self-employed persons, the Council shall, acting in accordance with the procedure referred to in Article 189b, issue directives for the mutual recognition of diplomas, certificates and other evidence of formal qualifications.

2. For the same purpose, the Council shall, before the end of the transitional period, issue directives for the coordination of the provisions laid down by law, regulation or administrative action in Member States concerning the taking up and pursuit of activities as self-employed persons. The Council, acting unanimously on a proposal from the Commission and after consulting the European Parliament, shall decide on directives the implementation of which involves in at least one Member State amendment of the existing principles laid down by law governing the professions with respect to training and conditions of access for natural persons. In other cases the Council shall act in accordance with the procedure referred to in Article 189b.

3. In the case of the medical and allied and pharmaceutical professions, the progressive abolition of restrictions shall be dependent upon coordination of the conditions for their exercise in the various Member States.'

(14) The title of Chapter 4 shall be replaced by the following:

'CHAPTER 4. CAPITAL AND PAYMENTS'

(15) The following Articles shall be inserted:

'Article 73a

As from 1 January 1994, Articles 67 to 73 shall be replaced by Articles 73b, c, d, e, f and g.

Article 73b

1. Within the framework of the provisions set out in this Chapter, all restrictions on the movement of capital between Member States and between Member States and third countries shall be prohibited.

2. Within the framework of the provisions set out in this Chapter, all restrictions on payments between Member States and between Member States and third countries shall be prohibited.

Article 73c

1. The provisions of Article 73b shall be without prejudice to the application to third countries of any restrictions which exist on 31 December 1993 under national or Community law adopted in respect of the movement of capital to or from third countries involving direct investment—including investment in real estate—establishment, the provision of financial services or the admission of securities to capital markets.

2. *Whilst endeavouring to achieve the objective of free movement of capital between Member States and third countries to the greatest extent possible and without prejudice to the other Chapters of this Treaty, the Council may, acting by a qualified majority on a proposal from the Commission, adopt measures on the movement of capital to or from third countries involving direct investment—including investment in real estate—establishment, the provision of financial services or the admission of securities to capital markets. Unanimity shall be required for measures under this paragraph which constitute a step back in Community law as regards the liberalization of the movement of capital to or from third countries.*

Article 73d

1. The provisions of Article 73b shall be without prejudice to the right of Member States:

(a) to apply the relevant provisions of their tax law which distinguish between tax-payers who are not in the same situation with regard to their place of residence or with regard to the place where their capital is invested;

(b) to take all requisite measures to prevent infringements of national law and regulations, in particular in the field of taxation and the prudential supervision of financial institutions, or to lay down procedures for the declaration of capital movements for purposes of administrative or statistical information, or to take measures which are justified on grounds of public policy or public security.

2. The provisions of this Chapter shall be without prejudice to the applicability of restrictions on the right of establishment which are compatible with this Treaty.

3. The measures and procedures referred to in paragraphs 1 and 2 shall not constitute a means of arbitrary discrimination or a disguised restriction on the free movement of capital and payments as defined in Article 73b.

Article 73e

By way of derogation from Article 73b, Member States which, on 31 December 1993, enjoy a derogation on the basis of existing Community law, shall be entitled to maintain, until 31 December 1995 at the latest, restrictions on movements of capital authorized by such derogations as exist on that date.

Article 73f

Where, in exceptional circumstances, movements of capital to or from third countries cause, or threaten to cause, serious difficulties for the operation of economic and monetary union, the Council, acting by a qualified majority on a proposal from the Commission and after consulting the ECB, may take safeguard measures with regard to third countries for a period not exceeding six months if such measures are strictly necessary.

Article 73g

1. If, in the cases envisaged in Article 228a, action by the Community is deemed necessary, the Council may, in accordance with the procedure provided for in Article 228a, take the necessary urgent measures on the movement of capital and on payments as regards the third countries concerned.

2. Without prejudice to Article 224 and as long as the Council has not taken measures pursuant to paragraph 1, a Member State may, for serious political reasons and on grounds of urgency, take unilateral measures against a third country with regard to capital movements and payments. The Commission and the other Member States shall be informed of such measures by the date of their entry into force at the latest.

The Council may, acting by a qualified majority on a proposal from the Commission, decide that the Member State concerned shall amend or abolish such measures. The President of the Council shall inform the European Parliament of any such decision taken by the Council.

Article 73h

Until 1 January 1994, the following provisions shall be applicable:

(1) Each Member State undertakes to authorize, in the currency of the Member State in which the creditor or the beneficiary resides, any payments connected with the movement of goods, services or capital, and any transfers of capital and earnings, to the extent that the movement of goods, services, capital and persons between Member States has been liberalized pursuant to this Treaty.

The Member States declare their readiness to undertake the liberalization of payments beyond the extent provided in the preceding subparagraph, in so far as their economic situation in general and the state of their balance of payments in particular so permit.

(2) In so far as movements of goods, services and capital are limited only by restrictions on payments connected therewith, these restrictions shall be progressively abolished by applying, mutatis mutandis, *the provisions of this Chapter and the Chapters relating to the abolition of quantitative restrictions and to the liberalization of services.*

(3) Member States undertake not to introduce between themselves any new restrictions on transfers connected with the invisible transactions listed in Annex III to this Treaty.

The progressive abolition of existing restrictions shall be effected in accordance with the provisions of Articles 63 to 65, in so far as such abolition is not governed by the provisions contained in paragraphs 1 and 2 or by the other provisions of this Chapter.

(4) If need be, Member States shall consult each other on the measures to be taken to enable the payments and transfers mentioned in this Article to be effected; such measures shall not prejudice the attainment of the objectives set out in this Treaty.'

(16) Article 75 shall be replaced by the following:

'Article 75

1. For the purpose of implementing Article 74, and taking into account the distinctive features of transport, the Council shall, acting in accordance with the procedure referred to in Article 189c and after consulting the Economic and Social Committee, lay down:

(a) common rules applicable to international transport to or from the territory of a Member State or passing across the territory of one or more Member States;

(b) the conditions under which non-resident carriers may operate transport services within a Member State;

(c) measures to improve transport safety;

(d) any other appropriate provisions.

2. The provisions referred to in (a) and (b) of paragraph 1 shall be laid down during the transitional period.

3. By way of derogation from the procedure provided for in paragraph 1, where the application of provisions concerning the principles of the regulatory system for transport would be liable to have a serious effect on the standard of living and on employment in certain areas and on the operation of transport facilities, they shall be laid down by the Council acting unanimously on a proposal from the Commission, after consulting the European Parliament and the Economic and Social Committee. In so doing, the Council shall take into account the need for adaptation to the economic development which will result from establishing the common market.'

(17) The title of Title I in Part Three shall be replaced by the following:

'TITLE V. COMMON RULES ON COMPETITION, TAXATION AND APPROXIMATION OF LAWS'

(18) In Article 92(3):

— the following point shall be inserted:

'(d) aid to promote culture and heritage conservation where such aid does not affect trading conditions and competition in the Community to an extent that is contrary to the common interest.'

— the present point (d) shall become (e).

(19) Article 94 shall be replaced by the following:

'Article 94

The Council, acting by a qualified majority on a proposal from the Commission and after consulting the European Parliament, may make any appropriate regulations for the application of Articles 92 and 93 and may in particular determine the conditions in which Article 93(3) shall apply and the categories of aid exempted from this procedure.'

(20) Article 99 shall be replaced by the following:

'Article 99

The Council shall, acting unanimously on a proposal from the Commission and after consulting the European Parliament and the Economic and Social Committee, adopt provisions for the harmonization of legislation concerning turnover taxes, excise duties and other forms of indirect taxation to the extent that such harmonization is necessary to ensure the establishment and the functioning of the internal market within the time-limit laid down in Article 7a.'

(21) Article 100 shall be replaced by the following:

'Article 100

The Council shall, acting unanimously on a proposal from the Commission and after consulting the European Parliament and the Economic and Social Committee, issue directives for the approximation of such laws, regulations or administrative provisions of the Member States as directly affect the establishment or functioning of the common market.'

(22) Article 100a(1) shall be replaced by the following:

'1. By way of derogation from Article 100 and save where otherwise provided in this Treaty, the following provisions shall apply for the achievement of the objectives set out in Article 7a. The Council shall, acting in accordance with the procedure referred to in Article 189b and after consulting the Economic and Social Committee, adopt the measures for the approximation of the provisions laid down by law, regulation or administrative action in Member States which have as their object the establishment and functioning of the internal market.'

(23) The following Article shall be inserted:

'Article 100c

1. The Council, acting unanimously on a proposal from the Commission and after consulting the European Parliament, shall determine the third countries whose nationals must be in possession of a visa when crossing the external borders of the Member States.

2. However, in the event of an emergency situation in a third country posing a threat of a sudden inflow of nationals from that country into the Community, the Council, acting by a qualified majority on a recommendation from the Commission, may introduce, for a period not exceeding six months, a visa requirement for nationals from the country in question. The visa requirement established under this paragraph may be extended in accordance with the procedure referred to in paragraph 1.

3. From 1 January 1996, the Council shall adopt the decisions referred to in paragraph 1 by a qualified majority. The Council shall, before that date, acting by a qualified majority on a proposal from the Commission and after consulting the European Parliament, adopt measures relating to a uniform format for visas.

4. In the areas referred to in this Article, the Commission shall examine any request made by a Member State that it submit a proposal to the Council.

5. This Article shall be without prejudice to the exercise of the responsibilities incumbent upon the Member States with regard to the maintenance of law and order and the safeguarding of internal security.

6. This Article shall apply to other areas if so decided pursuant to Article K.9 of the provisions of the Treaty on European Union which relate to cooperation in the fields of justice and home affairs, subject to the voting conditions determined at the same time.

7. The provisions of the conventions in force between the Member States governing areas covered by this Article shall remain in force until their content has been replaced by directives or measures adopted pursuant to this Article.'

(24) The following Article shall be inserted:

'Article 100d

The Coordinating Committee consisting of senior officials set up by Article K.4 of the Treaty on European Union shall contribute, without prejudice to the provisions of Article 151, to the preparation of the proceedings of the Council in the fields referred to in Article 100c.'

(25) Title II, Chapters 1, 2 and 3 in Part Three shall be replaced by the following:

TITLE VI. ECONOMIC AND MONETARY POLICY
CHAPTER 1. ECONOMIC POLICY
Article 102a

Member States shall conduct their economic policies with a view to contributing to the achievement of the objectives of the Community, as defined in Article 2, and in the context of the broad guidelines referred to in Article 103(2). The Member States and the Community shall act in accordance with the principle of an open market economy with free competition, favouring an efficient allocation of resources, and in compliance with the principles set out in Article 3a.

Article 103

1. Member States shall regard their economic policies as a matter of common concern and shall coordinate them within the Council, in accordance with the provisions of Article 102a.

2. The Council shall, acting by a qualified majority on a recommendation from the Commission, formulate a draft for the broad guidelines of the economic policies of the Member States and of the Community, and shall report its findings to the European Council.

The European Council shall, acting on the basis of the report from the Council, discuss a conclusion on the broad guidelines of the economic policies of the Member States and of the Community.

On the basis of this conclusion, the Council shall, acting by a qualified majority, adopt a recommendation setting out these broad guidelines. The Council shall inform the European Parliament of its recommendation.

3. In order to ensure closer coordination of economic policies and sustained convergence of the economic performances of the Member States, the Council shall, on the basis of reports submitted by the Commission, monitor economic developments in each of the Member States and in the Community as well as the consistency of economic policies with the broad guidelines referred to in paragraph 2, and regularly carry out an overall assessment.

For the purpose of this multilateral surveillance, Member States shall forward information to the Commission about important measures taken by them in the field of their economic policy and such other information as they deem necessary.

4. Where it is established, under the procedure referred to in paragraph 3, that the economic policies of a Member State are not consistent with the broad guidelines referred to in paragraph 2 or that they risk jeopardizing the proper functioning of economic and monetary union, the Council may, acting by a qualified majority on a recommendation from the Commission, make the necessary recommendations to the Member State concerned. The Council may, acting by a qualified majority on a proposal from the Commission, decide to make its recommendations public.

The President of the Council and the Commission shall report to the European Parliament on the results of multilateral surveillance. The President of the Council may be invited to appear before the competent Committee of the European Parliament if the Council has made its recommendations public.

5. The Council, acting in accordance with the procedure referred to in Article 189c, may adopt detailed rules for the multilateral surveillance procedure referred to in paragraphs 3 and 4 of this Article.

Article 103a

1. Without prejudice to any other procedures provided for in this Treaty, the Council may, acting unanimously on a proposal from the Commission, decide upon the measures appropriate to the economic situation, in particular if severe difficulties arise in the supply of certain products.

2. Where a Member State is in difficulties or is seriously threatened with severe difficulties caused by exceptional occurrences beyond its control, the Council may, acting unanimously on a proposal from the Commission, grant, under certain conditions, Community financial assistance to the Member State concerned. Where the severe difficulties are caused by natural disasters, the Council shall act by qualified majority. The President of the Council shall inform the European Parliament of the decision taken.

Article 104

1. Overdraft facilities or any other type of credit facility with the ECB or with the central banks of the Member States (hereinafter referred to as "national central banks") in favour of Community institutions or bodies, central governments, regional, local or other public authorities, other bodies governed by public law, or public undertakings of Member States shall be prohibited, as shall the purchase directly from them by the ECB or national central banks of debt instruments.

2. Paragraph 1 shall not apply to publicly owned credit institutions which, in the context of the supply of reserves by central banks, shall be given the same treatment by national central banks and the ECB as private credit institutions.

Article 104a

1. Any measure, not based on prudential considerations, establishing privileged access by Community institutions or bodies, central governments, regional, local or other public authorities, other bodies governed by public law, or public undertakings of Member States to financial institutions shall be prohibited.

2. *The Council, acting in accordance with the procedure referred to in Article 189c, shall, before 1 January 1994, specify definitions for the application of the prohibition referred to in paragraph 1.*

Article 104b

1. The Community shall not be liable for or assume the commitments of central governments, regional, local or other public authorities, other bodies governed by public law, or public undertakings of any Member State, without prejudice to mutual financial guarantees for the joint execution of a specific project. A Member State shall not be liable for or assume the commitments of central governments, regional, local or other public authorities, other bodies governed by public law or public undertakings of another Member State, without prejudice to mutual financial guarantees for the joint execution of a specific project.

2. If necessary, the Council, acting in accordance with the procedure referred to in Article 189c, may specify definitions for the application of the prohibitions referred to in Article 104 and in this Article.

Article 104c

1. Member States shall avoid excessive government deficits.

2. The Commission shall monitor the development of the budgetary situation and of the stock of government debt in the Member States with a view to identifying gross errors. In particular it shall examine compliance with budgetary discipline on the basis of the following two criteria:

(a) whether the ratio of the planned or actual government deficit to gross domestic product exceeds a reference value, unless

— *either the ratio has declined substantially and continuously and reached a level that comes close to the reference value;*

— *or, alternatively, the excess over the reference value is only exceptional and temporary and the ratio remains close to the reference value;*

(b) whether the ratio of government debt to gross domestic product exceeds a reference value, unless the ratio is sufficiently diminishing and approaching the reference value at a satisfactory pace.

The reference values are specified in the Protocol on the excessive deficit procedure annexed to this Treaty.

3. If a Member State does not fulfil the requirements under one or both of these criteria, the Commission shall prepare a report. The report of the Commission shall also take into account whether the government deficit exceeds government investment expenditure and take into account all other relevant factors, including the medium-term economic and budgetary position of the Member State.

The Commission may also prepare a report if, notwithstanding the fulfilment of the requirements under the criteria, it is of the opinion that there is a risk of an excessive deficit in a Member State.

4. The Committee provided for in Article 109c shall formulate an opinion on the report of the Commission.

5. If the Commission considers that an excessive deficit in a Member State exists or may occur, the Commission shall address an opinion to the Council.

6. The Council shall, acting by a qualified majority on a recommendation from the Commission, and having considered any observations which the Member State concerned may wish to make, decide after an overall assessment whether an excessive deficit exists.

7. Where the existence of an excessive deficit is decided according to paragraph 6, the Council shall make recommendations to the Member State concerned with a view to bringing that situation to an end within a given period. Subject to the provisions of paragraph 8, these recommendations shall not be made public.

8. Where it establishes that there has been no effective action in response to its recommendations within the period laid down, the Council may make its recommendations public.

9. If a Member State persists in failing to put into practice the recommendations of the Council, the Council may decide to give notice to the Member State to take, within a specified time-limit, measures for the deficit reduction which is judged necessary by the Council in order to remedy the situation.

In such a case, the Council may request the Member State concerned to submit reports in accordance with a specific timetable in order to examine the adjustment efforts of that Member State.

10. The rights to bring actions provided for in Articles 169 and 170 may not be exercised within the framework of paragraphs 1 to 9 of this Article.

11. As long as a Member State fails to comply with a decision taken in accordance with paragraph 9, the Council may decide to apply or, as the case may be, intensify one or more of the following measures:

— *to require the Member State concerned to publish additional information, to be specified by the Council, before issuing bonds and securities;*

— *to invite the European Investment Bank to reconsider its lending policy towards the Member State concerned;*

— to require the Member State concerned to make a non-interest-bearing deposit of an appropriate size with the Community until the excessive deficit has, in the view of the Council, been corrected;

— to impose fines of an appropriate size.

The President of the Council shall inform the European Parliament of the decisions taken.

12. The Council shall abrogate some or all of its decisions referred to in paragraphs 6 to 9 and 11 to the extent that the excessive deficit in the Member State concerned has, in the view of the Council, been corrected. If the Council has previously made public recommendations, it shall, as soon as the decision under paragraph 8 has been abrogated, make a public statement that an excessive deficit in the Member State concerned no longer exists.

13. When taking the decisions referred to in paragraphs 7 to 9, 11 and 12, the Council shall act on a recommendation from the Commission by a majority of two-thirds of the votes of its members weighted in accordance with Article 148(2), excluding the votes of the representative of the Member State concerned.

14. Further provisions relating to the implementation of the procedure described in this Article are set out in the Protocol on the excessive deficit procedure annexed to this Treaty.

The Council shall, acting unanimously on a proposal from the Commission and after consulting the European Parliament and the ECB, adopt the appropriate provisions which shall then replace the said Protocol.

Subject to the other provisions of this paragraph the Council shall, before 1 January 1994, acting by a qualified majority on a proposal from the Commission and after consulting the European Parliament, lay down detailed rules and definitions for the application of the provisions of the said Protocol.

CHAPTER 2. MONETARY POLICY

Article 105

1. The primary objective of the ESCB shall be to maintain price stability. Without prejudice to the objective of price stability, the ESCB shall support the general economic policies in the Community with a view to contributing to the achievement of the objectives of the Community as laid down in Article 2. The ESCB shall act in accordance with the principle of an open market economy with free competition, favouring an efficient allocation of resources, and in compliance with the principles set out in Article 3a.

2. The basic tasks to be carried out through the ESCB shall be:

— to define and implement the monetary policy of the Community;

— to conduct foreign-exchange operations consistent with the provisions of Article 109;

— to hold and manage the official foreign reserves of the Member States;

— to promote the smooth operation of payment systems.

3. The third indent of paragraph 2 shall be without prejudice to the holding and management by the governments of Member States of foreign-exchange working balances.

4. The ECB shall be consulted:

— on any proposed Community act in its fields of competence;

— by national authorities regarding any draft legislative provision in its fields of competence, but within the limits and under the conditions set out by the Council in accordance with the procedure laid down in Article 106(6).

The ECB may submit opinions to the appropriate Community institutions or bodies or to national authorities on matters in its fields of competence.

5. The ESCB shall contribute to the smooth conduct of policies pursued by the competent authorities relating to the prudential supervision of credit institutions and the stability of the financial system.

6. The Council may, acting unanimously on a proposal from the Commission and after consulting the ECB and after receiving the assent of the European Parliament, confer upon the ECB specific tasks concerning policies relating to the prudential supervision of credit institutions and other financial institutions with the exception of insurance undertakings.

Article 105a

1. The ECB shall have the exclusive right to authorize the issue of banknotes within the Community. The ECB and the national central banks may issue such notes. The banknotes issued by the ECB and the national central banks shall be the only such notes to have the status of legal tender within the Community.

2. Member States may issue coins subject to approval by the ECB of the volume of the issue. The Council may, acting in accordance with the procedure referred to in Article 189c and after consulting the ECB, adopt measures to harmonize the denominations and technical specifications of all coins intended for circulation to the extent necessary to permit their smooth circulation within the Community.

Article 106

1. The ESCB shall be composed of the ECB and of the national central banks.

2. The ECB shall have legal personality.

3. The ESCB shall be governed by the decision-making bodies of the ECB which shall be the Governing Council and the Executive Board.

4. The Statute of the ESCB is laid down in a Protocol annexed to this Treaty.

5. Articles 5.1, 5.2, 5.3, 17, 18, 19.1, 22, 23, 24, 26, 32.2, 32.3, 32.4, 32.6, 33.1(a) and 36 of the Statute of the ESCB may be amended by the Council, acting either by a qualified majority on a recommendation from the ECB and after consulting the Commission or unanimously on a proposal from the Commission and after consulting the ECB. In either case, the assent of the European Parliament shall be required.

6. The Council, acting by a qualified majority either on a proposal from the Commission and after consulting the European Parliament and the ECB or on a recommendation from the ECB and after consulting the European Parliament and the Commission, shall adopt the provisions referred to in Articles 4, 5.4, 19.2, 20, 28.1, 29.2, 30.4 and 34.3 of the Statute of the ESCB.

Article 107

When exercising the powers and carrying out the tasks and duties conferred upon them by this Treaty and the Statute of the ESCB, neither the ECB, nor a national central bank, nor any member of their decision-making bodies shall seek or take instructions from Community institutions or bodies, from any government of a Member State or from any other body. The Community institutions and bodies and the governments of the Member States undertake to respect this principle and not to seek to influence the members of the decision-making bodies of the ECB or of the national central banks in the performance of their tasks.

Article 108

Each Member State shall ensure, at the latest at the date of the establishment of the ESCB, that its national legislation including the statutes of its national central bank is compatible with this Treaty and the Statute of the ESCB.

Article 108a

1. In order to carry out the tasks entrusted to the ESCB, the ECB shall, in accordance with the provisions of this Treaty and under the conditions laid down in the Statute of the ESCB:

— make regulations to the extent necessary to implement the tasks defined in Article 3.1, first indent, Articles 19.1, 22 and 25.2 of the Statute of the ESCB and in cases which shall be laid down in the acts of the Council referred to in Article 106(6);

— take decisions necessary for carrying out the tasks entrusted to the ESCB under this Treaty and the Statute of the ESCB;

— make recommendations and deliver opinions.

2. *A regulation shall have general application. It shall be binding in its entirety and directly applicable in all Member States.*

Recommendations and opinions shall have no binding force.

A decision shall be binding in its entirety upon those to whom it is addressed.

Articles 190 to 192 shall apply to regulations and decisions adopted by the ECB.

The ECB may decide to publish its decisions, recommendations and opinions.

3. Within the limits and under the conditions adopted by the Council under the procedure laid down in Article 106(6), the ECB shall be entitled to impose fines or periodic penalty payments on undertakings for failure to comply with obligations under its regulations and decisions.

Article 109

1. By way of derogation from Article 228, the Council may, acting unanimously on a recommendation from the ECB or from the Commission, and after consulting the ECB in an endeavour to reach a consensus consistent with the objective of price stability, after consulting the European Parliament, in accordance with the procedure in paragraph 3 for determining the arrangements, conclude formal agreements on an exchange-rate system for the ecu in relation to non-Community currencies. The Council may, acting by a qualified majority on a recommendation from the ECB or from the Commission, and after consulting the ECB in an endeavour to reach a consensus consistent with the objective of price stability, adopt, adjust or abandon the central rates of the ecu within the exchange-rate system. The President of the Council shall inform the European Parliament of the adoption, adjustment or abandonment of the ecu central rates.

2. In the absence of an exchange-rate system in relation to one or more non-Community currencies as referred to in paragraph 1, the Council, acting by a qualified majority either on a recommendation from the Commission and after consulting the ECB or on a recommendation from the ECB, may formulate general orientations for exchange-rate policy in relation to these currencies. These general orientations shall be without prejudice to the primary objective of the ESCB to maintain price stability.

3. By way of derogation from Article 228, where agreements concerning monetary or foreign-exchange regime matters need to be negotiated by the Community with one or more States or international organizations, the Council, acting by a qualified majority on a recommendation from the Commission and after consulting the ECB, shall decide the arrangements for the negotiation and for the conclusion of such agreements. These arrangements shall ensure that the Community expresses a single position. The Commission shall be fully associated with the negotiations.

Agreements concluded in accordance with this paragraph shall be binding on the institutions of the Community, on the ECB and on Member States.

4. Subject to paragraph 1, the Council shall, on a proposal from the Commission and after consulting the ECB, acting by a qualified majority decide on the position of the Community at international level as regards issues of particular relevance to economic and monetary union and, acting unanimously, decide its representation in compliance with the allocation of powers laid down in Articles 103 and 105.

5. Without prejudice to Community competence and Community agreements as regards economic and monetary union, Member States may negotiate in international bodies and conclude international agreements.

CHAPTER 3. INSTITUTIONAL PROVISIONS
Article 109a

1. The Governing Council of the ECB shall comprise the members of the Executive Board of the ECB and the Governors of the national central banks.

2. (a) The Executive Board shall comprise the President, the Vice–President and four other members.

(b) The President, the Vice–President and the other members of the Executive Board shall be appointed from among persons of recognized standing and professional experience in monetary or banking matters by common accord of the governments of the Member States at the level of Heads of State or Government, on a recommendation from the Council, after it has consulted the European Parliament and the Governing Council of the ECB.

Their term of office shall be eight years and shall not be renewable.

Only nationals of Member States may be members of the Executive Board.

Article 109b

1. The President of the Council and a member of the Commission may participate, without having the right to vote, in meetings of the Governing Council of the ECB.

The President of the Council may submit a motion for deliberation to the Governing Council of the ECB.

2. The President of the ECB shall be invited to participate in Council meetings when the Council is discussing matters relating to the objectives and tasks of the ESCB.

3. The ECB shall address an annual report on the activities of the ESCB and on the monetary policy of both the previous and current year to the European Parliament, the Council and the Commission, and also to the European Council. The President of the ECB shall present this report to the Council and to the European Parliament, which may hold a general debate on that basis.

The President of the ECB and the other members of the Executive Board may, at the request of the European Parliament or on their own initiative, be heard by the competent Committees of the European Parliament.

Article 109c

1. In order to promote coordination of the policies of Member States to the full extent needed for the functioning of the internal market, a Monetary Committee with advisory status is hereby set up.

It shall have the following tasks:

— to keep under review the monetary and financial situation of the Member States and of the Community and the general payments system of the Member States and to report regularly thereon to the Council and to the Commission;

— to deliver opinions at the request of the Council or of the Commission, or on its own initiative for submission to those institutions;

— without prejudice to Article 151, to contribute to the preparation of the work of the Council referred to in Articles 73f, 73g, 103(2), (3), (4) and (5), 103a, 104a, 104b, 104c, 109e(2), 109f(6), 109h, 109i, 109j(2) and 109k(1);

— to examine, at least once a year, the situation regarding the movement of capital and the freedom of payments, as they result from the application of this Treaty and of measures adopted by the Council; the examination shall cover all measures relating to capital movements and payments; the Committee shall report to the Commission and to the Council on the outcome of this examination.

The Member States and the Commission shall each appoint two members of the Monetary Committee.

2. At the start of the third stage, an Economic and Financial Committee shall be set up. The Monetary Committee provided for in paragraph 1 shall be dissolved.

The Economic and Financial Committee shall have the following tasks:

— to deliver opinions at the request of the Council or of the Commission, or on its own initiative for submission to those institutions;

— to keep under review the economic and financial situation of the Member States and of the Community and to report regularly thereon to the Council and to the Commission, in particular on financial relations with third countries and international institutions;

— without prejudice to Article 151, to contribute to the preparation of the work of the Council referred to in Articles 73f, 73g, 103(2), (3), (4) and (5), 103a, 104a, 104b, 104c, 105(6), 105a(2), 106(5) and (6), 109, 109h, 109i(2) and (3), 109k(2), 109l(4) and (5), and to carry out other advisory and preparatory tasks assigned to it by the Council;

— to examine, at least once a year, the situation regarding the movement of capital and the freedom of payments, as they result from the application of this Treaty and of measures adopted by the Council; the examination shall cover all measures relating to capital movements and payments; the Committee shall report to the Commission and to the Council on the outcome of this examination.

The Member States, the Commission and the ECB shall each appoint no more than two members of the Committee.

3. The Council shall, acting by a qualified majority on a proposal from the Commission and after consulting the ECB and the Committee referred to in this Article, lay down detailed provisions concerning the composition of the Economic and Financial Committee. The President of the Council shall inform the European Parliament of such a decision.

4. In addition to the tasks set out in paragraph 2, if and as long as there are Member States with a derogation as referred to in Articles 109k and 109l, the Committee shall keep under review the monetary and financial situation and the general payments system of those Member States and report regularly thereon to the Council and to the Commission.

Article 109d

For matters within the scope of Articles 103(4), 104c with the exception of paragraph 14, 109, 109j, 109k and 109l(4) and (5), the Council or a Member State may request the Commission to make a recommendation or a proposal, as appropriate. The Commission shall examine this request and submit its conclusions to the Council without delay.

CHAPTER 4. TRANSITIONAL PROVISIONS

Article 109e

1. The second stage for achieving economic and monetary union shall begin on 1 January 1994.

2. Before that date

(a) each Member State shall:

— *adopt, where necessary, appropriate measures to comply with the prohibitions laid down in Article 73b, without prejudice to Article 73e, and in Articles 104 and 104a(1);*

— *adopt, if necessary, with a view to permitting the assessment provided for in subparagraph (b), multiannual programmes intended to ensure the lasting convergence necessary for the achievement of economic and monetary union, in particular with regard to price stability and sound public finances;*

(b) the Council shall, on the basis of a report from the Commission, assess the progress made with regard to economic and monetary convergence, in particular with regard to price stability and sound public finances, and the progress made with the implementation of Community law concerning the internal market.

3. The provisions of Articles 104, 104a(1), 104b(1) and 104c with the exception of paragraphs 1, 9, 11 and 14 shall apply from the beginning of the second stage.

The provisions of Articles 103a(2), 104c(1), (9) and (11), 105, 105a, 107, 109, 109a, 109b and 109c(2) and (4) shall apply from the beginning of the third stage.

4. In the second stage, Member States shall endeavour to avoid excessive government deficits.

5. During the second stage, each Member State shall, as appropriate, start the process leading to the independence of its central bank, in accordance with Article 108.

Article 109f

1. At the start of the second stage, a European Monetary Institute (hereinafter referred to as "EMI") shall be established and take up its duties; it shall have legal personality and be directed and managed by a Council, consisting of a President and the Governors of the national central banks, one of whom shall be Vice–President.

The President shall be appointed by common accord of the governments of the Member States at the level of Heads of State or Government, on a recommendation from, as the case may be, the Committee of Governors of the central banks of the Member States (hereinafter referred to as "Committee of Governors") or the Council of the EMI, and after consulting the European Parliament and the Council. The President shall be selected from among persons of recognized standing and professional experience in monetary or banking matters. Only nationals of Member States may be President of the EMI. The Council of the EMI shall appoint the Vice–President.

The Statute of the EMI is laid down in a Protocol annexed to this Treaty.

The Committee of Governors shall be dissolved at the start of the second stage.

2. The EMI shall:

— strengthen cooperation between the national central banks;

— strengthen the coordination of the monetary policies of the Member States, with the aim of ensuring price stability;

— monitor the functioning of the European Monetary System;

— hold consultations concerning issues falling within the competence of the national central banks and affecting the stability of financial institutions and markets;

— take over the tasks of the European Monetary Cooperation Fund, which shall be dissolved; the modalities of dissolution are laid down in the Statute of the EMI;

— facilitate the use of the ecu and oversee its development, including the smooth functioning of the ecu clearing system.

3. For the preparation of the third stage, the EMI shall:

— prepare the instruments and the procedures necessary for carrying out a single monetary policy in the third stage;

— promote the harmonization, where necessary, of the rules and practices governing the collection, compilation and distribution of statistics in the areas within its field of competence;

— prepare the rules for operations to be undertaken by the national central banks within the framework of the ESCB;

— promote the efficiency of cross-border payments;

— supervise the technical preparation of ecu banknotes.

At the latest by 31 December 1996, the EMI shall specify the regulatory, organizational and logistical framework necessary for the ESCB to perform its tasks in the third stage. This framework shall be submitted for decision to the ECB at the date of its establishment.

4. The EMI, acting by a majority of two-thirds of the members of its Council, may:

— formulate opinions or recommendations on the overall orientation of monetary policy and exchange-rate policy as well as on related measures introduced in each Member State;

— submit opinions or recommendations to governments and to the Council on policies which might affect the internal or external monetary situation in the Community and, in particular, the functioning of the European Monetary System;

— *make recommendations to the monetary authorities of the Member States concerning the conduct of their monetary policy.*

5. *The EMI, acting unanimously, may decide to publish its opinions and its recommendations.*

6. *The EMI shall be consulted by the Council regarding any proposed Community act within its field of competence.*

Within the limits and under the conditions set out by the Council, acting by a qualified majority on a proposal from the Commission and after consulting the European Parliament and the EMI, the EMI shall be consulted by the authorities of the Member States on any draft legislative provision within its field of competence.

7. *The Council may, acting unanimously on a proposal from the Commission and after consulting the European Parliament and the EMI, confer upon the EMI other tasks for the preparation of the third stage.*

8. *Where this Treaty provides for a consultative role for the ECB, references to the ECB shall be read as referring to the EMI before the establishment of the ECB.*

Where this Treaty provides for a consultative role for the EMI, references to the EMI shall be read, before 1 January 1994, as referring to the Committee of Governors.

9. *During the second stage, the term "ECB" used in Articles 173, 175, 176, 177, 180 and 215 shall be read as referring to the EMI.*

Article 109g

The currency composition of the ecu basket shall not be changed.

From the start of the third stage, the value of the ecu shall be irrevocably fixed in accordance with Article 109l(4).

Article 109h

1. *Where a Member State is in difficulties or is seriously threatened with difficulties as regards its balance of payments either as a result of an overall disequilibrium in its balance of payments, or as a result of the type of currency at its disposal, and where such difficulties are liable in particular to jeopardize the functioning of the common market or the progressive implementation of the common commercial policy, the Commission shall immediately investigate the position of the State in question and the action which, making use of all the means at its disposal, that State has taken or may take in accordance with the provisions of this Treaty. The Commission shall state what measures it recommends the State concerned to take.*

If the action taken by a Member State and the measures suggested by the Commission do not prove sufficient to overcome the difficulties which have arisen or which threaten, the Commission shall, after consulting the Committee referred to in Article 109c, recommend to the Council the granting of mutual assistance and appropriate methods therefor.

The Commission shall keep the Council regularly informed of the situation and of how it is developing.

2. The Council, acting by a qualified majority, shall grant such mutual assistance; it shall adopt directives or decisions laying down the conditions and details of such assistance, which may take such forms as:

(a) a concerted approach to or within any other international organizations to which Member States may have recourse;

(b) measures needed to avoid deflection of trade where the State which is in difficulties maintains or reintroduces quantitative restrictions against third countries;

(c) the granting of limited credits by other Member States, subject to their agreement.

3. If the mutual assistance recommended by the Commission is not granted by the Council or if the mutual assistance granted and the measures taken are insufficient, the Commission shall authorize the State which is in difficulties to take protective measures, the conditions and details of which the Commission shall determine.

Such authorization may be revoked and such conditions and details may be changed by the Council acting by a qualified majority.

4. Subject to Article 109k(6), this Article shall cease to apply from the beginning of the third stage.

Article 109i

1. Where a sudden crisis in the balance of payments occurs and a decision within the meaning of Article 109h(2) is not immediately taken, the Member State concerned may, as a precaution, take the necessary protective measures. Such measures must cause the least possible disturbance in the functioning of the common market and must not be wider in scope than is strictly necessary to remedy the sudden difficulties which have arisen.

2. The Commission and the other Member States shall be informed of such protective measures not later than when they enter into force. The Commission may recommend to the Council the granting of mutual assistance under Article 109h.

3. After the Commission has delivered an opinion and the Committee referred to in Article 109c has been consulted, the Council may, acting by a qualified majority, decide that the State concerned shall amend, suspend or abolish the protective measures referred to above.

4. Subject to Article 109k(6), this Article shall cease to apply from the beginning of the third stage.

Article 109j

1. The Commission and the EMI shall report to the Council on the progress made in the fulfilment by the Member States of their obligations regarding the achievement of economic and monetary union. These reports shall include an examination of the compatibility between each Member State's national legislation, including the statutes of its national central bank, and Articles 107 and 108 of this Treaty and the Statute of the ESCB. The reports shall also examine the achievement of a high degree of sustainable convergence by reference to the fulfilment by each Member State of the following criteria:

— *the achievement of a high degree of price stability; this will be apparent from a rate of inflation which is close to that of, at most, the three best performing Member States in terms of price stability;*

— *the sustainability of the government financial position; this will be apparent from having achieved a government budgetary position without a deficit that is excessive as determined in accordance with Article 104c(6);*

— *the observance of the normal fluctuation margins provided for by the exchange-rate mechanism of the European Monetary System, for at least two years, without devaluing against the currency of any other Member State;*

— *the durability of convergence achieved by the Member State and of its participation in the exchange-rate mechanism of the European Monetary System being reflected in the long-term interest-rate levels.*

The four criteria mentioned in this paragraph and the relevant periods over which they are to be respected are developed further in a Protocol annexed to this Treaty. The reports of the Commission and the EMI shall also take account of the development of the ecu, the results of the integration of markets, the situation and development of the balances of payments on current account and an examination of the development of unit labour costs and other price indices.

2. On the basis of these reports, the Council, acting by a qualified majority on a recommendation from the Commission, shall assess:

— *for each Member State, whether it fulfils the necessary conditions for the adoption of a single currency;*

— *whether a majority of the Member States fulfil the necessary conditions for the adoption of a single currency,*

and recommend its findings to the Council, meeting in the composition of the Heads of State or Government. The European

Parliament shall be consulted and forward its opinion to the Council, meeting in the composition of the Heads of State or Government.

3. Taking due account of the reports referred to in paragraph 1 and the opinion of the European Parliament referred to in paragraph 2, the Council, meeting in the composition of Heads of State or Government, shall, acting by a qualified majority, not later than 31 December 1996:

— *decide, on the basis of the recommendations of the Council referred to in paragraph 2, whether a majority of the Member States fulfil the necessary conditions for the adoption of a single currency;*

— *decide whether it is appropriate for the Community to enter the third stage,*

and if so

— *set the date for the beginning of the third stage.*

4. If by the end of 1997 the date for the beginning of the third stage has not been set, the third stage shall start on 1 January 1999. Before 1 July 1998, the Council, meeting in the composition of Heads of State or Government, after a repetition of the procedure provided for in paragraphs 1 and 2, with the exception of the second indent of paragraph 2, taking into account the reports referred to in paragraph 1 and the opinion of the European Parliament, shall, acting by a qualified majority and on the basis of the recommendations of the Council referred to in paragraph 2, confirm which Member States fulfil the necessary conditions for the adoption of a single currency.

Article 109k

1. If the decision has been taken to set the date in accordance with Article 109j(3), the Council shall, on the basis of its recommendations referred to in Article 109j(2), acting by a qualified majority on a recommendation from the Commission, decide whether any, and if so which, Member States shall have a derogation as defined in paragraph 3 of this Article. Such Member States shall in this Treaty be referred to as "Member States with a derogation".

If the Council has confirmed which Member States fulfil the necessary conditions for the adoption of a single currency, in accordance with Article 109j(4), those Member States which do not fulfil the conditions shall have a derogation as defined in paragraph 3 of this Article. Such Member States shall in this Treaty be referred to as "Member States with a derogation".

2. At least once every two years, or at the request of a Member State with a derogation, the Commission and the ECB shall report to the Council in accordance with the procedure laid down in

Article 109j(1). After consulting the European Parliament and after discussion in the Council, meeting in the composition of the Heads of State or Government, the Council shall, acting by a qualified majority on a proposal from the Commission, decide which Member States with a derogation fulfil the necessary conditions on the basis of the criteria set out in Article 109j(1), and abrogate the derogations of the Member States concerned.

3. A derogation referred to in paragraph 1 shall entail that the following Articles do not apply to the Member State concerned: Articles 104c(9) and (11), 105(1), (2), (3) and (5), 105a, 108a, 109, and 109a(2)(b). The exclusion of such a Member State and its national central bank from rights and obligations within the ESCB is laid down in Chapter IX of the Statute of the ESCB.

4. In Articles 105(1), (2) and (3), 105a, 108a, 109 and 109a(2)(b), "Member States" shall be read as "Member States without a derogation".

5. The voting rights of Member States with a derogation shall be suspended for the Council decisions referred to in the Articles of this Treaty mentioned in paragraph 3. In that case, by way of derogation from Articles 148 and 189a(1), a qualified majority shall be defined as two-thirds of the votes of the representatives of the Member States without a derogation weighted in accordance with Article 148(2), and unanimity of those Member States shall be required for an act requiring unanimity.

6. Articles 109h and 109i shall continue to apply to a Member State with a derogation.

Article 109l

1. Immediately after the decision on the date for the beginning of the third stage has been taken in accordance with Article 109j(3), or, as the case may be, immediately after 1 July 1998:

— *the Council shall adopt the provisions referred to in Article 106(6);*

— *the governments of the Member States without a derogation shall appoint, in accordance with the procedure set out in Article 50 of the Statute of the ESCB, the President, the Vice-President and the other members of the Executive Board of the ECB. If there are Member States with a derogation, the number of members of the Executive Board may be smaller than provided for in Article 11.1 of the Statute of the ESCB, but in no circumstances shall it be less than four.*

As soon as the Executive Board is appointed, the ESCB and the ECB shall be established and shall prepare for their full operation as described in this Treaty and the Statute of the ESCB. The full exercise of their powers shall start from the first day of the third stage.

2. As soon as the ECB is established, it shall, if necessary, take over tasks of the EMI. The EMI shall go into liquidation upon the establishment of the ECB; the modalities of liquidation are laid down in the Statute of the EMI.

3. If and as long as there are Member States with a derogation, and without prejudice to Article 106(3) of this Treaty, the General Council of the ECB referred to in Article 45 of the Statute of the ESCB shall be constituted as a third decision-making body of the ECB.

4. At the starting date of the third stage, the Council shall, acting with the unanimity of the Member States without a derogation, on a proposal from the Commission and after consulting the ECB, adopt the conversion rates at which their currencies shall be irrevocably fixed and at which irrevocably fixed rate the ecu shall be substituted for these currencies, and the ecu will become a currency in its own right. This measure shall by itself not modify the external value of the ecu. The Council shall, acting according to the same procedure, also take the other measures necessary for the rapid introduction of the ecu as the single currency of those Member States.

5. If it is decided, according to the procedure set out in Article 109k(2), to abrogate a derogation, the Council shall, acting with the unanimity of the Member States without a derogation and the Member State concerned, on a proposal from the Commission and after consulting the ECB, adopt the rate at which the ecu shall be substituted for the currency of the Member State concerned, and take the other measures necessary for the introduction of the ecu as the single currency in the Member State concerned.

Article 109m

1. Until the beginning of the third stage, each Member State shall treat its exchange-rate policy as a matter of common interest. In so doing, Member States shall take account of the experience acquired in cooperation within the framework of the European Monetary System (EMS) and in developing the ecu, and shall respect existing powers in this field.

2. From the beginning of the third stage and for as long as a Member State has a derogation, paragraph 1 shall apply by analogy to the exchange-rate policy of that Member State.'

(26) In Title II of Part Three, the title of Chapter 4 shall be replaced by the following:

'TITLE VII. COMMON COMMERCIAL POLICY'

(27) Article 111 shall be repealed.

(28) Article 113 shall be replaced by the following:

'*Article 113*

1. The common commercial policy shall be based on uniform principles, particularly in regard to changes in tariff rates, the conclusion of tariff and trade agreements, the achievement of uniformity in measures of liberalization, export policy and measures to protect trade such as those to be taken in the event of dumping or subsidies.

2. The Commission shall submit proposals to the Council for implementing the common commercial policy.

3. Where agreements with one or more States or international organizations need to be negotiated, the Commission shall make recommendations to the Council, which shall authorize the Commission to open the necessary negotiations.

The Commission shall conduct these negotiations in consultation with a special committee appointed by the Council to assist the Commission in this task and within the framework of such directives as the Council may issue to it.

The relevant provisions of Article 228 shall apply.

4. In exercising the powers conferred upon it by this Article, the Council shall act by a qualified majority.'

(29) Article 114 shall be repealed.

(30) Article 115 shall be replaced by the following:

'*Article 115*

In order to ensure that the execution of measures of commercial policy taken in accordance with this Treaty by any Member State is not obstructed by deflection of trade, or where differences between such measures lead to economic difficulties in one or more Member States, the Commission shall recommend the methods for the requisite cooperation between Member States. Failing this, the Commission may authorize Member States to take the necessary protective measures, the conditions and details of which it shall determine.

In case of urgency, Member States shall request authorization to take the necessary measures themselves from the Commission, which shall take a decision as soon as possible; the Member States concerned shall then notify the measures to the other Member States. The Commission may decide at any time that the Member States concerned shall amend or abolish the measures in question.

In the selection of such measures, priority shall be given to those which cause the least disturbance to the functioning of the common market.'

(31) Article 116 shall be repealed.

(32) In Part Three, the title of Title III shall be replaced by the following:

'TITLE VIII. SOCIAL POLICY, EDUCATION, VOCATIONAL TRAINING AND YOUTH'

(33) The first subparagraph of Article 118a(2) shall be replaced by the following:

'2. In order to help achieve the objective laid down in the first paragraph, the Council, acting in accordance with the procedure referred to in Article 189c and after consulting the Economic and Social Committee, shall adopt by means of directives, minimum requirements for gradual implementation, having regard to the conditions and technical rules obtaining in each of the Member States.'

(34) Article 123 shall be replaced by the following:

'Article 123

In order to improve employment opportunities for workers in the internal market and to contribute thereby to raising the standard of living, a European Social Fund is hereby established in accordance with the provisions set out below; it shall aim to render the employment of workers easier and to increase their geographical and occupational mobility within the Community, and to facilitate their adaptation to industrial changes and to changes in production systems, in particular through vocational training and retraining.'

(35) Article 125 shall be replaced by the following:

'Article 125

The Council, acting in accordance with the procedure referred to in Article 189c and after consulting the Economic and Social Committee, shall adopt implementing decisions relating to the European Social Fund.'

(36) Articles 126, 127 and 128 shall be replaced by the following:

'CHAPTER 3. EDUCATION, VOCATIONAL TRAINING AND YOUTH

Article 126

1. The Community shall contribute to the development of quality education by encouraging cooperation between Member States and, if necessary, by supporting and supplementing their action, while fully respecting the responsibility of the Member States for the content of teaching and the organization of education systems and their cultural and linguistic diversity.

2. Community action shall be aimed at:

— *developing the European dimension in education, particularly through the teaching and dissemination of the languages of the Member States;*

— *encouraging mobility of students and teachers,* inter alia *by encouraging the academic recognition of diplomas and periods of study;*

— *promoting cooperation between educational establishments;*

— *developing exchanges of information and experience on issues common to the education systems of the Member States;*

— *encouraging the development of youth exchanges and of exchanges of socio-educational instructors;*

— *encouraging the development of distance education.*

3. The Community and the Member States shall foster cooperation with third countries and the competent international organizations in the field of education, in particular the Council of Europe.

4. In order to contribute to the achievement of the objectives referred to in this Article, the Council:

— *acting in accordance with the procedure referred to in Article 189b, after consulting the Economic and Social Committee and the Committee of the Regions, shall adopt incentive measures, excluding any harmonization of the laws and regulations of the Member States;*

— *acting by a qualified majority on a proposal from the Commission, shall adopt recommendations.*

Article 127

1. The Community shall implement a vocational training policy which shall support and supplement the action of the Member States, while fully respecting the responsibility of the Member States for the content and organization of vocational training.

2. Community action shall aim to:

— *facilitate adaptation to industrial changes, in particular through vocational training and retraining;*

— *improve initial and continuing vocational training in order to facilitate vocational integration and reintegration into the labour market;*

— *facilitate access to vocational training and encourage mobility of instructors and trainees and particularly young people;*

— *stimulate cooperation on training between educational or training establishments and firms;*

— *develop exchanges of information and experience on issues common to the training systems of the Member States.*

3. The Community and the Member States shall foster cooperation with third countries and the competent international organizations in the sphere of vocational training.

4. The Council, acting in accordance with the procedure referred to in Article 189c and after consulting the Economic and Social Committee, shall adopt measures to contribute to the achievement of the objectives referred to in this Article, excluding any harmonization of the laws and regulations of the Member States.'

(37) The following shall be inserted:

'TITLE IX. CULTURE
Article 128

1. The Community shall contribute to the flowering of the cultures of the Member States, while respecting their national and regional diversity and at the same time bringing the common cultural heritage to the fore.

2. Action by the Community shall be aimed at encouraging cooperation between Member States and, if necessary, supporting and supplementing their action in the following areas:

— *improvement of the knowledge and dissemination of the culture and history of the European peoples;*

— *conservation and safeguarding of cultural heritage of European significance;*

— *non-commercial cultural exchanges;*

— *artistic and literary creation, including in the audiovisual sector.*

3. The Community and the Member States shall foster cooperation with third countries and the competent international organizations in the sphere of culture, in particular the Council of Europe.

4. The Community shall take cultural aspects into account in its action under other provisions of this Treaty.

5. In order to contribute to the achievement of the objectives referred to in this Article, the Council:

— *acting in accordance with the procedure referred to in Article 189b and after consulting the Committee of the Regions, shall adopt incentive measures, excluding any harmonization of the laws and regulations of the Member States. The Council shall act unanimously throughout the procedures referred to in Article 189b;*

— *acting unanimously on a proposal from the Commission, shall adopt recommendations.'*

(38) Titles IV, V, VI and VII shall be replaced by the following:

'TITLE X. PUBLIC HEALTH
Article 129

1. The Community shall contribute towards ensuring a high level of human health protection by encouraging cooperation between the Member States and, if necessary, lending support to their action.

Community action shall be directed towards the prevention of diseases, in particular the major health scourges, including drug dependence, by promoting research into their causes and their transmission, as well as health information and education.

Health protection requirements shall form a constituent part of the Community's other policies.

2. Member States shall, in liaison with the Commission, coordinate among themselves their policies and programmes in the areas referred to in paragraph 1. The Commission may, in close contact with the Member States, take any useful initiative to promote such coordination.

3. The Community and the Member States shall foster cooperation with third countries and the competent international organizations in the sphere of public health.

4. In order to contribute to the achievement of the objectives referred to in this Article, the Council:

— acting in accordance with the procedure referred to in Article 189b, after consulting the Economic and Social Committee and the Committee of the Regions, shall adopt incentive measures, excluding any harmonization of the laws and regulations of the Member States;

— acting by a qualified majority on a proposal from the Commission, shall adopt recommendations.

TITLE XI. CONSUMER PROTECTION
Article 129a

1. The Community shall contribute to the attainment of a high level of consumer protection through:

(a) measures adopted pursuant to Article 100a in the context of the completion of the internal market;

(b) specific action which supports and supplements the policy pursued by the Member States to protect the health, safety and economic interests of consumers and to provide adequate information to consumers.

2. The Council, acting in accordance with the procedure referred to in Article 189b and after consulting the Economic and Social Committee, shall adopt the specific action referred to in paragraph 1(b).

3. Action adopted pursuant to paragraph 2 shall not prevent any Member State from maintaining or introducing more stringent protective measures. Such measures must be compatible with this Treaty. The Commission shall be notified of them.

TITLE XII. TRANS–EUROPEAN NETWORKS
Article 129b

1. To help achieve the objectives referred to in Articles 7a and 130a and to enable citizens of the Union, economic operators and regional and local communities to derive full benefit from the setting up of an area without internal frontiers, the Community shall contribute to the establishment and development of trans-European networks in the areas of transport, telecommunications and energy infrastructures.

2. Within the framework of a system of open and competitive markets, action by the Community shall aim at promoting the interconnection and interoperability of national networks as well as access to such networks. It shall take account in particular of the need to link island, landlocked and peripheral regions with the central regions of the Community.

Article 129c

1. In order to achieve the objectives referred to in Article 129b, the Community:

— *shall establish a series of guidelines covering the objectives, priorities and broad lines of measures envisaged in the sphere of trans-European networks; these guidelines shall identify projects of common interest;*

— *shall implement any measures that may prove necessary to ensure the interoperability of the networks, in particular in the field of technical standardization;*

— *may support the financial efforts made by the Member States for projects of common interest financed by Member States, which are identified in the framework of the guidelines referred to in the first indent, particularly through feasibility studies, loan guarantees or interest-rate subsidies; the Community may also contribute, through the Cohesion Fund to be set up no later than 31 December 1993 pursuant to Article 130d, to the financing of specific projects in Member States in the area of transport infrastructure.*

The Community's activities shall take into account the potential economic viability of the projects.

2. Member States shall, in liaison with the Commission, coordinate among themselves the policies pursued at national level which may have a significant impact on the achievement of the objectives referred to in Article 129b. The Commission may, in close cooperation with the Member States, take any useful initiative to promote such coordination.

3. The Community may decide to cooperate with third countries to promote projects of mutual interest and to ensure the interoperability of networks.

Article 129d

The guidelines referred to in Article 129c(1) shall be adopted by the Council, acting in accordance with the procedure referred to in

Article 189b and after consulting the Economic and Social Committee and the Committee of the Regions.

Guidelines and projects of common interest which relate to the territory of a Member State shall require the approval of the Member State concerned.

The Council, acting in accordance with the procedure referred to in Article 189c and after consulting the Economic and Social Committee and the Committee of the Regions, shall adopt the other measures provided for in Article 129c(1).

TITLE XIII. INDUSTRY
Article 130

1. *The Community and the Member States shall ensure that the conditions necessary for the competitiveness of the Community's industry exist.*

For that purpose, in accordance with a system of open and competitive markets, their action shall be aimed at:

— *speeding up the adjustment of industry to structural changes;*

— *encouraging an environment favourable to initiative and to the development of undertakings throughout the Community, particularly small and medium-sized undertakings;*

— *encouraging an environment favourable to cooperation between undertakings;*

— *fostering better exploitation of the industrial potential of policies of innovation, research and technological development.*

2. *The Member States shall consult each other in liaison with the Commission and, where necessary, shall coordinate their action. The Commission may take any useful initiative to promote such coordination.*

3. *The Community shall contribute to the achievement of the objectives set out in paragraph 1 through the policies and activities it pursues under other provisions of this Treaty. The Council, acting unanimously on a proposal from the Commission, after consulting the European Parliament and the Economic and Social Committee, may decide on specific measures in support of action taken in the Member States to achieve the objectives set out in paragraph 1.*

This Title shall not provide a basis for the introduction by the Community of any measure which could lead to a distortion of competition.

TITLE XIV. ECONOMIC AND SOCIAL COHESION
Article 130a

In order to promote its overall harmonious development, the Community shall develop and pursue its actions leading to the strengthening of its economic and social cohesion.

In particular, the Community shall aim at reducing disparities between the levels of development of the various regions and the backwardness of the least favoured regions, including rural areas.

Article 130b

Member States shall conduct their economic policies and shall coordinate them in such a way as, in addition, to attain the objectives set out in Article 130a. The formulation and implementation of the Community's policies and actions and the implementation of the internal market shall take into account the objectives set out in Article 130a and shall contribute to their achievement. The Community shall also support the achievement of these objectives by the action it takes through the structural Funds (European Agricultural Guidance and Guarantee Fund—Guidance Section; European Social Fund; European Regional Development Fund), the European Investment Bank and the other existing financial instruments.

The Commission shall submit a report to the European Parliament, the Council, the Economic and Social Committee and the Committee of the Regions every three years on the progress made towards achieving economic and social cohesion and on the manner in which the various means provided for in this Article have contributed to it. This report shall, if necessary, be accompanied by appropriate proposals.

If specific actions prove necessary outside the Funds and without prejudice to the measures decided upon within the framework of the other Community policies, such actions may be adopted by the Council acting unanimously on a proposal from the Commission and after consulting the European Parliament, the Economic and Social Committee and the Committee of the Regions.

Article 130c

The European Regional Development Fund is intended to help to redress the main regional imbalances in the Community through participation in the development and structural adjustment of regions whose development is lagging behind and in the conversion of declining industrial regions.

Article 130d

Without prejudice to Article 130e, the Council, acting unanimously on a proposal from the Commission and after obtaining the assent of the European Parliament and consulting the Economic and Social Committee and the Committee of the Regions, shall define the tasks, priority objectives and the organization of the structural Funds, which may involve grouping the Funds. The Council, acting by the same procedure, shall also define the general rules applicable to them and the provisions necessary to ensure their effectiveness and the coordination of the Funds with one another and with the other existing financial instruments.

The Council, acting in accordance with the same procedure, shall before 31 December 1993 set up a Cohesion Fund to provide a financial contribution to projects in the fields of environment and trans-European networks in the area of transport infrastructure.

Article 130e

Implementing decisions relating to the European Regional Development Fund shall be taken by the Council, acting in accordance with the procedure referred to in Article 189c and after consulting the Economic and Social Committee and the Committee of the Regions.

With regard to the European Agricultural Guidance and Guarantee Fund—Guidance Section, and the European Social Fund, Articles 43 and 125 respectively shall continue to apply.

TITLE XV. RESEARCH AND TECHNOLOGICAL DEVELOPMENT

Article 130f

1. The Community shall have the objective of strengthening the scientific and technological bases of Community industry and encouraging it to become more competitive at international level, while promoting all the research activities deemed necessary by virtue of other Chapters of this Treaty.

2. For this purpose the Community shall, throughout the Community, encourage undertakings, including small and medium-sized undertakings, research centres and universities in their research and technological development activities of high quality; it shall support their efforts to cooperate with one another, aiming, notably, at enabling undertakings to exploit the internal market potential to the full, in particular through the opening up of national public contracts, the definition of common standards and the removal of legal and fiscal obstacles to that cooperation.

3. All Community activities under this Treaty in the area of research and technological development, including demonstration projects, shall be decided on and implemented in accordance with the provisions of this Title.

Article 130g

In pursuing these objectives, the Community shall carry out the following activities, complementing the activities carried out in the Member States:

(a) implementation of research, technological development and demonstration programmes, by promoting cooperation with and between undertakings, research centres and universities;

(b) promotion of cooperation in the field of Community research, technological development and demonstration with third countries and international organizations;

(c) dissemination and optimization of the results of activities in Community research, technological development and demonstration;

(d) stimulation of the training and mobility of researchers in the Community.

Article 130h

1. The Community and the Member States shall coordinate their research and technological development activities so as to ensure that national policies and Community policy are mutually consistent.

2. In close cooperation with the Member States, the Commission may take any useful initiative to promote the coordination referred to in paragraph 1.

Article 130i

1. A multiannual framework programme, setting out all the activities of the Community, shall be adopted by the Council, acting in accordance with the procedure referred to in Article 189b after consulting the Economic and Social Committee. The Council shall act unanimously throughout the procedures referred to in Article 189b.

The framework programme shall:

— *establish the scientific and technological objectives to be achieved by the activities provided for in Article 130g and fix the relevant priorities;*

— *indicate the broad lines of such activities;*

— *fix the maximum overall amount and the detailed rules for Community financial participation in the framework programme and the respective shares in each of the activities provided for.*

2. The framework programme shall be adapted or supplemented as the situation changes.

3. The framework programme shall be implemented through specific programmes developed within each activity. Each specific programme shall define the detailed rules for implementing it, fix its duration and provide for the means deemed necessary. The sum of the amounts deemed necessary, fixed in the specific programmes, may not exceed the overall maximum amount fixed for the framework programme and each activity.

4. The Council, acting by a qualified majority on a proposal from the Commission and after consulting the European Parliament and the Economic and Social Committee, shall adopt the specific programmes.

Article 130j

For the implementation of the multiannual framework programme the Council shall:

— determine the rules for the participation of undertakings, research centres and universities;

— lay down the rules governing the dissemination of research results.

Article 130k

In implementing the multiannual framework programme, supplementary programmes may be decided on involving the participation of certain Member States only, which shall finance them subject to possible Community participation.

The Council shall adopt the rules applicable to supplementary programmes, particularly as regards the dissemination of knowledge and access by other Member States.

Article 130l

In implementing the multiannual framework programme the Community may make provision, in agreement with the Member States concerned, for participation in research and development programmes undertaken by several Member States, including participation in the structures created for the execution of those programmes.

Article 130m

In implementing the multiannual framework programme the Community may make provision for cooperation in Community research, technological development and demonstration with third countries or international organizations.

The detailed arrangements for such cooperation may be the subject of agreements between the Community and the third parties concerned, which shall be negotiated and concluded in accordance with Article 228.

Article 130n

The Community may set up joint undertakings or any other structure necessary for the efficient execution of Community research, technological development and demonstration programmes.

Article 130o

The Council, acting unanimously on a proposal from the Commission and after consulting the European Parliament and the Economic and Social Committee, shall adopt the provisions referred to in Article 130n.

The Council, acting in accordance with the procedure referred to in Article 189c and after consulting the Economic and Social

Committee, shall adopt the provisions referred to in Articles 130j to l. Adoption of the supplementary programmes shall require the agreement of the Member States concerned.

Article 130p

At the beginning of each year the Commission shall send a report to the European Parliament and the Council. The report shall include information on research and technological development activities and the dissemination of results during the previous year, and the work programme for the current year.

TITLE XVI. ENVIRONMENT

Article 130r

1. Community policy on the environment shall contribute to pursuit of the following objectives:

— *preserving, protecting and improving the quality of the environment;*

— *protecting human health;*

— *prudent and rational utilization of natural resources;*

— *promoting measures at international level to deal with regional or worldwide environmental problems.*

2. Community policy on the environment shall aim at a high level of protection taking into account the diversity of situations in the various regions of the Community. It shall be based on the precautionary principle and on the principles that preventive action should be taken, that environmental damage should as a priority be rectified at source and that the polluter should pay. Environmental protection requirements must be integrated into the definition and implementation of other Community policies.

In this context, harmonization measures answering these requirements shall include, where appropriate, a safeguard clause allowing Member States to take provisional measures, for non-economic environmental reasons, subject to a Community inspection procedure.

3. In preparing its policy on the environment, the Community shall take account of:

— *available scientific and technical data;*

— *environmental conditions in the various regions of the Community;*

— *the potential benefits and costs of action or lack of action;*

— *the economic and social development of the Community as a whole and the balanced development of its regions.*

4. Within their respective spheres of competence, the Community and the Member States shall cooperate with third countries and with the competent international organizations. The arrange-

ments for Community cooperation may be the subject of agreements between the Community and the third parties concerned, which shall be negotiated and concluded in accordance with Article 228.

The previous subparagraph shall be without prejudice to Member States' competence to negotiate in international bodies and to conclude international agreements.

Article 130s

1. The Council, acting in accordance with the procedure referred to in Article 189c and after consulting the Economic and Social Committee, shall decide what action is to be taken by the Community in order to achieve the objectives referred to in Article 130r.

2. By way of derogation from the decision-making procedure provided for in paragraph 1 and without prejudice to Article 100a, the Council, acting unanimously on a proposal from the Commission and after consulting the European Parliament and the Economic and Social Committee, shall adopt:

— provisions primarily of a fiscal nature;

— measures concerning town and country planning, land use with the exception of waste management and measures of a general nature, and management of water resources;

— measures significantly affecting a Member State's choice between different energy sources and the general structure of its energy supply.

The Council may, under the conditions laid down in the preceding subparagraph, define those matters referred to in this paragraph on which decisions are to be taken by a qualified majority.

3. In other areas, general action programmes setting out priority objectives to be attained shall be adopted by the Council, acting in accordance with the procedure referred to in Article 189b and after consulting the Economic and Social Committee.

The Council, acting under the terms of paragraph 1 or paragraph 2 according to the case, shall adopt the measures necessary for the implementation of these programmes.

4. Without prejudice to certain measures of a Community nature, the Member States shall finance and implement the environment[al] policy.

5. Without prejudice to the principle that the polluter should pay, if a measure based on the provisions of paragraph 1 involves costs deemed disproportionate for the public authorities of a Member State, the Council shall, in the act adopting that measure, lay down appropriate provisions in the form of:

— temporary derogations, and/or

— *financial support from the Cohesion Fund to be set up no later than 31 December 1993 pursuant to Article 130d.*

Article 130t

The protective measures adopted pursuant to Article 130s shall not prevent any Member State from maintaining or introducing more stringent protective measures. Such measures must be compatible with this Treaty. They shall be notified to the Commission.

TITLE XVII. DEVELOPMENT COOPERATION

Article 130u

1. Community policy in the sphere of development cooperation, which shall be complementary to the policies pursued by the Member States, shall foster:

— the sustainable economic and social development of the developing countries and more particularly the most disadvantaged among them;

— the smooth and gradual integration of the developing countries into the world economy;

— the campaign against poverty in the developing countries.

2. Community policy in this area shall contribute to the general objective of developing and consolidating democracy and the rule of law, and to that of respecting human rights and fundamental freedoms.

3. The Community and the Member States shall comply with the commitments and take account of the objectives they have approved in the context of the United Nations and other competent international organizations.

Article 130v

The Community shall take account of the objectives referred to in Article 130u in the policies that it implements which are likely to affect developing countries.

Article 130w

1. Without prejudice to the other provisions of this Treaty the Council, acting in accordance with the procedure referred to in Article 189c, shall adopt the measures necessary to further the objectives referred to in Article 130u. Such measures may take the form of multiannual programmes.

2. The European Investment Bank shall contribute, under the terms laid down in its Statute, to the implementation of the measures referred to in paragraph 1.

3. The provisions of this Article shall not affect cooperation with the African, Caribbean and Pacific countries in the framework of the ACP–EEC Convention.

Article 130x

1. The Community and the Member States shall coordinate their policies on development cooperation and shall consult each other on their aid programmes, including in international organizations and during international conferences. They may undertake joint action. Member States shall contribute if necessary to the implementation of Community aid programmes.

2. The Commission may take any useful initiative to promote the coordination referred to in paragraph 1.

Article 130y

Within their respective spheres of competence, the Community and the Member States shall cooperate with third countries and with the competent international organizations. The arrangements for Community cooperation may be the subject of agreements between the Community and the third parties concerned, which shall be negotiated and concluded in accordance with Article 228.

The previous paragraph shall be without prejudice to Member States' competence to negotiate in international bodies and to conclude international agreements.'

E. In Part Five 'Institutions of the Community'

(39) Article 137 shall be replaced by the following:

'*Article 137*

The European Parliament, which shall consist of representatives of the peoples of the States brought together in the Community, shall exercise the powers conferred upon it by this Treaty.'

(40) Paragraph 3 of Article 138 shall be replaced by the following:

'3. *The European Parliament shall draw up proposals for elections by direct universal suffrage in accordance with a uniform procedure in all Member States.*

The Council shall, acting unanimously after obtaining the assent of the European Parliament, which shall act by a majority of its component members, lay down the appropriate provisions, which it shall recommend to Member States for adoption in accordance with their respective constitutional requirements.'

(41) The following Articles shall be inserted:

'*Article 138a*

Political parties at European level are important as a factor for integration within the Union. They contribute to forming a European awareness and to expressing the political will of the citizens of the Union.

Article 138b

In so far as provided in this Treaty, the European Parliament shall participate in the process leading up to the adoption of

Community acts by exercising its powers under the procedures laid down in Articles 189b and 189c and by giving its assent or delivering advisory opinions.

The European Parliament may, acting by a majority of its members, request the Commission to submit any appropriate proposal on matters on which it considers that a Community act is required for the purpose of implementing this Treaty.

Article 138c

In the course of its duties, the European Parliament may, at the request of a quarter of its members, set up a temporary Committee of Inquiry to investigate, without prejudice to the powers conferred by this Treaty on other institutions or bodies, alleged contraventions or maladministration in the implementation of Community law, except where the alleged facts are being examined before a court and while the case is still subject to legal proceedings.

The temporary Committee of Inquiry shall cease to exist on the submission of its report.

The detailed provisions governing the exercise of the right of inquiry shall be determined by common accord of the European Parliament, the Council and the Commission.

Article 138d

Any citizen of the Union, and any natural or legal person residing or having his registered office in a Member State, shall have the right to address, individually or in association with other citizens or persons, a petition to the European Parliament on a matter which comes within the Community's fields of activity and which affects him directly.

Article 138e

1. The European Parliament shall appoint an Ombudsman empowered to receive complaints from any citizen of the Union or any natural or legal person residing or having his registered office in a Member State concerning instances of maladministration in the activities of the Community institutions or bodies, with the exception of the Court of Justice and the Court of First Instance acting in their judicial role.

In accordance with his duties, the Ombudsman shall conduct inquiries for which he finds grounds, either on his own initiative or on the basis of complaints submitted to him direct or through a member of the European Parliament, except where the alleged facts are or have been the subject of legal proceedings. Where the Ombudsman establishes an instance of maladministration, he shall refer the matter to the institution concerned, which shall have a period of three months in which to inform him of its views. The Ombudsman shall then forward a report to the European

Parliament and the institution concerned. The person lodging the complaint shall be informed of the outcome of such inquiries.

The Ombudsman shall submit an annual report to the European Parliament on the outcome of his inquiries.

2. The Ombudsman shall be appointed after each election of the European Parliament for the duration of its term of office. The Ombudsman shall be eligible for reappointment.

The Ombudsman may be dismissed by the Court of Justice at the request of the European Parliament if he no longer fulfils the conditions required for the performance of his duties or if he is guilty of serious misconduct.

3. The Ombudsman shall be completely independent in the performance of his duties. In the performance of those duties he shall neither seek nor take instructions from any body. The Ombudsman may not, during his term of office, engage in any other occupation, whether gainful or not.

4. The European Parliament shall, after seeking an opinion from the Commission and with the approval of the Council acting by a qualified majority, lay down the regulations and general conditions governing the performance of the Ombudsman's duties.'

(42) The second subparagraph of Article 144 shall be supplemented by the following sentence:

'In this case, the term of office of the members of the Commission appointed to replace them shall expire on the date on which the term of office of the members of the Commission obliged to resign as a body would have expired.'

(43) The following Article shall be inserted:

'Article 146

The Council shall consist of a representative of each Member State at ministerial level, authorized to commit the government of that Member State.

The office of President shall be held in turn by each Member State in the Council for a term of six months, in the following order of Member States:

— *for a first cycle of six years: Belgium, Denmark, Germany, Greece, Spain, France, Ireland, Italy, Luxembourg, Netherlands, Portugal, United Kingdom;*

— *for the following cycle of six years: Denmark, Belgium, Greece, Germany, France, Spain, Italy, Ireland, Netherlands, Luxembourg, United Kingdom, Portugal.'*

(44) The following Article shall be inserted:

'Article 147

The Council shall meet when convened by its President on his own initiative or at the request of one of its members or of the Commission.'

(45) Article 149 shall be repealed.

(46) The following Article shall be inserted:

'Article 151

1. A committee consisting of the Permanent Representatives of the Member States shall be responsible for preparing the work of the Council and for carrying out the tasks assigned to it by the Council.

2. The Council shall be assisted by a General Secretariat, under the direction of a Secretary–General. The Secretary–General shall be appointed by the Council acting unanimously.

The Council shall decide on the organization of the General Secretariat.

3. The Council shall adopt its rules of procedure.'

(47) The following Article shall be inserted:

'Article 154

The Council shall, acting by a qualified majority, determine the salaries, allowances and pensions of the President and members of the Commission, and of the President, Judges, Advocates–General and Registrar of the Court of Justice. It shall also, again by a qualified majority, determine any payment to be made instead of remuneration.'

(48) The following Articles shall be inserted:

'Article 156

The Commission shall publish annually, not later than one month before the opening of the session of the European Parliament, a general report on the activities of the Community.

Article 157

1. The Commission shall consist of 17 members, who shall be chosen on the grounds of their general competence and whose independence is beyond doubt.

The number of members of the Commission may be altered by the Council, acting unanimously.

Only nationals of Member States may be members of the Commission.

The Commission must include at least one national of each of the Member States, but may not include more than two members having the nationality of the same State.

2. *The members of the Commission shall, in the general interest of the Community, be completely independent in the performance of their duties.*

In the performance of these duties, they shall neither seek nor take instructions from any government or from any other body. They shall refrain from any action incompatible with their duties. Each Member State undertakes to respect this principle and not to seek to influence the members of the Commission in the performance of their tasks.

The members of the Commission may not, during their term of office, engage in any other occupation, whether gainful or not. When entering upon their duties they shall give a solemn undertaking that, both during and after their term of office, they will respect the obligations arising therefrom and in particular their duty to behave with integrity and discretion as regards the acceptance, after they have ceased to hold office, of certain appointments or benefits. In the event of any breach of these obligations, the Court of Justice may, on application by the Council or the Commission, rule that the member concerned be, according to the circumstances, either compulsorily retired in accordance with Article 160 or deprived of his right to a pension or other benefits in its stead.

Article 158

1. The members of the Commission shall be appointed, in accordance with the procedure referred to in paragraph 2, for a period of five years, subject, if need be, to Article 144.

Their term of office shall be renewable.

2. The governments of the Member States shall nominate by common accord, after consulting the European Parliament, the person they intend to appoint as President of the Commission.

The governments of the Member States shall, in consultation with the nominee for President, nominate the other persons whom they intend to appoint as members of the Commission.

The President and the other members of the Commission thus nominated shall be subject as a body to a vote of approval by the European Parliament. After approval by the European Parliament, the President and the other members of the Commission shall be appointed by common accord of the governments of the Member States.

3. Paragraphs 1 and 2 shall be applied for the first time to the President and the other members of the Commission whose term of office begins on 7 January 1995.

The President and the other members of the Commission whose term of office begins on 7 January 1993 shall be appointed by common accord of the governments of the Member States. Their term of office shall expire on 6 January 1995.

Article 159

Apart from normal replacement, or death, the duties of a member of the Commission shall end when he resigns or is compulsorily retired.

The vacancy thus caused shall be filled for the remainder of the member's term of office by a new member appointed by common accord of the governments of the Member States. The Council may, acting unanimously, decide that such a vacancy need not be filled.

In the event of resignation, compulsory retirement or death, the President shall be replaced for the remainder of his term of office. The procedure laid down in Article 158(2) shall be applicable for the replacement of the President.

Save in the case of compulsory retirement under Article 160, members of the Commission shall remain in office until they have been replaced.

Article 160

If any member of the Commission no longer fulfils the conditions required for the performance of his duties or if he has been guilty of serious misconduct, the Court of Justice may, on application by the Council or the Commission, compulsorily retire him.

Article 161

The Commission may appoint a Vice-President or two Vice-Presidents from among its members.

Article 162

1. The Council and the Commission shall consult each other and shall settle by common accord their methods of cooperation.

2. The Commission shall adopt its rules of procedure so as to ensure that both it and its departments operate in accordance with the provisions of this Treaty. It shall ensure that these rules are published.

Article 163

The Commission shall act by a majority of the number of members provided for in Article 157.

A meeting of the Commission shall be valid only if the number of members laid down in its rules of procedure is present.'

(49) Article 165 shall be replaced by the following:

'Article 165

The Court of Justice shall consist of 13 Judges.

The Court of Justice shall sit in plenary session. It may, however, form chambers, each consisting of three or five Judges, either to undertake certain preparatory inquiries or to adjudicate on particular categories of cases in accordance with rules laid down for these purposes.

The Court of Justice shall sit in plenary session when a Member State or a Community institution that is a party to the proceedings so requests.

Should the Court of Justice so request, the Council may, acting unanimously, increase the number of Judges and make the necessary adjustments to the second and third paragraphs of this Article and to the second paragraph of Article 167.'

(50) Article 168a shall be replaced by the following:

'Article 168a

1. A Court of First Instance shall be attached to the Court of Justice with jurisdiction to hear and determine at first instance, subject to a right of appeal to the Court of Justice on points of law only and in accordance with the conditions laid down in the Statute, certain classes of action or proceeding defined in accordance with the conditions laid down in paragraph 2. The Court of First Instance shall not be competent to hear and determine questions referred for a preliminary ruling under Article 177.

2. At the request of the Court of Justice and after consulting the European Parliament and the Commission, the Council, acting unanimously, shall determine the classes of action or proceeding referred to in paragraph 1 and the composition of the Court of First Instance and shall adopt the necessary adjustments and additional provisions to the Statute of the Court of Justice. Unless the Council decides otherwise, the provisions of this Treaty relating to the Court of Justice, in particular the provisions of the Protocol on the Statute of the Court of Justice, shall apply to the Court of First Instance.

3. The members of the Court of First Instance shall be chosen from persons whose independence is beyond doubt and who possess the ability required for appointment to judicial office; they shall be appointed by common accord of the governments of the Member States for a term of six years. The membership shall be partially renewed every three years. Retiring members shall be eligible for reappointment.

4. The Court of First Instance shall establish its rules of procedure in agreement with the Court of Justice. Those rules shall require the unanimous approval of the Council.'

(51) Article 171 shall be replaced by the following:

'Article 171

1. If the Court of Justice finds that a Member State has failed to fulfil an obligation under this Treaty, the State shall be required to take the necessary measures to comply with the judgment of the Court of Justice.

2. If the Commission considers that the Member State concerned has not taken such measures it shall, after giving that State the opportunity to submit its observations, issue a reasoned opinion specifying the points on which the Member State concerned has not complied with the judgment of the Court of Justice.

If the Member State concerned fails to take the necessary measures to comply with the Court's judgment within the time-limit laid down by the Commission, the latter may bring the case before the Court of Justice. In so doing it shall specify the amount of the lump sum or penalty payment to be paid by the Member State concerned which it considers appropriate in the circumstances.

If the Court of Justice finds that the Member State concerned has not complied with its judgment it may impose a lump sum or penalty payment on it.

This procedure shall be without prejudice to Article 170.'

(52) Article 172 shall be replaced by the following:

'Article 172

Regulations adopted jointly by the European Parliament and the Council, and by the Council, pursuant to the provisions of this Treaty, may give the Court of Justice unlimited jurisdiction with regard to the penalties provided for in such regulations.'

(53) Article 173 shall be replaced by the following:

'Article 173

The Court of Justice shall review the legality of acts adopted jointly by the European Parliament and the Council, of acts of the Council, of the Commission and of the ECB, other than recommendations and opinions, and of acts of the European Parliament intended to produce legal effects vis-à-vis third parties.

It shall for this purpose have jurisdiction in actions brought by a Member State, the Council or the Commission on grounds of lack of competence, infringement of an essential procedural requirement, infringement of this Treaty or of any rule of law relating to its application, or misuse of powers.

The Court shall have jurisdiction under the same conditions in actions brought by the European Parliament and by the ECB for the purpose of protecting their prerogatives.

Any natural or legal person may, under the same conditions, institute proceedings against a decision addressed to that person or against a decision which, although in the form of a regulation *or a decision addressed to another person, is of direct and individual concern to the former.*

The proceedings provided for in this Article shall be instituted within two months of the publication of the measure, or of its notification to the plaintiff, or, in the absence thereof, of the day on which it came to the knowledge of the latter, as the case may be.'

(54) Article 175 shall be replaced by the following:

'Article 175

Should the European Parliament, the Council or the Commission, in infringement of this Treaty, fail to act, the Member States and the other institutions of the Community may bring an action before the Court of Justice to have the infringement established.

The action shall be admissible only if the institution concerned has first been called upon to act. If, within two months of being so called upon, the institution concerned has not defined its position, the action may be brought within a further period of two months.

Any natural or legal person may, under the conditions laid down in the preceding paragraphs, complain to the Court of Justice that an institution of the Community has failed to address to that person any act other than a recommendation or an opinion.

The Court of Justice shall have jurisdiction, under the same conditions, in actions or proceedings brought by the ECB in the areas falling within the latter's field of competence and in actions or proceedings brought against the latter.'

(55) Article 176 shall be replaced by the following:

'Article 176

The institution or institutions whose act has been declared void or whose failure to act has been declared contrary to this Treaty shall be required to take the necessary measures to comply with the judgment of the Court of Justice.

This obligation shall not affect any obligation which may result from the application of the second paragraph of Article 215.

This Article shall also apply to the ECB.'

(56) Article 177 shall be replaced by the following:

'Article 177

The Court of Justice shall have jurisdiction to give preliminary rulings concerning:

(a) the interpretation of this Treaty;

(b) the validity and interpretation of acts of the institutions of the Community and of the ECB;

(c) the interpretation of the statutes of bodies established by an act of the Council, where those statutes so provide.

Where such a question is raised before any court or tribunal of a Member State, that court or tribunal may, if it considers that a decision on the question is necessary to enable it to give judgment, request the Court of Justice to give a ruling thereon.

Where any such question is raised in a case pending before a court or tribunal of a Member State against whose decisions there is no judicial remedy under national law, that court or tribunal shall bring the matter before the Court of Justice.'

(57) Article 180 shall be replaced by the following:

'Article 180

The Court of Justice shall, within the limits hereinafter laid down, have jurisdiction in disputes concerning:

(a) the fulfilment by Member States of obligations under the Statute of the European Investment Bank. In this connection, the Board of Directors of the Bank shall enjoy the powers conferred upon the Commission by Article 169;

(b) measures adopted by the Board of Governors of the European Investment Bank. In this connection, any Member State, the Commission or the Board of Directors of the Bank may institute proceedings under the conditions laid down in Article 173;

(c) measures adopted by the Board of Directors of the European Investment Bank. Proceedings against such measures may be instituted only by Member States or by the Commission, under the conditions laid down in Article 173, and solely on the grounds of non-compliance with the procedure provided for in Article 21(2), (5), (6) and (7) of the Statute of the Bank;

(d) the fulfilment by national central banks of obligations under this Treaty and the Statute of the ESCB. In this connection the powers of the Council of the ECB in respect of national central banks shall be the same as those conferred upon the Commission in respect of Member States by Article 169. If the Court of Justice finds that a national central bank has failed to fulfil an obligation under this Treaty, that bank shall be required to take the necessary measures to comply with the judgment of the Court of Justice.'

(58) Article 184 shall be replaced by the following:

'Article 184

Notwithstanding the expiry of the period laid down in the fifth paragraph of Article 173, any party may, in proceedings in which a regulation adopted jointly by the European Parliament and the Council, or a regulation of the Council, of the Commission, or of the ECB is at issue, plead the grounds specified in the second paragraph of Article 173 in order to invoke before the Court of Justice the inapplicability of that regulation.'

(59) The following section shall be inserted:

'SECTION 5. THE COURT OF AUDITORS
Article 188a

The Court of Auditors shall carry out the audit.

Article 188b

1. *The Court of Auditors shall consist of 12 members.*

2. *The members of the Court of Auditors shall be chosen from among persons who belong or have belonged in their respective countries to external audit bodies or who are especially qualified for this office. Their independence must be beyond doubt.*

3. *The members of the Court of Auditors shall be appointed for a term of six years by the Council, acting unanimously after consulting the European Parliament.*

However, when the first appointments are made, four members of the Court of Auditors, chosen by lot, shall be appointed for a term of office of four years only.

The members of the Court of Auditors shall be eligible for reappointment.

They shall elect the President of the Court of Auditors from among their number for a term of three years. The President may be re-elected.

4. *The members of the Court of Auditors shall, in the general interest of the Community, be completely independent in the performance of their duties.*

In the performance of these duties, they shall neither seek nor take instructions from any government or from any other body. They shall refrain from any action incompatible with their duties.

5. *The members of the Court of Auditors may not, during their term of office, engage in any other occupation, whether gainful or not. When entering upon their duties they shall give a solemn undertaking that, both during and after their term of office, they will respect the obligations arising therefrom and in particular their duty to behave with integrity and discretion as regards the acceptance, after they have ceased to hold office, of certain appointments or benefits.*

6. *Apart from normal replacement, or death, the duties of a member of the Court of Auditors shall end when he resigns, or is compulsorily retired by a ruling of the Court of Justice pursuant to paragraph 7.*

The vacancy thus caused shall be filled for the remainder of the member's term of office.

Save in the case of compulsory retirement, members of the Court of Auditors shall remain in office until they have been replaced.

7. A member of the Court of Auditors may be deprived of his office or of his right to a pension or other benefits in its stead only if the Court of Justice, at the request of the Court of Auditors, finds that he no longer fulfils the requisite conditions or meets the obligations arising from his office.

8. The Council, acting by a qualified majority, shall determine the conditions of employment of the President and the members of the Court of Auditors and in particular their salaries, allowances and pensions. It shall also, by the same majority, determine any payment to be made instead of remuneration.

9. The provisions of the Protocol on the Privileges and Immunities of the European Communities applicable to the Judges of the Court of Justice shall also apply to the members of the Court of Auditors.

Article 188c

1. The Court of Auditors shall examine the accounts of all revenue and expenditure of the Community. It shall also examine the accounts of all revenue and expenditure of all bodies set up by the Community in so far as the relevant constituent instrument does not preclude such examination.

The Court of Auditors shall provide the European Parliament and the Council with a statement of assurance as to the reliability of the accounts and the legality and regularity of the underlying transactions.

2. The Court of Auditors shall examine whether all revenue has been received and all expenditure incurred in a lawful and regular manner and whether the financial management has been sound.

The audit of revenue shall be carried out on the basis both of the amounts established as due and the amounts actually paid to the Community.

The audit of expenditure shall be carried out on the basis both of commitments undertaken and payments made.

These audits may be carried out before the closure of accounts for the financial year in question.

3. The audit shall be based on records and, if necessary, performed on the spot in the other institutions of the Community and in the Member States. In the Member States the audit shall be carried out in liaison with the national audit bodies or, if these do not have the necessary powers, with the competent national departments. These bodies or departments shall inform the Court of Auditors whether they intend to take part in the audit.

The other institutions of the Community and the national audit bodies or, if these do not have the necessary powers, the competent national departments, shall forward to the Court of Auditors, at its request, any document or information necessary to carry out its task.

4. The Court of Auditors shall draw up an annual report after the close of each financial year. It shall be forwarded to the other institutions of the Community and shall be published, together with the replies of these institutions to the observations of the Court of Auditors, in the Official Journal of the European Communities.

The Court of Auditors may also, at any time, submit observations, particularly in the form of special reports, on specific questions and deliver opinions at the request of one of the other institutions of the Community.

It shall adopt its annual reports, special reports or opinions by a majority of its members.

It shall assist the European Parliament and the Council in exercising their powers of control over the implementation of the budget.'

(60) Article 189 shall be replaced by the following:

'Article 189

In order to carry out their task and in accordance with the provisions of this Treaty, the European Parliament acting jointly with the Council, the Council and the Commission shall make regulations and issue directives, take decisions, make recommendations or deliver opinions.

A regulation shall have general application. It shall be binding in its entirety and directly applicable in all Member States.

A directive shall be binding, as to the result to be achieved, upon each Member State to which it is addressed, but shall leave to the national authorities the choice of form and methods.

A decision shall be binding in its entirety upon those to whom it is addressed.

Recommendations and opinions shall have no binding force.'

(61) The following Articles shall be inserted:

'Article 189a

1. Where, in pursuance of this Treaty, the Council acts on a proposal from the Commission, unanimity shall be required for an act constituting an amendment to that proposal, subject to Article 189b(4) and (5).

2. As long as the Council has not acted, the Commission may alter its proposal at any time during the procedures leading to the adoption of a Community act.

Article 189b

1. Where reference is made in this Treaty to this Article for the adoption of an act, the following procedure shall apply.

2. The Commission shall submit a proposal to the European Parliament and the Council.

The Council, acting by a qualified majority after obtaining the opinion of the European Parliament, shall adopt a common position. The common position shall be communicated to the European Parliament. The Council shall inform the European Parliament fully of the reasons which led it to adopt its common position. The Commission shall inform the European Parliament fully of its position.

If, within three months of such communication, the European Parliament:

(a) approves the common position, the Council shall definitively adopt the act in question in accordance with that common position;

(b) has not taken a decision, the Council shall adopt the act in question in accordance with its common position;

(c) indicates, by an absolute majority of its component members, that it intends to reject the common position, it shall immediately inform the Council. The Council may convene a meeting of the Conciliation Committee referred to in paragraph 4 to explain further its position. The European Parliament shall thereafter either confirm, by an absolute majority of its component members, its rejection of the common position, in which event the proposed act shall be deemed not to have been adopted, or propose amendments in accordance with subparagraph (d) of this paragraph;

(d) proposes amendments to the common position by an absolute majority of its component members, the amended text shall be forwarded to the Council and to the Commission, which shall deliver an opinion on those amendments.

3. If, within three months of the matter being referred to it, the Council, acting by a qualified majority, approves all the amendments of the European Parliament, it shall amend its common position accordingly and adopt the act in question; however, the Council shall act unanimously on the amendments on which the Commission has delivered a negative opinion. If the Council does not approve the act in question, the President of the Council, in agreement with the President of the European Parliament, shall forthwith convene a meeting of the Conciliation Committee.

4. The Conciliation Committee, which shall be composed of the members of the Council or their representatives and an equal number of representatives of the European Parliament, shall have

the task of reaching agreement on a joint text, by a qualified majority of the members of the Council or their representatives and by a majority of the representatives of the European Parliament. The Commission shall take part in the Conciliation Committee's proceedings and shall take all the necessary initiatives with a view to reconciling the positions of the European Parliament and the Council.

5. If, within six weeks of its being convened, the Conciliation Committee approves a joint text, the European Parliament, acting by an absolute majority of the votes cast, and the Council, acting by a qualified majority, shall have a period of six weeks from that approval in which to adopt the act in question in accordance with the joint text. If one of the two institutions fails to approve the proposed act, it shall be deemed not to have been adopted.

6. Where the Conciliation Committee does not approve a joint text, the proposed act shall be deemed not to have been adopted unless the Council, acting by a qualified majority within six weeks of expiry of the period granted to the Conciliation Committee, confirms the common position to which it agreed before the conciliation procedure was initiated, possibly with amendments proposed by the European Parliament. In this case, the act in question shall be finally adopted unless the European Parliament, within six weeks of the date of confirmation by the Council, rejects the text by an absolute majority of its component members, in which case the proposed act shall be deemed not to have been adopted.

7. The periods of three months and six weeks referred to in this Article may be extended by a maximum of one month and two weeks respectively by common accord of the European Parliament and the Council. The period of three months referred to in paragraph 2 shall be automatically extended by two months where paragraph 2(c) applies.

8. The scope of the procedure under this Article may be widened, in accordance with the procedure provided for in Article N(2) of the Treaty on European Union, on the basis of a report to be submitted to the Council by the Commission by 1996 at the latest.

Article 189c

Where reference is made in this Treaty to this Article for the adoption of an act, the following procedure shall apply:

(a) The Council, acting by a qualified majority on a proposal from the Commission and after obtaining the opinion of the European Parliament, shall adopt a common position.

(b) The Council's common position shall be communicated to the European Parliament. The Council and the Commission shall inform the European Parliament fully of the reasons which

led the Council to adopt its common position and also of the Commission's position.

If, within three months of such communication, the European Parliament approves this common position or has not taken a decision within that period, the Council shall definitively adopt the act in question in accordance with the common position.

(c) *The European Parliament may, within the period of three months referred to in subparagraph (b), by an absolute majority of its component members, propose amendments to the Council's common position. The European Parliament may also, by the same majority, reject the Council's common position. The result of the proceedings shall be transmitted to the Council and the Commission.*

If the European Parliament has rejected the Council's common position, unanimity shall be required for the Council to act on a second reading.

(d) *The Commission shall, within a period of one month, re-examine the proposal on the basis of which the Council adopted its common position, by taking into account the amendments proposed by the European Parliament.*

The Commission shall forward to the Council, at the same time as its re-examined proposal, the amendments of the European Parliament which it has not accepted, and shall express its opinion on them. The Council may adopt these amendments unanimously.

(e) *The Council, acting by a qualified majority, shall adopt the proposal as re-examined by the Commission.*

Unanimity shall be required for the Council to amend the proposal as re-examined by the Commission.

(f) *In the cases referred to in subparagraphs (c), (d) and (e), the Council shall be required to act within a period of three months. If no decision is taken within this period, the Commission proposal shall be deemed not to have been adopted.*

(g) *The periods referred to in subparagraphs (b) and (f) may be extended by a maximum of one month by common accord between the Council and the European Parliament.'*

(62) Article 190 shall be replaced by the following:

'*Article 190*

Regulations, directives and decisions adopted jointly by the European Parliament and the Council, and such acts adopted by the Council or the Commission, shall state the reasons on which they are based and shall refer to any proposals or opinions which were required to be obtained pursuant to this Treaty.'

(63) Article 191 shall be replaced by the following:

'Article 191

1. Regulations, directives and decisions adopted in accordance with the procedure referred to in Article 189b shall be signed by the President of the European Parliament and by the President of the Council and published in the Official Journal of the European Communities. *They shall enter into force on the date specified in them or, in the absence thereof, on the 20th day following that of their publication.*

2. Regulations of the Council and of the Commission, as well as directives of those institutions which are addressed to all Member States, shall be published in the Official Journal of the European Communities. *They shall enter into force on the date specified in them or, in the absence thereof, on the 20th day following that of their publication.*

3. Other directives, and decisions, shall be notified to those to whom they are addressed and shall take effect upon such notification.'

(64) Article 194 shall be replaced by the following:

'Article 194

The number of members of the Economic and Social Committee shall be as follows:

Belgium	*12*
Denmark	*9*
Germany	*24*
Greece	*12*
Spain	*21*
France	*24*
Ireland	*9*
Italy	*24*
Luxembourg	*6*
Netherlands	*12*
Portugal	*12*
United Kingdom	*24*

The members of the Committee shall be appointed by the Council, acting unanimously, for four years. Their appointments shall be renewable.

The members of the Committee may not be bound by any mandatory instructions. They shall be completely independent in the performance of their duties, in the general interest of the Community.

The Council, acting by a qualified majority, shall determine the allowances of members of the Committee.'

(65) Article 196 shall be replaced by the following:

'Article 196

The Committee shall elect its chairman and officers from among its members for a term of two years.

It shall adopt its rules of procedure.

The Committee shall be convened by its chairman at the request of the Council or of the Commission. It may also meet on its own initiative.'

(66) Article 198 shall be replaced by the following:

'Article 198

The Committee must be consulted by the Council or by the Commission where this Treaty so provides. The Committee may be consulted by these institutions in all cases in which they consider it appropriate. It may issue an opinion on its own initiative in cases in which it considers such action appropriate.

The Council or the Commission shall, if it considers it necessary, set the Committee, for the submission of its opinion, a time-limit which may not be less than one month from the date on which the chairman receives notification to this effect. Upon expiry of the time-limit, the absence of an opinion shall not prevent further action.

The opinion of the Committee and that of the specialized section, together with a record of the proceedings, shall be forwarded to the Council and to the Commission.'

(67) The following Chapter shall be inserted:

'CHAPTER 4. THE COMMITTEE OF THE REGIONS

Article 198a

A Committee consisting of representatives of regional and local bodies, hereinafter referred to as "the Committee of the Regions", is hereby established with advisory status.

The number of members of the Committee of the Regions shall be as follows:

Belgium	*12*
Denmark	*9*
Germany	*24*
Greece	*12*
Spain	*21*
France	*24*
Ireland	*9*
Italy	*24*
Luxembourg	*6*
Netherlands	*12*
Portugal	*12*
United Kingdom	*24*

The members of the Committee and an equal number of alternate members shall be appointed for four years by the Council acting unanimously on proposals from the respective Member States. Their term of office shall be renewable.

The members of the Committee may not be bound by any mandatory instructions. They shall be completely independent in the performance of their duties, in the general interest of the Community.

Article 198b

The Committee of the Regions shall elect its chairman and officers from among its members for a term of two years.

It shall adopt its rules of procedure and shall submit them for approval to the Council, acting unanimously.

The Committee shall be convened by its chairman at the request of the Council or of the Commission. It may also meet on its own initiative.

Article 198c

The Committee of the Regions shall be consulted by the Council or by the Commission where this Treaty so provides and in all other cases in which one of these two institutions considers it appropriate.

The Council or the Commission shall, if it considers it necessary, set the Committee, for the submission of its opinion, a time-limit which may not be less than one month from the date on which the chairman receives notification to this effect. Upon expiry of the time-limit, the absence of an opinion shall not prevent further action.

Where the Economic and Social Committee is consulted pursuant to Article 198, the Committee of the Regions shall be informed by the Council or the Commission of the request for an opinion. Where it considers that specific regional interests are involved, the Committee of the Regions may issue an opinion on the matter.

It may issue an opinion on its own initiative in cases in which it considers such action appropriate.

The opinion of the Committee, together with a record of the proceedings, shall be forwarded to the Council and to the Commission.'

(68) The following chapter shall be inserted:

'CHAPTER 5. EUROPEAN INVESTMENT BANK

Article 198d

The European Investment Bank shall have legal personality.

The members of the European Investment Bank shall be the Member States.

The Statute of the European Investment Bank is laid down in a Protocol annexed to this Treaty.

Article 198e

The task of the European Investment Bank shall be to contribute, by having recourse to the capital market and utilizing its own resources, to the balanced and steady development of the common market in the interest of the Community. For this purpose the Bank shall, operating on a non-profit-making basis, grant loans and give guarantees which facilitate the financing of the following projects in all sectors of the economy:

(a) projects for developing less-developed regions;

(b) projects for modernizing or converting undertakings or for developing fresh activities called for by the progressive establishment of the common market, where these projects are of such a size or nature that they cannot be entirely financed by the various means available in the individual Member States;

(c) projects of common interest to several Member States which are of such a size or nature that they cannot be entirely financed by the various means available in the individual Member States.

In carrying out its task, the Bank shall facilitate the financing of investment programmes in conjunction with assistance from the structural Funds and other Community financial instruments.'

(69) Article 199 shall be replaced by the following:

'Article 199

All items of revenue and expenditure of the Community, including those relating to the European Social Fund, shall be included in estimates to be drawn up for each financial year and shall be shown in the budget.

Administrative expenditure occasioned for the institutions by the provisions of the Treaty on European Union relating to common foreign and security policy and to cooperation in the fields of justice and home affairs shall be charged to the budget. The operational expenditure occasioned by the implementation of the said provisions may, under the conditions referred to therein, be charged to the budget.

The revenue and expenditure shown in the budget shall be in balance.'

(70) Article 200 shall be repealed.

(71) Article 201 shall be replaced by the following:

'Article 201

Without prejudice to other revenue, the budget shall be financed wholly from own resources.

The Council, acting unanimously on a proposal from the Commission and after consulting the European Parliament, shall lay down provisions relating to the system of own resources of the Community, which it shall recommend to the Member States for adoption in accordance with their respective constitutional requirements.'

(72) The following Article shall be inserted:

'Article 201a

With a view to maintaining budgetary discipline, the Commission shall not make any proposal for a Community act, or alter its proposals, or adopt any implementing measure which is likely to have appreciable implications for the budget without providing the assurance that that proposal or that measure is capable of being financed within the limit of the Community's own resources arising under provisions laid down by the Council pursuant to Article 201.'

(73) Article 205 shall be replaced by the following:

'Article 205

The Commission shall implement the budget, in accordance with the provisions of the regulations made pursuant to Article 209, on its own responsibility and within the limits of the appropriations, having regard to the principles of sound financial management.

The regulations shall lay down detailed rules for each institution concerning its part in effecting its own expenditure.

Within the budget, the Commission may, subject to the limits and conditions laid down in the regulations made pursuant to Article 209, transfer appropriations from one chapter to another or from one subdivision to another.'

(74) Article 206 shall be replaced by the following:

'Article 206

1. The European Parliament, acting on a recommendation from the Council which shall act by a qualified majority, shall give a discharge to the Commission in respect of the implementation of the budget. To this end, the Council and the European Parliament in turn shall examine the accounts and the financial statement referred to in Article 205a, the annual report by the Court of Auditors together with the replies of the institutions under audit to the observations of the Court of Auditors and any relevant special reports by the Court of Auditors.

2. Before giving a discharge to the Commission, or for any other purpose in connection with the exercise of its powers over the implementation of the budget, the European Parliament may ask to hear the Commission give evidence with regard to the execution of expenditure or the operation of financial control systems. The Commission shall submit any necessary information to the European Parliament at the latter's request.

3. The Commission shall take all appropriate steps to act on the observations in the decisions giving discharge and on other observations by the European Parliament relating to the execution of expenditure, as well as on comments accompanying the recommendations on discharge adopted by the Council.

At the request of the European Parliament or the Council, the Commission shall report on the measures taken in the light of these observations and comments and in particular on the instructions given to the departments which are responsible for the implementation of the budget. These reports shall also be forwarded to the Court of Auditors.'

(75) Articles 206a and 206b shall be repealed.

(76) Article 209 shall be replaced by the following:

'Article 209

The Council, acting unanimously on a proposal from the Commission and after consulting the European Parliament and obtaining the opinion of the Court of Auditors, shall:

(a) make Financial Regulations specifying in particular the procedure to be adopted for establishing and implementing the budget and for presenting and auditing accounts;

(b) determine the methods and procedure whereby the budget revenue provided under the arrangements relating to the Community's own resources shall be made available to the Commission, and determine the measures to be applied, if need be, to meet cash requirements;

(c) lay down rules concerning the responsibility of financial controllers, authorizing officers and accounting officers, and concerning appropriate arrangements for inspection.'

(77) The following Article shall be inserted:

'Article 209a

Member States shall take the same measures to counter fraud affecting the financial interests of the Community as they take to counter fraud affecting their own financial interests.

Without prejudice to other provisions of this Treaty, Member States shall coordinate their action aimed at protecting the financial interests of the Community against fraud. To this end they shall organize, with the help of the Commission, close and regular cooperation between the competent departments of their administrations.'

(78) Article 215 shall be replaced by the following:

'Article 215

The contractual liability of the Community shall be governed by the law applicable to the contract in question.

In the case of non-contractual liability, the Community shall, in accordance with the general principles common to the laws of the Member States, make good any damage caused by its institutions or by its servants in the performance of their duties.

The preceding paragraph shall apply under the same conditions to damage caused by the ECB or by its servants in the performance of their duties.

The personal liability of its servants towards the Community shall be governed by the provisions laid down in their Staff Regulations or in the Conditions of Employment applicable to them.'

(79) Article 227 shall be amended as follows:

(a) paragraph 2 shall be replaced by the following:

'2. *With regard to the French overseas departments, the general and particular provisions of this Treaty relating to:*

— *the free movement of goods;*

— *agriculture, save for Article 40(4);*

— *the liberalization of services;*

— *the rules on competition;*

— *the protective measures provided for in Articles 109h, 109i and 226;*

— *the institutions,*

shall apply as soon as this Treaty enters into force.

The conditions under which the other provisions of this Treaty are to apply shall be determined, within two years of the entry into force of this Treaty, by decisions of the Council, acting unanimously on a proposal from the Commission.

The institutions of the Community will, within the framework of the procedures provided for in this Treaty, in particular Article 226, take care that the economic and social development of these areas is made possible.';

(b) in paragraph 5, subparagraph (a) shall be replaced by the following:

'(a) *this Treaty shall not apply to the Faeroe Islands.*'

(80) Article 228 shall be replaced by the following:

'Article 228

1. Where this Treaty provides for the conclusion of agreements between the Community and one or more States or international organizations, the Commission shall make recommendations to the Council, which shall authorize the Commission to open the necessary negotiations. The Commission shall conduct these negotiations in consultation with special committees appointed by the Council to assist it in this task and within the framework of such directives as the Council may issue to it.

In exercising the powers conferred upon it by this paragraph, the Council shall act by a qualified majority, except in the cases provided for in the second sentence of paragraph 2, for which it shall act unanimously.

2. Subject to the powers vested in the Commission in this field, the agreements shall be concluded by the Council, acting by a qualified majority on a proposal from the Commission. The Council shall act unanimously when the agreement covers a field for which unanimity is required for the adoption of internal rules, and for the agreements referred to in Article 238.

3. The Council shall conclude agreements after consulting the European Parliament, except for the agreements referred to in Article 113(3), including cases where the agreement covers a field for which the procedure referred to in Article 189b or that referred to in Article 189c is required for the adoption of internal rules. The European Parliament shall deliver its opinion within a time-limit which the Council may lay down according to the urgency of the matter. In the absence of an opinion within that time-limit, the Council may act.

By way of derogation from the previous subparagraph, agreements referred to in Article 238, other agreements establishing a specific institutional framework by organizing cooperation procedures, agreements having important budgetary implications for the Community and agreements entailing amendment of an act adopted under the procedure referred to in Article 189b shall be concluded after the assent of the European Parliament has been obtained.

The Council and the European Parliament may, in an urgent situation, agree upon a time-limit for the assent.

4. When concluding an agreement, the Council may, by way of derogation from paragraph 2, authorize the Commission to approve modifications on behalf of the Community where the agreement provides for them to be adopted by a simplified procedure or by a body set up by the agreement; it may attach specific conditions to such authorization.

5. When the Council envisages concluding an agreement which calls for amendments to this Treaty, the amendments must first be adopted in accordance with the procedure laid down in Article N of the Treaty on European Union.

6. The Council, the Commission or a Member State may obtain the opinion of the Court of Justice as to whether an agreement envisaged is compatible with the provisions of this Treaty. Where the opinion of the Court of Justice is adverse, the agreement may enter into force only in accordance with Article N of the Treaty on European Union.

7. Agreements concluded under the conditions set out in this Article shall be binding on the institutions of the Community and on Member States.'

(81) The following Article shall be inserted:

'Article 228a

Where it is provided, in a common position or in a joint action adopted according to the provisions of the Treaty on European Union relating to the common foreign and security policy, for an action by the Community to interrupt or to reduce, in part or completely, economic relations with one or more third countries, the Council shall take the necessary urgent measures. The Council shall act by a qualified majority on a proposal from the Commission.'

(82) Article 231 shall be replaced by the following:

'Article 231

The Community shall establish close cooperation with the Organization for Economic Cooperation and Development, the details of which shall be determined by common accord.'

(83) Articles 236 and 237 shall be repealed.

(84) Article 238 shall be replaced by the following:

'Article 238

The Community may conclude with one or more States or international organizations agreements establishing an association involving reciprocal rights and obligations, common action and special procedures.'

F. In Annex III:

(85) The title shall be replaced by the following:

'List of invisible transactions referred to in Article 73h of this Treaty'.

G. In the Protocol on the Statute of the European Investment Bank:

(86) The reference to Articles 129 and 130 shall be replaced by a reference to Articles 198d and 198e.

[Sections H and I, which contain the amendments to the ECSC and Eurotom treaties, are omitted.]

TITLE V

PROVISIONS ON A COMMON FOREIGN AND SECURITY POLICY

Article J

A common foreign and security policy is hereby established which shall be governed by the following provisions.

Article J.1

1. The Union and its Member States shall define and implement a common foreign and security policy, governed by the provisions of this Title and covering all areas of foreign and security policy.

2. The objectives of the common foreign and security policy shall be:

— to safeguard the common values, fundamental interests and independence of the Union;

— to strengthen the security of the Union and its Member States in all ways;

— to preserve peace and strengthen international security, in accordance with the principles of the United Nations Charter as well as the principles of the Helsinki Final Act and the objectives of the Paris Charter;

— to promote international cooperation;

— to develop and consolidate democracy and the rule of law, and respect for human rights and fundamental freedoms.

3. The Union shall pursue these objectives:

— by establishing systematic cooperation between Member States in the conduct of policy, in accordance with Article J.2;

— by gradually implementing, in accordance with Article J.3, joint action in the areas in which the Member States have important interests in common.

4. The Member States shall support the Union's external and security policy actively and unreservedly in a spirit of loyalty and mutual solidarity. They shall refrain from any action which is contrary to the interests of the Union or likely to impair its effectiveness as a cohesive force in international relations. The Council shall ensure that these principles are complied with.

Article J.2

1. Member States shall inform and consult one another within the Council on any matter of foreign and security policy of general interest in order to ensure that their combined influence is exerted as effectively as possible by means of concerted and convergent action.

2. Whenever it deems it necessary, the Council shall define a common position.

Member States shall ensure that their national policies conform to the common positions.

3. Member States shall coordinate their action in international organizations and at international conferences. They shall uphold the common positions in such forums.

In international organizations and at international conferences where not all the Member States participate, those which do take part shall uphold the common positions.

Article J.3

The procedure for adopting joint action in matters covered by the foreign and security policy shall be the following:

1. The Council shall decide, on the basis of general guidelines from the European Council, that a matter should be the subject of joint action.

Whenever the Council decides on the principle of joint action, it shall lay down the specific scope, the Union's general and specific objectives in carrying out such action, if necessary its duration, and the means, procedures and conditions for its implementation.

2. The Council shall, when adopting the joint action and at any stage during its development, define those matters on which decisions are to be taken by a qualified majority.

Where the Council is required to act by a qualified majority pursuant to the preceding subparagraph, the votes of its members shall be weighted in accordance with Article 148(2) of the Treaty establishing the European Community, and for their adoption, acts of the Council shall require at least 54 votes in favour, cast by at least eight members.

3. If there is a change in circumstances having a substantial effect on a question subject to joint action, the Council shall review the principles and objectives of that action and take the necessary decisions. As long as the Council has not acted, the joint action shall stand.

4. Joint actions shall commit the Member States in the positions they adopt and in the conduct of their activity.

5. Whenever there is any plan to adopt a national position or take national action pursuant to a joint action, information shall be provided in time to allow, if necessary, for prior consultations within the Council. The obligation to provide prior information shall not apply to measures which are merely a national transposition of Council decisions.

6. In cases of imperative need arising from changes in the situation and failing a Council decision, Member States may take the necessary measures as a matter of urgency having regard to the general objectives of the joint action. The Member State concerned shall inform the Council immediately of any such measures.

7. Should there be any major difficulties in implementing a joint action, a Member State shall refer them to the Council which shall discuss

them and seek appropriate solutions. Such solutions shall not counter to the objectives of the joint action or impair its effectiveness.

Article J.4

1. The common foreign and security policy shall include all questions related to the security of the Union, including the eventual framing of a common defence policy, which might in time lead to a common defence.

2. The Union requests the Western European Union (WEU), which is an integral part of the development of the Union, to elaborate and implement decisions and actions of the Union which have defence implications. The Council shall, in agreement with the institutions of the WEU, adopt the necessary practical arrangements.

3. Issues having defence implications dealt with under this Article shall not be subject to the procedures set out in Article J.3.

4. The policy of the Union in accordance with this Article shall not prejudice the specific character of the security and defence policy of certain Member States and shall respect the obligations of certain Member States under the North Atlantic Treaty and be compatible with the common security and defence policy established within that framework.

5. The provisions of this Article shall not prevent the development of closer cooperation between two or more Member States on a bilateral level, in the framework of the WEU and the Atlantic Alliance, provided such cooperation does not run counter to or impede that provided for in this Title.

6. With a view to furthering the objective of this Treaty, and having in view the date of 1998 in the context of Article XII of the Brussels Treaty, the provisions of this Article may be revised as provided for in Article N(2) on the basis of a report to be presented in 1996 by the Council to the European Council, which shall include an evaluation of the progress made and the experience gained until then.

Article J.5

1. The Presidency shall represent the Union in matters coming within the common foreign and security policy.

2. The Presidency shall be responsible for the implementation of common measures; in that capacity it shall in principle express the position of the Union in international organizations and international conferences.

3. In the tasks referred to in paragraphs 1 and 2, the Presidency shall be assisted if need be by the previous and next Member States to hold the Presidency. The Commission shall be fully associated in these tasks.

4. Without prejudice to Article J.2(3) and Article J.3(4), Member States represented in international organizations or international conferences where not all the Member States participate shall keep the latter informed of any matter of common interest.

Member States which are also members of the United Nations Security Council will concert and keep the other Member States fully informed. Member States which are permanent members of the Security Council will, in the execution of their functions, ensure the defence of the positions and the interests of the Union, without prejudice to their responsibilities under the provisions of the United Nations Charter.

Article J.6

The diplomatic and consular missions of the Member States and the Commission Delegations in third countries and international conferences, and their representations to international organizations, shall cooperate in ensuring that the common positions and common measures adopted by the Council are complied with and implemented.

They shall step up cooperation by exchanging information, carrying out joint assessments and contributing to the implementation of the provisions referred to in Article 8c of the Treaty establishing the European Community.

Article J.7

The Presidency shall consult the European Parliament on the main aspects and the basic choices of the common foreign and security policy and shall ensure that the views of the European Parliament are duly taken into consideration. The European Parliament shall be kept regularly informed by the Presidency and the Commission of the development of the Union's foreign and security policy.

The European Parliament may ask questions of the Council or make recommendations to it. It shall hold an annual debate on progress in implementing the common foreign and security policy.

Article J.8

1. The European Council shall define the principles of and general guidelines for the common foreign and security policy.

2. The Council shall take the decisions necessary for defining and implementing the common foreign and security policy on the basis of the general guidelines adopted by the European Council. It shall ensure the unity, consistency and effectiveness of action by the Union.

The Council shall act unanimously, except for procedural questions and in the case referred to in Article J.3(2).

3. Any Member State or the Commission may refer to the Council any question relating to the common foreign and security policy and may submit proposals to the Council.

4. In cases requiring a rapid decision, the Presidency, of its own motion, or at the request of the Commission or a Member State, shall convene an extraordinary Council meeting within 48 hours or, in an emergency, within a shorter period.

5. Without prejudice to Article 151 of the Treaty establishing the European Community, a Political Committee consisting of Political Di-

rectors shall monitor the international situation in the areas covered by common foreign and security policy and contribute to the definition of policies by delivering opinions to the Council at the request of the Council or on its own initiative. It shall also monitor the implementation of agreed policies, without prejudice to the responsibility of the Presidency and the Commission.

Article J.9

The Commission shall be fully associated with the work carried out in the common foreign and security policy field.

Article J.10

On the occasion of any review of the security provisions under Article J.4, the Conference which is convened to that effect shall also examine whether any other amendments need to be made to provisions relating to the common foreign and security policy.

Article J.11

1. The provisions referred to in Articles 137, 138, 139 to 142, 146, 147, 150 to 153, 157 to 163 and 217 of the Treaty establishing the European Community shall apply to the provisions relating to the areas referred to in this Title.

2. Administrative expenditure which the provisions relating to the areas referred to in this Title entail for the institutions shall be charged to the budget of the European Communities.

The Council may also:

— either decide unanimously that operational expenditure to which the implementation of those provisions gives rise is to be charged to the budget of the European Communities; in that event, the budgetary procedure laid down in the Treaty establishing the European Community shall be applicable;

— or determine that such expenditure shall be charged to the Member States, where appropriate in accordance with a scale to be decided.

TITLE VI

PROVISIONS ON COOPERATION IN THE FIELDS OF JUSTICE AND HOME AFFAIRS

Article K

Cooperation in the fields of justice and home affairs shall be governed by the following provisions.

Article K.1

For the purposes of achieving the objectives of the Union, in particular the free movement of persons, and without prejudice to the powers of the European Community, Member States shall regard the following areas as matters of common interest:

(1) asylum policy;

(2) rules governing the crossing by persons of the external borders of the Member States and the exercise of controls thereon;

(3) immigration policy and policy regarding nationals of third countries:

> (a) conditions of entry and movement by nationals of third countries on the territory of Member States;
>
> (b) conditions of residence by nationals of third countries on the territory of Member States, including family reunion and access to employment;
>
> (c) combating unauthorized immigration, residence and work by nationals of third countries on the territory of Member States;

(4) combating drug addiction in so far as this is not covered by (7) to (9);

(5) combating fraud on an international scale in so far as this is not covered by 7 to 9;

(6) judicial cooperation in civil matters;

(7) judicial cooperation in criminal matters;

(8) customs cooperation;

(9) police cooperation for the purposes of preventing and combating terrorism, unlawful drug trafficking and other serious forms of international crime, including if necessary certain aspects of customs cooperation, in connection with the organization of a Union-wide system for exchanging information within a European Police Office (Europol).

Article K.2

1. The matters referred to in Article K.1 shall be dealt with in compliance with the European Convention for the Protection of Human Rights and Fundamental Freedoms of 4 November 1950 and the Convention relating to the Status of Refugees of 28 July 1951 and having regard to the protection afforded by Member States to persons persecuted on political grounds.

2. This Title shall not affect the exercise of the responsibilities incumbent upon Member States with regard to the maintenance of law and order and the safeguarding of internal security.

Article K.3

1. In the areas referred to in Article K.1, Member States shall inform and consult one another within the Council with a view to coordinating their action. To that end, they shall establish collaboration between the relevant departments of their administrations.

2. The Council may:

— on the initiative of any Member State or of the Commission, in the areas referred to in Article K.1(1) to (6);

— on the initiative of any Member State, in the areas referred to in Article K.1(7) to (9):

(a) adopt joint positions and promote, using the appropriate form and procedures, any cooperation contributing to the pursuit of the objectives of the Union;

(b) adopt joint action in so far as the objectives of the Union can be attained better by joint action than by the Member States acting individually on account of the scale or effects of the action envisaged; it may decide that measures implementing joint action are to be adopted by a qualified majority;

(c) without prejudice to Article 220 of the Treaty establishing the European Community, draw up conventions which it shall recommend to the Member States for adoption in accordance with their respective constitutional requirements.

Unless otherwise provided by such conventions, measures implementing them shall be adopted within the Council by a majority of two-thirds of the High Contracting Parties.

Such conventions may stipulate that the Court of Justice shall have jurisdiction to interpret their provisions and to rule on any disputes regarding their application, in accordance with such arrangements as they may lay down.

Article K.4

1. A Coordinating Committee shall be set up consisting of senior officials. In addition to its coordinating role, it shall be the task of the Committee to:

— give opinions for the attention of the Council, either at the Council's request or on its own initiative;

— contribute, without prejudice to Article 151 of the Treaty establishing the European Community, to the preparation of the Council's discussions in the areas referred to in Article K.1 and, in accordance with the conditions laid down in Article 100d of the Treaty establishing the European Community, in the areas referred to in Article 100c of that Treaty.

2. The Commission shall be fully associated with the work in the areas referred to in this Title.

3. The Council shall act unanimously, except on matters of procedure and in cases where Article K.3 expressly provides for other voting rules.

Where the Council is required to act by a qualified majority, the votes of its members shall be weighted as laid down in Article 148(2) of the Treaty establishing the European Community, and for their adoption, acts of the Council shall require at least 54 votes in favour, cast by at least eight members.

Article K.5

Within international organizations and at international conferences in which they take part, Member States shall defend the common positions adopted under the provisions of this Title.

Article K.6

The Presidency and the Commission shall regularly inform the European Parliament of discussions in the areas covered by this Title.

The Presidency shall consult the European Parliament on the principal aspects of activities in the areas referred to in this Title and shall ensure that the views of the European Parliament are duly taken into consideration.

The European Parliament may ask questions of the Council or make recommendations to it. Each year, it shall hold a debate on the progress made in implementation of the areas referred to in this Title.

Article K.7

The provisions of this Title shall not prevent the establishment or development of closer cooperation between two or more Member States in so far as such cooperation does not conflict with, or impede, that provided for in this Title.

Article K.8

1. The provisions referred to in Articles 137, 138, 139 to 142, 146, 147, 150 to 153, 157 to 163 and 217 of the Treaty establishing the European Community shall apply to the provisions relating to the areas referred to in this Title.

2. Administrative expenditure which the provisions relating to the areas referred to in this Title entail for the institutions shall be charged to the budget of the European Communities.

The Council may also:

— either decide unanimously that operational expenditure to which the implementation of those provisions gives rise is to be charged to the budget of the European Communities; in that event, the budgetary procedure laid down in the Treaty establishing the European Community shall be applicable;

— or determine that such expenditure shall be charged to the Member States, where appropriate in accordance with a scale to be decided.

Article K.9

The Council, acting unanimously on the initiative of the Commission or a Member State, may decide to apply Article 100c of the Treaty establishing the European Community to action in areas referred to in Article K.1(1) to (6), and at the same time determine the relevant voting conditions relating to it. It shall recommend the Member States to adopt that decision in accordance with their respective constitutional requirements.

TITLE VII
FINAL PROVISIONS
Article L

The provisions of the Treaty establishing the European Community, the Treaty establishing the European Coal and Steel Community and the

Treaty establishing the European Atomic Energy Community concerning the powers of the Court of Justice of the European Communities and the exercise of those powers shall apply only to the following provisions of this Treaty:

(a) provisions amending the Treaty establishing the European Economic Community with a view to establishing the European Community, the Treaty establishing the European Coal and Steel Community and the Treaty establishing the European Atomic Energy Community;

(b) the third subparagraph of Article K.3(2)(c);

(c) Articles L to S.

Article M

Subject to the provisions amending the Treaty establishing the European Economic Community with a view to establishing the European Community, the Treaty establishing the European Coal and Steel Community and the Treaty establishing the European Atomic Energy Community, and to these final provisions, nothing in this Treaty shall affect the Treaties establishing the European Communities or the subsequent Treaties and Acts modifying or supplementing them.

Article N

1. The government of any Member State or the Commission may submit to the Council proposals for the amendment of the Treaties on which the Union is founded.

If the Council, after consulting the European Parliament and, where appropriate, the Commission, delivers an opinion in favour of calling a conference of representatives of the governments of the Member States, the conference shall be convened by the President of the Council for the purpose of determining by common accord the amendments to be made to those Treaties. The European Central Bank shall also be consulted in the case of institutional changes in the monetary area.

The amendments shall enter into force after being ratified by all the Member States in accordance with their respective constitutional requirements.

2. A conference of representatives of the governments of the Member States shall be convened in 1996 to examine those provisions of this Treaty for which revision is provided, in accordance with the objectives set out in Articles A and B.

Article O

Any European State may apply to become a Member of the Union. It shall address its application to the Council, which shall act unanimously after consulting the Commission and after receiving the assent of the European Parliament, which shall act by an absolute majority of its component members.

The conditions of admission and the adjustments to the Treaties on which the Union is founded which such admission entails shall be the subject of an agreement between the Member States and the applicant State. This agreement shall be submitted for ratification by all the contracting States in accordance with their respective constitutional requirements.

Article P

1. Articles 2 to 7 and 10 to 19 of the Treaty establishing a Single Council and a Single Commission of the European Communities, signed in Brussels on 8 April 1965, are hereby repealed.

2. Article 2, Article 3(2) and Title III of the Single European Act signed in Luxembourg on 17 February 1986 and in The Hague on 28 February 1986 are hereby repealed.

Article Q

This Treaty is concluded for an unlimited period.

Article R

1. This Treaty shall be ratified by the High Contracting Parties in accordance with their respective constitutional requirements. The instruments of ratification shall be deposited with the government of the Italian Republic.

2. This Treaty shall enter into force on 1 January 1993, provided that all the instruments of ratification have been deposited, or, failing that, on the first day of the month following the deposit of the instrument of ratification by the last signatory State to take this step.

Article S

This Treaty, drawn up in a single original in the Danish, Dutch, English, French, German, Greek, Irish, Italian, Portuguese and Spanish languages, the texts in each of these languages being equally authentic, shall be deposited in the archives of the government of the Italian Republic, which will transmit a certified copy to each of the governments of the other signatory States.

PROTOCOLS AND DECLARATIONS ANNEXED TO THE TREATY ON EUROPEAN UNION

[*Eds. Note*: Protocols are intended to have binding legal effect. Declarations represent the views and intentions of the intergovernmental conference delegates who prepared the TEU.

Space considerations limit the reproduction of Protocols and Declarations to those specifically indicated on the following list. Those not reproduced can be found in the sources indicated in the Eds. Note at page 104.]

PROTOCOLS

1. Protocol on the acquisition of property in Denmark
2. Protocol concerning Article 119 of the Treaty establishing the European Community [page 188]

3. Protocol on the Statute of the European System of Central Banks and of the European Central Bank

4. Protocol on the Statute of the European Monetary Institute

5. Protocol on the excessive deficit procedure [page 189]

6. Protocol on the convergence criteria referred to in Article 109j of the Treaty establishing the European Community [page 189]

7. Protocol amending the Protocol on the privileges and immunities of the European Communities

8. Protocol on Denmark

9. Protocol on Portugal

10. Protocol on the transition to the third stage of economic and monetary union [page 191]

11. Protocol on certain provisions relating to the United Kingdom of Great Britain and Northern Ireland [page 191]

12. Protocol on certain provisions relating to Denmark [page 193]

13. Protocol on France

14. Protocol on social policy, to which is annexed an agreement concluded between the Member States of the European Community with the exception of the United Kingdom of Great Britain and Northern Ireland, to which two declarations are attached [page 194]

15. Protocol on economic and social cohesion

16. Protocol on the Economic and Social Committee and the Committee of the Regions

17. Protocol annexed to the Treaty on European Union and to the Treaties establishing the European Communities [page 198]

DECLARATIONS

1. Declaration on civil protection, energy and tourism

2. Declaration on nationality of a Member State

3. Declaration on Part Three, Titles III and VI, of the Treaty establishing the European Community

4. Declaration on Part Three, Title VI, of the Treaty establishing the European Community

5. Declaration on monetary cooperation with non-Community countries

6. Declaration on monetary relations with the Republic of San Marino, the Vatican City and the Principality of Monaco

7. Declaration on Article 73d of the Treaty establishing the European Community

8. Declaration on Article 109 of the Treaty establishing the European Community

9. Declaration on Part Three, Title XVI, of the Treaty establishing the European Community

10. Declaration on Articles 109, 130r and 130y of the Treaty establishing the European Community
11. Declaration on the Directive of 24 November 1988 (Emissions)
12. Declaration on the European Development Fund
13. Declaration on the role of national parliaments in the European Union [page 198]
14. Declaration on the Conference of the Parliaments
15. Declaration on the number of members of the Commission and of the European Parliament [page 198]
16. Declaration on the hierarchy of Community Acts
17. Declaration on the right of access to information
18. Declaration on estimated costs under Commission proposals
19. Declaration on the implementation of Community law
20. Declaration on assessment of the environmental impact of Community measures
21. Declaration on the Court of Auditors
22. Declaration on the Economic and Social Committee
23. Declaration on cooperation with charitable associations
24. Declaration on the protection of animals
25. Declaration on the representation of the interests of the overseas countries and territories referred to in Article 227(3) and (5)(a) and (b) of the Treaty establishing the European Community
26. Declaration on the outermost regions of the Community
27. Declaration on voting in the field of the common foreign and security policy [page 199]
28. Declaration on practical arrangements in the field of the common foreign and security policy
29. Declaration on the use of languages in the field of the common foreign and security policy
30. Declaration on Western European Union [page 199]
31. Declaration on asylum
32. Declaration on police cooperation
33. Declaration on disputes between the ECB and the EMI and their servants

PROTOCOL

CONCERNING ARTICLE 119 OF THE TREATY ESTABLISHING THE EUROPEAN COMMUNITY

THE HIGH CONTRACTING PARTIES,

HAVE AGREED upon the following provision, which shall be annexed to the Treaty establishing the European Community:

For the purposes of Article 119 of this Treaty, benefits under occupational social security schemes shall not be considered as remuneration if and in so far as they are attributable to periods of employment prior to 17 May 1990, except in the case of workers or those claiming under them who have before that date initiated legal proceedings or introduced an equivalent claim under the applicable national law.

PROTOCOL
ON THE EXCESSIVE DEFICIT PROCEDURE

THE HIGH CONTRACTING PARTIES,

DESIRING to lay down the details of the excessive deficit procedure referred to in Article 104c of the Treaty establishing the European Community,

HAVE AGREED upon the following provisions, which shall be annexed to the Treaty establishing the European Community:

Article 1

The reference values referred to in Article 104c(2) of this Treaty are:

— 3% for the ratio of the planned or actual government deficit to gross domestic product at market prices;

— 60% for the ratio of government debt to gross domestic product at market prices.

Article 2

In Article 104c of this Treaty and in this Protocol:

— government means general government, that is central government, regional or local government and social security funds, to the exclusion of commercial operations, as defined in the European System of Integrated Economic Accounts;

— deficit means net borrowing as defined in the European System of Integrated Economic Accounts;

— investment means gross fixed capital formation as defined in the European System of Integrated Economic Accounts;

— debt means total gross debt at nominal value outstanding at the end of the year and consolidated between and within the sectors of general government as defined in the first indent.

Article 3

In order to ensure the effectiveness of the excessive deficit procedure, the governments of the Member States shall be responsible under this procedure for the deficits of general government as defined in the first indent of Article 2. The Member States shall ensure that national procedures in the budgetary area enable them to meet their obligations in this area deriving from this Treaty. The Member States shall report their planned and actual deficits and the levels of their debt promptly and regularly to the Commission.

Article 4

The statistical data to be used for the application of this Protocol shall be provided by the Commission.

PROTOCOL

ON THE CONVERGENCE CRITERIA REFERRED TO IN ARTICLE 109j OF THE TREATY ESTABLISHING THE EUROPEAN COMMUNITY

THE HIGH CONTRACTING PARTIES,

DESIRING to lay down the details of the convergence criteria which shall guide the Community in taking decisions on the passage to the third stage of economic and monetary union, referred to in Article 109j(1) of this Treaty,

HAVE AGREED upon the following provisions, which shall be annexed to the Treaty establishing the European Community:

Article 1

The criterion on price stability referred to in the first indent of Article 109j(1) of this Treaty shall mean that a Member State has a price performance that is sustainable and an average rate of inflation, observed over a period of one year before the examination, that does not exceed by more than 1½ percentage points that of, at most, the three best performing Member States in terms of price stability. Inflation shall be measured by means of the consumer price index on a comparable basis, taking into account differences in national definitions.

Article 2

The criterion on the government budgetary position referred to in the second indent of Article 109j(1) of this Treaty shall mean that at the time of the examination the Member State is not the subject of a Council decision under Article 104c(6) of this Treaty that an excessive deficit exists.

Article 3

The criterion on participation in the exchange-rate mechanism of the European Monetary System referred to in the third indent of Article 109j(1) of this Treaty shall mean that a Member State has respected the normal fluctuation margins provided for by the exchange-rate mechanism of the European Monetary System without severe tensions for at least the last two years before the examination. In particular, the Member State shall not have devalued its currency's bilateral central rate against any other Member State's currency on its own initiative for the same period.

Article 4

The criterion on the convergence of interest rates referred to in the fourth indent of Article 109j(1) of this Treaty shall mean that, observed over a period of one year before the examination, a Member State has had an average nominal long-term interest rate that does not exceed by more than two percentage points that of, at most, the three best performing Member States in terms of price stability. Interest rates shall be measured on the basis of long-term government bonds or comparable securities, taking into account differences in national definitions.

Article 5

The statistical data to be used for the application of this Protocol shall be provided by the Commission.

Article 6

The Council shall, acting unanimously on a proposal from the Commission and after consulting the European Parliament, the EMI or the ECB as the case may be, and the Committee referred to in Article 109c, adopt appropriate provisions to lay down the details of the convergence criteria referred to in Article 109j of this Treaty, which shall then replace this Protocol.

PROTOCOL
ON THE TRANSITION TO THE THIRD STAGE OF ECONOMIC AND MONETARY UNION

THE HIGH CONTRACTING PARTIES,

Declare the irreversible character of the Community's movement to the third stage of economic and monetary union by signing the new Treaty provisions on economic and monetary union.

Therefore all Member States shall, whether they fulfil the necessary conditions for the adoption of a single currency or not, respect the will for the Community to enter swiftly into the third stage, and therefore no Member State shall prevent the entering into the third stage.

If by the end of 1997 the date of the beginning of the third stage has not been set, the Member States concerned, the Community institutions and other bodies involved shall expedite all preparatory work during 1998, in order to enable the Community to enter the third stage irrevocably on 1 January 1999 and to enable the ECB and the ESCB to start their full functioning from this date.

This Protocol shall be annexed to the Treaty establishing the European Community.

PROTOCOL
ON CERTAIN PROVISIONS RELATING TO THE UNITED KINGDOM OF GREAT BRITAIN AND NORTHERN IRELAND

THE HIGH CONTRACTING PARTIES,

RECOGNIZING that the United Kingdom shall not be obliged or committed to move to the third stage of economic and monetary union without a separate decision to do so by its government and Parliament,

NOTING the practice of the government of the United Kingdom to fund its borrowing requirement by the sale of debt to the private sector,

HAVE AGREED the following provisions, which shall be annexed to the Treaty establishing the European Community:

1. The United Kingdom shall notify the Council whether it intends to move to the third stage before the Council makes its assessment under Article 109j(2) of this Treaty.

Unless the United Kingdom notifies the Council that it intends to move to the third stage, it shall be under no obligation to do so.

If no date is set for the beginning of the third stage under Article 109j(3) of this Treaty, the United Kingdom may notify its intention to move to the third stage before 1 January 1998.

2. Paragraphs 3 to 9 shall have effect if the United Kingdom notifies the Council that it does not intend to move to the third stage.

3. The United Kingdom shall not be included among the majority of Member States which fulfil the necessary conditions referred to in the second indent of Article 109j(2) and the first indent of Article 109j(3) of this Treaty.

4. The United Kingdom shall retain its powers in the field of monetary policy according to national law.

5. Articles 3a(2), 104c(1), (9) and (11), 105(1) to (5), 105a, 107, 108, 108a, 109, 109a(1) and (2)(b) and 109l(4) and (5) of this Treaty shall not apply to the United Kingdom. In these provisions references to the Community or the Member States shall not include the United Kingdom and references to national central banks shall not include the Bank of England.

6. Articles 109e(4) and 109h and i of this Treaty shall continue to apply to the United Kingdom. Articles 109c(4) and 109m shall apply to the United Kingdom as if it had a derogation.

7. The voting rights of the United Kingdom shall be suspended in respect of acts of the Council referred to in the Articles listed in paragraph 5. For this purpose the weighted votes of the United Kingdom shall be excluded from any calculation of a qualified majority under Article 109k(5) of this Treaty.

The United Kingdom shall also have no right to participate in the appointment of the President, the Vice–President and the other members of the Executive Board of the ECB under Articles 109a(2)(b) and 109l(1) of this Treaty.

8. Articles 3, 4, 6, 7, 9.2, 10.1, 10.3, 11.2, 12.1, 14, 16, 18 to 20, 22, 23, 26, 27, 30 to 34, 50 and 52 of the Protocol on the Statute of the European System of Central Banks and of the European Central Bank ('the Statute') shall not apply to the United Kingdom.

In those Articles, references to the Community or the Member States shall not include the United Kingdom and references to national central banks or shareholders shall not include the Bank of England.

References in Articles 10.3 and 30.2 of the Statute to 'subscribed capital of the ECB' shall not include capital subscribed by the Bank of England.

9. Article 109l(3) of this Treaty and Articles 44 to 48 of the Statute shall have effect, whether or not there is any Member State with a derogation, subject to the following amendments:

(a) References in Article 44 to the tasks of the ECB and the EMI shall include those tasks that still need to be performed in the third stage owing to any decision of the United Kingdom not to move to that stage.

(b) In addition to the tasks referred to in Article 47 the ECB shall also give advice in relation to and contribute to the preparation of any decision of the Council with regard to the United Kingdom taken in accordance with paragraphs 10(a) and 10(c).

(c) The Bank of England shall pay up its subscription to the capital of the ECB as a contribution to its operational costs on the same basis as national central banks of Member States with a derogation.

10. If the United Kingdom does not move to the third stage, it may change its notification at any time after the beginning of that stage. In that event:

(a) The United Kingdom shall have the right to move to the third stage provided only that it satisfies the necessary conditions. The Council, acting at the request of the United Kingdom and under the conditions and in accordance with the procedure laid down in Article 109k(2) of this Treaty, shall decide whether it fulfils the necessary conditions.

(b) The Bank of England shall pay up its subscribed capital, transfer to the ECB foreign reserve assets and contribute to its reserves on the same basis as the national central bank of a Member State whose derogation has been abrogated.

(c) The Council, acting under the conditions and in accordance with the procedure laid down in Article 109l(5) of this Treaty, shall take all other necessary decisions to enable the United Kingdom to move to the third stage.

If the United Kingdom moves to the third stage pursuant to the provisions of this Protocol, paragraphs 3 to 9 shall cease to have effect.

11. Notwithstanding Articles 104 and 109e(3) of this Treaty and Article 21.1 of the Statute, the government of the United Kingdom may maintain its 'ways and means' facility with the Bank of England if and so long as the United Kingdom does not move to the third stage.

PROTOCOL
ON CERTAIN PROVISIONS RELATING TO DENMARK

THE HIGH CONTRACTING PARTIES,

DESIRING to settle, in accordance with the general objectives of the Treaty establishing the European Community, certain particular problems existing at the present time,

TAKING INTO ACCOUNT that the Danish Constitution contains provisions which may imply a referendum in Denmark prior to Danish participation in the third stage of economic and monetary union,

HAVE AGREED on the following provisions, which shall be annexed to the Treaty establishing the European Community:

1. The Danish Government shall notify the Council of its position concerning participation in the third stage before the Council makes its assessment under Article 109j(2) of this Treaty.

2. In the event of a notification that Denmark will not participate in the third stage, Denmark shall have an exemption. The effect of the exemption shall be that all Articles and provisions of this Treaty and the Statute of the ESCB referring to a derogation shall be applicable to Denmark.

3. In such case, Denmark shall not be included among the majority of Member States which fulfil the necessary conditions referred to in the second indent of Article 109j(2) and the first indent of Article 109j(3) of this Treaty.

4. As for the abrogation of the exemption, the procedure referred to in Article 109k(2) shall only be initiated at the request of Denmark.

5. In the event of abrogation of the exemption status, the provisions of this Protocol shall cease to apply.

PROTOCOL
ON SOCIAL POLICY

THE HIGH CONTRACTING PARTIES,

NOTING that 11 Member States, that is to say the Kingdom of Belgium, the Kingdom of Denmark, the Federal Republic of Germany, the Hellenic Republic, the Kingdom of Spain, the French Republic, Ireland, the Italian Republic, the Grand Duchy of Luxembourg, the Kingdom of the Netherlands and the Portuguese Republic, wish to continue along the path laid down in the 1989 Social Charter; that they have adopted among themselves an Agreement to this end; that this Agreement is annexed to this Protocol; that this Protocol and the said Agreement are without prejudice to the provisions of this Treaty, particularly those relating to social policy which constitute an integral part of the *acquis communautaire:*

1. Agree to authorize those 11 Member States to have recourse to the institutions, procedures and mechanisms of the Treaty for the purposes of taking among themselves and applying as far as they are

concerned the acts and decisions required for giving effect to the above-mentioned Agreement.

2. The United Kingdom of Great Britain and Northern Ireland shall not take part in the deliberations and the adoption by the Council of Commission proposals made on the basis of this Protocol and the above-mentioned Agreement.

By way of derogation from Article 148(2) of the Treaty, acts of the Council which are made pursuant to this Protocol and which must be adopted by a qualified majority shall be deemed to be so adopted if they have received at least 44 votes in favour. The unanimity of the members of the Council, with the exception of the United Kingdom of Great Britain and Northern Ireland, shall be necessary for acts of the Council which must be adopted unanimously and for those amending the Commission proposal.

Acts adopted by the Council and any financial consequences other than administrative costs entailed for the institutions shall not be applicable to the United Kingdom of Great Britain and Northern Ireland.

3. This Protocol shall be annexed to the Treaty establishing the European Community.

AGREEMENT

ON SOCIAL POLICY CONCLUDED BETWEEN THE MEMBER STATES OF THE EUROPEAN COMMUNITY WITH THE EXCEPTION OF THE UNITED KINGDOM OF GREAT BRITAIN AND NORTHERN IRELAND

The undersigned 11 HIGH CONTRACTING PARTIES, that is to say the Kingdom of Belgium, the Kingdom of Denmark, the Federal Republic of Germany, the Hellenic Republic, the Kingdom of Spain, the French Republic, Ireland, the Italian Republic, the Grand Duchy of Luxembourg, the Kingdom of the Netherlands and the Portuguese Republic (hereinafter referred to as 'the Member States'),

WISHING to implement the 1989 Social Charter on the basis of the *acquis communautaire,*

CONSIDERING the Protocol on social policy,

HAVE AGREED as follows:

Article 1

The Community and the Member States shall have as their objectives the promotion of employment, improved living and working conditions, proper social protection, dialogue between management and labour, the development of human resources with a view to lasting high employment and the combating of exclusion. To this end the Community and the Member States shall implement measures which take account of the diverse forms of national practices, in particular in the field of contractual relations, and the need to maintain the competitiveness of the Community economy.

Article 2

1. With a view to achieving the objectives of Article 1, the Community shall support and complement the activities of the Member States in the following fields:

— improvement in particular of the working environment to protect workers' health and safety;

— working conditions;

— the information and consultation of workers;

— equality between men and women with regard to labour market opportunities and treatment at work;

— the integration of persons excluded from the labour market, without prejudice to Article 127 of the Treaty establishing the European Community (hereinafter referred to as 'the Treaty').

2. To this end, the Council may adopt, by means of directives, minimum requirements for gradual implementation, having regard to the conditions and technical rules obtaining in each of the Member States. Such directives shall avoid imposing administrative, financial and legal constraints in a way which would hold back the creation and development of small and medium-sized undertakings.

The Council shall act in accordance with the procedure referred to in Article 189c of the Treaty after consulting the Economic and Social Committee.

3. However, the Council shall act unanimously on a proposal from the Commission, after consulting the European Parliament and the Economic and Social Committee, in the following areas:

— social security and social protection of workers;

— protection of workers where their employment contract is terminated;

— representation and collective defence of the interests of workers and employers, including co-determination, subject to paragraph 6;

— conditions of employment for third-country nationals legally residing in Community territory;

— financial contributions for promotion of employment and job-creation, without prejudice to the provisions relating to the Social Fund.

4. A Member State may entrust management and labour, at their joint request, with the implementation of directives adopted pursuant to paragraphs 2 and 3.

In this case, it shall ensure that, no later than the date on which a directive must be transposed in accordance with Article 189, management and labour have introduced the necessary measures by agreement, the Member State concerned being required to take any necessary measure enabling it at any time to be in a position to guarantee the results imposed by that directive.

5. The provisions adopted pursuant to this Article shall not prevent any Member State from maintaining or introducing more stringent protective measures compatible with the Treaty.

6. The provisions of this Article shall not apply to pay, the right of association, the right to strike or the right to impose lock-outs.

Article 3

1. The Commission shall have the task of promoting the consultation of management and labour at Community level and shall take any relevant measure to facilitate their dialogue by ensuring balanced support for the parties.

2. To this end, before submitting proposals in the social policy field, the Commission shall consult management and labour on the possible direction of Community action.

3. If, after such consultation, the Commission considers Community action advisable, it shall consult management and labour on the content of the envisaged proposal. Management and labour shall forward to the Commission an opinion or, where appropriate, a recommendation.

4. On the occasion of such consultation, management and labour may inform the Commission of their wish to initiate the process provided for in Article 4. The duration of the procedure shall not exceed nine months, unless the management and labour concerned and the Commission decide jointly to extend it.

Article 4

1. Should management and labour so desire, the dialogue between them at Community level may lead to contractual relations, including agreements.

2. Agreements concluded at Community level shall be implemented either in accordance with the procedures and practices specific to management and labour and the Member States or, in matters covered by Article 2, at the joint request of the signatory parties, by a Council decision on a proposal from the Commission.

The Council shall act by qualified majority, except where the agreement in question contains one or more provisions relating to one of the areas referred to in Article 2(3), in which case it shall act unanimously.

Article 5

With a view to achieving the objectives of Article 1 and without prejudice to the other provisions of the Treaty, the Commission shall encourage cooperation between the Member States and facilitate the coordination of their action in all social policy fields under this Agreement.

Article 6

1. Each Member State shall ensure that the principle of equal pay for male and female workers for equal work is applied.

2. For the purpose of this Article, 'pay' means the ordinary basic or minimum wage or salary and any other consideration, whether in cash or in kind, which the worker receives directly or indirectly, in respect of his employment, from his employer.

Equal pay without discrimination based on sex means:

(a) that pay for the same work at piece rates shall be calculated on the basis of the same unit of measurement;

(b) that pay for work at time rates shall be the same for the same job.

3. This Article shall not prevent any Member State from maintaining or adopting measures providing for specific advantages in order to make it easier for women to pursue a vocational activity or to prevent or compensate for disadvantages in their professional careers.

Article 7

The Commission shall draw up a report each year on progress in achieving the objectives of Article 1, including the demographic situation in the Community. It shall forward the report to the European Parliament, the Council and the Economic and Social Committee.

The European Parliament may invite the Commission to draw up reports on particular problems concerning the social situation.

[Declarations omitted]

PROTOCOL

ANNEXED TO THE TREATY ON EUROPEAN UNION AND TO THE TREATIES ESTABLISHING THE EUROPEAN COMMUNITIES

THE HIGH CONTRACTING PARTIES,

HAVE AGREED upon the following provision, which shall be annexed to the Treaty on European Union and to the Treaties establishing the European Communities:

Nothing in the Treaty on European Union, or in the Treaties establishing the European Communities, or in the Treaties or Acts modifying or supplementing those Treaties, shall affect the application in Ireland of Article 40.3.3. of the Constitution of Ireland.

DECLARATION

ON THE ROLE OF NATIONAL PARLIAMENTS IN THE EUROPEAN UNION

The Conference considers that it is important to encourage greater involvement of national parliaments in the activities of the European Union.

To this end, the exchange of information between national parliaments and the European Parliament should be stepped up. In this context, the governments of the Member States will ensure, *inter alia,* that national parliaments receive Commission proposals for legislation in good time for information or possible examination.

Similarly, the Conference considers that it is important for contacts between the national parliaments and the European Parliament to be stepped up, in particular through the granting of appropriate reciprocal facilities and regular meetings between members of Parliament interested in the same issues.

DECLARATION
ON THE NUMBER OF MEMBERS OF THE COMMISSION AND OF THE EUROPEAN PARLIAMENT

The Conference agrees that the Member States will examine the questions relating to the number of members of the Commission and the number of members of the European Parliament no later than at the end of 1992, with a view to reaching an agreement which will permit the establishment of the necessary legal basis for fixing the number of members of the European Parliament in good time for the 1994 elections. The decisions will be taken in the light, *inter alia,* of the need to establish the overall size of the European Parliament in an enlarged Community.

DECLARATION
ON VOTING IN THE FIELD OF THE COMMON FOREIGN AND SECURITY POLICY

The Conference agrees that, with regard to Council decisions requiring unanimity, Member States will, to the extent possible, avoid preventing a unanimous decision where a qualified majority exists in favour of that decision.

DECLARATION
ON WESTERN EUROPEAN UNION

The Conference notes the following declarations:

I. DECLARATION
by Belgium, Germany, Spain, France, Italy, Luxembourg, the Netherlands, Portugal and the United Kingdom of Great Britain and Northern Ireland, which are members of the Western European Union and also members of the European Union

on

THE ROLE OF THE WESTERN EUROPEAN UNION AND ITS RELATIONS WITH THE EUROPEAN UNION AND WITH THE ATLANTIC ALLIANCE

Introduction

1. WEU Member States agree on the need to develop a genuine European security and defence identity and a greater European responsibility on defense matters. This identity will be pursued through a gradual process involving successive phases. WEU will form an integral

part of the process of the development of the European Union and will enhance its contribution to solidarity within the Atlantic Alliance. WEU Member States agree to strengthen the role of WEU, in the longer term perspective of a common defence policy within the European Union which might in time lead to a common defence, compatible with that of the Atlantic Alliance.

2. WEU will be developed as the defence component of the European Union and as a means to strengthen the European pillar of the Atlantic Alliance. To this end, it will formulate common European defence policy and carry forward its concrete implementation through the further development of its own operational role.

WEU Member States take note of Article J.4 relating to the common foreign and security policy of the Treaty on European Union which reads as follows:

'1. The common foreign and security policy shall include all questions related to the security of the Union, including the eventual framing of a common defence policy, which might in time lead to a common defence.

2. The Union requests the Western European Union (WEU), which is an integral part of the development of the Union, to elaborate and implement decisions and actions of the Union which have defence implications. The Council shall, in agreement with the institutions of the WEU, adopt the necessary practical arrangements.

3. Issues having defence implications dealt with under this Article shall not be subject to the procedures set out in Article J.3.

4. The policy of the Union in accordance with this Article shall not prejudice the specific character of the security and defence policy of certain Member States and shall respect the obligations of certain Member States under the North Atlantic Treaty and be compatible with the common security and defence policy established within that framework.

5. The provisions of this Article shall not prevent the development of closer cooperation between two or more Member States on a bilateral level, in the framework of the WEU and the Atlantic Alliance, provided such cooperation does not run counter to or impede that provided for in this Title.

6. With a view to furthering the objective of this Treaty, and having in view the date of 1998 in the context of Article XII of the Brussels Treaty, the provisions of this Article may be revised as provided for in Article N(2) on the basis of a report to be presented in 1996 by the Council to the European Council, which shall include an evaluation of the progress made and the experience gained until then.'

A. WEU's relations with European Union

3. The objective is to build up WEU in stages as the defence component of the European Union. To this end, WEU is prepared, at the request of the European Union, to elaborate and implement decisions and actions of the Union which have defence implications.

To this end, WEU will take the following measures to develop a close working relationship with the Union:

— as appropriate, synchronization of the dates and venues of meetings and harmonization of working methods;

— establishment of close cooperation between the Council and Secretariat-General of WEU on the one hand, and the Council of the Union and General Secretariat of the Council on the other;

— consideration of the harmonization of the sequence and duration of the respective Presidencies;

— arranging for appropriate modalities so as to ensure that the Commission of the European Communities is regularly informed and, as appropriate, consulted on WEU activities in accordance with the role of the Commission in the common foreign and security policy as defined in the Treaty on European Union;

— encouragement of closer cooperation between the Parliamentary Assembly of WEU and the European Parliament.

The WEU Council shall, in agreement with the competent bodies of the European Union, adopt the necessary practical arrangements.

B. WEU's relations with the Atlantic Alliance

4. The objective is to develop WEU as a means to strengthen the European pillar of the Atlantic Alliance. Accordingly WEU is prepared to develop further the close working links between WEU and the Alliance and to strengthen the role, responsibilities and contributions of WEU Member States in the Alliance. This will be undertaken on the basis of the necessary transparency and complementarity between the emerging European security and defence identity and the Alliance. WEU will act in conformity with the positions adopted in the Atlantic Alliance.

— WEU Member States will intensify their coordination on Alliance issues which represent an important common interest with the aim of introducing joint positions agreed in WEU into the process of consultation in the Alliance which will remain the essential forum for consultation among its members and the venue for agreement on policies bearing on the security and defence commitments of Allies under the North Atlantic Treaty.

— Where necessary, dates and venues of meetings will be synchronized and working methods harmonized.

— Close cooperation will be established between the Secretariats-General of WEU and NATO.

C. Operational role of WEU

5. WEU's operational role will be strengthened by examining and defining appropriate missions, structures and means, covering in particular:

— WEU planning cell;
— closer military cooperation complementary to the Alliance in particular in the fields of logistics, transport, training and strategic surveillance;
— meetings of WEU Chiefs of Defence Staff;
— military units answerable to WEU.

Other proposals will be examined further, including:

— enhanced cooperation in the field of armaments with the aim of creating a European armaments agency;
— development of the WEU Institute into a European Security and Defence Academy.

Arrangements aimed at giving WEU a stronger operational role will be fully compatible with the military dispositions necessary to ensure the collective defence of all Allies.

D. Other measures

6. As a consequence of the measures set out above, and in order to facilitate the strengthening of WEU's role, the seat of the WEU Council and Secretariat will be transferred to Brussels.

7. Representation on the WEU Council must be such that the Council is able to exercise its functions continuously in accordance with Article VIII of the modified Brussels Treaty. Member States may draw on a double-hatting formula, to be worked out, consisting of their representatives to the Alliance and to the European Union.

8. WEU notes that, in accordance with the provisions of Article J.4(6) concerning the common foreign and security policy of the Treaty on European Union, the Union will decide to review the provisions of this Article with a view to furthering the objective to be set by it in accordance with the procedure defined. The WEU will re-examine the present provisions in 1996. This re-examination will take account of the progress and experience acquired and will extend to relations between WEU and the Atlantic Alliance.

II. DECLARATION

by Belgium, Germany, Spain, France, Italy, Luxembourg, the Netherlands, Portugal and the United Kingdom of Great Britain and Northern Ireland which are members of the Western European Union

The Member States of WEU welcome the development of the European security and defence identity. They are determined, taking into account the role of WEU as the defence component of the European Union and as the means to strengthen the European pillar of the Atlantic Alliance, to put the relationship between WEU and the other European

States on a new basis for the sake of stability and security in Europe. In this spirit, they propose the following:

States which are members of the European Union are invited to accede to WEU on conditions to be agreed in accordance with Article XI of the modified Brussels Treaty, or to become observers if they so wish. Simultaneously, other European Member States of NATO are invited to become associate members of WEU in a way which will give them the possibility of participating fully in the activities of WEU.

The Member States of WEU assume that treaties and agreements corresponding with the above proposals will be concluded before 31 December 1992.

4. CONVENTION FOR THE PROTECTION OF HUMAN RIGHTS AND FUNDAMENTAL FREEDOMS *

(Signed at Rome, Nov. 4, 1950, effective Sept. 3, 1953)
1955 UNTS 220 (no. 2889)

The Governments signatory hereto,[1] being Members of the Council of Europe,

Considering the Universal Declaration of Human Rights proclaimed by the General Assembly of the United Nations on 10th December 1948;

Considering that this Declaration aims at securing the universal and effective recognition and observance of the Rights therein declared;

Considering that the aim of the Council of Europe is the achievement of greater unity between its Members and that one of the methods by which that aim is to be pursued is the maintenance and further realisation of Human Rights and Fundamental Freedoms;

Reaffirming their profound belief in those Fundamental Freedoms which are the foundation of justice and peace in the world and are best maintained on the one hand by an effective political democracy and on the other by a common understanding and observance of the Human Rights upon which they depend:

Being resolved, as the Governments of European countries which are like-minded and have a common heritage of political traditions, ideals, freedom and the rule of law, to take the first steps for the collective enforcement of certain of the Rights stated in the Universal Declaration;

Have agreed as follows:

Article 1

The High Contracting Parties shall secure to everyone within their jurisdiction the rights and freedoms defined in Section I of this Convention.

SECTION I

Article 2

(1) Everyone's right to life shall be protected by law. No one shall be deprived of his life intentionally save in the execution of a sentence of a court following his conviction of a crime for which this penalty is provided by law.

(2) Deprivation of life shall not be regarded as inflicted in contravention of this Article when it results from the use of force which is no more than absolutely necessary:

---

* Reservations omitted.

1. [Ed.] The original signatories were Belgium, Denmark, France, Federal Republic of Germany, Greece, Iceland, Ireland, Italy, Luxembourg, the Netherlands, Norway, the Saar, Sweden, Turkey and the United Kingdom. States that subsequently acceded to the Convention are Austria (1958), Cyprus (1962), Malta (1967), Switzerland (1974), Portugal (1978), Spain (1979), Liechtenstein (1982) and San Marino (1989).

(*a*) in defence of any person from unlawful violence;

(*b*) in order to effect a lawful arrest or to prevent the escape of a person lawfully detained;

(*c*) in action lawfully taken for the purpose of quelling a riot or insurrection.

Article 3

No one shall be subjected to torture or to inhuman or degrading treatment or punishment.

Article 4

(1) No one shall be held in slavery or servitude.

(2) No one shall be required to perform forced or compulsory labour.

(3) For the purpose of this Article the term "forced or compulsory labour" shall not include:

(*a*) any work required to be done in the ordinary course of detention imposed according to the provisions of Article 5 of this Convention or during conditional release from such detention;

(*b*) any service of a military character or, in case of conscientious objection in countries where they are recognised, service exacted instead of compulsory military service;

(*c*) any service exacted in case of an emergency or calamity threatening the life or well-being of the community;

(*d*) any work or service which forms part of normal civic obligations.

Article 5

(1) Everyone has the right to liberty and security of person.

No one shall be deprived of his liberty save in the following cases and in accordance with a procedure prescribed by law:

(*a*) the lawful detention of a person after conviction by a competent court;

(*b*) the lawful arrest or detention of a person for non-compliance with the lawful order of a court or in order to secure the fulfilment of any obligation prescribed by law;

(*c*) the lawful arrest or detention of a person effected for the purpose of bringing him before the competent legal authority on reasonable suspicion of having committed an offence or when it is reasonably considered necessary to prevent his committing an offence or fleeing after having done so;

(*d*) the detention of a minor by lawful order for the purpose of educational supervision or his lawful detention for the purpose of bringing him before the competent legal authority;

(*e*) the lawful detention of persons for the prevention of the spreading of infectious diseases, of persons of unsound mind, alcoholics or drug addicts or vagrants;

(*f*) the lawful arrest or detention of a person to prevent his effecting an unauthorized entry into the country or of a person against whom action is being taken with a view to deportation or extradition.

(2) Everyone who is arrested shall be informed promptly, in a language which he understands, of the reasons for his arrest and of any charge against him.

(3) Everyone arrested or detained in accordance with the provisions of paragraph 1(*c*) of this Article shall be brought promptly before a judge or other officer authorised by law to exercise judicial power and shall be entitled to trial within a reasonable time or to release pending trial. Release may be conditioned by guarantees to appear to trial.

(4) Everyone who is deprived of his liberty by arrest or detention shall be entitled to take proceedings by which the lawfulness of his detention shall be decided speedily by a court and his release ordered if the detention is not lawful.

(5) Everyone who has been the victim of arrest or detention in contravention of the provisions of this Article shall have an enforceable right to compensation.

Article 6

(1) In the determination of his civil rights and obligations or of any criminal charge against him, everyone is entitled to a fair and public hearing within a reasonable time by an independent and impartial tribunal established by law. Judgment shall be pronounced publicly but the press and public may be excluded from all or part of the trial in the interests of morals, public order or national security in a democratic society, where the interests of juveniles or the protection of the private life of the parties so require, or to the extent strictly necessary in the opinion of the court in special circumstances where publicity would prejudice the interests of justice.

(2) Everyone charged with a criminal offence shall be presumed innocent until proved guilty according to law.

(3) Everyone charged with a criminal offence has the following minimum rights:

(*a*) to be informed promptly, in a language which he understands and in detail, of the nature and cause of the accusation against him;

(*b*) to have adequate time and facilities for the preparation of his defence;

(*c*) to defend himself in person or through legal assistance of his own choosing or, if he has not sufficient means to pay for legal assistance, to be given it free when the interests of justice so require;

(*d*) to examine or have examined witnesses against him and to obtain the attendance and examination of witnesses on his behalf under the same conditions as witnesses against him;

(e) to have the free assistance of an interpreter if he cannot understand or speak the language used in court.

Article 7

(1) No one shall be held guilty of any criminal offence on account of any act or omission which did not constitute a criminal offence under national or international law at the time when it was committed. Nor shall a heavier penalty be imposed than the one that was applicable at the time the criminal offence was committed.

(2) This Article shall not prejudice the trial and punishment of any person for any act or omission which, at the time when it was committed, was criminal according to the general principles of law recognized by civilised nations.

Article 8

(1) Everyone has the right to respect for his private and family life, his home and his correspondence.

(2) There shall be no interference by a public authority with the exercise of this right except such as is in accordance with the law and is necessary in a democratic society in the interests of national security, public safety or the economic well-being of the country, for the prevention of disorder or crime, for the protection of health or morals, or for the protection of the rights and freedoms of others.

Article 9

(1) Everyone has the right to freedom of thought, conscience and religion; this right includes freedom to change his religion or belief and freedom, either alone or in community with others and in public or private, to manifest his religion or belief, in worship, teaching, practice and observance.

(2) Freedom to manifest one's religion or beliefs shall be subject only to such limitations as are prescribed by law and are necessary in a democratic society in the interests of public safety, for the protection of public order, health or morals, or for the protection of the rights and freedoms of others.

Article 10

(1) Everyone has the right to freedom of expression. This right shall include freedom to hold opinions and to receive and impart information and ideas without interference by public authority and regardless of frontiers. This Article shall not prevent States from requiring the licensing of broadcasting, television or cinema enterprises.

(2) The exercise of these freedoms, since it carries with it duties and responsibilities, may be subject to such formalities, conditions, restrictions or penalties as are prescribed by law and are necessary in a democratic society, in the interests of national security, territorial integrity or public safety, for the prevention of disorder or crime, for the protection of health or morals, for the protection of the reputation or rights of others, for

preventing the disclosure of information received in confidence, or for maintaining the authority and impartiality of the judiciary.

Article 11

(1) Everyone has the right to freedom of peaceful assembly and to freedom of association with others, including the right to form and to join trade unions for the protection of his interests.

(2) No restrictions shall be placed on the exercise of these rights other than such as are prescribed by law and are necessary in a democratic society in the interests of national security or public safety, for the prevention of disorder or crime, for the protection of health or morals or for the protection of the rights and freedoms of others. This Article shall not prevent the imposition of lawful restrictions on the exercise of these rights by members of the armed forces, of the police or of the administration of the State.

Article 12

Men and women of marriageable age have the right to marry and to found a family, according to the national laws governing the exercise of this right.

Article 13

Everyone whose rights and freedoms as set forth in this Convention are violated shall have an effective remedy before a national authority notwithstanding that the violation has been committed by persons acting in an official capacity.

Article 14

The enjoyment of rights and freedoms set forth in this Convention shall be secured without discrimination on any ground such as sex, race, colour, language, religion, political or other opinion, national or social origin, association with a national minority, property, birth or other status.

Article 15

(1) In time of war or other public emergency threatening the life of the nation any High Contracting Party may take measures derogating from its obligations under this Convention to the extent strictly required by the exigencies of the situation, provided that such measures are not inconsistent with its other obligations under international law.

(2) No derogation from Article 2, except in respect of deaths resulting from lawful acts of war, or from Articles 3, 4 (paragraph 1) and 7 shall be made under this provision.

(3) Any High Contracting Party availing itself of this right of derogation shall keep the Secretary-General of the Council of Europe fully informed of the measures which it has taken and the reasons therefor. It shall also inform the Secretary-General of the Council of Europe when such measures have ceased to operate and the provisions of the Convention are again being fully executed.

Article 16

Nothing in Articles 10, 11 and 14 shall be regarded as preventing the High Contracting Parties from imposing restrictions on the political activity of aliens.

Article 17

Nothing in this Convention may be interpreted as implying for any State, group or person any right to engage in any activity or perform any act aimed at the destruction of any of the rights and freedoms set forth herein or at their limitation to a greater extent than is provided for in the Convention.

Article 18

The restrictions permitted under this Convention to the said rights and freedoms shall not be applied for any purpose other than those for which they have been prescribed.

SECTION II

Article 19

To ensure the observance of the engagements undertaken by the High Contracting Parties in the present Convention, there shall be set up:

(1) A European Commission of Human Rights hereinafter referred to as "the Commission";

(2) A European Court of Human Rights, hereinafter referred to as "the Court".

> [Sections III (arts. 20–37) and IV (arts. 38–56) deal, respectively, with the organization and functioning of the Commission and Court provided for in Article 19. Section V (arts. 57–66) contains general and final provisions.]

PROTOCOL TO THE CONVENTION FOR THE PROTECTION OF HUMAN RIGHTS AND FUNDAMENTAL FREEDOMS

(signed at Paris, March 20, 1952, effective May 15, 1954)
1955 UNTS 260 (no. 2889)

The Governments signatory hereto,[2] being Members of the Council of Europe,

Being resolved to take steps to ensure the collective enforcement of certain rights and freedoms other than those already included in Section I of the Convention for the Protection of Human Rights and Fundamental Freedoms signed at Rome on 4th November, 1950 (hereinafter referred to as "the Convention"),

Have agreed as follows:

2. The signatory states are those listed in note 1 supra, at page 203.

Article 1

Every natural or legal person is entitled to the peaceful enjoyment of his possessions. No one shall be deprived of his possessions except in the public interest and subject to the conditions provided for by law and by the general principles of international law.

The preceding provisions shall not, however, in any way impair the right of a State to enforce such laws as it deems necessary to control the use of property in accordance with the general interest or to secure the payment of taxes or other contributions or penalties.

Article 2

No person shall be denied the right to education. In the exercise of any functions which it assumes in relation to education and to teaching, the State shall respect the right of parents to ensure such education and teaching in conformity with their own religious and philosophical convictions.

Article 3

The High Contracting Parties undertake to hold free elections at reasonable intervals by secret ballot, under conditions which will ensure the free expression of the opinion of the people in the choice of the legislature.

[Articles 4–6 are omitted]

PROTOCOL No. 4 TO THE CONVENTION FOR THE PROTECTION OF HUMAN RIGHTS AND FUNDAMENTAL FREEDOMS [3]
(Signed at Strasbourg, Sept. 16, 1963, effective May 2, 1968)
ETS no. 46

The Governments signatory hereto,[4] being Members of the Council of Europe,

Being resolved to take steps to ensure the collective enforcement of certain rights and freedoms other than those already included in Section I of the Convention for the Protection of Human Rights and Fundamental Freedoms signed at Rome on 4th November 1950 (hereinafter referred to as "the Convention") and in Articles 1 to 3 of the First Protocol to the Convention, signed at Paris on 20th March 1952,

Have agreed as follows:

Article 1

No one shall be deprived of his liberty merely on the ground of inability to fulfil a contractual obligation.

---

3. Declarations omitted.
4. [Ed.] The signatory governments are those listed in note 1 supra, with the exception of the Saar, Malta, Portugal, Spain, Liechtenstein and San Marino.

Article 2

1. Everyone lawfully within the territory of a State shall, within that territory, have the right to liberty of movement and freedom to choose his residence.

2. Everyone shall be free to leave any country, including his own.

3. No restrictions shall be placed on the exercise of these rights other than such as are in accordance with law and are necessary in a democratic society in the interests of national security or public safety, for the maintenance of *ordre public,* for the prevention of crime, for the protection of health or morals, or for the protection of the rights and freedoms of others.

4. The rights set forth in paragraph 1 may also be subject, in particular areas, to restrictions imposed in accordance with law and justified by the public interest in a democratic society.

Article 3

1. No one shall be expelled, by means either of an individual or of a collective measure, from the territory of the State of which he is a national.

2. No one shall be deprived of the right to enter the territory of the State of which he is a national.

Article 4

Collective expulsion of aliens is prohibited.

[Articles 5–7 are omitted.]

PROTOCOL No. 6 TO THE CONVENTION FOR THE PROTECTION OF HUMAN RIGHTS AND FUNDAMENTAL FREEDOMS

(Signed at Strasbourg, April 28, 1983, effective March 1, 1985)
ETS no. 114

The member States of the Council of Europe, signatory[5] to this Protocol to the Convention for the Protection of Human Rights and Fundamental Freedoms, signed at Rome on 4 November 1950 (hereinafter referred to as "the Convention"),

Considering that the evolution that has occurred in several member States of the Council of Europe expresses a general tendency in favour of abolition of the death penalty;

Have agreed as follows:

Article 1

The death penalty shall be abolished. No one shall be condemned to such penalty or executed.

---

5. [Ed.] The signatory states are those listed in note 1 supra, with the exception of the Saar and San Marino.

Article 2

A State may make provision in its law for the death penalty in respect of acts committed in time of war or of imminent threat of war; such penalty shall be applied only in the instances laid down in the law and in accordance with its provisions. The State shall communicate to the Secretary General of the Council of Europe the relevant provisions of that law.

Article 3

No derogation from the provisions of this Protocol shall be made under Article 15 of the Convention.

Article 4

No reservation may be made under Article 64 of the Convention in respect of the provisions of this Protocol.

[Articles 5–9 are omitted.]

PROTOCOL No. 7 TO THE CONVENTION FOR THE PROTECTION OF HUMAN RIGHTS AND FUNDAMENTAL FREEDOMS

(Signed at Strasbourg, Nov. 22, 1984, effective Nov. 1, 1988)
ETS no. 117

The member States of the Council of Europe signatory hereto,[6]

Being resolved to take further steps to ensure the collective enforcement of certain rights and freedoms by means of the Convention for the Protection of Human Rights and Fundamental Freedoms signed at Rome on 4 November 1950 (hereinafter referred to as "the Convention"),

Have agreed as follows:

Article 1

1. An alien lawfully resident in the territory of a State shall not be expelled therefrom except in pursuance of a decision reached in accordance with law and shall be allowed:

a. to submit reasons against his expulsion,

b. to have his case reviewed, and

c. to be represented for these purposes before the competent authority or a person or persons designated by that authority.

2. An alien may be expelled before the exercise of his rights under paragraph 1.*a*, *b* and *c* of this Article, when such expulsion is necessary in the interests of public order or is grounded on reasons of national security.

Article 2

1. Everyone convicted of a criminal offence by a tribunal shall have the right to have his conviction or sentence reviewed by a higher tribunal.

---

6. [Ed.] The signatory states are the same as those referred to in note 5 supra.

The exercise of this right, including the grounds on which it may be exercised, shall be governed by law.

2. This right may be subject to exceptions in regard to offences of a minor character, as prescribed by law, or in cases in which the person concerned was tried in the first instance by the highest tribunal or was convicted following an appeal against acquittal.

Article 3

When a person has by a final decision been convicted of a criminal offence and when subsequently his conviction has been reversed, or he has been pardoned, on the ground that a new or newly discovered fact shows conclusively that there has been a miscarriage of justice, the person who has suffered punishment as a result of such conviction shall be compensated according to the law or the practice of the State concerned, unless it is proved that the nondisclosure of the unknown fact in time is wholly or partly attributable to him.

Article 4

1. No one shall be liable to be tried or punished again in criminal proceedings under the jurisdiction of the same State for an offence for which he has already been finally acquitted or convicted in accordance with the law and penal procedure of that State.

2. The provisions of the preceding paragraph shall not prevent the reopening of the case in accordance with the law and penal procedure of the State concerned, if there is evidence of new or newly discovered facts, or if there has been a fundamental defect in the previous proceedings, which could affect the outcome of the case.

3. No derogation from this Article shall be made under Article 15 of the Convention.

Article 5

Spouses shall enjoy equality of rights and responsibilities of a private law character between them, and in their relations with their children, as to marriage, during marriage and in the event of its dissolution. This Article shall not prevent States from taking such measures as are necessary in the interests of the children.

[Articles 6–10 are omitted.]

5. JOINT DECLARATION BY THE EUROPEAN PARLIAMENT, THE COUNCIL AND THE COMMISSION

(Signed at Luxembourg, April 5, 1977)
O.J. C 103/1 (April 27, 1977)

THE EUROPEAN PARLIAMENT, THE COUNCIL AND THE COMMISSION,

Whereas the Treaties establishing the European Communities are based on the principle of respect for the law;

Whereas, as the Court of Justice has recognized, that law comprises, over and above the rules embodied in the treaties and secondary Community legislation, the general principles of law and in particular the fundamental rights, principles and rights on which the constitutional law of the Member States is based;

Whereas, in particular, all the Member States are Contracting Parties to the European Convention for the Protection of Human Rights and Fundamental Freedoms signed in Rome on 4 November 1950,

HAVE ADOPTED THE FOLLOWING DECLARATION:

1. The European Parliament, the Council and the Commission stress the prime importance they attach to the protection of fundamental rights, as derived in particular from the constitutions of the Member States and the European Convention for the Protection of Human Rights and Fundamental Freedoms.

2. In the exercise of their powers and in pursuance of the aims of the European Communities they respect and will continue to respect these rights.

6. PROTOCOL ON THE STATUTE OF THE COURT OF JUSTICE OF THE EUROPEAN ECONOMIC COMMUNITY

(Signed at Brussels, April 17, 1957)

298 UNTS 147 (1958), as amended by Council Decision 88/591, O.J. C 215/1 (Aug. 21, 1989)

The High Contracting Parties to the Treaty establishing the European Economic Community.

Desiring to lay down the Statute of the Court provided for in Article 188 of this Treaty.

* * *

Have agreed upon the following provisions, which shall be annexed to the Treaty establishing the European Economic Community.

Article 1

The Court established by Article 4 of this Treaty shall be constituted and shall function in accordance with the provisions of this Treaty and of this Statute.

TITLE I
JUDGES AND ADVOCATES–GENERAL

Article 2

Before taking up his duties each Judge shall, in open court, take an oath to perform his duties impartially and conscientiously and to preserve the secrecy of the deliberations of the Court.

Article 3

The Judges shall be immune from legal proceedings. After they have ceased to hold office, they shall continue to enjoy immunity in respect of acts performed by them in their official capacity including words spoken or written.

The Court, sitting in plenary session, may waive the immunity.

Where immunity has been waived and criminal proceedings are instituted against a Judge, he shall be tried, in any of the Member States, only by the Court competent to judge the members of the highest national judiciary.

Article 4

The Judges may not hold any political or administrative office.

They may not engage in any occupation, whether gainful or not, unless exemption is exceptionally granted by the Council.

When taking up their duties, they shall give a solemn undertaking that, both during and after their term of office, they will respect the obligations arising therefrom, in particular the duty to behave with integrity and discretion as regards the acceptance, after they have ceased to hold office, of certain appointments or benefits.

Any doubt on this point shall be settled by decision of the Court.

Article 5

Apart from normal replacement, or death, the duties of a Judge shall end when he resigns.

Where a Judge resigns, his letter of resignation shall be addressed to the President of the Court for transmission to the President of the Council. Upon this notification a vacancy shall arise on the bench.

Save where Article 6 applies, a Judge shall continue to hold office until his successor takes up his duties.

Article 6

A Judge may be deprived of his office or of his right to a pension or other benefits in its stead only if, in the unanimous opinion of the Judges and Advocates-General of the Court, he no longer fulfils the requisite conditions or meets the obligations arising from his office. The Judge concerned shall not take part in any such deliberations.

The Registrar of the Court shall communicate the decision of the Court to the President of the European Parliament and to the President of the Commission and shall notify it to the President of the Council.

In the case of a decision depriving a Judge of his office, a vacancy shall arise on the bench upon this latter notification.

Article 7

A Judge who is to replace a member of the Court whose term of office has not expired shall be appointed for the remainder of his predecessor's term.

Article 8

The provisions of Articles 2 to 7 shall apply to the Advocates-General.

TITLE II
ORGANIZATION

Article 9

The registrar shall take an oath before the Court to perform his duties impartially and conscientiously and to preserve the secrecy of the deliberations of the Court.

Article 10

The Court shall arrange for replacement of the Registrar on occasions when he is prevented from attending the Court.

Article 11

Officials and other servants shall be attached to the Court to enable it to function. They shall be responsible to the Registrar under the authority of the President.

Article 12

On a proposal from the Court, the Council may, acting unanimously, provide for the appointment of Assistant Rapporteurs and lay down the rules governing their service. The Assistant Rapporteurs may be required, under conditions laid down in the rules of procedure, to participate in preparatory inquiries in cases pending before the Court and to cooperate with the Judge who acts as Rapporteur.

The Assistant Rapporteurs shall be chosen from persons whose independence is beyond doubt and who possess the necessary legal qualifications; they shall be appointed by the Council. They shall take an oath before the Court to perform their duties impartially and conscientiously to preserve the secrecy of the deliberations of the Court.

Article 13

The Judges, the Advocates-General and the Registrar shall be required to reside at the place where the Court has its seat.

Article 14

The Court shall remain permanently in session. The duration of the judicial vacations shall be determined by the Court with due regard to the needs of its business.

Article 15

Decisions of the Court shall be valid only when an uneven number of its members is sitting in the deliberations. Decisions of the full Court shall be valid if seven members are sitting. Decisions of the Chambers shall be valid only if three Judges are sitting; in the event of one of the Judges of a Chamber being prevented from attending, a Judge of another Chamber may be called upon to sit in accordance with conditions laid down in the rules of procedure.

Article 16

No Judge or Advocate-General may take part in the disposal of any case in which he has previously taken part as agent or adviser or has acted for one of the parties, or in which he has been called upon to pronounce as a Member of a court or tribunal, of a commission of inquiry or in any other capacity.

If, for some special reason, any Judge or Advocate-General considers that he should not take part in the judgment or examination of a particular case, he shall so inform the President. If, for some special reason, the President considers that any Judge or Advocate-General should not sit or make submissions in a particular case, he shall notify him accordingly.

Any difficulty arising as to the application of this Article shall be settled by decision of the Court.

A party may not apply for a change in the composition of the Court or of one of its Chambers on the grounds of either the nationality of a Judge or the absence from the Court or from the Chamber of a Judge of the nationality of that party.

TITLE III
PROCEDURE

Article 17

The States and the institutions of the Community shall be represented before the Court by an agent appointed for each case; the agent may be assisted by an adviser or by a lawyer entitled to practise before a court of a Member State.

Other parties must be represented by a lawyer entitled to practise before a court of a Member State.

Such agents, advisers and lawyers shall, when they appear before the Court, enjoy the rights and immunities necessary to the independent exercise of their duties, under conditions laid down in the rules of procedure.

As regards such advisers and lawyers who appear before it, the Court shall have the powers normally accorded to courts of law, under conditions laid down in the rules of procedure.

University teachers being nationals of a Member State whose law accords them a right of audience shall have the same rights before the Court as are accorded by this Article to lawyers entitled to practice before a court of a Member State.

Article 18

The procedure before the Court shall consist of two parts: written and oral.

The written procedure shall consist of the communication to the parties and to the institutions of the Community whose decisions are in dispute, of applications, statements of case, defences and observations, and of replies, if any, as well as of all papers and documents in support or of certified copies of them.

Communications shall be made by the Registrar in the order and within the time laid down in the rules of procedure.

The oral procedure shall consist of the reading of the report presented by a Judge acting as Rapporteur, the hearing by the Court of agents, advisers and lawyers entitled to practise before a court of a Member State and of the submissions of the Advocate–General, as well as the hearing, if any, of witnesses and experts.

Article 19

A case shall be brought before the Court by a written application addressed to the Registrar. The application shall contain the applicant's name and permanent address and the description of the signatory, the name of the party against whom the application is made, the subject matter of the dispute, the submissions and a brief statement of the grounds on which the application is based.

The application shall be accompanied, where appropriate, by the measure the annulment of which is sought or, in the circumstances referred to in Article 175 of this Treaty, by documentary evidence of the date on which an institution was, in accordance with that Article, requested to act. If the documents are not submitted with the application, the Registrar shall ask the party concerned to produce them within a reasonable period, but in that event the rights of the party shall not lapse even if such documents are produced after the time limit for bringing proceedings.

Article 20

In the cases governed by Article 177 of this Treaty, the decision of the court or tribunal of a Member State which suspends its proceedings and refers a case to the Court shall be notified to the Court by the court or tribunal concerned. The decision shall then be notified by the Registrar of the Court to the parties, to the Member States and to the Commission, and also to the Council if the act the validity or interpretation of which is in dispute originates from the Council.

Within two months of this notification, the parties, the Member State, the Commission and, where appropriate, the Council, shall be entitled to submit statements of case or written observations to the Court.

Article 21

The Court may require the parties to produce all documents and to supply all information which the Court considers desirable. Formal note shall be taken of any refusal.

The Court may also require the Member States and institutions not being parties to the case to supply all information which the Court considers necessary for the proceedings.

Article 22

The Court may at any time entrust any individual, body authority, committee or other organization it chooses with the task of giving expert opinion.

Article 23

Witnesses may be heard under conditions laid down in the rules of procedure.

Article 24

With respect to defaulting witnesses the Court shall have the powers generally granted to courts and tribunals and may impose pecuniary penalties under conditions laid down in the rules of procedure.

Article 25

Witnesses and experts may be heard on oath taken in the form laid down in the rules of procedure or in the manner laid down by the law of the country of the witness or expert.

Article 26

The Court may order that a witness or expert be heard by the judicial authority of his place of permanent residence.

The order shall be sent for implementation to the competent judicial authority under conditions laid down in the rules of procedure. The documents drawn up in compliance with the letters rogatory shall be returned to the Court under the same conditions.

The Court shall defray the expenses, without prejudice to the right to charge them, where appropriate, to the parties.

Article 27

A Member State shall treat any violation of an oath by a witness or expert in the same manner as if the offence had been committed before one of its courts with jurisdiction in civil proceedings. At the instance of the Court, the Member State concerned shall prosecute the offender before its competent court.

Article 28

The hearing in court shall be in public, unless the Court, of its own motion or on application by the parties, decides otherwise for serious reasons.

Article 29

During the hearings the Court may examine the experts, the witnesses and the parties themselves. The latter, however, may address the Court only through their representatives.

Article 30

Minutes shall be made of each hearing and signed by the President and the Registrar.

Article 31

The case list shall be established by the President.

Article 32

The deliberations of the Court shall be and shall remain secret.

Article 33

Judgments shall state the reasons on which they are based. They shall contain the names of the Judges who took part in the deliberations.

Article 34

Judgments shall be signed by the President and the Registrar. They shall be read in open court.

Article 35

The Court shall adjudicate upon costs.

Article 36

The President of the Court may, by way of summary procedure, which may, in so far as necessary, differ from some of the rules contained in this

Statute and which shall be laid down in the rules of procedure, adjudicate upon applications to suspend execution, as provided for in Article 185 of this Treaty, or to prescribe interim measures in pursuance of Article 186, or to suspend enforcement in accordance with the last paragraph of Article 192.

Should the President be prevented from attending, his place shall be taken by another Judge under conditions laid down in the rules of procedure.

The ruling of the President or of the Judge replacing him shall be provisional and shall in no way prejudice the decision of the Court on the substance of the case.

Article 37

Member States and institutions of the Community may intervene in cases before the Court.

The same right shall be open to any other person establishing an interest in the result of any case submitted to the Court, save in cases between Member States, between institutions of the Community or between Member States and institutions of the Community.

Submissions made in an application to intervene shall be limited to supporting the submissions of one of the parties.

Article 38

Where the defending party, after having been duly summoned, fails to file written submissions in defence, judgment shall be given against that party by default. An objection may be lodged against the judgment within one month of it being notified. The objection shall not have the effect of staying enforcement of the judgment by default unless the Court decides otherwise.

Article 39

Member States, institutions of the Community and any other natural or legal persons may, in cases and under conditions to be determined by the rules of procedure, institute third-party proceedings to contest a judgment rendered without [their] being heard, where the judgment is prejudicial to their rights.

Article 40

If the meaning or scope of a judgment is in doubt, the Court shall construe it on application by any party or any institution of the Community establishing an interest therein.

Article 41

An application for revision of a judgment may be made to the Court only on discovery of a fact which is of such a nature as to be a decisive factor, and which, when the judgment was given, was unknown to the Court and to the party claiming the revision.

The revision shall be opened by a judgment of the Court expressly recording the existence of a new fact, recognizing that it is of such a character as to lay the case open to revision and declaring the application admissable on this ground.

No application for revision may be made after the lapse of ten years from the date of the judgment.

Article 42

Periods of grace based on considerations of distance shall be determined by the rules of procedure.

No right shall be prejudiced in consequence of the expiry of a time limit if the party concerned proves the existence of unforeseeable circumstances or of *force majeure*.

Article 43

Proceedings against the Community in matters arising from non-contractual liability shall be barred after a period of five years from the occurrence of the event giving rise thereto. The period of limitation shall be interrupted if proceedings are instituted before the Court or if prior to such proceedings an application is made by the aggrieved party to the relevant institution of the Community. In the latter event the proceedings must be instituted within the period of two months provided for in Article 173; the provisions of the second paragraph of Article 175 shall apply where appropriate.

TITLE IV
THE COURT OF FIRST INSTANCE OF THE EUROPEAN COMMUNITIES

Article 44

Articles 2 to 8, and 13 to 16 of this Statute shall apply to the Court of First Instance and its members. The oath referred to in Article 2 shall be taken before the Court of Justice and the decisions referred to in Articles 3, 4 and 6 shall be adopted by that Court after hearing the Court of First Instance.

Article 45

The Court of First Instance shall appoint its Registrar and lay down the rules governing his service. Articles 9, 10 and 13 of this Statute shall apply to the Registrar of the Court of First Instance *mutatis mutandis*.

The President of the Court of Justice and the President of the Court of First Instance shall determine, by common accord, the conditions under which officials and other servants attached to the Court of Justice shall render their services to the Court of First Instance to enable it to function. Certain officials or other servants shall be responsible to the Registrar of the Court of First Instance under the authority of the President of the Court of First Instance.

Article 46

The procedure before the Court of First Instance shall be governed by Title III of this Statute, with the exception of Article 20.

Such further and more detailed provisions as may be necessary shall be laid down in the Rules of Procedure established in accordance with Article 168a(4) of this Treaty.

Notwithstanding the fourth paragraph of Article 18 of this Statute, the Advocate-General may make his reasoned submissions in writing.

Article 47

Where an application or other procedural document addressed to the Court of First Instance is lodged by mistake with the Registrar of the Court of Justice it shall be transmitted immediately by that Registrar to the Registrar of the Court of First Instance; likewise, where an application or other procedural document addressed to the Court of Justice is lodged by mistake with the Registrar of the Court of First Instance, it shall be transmitted immediately by that Registrar to the Registrar of the Court of Justice.

Where the Court of First Instance finds that it does not have jurisdiction to hear and determine an action in respect of which the Court of Justice has jurisdiction, it shall refer that action to the Court of Justice; likewise, where the Court of Justice finds that an action falls within the jurisdiction of the Court of First Instance, it shall refer that action to the Court of First Instance, whereupon that Court may not decline jurisdiction.

Where the Court of Justice and the Court of First Instance are seised of cases in which the same relief is sought, the same issue of interpretation is raised or the validity of the same act is called in question, the Court of First Instance may, after hearing the parties, stay the proceedings before it until such time as the Court of Justice shall have delivered judgment. Where applications are made for the same act to be declared void, the Court of First Instance may also decline jurisdiction in order that the Court of Justice may rule on such applications. In the cases referred to in this sub-paragraph, the Court of Justice may also decide to stay the proceedings before it; in that event, the proceedings before the Court of First Instance shall continue.

Article 48

Final decisions of the Court of First Instance, decisions disposing of the substantive issues in part only or disposing of a procedural issue concerning a plea of lack of competence or inadmissibility, shall be notified by the Registrar of the Court of First Instance to all parties as well as all Member States and the Community institutions even if they did not intervene in the case before the Court of First Instance.

Article 49

An appeal may be brought before the Court of Justice, within two months of the notification of the decision appealed against, against final decisions of the Court of First Instance and decisions of that Court disposing of the substantive issues in part only or disposing of a procedural issue concerning a plea of lack of competence or inadmissibility.

Such an appeal may be brought by any party which has been unsuccessful, in whole or in part, in its submissions. However, interveners other than the Member States and the Community institutions may bring such an appeal only where the decision of the Court of First Instance directly affects them.

With the exception of cases relating to disputes between the Community and its servants, an appeal may also be brought by Member States and Community institutions which did not intervene in the proceedings before the Court of First Instance. Such Member States and institutions shall be in the same position as Member States or institutions which intervened at first instance.

Article 50

Any person whose application to intervene has been dismissed by the Court of First Instance may appeal to the Court of Justice within two weeks of the notification of the decision dismissing the application.

The parties to the proceedings may appeal to the Court of Justice against any decision of the Court of First Instance made pursuant to Article 185 or 186 or the fourth paragraph of Article 192 of this Treaty within two months from their notification.

The appeal referred to in the first two paragraphs of this Article shall be heard and determined under the procedure referred to in Article 36 of this Statute.

Article 51

An appeal to the Court of Justice shall be limited to points of law. It shall lie on the grounds of lack of competence of the Court of First Instance, a breach of procedure before it which adversely affects the interests of the appellant as well as the infringement of Community law by the Court of First Instance.

No appeal shall lie regarding only the amount of the costs or the party ordered to pay them.

Article 52

Where an appeal is brought against a decision of the Court of First Instance, the procedure before the Court of Justice shall consist of a written part and an oral part. In accordance with conditions laid down in the Rules of Procedure the Court of Justice, having heard the Advocate-General and the parties, may dispense with the oral procedure.

Article 53

Without prejudice to Articles 185 and 186 of this Treaty, an appeal shall not have suspensory effect.

By way of derogation from Article 187 of this Treaty, decisions of the Court of First Instance declaring a regulation to be void shall take effect only as from the date of expiry of the period referred to in the first paragraph of Article 49 of this Statute or, if an appeal shall have been brought within that period, as from the date of dismissal of the appeal, without prejudice, however, to the right of a party to apply to the Court of Justice, pursuant to Articles 185 and 186 of this Treaty, for the suspension of the effects of the regulation which has been declared void or for the prescription of any other interim measure.

Article 54

If the appeal is well founded, the Court of Justice shall quash the decision of the Court of First Instance. It may itself give final judgment in the matter, where the state of the proceedings so permits, or refer the case back to the Court of First Instance for judgment.

Where a case is referred back to the Court of First Instance, that Court shall be bound by the decision of the Court of Justice on points of law.

When an appeal brought by a Member State or a Community institution, which did not intervene in the proceedings before the court of First Instance, is well founded the Court of Justice may, if it considers this necessary, state which of the effects of the decision of the Court of First Instance which has been quashed shall be considered as definitive in respect of the parties to the litigation.

Article 55

The rules of procedure of the Court provided for in Article 188 of this Treaty shall contain, apart from the provisions contemplated by this Statute, any other provisions necessary for applying and, where required, supplementing it.

Article 56

The Council may, acting unanimously, make such further adjustments to the provisions of this Statute as may be required by reason of measures taken by the Council in accordance with the last paragraph of Article 165 of this Treaty.

Article 57

Immediately after the oath has been taken, the President of the Council shall proceed to choose by lot the Judges and the Advocates-General whose terms of office are to expire at the end of the first three years in accordance with the second and third paragraphs of Article 167 of this Treaty.

7. RULES OF PROCEDURE OF THE COURT OF JUSTICE OF THE EUROPEAN COMMUNITIES

June 19, 1991

O.J. L 176/7 (July 4, 1991)

[*Eds. Note:* The Rules of Procedure of the Court of Justice, adopted on Dec. 4, 1974, were amended successively on Sept. 12, 1979, May 27, 1981, May 8, 1987, June 7, 1989, and May 15, 1991. They were republished in their entirety on June 19, 1991.

Due to scarcity of space, the Rules of Procedure cannot be reproduced in full. There follows their table of contents and selected articles only.]

Contents

Interpretation (Article 1)

Title I. Organization of the Court

Ch.
1. Judges and Advocates–General (Articles 2 to 6)
2. Presidency of the Court and constitution of the Chambers (Articles 7 to 11)
3. Registry
    1. The Registrar and Assistant Registrars (Articles 12 to 19)
    2. Other departments (Articles 20 to 23)
4. Assistant Rapporteurs (Article 24)
5. The working of the Court (Articles 25 to 28)
6. Languages (Articles 29 to 31)
7. Rights and obligations of agents, advisers and lawyers (Articles 32 to 36)

Title II. Procedure

1. Written procedure (Articles 37 to 44a)
2. Preparatory inquiries
    1. Measures of inquiry (Articles 45 and 46)
    2. The summoning and examination of witnesses and experts (Articles 47 to 53)
    3. Closure of the preparatory inquiry (Article 54)
3. Oral procedure (Articles 55 to 62)
4. Judgments (Articles 63 to 68)
5. Costs (Articles 69 to 75)
6. Legal aid (Article 76)
7. Discontinuance (Articles 77 and 78)
8. Service (Article 79)
9. Time limits (Articles 80 to 82)
10. Stay of proceedings (Article 82a)

Title III. Special forms of procedure

1. Suspension of operation or enforcement and other interim measures (Articles 83 to 90)
2. Preliminary issues (Articles 91 and 92)
3. Intervention (Article 93)
4. Judgments by default and applications to set them aside (Article 94)
5. Cases assigned to Chambers (Article 95)
6. Exceptional review proceedings
    1. Third-party proceedings (Article 97)
    2. Revision (Articles 98 to 100)

Ch.
7. Appeals against decisions of the Arbitration Committee (Article 101)
8. Interpretation of judgments (Article 102)
9. Preliminary rulings and other references for interpretation (Articles 103 and 104)
10. Special procedures under Articles 103 to 105 of the Euratom Treaty (Articles 105 and 106)
11. Opinions (Articles 107 to 109)

Title IV. Appeals against decisions of the Court of First Instance (Articles 110 to 123)

Miscellaneous provisions (Articles 124 to 127)
Annex I   Decision on official holidays
Annex II Decision on extension on time-limits on account of distance

TITLE I
ORGANIZATION OF THE COURT

* * *

Chapter 2. Presidency of the Court and Constitution of the Chambers

Article 7

1. The Judges shall, immediately after the partial replacement provided for in * * * Article 167 of the EEC Treaty * * *, elect one of their number as President of the Court for a term of three years.

2. If the office of the President of the Court falls vacant before the normal date of expiry thereof, the Court shall elect a successor for the remainder of the term.

3. The elections provided for in this Article shall be by secret ballot. If a Judge obtains an absolute majority he shall be elected. If no Judge obtains an absolute majority, a second ballot shall be held and the Judge obtaining the most votes shall be elected. Where two or more Judges obtain an equal number of votes the oldest of them shall be deemed elected.

Article 8

The President shall direct the judicial business and the administration of the Court; he shall preside at hearings and deliberations.

Article 9

1. The Court shall set up Chambers in accordance with the provisions of * * * the second paragraph of Article 165 of the EEC Treaty * * * and shall decide which Judges shall be attached to them.

* * *

2. As soon as an application initiating proceedings has been lodged, the President shall assign the case to one of the Chambers for any preparatory inquiries and shall designate a Judge from that Chamber to act as Rapporteur.

3. The Court shall lay down criteria by which, as a rule, cases are to be assigned to Chambers.

4. These Rules shall apply to proceedings before the Chambers.

In cases assigned to a Chamber the powers of the President of the Court shall be exercised by the President of the Chamber.

Article 10

1. The Court shall appoint for a period of one year the Presidents of the Chambers and the First Advocate–General.

The provisions of Article 7(2) and (3) shall apply.

* * *

2. The First Advocate–General shall assign each case to an Advocate–General as soon as the Judge–Rapporteur has been designated by the President. He shall take the necessary steps if an Advocate–General is absent or prevented from acting.

* * *

Chapter 5. The Working of the Court

Article 25

1. The dates and times of the sittings of the Court shall be fixed by the President.

2. The dates and times of the sittings of the Chambers shall be fixed by their respective Presidents.

3. The Court and the Chambers may choose to hold one or more sittings in a place other than that in which the Court has its seat.

Article 26

1. Where, by reason of a Judge being absent or prevented from attending, there is an even number of Judges, the most junior Judge within the meaning of Article 6 of these Rules shall abstain from taking part in the deliberations unless he is the Judge–Rapporteur. In that case the Judge immediately senior to him shall abstain from taking part in the deliberations.

2. If after the Court has been convened it is found that the quorum of seven Judges has not been attained, the President shall adjourn the sitting until there is a quorum.

3. If in any Chamber the quorum of three Judges has not been attained, the President of that Chamber shall so inform the President of the Court who shall designate another Judge to complete the Chamber.

Article 27

1. The Court and Chambers shall deliberate in closed session.

2. Only those Judges who were present at the oral proceedings and the Assistant Rapporteur, if any, entrusted with the consideration of the case may take part in the deliberations.

3. Every judge taking part in the deliberations shall state his opinion and the reasons for it.

4. Any Judge may require that any questions be formulated in the language of his choice and communicated in writing to the Court or Chamber before being put to the vote.

5. The conclusions reached by the majority of the Judges after final discussion shall determine the decision of the Court. Votes shall be cast in reverse order to the order of precedence laid down in Article 6 of these Rules.

6. Differences of view on the substance, wording or order of questions, or on the interpretation of the voting shall be settled by decision of the Court or Chamber.

7. Where the deliberations of the Court concern questions of its own administration, the Advocates-General shall take part and have a vote. The Registrar shall be present, unless the Court decides to the contrary.

8. Where the court sits without the Registrar being present it shall, if necessary, instruct the most junior Judge within the meaning of Article 6 of these rules to draw up minutes. The minutes shall be signed by this Judge and by the President.

* * *

Chapter 6. Languages

Article 29

1. The language of a case shall be Danish, Dutch, English, French, German, Greek, Irish, Italian, Portuguese or Spanish.

2. The language of a case shall be chosen by the applicant, except that:

(a) where the defendant is a Member State or a natural or legal person having the nationality of a Member State, the language of the case shall be the official language of that State; where that State has more than one official language, the applicant may choose between them;

(b) at the joint request of the parties the Court may authorize another of the languages mentioned in paragraph (1) of this Article to be used as the language of the case for all or part of the proceedings;

(c) at the request of one of the parties, and after the opposite party and the Advocate-General have been heard, the Court, may, by way of derogation from subparagraphs (a) and (b), authorize another of the languages mentioned in paragraph (1) of this Article to be used as the language of the case for all or part of the proceedings; such a request may not be submitted by an institution of the European Communities.

In cases to which Article 103 of these Rules applies, the language of the case shall be the language of the national court or tribunal which refers the matter to the Court.

3. The language of the case shall be used in the written and oral pleadings of the parties and in supporting documents, and also in the minutes and decisions of the Court.

Any supporting documents expressed in another language must be accompanied by a translation into the language of the case.

In the case of lengthy documents, translations may be confined to extracts. However, the Court or Chamber may, of its own motion or at the request of a party, at any time call for a complete or fuller translation.

Notwithstanding the foregoing provisions, a Member State shall be entitled to use its official language when intervening in a case before the Court or when taking part in any reference of a kind mentioned in Article 103. This provision shall apply both to written statements and to oral addresses. The Registrar shall cause any such statement or address to be translated into the language of the case.

4. Where a witness or expert states that he is unable adequately to express himself in one of the languages referred to in paragraph (1) of this Article, the Court or Chamber may authorize him to give his evidence in another language. The Registrar shall arrange for translation into the language of the case.

5. The President of the Court and the Presidents of Chambers in conducting oral proceedings, the Judge-Rapporteur both in his preliminary report and in his report for the hearing, Judges and Advocates-General in putting questions and Advocates-General in delivering their opinions may use one of the languages referred to in paragraph (1) of this Article other than the language of the case. The Registrar shall arrange for translation into the language of the case.

Article 30

1. The Registrar shall, at the request of any Judge, of the Advocate-General or of a party, arrange for anything said or written in the course of the proceedings before the Court or a Chamber to be translated into the languages he chooses from those referred to in Article 29(1).

2. Publications of the Court shall be issued in the languages referred to in Article 1 of Council Regulation No. 1.

Article 31

The texts of documents drawn up in the language of the case or in any other language authorized by the Court pursuant to Article 29 of these rules shall be authentic.

* * *

TITLE II
PROCEDURE
Chapter 1. Written Procedure
Article 37

1. The original of every pleading must be signed by the party's agent or lawyer.

The original, accompanied by all annexes referred to therein, shall be lodged together with five copies for the Court and a copy for every other party to the proceedings. Copies shall be certified by the party lodging them.

2. Institutions shall in addition produce, within time-limits laid down by the Court, translations of all pleadings into the other languages provided for by Article 1 of Council Regulation No. 1. The second subparagraph of paragraph (1) of this Article shall apply.

3. All pleadings shall bear a date. In the reckoning of time-limits for taking steps in proceedings, only the date of lodgment at the Registry shall be taken into account.

4. To every pleading there shall be annexed a file containing the documents relied on in support of it, together with a schedule listing them.

5. Where in view of the length of a document only extracts from it are annexed to the pleading, the whole document or a full copy of it shall be lodged at the Registry.

* * *

Article 38

1. An application of the kind referred to in * * * Article 19 of the [Statute of the Court of Justice] shall state:

(a) the name and address of the applicant;

(b) the designation of the party against whom the application is made;

(c) the subject-matter of the proceedings and a summary of the pleas in law on which the application is based;

(d) the form of order sought by the applicant;

(e) where appropriate, the nature of any evidence offered in support.

* * *

3. The lawyer acting for a party must lodge at the Registry a certificate that he is entitled to practise before a Court of a Member State.

4. The application shall be accompanied, where appropriate, by the documents specified in the second paragraph of * * * Article 19 of the [Statute of the Court of Justice].

* * *

Article 40

1. Within one month after service on him of the application, the defendant shall lodge a defence, stating:

(a) the name and address of the defendant;

(b) the arguments of fact and law relied on;

(c) the form of order sought by the defendant;

(d) the nature of any evidence offered by him.

The provisions of Article 38(2) to (5) of these Rules shall apply to the defence.

2. The time-limit laid down in paragraph (1) of this Article may be extended by the President on a reasoned application by the defendant.

Article 41

1. The application initiating the proceedings and the defence may be supplemented by a reply from the applicant and by a rejoinder from the defendant.

2. The President shall fix the time-limits within which these pleadings are to be lodged.

Article 42

1. In reply or rejoinder a party may offer further evidence. The party must, however, give reasons for the delay in offering it.

2. No new plea in law may be introduced in the course of proceedings unless it is based on matters of law or of fact which come to light in the course of the procedure.

* * *

Article 43

The Court may, at any time, after hearing the parties and the Advocate–General, if the assignment referred to in Article 10(2) has taken place, order that two or more cases concerning the same subject-matter shall, on account of the connection between them, be joined for the purposes of the written or oral procedure or of the final judgment. The cases may subsequently be disjoined.

Article 44

1. After the rejoinder provided for in Article 41(1) of these Rules has been lodged, the President shall fix a date on which the Judge–Rapporteur is to present his preliminary report to the Court. The report shall contain recommendations as to whether a preparatory inquiry or any other preparatory step should be undertaken and whether the case should be referred to the Chamber to which it has been assigned under Article 9(2).

The Court shall decide, after hearing the Advocate–General, what action to take upon the recommendations of the Judge–Rapporteur.

* * *

2. Where the Court orders a preparatory inquiry and does not undertake it itself, it shall assign the inquiry to the Chamber.

Where the Court decides to open the oral procedure without an inquiry, the President shall fix the opening date.

Article 44(a)

Without prejudice to any special provisions laid down in these Rules, and except in the specific cases in which * * * the Court, acting on a report from the Judge–Rapporteur, after hearing the Advocate–General and with the express consent of the parties, decides otherwise, the procedure before the Court shall also include an oral part.

Chapter 2. Preparatory Inquiries
Section 1. Measures of Inquiry

Article 45

1. The Court, after hearing the Advocate–General, shall prescribe the measures of inquiry that it considers appropriate by means of an order setting out the facts to be proved. Before the Court decides on the measures of inquiry referred to in paragraph (2)(c), (d) and (e) the parties shall be heard.

The order shall be served on the parties.

2. Without prejudice to * * * Articles 21 and 22 of the [Statute of the Court of Justice], the following measures of inquiry may be adopted:

(a) the personal appearance of the parties;

(b) a request for information and production of documents;

(c) oral testimony;

(d) the commissioning of an expert's report;

(e) an inspection of the place or thing in question.

3. The measures of inquiry which the Court has ordered may be conducted by the Court itself, or be assigned to the Judge–Rapporteur.

The Advocate–General shall take part in the measures of inquiry.

4. Evidence may be submitted in rebuttal and previous evidence may be amplified.

Article 46

1. A Chamber to which a preparatory inquiry has been assigned may exercise the powers vested in the Court by Articles 45 and 47 to 53 of these Rules; the powers vested in the President of the Court may be exercised by the President of the Chamber.

* * *

Section 2. The Summoning and Examination of Witnesses and Experts

Article 47

1. The Court may, either of its own motion or [on] application by a party, and after hearing the Advocate–General, order that certain facts be proved by witnesses. The order of the Court shall set out the facts to be established.

The Court may summon a witness of its own motion or on application by a party or at the instance of the Advocate-General.

An application by a party for the examination of a witness shall state precisely about what facts and for what reasons the witness should be examined.

2. The witness shall be summoned by an order of the Court containing the following information:

(a) the surname, forenames, description and address of the witness;

(b) an indication of the facts about which the witness is to be examined;

(c) where appropriate, particulars of the arrangements made by the Court for reimbursement of expenses incurred by the witness, and of the penalties which may be imposed on defaulting witnesses.

The order shall be served on the parties and the witnesses.

* * *

4. After the identity of the witness has been established, the President shall inform him that he will be required to vouch the truth of his evidence in the manner laid down in these Rules.

The witness shall give his evidence to the Court, the parties having been given notice to attend. After the witness has given his main evidence the President may, at the request of a party or of his own motion, put questions to him.

The other Judges and the Advocate-General may do likewise.

Subject to the control of the President, questions may be put to witnesses by the representatives of the parties.

* * *

6. The Registrar shall draw up minutes in which the evidence of each witness is reproduced.

The minutes shall be signed by the President or by the Judge-Rapporteur responsible for conducting the examination of the witness, and by the Registrar. Before the minutes are thus signed, witnesses must be given an opportunity to check the content of the minutes and to sign them.

The minutes shall constitute an official record.

* * *

Article 49

1. The Court may order that an expert's report be obtained. The order appointing the expert shall define his task and set a time-limit within which he is to make his report.

2. The expert shall receive a copy of the order, together with all the documents necessary for carrying out his task. He shall be under the

supervision of the Judge–Rapporteur, who may be present during his investigation and who shall be kept informed of his progress in carrying out his task.

The Court may request the parties or one of them to lodge security for the costs of the expert's report.

3. At the request of the expert, the Court may order the examination of witnesses. Their examination shall be carried out in accordance with Article 47 of these Rules.

4. The expert may give his opinion only on points which have been expressly referred to him.

5. After the expert has made his report, the Court may order that he be examined, the parties having been given notice to attend.

Subject to the control of the President, questions may be put to the expert by the representatives of the parties.

* * *

Article 52

The Court may, on application by a party or of its own motion, issue letters rogatory for the examination of witnesses or experts, as provided for in the supplementary rules mentioned in Article 125 of these Rules.

Article 53

1. The Registrar shall draw up minutes of every hearing. The minutes shall be signed by the President and by the Registrar and shall constitute an official record.

* * *

Section 3. Closure of the Preparatory Inquiry

Article 54

Unless the Court prescribes a period within which the parties may lodge written observations, the President shall fix the date for the opening of the oral procedure after the preparatory inquiry has been completed.

Where a period had been prescribed for the lodging of written observations, the President shall fix the date for the opening of the oral procedure after that period has expired.

Chapter 3. Oral Procedure

* * *

Article 56

1. The proceedings shall be opened and directed by the President, who shall be responsible for the proper conduct of the hearing.

2. The oral proceedings in cases heard *in camera* shall not be published.

Article 57

The President may in the course of the hearing put questions to the agents, advisers or lawyers of the parties.

The other Judges and the Advocate-General may do likewise.

Article 58

A party may address the Court only through his agent, adviser or lawyer.

Article 59

1. The Advocate-General shall deliver his opinion orally at the end of the oral procedure.

2. After the Advocate-General has delivered his opinion, the President shall declare the oral procedure closed.

Article 60

The Court may at any time, in accordance with Article 45(1), after hearing the Advocate-General, order any measure of inquiry to be taken or that a previous inquiry be repeated or expanded. The Court may direct the Chamber or the Judge-Rapporteur to carry out the measures so ordered.

Article 61

The Court may after hearing the Advocate-General order the reopening of the oral procedure.

Article 62

1. The Registrar shall draw up minutes of every hearing. The minutes shall be signed by the President and by the Registrar and shall constitute an official record.

2. The parties may inspect the minutes at the Registry and obtain copies at their own expense.

Chapter 4. Judgments

Article 63

The judgment shall contain:

— a statement that it is the judgment of the Court,
— the date of its delivery,
— the names of the President and of the Judges taking part in it,
— the name of the Advocate-General,
— the name of the Registrar,
— the description of the parties,
— the names of the agents, advisers and lawyers of the parties,
— a statement of the forms of order sought by the parties,
— a statement that the Advocate-General has been heard,
— a summary of the facts,

— the grounds for the decision,

— the operative part of the judgment, including the decision as to costs.

Article 64

1. The judgment shall be delivered in open court; the parties shall be given notice to attend to hear it.

* * *

Article 65

The judgment shall be binding from the date of its delivery.

* * *

Chapter 5. Costs

Article 69

1. A decision as to costs shall be given in the final judgment or in the order which closes the proceedings.

2. The unsuccessful party shall be ordered to pay the costs if they have been applied for in the successful party's pleadings.

Where there are several unsuccessful parties the Court shall decide how the costs are to be shared.

3. Where each party succeeds on some and fails on other heads, or where the circumstances are exceptional, the Court may order that the costs be shared or that the parties bear their own costs.

The Court may order a party, even if successful, to pay costs which the Court considers that party to have unreasonably or vexatiously caused the opposite party to incur.

4. The Member States and institutions which intervene in the proceedings shall bear their own costs.

* * *

6. Where a case does not proceed to judgment the costs shall be in the discretion of the Court.

Article 70

Without prejudice to the second subparagraph of Article 69(3) of these Rules, in proceedings between the Communities and their servants the institutions shall bear their own costs.

* * *

Article 72

Proceedings before the Court shall be free of charge, except that:

(a) where a party has caused the Court to incur avoidable costs the Court may, after hearing the Advocate-General, order that party to refund them;

(b) where copying or translation work is carried out at the request of a party, the cost shall, in so far as the Registrar considers it excessive, be paid for by that party on the scale of charges referred to in Article 16(5) of these Rules.

Article 73

Without prejudice to the proceeding Article, the following shall be regarded as recoverable costs:

(a) sums payable to witnesses and experts under Article 51 of these Rules;

(b) expenses necessarily incurred by the parties for the purpose of the proceedings, in particular the travel and subsistence expenses and the remuneration of agents, advisers or lawyers.

* * *

Chapter 6. Legal Aid

Article 76

1. A party who is wholly or in part unable to meet the costs of the proceedings may at any time apply for legal aid.

The application shall be accompanied by evidence of the applicant's need of assistance, and in particular by a document from the competent authority certifying his lack of means.

2. If the application is made prior to proceedings which the applicant wishes to commence, it shall briefly state the subject of such proceedings.

The application need not be made through a lawyer.

3. The President shall designate a Judge to act as Rapporteur. The Chamber to which the latter belongs shall, after considering the written observations of the opposite party and after hearing the Advocate–General, decide whether legal aid should be granted in full or in part, or whether it should be refused. The Chamber shall consider whether there is manifestly no cause of action.

* * *

TITLE III

SPECIAL FORMS OF PROCEDURE

Chapter 1. Suspension of Operation or Enforcement and Other Interim Measures

Article 83

1. An application to suspend the operation of any [suspensive] measure adopted by an institution, made pursuant to * * * Article 185 of the EEC Treaty * * * shall be admissible only if the applicant is challenging that measure in proceedings before the Court.

An application for the adoption of any other interim measure referred to in * * * Article 186 of the EEC Treaty * * * shall be admissible only if it is made by a party to a case before the Court and relates to that case.

2. An application of a kind referred to in paragraph (1) of this Article shall state the subject-matter of the proceedings, the circumstances giving rise to urgency and the pleas of fact and law establishing a *prima facie* case for the interim measures applied for.

* * *

Article 84

1. The application shall be served on the opposite party, and the President shall prescribe a short period within which that party may submit written or oral observations.

2. The President may order a preparatory inquiry.

The President may grant the application even before the observations of the opposite party have been submitted. This decision may be varied or cancelled even without any application being made by any party.

Article 85

The President shall either decide on the application himself or refer it to the Court.

* * *

Article 86

1. The decision on the application shall take the form of a reasoned order, from which no appeal shall lie. The order shall be served on the parties forthwith.

2. The enforcement of the order may be made conditional on the lodging by the applicant of security, of an amount and nature to be fixed in the light of the circumstances.

* * *

4. The order shall have only an interim effect, and shall be without prejudice to the decision of the Court on the substance of the case.

Article 87

On application by a party, the order may at any time be varied or cancelled on account of a change in circumstances.

Article 88

Rejection of an application for an interim measure shall not bar the party who made it from making a further application on the basis of new facts.

Article 89

The provisions of this Chapter shall apply to applications to suspend the enforcement of a decision of the Court or of any measure adopted by another institution, submitted pursuant to * * * Articles 187 and 192 of the EEC Treaty * * *. The order granting the application shall fix, where appropriate, a date on which [the] interim measure is to lapse.

* * *

Chapter 2. Preliminary Issues

Article 91

1. A party applying to the Court for a decision on a preliminary objection or other preliminary plea not going to the substance of the case shall make the application by a separate document.

The application must state the pleas of fact and law relied on and the form of order sought by the applicant; any supporting documents must be annexed to it.

2. As soon as the application has been lodged, the President shall prescribe a period within which the opposite party may lodge a document containing a statement of the form of order sought by that party and its pleas in law.

3. Unless the Court decides otherwise, the remainder of the proceedings shall be oral.

4. The Court shall, after hearing the Advocate–General, decide on the application or reserve its decision for the final judgment.

* * *

Article 92

1. Where it is clear that the Court has no jurisdiction to take cognizance of an action or where the action is manifestly inadmissible, the Court may, by reasoned order, after hearing the Advocate–General and without taking further steps in the proceedings, give a decision on the action.

2. The Court may at any time of its own motion consider whether there exists any absolute bar to proceeding with a case, and shall give its decision in accordance with Article 91(3) and (4) of these Rules.

> [See the Table of Contents, supra page 225, for coverage of the other chapters of Title III (such as intervention, assignment of cases to chambers, revision of judgments and interpretation of judgments).]
>
> [Title IV, on appeals against decisions of the Court of First Instance, is omitted.]

8. CONVENTION ON JURISDICTION AND THE ENFORCEMENT OF JUDGMENTS IN CIVIL AND COMMERCIAL MATTERS

(Signed at Brussels, Sept. 27, 1968, effective Feb. 1, 1973)
(as amended)
O.J. L304/77 (Oct. 30, 1978)

[*Eds. Note*: This Convention, commonly known as the "Brussels" or "Judgments" Convention, was entered into by the then six EC Member States pursuant to Article 220 of the EEC Treaty. It sought to harmonize and regularize the rules governing the international jurisdiction of the courts of the signatory states, and to promote the mutual recognition and enforcement of their judgments. Only a few provisions of the protocol attached to the 1968 Convention are reproduced here.

In 1971, the same six states entered into a Protocol conferring on the Court of Justice jurisdiction to interpret the Brussels Convention and its protocol, and more particularly to give preliminary rulings on them. Protocol 75/464, O.J. L 204/28 (Aug. 2, 1975), republished as amended at O.J. L 304/97 (Oct. 30, 1978). The 1971 Protocol immediately follows the Brussels Convention in this Supplement.

The Brussels Convention itself was amended by a series of conventions of accession by new EC Member States. Convention on the Accession to the [Brussels] Convention of the Kingdom of Denmark, Ireland and the United Kingdom of Great Britain and Northern Ireland, O.J. L 304/1 (Oct. 30, 1978); Convention on the Accession of Greece to the [Brussels] Convention, O.J. L 388/1 (Dec. 31, 1982); Convention on the Accession of the Kingdom of Spain and the Portuguese Republic to the [Brussels] Convention, O.J. L 285/1 (Oct. 3, 1989). The text of the Brussels Convention reprinted below reflects the amendments made by these conventions of accession. (The accession conventions also amended the 1971 Protocol on the Court of Justice's preliminary reference jurisdiction.)

In September 1988, the then 12 EC Member States and the EFTA states of Austria, Finland, Iceland, Norway, Sweden and Switzerland signed the so-called Lugano Convention on Jurisdiction and the Enforcement of Judgments in Civil and Commercial Matters, 88/592, O.J. L 319/9 (Nov. 25, 1988). This Convention essentially aims at extending the Brussels Convention principles to a wider circle of states. In declarations annexed to the Lugano Convention, the EC Member States effectively call upon the Court of Justice when interpreting the Brussels Convention to "pay due account" to rulings under the Lugano Convention, and the EFTA States call upon their own courts when interpreting the Lugano Convention to "pay due account" to Court of Justice and EC Member State rulings on provisions of the Brussels Convention that are substantially identical to those of the Lugano Convention.

The Lugano Convention, which is not yet in force, is not reproduced in this Supplement.]

PREAMBLE

THE HIGH CONTRACTING PARTIES TO THE TREATY ESTABLISHING THE EUROPEAN ECONOMIC COMMUNITY,

Desiring to implement the provisions of Article 220 of that Treaty by virtue of which they undertook to secure the simplification of formalities governing the reciprocal recognition and enforcement of judgments of courts or tribunals;

Anxious to strengthen in the Community the legal protection of persons therein established;

Considering that it is necessary for this purpose to determine the international jurisdiction of their courts, to facilitate recognition and to introduce an expeditious procedure for securing the enforcement of judgments, authentic instruments and court settlements;

* * *

HAVE AGREED AS FOLLOWS:

TITLE I
SCOPE
Article 1

This Convention shall apply in civil and commercial matters whatever the nature of the court or tribunal. It shall not extend, in particular, to revenue, customs or administrative matters

The Convention shall not apply to:

1. the status or legal capacity of natural persons, rights in property arising out of a matrimonial relationship, wills and succession;
2. bankruptcy, proceedings relating to the winding-up of insolvent companies or other legal persons, judicial arrangements, compositions and analogous proceedings;
3. social security;
4. arbitration.

TITLE II
JURISDICTION
Section 1. General Provisions
Article 2

Subject to the provisions of this Convention, persons domiciled in a Contracting State shall, whatever their nationality, be sued in the courts of that State.

Persons who are not nationals of the State in which they are domiciled shall be governed by the rules of jurisdiction applicable to nationals of that State.

Article 3

Persons domiciled in a Contracting State may be sued in the courts of another Contracting State only by virtue of the rules set out in Sections 2 to 6 of this Title.

In particular the following provisions shall not be applicable as against them:

— in Belgium: Article 15 of the civil code and Article 638 of the judicial code,

— in Denmark: Article 248(2) of the law on civil procedure and Chapter 3, Article 3 of the Greenland law on civil procedure,

— in the Federal Republic of Germany: Article 23 of the code of civil procedure,

— in Greece, Article 40 of the code of civil procedure,

— in France: Articles 14 and 15 of the civil code,

— in Ireland: the rules which enable jurisdiction to be founded on the document instituting the proceedings having been served on the defendant during his temporary presence in Ireland,

— in Italy: Articles 2 and 4, Nos 1 and 2 of the code of civil procedure,

— in Luxembourg: Articles 14 and 15 of the civil code,

— in the Netherlands: Articles 126(3) and 127 of the code of civil procedure,

— in Portugal: Article 65(1)(c), Article 65(2) and Article 65A(c) of the code of civil procedure and Article 11 of the code of labour procedure,

— in the United Kingdom: the rules which enable jurisdiction to be founded on:

  (a) the document instituting the proceedings having been served on the defendant during his temporary presence in the United Kingdom; or

  (b) the presence within the United Kingdom of property belonging to the defendant; or

  (c) the seizure by the plaintiff of property situated in the United Kingdom.

Article 4

If the defendant is not domiciled in a Contracting State, the jurisdiction of the courts of each Contracting State shall, subject to the provisions of Article 16, be determined by the law of that State.

As against such a defendant, any person domiciled in a Contracting State may, whatever his nationality, avail himself in that State of the rules of jurisdiction there in force, and in particular those specified in the second paragraph of Article 3, in the same way as the nationals of that State.

Section 2. Special Jurisdiction
Article 5

A person domiciled in a Contracting State may, in another Contracting State, be sued:

1. in matters relating to a contract, in the courts for the place of performance of the obligation in question; in matters relating to individual contracts of employment, this place is that where the employee habitually carries out his work, or if the employee does not habitually carry out his work in any one country, the employer may also be sued in the courts for the place where the business which engaged the employee was or is now situated;

2. in matters relating to maintenance, in the courts for the place where the maintenance creditor is domiciled or habitually resident or, if the matter is ancillary to proceedings concerning the status of a person, in the court which, according to its own law, has jurisdiction to entertain those proceedings, unless that jurisdiction is based solely on the nationality of one of the parties;

3. in matters relating to tort, delict or quasi-delict, in the courts for the place where the harmful event occurred;

4. as regards a civil claim for damages or restitution which is based on an act giving rise to criminal proceedings, in the court seised of those proceedings, to the extent that that court has jurisdiction under its own law to entertain civil proceedings;

5. as regards a dispute arising out of the operations of a branch, agency or other establishment, in the courts for the place in which the branch, agency or other establishment is situated;

6. as settlor, trustee or beneficiary of a trust created by the operation of a statute, or by a written instrument, or created orally and evidenced in writing, in the courts of the Contracting State in which the trust is domiciled;

7. as regards a dispute concerning the payment of remuneration claimed in respect of the salvage of a cargo or freight, in the court under the authority of which the cargo or freight in question:

   (a) has been arrested to secure such payment, or

   (b) could have been so arrested, but bail or other security has been given;

provided that this provision shall apply only if it is claimed that the defendant has an interest in the cargo or freight or had such an interest at the time of salvage.

Article 6

A person domiciled in a Contracting State may also be sued:

1. where he is one of a number of defendants, in the courts for the place where any one of them is domiciled;

2. as a third party in an action on a warranty or guarantee or in any other third party proceedings, in the court seised of the original proceedings, unless these were instituted solely with the object of removing him from the jurisdiction of the court which would be competent in his case;

3. on a counter-claim arising from the same contract or facts on which the original claim was based, in the court in which the original claim is pending;

4. in matters relating to a contract, if the action may be combined with an action against the same defendant in matters relating to rights *in rem* in immovable property, in the court of the Contracting State in which the property is situated.

Article 6a

Where by virtue of this Convention a court of a Contracting State has jurisdiction in actions relating to liability arising from the use or operation of a ship, that court, or any other court substituted for this purpose by the internal law of that State, shall also have jurisdiction over claims for limitation of such liability.

Section 3. Jurisdiction in Matters Relating to Insurance

[omitted]

Section 4. Jurisdiction Over Consumer Contracts

Article 13

In proceedings concerning a contract concluded by a person for a purpose which can be regarded as being outside his trade or profession, hereinafter called 'the consumer', jurisdiction shall be determined by this Section, without prejudice to the provisions of Articles 4 and 5(5), if it is:

1. a contract for the sale of goods on instalment credit terms, or

2. a contract for a loan repayable by instalments, or for any other form of credit, made to finance the sale of goods, or

3. any other contract for the supply of goods or a contract for the supply of services, and

   (a) in the State of the consumer's domicile the conclusion of the contract was preceded by a specific invitation addressed to him or by advertising, and

   (b) the consumer took in that State the steps necessary for the conclusion of the contract.

Where a consumer enters into a contract with a party who is not domiciled in a Contracting State but has a branch, agency or other establishment in one of the Contracting States, that party shall, in disputes arising out of the operations of the branch, agency or establishment, be deemed to be domiciled in that State.

This Section shall not apply to contracts of transport.

Article 14

A consumer may bring proceedings against the other party to a contract either in the courts of the Contracting State in which that party is domiciled or in the courts of the Contracting State in which he is himself domiciled.

Proceedings may be brought against a consumer by the other party to the contract only in the courts of the Contracting State in which the consumer is domiciled.

These provisions shall not affect the right to bring a counterclaim in the court in which, in accordance with this Section, the original claim is pending.

Article 15

The provisions of this Section may be departed from only by an agreement:

1. which is entered into after the dispute has arisen, or

2. which allows the consumer to bring proceedings in courts other than those indicated in this Section, or

3. which is entered into by the consumer and the other party to the contract, both of whom are at the time of conclusion of the contract domiciled or habitually resident in the same Contracting State, and which confers jurisdiction on the courts of that State, provided that such an agreement is not contrary to the law of that State.

Section 5. Exclusive Jurisdiction

Article 16

The following courts shall have exclusive jurisdiction, regardless of domicile:

1. (a) in proceedings which have as their object rights *in rem* in immovable property or tenancies of immovable property, the courts of the Contracting State in which the property is situated;

(b) however, in proceedings which have as their object tenancies of immovable property concluded for temporary private use for a maximum period of six consecutive months, the courts of the Contracting State in which the defendant is domiciled shall also have jurisdiction, provided that the landlord and the tenant are natural persons and are domiciled in the same Contracting State;

2. in proceedings which have as their object the validity of the constitution, the nullity or the dissolution of companies or other legal persons or associations of natural or legal persons, or the decisions of their organs, the courts of the Contracting State in which the company, legal person or association has its seat;

3. in proceedings which have as their object the validity of entries in public registers, the courts of the Contracting State in which the register is kept;

4. in proceedings concerned with the registration or validity of patents, trade marks, designs, or other similar rights required to be deposited or registered, the courts of the Contracting State in which the deposit or registration has been applied for, has taken place or is under the terms of an international convention deemed to have taken place;

5. in proceedings concerned with the enforcement of judgments, the courts of the Contracting State in which the judgment has been or is to be enforced.

Section 6. Prorogation of Jurisdiction
Article 17

If the parties, one or more of whom is domiciled in a Contracting State, have agreed that a court or the courts of a Contracting State are to have jurisdiction to settle any disputes which have arisen or which may arise in connection with a particular legal relationship, that court or those courts shall have exclusive jurisdiction. Such an agreement conferring jurisdiction shall be either:

(a) in writing or evidenced in writing, or

(b) in a form which accords with practices which the parties have established between themselves, or

(c) in international trade or commerce, in a form which accords with a usage of which the parties are or ought to have been aware and which in such trade or commerce is widely known to, and regularly observed by, parties to contracts of the type involved in the particular trade or commerce concerned.

Where such an agreement is concluded by parties, none of whom is domiciled in a Contracting State, the courts of other Contracting States shall have no jurisdiction over their disputes unless the court or courts chosen have declined jurisdiction.

> [Paragraphs 3 and 4 of Article 17, on jurisdiction conferred by trust instruments, are omitted.]

If an agreement conferring jurisdiction was concluded for the benefit of only one of the parties, that party shall retain the right to bring proceedings in any other court which has jurisdiction by virtue of this Convention.

> [Paragraph 6 of Article 17, on agreements conferring jurisdiction over employment contract disputes, is omitted.]

Article 18

Apart from jurisdiction derived from other provisions of this Convention, a court of a Contracting State before whom a defendant enters an appearance shall have jurisdiction. This rule shall not apply where appearance was entered solely to contest the jurisdiction, or where another court has exclusive jurisdiction by virtue of Article 16.

Section 7. Examination as to Jurisdiction and Admissibility

Article 19

Where a court of a Contracting State is seised of a claim which is principally concerned with a matter over which the courts of another Contracting State have exclusive jurisdiction by virtue of Article 16, it shall declare of its own motion that it has no jurisdiction.

Article 20

Where a defendant domiciled in one Contracting State is sued in a court of another Contracting State and does not enter an appearance, the court shall declare of its own motion that it has no jurisdiction unless its jurisdiction is derived from the provisions of this Convention.

The court shall stay the proceedings so long as it is not shown that the defendant has been able to receive the document instituting the proceedings or an equivalent document in sufficient time to enable him to arrange for his defence, or that all necessary steps have been taken to this end.

The provisions of the foregoing paragraph shall be replaced by those of Article 15 of the Hague Convention of 15 November 1965 on the service abroad of judicial and extrajudicial documents in civil or commercial matters, if the document instituting the proceedings or notice thereof had to be transmitted abroad in accordance with that Convention.

Section 8. Lis Pendens—Related Actions

Article 21

Where proceedings involving the same cause of action and between the same parties are brought in the courts of different Contracting States, any court other than the court first seised shall of its own motion stay its proceedings until such time as the jurisdiction of the court first seised is established.

Where the jurisdiction of the court first seised is established, any court other than the court first seised shall decline jurisdiction in favour of that court.

Article 22

Where related actions are brought in the courts of different Contracting States, any court other than the court first seised may, while the actions are pending at first instance, stay its proceedings.

A court other than the court first seised may also, on the application of one of the parties, decline jurisdiction if the law of that court permits the consolidation of related actions and the court first seised has jurisdiction over both actions.

For the purposes of this Article, actions are deemed to be related where they are so closely connected that it is expedient to hear and determine them together to avoid the risk of irreconcilable judgments resulting from separate proceedings.

Article 23

Where actions come within the exclusive jurisdiction of several courts, any court other than the court first seised shall decline jurisdiction in favour of that court.

Section 9. Provisional, Including Protective, Measures

Article 24

Application may be made to the courts of a Contracting State for such provisional, including protective, measures as may be available under the law of that State, even if, under this Convention, the courts of another Contracting State have jurisdiction as to the substance of the matter.

TITLE III

RECOGNITION AND ENFORCEMENT

Article 25

For the purposes of this Convention, 'judgment' means any judgment given by a court or tribunal of a Contracting State, whatever the judgment may be called, including a decree, order, decision or writ of execution, as well as the determination of costs or expenses by an officer of the court.

Section 1. Recognition

Article 26

A judgment given in a Contracting State shall be recognized in the other Contracting States without any special procedure being required.

Any interested party who raises the recognition of a judgment as the principal issue in a dispute may, in accordance with the procedures provided for in Sections 2 and 3 of this Title, apply for a decision that the judgment be recognized.

If the outcome of proceedings in a court of a Contracting State depends on the determination of an incidental question of recognition that court shall have jurisdiction over that question.

Article 27

A judgment shall not be recognized:

1. if such recognition is contrary to public policy in the State in which recognition is sought;

2. where it was given in default of appearance, if the defendant was not duly served with the document which instituted the proceedings or with an equivalent document in sufficient time to enable him to arrange for his defence;

3. if the judgment is irreconcilable with a judgment given in a dispute between the same parties in the State in which recognition is sought;

4. if the court of the State in which the judgment was given, in order to arrive at its judgment, has decided a preliminary question concerning

the status or legal capacity of natural persons, rights in property arising out of a matrimonial relationship, wills or succession in a way that conflicts with a rule of the private international law of the State in which the recognition is sought, unless the same result would have been reached by the application of the rules of private international law of that State;

5. if the judgment is irreconcilable with an earlier judgment given in a non-Contracting State involving the same cause of action and between the same parties, provided that this latter judgment fulfils the conditions necessary for its recognition in the State addressed.

Article 28

Moreover, a judgment shall not be recognized if it conflicts with the provisions of Section 3, 4 or 5 of Title II, or in a case provided for in Article 59.

In its examination of the grounds of jurisdiction referred to in the foregoing paragraph, the court or authority applied to shall be bound by the findings of fact on which the court of the State in which the judgment was given based its jurisdiction.

Subject to the provisions of the first paragraph, the jurisdiction of the court of the State in which the judgment was given may not be reviewed; the test of public policy referred to in Article 27(1) may not be applied to the rules relating to jurisdiction.

Article 29

Under no circumstances may a foreign judgment be reviewed as to its substance.

Article 30

A court of a Contracting State in which recognition is sought of a judgment given in another Contracting State may stay the proceedings if an ordinary appeal against the judgment has been lodged.

A court of a Contracting State in which recognition is sought of a judgment given in Ireland or the United Kingdom may stay the proceedings if enforcement is suspended in the State in which the judgment was given by reason of an appeal.

Section 2. Enforcement

Article 31

A judgment given in a Contracting State and enforceable in that State shall be enforced in another Contracting State when, on the application of any interested party, it has been declared enforceable there.

However, in the United Kingdom, such a judgment shall be enforced in England and Wales, in Scotland, or in Northern Ireland when, on the application of any interested party, it has been registered for enforcement in that part of the United Kingdom.

> [Article 32 recites for each state the level of court in which applications for enforcement must be filed.]

Article 33

The procedure for making the application shall be governed by the law of the State in which enforcement is sought.

* * *

Article 34

The court applied to shall give its decision without delay; the party against whom enforcement is sought shall not at this stage of the proceedings be entitled to make any submissions on the application.

The application may be refused only for one of the reasons specified in Articles 27 and 28.

Under no circumstances may the foreign judgment be reviewed as to its substance.

Article 35

The appropriate officer of the court shall without delay bring the decision given on the application to the notice of the applicant in accordance with the procedure laid down by the law of the State in which enforcement is sought.

Article 36

If enforcement is authorized, the party against whom enforcement is sought may appeal against the decision within one month of service thereof.

If that party is domiciled in a Contracting State other than that in which the decision authorizing enforcement was given, the time for appealing shall be two months and shall run from the date of service, either on him in person or at his residence. No extension of time may be granted on account of distance.

> [Article 37 recites for each state the level of court in which appeals against decisions authorizing enforcement must be filed, as well as the means for contesting the judgment given on appeal.]

Article 38

The court with which the appeal under the first paragraph of Article 37 is lodged may, on the application of the appellant, stay the proceedings if an ordinary appeal has been lodged against the judgment in the State in which that judgment was given or if the time for such an appeal has not yet expired; in the latter case, the court may specify the time within which such an appeal is to be lodged.

Where the judgment was given in Ireland or the United Kingdom, any form of appeal available in the State in which it was given shall be treated as an ordinary appeal for the purposes of the first paragraph.

The court may also make enforcement conditional on the provision of such security as it shall determine.

Article 39

During the time specified for an appeal pursuant to Article 36 and until any such appeal has been determined, no measures of enforcement may be taken other than protective measures taken against the property of the party against whom enforcement is sought.

The decision authorizing enforcement shall carry with it the power to proceed to any such protective measures.

> [Article 40 recites for each state the level of court in which appeals against decisions refusing enforcement must be filed. Article 41 recites the means in each state for contesting the judgment given on appeal.]

Article 42

Where a foreign judgment has been given in respect of several matters and enforcement cannot be authorized for all of them, the court shall authorize enforcement for one or more of them.

An applicant may request partial enforcement of a judgment.

Article 43

A foreign judgment which orders a periodic payment by way of a penalty shall be enforceable in the State in which enforcement is sought only if the amount of the payment has been finally determined by the courts of the State in which the judgment was given.

> [Article 44, dealing with exemption from costs or expenses, is omitted.]

Article 45

No security, bond or deposit, however described, shall be required of a party who in one Contracting State applies for enforcement of a judgment given in another Contracting State on the ground that he is a foreign national or that he is not domiciled or resident in the State in which enforcement is sought.

Section 3. Common Provisions

Article 46

A party seeking recognition or applying for enforcement of a judgment shall produce:

1. a copy of the judgment which satisfies the conditions necessary to establish its authenticity;
2. in the case of a judgment given in default, the original or a certified true copy of the document which establishes that the party in default was served with the document instituting the proceedings or with an equivalent document.

> [Articles 47 through 49, on additional documentary requirements, are omitted.]

TITLE IV
AUTHENTIC INSTRUMENTS AND COURT SETTLEMENTS

Article 50

A document which has been formally drawn up or registered as an authentic instrument and is enforceable in one Contracting State shall, in another Contracting State, be declared enforceable there, on application made in accordance with the procedures provided for in Article 31 *et seq.* The application may be refused only if enforcement of the instrument is contrary to public policy in the State addressed.

The instrument produced must satisfy the conditions necessary to establish its authenticity in the State of origin.

The provisions of Section 3 of Title III shall apply as appropriate.

Article 51

A settlement which has been approved by a court in the course of proceedings and is enforceable in the State in which it was concluded shall be enforceable in the State in which enforcement is sought under the same conditions as authentic instruments.

TITLE V
GENERAL PROVISIONS

Article 52

In order to determine whether a party is domiciled in the Contracting State whose courts are seised of a matter, the Court shall apply its internal law.

If a party is not domiciled in the State whose courts are seised of the matter, then, in order to determine whether the party is domiciled in another Contracting State, the court shall apply the law of that State.

Article 53

For the purposes of this Convention, the seat of a company or other legal person or association of natural or legal persons shall be treated as its domicile. However, in order to determine that seat, the court shall apply its rules of private international law.

In order to determine whether a trust is domiciled in the Contracting State whose courts are seised of the matter, the court shall apply its rules of private international law.

TITLE VI
TRANSITIONAL PROVISIONS

[omitted]

TITLE VII
RELATIONSHIP TO OTHER CONVENTIONS

* * *

Article 57

1. This Convention shall not affect any conventions to which the Contracting States are or will be parties and which in relation to particular matters, govern jurisdiction or the recognition or enforcement of judgments.

2. With a view to its uniform interpretation, paragraph 1 shall be applied in the following manner:

(a) this Convention shall not prevent a court of a Contracting State which is a party to a convention on a particular matter from assuming jurisdiction in accordance with that Convention, even where the defendant is domiciled in another Contracting State which is not a party to that Convention. The court hearing the action shall, in any event, apply Article 20 of this Convention;

(b) judgments given in a Contracting State by a court in the exercise of jurisdiction provided for in a convention on a particular matter shall be recognized and enforced in the other Contracting State in accordance with this Convention.

Where a convention on a particular matter to which both the State of origin and the State addressed are parties lays down conditions for the recognition or enforcement of judgments, those conditions shall apply. In any event, the provisions of this Convention which concern the procedure for recognition and enforcement of judgments may be applied.

3. This Convention shall not affect the application of provisions which, in relation to particular matters, govern jurisdiction or the recognition or enforcement of judgments and which are or will be contained in acts of the institutions of the European Communities or in national laws harmonized in implementation of such acts.

* * *

Article 59

This Convention shall not prevent a Contracting State from assuming, in a convention on the recognition and enforcement of judgments, an obligation towards a third State not to recognize judgments given in other Contracting States against defendants domiciled or habitually resident in the third State where, in cases provided for in Article 4, the judgment could only be founded on a ground of jurisdiction specified in the second paragraph of Article 3.

However, a Contracting State may not assume an obligation towards a third State not to recognize a judgment given in another Contracting State by a court basing its jurisdiction on the presence within that State of property belonging to the defendant, or the seizure by the plaintiff of property situated there:

1. if the action is brought to assert or declare proprietary or possessory rights in that property, seeks to obtain authority to dispose of it, or arises from another issue relating to such property, or,

2. if the property constitutes the security for a debt which is the subject-matter of the action.

TITLE VIII
FINAL PROVISIONS

* * *

Article 63

The Contracting States recognize that any State which becomes a member of the European Economic Community shall be required to accept this Convention as a basis for the negotiations between the Contracting States and that State necessary to ensure the implementation of the last paragraph of Article 220 of the Treaty establishing the European Economic Community.

The necessary adjustments may be the subject of a special convention between the Contracting States of the one part and the new Member States of the other part.

* * *

Article 65

The Protocol annexed to this Convention by common accord of the Contracting States shall form an integral part thereof.

Article 66

This Convention is concluded for an unlimited period.

* * *

PROTOCOL
annexed to the 1968 Convention

The High Contracting Parties have agreed upon the following provisions, which shall be annexed to the Convention:

Article I

Any person domiciled in Luxembourg who is sued in a court of another Contracting State pursuant to Article 5(1) may refuse to submit to the jurisdiction of that court. If the defendant does not enter an appearance the court shall declare of its own motion that it has no jurisdiction.

An agreement conferring jurisdiction, within the meaning of Article 17, shall be valid with respect to a person domiciled in Luxembourg only if that person has expressly and specifically so agreed.

* * *

Article III

In proceedings for the issue of an order for enforcement, no charge, duty or fee calculated by reference to the value of the matter in issue may be levied in the State in which enforcement is sought.

* * *

Article Vd

Without prejudice to the jurisdiction of the European Patent Office under the Convention on the grant of European patents, signed at Munich on 5 October 1973, the courts of each Contracting State shall have exclusive jurisdiction, regardless of domicile, in proceedings concerned with the registration or validity of any European patent granted for that State which is not a Community patent by virtue of the provisions of Article 86 of the Convention for the European patent for the common market, signed at Luxembourg on 15 December 1975.

[Articles II, IV–Vc and VI of the Protocol are omitted.]

PROTOCOL

on the interpretation by the Court of Justice of the Convention of 27 September 1968 on jurisdiction and the enforcement of judgments in civil and commercial matters

(Signed at Luxembourg, June 3, 1971, effective Sept. 1, 1975)
(as amended)
O.J. L 304/97 (Oct. 30, 1978)

THE HIGH CONTRACTING PARTIES TO THE TREATY ESTABLISHING THE EUROPEAN ECONOMIC COMMUNITY,

Having regard to the Declaration annexed to the Convention on jurisdiction and the enforcement of judgments in civil and commercial matters, signed at Brussels on 27 September 1968,

Have decided to conclude a Protocol conferring jurisdiction on the Court of Justice of the European Communities to interpret that Convention, and * * *

HAVE AGREED AS FOLLOWS:

Article 1

The Court of Justice of the European Communities shall have jurisdiction to give rulings on the interpretation of the Convention on jurisdiction and the enforcement of judgments in civil and commercial matters and of the Protocol annexed to that Convention, signed at Brussels on 27 September 1968, and also on the interpretation of the present Protocol.

[The remaining paragraphs of Article 1 confer preliminary ruling jurisdiction on the Court of Justice regarding the Convention on Accession to the Brussels Convention of Denmark, Ireland and the UK (¶ 2), Greece (¶ 3), and Spain and Portugal (¶ 4).]

Article 2

The following courts may request the Court of Justice to give preliminary rulings on questions of interpretation:

[Paragraph 1 of Article 2 essentially recites the supreme courts of each state, including for the UK "the House of

Lords and courts to which application has been made under the second paragraph of Article 37 or under Article 41 of the Convention."]

2. the courts of the Contracting States when they are sitting in an appellate capacity;

3. in the cases provided for in Article 37 of the Convention, the courts referred to in that Article.

Article 3

1. Where a question of interpretation of the Convention or of one of the other instruments referred to in Article 1 is raised in a case pending before one of the courts listed in Article 2(1), that court shall, if it considers that a decision on the question is necessary to enable it to give judgment, request the Court of Justice to give a ruling thereon.

2. Where such a question is raised before any court referred to in Article 2 (2) or (3), that court may, under the conditions laid down in paragraph 1, request the Court of Justice to give a ruling thereon.

Article 4

1. The competent authority of a Contracting State may request the Court of Justice to give a ruling on a question of interpretation of the Convention or of one of the other instruments referred to in Article 1 if judgments given by courts of that State conflict with the interpretation given either by the Court of Justice or in a judgment of one of the courts of another Contracting State referred to in Article 2 (1) or (2). The provisions of this paragraph shall apply only to judgments which have become *res judicata.*

2. The interpretation given by the Court of Justice in response to such a request shall not affect the judgments which gave rise to the request for interpretation.

3. The Procurators–General of the Courts of Cassation of the Contracting States, or any other authority designated by a Contracting State, shall be entitled to request the Court of Justice for a ruling on interpretation in accordance with paragraph 1.

4. The Registrar of the Court of Justice shall give notice of the request to the Contracting States, to the Commission and to the Council of the European Communities; they shall then be entitled within two months of the notification to submit statements of case or written observations to the Court.

5. No fees shall be levied or any costs or expenses awarded in respect of the proceedings provided for in this Article.

Article 5

1. Except where this Protocol otherwise provides, the provisions of the Treaty establishing the European Economic Community and those of the Protocol on the Statute of the Court of Justice annexed thereto, which are applicable when the Court is requested to give a preliminary ruling,

shall also apply to any proceedings for the interpretation of the Convention and the other instruments referred to in Article 1.

2. The Rules of Procedure of the Court of Justice shall, if necessary, be adjusted and supplemented in accordance with Article 188 of the Treaty establishing the European Economic Community.

Article 6

[deleted]

* * *

Article 9

The Contracting States recognize that any State which becomes a member of the European Economic Community, and to which Article 63 of the Convention on jurisdiction and the enforcement of judgments in civil and commercial matters applies, must accept the provisions of this Protocol, subject to such adjustments as may be required.

* * *

Article 12

This Protocol is concluded for an unlimited period.

* * *

[In a Joint Declaration attached to this Protocol, the original signatory states declared their readiness to organize, in cooperation with the Court of Justice, an exchange of information on the judgments concerning the Convention and the 1968 Protocol given by the courts referred to in Article 2(1) of this Protocol.]

Part II

THE FOUR FREEDOMS AND THE INTERNAL MARKET

INTRODUCTION

The process of harmonization to achieve the free movement of goods, persons, services and capital and thereby to attain an integrated internal market has produced a tremendous volume of legislation, chiefly in the form of directives. As described in Chapter 12 of the casebook, a substantial number of such directives were adopted in the 1960s and 1970s.

The program of legislation outlined in the Commission White Paper on Completing the Internal Market, COM (85) 310 (June 1985), discussed in the casebook at page 432, has engendered another substantial body of legislation. Rather than reproducing the White Paper, which is now largely of historical interest, a number of the more important achievements of the White Paper program are printed hereafter. The steady progress toward completing the internal market by 1992 is summarized in the Commission's annual General Reports to Parliament and in greater detail in special Annual Progress Reports, e.g., the Seventh Report on the Implementation of the White Paper, COM (92) 383 final, Sept. 2, 1992.

The legislation reproduced hereafter represents the most important items discussed in the casebook, presented in the sequence of the casebook chapters. To achieve the widest possible sampling of legislation, some items have been lightly excerpted. Whereas clauses which essentially duplicate specific articles in the legislation, and text which is too detailed or technical to be of pedagogical interest, have been deleted. Footnote references in recent legislation to the initial Commission proposal and reports of Parliament and the Economic and Social Council have been retained to facilitate further research.

The significance of each of the printed documents is indicated in its coverage in the casebook. We indicate here only the reason for the selection of the reproduced documents and make cross-references to casebook coverage or citation of related documents, sector by sector.

Free movement of goods. Directive 70/50 provides a valuable illustrative list of Member State measures which restrict the free movement of goods. The Commission Communication on *Cassis de Dijon* constitutes a policy view on the implications of that judgment.

Intellectual property rights. The trademark harmonization Directive 89/104 is the first measure adopted in the effort to produce an integrated system of intellectual property rights, thus reducing the tendency of national rights to partition the market for goods and services. Major pending proposals, such as the draft Community Trademark Regulation, the Community Patent Convention, and a series of new initiatives in copyright law, are reviewed in Chapter 11(D).

Technical and safety legislation. The dangerous substances directive 79/831 is a model illustrating the early wave of harmonization legislation covering dangerous solvents, pharmaceuticals, paints and varnishes, cosmetics, etc., reviewed in Chapter 12(A). Directive 83/189 is an important part of the program for a new approach to technical harmonization, covered in Chapter 12(C), because it serves to reduce the risk that newly adopted national regulations or standards will hinder the free movement of goods. The machinery safety directive 89/392 is a model of the new form of "framework" technical quality and safety directive, with other examples (toys, pressure vessels) being covered in Chapter 12(C).

Free movement of workers. Regulation 1612/68 is the fundamental expression of the rules enabling workers and their families to achieve complete integration into the host State employment and social environment. It is supplemented by Directive 68/360 on rights of residence and Directive 64/221, which narrowly limits the Member States' power to restrict free movement on grounds of public policy, public security or public health. Accessory regulations, as the right to continued residence after ceasing work and the right of education for dependent children, are mentioned in Chapter 13(C). Review of the social security benefits legislation is to be found in Chapter 14(C).

The People's Europe program. The three directives 90/366, 90/365 and 90/364, covering respectively a right of residence for students, for retired persons, and for virtually all persons not engaged in an occupational activity, represent the principal achievement of the People's Europe program. Chapter 14(A) reviews other important legislation in this program, such as the directives harmonizing conditions for drivers' licenses and for the control of the sale and ownership of weapons, as well as the proposal for voting in local elections. Chapter 14(B)2 describes the Erasmus and related programs to encourage student mobility and cooperation among higher education institutions.

Right of establishment and freedom to provide services. The General Programme for the abolition of restrictions on the freedom of establishment remains important because of its descriptive list of discriminatory Member State rules, practices and conditions. The corresponding program with regard to services is mentioned in Chapter 15(A). Directive 86/653 on commercial agents is an excellent illustration of harmonization directives intended to facilitate establishment by creating common rules in a particular sector. Directive 89/552 on television broadcasting is not only a rare example of harmonizing rules in a trans-border services sector; it also illustrates the Community's efforts to promote cultural interests, as discussed in Chapter 15(B)3.

Company law. Harmonization in this field is important because it promotes commercial enterprise by reducing disparities in the structure and operations of companies, particularly those created in the larger stock corporation form. The First and Second Directives, 68/151 and 77/91, provide rules on the capital and shareholding structure of companies, as well as on mandatory disclosures to shareholders and third parties. The Third Directive 78/855 is likewise a key one since it creates a modern system for executing corporate mergers. Chapter 15(D) mentions other company law directives, as well as the well-known draft Fifth directive on internal shareholding and management structure and the proposal for a Community stock corporation, both unfortunately too long for reproduction. Chapter 15(D) also discusses the Fourth Directive 78/660 on annual accounts and the accessory Seventh and Eighth directives. Finally, the European Economic Interest Grouping Regulation is printed, because it constitutes a useful initiative in facilitating joint ventures.

Professional rights. Directive 89/48 on the recognition of higher education diplomas is a major internal market program achievement, facilitating the right of establishment for a wide variety of professions, including lawyers. It follows a new approach of mutual trust, making no attempt to harmonize educational standards, the approach used for earlier directives for the medical and accessory professions. The earlier directives are discussed in Chapter 16(A). Directive 77/249 on lawyers' trans-border services is not only important in facilitating rights of practice by Community lawyers; it is also a rare example of a directive limited to services.

Capital movements. Directive 88/361 on free movement of capital is critical in enabling market integration for financial services, as well as serving as a key element in the first stage toward an economic and monetary union. The earlier 1961 and 1962 directives which represented an important but limited initial stage in facilitating many types of capital movements are described in Chapter 17(A).

Securities harmonization. The program for harmonization of securities law, commenced in the late 1970s, but with new impetus in the internal market program, is now largely complete. The initial key directives 79/279, 80/390, and 82/121, covering the access of securities to stock exchanges, and the initial and ongoing regular disclosure requirements placed upon issuers of listed securities, provide the ground rules which enable a Community-wide market in securities. Directive 89/298 supplements these by setting the rules for a prospectus for securities which are not quoted. Also accessory is the UCITS, or mutual fund directive, discussed in Chapter 17(D)1. The significant second-generation directives 89/592 on insider trading and 88/627 on disclosure of major shareholdings promote the proper functioning of securities markets by protecting investor confidence in the reliability of the markets. Finally, the pending draft directive on the regulation of investment advisors and brokers is discussed in Chapter 17(D)1.

Banking harmonization. The initial stage of harmonization occurred with the First Directive 77/780, parts of which are still relevant. Probably no other internal market program directive is more important than the Second Banking Directive 89/646, which is accordingly presented virtually without excerpts. Chapter 17(D)2 mentions the useful technical directives on own funds and solvency ratios as well as the directive on consolidated supervision of trans-border subsidiaries.

Table of Contents

PART II. THE FOUR FREEDOMS AND THE INTERNAL MARKET

Doc.
1. Commission Directive 70/50 on the abolition of measures which have an effect equivalent to quantitative restrictions on imports.
2. Commission Communication concerning the consequences of the judgment in Case 120/78 ("Cassis de Dijon").
3. First Council Directive 89/104 to approximate the laws of the Member States relating to trade marks.
4. Council Directive 79/831 on the approximation of the laws relating to the classification, packaging and labelling of dangerous substances.
5. Council Directive 83/189 laying down a procedure for the provision of information in the field of technical standards and regulations.
6. Council Directive 89/392 on the approximation of the laws of Member States relating to machinery.
7. Council Regulation 1612/68 on freedom of movement for workers within the Community.
8. Council Directive 68/360 on the abolition of restrictions on movement and residence within the Community for workers of Member States and their families.
9. Council Directive 64/221 on the coordination of special measures concerning the movement and residence of foreign nationals which are justified on grounds of public policy, public security or public health.
10. Council Directive 90/365 on the right of residence for employees and self-employed persons who have ceased their occupational activity.
11. Council Directive 90/364 on the right of residence.
12. Council Directive 90/366 on the right of residence for students.
13. General Programme for the abolition of restrictions on freedom of establishment.
14. Council Directive 86/653 on the coordination of the laws of the Member States relating to self-employed commercial agents.
15. Council Directive 89/552 on the coordination of certain provisions laid down by law, regulation or administrative action in Member States concerning the pursuit of television broadcasting activities.
16. First Council Directive 68/151 on coordination of safeguards which are required by Member States of companies with a view to making such safeguards equivalent throughout the Community.
17. Second Council Directive 77/91 on coordination of safeguards which are required by Member States in respect of the formation of public limited liability companies and the maintenance and alteration of their capital.

Doc.

18. Third Council Directive 78/855 concerning mergers of public limited liability companies.
19. Fourth Council Directive 78/660 on the annual accounts of certain types of companies.
20. Council Regulation 2137/85 on the European Economic Interest Grouping.
21. Council Directive 89/48 on a general system for the recognition of higher-education diplomas awarded on completion of profession education and training.
22. Council Recommendation 89/49 concerning nationals of Member States who hold a diploma conferred in a third State.
23. Council Directive 77/249 to facilitate the effective exercise by lawyers of freedom to provide services.
24. Council Directive 88/361 for the implementation of Article 67 [free movement of capital].
25. Council Directive 79/279 coordinating the conditions for the admission of securities to official stock exchange listing.
26. Council Directive 80/390 coordinating the requirements for the drawing-up, scrutiny and distribution of the listing particulars to be published for the admission of securities to official stock exchange listing.
27. Council Directive 87/345 amending Directive 80/390.
28. Council Directive 82/121 on information to be published by companies to shares of which have been admitted to official stock-exchange listing.
29. Council Directive 89/298 coordinating the requirements for the prospectus to be published when transferable securities are offered to the public.
30. Council Directive 89/592 coordinating regulations on insider dealing.
31. Council Directive 88/627 on the information to be published when a major holding in a listed company is acquired or disposed of.
32. First Council Directive 77/780 on the coordination of laws, regulations and administrative provisions relating to the taking up and pursuit of the business of credit institutions.
33. Second Council Directive 89/646 on the coordination of laws relating to the business of credit institutions.

1. COMMISSION DIRECTIVE 70/50/EEC

of 22 December 1969

based on the provisions of Article 33(7), on the abolition of measures which have an effect equivalent to quantitative restrictions on imports and are not covered by other provisions adopted in pursuance of the EEC Treaty

J.O. L 13/29 (Jan. 19, 1970), English Spec. Ed. 1970–I, 17

THE COMMISSION OF THE EUROPEAN COMMUNITIES,

Having regard to the provisions of the Treaty establishing the European Economic Community, and in particular Article 33(7) thereof;

Whereas for the purpose of Article 30 *et seq.* 'measures' means laws, regulations, administrative provisions, administrative practices, and all instruments issuing from a public authority, including recommendations;

Whereas for the purposes of this Directive 'administrative practices' means any standard and regularly followed procedure of a public authority; whereas 'recommendations' means any instruments issuing from a public authority which, while not legally binding on the addressees thereof, cause them to pursue a certain conduct;

Whereas the formalities to which imports are subject do not as a general rule have an effect equivalent to that of quantitative restrictions and, consequently, are not covered by this Directive;

Whereas certain measures adopted by Member States, other than those applicable equally to domestic and imported products, which were operative at the date of entry into force of the Treaty and are not covered by other provisions adopted in pursuance of the Treaty, either preclude importation or make it more difficult or costly than the disposal of domestic production;

* * *

Whereas such measures hinder imports which could otherwise take place, and thus have an effect equivalent to quantitative restrictions on imports;

Whereas effects on the free movement of goods of measures which relate to the marketing of products and which apply equally to domestic and imported products are not as a general rule equivalent to those of quantitative restrictions, since such effects are normally inherent in the disparities between rules applied by Member States in this respect;

Whereas, however, such measures may have a restrictive effect on the free movement of goods over and above that which is intrinsic to such rules;

Whereas such is the case where imports are either precluded or made more difficult or costly than the disposal of domestic production and where such effect is not necessary for the attainment of an objective within the scope of the powers for the regulation of trade left to Member States by the Treaty; whereas such is in particular the case where the said objective can be attained just as effectively by other means which are less of a hindrance to trade; whereas such is also the case where the restrictive effect of these provisions on the free movement of goods is out of proportion to their purpose;

Whereas these measures accordingly have an effect equivalent to that of quantitative restrictions on imports;

* * *

Whereas the provisions concerning the abolition of quantitative restrictions and measures having equivalent effect between Member States apply both to products originating in and exported by Member States and to products originating in third countries and put into free circulation in the other Member States;

* * *

HAS ADOPTED THIS DIRECTIVE:

Article 1

The purpose of this Directive is to abolish the measures referred to in Articles 2 and 3, which were operative at the date of entry into force of the EEC Treaty.

Article 2

1. This Directive covers measures, other than those applicable equally to domestic or imported products, which hinder imports which could otherwise take place, including measures which make importation more difficult or costly than the disposal of domestic production.

2. In particular, it covers measures which make imports or the disposal, at any marketing stage, of imported products subject to a condition—other than a formality—which is required in respect of imported products only, or a condition differing from that required for domestic products and more difficult to satisfy. Equally, it covers, in particular, measures which favour domestic products or grant them a preference, other than an aid, to which conditions may or may not be attached.

3. The measures referred to must be taken to include those measures which:

(a) lay down, for imported products only, minimum or maximum prices below or above which imports are prohibited, reduced or made subject to conditions liable to hinder importation;

(b) lay down less favourable prices for imported products than for domestic products;

(c) fix profit margins or any other price components for imported products only or fix these differently for domestic products and for imported products, to the detriment of the latter;

(d) preclude any increase in the price of the imported product corresponding to the supplementary costs and charges inherent in importation;

(e) fix the prices of products solely on the basis of the cost price or the quality of domestic products at such a level as to create a hindrance to importation;

(f) lower the value of an imported product, in particular by causing a reduction in its intrinsic value, or increase its costs;

(g) make access of imported products to the domestic market conditional upon having an agent or representative in the territory of the importing Member State;

(h) lay down conditions of payment in respect of imported products only, or subject imported products to conditions which are different from those laid down for domestic products and more difficult to satisfy;

(i) require for imports only, the giving of guarantees or making of payments on account;

(j) subject imported products only to conditions, in respect in particular of shape, size, weight, composition, presentation, identification or putting up, or subject imported products to conditions which are different from those for domestic products and more difficult to satisfy;

(k) hinder the purchase by private individuals of imported products only, or encourage, require or give preference to the purchase of domestic products only;

(*l*) totally or partially preclude the use of national facilities or equipment in respect of imported products only, or totally or partially confine the use of such facilities or equipment to domestic products only;

(m) prohibit or limit publicity in respect of imported products only, or totally or partially confine publicity to domestic products only;

(n) prohibit, limit or require stocking in respect of imported products only; totally or partially confine the use of stocking facilities to domestic products only, or make the stocking of imported products subject to conditions which are different from those required for domestic products and more difficult to satisfy;

(*o*) make importation subject to the granting of reciprocity by one or more Member States;

(p) prescribe that imported products are to conform, totally or partially, to rules other than those of the importing country;

(q) specify time limits for imported products which are insufficient or excessive in relation to the normal course of the various transactions to which these time limits apply;

(r) subject imported products to controls or, other than those inherent in the customs clearance procedure, to which domestic products are not subject or which are stricter in respect of imported products than they are in respect of domestic products, without this being necessary in order to ensure equivalent protection;

(s) confine names which are not indicative of origin or source to domestic products only.

Article 3

This Directive also covers measures governing the marketing of products which deal, in particular, with shape, size, weight, composition, presentation, identification or putting up and which are equally applicable to domestic and imported products, where the restrictive effect of such measures on the free movement of goods exceeds the effects intrinsic to trade rules.

This is the case, in particular, where:

—the restrictive effects on the free movement of goods are out of proportion to their purpose;

—the same objective can be attained by other means which are less of a hindrance to trade.

Article 4

1. Member States shall take all necessary steps in respect of products which must be allowed to enjoy free movement pursuant to Articles 9 and 10 of the Treaty to abolish measures having an effect equivalent to quantitative restrictions on imports and covered by this Directive.

2. Member States shall inform the Commission of measures taken pursuant to this Directive.

Article 5

1. This Directive does not apply to measures:

(a) which fall under Article 37(1) of the EEC Treaty;

(b) which are referred to in Article 44 of the EEC Treaty or form an integral part of a national organization of an agricultural market not yet replaced by a common organization.

2. This Directive shall apply without prejudice to the application, in particular, of Articles 36 and 223 of the EEC Treaty.

Article 6

This Directive is addressed to the Member States.

2. COMMUNICATION FROM THE COMMISSION CONCERNING THE CONSEQUENCES OF THE JUDGMENT GIVEN BY THE COURT OF JUSTICE ON 20 FEBRUARY 1979 IN CASE 120/78 ('CASSIS DE DIJON')

O.J. C 256/2 (Mar. 10, 1980)

The following is the text of a letter which has been sent to the Member States; the European Parliament and the Council have also been notified of it.

In the Commission's Communication of 6 November 1978 on 'Safeguarding free trade within the Community', it was emphasized that the free movement of goods is being affected by a growing number of restrictive measures.

The judgment delivered by the Court of Justice on 20 February 1979 in Case 120/78 (the 'Cassis de Dijon' case), * * * has given the Commission some interpretative guidance enabling it to monitor more strictly the application of the Treaty rules on the free movement of goods, particularly Articles 30 to 36 of the EEC Treaty.

The Court gives a very general definition of the barriers to free trade which are prohibited by the provisions of Article 30 *et seq.* of the EEC Treaty. These are taken to include 'any national measure capable of hindering, directly or indirectly, actually or potentially, intra-Community trade'.

In its judgment of 20 February 1979 the Court indicates the scope of this definition as it applies to technical and commercial rules.

Any product lawfully produced and marketed in one Member State must, in principle, be admitted to the market of any other Member State.

Technical and commercial rules, even those equally applicable to national and imported products, may create barriers to trade only where those rules are necessary to satisfy mandatory requirements and to serve a purpose which is in the general interest and for which they are an essential guarantee. This purpose must be such as to take precedence over the requirements of the free movement of goods, which constitutes one of the fundamental rules of the Community.

The conclusions in terms of policy which the Commission draws from this new guidance are set out below.

—Whereas Member States may, with respect to domestic products and in the absence of relevant Community provisions, regulate the terms on which such products are marketed, the case is different for products imported from other Member States.

Any product imported from another Member State must in principle be admitted to the territory of the importing Member State if it has been lawfully produced, that is, conforms to rules and processes of manufacture that are customarily and traditionally accepted in the exporting country, and is marketed in the territory of the latter.

This principle implies that Member States, when drawing up commercial or technical rules liable to affect the free movement of goods, may not take an exclusively national viewpoint and take account only of requirements confined to domestic products. The proper functioning of the common market demands that each Member State also give consideration to the legitimate requirements of the other Member States.

—Only under very strict conditions does the Court accept exceptions to this principle; barriers to trade resulting from differences between commercial and technical rules are only admissible:

- if the rules are necessary, that is appropriate and not excessive, in order to satisfy mandatory requirements (public health, protection of consumers or the environment, the fairness of commercial transactions, etc.);
- if the rules serve a purpose in the general interest which is compelling enough to justify an exception to a fundamental rule of the Treaty such as the free movement of goods;
- if the rules are essential for such a purpose to be attained, i.e. are the means which are the most appropriate and at the same time least hinder trade.

The Court's interpretation has induced the Commission to set out a number of guidelines.

—The principles deduced by the Court imply that a Member State may not in principle prohibit the sale in its territory of a product lawfully produced and marketed in another Member State even if the product is produced according to technical or quality requirements which differ from those imposed on its domestic products. Where a product 'suitably and satisfactorily' fulfils the legitimate objective of a Member State's own rules (public safety, protection of the consumer or the environment, etc.), the importing country cannot justify prohibiting its sale in its territory by claiming that the way it fulfils the objective is different from that imposed on domestic products.

In such a case, an absolute prohibition of sale could not be considered 'necessary' to satisfy a 'mandatory requirement' because it would not be an 'essential guarantee' in the sense defined in the Court's judgment.

The Commission will therefore have to tackle a whole body of commercial rules which lay down that products manufactured and marketed in one Member State must fulfil technical or qualitative conditions in order to be admitted to the market of another and specifically in all cases where the trade barriers occasioned by such rules are inadmissible according to the very strict criteria set out by the Court.

The Commission is referring in particular to rules covering the composition, designation, presentation and packaging of products as well as rules requiring compliance with certain technical standards.

—The Commission's work of harmonization will henceforth have to be directed mainly at national laws having an impact on the functioning of the common market where barriers to trade to be removed arise from national provisions which are admissible under the criteria set by the Court.

The Commission will be concentrating on sectors deserving priority because of their economic relevance to the creation of a single internal market.

To forestall later difficulties, the Commission will be informing Member States of potential objections, under the terms of Community law, to provisions they may be considering introducing which come to the attention of the Commission.

It will be producing suggestions soon on the procedures to be followed in such cases.

The Commission is confident that this approach will secure greater freedom of trade for the Community's manufacturers, so strengthening the industrial base of the Community, while meeting the expectations of consumers.

3. FIRST COUNCIL DIRECTIVE 89/104/EEC

of 21 December 1988
to approximate the laws of the Member States relating to trade marks

O.J. L 40/1 (Feb. 11, 1989)

THE COUNCIL OF THE EUROPEAN COMMUNITIES,

Having regard to the Treaty establishing the European Economic Community, and in particular Article 100a thereof,

Having regard to the proposal from the Commission [1],

In cooperation with the European Parliament [2],

Having regard to the opinion of the Economic and Social Committee [3],

Whereas the trade mark laws at present applicable in the Member States contain disparities which may impede the free movement of goods and freedom to provide services and may distort competition within the common market; whereas it is therefore necessary, in view of the establishment and functioning of the internal market, to approximate the laws of Member States;

Whereas it is important not to disregard the solutions and advantages which the Community trade mark system may afford to undertakings wishing to acquire trade marks;

Whereas it does not appear to be necessary at present to undertake full-scale approximation of the trade mark laws of the Member States and it will be sufficient if approximation is limited to those national provisions of law which most directly affect the functioning of the internal market;

Whereas the Directive does not deprive the Member States of the right to continue to protect trade marks acquired through use but takes them into account only in regard to the relationship between them and trade marks acquired by registration;

Whereas Member States also remain free to fix the provisions of procedure concerning the registration, the revocation and the invalidity of trade marks acquired by registration; whereas they can, for example, determine the form of trade mark registration and invalidity procedures, decide whether earlier rights should be invoked either in the registration procedure or in the invalidity procedure or in both and, if they allow earlier rights to be invoked in the registration procedure, have an opposition procedure or an *ex officio* examination procedure or both; whereas Member States remain free to determine the effects of revocation or invalidity of trade marks;

Whereas this Directive does not exclude the application to trade marks of provisions of law of the Member States other than trade mark

---

1. OJ No C 351, 31. 12. 1980, p. 1 and OJ No C 351, 31. 12. 1985, p. 4.
2. OJ No C 307, 14. 11. 1983, p. 66 and OJ No C 309, 5. 12. 1988.
3. OJ No C 310, 30. 11. 1981, p. 22.

law, such as the provisions relating to unfair competition, civil liability or consumer protection;

Whereas attainment of the objectives at which this approximation of laws is aiming requires that the conditions for obtaining and continuing to hold a registered trade mark are, in general, identical in all Member States; whereas, to this end, it is necessary to list examples of signs which may constitute a trade mark, provided that such signs are capable of distinguishing the goods or services of one undertaking from those of other undertakings; whereas the grounds for refusal or invalidity concerning the trade mark itself, for example, the absence of any distinctive character, or concerning conflicts between the trade mark and earlier rights, are to be listed in an exhaustive manner, even if some of these grounds are listed as an option for the Member States which will therefore be able to maintain or introduce those grounds in their legislation; whereas Member States will be able to maintain or introduce into their legislation grounds of refusal or invalidity linked to conditions for obtaining and continuing to hold a trade mark for which there is no provision of approximation, concerning, for example, the eligibility for the grant of a trade mark, the renewal of the trade mark or rules on fees, or related to the non-compliance with procedural rules;

Whereas in order to reduce the total number of trade marks registered and protected in the Community and, consequently, the number of conflicts which arise between them, it is essential to require that registered trade marks must actually be used or, if not used, be subject to revocation; whereas it is necessary to provide that a trade mark cannot be invalidated on the basis of the existence of a non-used earlier trade mark, while the Member States remain free to apply the same principle in respect of the registration of a trade mark or to provide that a trade mark may not be successfully invoked in infringement proceedings if it is established as a result of a plea that the trade mark could be revoked; whereas in all these cases it is up to the Member States to establish the applicable rules of procedure;

Whereas it is fundamental, in order to facilitate the free circulation of goods and services, to ensure that henceforth registered trade marks enjoy the same protection under the legal systems of all the Member States; whereas this should however not prevent the Member States from granting at their option extensive protection to those trade marks which have a reputation;

Whereas the protection afforded by the registered trade mark, the function of which is in particular to guarantee the trade mark as an indication of origin, is absolute in the case of identity between the mark and the sign and goods or services; whereas the protection applies also in case of similarity between the mark and the sign and the goods or services; whereas it is indispensable to give an interpretation of the concept of similarity in relation to the likelihood of confusion; whereas the likelihood of confusion, the appreciation of which depends on numerous elements and, in particular, on the recognition of the trade mark on the market, of the association which can be made with the used or registered sign, of the degree of similarity between the trade mark and the sign and between the goods or services identified, constitutes the specific condition for such protection; whereas the ways in which likelihood of confusion may be established, and in particular the onus of proof, are a matter for national procedural rules which are not prejudiced by the Directive;

Whereas it is important, for reasons of legal certainty and without inequitably prejudicing the interests of a proprietor of an earlier trade mark, to provide that the latter may no longer request a declaration of invalidity nor may he oppose the use of a trade mark subsequent to his own of which he has knowingly tolerated the use for a substantial length of time, unless the application for the subsequent trade mark was made in bad faith;

Whereas all Member States of the Community are bound by the Paris Convention for the Protection of Industrial Property; whereas it is necessary that the provisions of this Directive are entirely consistent with those of the Paris Convention; whereas the obligations of the Member States resulting from this Convention are not affected by this Directive; whereas, where appropriate, the second subparagraph of Article 234 of the Treaty is applicable,

HAS ADOPTED THIS DIRECTIVE:

Article 1
Scope

This Directive shall apply to every trade mark in respect of goods or services which is the subject of registration or of an application in a Member State for registration as an individual trade mark, a collective mark or a guarantee or certification mark, or which is the subject of a registration or an application for registration in the Benelux Trade Mark Office or of an international registration having effect in a Member State.

Article 2
Signs of which a trade mark may consist

A trade mark may consist of any sign capable of being represented graphically, particularly words, including personal names, designs, letters, numerals, the shape of goods or of their packaging, provided that such signs are capable of distinguishing the goods or services of one undertaking from those of other undertakings.

Article 3
Grounds for refusal or invalidity

1. The following shall not be registered or if registered shall be liable to be declared invalid:

   (a) signs which cannot constitute a trade mark;

   (b) trade marks which are devoid of any distinctive character;

(c) trade marks which consist exclusively of signs or indications which may serve, in trade, to designate the kind, quality, quantity, intended purpose, value, geographical origin, or the time of production of the goods or of rendering of the service, or other characteristics of the goods or service;

(d) trade marks which consist exclusively of signs or indications which have become customary in the current language or in the *bona fide* and established practices of the trade;

(e) signs which consist exclusively of:

— the shape which results from the nature of the goods themselves, or

— the shape of goods which is necessary to obtain a technical result, or

— the shape which gives substantial value to the goods;

(f) trade marks which are contrary to public policy or to accepted principles of morality;

(g) trade marks which are of such a nature as to deceive the public, for instance as to the nature, quality or geographical origin of the goods or service;

(h) trade marks which have not been authorized by the competent authorities and are to be refused or invalidated pursuant to Article 6 *ter* of the Paris Convention for the Protection of Industrial Property, hereinafter referred to as the 'Paris Convention'.

2. Any Member State may provide that a trade mark shall not be registered or, if registered, shall be liable to be declared invalid where and to the extent that:

(a) the use of that trade mark may be prohibited pursuant to provisions of law other than trade mark law of the Member State concerned or of the Community;

(b) the trade mark covers a sign of high symbolic value, in particular a religious symbol;

(c) the trade mark includes badges, emblems and escutcheons other than those covered by Article 6 *ter* of the Paris Convention and which are of public interest, unless the consent of the appropriate authorities to its registration has been given in conformity with the legislation of the Member State;

(d) the application for registration of the trade mark was made in bad faith by the applicant.

3. A trade mark shall not be refused registration or be declared invalid in accordance with paragraph 1(b), (c) or (d) if, before the date of application for registration and following the use which has been made of it, it has acquired a distinctive character. Any Member State may in addition provide that this provision shall also apply where the distinctive

character was acquired after the date of application for registration or after the date of registration.

4. Any Member State may provide that, by derogation from the preceding paragraphs, the grounds of refusal of registration or invalidity in force in that State prior to the date on which the provisions necessary to comply with this Directive enter into force, shall apply to trade marks for which application has been made prior to that date.

Article 4

Further grounds for refusal or invalidity concerning conflicts with earlier rights

1. A trade mark shall not be registered or, if registered, shall be liable to be declared invalid:

(a) if it is identical with an earlier trade mark, and the goods or services for which the trade mark is applied for or is registered are identical with the goods or services for which the earlier trade mark is protected;

(b) if because of its identity with, or similarity to, the earlier trade mark and the identity or similarity of the goods or services covered by the trade marks, there exists a likelihood of confusion on the part of the public, which includes the likelihood of association with the earlier trade mark.

2. 'Earlier trade marks' within the meaning of paragraph 1 means:

(a) trade marks of the following kinds with a date of application for registration which is earlier than the date of application for registration of the trade mark, taking account, where appropriate, of the priorities claimed in respect of those trade marks:

(i) Community trade marks;
(ii) trade marks registered in the Member State or, in the case of Belgium, Luxembourg or the Netherlands, at the Benelux Trade Mark Office;
(iii) trade marks registered under international arrangements which have effect in the Member State;

(b) Community trade marks which validly claim seniority, in accordance with the Regulation on the Community trade mark, from a trade mark referred to in (a)(ii) and (iii), even when the latter trade mark has been surrendered or allowed to lapse;

(c) applications for the trade marks referred to in (a) and (b), subject to their registration;

(d) trade marks which, on the date of application for registration of the trade mark, or, where appropriate, of the priority claimed in respect of the application for registration of the trade mark, are well known in a Member State, in the sense in which the words 'well known' are used in Article 6 *bis* of the Paris Convention;

3. A trade mark shall furthermore not be registered or, if registered, shall be liable to be declared invalid if it is identical with, or similar to, an earlier Community trade mark within the meaning of paragraph 2 and is to be, or has been, registered for goods or services which are not similar to those for which the earlier Community trade mark is registered, where the earlier Community trade mark has a reputation in the Community and where the use of the later trade mark without due cause would take unfair advantage of, or be detrimental to, the distinctive character or the repute of the earlier Community trade mark.

4. Any Member State may furthermore provide that a trade mark shall not be registered or, if registered, shall be liable to be declared invalid where, and to the extent that:

(a) the trade mark is identical with, or similar to, an earlier national trade mark within the meaning of paragraph 2 and is to be, or has been, registered for goods or services which are not similar to those for which the earlier trade mark is registered, where the earlier trade mark has a reputation in the Member State concerned and where the use of the later trade mark without due cause would take unfair advantage of, or be detrimental to, the distinctive character or the repute of the earlier trade mark;

(b) rights to a non-registered trade mark or to another sign used in the course of trade were acquired prior to the date of application for registration of the subsequent trade mark, or the date of the priority claimed for the application for registration of the subsequent trade mark and that non-registered trade mark or other sign confers on its proprietor the right to prohibit the use of a subsequent trade mark;

(c) the use of the trade mark may be prohibited by virtue of an earlier right other than the rights referred to in paragraphs 2 and 4(b) and in particular:

   (i) a right to a name;
   (ii) a right of personal portrayal;
   (iii) a copyright;
   (iv) an industrial property right;

(d) the trade mark is identical with, or similar to, an earlier collective trade mark conferring a right which expired within a period of a maximum of three years preceding application;

(e) the trade mark is identical with, or similar to, an earlier guarantee or certification mark conferring a right which expired within a period preceding application the length of which is fixed by the Member State;

(f) the trade mark is identical with, or similar to, an earlier trade mark which was registered for identical or similar goods or services and conferred on them a right which has expired for failure to renew within a period of a maximum of two years preceding application, unless the proprietor of the earlier trade mark gave his agreement for the registration of the later mark or did not use his trade mark;

(g) the trade mark is liable to be confused with a mark which was in use abroad on the filing date of the application and which is still in use there, provided that at the date of the application the applicant was acting in bad faith.

5. The Member States may permit that in appropriate circumstances registration need not be refused or the trade mark need not be declared invalid where the proprietor of the earlier trade mark or other earlier right consents to the registration of the later trade mark.

6. Any Member State may provide that, by derogation from paragraphs 1 to 5, the grounds for refusal of registration or invalidity in force in that State prior to the date on which the provisions necessary to comply with this Directive enter into force, shall apply to trade marks for which application has been made prior to that date.

Article 5
Rights conferred by a trade mark

1. The registered trade mark shall confer on the proprietor exclusive rights therein. The proprietor shall be entitled to prevent all third parties not having his consent from using in the course of trade:

(a) any sign which is identical with the trade mark in relation to goods or services which are identical with those for which the trade mark is registered;

(b) any sign where, because of its identity with, or similarity to, the trade mark and the identity or similarity of the goods or services covered by the trade mark and the sign, there exists a likelihood of confusion on the part of the public, which includes the likelihood of association between the sign and the trade mark.

2. Any Member State may also provide that the proprietor shall be entitled to prevent all third parties not having his consent from using in the course of trade any sign which is identical with, or similar to, the trade mark in relation to goods or services which are not similar to those for which the trade mark is registered, where the latter has a reputation in the Member State and where use of that sign without due cause takes unfair advantage of, or is detrimental to, the distinctive character or the repute of the trade mark.

3. The following, *inter alia,* may be prohibited under paragraphs 1 and 2:

(a) affixing the sign to the goods or to the packaging thereof;

(b) offering the goods, or putting them on the market or stocking them for those purposes under that sign, or offering or supplying services thereunder;

(c) importing or exporting the goods under the sign;

(d) using the sign on business papers and in advertising.

4. Where, under the law of the Member State, the use of a sign under the conditions referred to in 1(b) or 2 could not be prohibited before

the date on which the provisions necessary to comply with this Directive entered into force in the Member State concerned, the rights conferred by the trade mark may not be relied on to prevent the continued use of the sign.

5. Paragraphs 1 to 4 shall not affect provisions in any Member State relating to the protection against the use of a sign other than for the purposes of distinguishing goods or services, where use of that sign without due cause takes unfair advantage of, or is detrimental to, the distinctive character or the repute of the trade mark.

Article 6

Limitation of the effects of a trade mark

1. The trade mark shall not entitle the proprietor to prohibit a third party from using, in the course of trade,

(a) his own name or address;

(b) indications concerning the kind, quality, quantity, intended purpose, value, geographical origin, the time of production of goods or of rendering of the service, or other characteristics of goods or services;

(c) the trade mark where it is necessary to indicate the intended purpose of a product or service, in particular as accessories or spare parts;

provided he uses them in accordance with honest practices in industrial or commercial matters.

2. The trade mark shall not entitle the proprietor to prohibit a third party from using, in the course of trade, an earlier right which only applies in a particular locality if that right is recognized by the laws of the Member State in question and within the limits of the territory in which it is recognized.

Article 7

Exhaustion of the rights conferred by a trade mark

1. The trade mark shall not entitle the proprietor to prohibit its use in relation to goods which have been put on the market in the Community under that trade mark by the proprietor or with his consent.

2. Paragraph 1 shall not apply where there exist legitimate reasons for the proprietor to oppose further commercialization of the goods, especially where the condition of the goods is changed or impaired after they have been put on the market.

Article 8

Licensing

1. A trade mark may be licensed for some or all of the goods or services for which it is registered and for the whole or part of the Member State concerned. A license may be exclusive or non-exclusive.

2. The proprietor of a trade mark may invoke the rights conferred by that trade mark against a licensee who contravenes any provision in his licensing contract with regard to its duration, the form covered by the

registration in which the trade mark may be used, the scope of the goods or services for which the licence is granted, the territory in which the trade mark may be affixed, or the quality of the goods manufactured or of the services provided by the licensee.

Article 9
Limitation in consequence of acquiescence

1. Where, in a Member State, the proprietor of an earlier trade mark as referred to in Article 4(2) has acquiesced, for a period of five successive years, in the use of a later trade mark registered in that Member State while being aware of such use, he shall no longer be entitled on the basis of the earlier trade mark either to apply for a declaration that the later trade mark is invalid or to oppose the use of the later trade mark in respect of the goods or services for which the later trade mark has been used, unless registration of the later trade mark was applied for in bad faith.

2. Any Member State may provide that paragraph 1 shall apply *mutatis mutandis* to the proprietor of an earlier trade mark referred to in Article 4(4)(a) or an other earlier right referred to in Article 4(4)(b) or (c).

3. In the cases referred to in paragraphs 1 and 2, the proprietor of a later registered trade mark shall not be entitled to oppose the use of the earlier right, even though that right may no longer be invoked against the later trade mark.

Article 10
Use of trade marks

1. If, within a period of five years following the date of the completion of the registration procedure, the proprietor has not put the trade mark to genuine use in the Member State in connection with the goods or services in respect of which it is registered, or if such use has been suspended during an uninterrupted period of five years, the trade mark shall be subject to the sanctions provided for in this Directive, unless there are proper reasons for non-use.

2. The following shall also constitute use within the meaning of paragraph 1:

(a) use of the trade mark in a form differing in elements which do not alter the distinctive character of the mark in the form in which it was registered;

(b) affixing of the trade mark to goods or to the packaging thereof in the Member State concerned solely for export purposes.

3. Use of the trade mark with the consent of the proprietor or by any person who has authority to use a collective mark or a guarantee or certification mark shall be deemed to constitute use by the proprietor.

4. In relation to trade marks registered before the date on which the provisions necessary to comply with this Directive enter into force in the Member State concerned:

(a) where a provision in force prior to that date attaches sanctions to non-use of a trade mark during an uninterrupted period, the relevant period of five years mentioned in paragraph 1 shall be deemed to have begun to run at the same time as any period of non-use which is already running at that date;

(b) where there is no use provision in force prior to that date, the periods of five years mentioned in paragraph 1 shall be deemed to run from that date at the earliest.

Article 11
Sanctions for non-use of a trade mark in legal or administrative proceedings

1. A trade mark may not be declared invalid on the ground that there is an earlier conflicting trade mark if the latter does not fulfil the requirements of use set out in Article 10(1), (2) and (3) or in Article 10(4), as the case may be.

2. Any Member State may provide that registration of a trade mark may not be refused on the ground that there is an earlier conflicting trade mark if the latter does not fulfil the requirements of use set out in Article 10(1), (2) and (3) or in Article 10(4), as the case may be.

3. Without prejudice to the application of Article 12, where a counter-claim for revocation is made, any Member State may provide that a trade mark may not be successfully invoked in infringement proceedings if it is established as a result of a plea that the trade mark could be revoked pursuant to Article 12(1).

4. If the earlier trade mark has been used in relation to part only of the goods or services for which it is registered, it shall, for purposes of applying paragraphs 1, 2 and 3, be deemed to be registered in respect only of that part of the goods or services.

Article 12
Grounds for revocation

1. A trade mark shall be liable to revocation if, within a continuous period of five years, it has not been put to genuine use in the Member State in connection with the goods or services in respect of which it is registered, and there are no proper reasons for non-use; however, no person may claim that the proprietor's rights in a trade mark should be revoked where, during the interval between expiry of the five-year period and filing of the application for revocation, genuine use of the trade mark has been started or resumed; the commencement or resumption of use within a period of three months preceding the filing of the application for revocation which began at the earliest on expiry of the continuous period of five years of non-use, shall, however, be disregarded where preparations for the commencement or resumption occur only after the proprietor becomes aware that the application for revocation may be filed.

2. A trade mark shall also be liable to revocation if, after the date on which it was registered,

(a) in consequence of acts or inactivity of the proprietor, it has become the common name in the trade for a product or service in respect of which it is registered;

(b) in consequence of the use made of it by the proprietor of the trade mark or with his consent in respect of the goods or services for which it is registered, it is liable to mislead the public, particularly as to the nature, quality or geographical origin of those goods or services.

Article 13
Grounds for refusal or revocation or invalidity relating to only some of the goods or services

Where grounds for refusal of registration or for revocation or invalidity of a trade mark exist in respect of only some of the goods or services for which that trade mark has been applied for or registered, refusal of registration or revocation or invalidity shall cover those goods or services only.

Article 14
Establishment *a posteriori* of invalidity or revocation of a trade mark

Where the seniority of an earlier trade mark which has been surrendered or allowed to lapse, is claimed for a Community trade mark, the invalidity or revocation of the earlier trade mark may be established *a posteriori*.

Article 15
Special provisions in respect of collective marks, guarantee marks and certification marks

1. Without prejudice to Article 4, Member States whose laws authorize the registration of collective marks or of guarantee or certification marks may provide that such marks shall not be registered, or shall be revoked or declared invalid, on grounds additional to those specified in Articles 3 and 12 where the function of those marks so requires.

2. By way of derogation from Article 3(1)(c), Member States may provide that signs or indications which may serve, in trade, to designate the geographical origin of the goods or services may constitute collective, guarantee or certification marks. Such a mark does not entitle the proprietor to prohibit a third party from using in the course of trade such signs or indications, provided he uses them in accordance with honest practices in industrial or commercial matters; in particular, such a mark may not be invoked against a third party who is entitled to use a geographical name.

Article 16
National provisions to be adopted pursuant to this Directive

1. The Member States shall bring into force the laws, regulations and administrative provisions necessary to comply with this Directive not later than 28 December 1991. They shall immediately inform the Commission thereof.

2. Acting on a proposal from the Commission, the Council, acting by qualified majority, may defer the date referred to in paragraph 1 until 31 December 1992 at the latest.

3. Member States shall communicate to the Commission the text of the main provisions of national law which they adopt in the field governed by this Directive.

Article 17
Addressees

This Directive is addressed to the Member States.

4. COUNCIL DIRECTIVE 79/831/EEC

of 18 September 1979

amending for the sixth time Directive 67/548/EEC on the approximation of the laws, regulations and administrative provisions relating to the classification, packaging and labelling of dangerous substances

O.J. L 259/10 (Oct. 15, 1979)

THE COUNCIL OF THE EUROPEAN COMMUNITIES,

Having regard to the Treaty establishing the European Economic Community, and in particular Article 100 thereof,

Having regard to the proposal from the Commission,

Having regard to the opinion of the European Parliament,[1]

Having regard to the opinion of the Economic and Social Committee,[2]

Whereas to protect man and the environment against potential risks which could arise from the placing on the market of new substances, it is necessary to lay down appropriate measures and in particular to reinforce the recommendations provided in Council Directive 67/548/EEC of 27 June 1967 on the approximation of the laws, regulations and administrative provisions relating to the classification, packaging and labelling of dangerous substances,[3] as last amended by Directive 75/409/EEC;[4]

Whereas it is necessary for these reasons to amend Directive 67/548/EEC which at the moment by an adequate classification, packaging and labelling of dangerous substances protects the population and principally the workers using them;

Whereas in order to control the effects on man and the environment it is advisable that any new substance placed on the market be subjected to a prior study by the manufacturer or importer and a notification to the competent authorities conveying mandatorily certain information; whereas it is, moreover, important to follow closely the evolution and use of new substances placed on the market, and that in order to do this it is necessary to institute a system which allows all new substances to be listed;

* * *

Whereas it is necessary to provide for measures making it possible to introduce a procedure of notification to one Member State which is then valid for the Community; whereas, it is, moreover, necessary to provide that the measures relating to the classification and labelling of substances may be laid down at Community level;

1. OJ No C 30, 7.2.1977, p. 35.
2. OJ No C 114, 11.5.1977, p. 20.
3. OJ No 196, 16.8.1967, p. 1.
4. OJ No L 183, 14.7.1975, p. 22.

Whereas it is necessary to introduce measures for the packaging and provisional labelling of dangerous substances not yet appearing in Annex 1 to Directive 67/548/EEC;

Whereas it is necessary to make the indication of safety advice obligatory;

* * *

HAS ADOPTED THIS DIRECTIVE:

Article 1

Articles 1 to 8 of Directive 67/548/EEC are hereby replaced by the following Articles:

'*Article 1*

1. The purpose of this Directive is to approximate the laws, regulations and administrative provisions of the Member States on:

(a) the notification of substances, and

(b) the classification, packaging and labelling of substances dangerous to man and the environment,

which are placed on the market in the Member States.

2. This Directive does not apply to the provisions relating to:

(a) medicinal products, narcotics and radioactive substances;

(b) the carriage of dangerous substances by rail, road, inland waterway, sea or air;

(c) foodstuffs or feedingstuffs;

(d) substances in the form of waste which are covered by Council Directive 75/442/EEC of 15 July 1975 relating to waste [1] and Council Directive 78/319/EEC of 20 March 1978 relating to toxic and dangerous waste;[2]

* * *

Article 2

1. For the purpose of this Directive:

(a) "substances" means chemical elements and their compounds as they occur in the natural state or as produced by industry, including any additives required for the purpose of placing them on the market;

(b) "preparations" means mixtures or solutions composed of two or more substances;

(c) "environment" means water, air and land and their interrelationship as well as relationships between them and any living organisms;

1. OJ No L 194, 15.7.1975, p. 39.   2. OJ No L 84, 31.3.1978, p. 43.

(d) "notification" means the documents whereby the manufacturer or any other person established in the Community who places a substance on its own or in a preparation on the market presents the requisite information to the competent authority of a Member State. The person so doing shall hereinafter be referred to as "the notifier";

(e) "placing on the market" means supplying or making available to third parties.

Importation into Community customs territory shall be deemed to be placing on the market for the purposes of this Directive.

2. The following substances and preparations are "dangerous" within the meaning of this Directive:

(a) explosive:

substances and preparations which may explode under the effect of flame or which are more sensitive to shocks or friction than dinitrobenzene;

(b) oxidizing:

substances and preparations which give rise to highly exothermic reaction when in contact with other substances, particularly flammable substances;

(c) extremely flammable:

liquid substances and preparations having a flash point lower than 0° C and a boiling point lower than or equal to 35° C;

(d) highly flammable:

— substances and preparations which may become hot and finally catch fire in contact with air at ambient temperature without any application of energy, or

— solid substances and preparations which may readily catch fire after brief contact with a source of ignition and which continue to burn or to be consumed after removal of the source of ignition, or

— liquid substances and preparations having a flash point below 21° C, or

— gaseous substances and preparations which are flammable in air at normal pressure, or

— substances and preparations which, in contact with water or damp air, evolve highly flammable gases in dangerous quantities;

(e) flammable:

liquid substances and preparations having a flash point equal to or greater than 21° C and less than or equal to 55° C;

(f) very toxic:

substances and preparations which, if they are inhaled or ingested or if they penetrate the skin, may involve extremely serious, acute or chronic health risks and even death;

(g) toxic:

substances and preparations which, if they are inhaled or ingested or if they penetrate the skin, may involve serious, acute or chronic health risks and even death;

(h) harmful:

substances and preparations which, if they are inhaled or ingested or if they penetrate the skin, may involve limited health risks;

(i) corrosive:

substances and preparations which may, on contact with living tissues, destroy them;

(j) irritant:

non-corrosive substances and preparations which, through immediate, prolonged or repeated contact with the skin or mucous membrane, can cause inflammation;

(k) dangerous for the environment:

substances and preparations the use of which presents or may present immediate or delayed risks for the environment;

(*l*) carcinogenic:

substances or preparations which, if they are inhaled or ingested or if they penetrate the skin, may induce cancer in man or increase its incidence;

(m) teratogenic;

(n) mutagenic.

Article 3

1. The physico-chemical properties of the substances and preparations shall be determined according to the methods specified in Annex V(A); their toxicity shall be determined according to the methods specified in Annex V(B) and their ecotoxicity according to those specified in Annex V(C).

2. The real or potential environmental hazard shall be assessed according to the characteristics set out in Annexes VII and VIII, on the basis of any existing internationally recognized parameters.

3. The general principles of the classification and labelling of substances and preparations shall be applied according to the criteria in Annex VI, save where contrary requirements for dangerous preparations are specified in separate Directives.

Article 4

1. The classification of dangerous substances according to the degree of hazard and to the specific nature of the risks involved shall be based on the categories laid down in Article 2(2). For categories (a) to (j) the substances shall be classified according to the greatest degree of hazard, in accordance with Article 16(4).

2. The dangerous substances listed in Annex I shall, where appropriate, be given a rating enabling the health hazard of preparations to be assessed. The ratings shall be determined in accordance with the criteria established by a subsequent Council Directive.

Article 5

1. The Member States shall take all the measures necessary to ensure that without prejudice to Article 8 substances cannot be placed on the market on their own or in preparations unless the substances have been:

— notified to the competent authority of one of the Member States in accordance with this Directive,

— packaged and labelled in accordance with Articles 15 to 18 and with the criteria in Annex VI, and in accordance with the results of the tests provided for in Article 6.

* * *

Article 6

1. Without prejudice to Articles 1(4) and 8(1), any manufacturer or importer into the Community of a substance within the meaning of this Directive shall be required to submit to the competent authority referred to in Article 7 of the Member State in which the substance is produced or into which it is imported into the Community, at the latest 45 days before the substance is placed on the market, a notification including:

— a technical dossier supplying the information necessary for evaluating the foreseeable risks, whether immediate or delayed, which the substance may entail for man and the environment, and containing at least the information and results of the studies referred to in Annex VII, together with a detailed and full description of the studies conducted and of the methods used or a bibliographical reference to them,

— a declaration concerning the unfavourable effects of the substance in terms of the various uses envisaged,

— the proposed classification and labelling of the substance in accordance with this Directive,

— proposals for any recommended precautions relating to the safe use of the substance.

* * *

4. Any notifier of a substance already notified shall be required to inform the competent authority of:

— changes in the annual or total quantities placed on the market by him in accordance with the tonnage range laid down in Annex VII, point 2.2.1,

— new knowledge of the effects of the substance on man and/or the environment of which he may reasonably be expected to have become aware,

— new uses for which the substance is placed on the market (within the meaning of Annex VII, point 2.1.2) of which he may reasonably be expected to have become aware,

— any change in the properties resulting from a modification of the substance referred to in Annex VII, point 1.3.

5. The notifier shall also be required to inform the competent authority of the results of the studies carried out in accordance with Annex VIII.

Article 7

1. Member States shall appoint the competent authority or authorities responsible for receiving the information provided for in Article 6 and examining its conformity with the requirements of the Directive, and in particular:

— the notifier's proposed findings on any foreseeable risks which the substance may entail,

— classification and labelling,

— the proposals for any recommended precautions relating to safe use submitted by the notifier.

Moreover, if it can be shown to be necessary for the evaluation of the hazard which may be caused by a substance, the competent authorities may:

— ask for further information and/or verification tests concerning the substances of which they have been notified; this may also include requesting the information referred to in Annex VIII earlier than provided for therein,

— carry out such sampling as is necessary for control purposes,

— take appropriate measures relating to safe use of a substance pending the introduction of Community provisions.

2. The procedure laid down in Article 21 shall be followed in confirming or amending proposals for:

— classification,

— labelling, and

— the recommended precautionary measures provided for in Annex VII, points 2.3, 2.4 and 2.5.

3. Member States and the Commission shall ensure that any information concerning commercial exploitation or manufacturing is kept secret.

Article 8

[Omitted. Covers principally minor quantities marketed for research or analysis purposes.]

Article 9

When a Member State has received the notification dossier or additional information referred to in Article 6 it shall forthwith send to the Commission a copy of the dossier or a summary thereof together with any relevant comments; in the case of the further information referred to in Article 7(1) and the additional information or studies provided for in Annex VIII, the competent authority shall notify the Commission of the tests chosen, the reasons for their choice, and the assessment of their results.

Article 10

1. On receipt of the copy of the notification dossier, the summary thereof or the additional information sent by a Member State, the Commission shall forward:

— the notification dossier or the summary thereof to the other Member States,

— any other relevant information it has collected pursuant to this Directive to all Member States.

2. The competent authority of any Member State may consult direct the competent authority which received the original notification, or the Commission, on specific details of the data contained in the dossier required under this Directive; it may also suggest that further tests or information be requested. If the competent authority which received the original notification fails to comply with the suggestions of other authorities regarding further information or amendments in the study programmes provided for in Annex VIII, it shall give its reasons to the other authorities concerned. Should it not be possible for the authorities concerned to reach agreement and should any one authority feel, on the basis of detailed reasons, that additional information or amendments in the study programmes are nevertheless really necessary to protect man and the environment, it may ask the Commission to take a decision in accordance with the procedure laid down in Article 21.

Article 11

1. If he considers that there is a confidentiality problem, the notifier may indicate the information provided for in Article 6 which he considers to be commercially sensitive and disclosure of which might harm him industrially or commercially, and which he therefore wishes to be kept secret from all persons other than the competent

authorities and the Commission. Full justification must be given in such cases.

Industrial and commercial secrecy shall not apply to:

— the trade name of the substance,

— physico-chemical data concerning the substance in connection with Annex VII, point 3,

— the possible ways of rendering the substance harmless,

— the interpretation of the toxicological and ecotoxicological tests and the name of the body responsible for the tests,

— the recommended methods and precautions referred to in Annex VII, point 2.3 and the emergency measures referred to in Annex VII, points 2.4 and 2.5.

* * *

2. The authority receiving the notification shall decide on its own responsibility which information is covered by industrial and commercial secrecy in accordance with paragraph 1.

* * *

4. Confidential information brought to the attention either of the Commission or of a Member State shall be kept secret.

* * *

Article 12

[Omitted. Covers summaries of data in Articles 9 and 10.]

Article 13

1. The Commission shall, on the basis in particular of information provided by the Member States, draw up an inventory of substances on the Community market by 18 September 1981.

In so doing it shall have regard to Articles 1(4) and 8.

The inventory shall give the chemical name under an internationally recognized chemical nomenclature (preferably IUPAC), the CAS number and the common name or ISO abbreviation, if any.

2. The Commission shall keep a list of all substances notified under this Directive.

* * *

Article 14

Annex I contains the list of substances classified in accordance with Article 4 and any recommendations relating to safe use.

Article 15

1. Member States shall take all necessary measures to ensure that dangerous substances cannot be placed on the market unless their packaging satisfies the following requirements:

(a) it shall be so designed and constructed that its contents cannot escape; this requirement shall not apply where special safety devices are prescribed;

(b) the materials constituting the packaging and fastenings must not be susceptible to adverse attack by the contents, or liable to form harmful or dangerous compounds with the contents;

(c) packaging and fastenings must be strong and solid throughout to ensure that they will not loosen and will safely meet the normal stresses and strains of handling;

(d) containers fitted with replaceable fastening devices shall be so designed that the packaging can be repeatedly refastened without the contents escaping.

2. The Member States may also prescribe that:

— packages shall initially be closed with a seal in such a way that when the package is opened for the first time the seal is irreparably damaged,

— containers with a capacity not exceeding three litres which contain dangerous substances intended for domestic use shall have child-resistant fastenings,

— containers with a capacity not exceeding one litre which contain very toxic, toxic or corrosive liquids intended for domestic use shall carry a tactile warning of danger.

* * *

Article 16

1. Member States shall take all necessary measures to ensure that dangerous substances cannot be placed on the market unless the labelling on their packaging satisfies the following requirements.

2. Every package shall show clearly and indelibly the following:

— the name of the substance,

— the origin of the substance,

— the danger symbol, when laid down, and indication of danger involved in the use of the substance,

— standard phrases indicating the special risks arising from such dangers,

— standard phrases indicating the safety advice relating to the use of the substance.

(a) The name of the substance shall be one of the terms listed in Annex I; if this is not the case the name must be given in accordance with internationally recognized nomenclature.

(b) The indication of origin shall include the name and address of the manufacturer, the distributor or the importer.

(c) The following symbols and indications of danger are to be used:

- explosive:
an exploding bomb (E)
- oxidizing: a flame over a circle (O)
- extremely flammable: a flame (F)
- highly flammable: a flame (F)
- very toxic: a skull and cross-bones (T)
- toxic: a skull and cross-bones (T)
- harmful: a St. Andrew's cross (Xn)
- corrosive: the symbol showing the damaging effect of an acid (C)
- irritant: a St. Andrew's cross (Xi)

The symbols must conform to those in Annex II; they shall be printed in black on an orange-yellow background.

(d) The special risks involved in using the substances shall be indicated by one or more of the standard phrases which, in accordance with the references contained in the list in Annex I, are set out in Annex III. In the case of a substance not listed in Annex I, the reference to the special risks attributed to the dangerous substances shall comply with appropriate indications given in Annex III.

* * *

(e) The safety advice relating to the use of the substances shall be indicated by standard phrases which, in accordance with the references contained in the list in Annex I, are set out in Annex IV.

* * *

(f) Indications such as "non-toxic", "non-harmful" or any other similar indications must not appear on the label or packaging of substances subject to this Directive.

* * *

4. When more than one danger symbol is assigned to a substance:

- the obligation to indicate the symbol T makes the symbols X and C optional, unless Annex I includes provision to the contrary,
- the obligation to indicate the symbol C makes the symbol X optional,
- the obligation to indicate the symbol E makes the symbols F and O optional.

Article 17

1. Where the particulars required by Article 16 appear on a label, that label shall be firmly affixed to one or more surfaces of the packaging so that these particulars can be read horizontally when the package is set down normally. The dimensions of the label shall be as follows:

Capacity of the package	*Dimensions (in millimetres)*
— not exceeding three litres:	if possible at least 52 × 74
— greater than three litres but not exceeding 50 litres:	at least 74 × 105
— greater than 50 litres but not exceeding 500 litres:	at least 105 × 148
— greater than 500 litres:	at least 148 × 210

Each symbol shall cover at least one tenth of the surface area of the label but not be less than 1 cm^2. The entire surface of the label shall adhere to the package immediately containing the substance.

* * *

3. The colour and presentation of the label—or, in the case of paragraph 2, of the package—shall be such that the danger symbol and its background stand out clearly from it.

4. Member States may make the placing on the market of dangerous substances in their territories subject to the use of the official language or languages in respect of the labelling thereof.

* * *

Article 18

[Omitted. Covers the handling of small quantity packages.]

Article 19

The amendments necessary for adapting the Annexes * * * to technical progress shall be adopted in accordance with the procedure laid down in Article 21.

Article 20

1. A Committee (hereinafter called "the Committee") is hereby set up to adapt to technical progress the Directives concerning the elimination of technical barriers to trade in dangerous substances and preparations. It shall consist of representatives of the Member States, with a Commission representative as chairman.

2. The Committee shall adopt its own rules of procedure.

Article 21

[Omitted: Describes the procedure for adopting technical amendments to the Annexes to be followed by the Commission, the Committee and the Council.]

Article 22

The Member States may not, on grounds relating to notification, classification, packaging or labelling within the meaning of this Directive, prohibit, restrict or impede the placing on the market of substances which comply with the requirements of this Directive and the Annexes thereto.

Article 23

1. Where a Member State has detailed evidence that a substance, although satisfying the requirements of this Directive, constitutes a hazard for man or the environment by reason of its classification packaging or labelling, it may provisionally prohibit the sale of that substance or subject it to special conditions in its territory. It shall immediately inform the Commission and the other Member States of such action and give reasons for its decision.

2. The Commission shall consult the Member States concerned within six weeks, then give its view without delay and take the appropriate measures.

3. If the Commission considers that technical adaptations to this Directive are necessary, such adaptations shall be adopted, either by the Commission or by the Council, in accordance with the procedure laid down in Article 21; in such case, the Member State which has adopted safeguard measures may maintain them until the adaptations enter into force.

Article 2

Articles 9, 10 and 11 of Directive 67/548/EEC hereby become Articles 24, 25 and 26.

Article 24

Member States shall inform the Commission of all laws, regulations and administrative provisions which they adopt in the field covered by this Directive.

Article 25

Member States shall adopt the measures needed in order to comply with this Directive and shall apply them by 1 January 1970 at the latest.

They shall forthwith inform the Commission thereof.

Article 26

This Directive is addressed to the Member States.

[Annexes omitted, except for Annex II]

ANNEXE II – ANLAGE II – BIJLAGE II – ALLEGATO II – ANNEX II

E

Explosif
Explosionsgefährlich
Ontplofbaar
Esplosivo
Explosive

O

Comburant
Brandfördernd
Oxyderend
Comburente
Oxidising

F

Facilement inflammable
Leicht entzündlich
Licht ontvlambaar
Facilmente infiammabile
Easily flammable

T

Toxique
Gift
Vergiftig
Tossico
Toxic

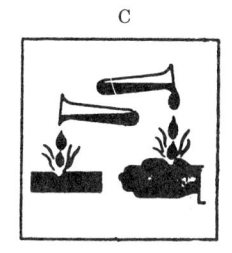

C

Corrosif
Ätzend
Corrosief
Corrosivo
Corrosive

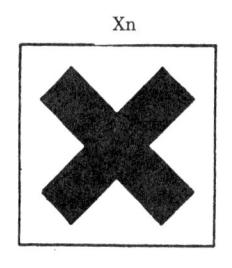

Xn

Nocif
Gesundheitsschädlich
Schadelijk
Nocivo
Harmful

Xi

Irritant
Reizstoff
Irriterend
Irritante
Irritant

N.B. The current text of Annex II provides also the Greek, Portugese and Spanish equivalents of these words.

5. COUNCIL DIRECTIVE 83/189/EEC

of 28 March 1983

laying down a procedure for the provision of information in the field of technical standards and regulations

O.J. L 109/8 (Apr. 26, 1983)

THE COUNCIL OF THE EUROPEAN COMMUNITIES.

Having regard to the Treaty establishing the European Economic Community, and in particular Articles 100 and 213 thereof,

Having regard to the proposal from the Commission,

Having regard to the opinion of the European Parliament,

Having regard to the opinion of the Economic and Social Committee,

Whereas the prohibition of quantitative restrictions on the movement of goods and of measures having an equivalent effect is one of the basic principles of the Community;

Whereas barriers to trade resulting from technical regulations relating to products may be allowed only where they are necessary in order to meet essential requirements and have an objective in the public interest of which they constitute the main guarantee;

Whereas it is essential for the Commission to have the necessary information at its disposal before the adoption of technical provisions; whereas, consequently, the Member States which are required to facilitate the achievement of its task pursuant to Article 5 of the Treaty must notify it of their projects in the field of technical regulations;

* * *

Whereas, * * * the Member State in question must, pursuant to the general obligations laid down in Article 5 of the Treaty, defer implementation of the contemplated measure for a period sufficient to allow either a joint examination of * * * amendments [proposed by the Commission or other Member States] or the preparation of the proposal for a Council Directive or of the Commission Directive; whereas the time limits laid down in the Agreement of the representatives of the Governments of the Member States meeting within the Council of 28 May 1969 providing for standstill and notification to the Commission, as amended by the Agreement of 5 March 1973, have proved inadequate in the cases concerned and should accordingly be extended;

Whereas the procedure concerning the standstill arrangement and notification of the Commission contained in the abovementioned Agreement of 28 May 1969 remains applicable to products subject to that procedure which are not covered by this Directive;

Whereas, in practice, national technical standards may have the same effects on the free movement of goods as technical regulations;

Whereas it would therefore appear necessary to inform the Commission of draft standards under similar conditions to those which apply to technical regulations; whereas, pursuant to Article 213 of the Treaty, the Commission may, within the limits and under the conditions laid down by the Council in accordance with the provisions of the Treaty, collect any information and carry out any checks required for the performance of the tasks entrusted to it;

* * *

HAS ADOPTED THIS DIRECTIVE:

Article 1

For the purposes of this Directive, the following meanings shall apply:

1. 'technical specification', a specification contained in a document which lays down the characteristics required of a product such as levels of quality, performance, safety or dimensions, including the requirements applicable to the product as regards terminology, symbols, testing and test methods, packaging, marking or labeling;

2. 'standard', a technical specification approved by a recognized standardizing body for repeated or continuous application, with which compliance is not compulsory;

3. 'standards programme', document listing the subjects for which it is intended to draw up or alter a standard;

4. 'draft standard', document containing the text of the technical specifications concerning a given subject, which is being considered for adoption in accordance with the national standards procedure, as that document stands after the preparatory work and as circulated for public comment or scrutiny;

5. 'technical regulation', technical specifications, including the relevant administrative provisions, the observance of which is compulsory, *de jure* or *de facto,* in the case of marketing or use in a Member State or a major part thereof, except those laid down by local authorities;

6. 'draft technical regulation', the text of a technical specification including administrative provisions, formulated with the aim of enacting it or of ultimately having it enacted as a technical regulation, the text being at a stage or preparation at which substantial amendments can still be made;

7. 'product', any industrially manufactured product and any agricultural product.

> [Directive 88/182, O.J. L 81/75 (Mar. 26, 1988), amended the definition to include agricultural products, medicinal products and cosmetics.]

Article 2

1. The Commission and the standards institutions in List 1 annexed hereto shall be informed each year, not later than 31 January, of the

standards programmes drawn up by the national institutions in List 2 annexed hereto. This information shall be brought up to date every quarter. The Commission may amend or supplement these lists on the basis of communications from the Member States.

2. Standards programmes shall indicate in particular whether the standard:

— will be the transposition in full of an existing international or European standard,

— will be the transposition of an international or European standard incorporating certain national divergences or amendments,

— will be a new national standard,

— will constitute an amendment of a national standard.

* * *

3. The Commission shall keep this information at the disposal of the Member States in a form in which the different programmes can be compared.

Article 3

The Commission and the standards institutions shall be informed if one or more standards institutions:

— wish to be involved passively or actively (by sending an observer) in activities planned by other standards institutions,

— wish a European standard or any other document leading to uniform technical specifications to be drawn up.

Article 4

At least every four months the standards institutions referred to in List 1 and the Commission shall receive all new draft standards, except where such standards merely transpose the full text of an international or European standard.

When a draft is communicated it shall be indicated whether the standard will be:

— the transposition of an international or European standard incorporating certain national divergences or amendments,

— a new national standard, or

— an amendment of a national standard.

Article 5

A Standing Committee shall be set up consisting of representatives appointed by the Member States who may call on the assistance of experts or advisers; its chairman shall be a representative of the Commission.

The Committee shall draw up its own rules of procedure.

Article 6

1. The Committee shall meet at least twice a year with the representatives of the standards institutions referred to in List 1.

2. The Commission shall submit to the Committee a report on the implementation and application of the abovementioned procedures and proposals aimed at eliminating existing or foreseeable barriers to trade.

3. The Committee shall express its opinion on the communications and proposals referred to in paragraph 2 and may in this connection propose, in particular, that the Commission:

— request the European standards institutions to draw up a European standard within a given time limit,

— ensure where necessary, in order to avoid the risk of barriers to trade, that initially the Member States concerned decide amongst themselves on appropriate measures,

— take all appropriate measures.

* * *

5. The Committee may be consulted by the Commission on any preliminary draft technical regulation received by the latter.

* * *

7. The proceedings of the Committee and the information to be submitted to it shall be confidential.

However, the Committee and the national authorities may, provided that the necessary precautions are taken, consult, for an expert opinion, natural or legal persons, including persons in the private sector.

Article 7

1. Member States shall take all appropriate measures to ensure that their standards institutions do not draw up or introduce standards in the field in question while the European standard referred to in the first indent of Article 6(3) is being drawn up. This undertaking shall lapse unless a European standard has been introduced within six months following expiry of the time limit fixed in accordance with the said indent.

* * *

Article 8

1. Member States shall immediately communicate to the Commission any draft technical regulation, except where such technical regulation merely transposes the full text of an international or European standard, in which case information regarding the relevant standard shall suffice; they shall also let the Commission have a brief statement of the grounds which make the enactment of such a technical regulation necessary, where these are not already made clear in the draft.

The Commission shall immediately notify the other Member States of any draft it has received; it may also refer this draft to the Committee for its opinion.

2. The Commission and the Member States may make comments to the Member State which has forwarded a draft technical regulation, that Member State shall take such comments into account as far as possible in the subsequent preparation of the technical regulation.

3. At the express request of a Member State or the Commission, Member States shall communicate to them, without delay, the definitive text of a technical regulation.

4. The information supplied under this Article shall be confidential.

However, the Committee and the national authorities may, provided that the necessary precautions are taken, consult, for an expert opinion, natural or legal persons, including persons in the private sector.

Article 9

1. Without prejudice to paragraph 2, Member States shall postpone the adoption of a draft technical regulation for six months from the date of the notification referred to in Article 8(1) if the Commission or another Member State delivers a detailed opinion, within three months of that date, to the effect that the measure envisaged must be amended in order to eliminate or reduce any barriers which it might create to the free movement of goods.

2. The period in paragraph 1 shall be 12 months if, within three months following the notification referred to in Article 8(1), the Commission gives notice of its intention of proposing or adopting a Directive on the subject.

3. Paragraphs 1 and 2 shall not apply in those cases where, for urgent reasons relating to the protection of public health or safety, a Member State is obliged to prepare technical regulations in a very short space of time in order to enact and introduce them immediately without any consultations being possible. In such cases the Member State in question shall in the notification provided for in Article 8 state the grounds warranting the urgent adoption of the measures.

Article 10

Articles 8 and 9 shall not apply where Member States honour their obligations arising out of Community Directives or commitments arising out of an international agreement where they result in the adoption of uniform technical specifications in the Community.

Article 11

No later than four years following the date of notification of this Directive the Commission, in close cooperation with the Committee referred to in Article 5, shall review the operation of the procedures laid down in this Directive and, if need be, submit any relevant proposals for amending them.

Article 12

1. Member States shall bring into force the measures necessary in order to comply with this Directive within 12 months following its notification and shall forthwith inform the Commission thereof.

2. Member States shall ensure that the texts of the main provisions of national law which they adopt in the field governed by this Directive are communicated to the Commission.

Article 13

This Directive is addressed to the Member States.

[Annexes omitted.]

6. COUNCIL DIRECTIVE 89/392/EEC

of 14 June 1989

on the approximation of the laws of the Member States relating to machinery

O.J. L 183/9 (June 29, 1989)

THE COUNCIL OF THE EUROPEAN COMMUNITIES,

Having regard to the Treaty establishing the European Economic Community, and in particular Article 100a thereof,

Having regard to the proposal from the Commission,

In cooperation with the European Parliament,

Having regard to the opinion of the Economic and Social Committee,

Whereas Member States are responsible for ensuring the health and safety on their territory of their people and, where appropriate, of domestic animals and goods and, in particular, of workers notably in relation to the risks arising out of the use of machinery;

Whereas, in the Member States, the legislative systems regarding accident prevention are very different; whereas the relevant compulsory provisions, frequently supplemented by *de facto* mandatory technical specifications and/or voluntary standards, do not necessarily lead to different levels of health and safety, but nevertheless, owing to their disparities, constitute barriers to trade within the Community; whereas, furthermore, conformity certification and national certification systems for machinery differ considerably;

Whereas the maintenance or improvement of the level of safety attained by the Member States constitutes one of the essential aims of this Directive and of the principle of safety as defined by the essential requirements;

Whereas existing national health and safety provisions providing protection against the risks caused by machinery must be approximated to ensure free movement of machinery without lowering existing justified levels of protection in the Member States; whereas the provisions of this Directive concerning the design and construction of machinery, essential for a safer working environment shall be accompanied by specific provisions concerning the prevention of certain risks to which workers can be exposed at work, as well as by provisions based on the organization of safety of workers in the working environment;

Whereas the machinery sector is an important part of the engineering industry and is one of the industrial mainstays of the Community economy;

Whereas paragraphs 65 and 68 of the White Paper on the completion of the internal market, approved by the European Council in June 1985, provide for a new approach to legislative harmonization;

Whereas the social cost of the large number of accidents caused directly by the use of machinery can be reduced by inherently safe design and construction of machinery and by proper installations and maintenance;

* * *

Whereas specific Directives containing design and construction provisions for certain categories of machinery are now envisaged; whereas the very broad scope of this Directive must be limited in relation to these Directives and also existing Directives where they contain design and construction provisions;

Whereas Community law, in its present form, provides—by way of derogation from one of the fundamental rules of the Community, namely the free movement of goods—that obstacles to movement within the Community resulting from disparities in national legislation relating to the marketing of products must be accepted in so far as the provisions concerned can be recognized as being necessary to satisfy imperative requirements; whereas, therefore, the harmonization of laws in this case must be limited only to those requirements necessary to satisfy the imperative and essential health and safety requirements relating to machinery; whereas these requirements must replace the relevant national provisions because they are essential;

* * *

Whereas, therefore, this Directive defines only the essential health and safety requirements of general application, supplemented by a number of more specific requirements for certain categories of machinery; whereas, in order to help manufacturers to prove conformity to these essential requirements and in order to allow inspection for conformity to the essential requirements, it is desirable to have standards harmonized at European level for the prevention of risks arising out of the design and construction of machinery; whereas these standards harmonized at European level are drawn up by private-law bodies and must retain their non-binding status; whereas for this purpose the European Committee for Standardization (CEN) and the European Committee for Electrotechnical Standardization (Cenelec) are the bodies recognized as competent to adopt harmonized standards in accordance with the general guidelines for cooperation between the Commission and these two bodies signed on 13 November 1984; whereas, within the meaning of this Directive, a harmonized standard is a technical specification (European standard or harmonization document) adopted by either or both of these bodies, on the basis of a remit from the Commission in accordance with the provisions of Council Directive 83/189/EEC of 28 March 1983 laying down a procedure for the provision of information in the field of technical standards and regulations;

* * *

HAS ADOPTED THIS DIRECTIVE:

CHAPTER I

SCOPE, PLACING ON THE MARKET AND FREEDOM OF MOVEMENT

Article 1

1. This Directive applies to machinery and lays down the essential health and safety requirements therefor, as defined in Annex I.

2. For the purposes of this Directive, 'machinery' means an assembly of linked parts or components, at least one of which moves, with the appropriate actuators, control and power circuits, etc., joined together for a specific application, in particular for the processing, treatment, moving or packaging of a material.

The term 'machinery' also covers an assembly of machines which, in order to achieve the same end, are arranged and controlled so that they function as an integral whole.

3. The following are excluded from the scope of this Directive:

— mobile equipment,

— lifting equipment,

— machinery whose only power source is directly applied manual effort,

— machinery for medical use used in direct contact with patients,

— special equipment for use in fairgrounds and/or amusement parks,

— steam boilers, tanks and pressure vessels,

— machinery specially designed or put into service for nuclear purposes which, in the event of failure, may result in an emission of radioactivity,

— radioactive sources forming part of a machine,

— firearms,

— storage tanks and pipelines for petrol, diesel fuel, inflammable liquids and dangerous substances.

* * *

Article 2

1. Member States shall take all appropriate measures to ensure that machinery covered by this Directive may be placed on the market and put into service only if it does not endanger the health or safety of persons and, where appropriate, domestic animals or property, when properly installed and maintained and used for its intended purpose.

2. The provisions of this Directive shall not affect Member States' entitlement to lay down, in due observance of the Treaty, such requirements as they may deem necessary to ensure that persons and in particular workers are protected when using the machines in question, provided that this does not mean that the machinery is modified in a way not specified in the Directive.

3. At trade fairs, exhibitions, demonstrations, etc., Member States shall not prevent the showing of machinery which does not conform to the provisions of this Directive, provided that a visible sign clearly indicates that such machinery does not conform and that it is not for sale until it has been brought into conformity by the manufacturer or his authorized representative established in the Community. During demonstrations, adequate safety measures shall be taken to ensure the protection of persons.

Article 3

Machinery covered by this Directive shall satisfy the essential health and safety requirements set out in Annex I.

Article 4

1. Member States shall not prohibit, restrict or impede the placing on the market and putting into service in their territory of machinery which complies with the provisions of this Directive.

2. Member States shall not prohibit, restrict or impede the placing on the market of machinery where the manufacturer or his authorized representative established in the Community declares in accordance with Annex II.B that it is intended to be incorporated into machinery or assembled with other machinery to constitute machinery covered by this Directive except where it can function independently.

Article 5

1. Member States shall regard machinery bearing the EC mark and accompanied by the EC declaration of conformity referred to in Annex II as conforming to the essential health and safety requirements referred to in Article 3.

In the absence of harmonized standards, Member States shall take any steps they deem necessary to bring to the attention of the parties concerned the existing national technical standards and specifications which are regarded as important or relevant to the proper implementation of the essential safety and health requirements in Annex I.

2. Where a national standard transposing a harmonized standard, the reference for which has been published in the *Official Journal of the European Communities,* covers one or more of the essential safety requirements, machinery constructed in accordance with this standard shall be presumed to comply with the relevant essential requirements.

* * *

Article 6

[Omitted. Describes the role of an advisory committee.]

Article 7

1. Where a Member State ascertains that machinery bearing the EC mark and used in accordance with its intended purpose is liable to endanger the safety of persons, and, where appropriate, domestic animals

or property, it shall take all appropriate measures to withdraw such machinery from the market, to prohibit the placing on the market, putting into service or use thereof, or to restrict free movement thereof.

The Member State shall immediately inform the Commission of any such measure, indicating the reasons for its decision and, in particular, whether non-conformity is due to:

(a) failure to satisfy the essential requirements referred to in Article 3;

(b) incorrect application of the standards referred to in Article 5(2);

(c) shortcomings in the standards referred to in Article 5(2) themselves.

2. The Commission shall enter into consultation with the parties concerned without delay. Where the Commission considers, after this consultation, that the measure is justified, it shall immediately so inform the Member State which took the initiative and the other Member States. Where the Commission considers, after this consultation, that the action is unjustified, it shall immediately so inform the Member State which took the initiative and the manufacturer or his authorized representative established within the Community. Where the decision referred to in paragraph 1 is based on a shortcoming in the standards, and where the Member State at the origin of the decision maintains its position, the Commission shall immediately inform the Committee in order to initiate the procedures referred to in Article 6(1).

* * *

CHAPTER II

CERTIFICATION PROCEDURE

Article 8

1. The manufacturer, or his authorized representative established in the Community, shall, in order to certify the conformity of machinery with the provisions of this Directive, draw up an EC declaration of conformity based on the model given in Annex II for each machine manufactured and shall affix to the machinery the EC mark referred to in Article 10.

> [Omitted text describes the mode of review of machinery.]

* * *

6. Where neither the manufacturer nor his authorized representative established in the Community fulfils the obligations of the preceding paragraphs, these obligations shall fall to any person placing the machinery on the market in the Community. The same obligations shall apply to any person assembling machinery or parts thereof of various origins or constructing machinery for his own use.

Article 9

1. Each Member State shall notify the Commission and the other Member States of the approved bodies responsible for carrying out the certification procedures referred to in Article 8(2)(b) and (c). The Commission shall publish a list of these bodies in the *Official Journal of the European Communities* for information and shall ensure that the list is kept up to date.

* * *

CHAPTER III

EC MARK

Article 10

1. The 'EC' mark shall consist of the EC symbol followed by the last two digits of the year in which the mark was affixed.

* * *

3. Marks or inscriptions liable to be confused with the EC mark shall not be put on machinery.

CHAPTER IV

FINAL PROVISIONS

Article 11

Any decision taken pursuant to this Directive which restricts the marketing and putting into service of machinery shall state the exact grounds on which it is based. Such a decision shall be notified as soon as possible to the party concerned, who shall at the same time be informed of the legal remedies available to him under the laws in force in the Member State concerned and of the time limits to which such remedies are subject.

* * *

Article 13

1. Member States shall adopt and publish the laws, regulations and administrative provisions necessary in order to comply with this Directive by 1 January 1992 at the latest. They shall forthwith inform the Commission thereof.

They shall apply these provisions with effect from 31 December 1992.

* * *

Article 14

This Directive is addressed to the Member States.

ANNEX III
EC MARK

The EC mark consists of the symbol shown below and the last two figures of the year in which the mark was affixed.

CE

7. REGULATION (EEC) 1612/68 OF THE COUNCIL

of 15 October 1968

on freedom of movement for workers within the Community

O.J. English Spec. Ed. 1968–II, 475

THE COUNCIL OF THE EUROPEAN COMMUNITIES,

Having regard to the Treaty establishing the European Economic Community, and in particular Article 49 thereof;

Having regard to the proposal from the Commission;

Having regard to the Opinion of the European Parliament;[1]

Having regard to the Opinion of the Economic and Social Committee;[2]

Whereas freedom of movement for workers should be secured within the Community by the end of the transitional period at the latest; whereas the attainment of this objective entails the abolition of any discrimination based on nationality between workers of the Member States as regards employment, remuneration and other conditions of work and employment, as well as the right of such workers to move freely within the Community in order to pursue activities as employed persons subject to any limitations justified on grounds of public policy, public security or public health;

Whereas by reason in particular of the early establishment of the customs union and in order to ensure the simultaneous completion of the principal foundations of the Community, provisions should be adopted to enable the objectives laid down in Articles 48 and 49 of the Treaty in the field of freedom of movement to be achieved and to perfect measures adopted successively under Regulation No 15[3] on the first steps for attainment of freedom of movement and under Council Regulation No 38/54/EEC[4] of 25 March 1964 on freedom of movement for workers within the Community;

Whereas freedom of movement constitutes a fundamental right of workers and their families; whereas mobility of labour within the Community must be one of the means by which the worker is guaranteed the possibility of improving his living and working conditions and promoting his social advancement, while helping to satisfy the requirements of the economies of the Member States; whereas the right of all workers in the Member States to pursue the activity of their choice within the Community should be affirmed;

Whereas such right must be enjoyed without discrimination by permanent, seasonal and frontier workers and by those who pursue their activities for the purpose of providing services;

1. OJ No 268, 6.11.1967, p. 9.
2. OJ No 298, 7.12.1967, p. 10.
3. OJ No 57, 26.8.1961, p. 1073/61.
4. OJ No 62, 17.4.1964, p. 965/64.

Whereas the right of freedom of movement, in order that it may be exercised, by objective standards, in freedom and dignity, requires that equality of treatment shall be ensured in fact and in law in respect of all matters relating to the actual pursuit of activities as employed persons and to eligibility for housing, and also that obstacles to the mobility of workers shall be eliminated, in particular as regards the worker's right to be joined by his family and the conditions for the integration of that family into the host country;

Whereas the principle of non-discrimination between Community workers entails that all nationals of Member States have the same priority as regards employment as is enjoyed by national workers;

* * *

HAS ADOPTED THIS REGULATION:

PART I
EMPLOYMENT AND WORKERS' FAMILIES
Title I. Eligibility for employment
Article 1

1. Any national of a Member State, shall, irrespective of his place of residence, have the right to take up an activity as an employed person, and to pursue such activity, within the territory of another Member State in accordance with the provisions laid down by law, regulation or administrative action governing the employment of nationals of that State.

2. He shall, in particular, have the right to take up available employment in the territory of another Member State with the same priority as nationals of that State.

Article 2

Any national of a Member State and any employer pursuing an activity in the territory of a Member State may exchange their applications for and offers of employment, and may conclude and perform contracts of employment in accordance with the provisions in force laid down by law, regulation or administrative action, without any discrimination resulting therefrom.

Article 3

1. Under this Regulation, provisions laid down by law, regulation or administrative action or administrative practices of a Member State shall not apply:

— where they limit application for and offers of employment, or the right of foreign nationals to take up and pursue employment or subject these to conditions not applicable in respect of their own nationals; or

— where, though applicable irrespective of nationality, their exclusive or principal aim or effect is to keep nationals of other Member States away from the employment offered.

This provision shall not apply to conditions relating to linguistic knowledge required by reason of the nature of the post to be filled.

2. There shall be included in particular among the provisions or practices of a Member State referred to in the first subparagraph of paragraph 1 those which:

(a) prescribe a special recruitment procedure for foreign nationals;

(b) limit or restrict the advertising of vacancies in the press or through any other medium or subject it to conditions other than those applicable in respect of employers pursuing their activities in the territory of that Member State;

(c) subject eligibility for employment to conditions of registration with employment offices or impede recruitment of individual workers, where persons who do not reside in the territory of that State are concerned.

Article 4

1. Provisions laid down by law, regulation or administrative action of the Member States which restrict by number or percentage the employment of foreign nationals in any undertaking, branch of activity or region, or at a national level, shall not apply to nationals of the other Member States.

2. When in a Member State the granting of any benefit to undertakings is subject to a minimum percentage of national workers being employed, nationals of the other Member States shall be counted as national workers, subject to the provisions of the Council Directive of 15 October 1963.[2]

Article 5

A national of a Member State who seeks employment in the territory of another Member State shall receive the same assistance there as that afforded by the employment offices in that State to their own nationals seeking employment.

Article 6

1. The engagement and recruitment of a national of one Member State for a post in another Member State shall not depend on medical, vocational or other criteria which are discriminatory on grounds of nationality by comparison with those applied to nationals of the other Member State who wish to pursue the same activity.

2. Nevertheless, a national who holds an offer in his name from an employer in a Member State other than that of which he is a national may have to undergo a vocational test, if the employer expressly requests this when making his offer of employment.

2. OJ No 159, 2.11.1963, p. 2661/63.

Title II. Employment and equality of treatment

Article 7

1. A worker who is a national of a Member State may not, in the territory of another Member State, be treated differently from national workers by reason of his nationality in respect of any conditions of employment and work, in particular as regards remuneration, dismissal, and should he become unemployed, reinstatement or re-employment;

2. He shall enjoy the same social and tax advantages as national workers.

3. He shall also, by virtue of the same right and under the same conditions as national workers, have access to training in vocational schools and retraining centres.

4. Any clause of a collective or individual agreement or of any other collective regulation concerning eligibility for employment, employment, remuneration and other conditions of work or dismissal shall be null and void in so far as it lays down or authorises discriminatory conditions in respect of workers who are nationals of the other Member States.

Article 8

1. A worker who is a national of a Member State and who is employed in the territory of another Member State shall enjoy equality of treatment as regards membership of trade unions and the exercise of rights attaching thereto, including the right to vote [and to be eligible for the administration or management posts of a trade union]; he may be excluded from taking part in the management of bodies governed by public law and from holding an office governed by public law. Furthermore, he shall have the right of eligibility for workers' representative bodies in the undertaking. The provisions of this Article shall not affect laws or regulations in certain Member States which grant more extensive rights to workers coming from the other Member States. [Insert added by Council Regulation 312/76, O.J. L39/2 (Feb. 14, 1976).]

* * *

Article 9

1. A worker who is a national of a Member State and who is employed in the territory of another Member State shall enjoy all the rights and benefits accorded to national workers in matters of housing, including ownership of the housing he needs.

2. Such worker may, with the same right as nationals, put his name down on the housing lists in the region in which he is employed, where such lists exist; he shall enjoy the resultant benefits and priorities.

If his family has remained in the country whence he came, they shall be considered for this purpose as residing in the said region, where national workers benefit from a similar presumption.

Title III. Workers' families

Article 10

1. The following shall, irrespective of their nationality, have the right to install themselves with a worker who is a national of one Member State and who is employed in the territory of another Member State:

(a) his spouse and their descendants who are under the age of 21 years or are dependents;

(b) dependent relatives in the ascending line of the worker and his spouse.

2. Member States shall facilitate the admission of any member of the family not coming within the provisions of paragraph 1 if dependent on the worker referred to above or living under his roof in the country whence he comes.

3. For the purposes of paragraphs 1 and 2, the worker must have available for his family housing considered as normal for national workers in the region where he is employed; this provision, however must not give rise to discrimination between national workers and workers from the other Member States.

Article 11

Where a national of a Member State is pursuing an activity as an employed or self-employed person in the territory of another Member State, his spouse and those of the children who are under the age of 21 years or dependent on him shall have the right to take up any activity as an employed person throughout the territory of that same State, even if they are not nationals of any Member State.

Article 12

The children of a national of a Member State who is or has been employed in the territory of another Member State shall be admitted to that State's general educational, apprenticeship and vocational training courses under the same conditions as the nationals of that State, if such children are residing in its territory.

Member States shall encourage all efforts to enable such children to attend these courses under the best possible conditions.

PART II
CLEARANCE OF VACANCIES AND APPLICATIONS FOR EMPLOYMENT

Title I. Co-operation between the Member States and with the Commission

Article 13

1. The Member States or the Commission shall instigate or together undertake any study of employment or unemployment which they consider necessary for securing freedom of movement for workers within the Community.

The central employment services of the Member States shall co-operate closely with each other and with the Commission with a view to acting jointly as regards the clearing of vacancies and applications for employment within the Community and the resultant placing of workers in employment.

2. To this end the Member States shall designate specialist services which shall be entrusted with organising work in the fields referred to above and co-operating with each other and with the departments of the Commission.

> [Omitted articles 14–48 describe the composition, role and operating procedures of specialist services, the European Co-ordination Office for vacancy clearance, and Advisory and Technical committees.]

8. COUNCIL DIRECTIVE 68/360/EEC

of 15 October 1968
on the abolition of restrictions on movement and residence within the Community for workers of Member States and their families

O.J. English Spec. Ed. 1968–II, 485

THE COUNCIL OF THE EUROPEAN COMMUNITIES,

Having regard to the Treaty establishing the European Economic Community, and in particular Article 49 thereof;

Having regard to the proposal from the Commission;

Having regard to the Opinion of the European Parliament;

Having regard to the Opinion of the Economic and Social Committee;

Whereas Council Regulation (EEC) No 1612/68 fixed the provisions governing freedom of movement for workers within the Community; whereas, consequently, measures should be adopted for the abolition of restrictions which still exist concerning movement and residence within the Community, which conform to the rights and privileges accorded by the said Regulation to nationals of any Member State who move in order to pursue activities as employed persons and to members of their families;

Whereas the rules applicable to residence should, as far as possible, bring the position of workers from other Member States and members of their families into line with that of nationals;

* * *

HAS ADOPTED THIS DIRECTIVE:

Article 1

Member States shall, acting as provided in this Directive, abolish restrictions on the movement and residence of nationals of the said States and of members of their families to whom Regulation (EEC) No 1612/68 applies.

Article 2

1. Member States shall grant the nationals referred to in Article 1 the right to leave their territory in order to take up activities as employed persons and to pursue such activities in the territory of another Member State. Such right shall be exercised simply on production of a valid identity card or passport. Members of the family shall enjoy the same right as the national on whom they are dependent.

2. Member States shall, acting in accordance with their laws, issue to such nationals, or renew, an identity card or passport, which shall state in particular the holder's nationality.

3. The passport must be valid at least for all Member States and for countries through which the holder must pass when travelling between Member States. Where a passport is the only document on which the

holder may lawfully leave the country, its period of validity shall be not less than five years.

4. Member States may not demand from the nationals referred to in Article 1 any exit visa or any equivalent document.

Article 3

1. Member States shall allow the persons referred to in Article 1 to enter their territory simply on production of a valid identity card or passport.

2. No entry visa or equivalent document may be demanded save from members of the family who are not nationals of a Member State. Member States shall accord to such persons every facility for obtaining any necessary visas.

Article 4

1. Member States shall grant the right of residence in their territory to the persons referred to in Article 1 who are able to produce the documents listed in paragraph 3.

2. As proof of the right of residence, a document entitled 'Residence Permit for a National of a Member State of the EEC' shall be issued. This document must include a statement that it has been issued pursuant to Regulation (EEC) No 1612/68 and to the measures taken by the Member States for the implementation of the present Directive. The text of such statement is given in the Annex to this Directive.

3. For the issue of a Residence Permit for a National of a Member State of the EEC, Member States may require only the production of the following documents;

— by the worker;
  (a) the document with which he entered their territory;
  (b) a confirmation of engagement from the employer or a certificate of employment;
— by the members of the worker's family:
  (c) the document with which they entered the territory;
  (d) a document issued by the competent authority of the State of origin or the State whence they came, proving their relationship;
  (e) in the cases referred to in Article 10(1) and (2) of Regulation (EEC) No 1612/68, a document issued by the competent authority of the State of origin or the State whence they came, testifying that they are dependent on the worker or that they live under his roof in such country.

4. A member of the family who is not a national of a Member State shall be issued with a residence document which shall have the same validity as that issued to the worker on whom he is dependent.

Article 5

Completion of the formalities for obtaining a residence permit shall not hinder the immediate beginning of employment under a contract concluded by the applicants.

Article 6

1. The residence permit:

(a) must be valid throughout the territory of the Member State which issued it;

(b) must be valid for at least five years from the date of issue and be automatically renewable.

2. Breaks in residence not exceeding six consecutive months and absence on military service shall not affect the validity of a residence permit.

3. Where a worker is employed for a period exceeding three months but not exceeding a year in the service of an employer in the host State or in the employ of a person providing services, the host Member State shall issue him a temporary residence permit, the validity of which may be limited to the expected period of the employment.

Subject to the provisions of Article 8(1)(c), a temporary residence permit shall be issued also to a seasonal worker employed for a period of more than three months. The period of employment must be shown in the documents referred to in paragraph 4(3)(b).

Article 7

1. A valid residence permit may not be withdrawn from a worker solely on the grounds that he is no longer in employment, either because he is temporarily incapable of work as a result of illness or accident, or because he is involuntarily unemployed, this being duly confirmed by the competent employment office.

2. When the residence permit is renewed for the first time, the period of residence may be restricted, but not to less than twelve months, where the worker has been involuntarily unemployed in the Member State for more than twelve consecutive months.

Article 8

1. Member States shall, without issuing a residence permit, recognise the right of residence in their territory of:

(a) a worker pursuing an activity as an employed person, where the activity is not expected to last for more than three months. The document with which the person concerned entered the territory and a statement by the employer on the expected duration of the employment shall be sufficient to cover his stay * * *.

(b) a worker who, while having his residence in the territory of a Member State to which he returns as a rule, each day or at least once a week, is employed in the territory of another Member State. The competent authority of the State where he is employed may issue such worker with a special permit valid for five years and automatically renewable;

(c) a seasonal worker who holds a contract of employment stamped by the competent authority of the Member State on whose territory he has come to pursue his activity.

* * *

Article 9

1. The residence documents granted to nationals of a Member State of the EEC referred to in this Directive shall be issued and renewed free of charge or on payment of an amount not exceeding the dues and taxes charged for the issue of identity cards to nationals.

* * *

Article 10

Member States shall not derogate from the provisions of this Directive save on grounds of public policy, public security or public health.

* * *

Article 14

This Directive is addressed to the Member States.

ANNEX

Text of the statement referred to in Article 4(2):

'This permit is issued pursuant to Regulation (EEC) No 1612/68 of the Council of the European Communities of 15 October 1968 and to the measures taken in implementation of the Council Directive of 15 October 1968.

In accordance with the provisions of the above-mentioned Regulation, the holder of this permit has the right to take up and pursue an activity as an employed person in _____[1] territory under the same conditions as _____[1] workers.'

---

1. Belgian, German, French, Italian, Luxembourg, Netherlands, according to the country issuing the permit.

9. COUNCIL DIRECTIVE 64/221/EEC

of 25 February 1964

on the co-ordination of special measures concerning the movement and residence of foreign nationals which are justified on grounds of public policy, public security or public health

O.J. English Spec. Ed. 1963–1964, 117

THE COUNCIL OF THE EUROPEAN ECONOMIC COMMUNITY,

Having regard to the Treaty establishing the European Economic Community, and in particular Article 56(2) thereof;

Having regard to Council Regulation No 15 of 16 August 1961[1] on initial measures to bring about free movement of workers within the Community, and in particular Article 47 thereof;

* * *

Having regard to the General Programmes for the abolition of restrictions on freedom of establishment and on freedom to provide services, and in particular Title II of each such programme;

* * *

Whereas co-ordination of provisions laid down by law, regulation or administrative action which provide for special treatment for foreign nationals on grounds of public policy, public security or public health should in the first place deal with the conditions for entry and residence of nationals of Member States moving within the Community either in order to pursue activities as employed or self-employed persons, or as recipients of services;

* * *

Whereas, in each Member State, nationals of other Member States should have adequate legal remedies available to them in respect of the decisions of the administration in such matters;

* * *

HAS ADOPTED THIS DIRECTIVE:

Article 1

1. The provisions of this Directive shall apply to any national of a Member State who resides in or travels to another Member State of the Community, either in order to pursue an activity as an employed or self-employed person, or as a recipient of services.

2. These provisions shall apply also to the spouse and to members of the family who come within the provisions of the regulations and directives adopted in this field in pursuance of the Treaty.

---

1. OJ No 57, 26.8.1961, p. 1073/61.

Article 2

1. This Directive relates to all measures concerning entry into their territory, issue or renewal of residence permits, or expulsion from their territory, taken by Member States on grounds of public policy, public security or public health.

2. Such grounds shall not be invoked to service economic ends.

Article 3

1. Measures taken on grounds of public policy or of public security shall be based exclusively on the personal conduct of the individual concerned.

2. Previous criminal convictions shall not in themselves constitute grounds for the taking of such measures.

3. Expiry of the identity card or passport used by the person concerned to enter the host country and to obtain a residence permit shall not justify expulsion from the territory.

4. The State which issued the identity card or passport shall allow the holder of such document to re-enter its territory without any formality even if the document is no longer valid or the nationality of the holder is in dispute.

Article 4

1. The only diseases or disabilities justifying refusal of entry into a territory or refusal to issue a first residence permit shall be those listed in the Annex to this Directive.

2. Diseases or disabilities occurring after a first residence permit has been issued shall not justify refusal to renew the residence permit or expulsion from the territory.

3. Member States shall not introduce new provisions or practices which are more restrictive than those in force at the date of notification of this Directive.

Article 5

1. A decision to grant or to refuse a first residence permit shall be taken as soon as possible and in any event not later than six months from the date of application for the permit.

The person concerned shall be allowed to remain temporarily in the territory pending a decision either to grant or to refuse a residence permit.

2. The host country may, in cases where this is considered essential, request the Member State of origin of the applicant, and if need be other Member States, to provide information concerning any previous police record. Such enquiries shall not be made as a matter of routine. The Member State consulted shall give its reply within two months.

Article 6

The person concerned shall be informed of the grounds of public policy, public security, or public health upon which the decision taken in his case is based, unless this is contrary to the interests of the security of the State involved.

Article 7

The person concerned shall be officially notified of any decision to refuse the issue or renewal of a residence permit or to expel him from the territory. The period allowed for leaving the territory shall be stated in this notification. Save in cases of urgency, this period shall be not less than fifteen days if the person concerned has not yet been granted a residence permit and not less than one month in all other cases.

Article 8

The person concerned shall have the same legal remedies in respect of any decision concerning entry, or refusing the issue or renewal of a residence permit, or ordering expulsion from the territory, as are available to nationals of the State concerned in respect of acts of the administration.

Article 9

1. Where there is no right of appeal to a court of law, or where such appeal may be only in respect of the legal validity of the decision, or where the appeal cannot have suspensory effect, a decision refusing renewal of a residence permit or ordering the expulsion of the holder of a residence permit from the territory shall not be taken by the administrative authority, save in cases of urgency, until an opinion has been obtained from a competent authority of the host country before which the person concerned enjoys such rights of defence and of assistance or representation as the domestic law of that country provides for.

This authority shall not be the same as that empowered to take the decision refusing renewal of the residence permit or ordering expulsion.

2. Any decision refusing the issue of a first residence permit or ordering expulsion of the person concerned before the issue of the permit shall, where that person so requests, be referred for consideration to the authority whose prior opinion is required under paragraph I. The person concerned shall then be entitled to submit his defence in person, except where this would be contrary to the interests of national security.

* * *

Article 11

This Directive is addressed to the Member States.

ANNEX

A. *Diseases which might endanger public health:*

1. Diseases subject to quarantine listed in International Health Regulation No 2 of the World Health Organisation of 25 May 1951;

2. Tuberculosis of the respiratory system in an active state or showing a tendency to develop;

3. Syphilis;

4. Other infectious diseases or contagious parasitic diseases if they are the subject of provisions for the protection of nationals of the host country.

B. *Diseases and disabilities which might threaten public policy or public security:*

1. Drug addiction;

2. Profound mental disturbance; manifest conditions of psychotic disturbance with agitation, delirium, hallucinations or confusion.

10. COUNCIL DIRECTIVE 90/365/EEC

of 28 June 1990

on the right of residence for employees and self-employed persons who have ceased their occupational activity

O.J. L 180/28 (July 13, 1990)

THE COUNCIL OF THE EUROPEAN COMMUNITIES,

Having regard to the Treaty establishing the European Economic Community, and in particular Article 235 thereof,

Having regard to the proposal from the Commission,[1]

Having regard to the opinion of the European Parliament,[2]

Having regard to the opinion of the Economic and Social Committee,[3]

Whereas Article 3(c) of the Treaty provides that the activities of the Community shall include, as provided in the Treaty, the abolition, as between Member States, of obstacles to freedom of movement for persons;

Whereas Article 8a of the Treaty provides that the internal market must be established by 31 December 1992; whereas the internal market comprises an area without internal frontiers in which the free movement of goods, persons, services and capital is ensured, in accordance with the provisions of the Treaty;

Whereas Articles 48 and 52 of the Treaty provide for freedom of movement for workers and self-employed persons, which entails the right of residence in the Member States in which they pursue their occupational activity; whereas it is desirable that this right of residence also be granted to persons who have ceased their occupational activity even if they have not exercised their right to freedom of movement during their working life;

Whereas beneficiaries of the right of residence must not become an unreasonable burden on the public finances of the host Member State;

Whereas under Article 10 of Regulation (EEC) No 1408/71,[4] as amended by Regulation (EEC) No 1390/81,[5] recipients of invalidity or old age cash benefits or pensions for accidents at work or occupational diseases are entitled to continue to receive these benefits and pensions even if they reside in the territory of a Member State other than that in which the institution responsible for payment is situated;

Whereas this right can only be genuinely exercised if it is also granted to members of the family;

* * *

1. OJ No C 191, 28.7.1989, p. 3; and OJ No C 26, 3.2.1990, p. 19.
2. Opinion delivered on 13 June 1990 (not yet published in the Official Journal).
3. OJ No C 329, 30. 12. 1989, p. 25.
4. OJ No L 149, 5.7.1971, p. 2.
5. OJ No L 143, 29. 5. 1981, p. 1.

Whereas the Treaty does not provide, for the action concerned, powers other than those of Article 235,

HAS ADOPTED THIS DIRECTIVE:

Article 1

1. Member States shall grant the right of residence to nationals of Member States who have pursued an activity as an employee or self-employed person and to members of their families as defined in paragraph 2, provided that they are recipients of an invalidity or early retirement pension, or old age benefits, or of a pension in respect of an industrial accident or disease of an amount sufficient to avoid becoming a burden on the social security system of the host Member State during their period of residence and provided they are covered by sickness insurance in respect of all risks in the host Member State.

The resources of the applicant shall be deemed sufficient where they are higher than the level of resources below which the host Member State may grant social assistance to its nationals, taking into account the personal circumstances of persons admitted pursuant to paragraph 2.

Where the second subparagraph cannot be applied in a Member State the resources of the applicant shall be deemed sufficient if they are higher than the level of the minimum social security pension paid by the host Member State.

2. The following shall, irrespective of their nationality, have the right to install themselves in another Member State with the holder of the right of residence:

(a) his or her spouse and their descendants who are dependents;

(b) dependent relatives in the ascending line of the holder of the right of residence and his or her spouse.

Article 2

1. Exercise of the right of residence shall be evidenced by means of the issue of a document known as a 'Residence permit for a national of a Member State of the EEC', whose validity may be limited to five years on a renewable basis. However, the Member States may, when they deem it to be necessary, require revalidation of the permit at the end of the first two years of residence. Where a member of the family does not hold the nationality of a Member State, he or she shall be issued with a residence document of the same validity as that issued to the national on whom he or she depends.

For the purposes of issuing the residence permit or document, the Member State may require only that the applicant present a valid identity card or passport and provide proof that he or she meets the conditions laid down in Article 1.

2. Articles 2, 3, 6(1)(a) and (2) and Article 9 of Directive 68/360/EEC shall apply *mutatis mutandis* to the beneficiaries of this Directive.

The spouse and the dependent children of a national of a Member State entitled to the right of residence within the territory of a Member State shall be entitled to take up any employed or self-employed activity anywhere within the territory of that Member State, even if they are not nationals of a Member State.

Member States shall not derogate from the provisions of this Directive save on grounds of public policy, public security or public health. In that event, Directive 64/221/EEC shall apply.

3. This Directive shall not affect existing law on the acquisition of second homes.

Article 3

The right of residence shall remain for as long as beneficiaries of that right fulfil the conditions laid down in Article 1.

Article 4

The Commission shall, not more than three years after the date of implementation of this Directive, and at three-yearly intervals thereafter, draw up a report on the application of this Directive and submit it to the European Parliament and the Council.

Article 5

Member States shall bring into force the laws, regulations and administrative provisions necessary to comply with this Directive not later than 30 June 1992. They shall forthwith inform the Commission thereof.

Article 6

This Directive is addressed to the Member States.

11. COUNCIL DIRECTIVE 90/364/EEC

of 28 June 1990
on the right of residence
O.J. L 180/26 (July 13, 1990)

THE COUNCIL OF THE EUROPEAN COMMUNITIES,

Having regard to the Treaty establishing the European Economic Community, and in particular Article 235 thereof,

Having regard to the proposal from the Commission,

Having regard to the opinion of the European Parliament,

Having regard to the opinion of the Economic and Social Committee,

Whereas Article 3(c) of the Treaty provides that the activities of the Community shall include, as provided in the Treaty, the abolition, as between Member States, of obstacles to freedom of movement for persons;

Whereas Article 8a of the Treaty provides that the internal market must be established by 31 December 1992; whereas the internal market comprises an area without internal frontiers in which the free movement of goods, persons, services and capital is ensured in accordance with the provisions of the Treaty;

Whereas national provisions on the right of nationals of the Member States to reside in a Member State other than their own must be harmonized to ensure such freedom of movement;

Whereas beneficiaries of the right of residence must not become an unreasonable burden on the public finances of the host Member State;

Whereas this right can only be genuinely exercised if it is also granted to members of the family;

* * *

Whereas the Treaty does not provide, for the action concerned, powers other than those of Article 235,

HAS ADOPTED THIS DIRECTIVE:

Article 1

1. Member States shall grant the right of residence to nationals of Member States who do not enjoy this right under other provisions of Community law and to members of their families as defined in paragraph 2, provided that they themselves and the members of their families are covered by sickness insurance in respect of all risks in the host Member State and have sufficient resources to avoid becoming a burden on the social assistance system of the host Member State during their period of residence.

The resources referred to in the first subparagraph shall be deemed sufficient where they are higher than the level of resources below which the host Member State may grant social assistance to its nationals, taking into account the personal circumstances of the applicant and, where appropriate, the personal circumstances of persons admitted pursuant to paragraph 2.

Where the second subparagraph cannot be applied in a Member State, the resources of the applicant shall be deemed sufficient if they are higher than the level of the minimum social security pension paid by the host Member State.

2. The following shall, irrespective of their nationality, have the right to install themselves in another Member State with the holder of the right of residence:

(a) his or her spouse and their descendants who are dependents;

(b) dependent relatives in the ascending line of the holder of the right of residence and his or her spouse.

Article 2

1. Exercise of the right of residence shall be evidenced by means of the issue of a document known as a 'Residence permit for a national of a Member State of the EEC', the validity of which may be limited to five years on a renewable basis. However, the Member States may, when they deem it to be necessary, require revalidation of the permit at the end of the first two years of residence. Where a member of the family does not hold the nationality of a Member State, he or she shall be issued with a residence document of the same validity as that issued to the national on whom he or she depends.

For the purpose of issuing the residence permit or document, the Member State may require only that the applicant present a valid identity card or passport and provide proof that he or she meets the conditions laid down in Article 1.

2. Articles 2, 3, 6(1)(a) and (2) and Article 9 of Directive 68/360/EEC shall apply *mutatis mutandis* to the beneficiaries of this Directive.

The spouse and the dependent children of a national of a Member State entitled to the right of residence within the territory of a Member State shall be entitled to take up any employed or self-employed activity anywhere within the territory of that Member State, even if they are not nationals of a Member State.

Member States shall not derogate from the provisions of this Directive save on grounds of public policy, public security or public health. In that event, Directive 64/221/EEC shall apply.

3. This Directive shall not affect existing law on the acquisition of second homes.

Article 3

The right of residence shall remain for as long as beneficiaries of that right fulfil the conditions laid down in Article 1.

Article 4

The Commission shall, not more than three years after the date of implementation of this Directive, and at three-yearly intervals thereafter, draw up a report on the application of this Directive and submit it to the European Parliament and the Council.

Article 5

Member States shall bring into force the laws, regulations and administrative provisions necessary to comply with this Directive not later than 30 June 1992. They shall forthwith inform the Commission thereof.

Article 6

This Directive is addressed to the Member States.

12. COUNCIL DIRECTIVE 90/366/EEC

of 28 June 1990

on the right of residence for students

O.J. L 180/30 (July 13, 1990)

THE COUNCIL OF THE EUROPEAN COMMUNITIES,

Having regard to the Treaty establishing the European Economic Community, and in particular Article 235 thereof,

Having regard to the proposal from the Commission,[1]

Having regard to the opinion of the European Parliament,[2]

Having regard to the opinion of the Economic and Social Committee,[3]

Whereas Article 3(c) of the Treaty provides that the activities of the Community shall include, as provided in the Treaty, the abolition, as between Member States, of obstacles to freedom of movement for persons;

Whereas Article 8a of the Treaty provides that the internal market must be established by 31 December 1992; whereas the internal market comprises an area without internal frontiers in which the free movement of goods, persons, services and capital is ensured in accordance with the provisions of the Treaty;

Whereas, as the Court of Justice has ruled, Articles 128 and 7 of the Treaty prohibit any discrimination between nationals of the Member States as regards access to vocational training in the Community;

Whereas the right of residence for students forms part of a set of related measures designed to promote vocational training;

Whereas beneficiaries of the right of residence must not become an unreasonable burden on the public finances of the host Member State;

Whereas, in the present state of Community law, assistance granted to students, as established by the case law of the Court of Justice, does not fall within the scope of the Treaty within the meaning of Article 7 thereof;

Whereas it is necessary for the Member States to adopt administrative measures to facilitate residence without discrimination;

Whereas the right of residence can only be genuinely exercised if it is granted to the spouse and their dependent children;

* * *

Whereas this Directive does not apply to students who enjoy the right of residence by virtue of the fact that they are or have been effectively engaged in economic activities or are members of the family of a migrant worker;

---

1. OJ No C 191, 28. 7. 1989, p. 2; and OJ No C 26, 3.2.1990, p. 15.
2. Opinion delivered on 13 June 1990 (not yet published in the Official Journal).
3. OJ No C 329, 30. 12. 1989, p. 25.

Whereas the Treaty does not provide, for the action concerned, powers other than those of Article 235,

HAS ADOPTED THIS DIRECTIVE:

Article 1

Member States shall, in order to facilitate access to vocational training, grant the right of residence to any student who is a national of a Member State and who does not enjoy this right under other provisions of Community law, and to the student's spouse and their dependent children, where the student assures the relevant national authority, by means of a declaration or by such alternative means as the student may choose that are at least equivalent, that he has sufficient resources to avoid becoming a burden on the social assistance system of the host Member State during their period of residence, provided that the student is enrolled in a recognized educational establishment for the principal purpose of following a vocational training course there and that they are covered by sickness insurance in respect of all risks in the host Member State.

Article 2

1. The right of residence shall be restricted to the duration of the course of studies in question.

The right of residence shall be evidenced by means of the issue of a document known as a 'Residence permit for a national of a Member State of the EEC', the validity of which may be limited to the duration of the course of studies or to one year where the course lasts longer; in the latter event it shall be renewable annually. Where a member of the family does not hold the nationality of a Member State, he or she shall be issued with a residence document of the same validity as that issued to the national on whom he or she depends.

For the purpose of issuing the residence permit or document, the Member State may require only that the applicant present a valid identity card or passport and provide proof that he or she meets the conditions laid down in Article 1.

2. Articles 2, 3 and 9 of Directive 68/360/EEC shall apply *mutatis mutandis* to the beneficiaries of this Directive.

The spouse and the dependent children of a national of a Member State entitled to the right of residence within the territory of a Member State shall be entitled to take up any employed or self-employed activity anywhere within the territory of that Member State, even if they are not nationals of a Member State.

Member States shall not derogate from the provisions of this Directive save on grounds of public policy, public security or public health: in that event, Articles 2 to 9 of Directive 64/221/EEC shall apply.

Article 3

This Directive shall not establish any entitlement to the payment of maintenance grants by the host Member State on the part of students benefiting from the right of residence.

Article 4

The right of residence shall remain for as long as beneficiaries of that right fulfil the conditions laid down in Article 1.

Article 5

The Commission shall, not more than three years after the date of implementation of this Directive, and at three-yearly intervals thereafter, draw up a report on the application of this Directive and submit it to the European Parliament and the Council.

The Commission shall pay particular attention to any difficulties to which the implementation of Article 1 might give rise in the Member States; it shall, if appropriate, submit proposals to the Council with the aim of remedying such difficulties.

Article 6

Member States shall bring into force the law, regulations and administrative provisions necessary to comply with this Directive not later than 30 June 1992. They shall forthwith inform the Commission thereof.

Article 7

This Directive is addressed to the Member States.

13. GENERAL PROGRAMME

for the abolition of restrictions on freedom of establishment
O.J. English Spec. Ed. 1974, IX, 7

THE COUNCIL OF THE EUROPEAN ECONOMIC COMMUNITY,

Having regard to the provisions of the Treaty, and in particular Articles 54 and 132(5) thereof;

Having regard to the proposal from the Commission;

Having regard to the Opinion of the Economic and Social Committee;

Having regard to the Opinion of the European Parliament;

Has adopted this General Programme for the abolition of restrictions on freedom of establishment within the European Economic Community.

Title I
Beneficiaries

[T]he persons entitled to benefit from the abolition of restrictions on freedom of establishment as set out in this General Programme are:

— nationals of Member States or of the overseas countries and territories, and

— companies and firms formed under the law of a Member State or of an overseas country or territory and having either the seat prescribed by their statutes, or their centre of administration, or their main establishment situated within the Community or in an overseas country or territory,

who wish to establish themselves in order to pursue activities as self-employed persons in a Member State; and

— nationals of Member States or of the overseas countries and territories who are established in a Member State or in an overseas country or territory, and

— companies and firms as above, provided that, where only the seat prescribed by their statutes is situated within the Community or in an overseas country or territory, their activity shows a real and continuous link with the economy of a Member State or of an overseas country or territory; such link shall not be one of nationality, whether of the members of the company or firm, or of the persons holding managerial or supervisory posts therein, or of the holders of the capital,

who wish to set up agencies, branches or subsidiaries in a Member State.

Title II
Entry and Residence

The following steps are to be taken before the end of the second year of the second stage of the transitional period:

A. The provisions laid down by law, Regulation or administrative action which in any Member State govern the entry and residence of nationals of other Member States will, where such provisions are not justified on grounds of public policy, public security or public health, and are liable to hinder those nationals in taking up or pursuing activities as self-employed persons, be so amended, in particular by the abrogation of those having an economic purpose, as to eliminate this source of hindrance;

B. The abolition of provisions laid down by law, Regulation or administrative action which in a Member State prohibit nationals of other Member States working in paid employment in that State from staying on and taking up an activity there in a self-employed capacity even though such nationals satisfy the requirements which they would have to meet if they were entering the Member State in question at the time when they wished to take up the activity concerned.

Title III
Restrictions

Subject to the exceptions or special provisions laid down in the Treaty and in particular to:

— Article 55 concerning activities which are connected with the exercise of official authority in a Member State; and to

— Article 56 concerning provisions on special treatment for foreign nationals on grounds of public policy, public security or public health,

the following restrictions are to be eliminated in accordance with the timetable laid down under Title IV:

A. Any measure which, pursuant to any provision laid down by law, Regulation or administrative action in a Member State, or as the result of the application of such a provision, or of administrative practices, prohibits or hinders nationals of other Member States in their pursuit of an activity as a self-employed person by treating nationals of other Member States differently from nationals of the country concerned.

Such restrictive provisions and practices are in particular those which, in respect of foreign nationals only:

(a) prohibit the taking up or pursuit of an activity as a self-employed person;

(b) make the taking up or pursuit of an activity as a self-employed person subject to an authorization or to the issue of a document such as a foreign trader's permit;

(c) impose additional conditions in respect of the granting of any authorization required for the taking up or pursuit of an activity as a self-employed person;

(d) make the taking up or pursuit of an activity as a self-employed person subject to a period of prior residence or training in the host country;

(e) make the taking up or pursuit of an activity as a self-employed person more costly by through (sic) taxation or other financial burdens, such as a requirement that the person concerned shall lodge a deposit or provide security in the host country;

(f) limit or hinder, by making it more costly or more difficult, access to sources of supply or to distribution outlets;

(g) prohibit or hinder access to any vocational training which is necessary or useful for the pursuit of an activity as a self-employed person;

(h) prohibit foreign nationals from becoming members of companies or firms, or restrict their rights as members, in particular as regards the functions which they may perform within the company or firm;

(i) deny or restrict the right to participate in social security schemes, in particular sickness, accident, invalidity or old age insurance schemes, or the right to receive family allowances;

(j) grant less favourable treatment in the event of nationalization, expropriation or requisition.

The like shall apply to provisions and practices which, in respect of foreign nationals only, exclude, limit or impose conditions on the power to exercise rights normally attaching to an activity as a self-employed person, and in particular the power:

(a) to enter into contracts, in particular contracts for work, business or agricultural tenancies, and contracts of employment, and to enjoy all rights arising under such contracts;

(b) to submit tenders for or to act directly as a party or as a subcontractor in contracts with the State or with any other legal person governed by public law;

(c) to obtain licences or authorizations issued by the State or by any other legal person governed by public law;

(d) to acquire, use or dispose of movable or immovable property or rights therein;

(e) to acquire, use or dispose of intellectual property and all rights deriving therefrom;

(f) to borrow, and in particular to have access to the various forms of credit;

(g) to receive aids granted by the State, whether direct or indirect;

(h) to be a party to legal or administrative proceedings;

(i) to join professional or trade organizations;

where the professional or trade activities of the person concerned necessarily involve the exercise of such power.

Furthermore, included among the abovementioned provisions and practices are those which limit or impair the freedom of personnel belonging to the main establishment in one Member State to take up managerial or supervisory posts in agencies, branches or subsidiaries in another Member State.

B. Any requirements imposed, pursuant to any provision laid down by law, Regulation or administrative action or in consequence of any administrative practice, in respect of the taking up or pursuit of an activity as a self-employed person where, although applicable irrespective of nationality, their effect is exclusively or principally, to hinder the taking up or pursuit of such activity by foreign nationals.

Title IV
Timetable

[The omitted text in Titles IV–VII, together with annexes, sets forth the timetable for legislative action, sector by sector.]

14. COUNCIL DIRECTIVE 86/653/EEC

of 18 December 1986
on the coordination of the laws of the Member States relating to self-employed commercial agents
O.J. L 382/17 (Dec. 31, 1986)

THE COUNCIL OF THE EUROPEAN COMMUNITIES,

Having regard to the Treaty establishing the European Economic Community, and in particular Articles 57(2) and 100 thereof,

Having regard to the proposal from the Commission,[1]

Having regard to the opinion of the European Parliament,[2]

Having regard to the opinion of the Economic and Social Committee,[3]

Whereas the restrictions on the freedom of establishment and the freedom to provide services in respect of activities of intermediaries in commerce, industry and small craft industries were abolished by Directive 64/224/EEC;[4]

Whereas the differences in national laws concerning commercial representation substantially affect the conditions of competition and the carrying-on of that activity within the Community and are detrimental both to the protection available to commercial agents *vis-à-vis* their principals and to the security of commercial transactions; whereas moreover those differences are such as to inhibit substantially the conclusion and operation of commercial representation contracts where principal and commercial agent are established in different Member States;

Whereas trade in goods between Member States should be carried on under conditions which are similar to those of a single market, and this necessitates approximation of the legal systems of the Member States to the extent required for the proper functioning of the common market; whereas in this regard the rules concerning conflict of laws do not, in the matter of commercial representation, remove the inconsistencies referred to above, nor would they even if they were made uniform, and accordingly the proposed harmonization is necessary notwithstanding the existence of those rules;

Whereas in this regard the legal relationship between commercial agent and principal must be given priority;

Whereas it is appropriate to be guided by the principles of Article 117 of the Treaty and to maintain improvements already made, when harmonizing the laws of the Member States relating to commercial agents;

Whereas additional transitional periods should be allowed for certain Member States which have to make a particular effort to adapt their regulations, especially those concerning indemnity for termination of

1. OJ No C 13, 18.1.1977, p. 2; OJ No C 56, 2. 3. 1979, p. 5.
2. OJ No C 239, 9. 10. 1978, p. 17.
3. OJ No C 59, 8. 3. 1978, p. 31.
4. OJ No 56, 4. 4. 1964, p. 869/64.

contract between the principal and the commercial agent, to the requirements of this Directive,

HAS ADOPTED THIS DIRECTIVE:

CHAPTER I
SCOPE
Article 1

1. The harmonization measures prescribed by this Directive shall apply to the laws, regulations and administrative provisions of the Member States governing the relations between commercial agents and their principals.

2. For the purposes of this Directive, 'commercial agent' shall mean a self-employed intermediary who has continuing authority to negotiate the sale or the purchase of goods on behalf of another person, hereinafter called the 'principal', or to negotiate and conclude such transactions on behalf of and in the name of that principal.

3. A commercial agent shall be understood within the meaning of this Directive as not including in particular:

— a person who, in his capacity as an officer, is empowered to enter into commitments binding on a company or association,

— a partner who is lawfully authorized to enter into commitments binding on his partners,

— a receiver, a receiver and manager, a liquidator or a trustee in bankruptcy.

Article 2

1. This Directive shall not apply to:

— commercial agents whose activities are unpaid,

— commercial agents when they operate on commodity exchanges or in the commodity market, or

— the body known as the Crown Agents for Overseas Governments and Administrations, as set up under the Crown Agents Act 1979 in the United Kingdom, or its subsidiaries.

2. Each of the Member States shall have the right to provide that the Directive shall not apply to those persons whose activities as commercial agents are considered secondary by the law of that Member State.

CHAPTER II
RIGHTS AND OBLIGATIONS
Article 3

1. In performing his activities, a commercial agent must look after his principal's interests and act dutifully and in good faith.

2. In particular, a commercial agent must:

(a) make proper efforts to negotiate and, where appropriate, conclude the transactions he is instructed to take care of;

(b) communicate to his principal all the necessary information available to him;

(c) comply with reasonable instructions given by his principal.

Article 4

1. In his relations with his commercial agent, a principal must act dutifully and in good faith.

2. A principal must in particular:

(a) provide his commercial agent with the necessary documentation relating to the goods concerned;

(b) obtain for his commercial agent the information necessary for the performance of the agency contract, and in particular notify the commercial agent within a reasonable period once he anticipates that the volume of commercial transactions will be significantly lower than that which the commercial agent could normally have expected.

3. A principal must, in addition, inform the commercial agent within a reasonable period of his acceptance, refusal, and of any non-execution of a commercial transaction which the commercial agent has procured for the principal.

Article 5

The parties may not derogate from the provisions of Articles 3 and 4.

CHAPTER III
REMUNERATION

Article 6

1. In the absence of any agreement on this matter between the parties, and without prejudice to the application of the compulsory provisions of the Member States concerning the level of remuneration, a commercial agent shall be entitled to the remuneration that commercial agents appointed for the goods forming the subject of his agency contract are customarily allowed in the place where he carries on his activities. If there is no such customary practice a commercial agent shall be entitled to reasonable remuneration taking into account all the aspects of the transaction.

2. Any part of the remuneration which varies with the number or value of business transactions shall be deemed to be commission within the meaning of this Directive.

3. Articles 7 to 12 shall not apply if the commercial agent is not remunerated wholly or in part by commission.

Article 7

1. A commercial agent shall be entitled to commission on commercial transactions concluded during the period covered by the agency contract:

(a) where the transaction has been concluded as a result of his action; or

(b) where the transaction is concluded with a third party whom he has previously acquired as a customer for transactions of the same kind.

2. A commercial agent shall also be entitled to commission on transactions concluded during the period covered by the agency contract:

— either where he is entrusted with a specific geographical area or group of customers,

— or where he has an exclusive right to a specific geographical area or group of customers,

and where the transaction has been entered into with a customer belonging to that area or group.

Member States shall include in their legislation one of the possibilities referred to in the above two indents.

Article 8

A commercial agent shall be entitled to commission on commercial transactions concluded after the agency contract has terminated:

(a) if the transaction is mainly attributable to the commercial agent's efforts during the period covered by the agency contract and if the transaction was entered into within a reasonable period after that contract terminated; or

(b) if, in accordance with the conditions mentioned in Article 7, the order of the third party reached the principal or the commercial agent before the agency contract terminated.

Article 9

A commercial agent shall not be entitled to the commission referred to in Article 7, if that commission is payable, pursuant to Article 8, to the previous commercial agent, unless it is equitable because of the circumstances for the commission to be shared between the commercial agents.

Article 10

1. The commission shall become due as soon as and to the extent that one of the following circumstances obtains:

(a) the principal has executed the transaction; or

(b) the principal should, according to his agreement with the third party, have executed the transaction; or

(c) the third party has executed the transaction.

2. The commission shall become due at the latest when the third party has executed his part of the transaction or should have done so if the principal had executed his part of the transaction, as he should have.

3. The commission shall be paid not later than on the last day of the month following the quarter in which it became due.

4. Agreements to derogate from paragraphs 2 and 3 to the detriment of the commercial agent shall not be permitted.

Article 11

1. The right to commission can be extinguished only if and to the extent that:

— it is established that the contract between the third party and the principal will not be executed, and

— that face is due to a reason for which the principal is not to blame.

2. Any commission which the commercial agent has already received shall be refunded if the right to it is extinguished.

3. Agreements to derogate from paragraph 1 to the detriment of the commercial agent shall not be permitted.

Article 12

1. The principal shall supply his commercial agent with a statement of the commission due, not later than the last day of the month following the quarter in which the commission has become due. This statement shall set out the main components used in calculating the amount of commission.

2. A commercial agent shall be entitled to demand that he be provided with all the information, and in particular an extract from the books, which is available to his principal and which he needs in order to check the amount of the commission due to him.

3. Agreements to derogate from paragraphs 1 and 2 to the detriment of the commercial agent shall not be permitted.

4. This Directive shall not conflict with the internal provisions of Member States which recognize the right of a commercial agent to inspect a principal's books.

CHAPTER IV

CONCLUSION AND TERMINATION OF THE AGENCY CONTRACT

Article 13

1. Each party shall be entitled to receive from the other on request a signed written document setting out the terms of the agency contract including any terms subsequently agreed. Waiver of this right shall not be permitted.

2. Notwithstanding paragraph 1 a Member State may provide that an agency contract shall not be valid unless evidenced in writing.

Article 14

An agency contract for a fixed period which continues to be performed by both parties after that period has expired shall be deemed to be converted into an agency contract for an indefinite period.

Article 15

1. Where an agency contract is concluded for an indefinite period either party may terminate it by notice.

2. The period of notice shall be one month for the first year of the contract, two months for the second year commenced, and three months for the third year commenced and subsequent years. The parties may not agree on shorter periods of notice.

3. Member States may fix the period of notice at four months for the fourth year of the contract, five months for the fifth year and six months for the sixth and subsequent years. They may decide that the parties may not agree to shorter periods.

4. If the parties agree on longer periods than those laid down in paragraphs 2 and 3, the period of notice to be observed by the principal must not be shorter than that to be observed by the commercial agent.

5. Unless otherwise agreed by the parties, the end of the period of notice must coincide with the end of a calendar month.

6. The provisions of this Article shall apply to an agency contract for a fixed period where it is converted under Article 14 into an agency contract for an indefinite period, subject to the proviso that the earlier fixed period must be taken into account in the calculation of the period of notice.

Article 16

Nothing in this Directive shall affect the application of the law of the Member States where the latter provides for the immediate termination of the agency contract:

(a) because of the failure of one party to carry out all or part of his obligations;

(b) where exceptional circumstances arise.

Article 17

1. Member States shall take the measures necessary to ensure that the commercial agent is, after termination of the agency contract, indemnified in accordance with paragraph 2 or compensated for damage in accordance with paragraph 3.

    2. (a) The commercial agent shall be entitled to an indemnity if and to the extent that:
— he has brought the principal new customers or has significantly increased the volume of business with existing customers and the principal continues to derive substantial benefits from the business with such customers, and
— the payment of this indemnity is equitable having regard to all the circumstances and, in particular, the commission lost by the commercial agent on the business transacted with such customers. Member States may provide for such circumstances also to include the application or otherwise of a restraint of trade clause, within the meaning of Article 20;

    (b) The amount of the indemnity may not exceed a figure equivalent to an indemnity for one year calculated from the commercial agent's average annual remuneration over the preceding five years and if the contract goes back less than five years the indemnity shall be calculated on the average for the period in question;

(c) The grant of such an indemnity shall not prevent the commercial agent from seeking damages.

3. The commercial agent shall be entitled to compensation for the damage he suffers as a result of the termination of his relations with the principal.

Such damage shall be deemed to occur particularly when the termination takes place in circumstances:

— depriving the commercial agent of the commission which proper performance of the agency contract would have procured him whilst providing the principal with substantial benefits linked to the commercial agent's activities,

— and/or which have not enabled the commercial agent to amortize the costs and expenses that he had incurred for the performance of the agency contract on the principal's advice.

4. Entitlement to the indemnity as provided for in paragraph 2 or to compensation for damage as provided for under paragraph 3, shall also arise where the agency contract is terminated as a result of the commercial agent's death.

5. The commercial agent shall lose his entitlement to the indemnity in the instances provided for in paragraph 2 or to compensation for damage in the instances provided for in paragraph 3, if within one year following termination of the contract he has not notified the principal that he intends pursuing his entitlement.

6. The Commission shall submit to the Council, within eight years following the date of notification of this Directive, a report on the implementation of this Article, and shall if necessary submit to it proposals for amendments.

Article 18

The indemnity or compensation referred to in Article 17 shall not be payable:

(a) where the principal has terminated the agency contract because of default attributable to the commercial agent which would justify immediate termination of the agency contract under national law;

(b) where the commercial agent has terminated the agency contract, unless such termination is justified by circumstances attributable to the principal or on grounds of age, infirmity or illness of the commercial agent in consequence of which he cannot reasonably be required to continue his activities;

(c) where, with the agreement of the principal, the commercial agent assigns his rights and duties under the agency contract to another person.

Article 19

The parties may not derogate from Articles 17 and 18 to the detriment of the commercial agent before the agency contract expires.

Article 20

1. For the purposes of this Directive, an agreement restricting the business activities of a commercial agent following termination of the agency contract is hereinafter referred to as a restraint of trade clause.

2. A restraint of trade clause shall be valid only if and to the extent that:

(a) it is concluded in writing; and

(b) it relates to the geographical area or the group of customers and the geographical area entrusted to the commercial agent and to the kind of goods covered by his agency under the contract.

3. A restraint of trade clause shall be valid for not more than two years after termination of the agency contract.

4. This Article shall not affect provisions of national law which impose other restrictions on the validity or enforceability of restraint of trade clauses or which enable the courts to reduce the obligations on the parties resulting from such an agreement.

CHAPTER V
GENERAL AND FINAL PROVISIONS

Article 21

Nothing in this Directive shall require a Member State to provide for the disclosure of information where such disclosure would be contrary to public policy.

Article 22

1. Member States shall bring into force the provisions necessary to comply with this Directive before 1 January 1990. They shall forthwith inform the Commission thereof. Such provisions shall apply at least to contracts concluded after their entry into force. They shall apply to contracts in operation by 1 January 1994 at the latest.

2. As from the notification of this Directive, Member States shall communicate to the Commission the main laws, regulations and administrative provisions which they adopt in the field governed by this Directive.

3. However, with regard to Ireland and the United Kingdom, 1 January 1990 referred to in paragraph 1 shall be replaced by 1 January 1994.

With regard to Italy, 1 January 1990 shall be replaced by 1 January 1993 in the case of the obligations deriving from Article 17.

Article 23

This Directive is addressed to the Member States.

15. COUNCIL DIRECTIVE 89/552/EEC

of 3 October 1989

on the coordination of certain provisions laid down by law, regulation or administrative action in Member States concerning the pursuit of television broadcasting activities

O.J. L 298/23 (Oct. 17, 1989)

THE COUNCIL OF THE EUROPEAN COMMUNITIES,

Having regard to the Treaty establishing the European Economic Community, and in particular Articles 57(2) and 66 thereof,

Having regard to the proposal from the Commission,[1]

In cooperation with the European Parliament,[2]

Having regard to the opinion of the Economic and Social Committee,[3]

Whereas the objectives of the Community as laid down in the Treaty include establishing an even closer union among the peoples of Europe, fostering closer relations between the States belonging to the Community, ensuring the economic and social progress of its countries by common action to eliminate the barriers which divide Europe, encouraging the constant improvement of the living conditions of its peoples as well as ensuring the preservation and strengthening of peace and liberty;

Whereas the Treaty provides for the establishment of a common market, including the abolition, as between Member States, of obstacles to freedom of movement for services and the institution of a system ensuring that competition in the common market is not distorted;

Whereas broadcasts transmitted across frontiers by means of various technologies are one of the ways of pursuing the objectives of the Community; whereas measures should be adopted to permit and ensure the transition from national markets to a common programme production and distribution market and to establish conditions of fair competition without prejudice to the public interest role to be discharged by the television broadcasting services;

* * *

Whereas television broadcasting constitutes, in normal circumstances, a service within the meaning of the Treaty;

Whereas the Treaty provides for free movement of all services normally provided against payment, without exclusion on grounds of their cultural or other content and without restriction of nationals of Member States established in a Community country other than that of the person for whom the services are intended;

---

1. OJ No C 179, 17.7. 1986, p. 4.
2. OJ No C 49, 22.2. 1988, p. 53, and OJ No C 158, 26.6.1989.
3. OJ No C 232, 31.8.1987, p. 29.

Whereas this right as applied to the broadcasting and distribution of television services is also a specific manifestation in Community law of a more general principle, namely the freedom of expression as enshrined in Article 10(1) of the Convention for the Protection of Human Rights and Fundamental Freedoms ratified by all Member States; whereas for this reason the issuing of directives on the broadcasting and distribution of television programmes must ensure their free movement in the light of the said Article and subject only to the limits set by paragraph 2 of that Article and by Article 56(1) of the Treaty;

Whereas the laws, regulations and administrative measures in Member States concerning the pursuit of activities as television broadcasters and cable operators contain disparities, some of which may impede the free movement of broadcasts within the Community and may distort competition within the common market;

Whereas all such restrictions on freedom to provide broadcasting services within the Community must be abolished under the Treaty;

Whereas such abolition must go hand in hand with coordination of the applicable laws; whereas this coordination must be aimed at facilitating the pursuit of the professional activities concerned and, more generally, the free movement of information and ideas within the Community;

Whereas it is consequently necessary and sufficient that all broadcasts comply with the law of Member State from which they emanate;

Whereas this Directive lays down the minimum rules needed to guarantee freedom of transmission in broadcasting; whereas, therefore, it does not affect the responsibility of the Member States and their authorities with regard to the organization—including the systems of licensing, administrative authorization or taxation—financing and the content of programmes; whereas the independence of cultural developments in the Member States and the preservation of cultural diversity in the Community therefore remain unaffected;

* * *

Whereas this Directive, being confined specifically to television broadcasting rules, is without prejudice to existing or future Community acts of harmonization, in particular to satisfy mandatory requirements concerning the protection of consumers and the fairness of commercial transactions and competition;

Whereas co-ordination is nevertheless needed to make it easier for persons and industries producing programmes having a cultural objective to take up and pursue their activities;

Whereas minimum requirements in respect of all public or private Community television programmes for European audio-visual productions have been a means of promoting production, independent production and distribution in the abovementioned industries and are complementary to other instruments which are already or will be proposed to favour the same objective;

Whereas it is therefore necessary to promote markets of sufficient size for television productions in the Member States to recover necessary investments not only by establishing common rules opening up national markets but also by envisaging for European productions where practicable and by appropriate means a majority proportion in television programmes of all Member States;

* * *

Whereas in order to ensure that the interests of consumers as television viewers are fully and properly protected, it is essential for television advertising to be subject to a certain number of minimum rules and standards and that the Member States must maintain the right to set more detailed or stricter rules and in certain circumstances to lay down different conditions for television broadcasters under their jurisdiction;

* * *

HAS ADOPTED THIS DIRECTIVE:

CHAPTER I

DEFINITIONS

Article 1

For the purpose of this Directive:

(a) 'television broadcasting' means the initial transmission by wire or over the air, including that by satellite, in unencoded or encoded form, of television programmes intended for reception by the public. It includes the communication of programmes between undertakings with a view to their being relayed to the public. It does not include communication services providing items of information or other messages on individual demand such as telecopying, electronic data banks and other similar services;

(b) 'television advertising' means any form of announcement broadcast in return for payment or for similar consideration by a public or private undertaking in connection with a trade, business, craft or profession in order to promote the supply of goods or services, including immovable property, or rights and obligations, in return for payment.

Except for the purposes of Article 18, this does not include direct offers to the public for the sale, purchase or rental of products or for the provision of services in return for payment;

(c) 'surreptitious advertising' means the representation in words or pictures of goods, services, the name, the trade mark or the activities of a producer of goods or a provider of services in programmes when such representation is intended by the broadcaster to serve advertising and might mislead the public as to its nature. Such representation is considered to be intentional in particular if it is done in return for payment or for similar consideration;

(d) 'sponsorship' means any contribution made by a public or private undertaking not engaged in television broadcasting activities or in the production of audio-visual works, to the financing of television programmes with a view to promoting its name, its trade mark, its image, its activities or its products.

CHAPTER II
GENERAL PROVISIONS

Article 2

1. Each Member State shall ensure that all television broadcasts transmitted

— by broadcasters under its jurisdiction, or

— by broadcasters who, while not being under the jurisdiction of any Member State, make use of a frequency or a satellite capacity granted by, or a satellite up-link situated in, that Member State,

comply with the law applicable to broadcasts intended for the public in that Member State.

2. Member States shall ensure freedom of reception and shall not restrict retransmission on their territory of television broadcasts from other Member States for reasons which fall within the fields coordinated by this Directive.

* * *

Article 3

1. Member States shall remain free to require television broadcasters under their jurisdiction to lay down more detailed or stricter rules in the areas covered by this Directive.

2. Member States shall, by appropriate means, ensure, within the framework of their legislation, that television broadcasters under their jurisdiction comply with the provisions of this Directive.

CHAPTER III
PROMOTION OF DISTRIBUTION AND PRODUCTION OF TELEVISION PROGRAMMES

Article 4

1. Member States shall ensure where practicable and by appropriate means, that broadcasters reserve for European works, within the meaning of Article 6, a majority proportion of their transmission time, excluding the time appointed to news, sports events, games, advertising and teletext services. This proportion, having regard to the broadcaster's informational, educational, cultural and entertainment responsibilities to its viewing public, should be achieved progressively, on the basis of suitable criteria.

2. Where the proportion laid down in paragraph 1 cannot be attained, it must not be lower than the average for 1988 in the Member State concerned.

However, in respect of the Hellenic Republic and the Portuguese Republic, the year 1988 shall be replaced by the year 1990.

3. From 3 October 1991, the Member States shall provide the Commission every two years with a report on the application of this Article and Article 5.

That report shall in particular include a statistical statement on the achievement of the proportion referred to in this Article and Article 5 for each of the television programmes falling within the jurisdiction of the Member State concerned, the reasons, in each case, for the failure to attain that proportion and the measures adopted or envisaged in order to achieve it.

The Commission shall inform the other Member States and the European Parliament of the reports, which shall be accompanied, where appropriate, by an opinion. * * *

4. The Council shall review the implementation of this Article on the basis of a report from the Commission accompanied by any proposals for revision that it may deem appropriate no later than the end of the fifth year from the adoption of the Directive.

* * *

Article 5

Member States shall ensure, where practicable and by appropriate means, that broadcasters reserve at least 10% of their transmission time, excluding the time appointed to news, sports events, games, advertising and teletext services, or alternately, at the discretion of the Member State, at least 10% of their programming budget, for European works created by producers who are independent of broadcasters. * * *

Article 6

1. Within the meaning of this chapter, 'European works' means the following:

(a) works originating from Member States of the Community and, as regards television broadcasters falling within the jurisdiction of the Federal Republic of Germany, works from German territories where the Basic Law does not apply and fulfilling the conditions of paragraph 2;

(b) works originating from European third States party to the European Convention on Transfrontier Television of the Council of Europe and fulfilling the conditions of paragraph 2;

(c) works originating from other European third countries and fulfilling the conditions of paragraph 3.

2. The works referred to in paragraph 1(a) and (b) are works mainly made with authors and workers residing in one or more States referred to in paragraph 1(a) and (b) provided that they comply with one of the following three conditions:

(a) they are made by one or more producers established in one or more of those States; or

(b) production of the works is supervised and actually controlled by one or more producers established in one or more of those States; or

(c) the contribution of co-producers of those States to the total co-production costs is preponderant and the co-production is not controlled by one or more producers established outside those States.

3. The works referred to in paragraph 1(c) are works made exclusively or in co-production with producers established in one or more Member State by producers established in one or more European third countries with which the Community will conclude agreements in accordance with the procedures of the Treaty, if those works are mainly made with authors and workers residing in one or more European States.

* * *

Article 7

Member States shall ensure that the television broadcasters under their jurisdiction do not broadcast any cinematographic work, unless otherwise agreed between its rights holders and the broadcaster, until two years have elapsed since the work was first shown in cinemas in one of the Member States of the Community; in the case of cinematographic works co-produced by the broadcaster, this period shall be one year.

Article 8

Where they consider it necessary for purposes of language policy, the Member States, whilst observing Community law, may as regards some or all programmes of television broadcasters under their jurisdiction, lay down more detailed or stricter rules in particular on the basis of language criteria.

Article 9

This chapter shall not apply to local television broadcasts not forming part of a national network.

CHAPTER IV

TELEVISION ADVERTISING AND SPONSORSHIP

Article 10

1. Television advertising shall be readily recognizable as such and kept quite separate from other parts of the programme service by optical and/or acoustic means.

2. Isolated advertising spots shall remain the exception.

3. Advertising shall not use subliminal techniques.

4. Surreptitious advertising shall be prohibited.

Article 11

1. Advertisements shall be inserted between programmes. Provided the conditions contained in paragraphs 2 to 5 of this Article are fulfilled,

advertisements may also be inserted during programmes in such a way that the integrity and value of the programme, taking into account natural breaks in and the duration and nature of the programme, and the rights of the rights holders are not prejudiced.

* * *

3. The transmission of audiovisual works such as feature films and films made for television (excluding series, serials, light entertainment programmes and documentaries), provided their programmed duration is more than 45 minutes, may be interrupted once for each complete period of 45 minutes. * * *

* * *

5. Advertisements shall not be inserted in any broadcast of a religious service. News and current affairs programmes, documentaries, religious programmes, and children's programmes, when their programmed duration is less than 30 minutes shall not be interrupted by advertisements. If their programmed duration is of 30 minutes or longer, the provisions of the previous paragraphs shall apply.

Article 12

Television advertising shall not:

(a) prejudice respect for human dignity;

(b) include any discrimination on grounds of race, sex or nationality;

(c) be offensive to religious or political beliefs;

(d) encourage behaviour prejudicial to health or to safety;

(e) encourage behaviour prejudicial to the protection of the environment.

Article 13

All forms of television advertising for cigarettes and other tobacco products shall be prohibited.

Article 14

Television advertising for medicinal products and medical treatment available only on prescription in the Member State within whose jurisdiction the broadcaster falls shall be prohibited.

Article 15

Television advertising for alcoholic beverages shall comply with the following criteria:

(a) it may not be aimed specifically at minors or, in particular, depict minors consuming these beverages;

(b) it shall not link the consumption of alcohol to enhanced physical performance or to driving;

(c) it shall not create the impression that the consumption of alcohol contributes towards social or sexual success;

(d) it shall not claim that alcohol has therapeutic qualities or that it is a stimulant, a sedative or a means of resolving personal conflicts;

(e) it shall not encourage immoderate consumption of alcohol or present abstinence or moderation in a negative light;

(f) it shall not place emphasis on high alcoholic content as being a positive quality of the beverages.

Article 16

Television advertising shall not cause moral or physical detriment to minors, and shall therefore comply with the following criteria for their protection:

(a) it shall not directly exhort minors to buy a product or a service by exploiting their inexperience or credulity;

(b) it shall not directly encourage minors to persuade their parents or others to purchase the goods or services being advertised;

(c) it shall not exploit the special trust minors place in parents, teachers or other persons;

(d) it shall not unreasonably show minors in dangerous situations.

Article 17

1. Sponsored television programmes shall meet the following requirements:

(a) the content and scheduling of sponsored programmes may in no circumstances be influenced by the sponsor in such a way as to affect the responsibility and editorial independence of the broadcaster in respect of programmes;

(b) they must be clearly identified as such by the name and/or logo of the sponsor at the beginning and/or the end of the programmes;

(c) they must not encourage the purchase or rental of the products or services of the sponsor or a third party, in particular by making special promotional references to those products or services.

2. Television programmes may not be sponsored by natural or legal persons whose principal activity is the manufacture or sale of products, or the provision of services, the advertising of which is prohibited by Article 13 or 14.

3. News and current affairs programmes may not be sponsored.

Article 18

1. The amount of advertising shall not exceed 15% of the daily transmission time. * * *

2. The amount of spot advertising within a given one-hour period shall not exceed 20%.

* * *

Article 19

Member States may lay down stricter rules than those in Article 18 for programming time and the procedures for television broadcasting for television broadcasters under their jurisdiction, so as to reconcile demand for televised advertising with the public interest, taking account in particular of:

(a) the role of television in providing information, education, culture and entertainment;

(b) the protection of pluralism of information and of the media.

* * *

CHAPTER V
PROTECTION OF MINORS
Article 22

Member States shall take appropriate measures to ensure that television broadcasts by broadcasters under their jurisdiction do not include programmes which might seriously impair the physical, mental or moral development of minors, in particular those that involve pornography or gratuitous violence. This provision shall extend to other programmes which are likely to impair the physical, mental or moral development of minors, except where it is ensured, by selecting the time of the broadcast or by any technical measure, that minors in the area of transmission will not normally hear or see such broadcasts.

Member States shall also ensure that broadcasts do not contain any incitement to hatred on grounds of race, sex, religion or nationality.

CHAPTER VI
RIGHT OF REPLY
Article 23

1. Without prejudice to other provisions adopted by the Member States under civil, administrative or criminal law, any natural or legal person, regardless of nationality, whose legitimate interests, in particular reputation and good name, have been damaged by an assertion of incorrect facts in a television programme must have a right of reply or equivalent remedies.

2. A right of reply or equivalent remedies shall exist in relation to all broadcasters under the jurisdiction of a Member State.

3. Member States shall adopt the measures needed to establish the right of reply or the equivalent remedies and shall determine the procedure to be followed for the exercise thereof. In particular, they shall ensure that a sufficient time span is allowed and that the procedures are such that the right or equivalent remedies can be exercised appropriately by natural or legal persons resident or established in other Member States.

* * *

CHAPTER VII
FINAL PROVISIONS

* * *

Article 25

1. Member States shall bring into force the laws, regulations and administrative provisions necessary to comply with this Directive not later than 3 October 1991.

* * *

Article 26

Not later than the end of the fifth year after the date of adoption of this Directive and every two years thereafter, the Commission shall submit to the European Parliament, the Council, and the Economic and Social Committee a report on the application of this Directive and, if necessary, make further proposals to adapt it to developments in the field of television broadcasting.

Article 27

This Directive is addressed to the Member States.

16. FIRST COUNCIL DIRECTIVE 68/151/EEC

of 9 March 1968

on coordination of safeguards which, for the protection of the interests of members and others, are required by Member States of companies within the meaning of the second paragraph of Article 58 of the Treaty, with a view to making such safeguards equivalent throughout the Community

O.J. English Spec. Ed.1968–I, 41

THE COUNCIL OF THE EUROPEAN COMMUNITIES,

Having regard to the Treaty establishing the European Economic Community, and in particular Article 54(3)(g) thereof;

Having regard to the General Programme for the abolition of restrictions on freedom of establishment, and in particular Title VI thereof;

Having regard to the proposal from the Commission;

Having regard to the Opinion of the European Parliament;

Having regard to the Opinion of the Economic and Social Committee;

Whereas the co-ordination provided for in Article 54(3)(g) and in the General Programme for the abolition of restrictions on freedom of establishment is a matter of urgency, especially in regard to companies limited by shares or otherwise having limited liability, since the activities of such companies often extend beyond the frontiers of national territories;

* * *

HAS ADOPTED THIS DIRECTIVE:

Article 1

The co-ordination measures prescribed by this Directive shall apply to the laws, regulations and administrative provisions of the Member States relating to the following types of company:

— *In Germany:*

die Aktiengesellschaft, die Kommanditgesellschaft auf Aktien, die Gesellschaft mit beschränkter Haftung;

— *In Belgium:*

de naamloze vennootschap	la société anonyme,
de commanditaire vennootschap op aandelen	la société en commandite par actions,
de personen vennootschap met beperkte aansprakelijkheid;	la société de personnes a responsabilité limitée;

— *In France:*

la société anonyme, la société en commandite par actions, la société a responsabilité limitée;

— *In Italy:*

società per azioni, società in accomandita per azioni, società a responsabilità limitata;

— *In Luxembourg:*

la société anonyme, la société en commandite par actions, la société a responsabilité limitée;

— *In the Netherlands:*

de naamloze vennootschap, de commanditaire vennootschap op aandelen.

SECTION 1
DISCLOSURE
Article 2

1. Member States shall take the measures required to ensure compulsory disclosure by companies of at least the following documents and particulars:

(a) The instrument of constitution, and the statutes if they are contained in a separate instrument;

(b) Any amendments to the instruments mentioned in (a), including any extension of the duration of the company;

(c) After every amendment of the instrument of constitution or of the statutes, the complete text of the instrument or statutes as amended to date;

(d) The appointment, termination of office and particulars of the persons who either as a body constituted pursuant to law or as members of any such body:

(i) are authorised to represent the company in dealings with third parties and in legal proceedings;

(ii) take part in the administration, supervision or control of the company.

It must appear from the disclosure whether the persons authorised to represent the company may do so alone or must act jointly;

(e) At least once a year, the amount of the capital subscribed, where the instrument of constitution or the statutes mention an authorised capital, unless any increase in the capital subscribed necessitates an amendment of the statutes;

(f) The balance sheet and the profit and loss account for each financial year. The document containing the balance sheet shall give particulars of the persons who are required by law to certify it.

[Modified by the Fourth Company Directive]

* * *

(g) Any transfer of the seat of the company;

(h) The winding up of the company;

(i) Any declaration of nullity of the company by the courts;

(j) The appointment of liquidators, particulars concerning them, and their respective powers, unless such powers are expressly and exclusively derived from law or from the statutes of the company;

(k) The termination of the liquidation and, in Member States where striking off the register entails legal consequences, the fact of any such striking off.

* * *

Article 3

1. In each Member State a file shall be opened in a central register, commercial register or companies register, for each of the companies registered therein.

2. All documents and particulars which must be disclosed in pursuance of Article 2 shall be kept in the file or entered in the register; the subject matter of the entries in the register must in every case appear in the file.

3. A copy of the whole or any part of the documents or particulars referred to in Article 2 must be obtainable by application in writing at a price not exceeding the administrative cost thereof.

Copies supplied shall be certified as 'true copies', unless the applicant dispenses with such certification.

4. Disclosure of the documents and particulars referred to in paragraph 2 shall be effected by publication in the national gazette appointed for that purpose by the Member State, either of the full or partial text, or by means of a reference to the document which has been deposited in the file or entered in the register.

* * *

Article 4

Member States shall prescribe that letters and order forms shall state the following particulars:

— the register in which the file mentioned in Article 3 is kept, together with the number of the company in that register;

— the legal form of the company, the location of its seat and, where appropriate, the fact that the company is being wound up.

Where in these documents mention is made of the capital of the company, the reference shall be to the capital subscribed and paid up.

Article 5

Each Member State shall determine by which persons the disclosure formalities are to be carried out.

Article 6

Member States shall provide for appropriate penalties in case of:

— failure to disclose the balance sheet and profit and loss account as required by Article 2(1)(f);
— omission from commercial documents of the compulsory particulars provided for in Article 4.

SECTION II
VALIDITY OF OBLIGATIONS ENTERED INTO BY A COMPANY

Article 7

If, before a company being formed has acquired legal personality, action has been carried out in its name and the company does not assume the obligations arising from such action, the persons who acted shall, without limit, be jointly and severally liable therefor, unless otherwise agreed.

* * *

Article 9

1. Acts done by the organs of the company shall be binding upon it even if those acts are not within the objects of the company, unless such acts exceed the powers that the law confers or allows to be conferred on those organs.

However, Member States may provide that the company shall not be bound where such acts are outside the objects of the company, if it proves that the third party knew that the act was outside those objects or could not in view of the circumstances have been unaware of it; disclosure of the statutes shall not of itself be sufficient proof thereof.

2. The limits on the powers of the organs of the company, arising under the statutes or from a decision of the competent organs, may never be relied on as against third parties, even if they have been disclosed.

* * *

SECTION III
NULLITY OF THE COMPANY

Article 10

In all Member States whose laws do not provide for preventive control, administrative or judicial, at the time of formation of a company, the instrument of constitution, the company statutes and any amendments to those documents shall be drawn up and certified in due legal form.

Article 11

The laws of the Member States may not provide for the nullity of companies otherwise than in accordance with the following provisions:

1. Nullity must be ordered by decision of a court of law;

2. Nullity may be ordered only on the following grounds:

(a) that no instrument of constitution was executed or that the rules of preventive control or the requisite legal formalities were not complied with;

(b) that the objects of the company are unlawful or contrary to public policy;

(c) that the instrument of constitution or the statutes do not state the name of the company, the amount of the individual subscriptions of capital, the total amount of the capital subscribed or the objects of the company;

(d) failure to comply with the provisions of the national law concerning the minimum amount of capital to be paid up;

(e) the incapacity of all the founder members;

* * *

Article 12

* * *

2. Nullity shall entail the winding up of the company, as may dissolution.

* * *

SECTION IV
GENERAL PROVISIONS

* * *

Article 14

This Directive is addressed to the Member States.

17. SECOND COUNCIL DIRECTIVE 77/91/EEC

of 13 December 1976

on coordination of safeguards which, for the protection of the interests of members and others, are required by Member States of companies within the meaning of the second paragraph of Article 58 of the Treaty, in respect of the formation of public limited liability companies and the maintenance and alteration of their capital, with a view to making such safeguards equivalent

O.J. L. 26/1 (Jan. 31, 1977)

THE COUNCIL OF THE EUROPEAN COMMUNITIES,

Having regard to the Treaty establishing the European Economic Community, and in particular Article 54(3)(g) thereof,

Having regard to the proposal from the Commission,

Having regard to the opinion of the European Parliament,

Having regard to the opinion of the Economic and Social Committee,

Whereas the coordination provided for in Article 54(3)(g) and in the General Programme for the abolition of restrictions on freedom of establishment, which was begun by Directive 68/151/EEC, is especially important in relation to public limited liability companies, because their activities predominate in the economy of the Member States and frequently extend beyond their national boundaries;

Whereas in order to ensure minimum equivalent protection for both shareholders and creditors of public limited liability companies, the coordination of national provisions relating to their formation and to the maintenance, increase or reduction of their capital is particularly important;

* * *

Whereas Community provisions should be adopted for maintaining the capital, which constitutes the creditors' security, in particular by prohibiting any reduction thereof by distribution to shareholders where the latter are not entitled to it and by imposing limits on the company's right to acquire its own shares;

Whereas it is necessary, having regard to the objectives of Article 54(3)(g), that the Member States' laws relating to the increase or reduction of capital ensure that the principles of equal treatment of shareholders in the same position and of protection of creditors whose claims exist prior to the decision on reduction are observed and harmonized,

HAS ADOPTED THIS DIRECTIVE:

Article 1

1. The coordination measures prescribed by this Directive shall apply to the provisions laid down by law, regulation or administrative action in Member States relating to the following types of company:

— *in Belgium:*
la société anonyme / de naamloze vennootschap;
— *in Denmark:*
aktieselskabet;
— *in France:*
la société anonyme;
— *in Germany:*
die Aktiengesellschaft;
— *in Ireland:*
the public company limited by shares,
the public company limited by guarantee and having a share capital;
— *in Italy:*
la società per azioni;
— *in Luxembourg:*
la société anonyme;
— *in the Netherlands:*
de naamloze vennootschap;
— *in the United Kingdom:*
the public company limited by shares,
the public company limited by guarantee and having a share capital.

The name for any company of the above types shall comprise or be accompanied by a description which is distinct from the description required of other types of companies.

* * *

Article 2

The statutes or the instrument of incorporation of the company shall always give at least the following information:

(a) the type and name of the company;
(b) the objects of the company;
(c) — when the company has no authorized capital, the amount of the subscribed capital,
— when the company has an authorized capital, the amount thereof and also the amount of the capital subscribed at the time the company is incorporated or is authorized to commence business, and at the time of any change in the authorized capital, without prejudice to Article 2(1)(e) of Directive 68/151/EEC;
(d) in so far as they are not legally determined, the rules governing the number of and the procedure for appointing members of the bodies responsible for representing the company with regard to third parties, administration, management, supervision or control of the company and the allocation of powers among those bodies;
(e) the duration of the company, except where this is indefinite.

Article 3

The following information at least must appear in either the statutes or the instrument of incorporation or a separate document published in accordance with the procedure laid down in the laws of each Member State in accordance with Article 3 of Directive 68/151/EEC:

(a) the registered office;

(b) the nominal value of the shares subscribed and, at least once a year, the number thereof;

(c) the number of shares subscribed without stating the nominal value, where such shares may be issued under national law;

(d) the special conditions if any limiting the transfer of shares;

(e) where there are several classes of shares, the information under (b), (c) and (d) for each class and the rights attaching to the shares of each class;

(f) whether the shares are registered or bearer, where national law provides for both types, and any provisions relating to the conversion of such shares unless the procedure is laid down by law;

(g) the amount of the subscribed capital paid up at the time the company is incorporated or is authorized to commence business;

(h) the nominal value of the shares or, where there is not nominal value, the number of shares issued for a consideration other than in cash, together with the nature of the consideration and the name of the person providing this consideration;

(i) the identity of the natural or legal persons or companies or firms by whom or in whose name the statutes or the instrument of incorporation, or where the company was not formed at the same time, the drafts of these documents, have been signed;

(j) the total amount, or at least an estimate, of all the costs payable by the company or chargeable to it by reason of its formation and, where appropriate, before the company is authorized to commence business;

(k) any special advantage granted, at the time the company is formed or up to the time it receives authorization to commence business, to anyone who has taken part in the formation of the company or in transactions leading to the grant of such authorization.

* * *

Article 6

1. The laws of the Member States shall require that, in order that a company may be incorporated or obtain authorization to commence business, a minimum capital shall be subscribed the amount of which shall be not less than 25,000 European [currency units (ECUs)].

* * *

Article 7

The subscribed capital may be formed only of assets capable of economic assessment. However, an undertaking to perform work or supply services may not form part of these assets.

Article 8

1. Shares may not be issued at a price lower than their nominal value, or, where there is no nominal value, their accountable par.

* * *

Article 9

1. Shares issued for a consideration must be paid up at the time the company is incorporated or is authorized to commence business at not less than 25% of their nominal value or, in the absence of a nominal value, their accountable par.

2. However, where shares are issued for a consideration other than in cash at the time the company is incorporated or is authorized to commence business, the consideration must be transferred in full within five years of that time.

Article 10

1. A report on any consideration other than in cash shall be drawn up before the company is incorporated or is authorized to commence business, by one or more independent experts appointed or approved by an administrative or judicial authority. Such experts may be natural persons as well as legal persons and companies or firms under the laws of each Member State.

2. The experts' report shall contain at least a description of each of the assets comprising the consideration as well as of the methods of valuation used and shall state whether the values arrived at by the application of these methods correspond at least to the number and nominal value or, where there is no nominal value, to the accountable par and, where appropriate, to the premium on the shares to be issued for them.

3. The expert's report shall be published in the manner laid down by the laws of each Member State, in accordance with Article 3 of Directive 68/151/EEC.

* * *

Article 15

1. (a) Except for cases of reductions of subscribed capital, no distribution to shareholders may be made when on the closing date of the last financial year the net assets as set out in the company's annual accounts are, or following such a distribution would become, lower than the amount of the subscribed capital plus those reserves which may not be distributed under the law or the statutes.

* * *

(c) The amount of a distribution to shareholders may not exceed the amount of the profits at the end of the last financial year plus any profits brought forward and sums drawn from reserves available for this purpose, less any losses brought forward and sums placed to reserve in accordance with the law or the statutes.

(d) The expression 'distribution' used in subparagraphs (a) and (c) includes in particular the payment of dividends and of interest relating to shares.

* * *

Article 17

1. In the case of a serious loss of the subscribed capital, a general meeting of shareholders must be called within the period laid down by the laws of the Member States, to consider whether the company should be wound up or any other measures taken.

2. The amount of a loss deemed to be serious within the meaning of paragraph 1 may not be set by the laws of Member States at a figure higher than half the subscribed capital.

Article 18

1. The shares of a company may not be subscribed for by the company itself.

* * *

Article 19

1. Where the laws of a Member State permit a company to acquire its own shares, either itself or through a person acting in his own name but on the company's behalf, they shall make such acquisitions subject to at least the following conditions:

(a) authorization shall be given by the general meeting, which shall determine the terms and conditions of such acquisitions, and in particular the maximum number of shares to be acquired, the duration of the period for which the authorization is given and which may not exceed 18 months, and, in the case of acquisition for value, the maximum and minimum consideration. Members of the administrative or management body shall be required to satisfy themselves that at the time when each authorized acquisition is effected the conditions referred to in subparagraphs (b), (c) and (d) are respected;

(b) the nominal value or, in the absence thereof, the accountable par of the acquired shares, including shares previously acquired by the company and held by it, and shares acquired by a person acting in his own name but on the company's behalf, may not exceed 10% of the subscribed capital;

(c) the acquisitions may not have the effect of reducing the net assets below the amount mentioned in Article 15(1)(a);

(d) only fully paid-up shares may be included in the transaction.

2. The laws of a Member State may provide for derogations from the first sentence of paragraph 1(a) where the acquisition of a company's own

shares is necessary to prevent serious and imminent harm to the company. * * *

3. Member States may decide not to apply the first sentence of paragraph 1(a) to shares acquired by either the company itself or by a person acting in his own name but on the company's behalf, for distribution to that company's employees or to the employees of an associate company. Such shares must be distributed within 12 months of their acquisition.

* * *

Article 21

Shares acquired in contravention of Articles 19 and 20 shall be disposed of within one year of their acquisition. Should they not be disposed of within that period, Article 20(3) shall apply.

Article 22

1. Where the laws of a Member State permit a company to acquire its own shares, either itself or through a person acting in his own name but on the company's behalf, they shall make the holding of these shares at all times subject to at least the following conditions:

(a) among the rights attaching to the shares, the right to vote attaching to the company's own shares shall in any event be suspended;

(b) if the shares are included among the assets shown in the balance sheet, a reserve of the same amount, unavailable for distribution, shall be included among the liabilities.

* * *

Article 23

1. A company may not advance funds, nor make loans, nor provide security, with a view to the acquisition of its shares by a third party.

2. Paragraph 1 shall not apply to transactions concluded by banks and other financial institutions in the normal course of business, nor to transactions effected with a view to the acquisition of shares by or for the company's employees or the employees of an associate company. However, these transactions may not have the effect of reducing the net assets below the amount specified in Article 15(1)(a).

* * *

Article 25

1. Any increase in capital must be decided upon by the general meeting. Both this decision and the increase in the subscribed capital shall be published in the manner laid down by the laws of each Member State, in accordance with Article 3 of Directive 68/151/EEC.

2. Nevertheless, the statutes or instrument of incorporation or the general meeting, the decision of which must be published in accordance with the rules referred to in paragraph 1, may authorize an increase in

the subscribed capital up to a maximum amount which they shall fix with due regard for any maximum amount provided for by law. Where appropriate, the increase in the subscribed capital shall be decided on within the limits of the amount fixed, by the company body empowered to do so. The power of such body in this respect shall be for a maximum period of five years and may be renewed one or more times by the general meeting, each time for a period not exceeding five years.

3. Where there are several classes of shares, the decision by the general meeting concerning the increase in capital referred to in paragraph 1 or the authorization to increase the capital referred to in paragraph 2, shall be subject to a separate vote at least for each class of shareholder whose rights are affected by the transaction.

4. This Article shall apply to the issue of all securities which are convertible into shares or which carry the right to subscribe for shares, but not to the conversion of such securities, nor to the exercise of the right to subscribe.

Article 26

Shares issued for a consideration, in the course of an increase in subscribed capital, must be paid up to at least 25% of their nominal value or, in the absence of a nominal value, of their accountable par. Where provision is made for an issue premium, it must be paid in full.

Article 27

1. Where shares are issued for a consideration other than in cash in the course of an increase in the subscribed capital the consideration must be transferred in full within a period of five years from the decision to increase the subscribed capital.

2. The consideration referred to in paragraph 1 shall be the subject of a report drawn up before the increase in capital is made by one or more experts who are independent of the company and appointed or approved by an administrative or judicial authority. Such experts may be natural persons as well as legal persons and companies and firms under the laws of each Member State.

Article 10(2) and (3) shall apply.

* * *

Article 28

Where an increase in capital is not fully subscribed, the capital will be increased by the amount of the subscriptions received only if the conditions of the issue so provide.

Article 29

1. Whenever the capital is increased by consideration in cash, the shares must be offered on a pre-emptive basis to shareholders in proportion to the capital represented by their shares.

2. The laws of a Member State:

(a) need not apply paragraph 1 above to shares which carry a limited right to participate in distributions within the meaning of Article 15 and/or in the company's assets in the event of liquidation; or

(b) may permit, where the subscribed capital of a company having several classes of shares carrying different rights with regard to voting, or participation in distributions within the meaning of Article 15 or in assets in the event of liquidation, is increased by issuing new shares in only one of these classes, the right of pre-emption of shareholders of the other classes to be exercised only after the exercise of this right by the shareholders of the class in which the new shares are being issued.

* * *

4. The right of pre-emption may not be restricted or withdrawn by the statutes or instrument of incorporation. This may, however, be done by decision of the general meeting. The administrative or management body shall be required to present to such a meeting a written report indicating the reasons for restriction or withdrawal of the right of pre-emption, and justifying the proposed issue price. * * *

* * *

Article 30

Any reduction in the subscribed capital, except under a court order, must be subject at least to a decision of the general meeting acting in accordance with the rules for a quorum and a majority laid down in Article 40 without prejudice to Articles 36 and 37. * * *

Article 31

Where there are several classes of shares, the decision by the general meeting concerning a reduction in the subscribed capital shall be subject to a separate vote, at least for each class of shareholders whose rights are affected by the transaction.

* * *

Article 39

Where the laws of a Member State authorize companies to issue redeemable shares, they shall require that the following conditions, at least, are complied with for the redemption of such shares:

(a) redemption must be authorized by the company's statutes or instrument of incorporation before the redeemable shares are subscribed for;

(b) the shares must be fully paid up;

(c) the terms and the manner of redemption must be laid down in the company's statutes or instrument of incorporation;

(d) redemption can be only effected by using sums available for distribution in accordance with Article 15(1) or the proceeds of a new issue made with a view to effecting such redemption;

* * *

Article 40

1. The laws of the Member States shall provide that the decisions referred to in Articles 29(4) and (5), 30, 31, 35 and 38 must be taken at least by a majority of not less than two-thirds of the votes attaching to the securities or the subscribed capital represented.

2. The laws of the Member States may, however, lay down that a simple majority of the votes specified in paragraph 1 is sufficient when at least half the subscribed capital is represented.

Article 41

1. Member States may derogate from Article 9(1), Article 19(1)(a), first sentence, and (b) and from Articles 25, 26 and 29 to the extent that such derogations are necessary for the adoption or application of provisions designed to encourage the participation of employees, or other groups of persons defined by national law, in the capital of undertakings.

* * *

Article 42

For the purposes of the implementation of this Directive, the laws of the Member States shall ensure equal treatment to all shareholders who are in the same position.

* * *

Article 44

This Directive is addressed to the Member States.

18. THIRD COUNCIL DIRECTIVE 78/855/EEC

of 9 October 1978
based on Article 54(3)(g) of the Treaty concerning mergers of public limited liability companies
O.J.L. 295/36 (Oct. 20, 1978)

THE COUNCIL OF THE EUROPEAN COMMUNITIES.

Having regard to the Treaty establishing the European Economic Community, and in particular Article 54(3)(g) thereof,

Having regard to the proposal from the Commission,

Having regard to the opinion of the European Parliament,

Having regard to the opinion of the Economic and Social Committee,

* * *

Whereas the protection of the interests of members and third parties requires that the laws of the Member States relating to mergers of public limited liability companies be coordinated and that provision for mergers should be made in the laws of all the Member States;

Whereas in the context of such coordination it is particularly important that the shareholders of merging companies be kept adequately informed in as objective a manner as possible and that their rights be suitably protected;

Whereas the protection of employees' rights in the event of transfers of undertakings, businesses or parts of businesses is at present regulated by Directive 77/187/EEC [8];

Whereas creditors, including debenture holders, and persons having other claims on the merging companies must be protected so that the merger does not adversely affect their interests;

Whereas the disclosure requirements of Directive 68/151/EEC must be extended to include mergers so that third parties are kept adequately informed;

* * *

HAS ADOPTED THIS DIRECTIVE:

Article 1
Scope

1. The coordination measures laid down by this Directive shall apply to the laws, regulations and administrative provisions of the Member States relating to the following types of company:

— Germany:
die Aktiengesellschaft,

---

8. OJ No L 61, 5. 3. 1977, p. 26.

— Belgium:
la société anonyme/de naamloze vennootschap,
— Denmark:
aktieselskaber,
— France:
la société anonyme,
— Ireland:
public companies limited by shares, and public companies limited by guarantee having a share capital,
— Italy:
la società per azioni,
— Luxembourg:
la société anonyme,
— the Netherlands:
de naamloze vennootschap,
— the United Kingdom:
public companies limited by shares, and public companies limited by guarantee having a share capital.

* * *

CHAPTER I
REGULATION OF MERGER BY THE ACQUISITION OF ONE OR MORE COMPANIES BY ANOTHER AND OF MERGER BY THE FORMATION OF A NEW COMPANY

Article 2

The Member States shall, as regards companies governed by their national laws, make provision for rules governing merger by the acquisition of one or more companies by another and merger by the formation of a new company.

Article 3

1. For the purposes of this Directive, 'merger by acquisition' shall mean the operation whereby one or more companies are wound up without going into liquidation and transfer to another all their assets and liabilities in exchange for the issue to the shareholders of the company or companies being acquired of shares in the acquiring company and a cash payment, if any, not exceeding 10% of the nominal value of the shares so issued or, where they have no nominal value, of their accounting par value.

2. A Member State's laws may provide that merger by acquisition may also be effected where one or more of the companies being acquired is in liquidation, provided that this option is restricted to companies which have not yet begun to distribute their assets to their shareholders.

Article 4

1. For the purposes of this Directive, 'merger by the formation of a new company' shall mean the operation whereby several companies are wound up without going into liquidation and transfer to a company that they set up all their assets and liabilities in exchange for the issue to their shareholders of shares in the new company and a cash payment, if any,

not exceeding 10% of the nominal value of the shares so issued or, where they have no nominal value, of their accounting par value.

2. A Member State's laws may provide that merger by the formation of a new company may also be effected where one or more of the companies which are ceasing to exist is in liquidation, provided that this option is restricted to companies which have not yet begun to distribute their assets to their shareholders.

CHAPTER II
MERGER BY ACQUISITION
Article 5

1. The administrative or management bodies of the merging companies shall draw up draft terms of merger in writing.

2. Draft terms of merger shall specify at least:

(a) the type, name and registered office of each of the merging companies;

(b) the share exchange ratio and the amount of any cash payment;

(c) the terms relating to the allotment of shares in the acquiring company;

(d) the date from which the holding of such shares entitles the holders to participate in profits and any special conditions affecting that entitlement;

(e) the date from which the transactions of the company being acquired shall be treated for accounting purposes as being those of the acquiring company;

(f) the rights conferred by the acquiring company on the holders of shares to which special rights are attached and the holders of securities other than shares, or the measures proposed concerning them;

(g) any special advantage granted to the experts referred to in Article 10(1) and members of the merging companies' administrative, management, supervisory or controlling bodies.

Article 6

Draft terms of merger must be published in the manner prescribed by the laws of each Member State in accordance with Article 3 of Directive 68/151/EEC, for each of the merging companies, at least one month before the date fixed for the general meeting which is to decide thereon.

Article 7

1. A merger shall require at least the approval of the general meeting of each of the merging companies. The laws of the Member States shall provide that this decision shall require a majority of not less than two thirds of the votes attaching either to the shares or to the subscribed capital represented.

The laws of a Member State may, however, provide that a simple majority of the votes specified in the first subparagraph shall be sufficient when at least half of the subscribed capital is represented. Moreover, where appropriate, the rules governing alterations to the memorandum and articles of association shall apply.

2. Where there is more than one class of shares, the decision concerning a merger shall be subject to a separate vote by at least each class of shareholders whose rights are affected by the transaction.

3. The decision shall cover both the approval of the draft terms of merger and any alterations to the memorandum and articles of association necessitated by the merger.

Article 8

The laws of a Member State need not require approval of the merger by the general meeting of the acquiring company if the following conditions are fulfilled:

(a) the publication provided for in Article 6 must be effected, for the acquiring company, at least one month before the date fixed for the general meeting of the company or companies being acquired which are to decide on the draft terms of merger;

(b) at least one month before the date specified in (a), all shareholders of the acquiring company must be entitled to inspect the documents specified in Article 11(1) at the registered office of the acquiring company;

(c) one or more shareholders of the acquiring company holding a minimum percentage of the subscribed capital must be entitled to require that a general meeting of the acquiring company be called to decide whether to approve the merger. This minimum percentage may not be fixed at more than 5%. The Member States may, however, provide for the exclusion of non-voting shares from this calculation.

Article 9

The administration or management bodies of each of the merging companies shall draw up a detailed written report explaining the draft terms of merger and setting out the legal and economic grounds for them, in particular the share exchange ratio.

The report shall also describe any special valuation difficulties which have arisen.

Article 10

1. One or more experts, acting on behalf of each of the merging companies but independent of them, appointed or approved by a judicial or administrative authority, shall examine the draft terms of merger and draw up a written report to the shareholders. However, the laws of a Member State may provide for the appointment of one or more independent experts for all the merging companies, if such appointment is made by a judicial or administrative authority at the joint request of those companies. Such experts may, depending on the laws of each Member State, be natural or legal persons or companies or firms.

2. In the report mentioned in paragraph 1 the experts must in any case state whether in their opinion the share exchange ratio is fair and reasonable. Their statement must at least:

(a) indicate the method or methods used to arrive at the share exchange ratio proposed;

(b) state whether such method or methods are adequate in the case in question, indicate the values arrived at using each such method and give an opinion on the relative importance attributed to such methods in arriving at the value decided on.

The report shall also describe any special valuation difficulties which have arisen.

3. Each expert shall be entitled to obtain from the merging companies all relevant information and documents and to carry out all necessary investigations.

Article 11

1. All shareholders shall be entitled to inspect at least the following documents at the registered office at least one month before the date fixed for the general meeting which is to decide on the draft terms of merger:

(a) the draft terms of merger;

(b) the annual accounts and annual reports of the merging companies for the preceding three financial years;

(c) an accounting statement drawn up as at a date which must not be earlier than the first day of the third month preceding the date of the draft terms of merger, if the latest annual accounts relate to a financial year which ended more than six months before that date;

(d) the reports of the administrative or management bodies of the merging companies provided for in Article 9;

(e) the reports provided for in Article 10.

2. The accounting statement provided for in paragraph 1(c) shall be drawn up using the same methods and the same layout as the last annual balance sheet.

However, the laws of a Member State may provide that:

(a) it shall not be necessary to take a fresh physical inventory;

(b) the valuations shown in the last balance sheet shall be altered only to reflect entries in the books of account; the following shall nevertheless be taken into account:

— interim depreciation and provisions,

— material changes in actual value not shown in the books.

3. Every shareholder shall be entitled to obtain, on request and free of charge, full or, if so desired, partial copies of the documents referred to in paragraph 1.

Article 12

Protection of the rights of the employees of each of the merging companies shall be regulated in accordance with Directive 77/187/EEC.

Article 13

1. The laws of the Member States must provide for an adequate system of protection of the interests of creditors of the merging companies whose claims antedate the publication of the draft terms of merger and have not fallen due at the time of such publication.

2. To this end, the laws of the Member States shall at least provide that such creditors shall be entitled to obtain adequate safeguards where the financial situation of the merging companies makes such protection necessary and where those creditors do not already have such safeguards.

3. Such protection may be different for the creditors of the acquiring company and for those of the company being acquired.

Article 14

Without prejudice to the rules governing the collective exercise of their rights, Article 13 shall apply to the debenture holders of the merging companies, except where the merger has been approved by a meeting of the debenture holders, if such a meeting is provided for under national laws, or by the debenture holders individually.

Article 15

Holders of securities, other than shares, to which special rights are attached, must be given rights in the acquiring company at least equivalent to those they possessed in the company being acquired, unless the alteration of those rights has been approved by a meeting of the holders of such securities, if such a meeting is provided for under national laws, or by the holders of those securities individually, or unless the holders are entitled to have their securities repurchased by the acquiring company.

Article 16

1. Where the laws of a Member State do not provide for judicial or administrative preventive supervision of the legality of mergers, or where such supervision does not extend to all the legal acts required for a merger, the minutes of the general meetings which decide on the merger and, where appropriate, the merger contract subsequent to such general meetings shall be drawn up and certified in due legal form. In cases where the merger need not be approved by the general meetings of all the merging companies, the draft terms of merger must be drawn up and certified in due legal form.

2. The notary or the authority competent to draw up and certify the document in due legal form must check and certify the existence and validity of the legal acts and formalities required of the company for which he or it is acting and of the draft terms of merger.

Article 17

The laws of the Member States shall determine the date on which a merger takes effect.

Article 18

1. A merger must be publicized in the manner prescribed by the laws of each Member State, in accordance with Article 3 of Directive 68/151/EEC, in respect of each of the merging companies.

2. The acquiring company may itself carry out the publication formalities relating to the company or companies being acquired.

Article 19

1. A merger shall have the following consequences *ipso jure* and simultaneously:

(a) the transfer, both as between the company being acquired and the acquiring company and as regards third parties, to the acquiring company of all the assets and liabilities of the company being acquired;

(b) the shareholders of the company being acquired become shareholders of the acquiring company;

(c) the company being acquired ceases to exist.

2. No shares in the acquiring company shall be exchanged for shares in the company being acquired held either:

(a) by the acquiring company itself or through a person acting in his own name but on its behalf;

or

(b) by the company being acquired itself or through a person acting in his own name but on its behalf.

* * *

Article 20

The laws of the Member States shall at least lay down rules governing the civil liability towards the shareholders of the company being acquired of the members of the administrative or management bodies of that company in respect of misconduct on the part of members of those bodies in preparing and implementing the merger.

Article 21

The laws of the Member States shall at least lay down rules governing the civil liability towards the shareholders of the company being acquired of the experts responsible for drawing up on behalf of that company the report referred to in Article 10(1) in respect of misconduct on the part of those experts in the performance of their duties.

Article 22

1. The laws of the Member States may lay down nullity rules for mergers in accordance with the following conditions only:

(a) nullity must be ordered in a court judgment;

(b) mergers which have taken effect pursuant to Article 17 may be declared void only if there has been no judicial or administrative preventive supervision of their legality, or if they have not been drawn up and certified in due legal form, or if it is shown that the decision of the general meeting is void or voidable under national law;

(c) nullification proceedings may not be initiated more than six months after the date on which the merger becomes effective as against the person alleging nullity or if the situation has been rectified;

(d) where it is possible to remedy a defect liable to render a merger void, the competent court shall grant the companies involved a period of time within which to rectify the situation;

(e) a judgment declaring a merger void shall be published in the manner prescribed by the laws of each Member State in accordance with Article 3 of Directive 68/151/EEC;

(f) where the laws of a Member State permit a third party to challenge such a judgment, he may do so only within six months of publication of the judgment in the manner prescribed by Directive 68/151/EEC;

(g) a judgment declaring a merger void shall not of itself affect the validity of obligations owed by or in relation to the acquiring company which arose before the judgment was published and after the date referred to in Article 17;

(h) companies which have been parties to a merger shall be jointly and severally liable in respect of the obligations of the acquiring company referred to in (g).

2. By way of derogation from paragraph 1(a), the laws of a Member State may also provide for the nullity of a merger to be ordered by an administrative authority if an appeal against such a decision lies to a court. Subparagraphs (b), (d), (e), (f), (g) and (h) shall apply by analogy to the administrative authority. Such nullification proceedings may not be initiated more than six months after the date referred to in Article 17.

3. The foregoing shall not affect the laws of the Member States on the nullity of a merger pronounced following any supervision other than judicial or administrative preventive supervision of legality.

CHAPTER III
MERGER BY FORMATION OF A NEW COMPANY
Article 23

1. Articles 5, 6, 7 and 9 to 22 shall apply, without prejudice to Articles 11 and 12 of Directive 68/151/EEC, to merger by formation of a new company. For this purpose, 'merging companies' and 'company being acquired' shall mean the companies which will cease to exist, and 'acquiring company' shall mean the new company.

2. Article 5(2)(a) shall also apply to the new company.

3. The draft terms of merger and, if they are contained in a separate document, the memorandum or draft memorandum of association and the articles or draft articles of association of the new company shall be approved at a general meeting of each of the companies that will cease to exist.

4. The Member States need not apply to the formation of a new company the rules governing the verification of any consideration other than cash which are laid down in Article 10 of Directive 77/91/EEC.

CHAPTER IV
ACQUISITION OF ONE COMPANY BY ANOTHER WHICH HOLDS 90% OR MORE OF ITS SHARES

Article 24

The Member States shall make provision, in respect of companies governed by their laws, for the operation whereby one or more companies are wound up without going into liquidation and transfer all their assets and liabilities to another company which is the holder of all their shares and other securities conferring the right to vote at general meetings. Such operations shall be regulated by the provisions of Chapter II, with the exception of Articles 5(2)(b), (c) and (d), 9, 10, 11(1)(d) and (e), 19(1)(b), 20 and 21.

Article 25

The Member States need not apply Article 7 to the operations specified in Article 24 if the following conditions at least are fulfilled:

(a) the publication provided for in Article 6 must be effected, as regards each company involved in the operation, at least one month before the operation takes effect;

(b) at least one month before the operation takes effect, all shareholders of the acquiring company must be entitled to inspect the documents specified in Article 11(1)(a), (b) and (c) at the company's registered office. Article 11(2) and (3) must apply;

(c) Article 8(c) must apply.

Article 26

The Member States may apply Articles 24 and 25 to operations whereby one or more companies are wound up without going into liquidation and transfer all their assets and liabilities to another company, if all the shares and other securities specified in Article 24 of the company or companies being acquired are held by the acquiring company and/or by persons holding those shares and securities in their own names but on behalf of that company.

Article 27

In cases of merger where one or more companies are acquired by another company which holds 90% or more, but not all, of the shares and other securities of each of those companies the holding of which confers the right to vote at general meetings, the Member States need not require approval of the merger by the general meeting of the acquiring company, provided that the following conditions at least are fulfilled:

(a) the publication provided for in Article 6 must be effected, as regards the acquiring company, at least one month before the date fixed for the general meeting of the company or companies being acquired which is to decide on the draft terms of merger;

(b) at least one month before the date specified in (a), all shareholders of the acquiring company must be entitled to inspect the documents specified in Article 11(1)(a), (b) and (c) at the company's registered office. Article 11(2) and (3) must apply;

(c) Article 8(c) must apply.

Article 28

The Member States need not apply Articles 9 to 11 to a merger within the meaning of Article 27 if the following conditions at least are fulfilled:

(a) the minority shareholders of the company being acquired must be entitled to have their shares acquired by the acquiring company;

(b) if they exercise that right, they must be entitled to receive consideration corresponding to the value of their shares;

(c) in the event of disagreement regarding such consideration, it must be possible for the value of the consideration to be determined by a court.

Article 29

The Member States may apply Articles 27 and 28 to operations whereby one or more companies are wound up without going into liquidation and transfer all their assets and liabilities to another company if 90% or more, but not all, of the shares and other securities referred to in Article 27 of the company or companies being acquired are held by that acquiring company and/or by persons holding those shares and securities in their own names but on behalf of that company.

CHAPTER V
OTHER OPERATIONS TREATED AS MERGERS

Article 30

Where in the case of one of the operations referred to in Article 2 the laws of a Member State permit a cash payment to exceed 10%, Chapters II and III and Articles 27, 28 and 29 shall apply.

Article 31

Where the laws of a Member State permit one of the operations referred to in Articles 2, 24 and 30, without all of the transferring companies thereby ceasing to exist, Chapter II, except for Article 19(1)(c), Chapter III or Chapter IV shall apply as appropriate.

CHAPTER VI
FINAL PROVISIONS

* * *

Article 33

This Directive is addressed to the Member States.

19. FOURTH COUNCIL DIRECTIVE 78/660/EEC

of 25 July 1978
based on Article 54(3)(g) of the Treaty on the annual accounts of certain types of companies
O.J. L 222/11 (Aug. 14, 1978)

THE COUNCIL OF THE EUROPEAN COMMUNITIES,

Having regard to the Treaty establishing the European Economic Community, and in particular Article 54(3)(g) thereof,

Having regard to the proposal from the Commission,

Having regard to the opinion of the European Parliament,

Having regard to the opinion of the Economic and Social Committee,

Whereas the coordination of national provisions concerning the presentation and content of annual accounts and annual reports, the valuation methods used therein and their publication in respect of certain companies with limited liability is of special importance for the protection of members and third parties;

Whereas simultaneous coordination is necessary in these fields for these forms of company because, on the one hand, these companies' activities frequently extend beyond the frontiers of their national territories and, on the other, they offer no safeguards to third parties beyond the amounts of their net assets; * * *

Whereas it is necessary, moreover, to establish in the Community minimum equivalent legal requirements as regards the extent of the financial information that should be made available to the public by companies that are in competition with one another;

Whereas annual accounts must give a true and fair view of a company's assets and liabilities, financial position and profit or loss; whereas to this end a mandatory layout must be prescribed for the balance sheet and the profit and loss account and whereas the minimum content of the notes on the accounts and the annual report must be laid down; whereas, however, derogations may be granted for certain companies of minor economic or social importance;

Whereas the different methods for the valuation of assets and liabilities must be coordinated to the extent necessary to ensure that annual accounts disclose comparable and equivalent information;

Whereas the annual accounts of all companies to which this Directive applies must be published in accordance with Directive 68/151/EEC; whereas, however, certain derogations may likewise be granted in this area for small and medium-sized companies;

Whereas annual accounts must be audited by authorized persons whose minimum qualifications will be the subject of subsequent coordination; whereas only small companies may be relieved of this audit obligation;

Whereas, when a company belongs to a group, it is desirable that group accounts giving a true and fair view of the activities of the group as a whole be published; whereas, however, pending the entry into force of a Council Directive on consolidated accounts, derogations from certain provisions of this Directive are necessary;

Whereas, in order to meet the difficulties arising from the present position regarding legislation in certain Member States, the period allowed for the implementation of certain provisions of this Directive must be longer than the period generally laid down in such cases,

HAS ADOPTED THIS DIRECTIVE:

Article 1

1. The coordination measures prescribed by this Directive shall apply to the laws, regulations and administrative provisions of the Member States relating to the following types of companies:

— in Germany:
die Aktiengesellschaft, die Kommanditgesellschaft auf Aktien, die Gesellschaft mit beschränkter Haftung;
— in Belgium:
la société anonyme/de naamloze vennootschap, la société en commandite par actions/de commanditaire vennootschap op aandelen, la société de personnes à responsabilité limitée/de personenvennootschap met beperkte aansprakelijkheid;
— in Denmark:
aktieselskaber, kommanditaktieselskaber, anpartsselskaber;
— in France:
la société anonyme, la société en commandite par actions, la société à responsabilité limitée;
— in Ireland:
public companies limited by shares or by guarantee, private companies limited by shares or by guarantee;
— in Italy:
la società per azioni, la società in accomandita per azioni, la società a responsabilità limitata;
— in Luxembourg:
la société anonyme, la société en commandite par actions, la société à responsabilité limitée;
— in the Netherlands:
de naamloze vennootschap, de besloten vennootschap met beperkte aansprakelijkheid;
— in the United Kingdom:
public companies limited by shares or by guarantee, private companies limited by shares or by guarantee.

2. Pending subsequent coordination, the Member States need not apply the provisions of this Directive to banks and other financial institutions or to insurance companies.

SECTION 1
GENERAL PROVISIONS
Article 2

1. The annual accounts shall comprise the balance sheet, the profit and loss account and the notes on the accounts. These documents shall constitute a composite whole.

2. They shall be drawn up clearly and in accordance with the provisions of this Directive.

3. The annual accounts shall give a true and fair view of the company's assets, liabilities, financial position and profit or loss.

4. Where the application of the provisions of this Directive would not be sufficient to give a true and fair view within the meaning of paragraph 3, additional information must be given.

5. Where in exceptional cases the application of a provision of this Directive is incompatible with the obligation laid down in paragraph 3, that provision must be departed from in order to give a true and fair view within the meaning of paragraph 3. Any such departure must be disclosed in the notes on the accounts together with an explanation of the reasons for it and a statement of its effect on the assets, liabilities, financial position and profit or loss. The Member States may define the exceptional cases in question and lay down the relevant special rules.

6. The Member States may authorize or require the disclosure in the annual accounts of other information as well as that which must be disclosed in accordance with this Directive.

SECTION 2
GENERAL PROVISIONS CONCERNING THE BALANCE SHEET AND THE PROFIT AND LOSS ACCOUNT
Article 3

The layout of the balance sheet and of the profit and loss account, particularly as regards the form adopted for their presentation, may not be changed from one financial year to the next. Departures from this principle shall be permitted in exceptional cases. Any such departure must be disclosed in the notes on the accounts together with an explanation of the reasons therefor.

Article 4

1. In the balance sheet and in the profit and loss account the items prescribed in Articles 9, 10 and 23 to 26 must be shown separately in the order indicated.

* * *

4. In respect of each balance sheet and profit and loss account item the figure relating to the corresponding item for the preceding financial year must be shown. The Member States may provide that, where these figures are not comparable, the figure for the preceding financial year

must be adjusted. In any case, non-comparability and any adjustment of the figures must be disclosed in the notes on the accounts, with relevant comments.

5. Save where there is a corresponding item for the preceding financial year within the meaning of paragraph 4, a balance sheet or profit and loss account item for which there is no amount shall not be shown.

* * *

Article 6

The Member States may authorize or require adaptation of the layout of the balance sheet and profit and loss account in order to include the appropriation of profit or the treatment of loss.

Article 7

Any set-off between asset and liability items, or between income and expenditure items, shall be prohibited.

[Omitted Articles 8-10 describe in detail the lay-out of items in the balance sheet.]

Article 11

The Member States may permit companies which on their balance sheet dates do not exceed the limits of two of the three following criteria:

—balance sheet total: [2,000,000 ECU]

—net turnover: [4,000,000 ECU]

—average number of employees during the financial year: 50

to draw up abridged balance sheets showing only [certain identified items] * * *.

[Figures within brackets represent an amendment made by Directive 90/604, O.J.L. 317/57 (Nov. 16, 1990).]

[Omitted Articles 12-21 state rules for describing balance sheet items. Omitted Articles 22-26 describe in detail the lay-out of items in the profit and loss statement. Article 27 permits smaller companies to draw up abridged profit and loss statements. Omitted Articles 28-30 state rules for certain items.]

SECTION 7
VALUATION RULES

Article 31

1. The Member States shall ensure that the items shown in the annual accounts are valued in accordance with the following general principles:

(a) the company must be presumed to be carrying on its business as a going concern;

(b) the methods of valuation must be applied consistently from one financial year to another;

(c) valuation must be made on a prudent basis, and in particular:

(aa) only profits made at the balance sheet date may be included,

(bb) account must be taken of all foreseeable liabilities and potential losses arising in the course of the financial year concerned or of a previous one, even if such liabilities or losses become apparent only between the date of the balance sheet and the date on which it is drawn up,

(cc) account must be taken of all depreciation, whether the result of the financial year is a loss or a profit;

(d) account must be taken of income and charges relating to the financial year, irrespective of the date of receipt or payment of such income or charges;

(e) the components of asset and liability items must be valued separately;

(f) the opening balance sheet for each financial year must correspond to the closing balance sheet for the preceding financial year.

2. Departures from these general principles shall be permitted in exceptional cases. Any such departures must be disclosed in the notes on the accounts and the reasons for them given together with an assessment of their effect on the assets, liabilities, financial position and profit or loss.

Article 32

The items shown in the annual accounts shall be valued in accordance with Articles 34 to 42, which are based on the principle of purchase price or production cost.

* * *

Article 35

1. (a) Fixed assets must be valued at purchase price or production cost, without prejudice to (b) and (c) below.

(b) The purchase price or production cost of fixed assets with limited useful economic lives must be reduced by value adjustments calculated to write off the value of such assets systematically over their useful economic lives.

(c) (aa) Value adjustments may be made in respect of financial fixed assets, so that they are valued at the lower figure to be attributed to them at the balance sheet date.

(bb) Value adjustments must be made in respect of fixed assets, whether their useful economic lives are limited or not, so that they are valued at the lower figure to be attributed to them at the balance sheet date if it is expected that the reduction in their value will be permanent.

(cc) The value adjustments referred to in (aa) and (bb) must be charged to the profit and loss account and disclosed separately in the notes on the accounts if they have not been shown separately in the profit and loss account.

(dd) Valuation at the lower of the values provided for in (aa) and (bb) may not be continued if the reasons for which the value adjustments were made have ceased to apply.

(d) If fixed assets are the subject of exceptional value adjustments for taxation purposes alone, the amount of the adjustments and the reasons for making them shall be indicated in the notes on the accounts.

2. The purchase price shall be calculated by adding to the price paid the expenses incidental thereto.

3. (a) The production cost shall be calculated by adding to the purchasing price of the raw materials and consumables the costs directly attributable to the product in question.

(b) A reasonable proportion of the costs which are only indirectly attributable to the product in question may be added into the production costs to the extent that they relate to the period of production.

4. Interest on capital borrowed to finance the production of fixed assets may be included in the production costs to the extent that it relates to the period of production. In that event, the inclusion of such interest under 'Assets' must be disclosed in the notes on the accounts.

* * *

Article 37

1. Article 34 shall apply to costs of research and development. In exceptional cases, however, the Member States may permit derogations from Article 34(1)(a). In that case, they may also provide for derogations from Article 34(1)(b). Such derogations and the reasons for them must be disclosed in the notes on the accounts.

2. Article 34(1)(a) shall apply to goodwill. The Member States may, however, permit companies to write goodwill off systematically over a limited period exceeding five years provided that this period does not exceed the useful economic life of the asset and is disclosed in the notes on the accounts together with the supporting reasons therefor.

Article 38

Tangible fixed assets, raw materials and consumables which are constantly being replaced and the overall value of which is of secondary importance to the undertaking may be shown under 'Assets' at a fixed quantity and value, if the quantity, value and composition thereof do not vary materially.

Article 39

1. (a) Current assets must be valued at purchase price or production cost, without prejudice to (b) and (c) below.

(b) Value adjustments shall be made in respect of current assets with a view to showing them at the lower market value or, in particular circumstances, another lower value to be attributed to them at the balance sheet date.

(c) The Member States may permit exceptional value adjustments where, on the basis of a reasonable commercial assessment, these are necessary if the valuation of these items is not to be modified in the near future because of fluctuations in value. The amount of these value adjustments must be disclosed separately in the profit and loss account or in the notes on the accounts.

(d) Valuation at the lower value provided for in (b) and (c) may not be continued if the reasons for which the value adjustments were made have ceased to apply.

(e) If current assets are the subject of exceptional value adjustments for taxation purposes alone, the amount of the adjustments and the reasons for making them must be disclosed in the notes on the accounts.

2. The definitions of purchase price and of production cost given in Article 35(2) and (3) shall apply. The Member States may also apply Article 35(4). Distribution costs may not be included in production costs.

Article 40

1. The Member States may permit the purchase price or production cost of stocks of goods of the same category and all fungible items including investments to be calculated either on the basis of weighted average prices or by the 'first in, first out' (FIFO) method, the 'last in, first out' (LIFO) method, or some similar method.

* * *

Article 41

1. Where the amount repayable on account of any debt is greater than the amount received, the difference may be shown as an asset. It must be shown separately in the balance sheet or in the notes on the accounts.

2. The amount of this difference must be written off by a reasonable amount each year and completely written off no later than the time of repayment of the debt.

Article 42

Provisions for liabilities and charges may not exceed in amount the sums which are necessary.

The provisions shown in the balance sheet under 'Other provisions' must be disclosed in the notes on the accounts if they are material.

SECTION 8
CONTENTS OF THE NOTES ON THE ACCOUNTS

* * *

SECTION 9
CONTENTS OF THE ANNUAL REPORT
Article 46

1. The annual report must include at least a fair review of the development of the company's business and of its position.

2. The report shall also give an indication of:

(a) any important events that have occurred since the end of the financial year;

(b) the company's likely future development;

(c) activities in the field of research and development;

(d) the information concerning acquisitions of own shares prescribed by Article 22(2) of Directive 77/91/EEC.

SECTION 10
PUBLICATION
Article 47

1. The annual accounts, duly approved, and the annual report, together with the opinion submitted by the person responsible for auditing the accounts, shall be published as laid down by the laws of each Member State in accordance with Article 3 of Directive 68/151/EEC.

The laws of a Member State may, however, permit the annual report not to be published as stipulated above. In that case, it shall be made available to the public at the company's registered office in the Member State concerned. It must be possible to obtain a copy of all or part of any such report free of charge upon request.

2. By way of derogation from paragraph 1, the Member States may permit the companies referred to in Article 11 to publish:

(a) abridged balance sheets * * *.

In addition, the Member States may relieve such companies from the obligation to publish their profit and loss accounts and annual reports and the opinions of the persons responsible for auditing the accounts.

* * *

Article 48

Whenever the annual accounts and the annual report are published in full, they must be reproduced in the form and text on the basis of which the person responsible for auditing the accounts has drawn up his opinion. They must be accompanied by the full text of his report. If the person responsible for auditing the accounts has made any qualifications or refused to report upon the accounts, that fact must be disclosed and the reasons given.

* * *

SECTION 11
AUDITING
Article 51

1. (a) Companies must have their annual accounts audited by one or more persons authorized by national law to audit accounts.
   (b) The person or persons responsible for auditing the accounts must also verify that the annual report is consistent with the annual accounts for the same financial year.

2. The Member States may relieve the companies referred to in Article 11 from the obligation imposed by paragraph 1.

* * *

SECTION 12
FINAL PROVISIONS
Article 52

1. A Contact Committee shall be set up under the auspices of the Commission. Its function shall be:

(a) to facilitate, without prejudice to the provisions of Articles 169 and 170 of the Treaty, harmonized application of this Directive through regular meetings dealing in particular with practical problems arising in connection with its application;

(b) to advise the Commission, if necessary, on additions or amendments to this Directive.

2. The Contact Committee shall be composed of representatives of the Member States and representatives of the Commission. The chairman shall be a representative of the Commission. The Commission shall provide the secretariat.

3. The Committee shall be convened by the chairman either on his own initiative or at the request of one of its members.

* * *

20. COUNCIL REGULATION (EEC) 2137/85

of 25 July 1985
on the European Economic Interest Grouping (EEIG)
O.J. L 199/1 (July 31, 1985)

THE COUNCIL OF THE EUROPEAN COMMUNITIES,

Having regard to the Treaty establishing the European Economic Community, and in particular Article 235 thereof,

Having regard to the proposal from the Commission,[1]

Having regard to the opinion of the European Parliament,[2]

Having regard to the opinion of the Economic and Social Committee,[3]

Whereas a harmonious development of economic activities and a continuous and balanced expansion throughout the Community depend on the establishment and smooth functioning of a common market offering conditions analogous to those of a national market; whereas to bring about this single market and to increase its unity a legal framework which facilitates the adaptation of their activities to the economic conditions of the Community should be created for natural persons, companies, firms and other legal bodies in particular; whereas to that end it is necessary that those natural persons, companies, firms and other legal bodies should be able to cooperate effectively across frontiers;

Whereas cooperation of this nature can encounter legal, fiscal or psychological difficulties; whereas the creation of an appropriate Community legal instrument in the form of a European Economic Interest Grouping would contribute to the achievement of the abovementioned objectives and therefore proves necessary;

Whereas the Treaty does not provide the necessary powers for the creation of such a legal instrument;

Whereas a grouping's ability to adapt to economic conditions must be guaranteed by the considerable freedom for its members in their contractual relations and the internal organization of the grouping;

Whereas a grouping differs from a firm or company principally in its purpose, which is only to facilitate or develop the economic activities of its members to enable them to improve their own results; whereas, by reason of that ancillary nature, a grouping's activities must be related to the economic activities of its members but not replace them so that, to that extent, for example, a grouping may not itself, with regard to third parties, practise a profession, the concept of economic activities being interpreted in the widest sense;

Whereas access to grouping form must be made as widely available as possible to natural persons, companies, firms and other legal bodies, in keeping with the aims of this Regulation; whereas this Regulation shall

---

1. OJ No C 14, 15. 2. 1974, p. 30 and OJ No C 103, 28. 4. 1978, p. 4.
2. OJ No C 163, 11. 7. 1977, p. 17.
3. OJ No C 108, 15. 5. 1975, p. 46.

not, however, prejudice the application at national level of legal rules and/or ethical codes concerning the conditions for the pursuit of business and professional activities;

* * *

Whereas this Regulation provides that the profits or losses resulting from the activities of a grouping shall be taxable only in the hands of its members; whereas it is understood that otherwise national tax laws apply, particularly as regards the apportionment of profits, tax procedures and any obligations imposed by national tax law;

Whereas in matters not covered by this Regulation the laws of the Member States and Community law are applicable, for example with regard to:

— social and labour laws,

— competition law,

— intellectual property law;

* * *

HAS ADOPTED THIS REGULATION:

Article 1

1. European Economic Interest Groupings shall be formed upon the terms, in the manner and with the effects laid down in this Regulation.

Accordingly, parties intending to form a grouping must conclude a contract and have the registration provided for in Article 6 carried out.

2. A grouping so formed shall, from the date of its registration as provided for in Article 6, have the capacity, in its own name, to have rights and obligations of all kinds, to make contracts or accomplish other legal acts, and to sue and be sued.

3. The Member States shall determine whether or not groupings registered at their registries, pursuant to Article 6, have legal personality.

Article 2

1. Subject to the provisions of this Regulation, the law applicable, on the one hand, to the contract for the formation of a grouping, except as regards matters relating to the status or capacity of natural persons and to the capacity of legal persons and, on the other hand, to the internal organization of a grouping shall be the internal law of the State in which the official address is situated, as laid down in the contract for the formation of the grouping.

2. Where a State comprises several territorial units, each of which has its own rules of law applicable to the matters referred to in paragraph 1, each territorial unit shall be considered as a State for the purposes of identifying the law applicable under this Article.

Article 3

1. The purpose of a grouping shall be to facilitate or develop the economic activities of its members and to improve or increase the results of those activities; its purpose is not to make profits for itself.

Its activity shall be related to the economic activities of its members and must not be more than ancillary to those activities.

2. Consequently, a grouping may not:

(a) exercise, directly or indirectly, a power of management or supervision over its members' own activities or over the activities of another undertaking, in particular in the fields of personnel, finance and investment;

(b) directly or indirectly, on any basis whatsoever, hold shares of any kind in a member undertaking; the holding of shares in another undertaking shall be possible only in so far as it is necessary for the achievement of the grouping's objects and if it is done on its members' behalf;

(c) employ more than 500 persons;

(d) be used by a company to make a loan to a director of a company, or any person connected with him, when the making of such loans is restricted or controlled under the Member States' laws governing companies. Nor must a grouping be used for the transfer of any property between a company and a director, or any person connected with him, except to the extent allowed by the Member States' laws governing companies. For the purposes of this provision the making of a loan includes entering into any transaction or arrangement of similar effect, and property includes moveable and immoveable property;

(e) be a member of another European Economic Interest Grouping.

Article 4

1. Only the following may be members of a grouping:

(a) companies or firms within the meaning of the second paragraph of Article 58 of the Treaty and other legal bodies governed by public or private law, which have been formed in accordance with the law of a Member State and which have their registered or statutory office and central administration in the Community; where, under the law of a Member State, a company, firm or other legal body is not obliged to have a registered or statutory office, it shall be sufficient for such a company, firm or other legal body to have its central administration in the Community;

(b) natural persons who carry on any industrial, commercial, craft or agricultural activity or who provide professional or other services in the Community.

2. A grouping must comprise at least:

(a) two companies, firms or other legal bodies, within the meaning of paragraph 1, which have their central administrations in different Member States, or

(b) two natural persons, within the meaning of paragraph 1, who carry on their principal activities in different Member States, or

(c) a company, firm or other legal body within the meaning of paragraph 1 and a natural person, of which the first has its central administration in one Member State and the second carries on his principal activity in another Member State.

3. A Member State may provide that groupings registered at its registries in accordance with Article 6 may have no more than 20 members. For this purpose, that Member State may provide that, in accordance with its laws, each member of a legal body formed under its laws, other than a registered company, shall be treated as a separate member of a grouping.

4. Any Member State may, on grounds of that State's public interest, prohibit or restrict participation in groupings by certain classes of natural persons, companies, firms, or other legal bodies.

Article 5

A contract for the formation of a grouping shall include at least:

(a) the name of the grouping preceded or followed either by the words 'European Economic Interest Grouping' or by the initials 'EEIG', unless those words or initials already form part of the name;

(b) the official address of the grouping;

(c) the objects for which the grouping is formed;

(d) the name, business name, legal form, permanent address or registered office, and the number and place of registration, if any, of each member of the grouping;

(e) the duration of the grouping, except where this is indefinite.

Article 6

A grouping shall be registered in the State in which it has its official address, at the registry designated pursuant to Article 39(1).

Article 7

A contract for the formation of a grouping shall be filed at the registry referred to in Article 6.

The following documents and particulars must also be filed at that registry:

(a) any amendment to the contract for the formation of a grouping, including any change in the composition of a grouping;

(b) notice of the setting up or closure of any establishment of the grouping;

(c) any judicial decision establishing or declaring the nullity of a grouping, in accordance with Article 15;

(d) notice of the appointment of the manager or managers of a grouping, their names and any other identification particulars required by the law of the Member State in which the register is kept, notification that they may act alone or must act jointly, and the termination of any manager's appointment;

(e) notice of a member's assignment of his participation in a grouping or a proportion thereof, in accordance with Article 22(1);

* * *

Article 8

The following must be published, as laid down in Article 39, in the gazette referred to in paragraph 1 of that Article:

(a) the particulars which must be included in the contract for the formation of a grouping, pursuant to Article 5, and any amendments thereto;

(b) the number, date and place of registration as well as notice of the termination of that registration;

(c) the documents and particulars referred to in Article 7(b) to (j).

* * *

Article 9

1. The documents and particulars which must be published pursuant to this Regulation may be relied on by a grouping as against third parties under the conditions laid down by the national law applicable pursuant to Article 3(5) and (7) of Council Directive 68/151/EEC of 9 March 1968 * * *.

* * *

Article 10

Any grouping establishment situated in a Member State other than that in which the official address is situated shall be registered in that State. For the purpose of such registration, a grouping shall file, at the appropriate registry in that Member State, copies of the documents which must be filed at the registry of the Member State in which the official address is situated, together, if necessary, with a translation which conforms with the practice of the registry where the establishment is registered.

Article 11

Notice that a grouping has been formed or that the liquidation of a grouping has been concluded stating the number, date and place of registration and the date, place and title of publication, shall be given in the *Official Journal of the European Communities* after it has been published in the gazette referred to in Article 39(1).

Article 12

The official address referred to in the contract for the formation of a grouping must be situated in the Community.

The official address must be fixed either:

(a) where the grouping has its central administration, or

(b) where one of the members of the grouping has its central administration or, in the case of a natural person, his principal activity, provided that the grouping carries on an activity there.

* * *

Article 16

1. The organs of a grouping shall be the members acting collectively and the manager or managers.

A contract for the formation of a grouping may provide for other organs; if it does it shall determine their powers.

2. The members of a grouping, acting as a body, may take any decision for the purpose of achieving the objects of the grouping.

Article 17

1. Each member shall have one vote. The contract for the formation of a grouping may, however, give more than one vote to certain members, provided that no one member holds a majority of the votes.

2. A unanimous decision by the members shall be required to:

(a) alter the objects of a grouping;

(b) alter the number of votes allotted to each member;

(c) alter the conditions for the taking of decisions;

(d) extend the duration of a grouping beyond any period fixed in the contract for the formation of the grouping;

(e) alter the contribution by every member or by some members to the grouping's financing;

(f) alter any other obligation of a member, unless otherwise provided by the contract for the formation of the grouping;

(g) make any alteration to the contract for the formation of the grouping not covered by this paragraph, unless otherwise provided by that contract.

3. Except where this Regulation provides that decisions must be taken unanimously, the contract for the formation of a grouping may prescribe the conditions for a quorum and for a majority, in accordance with which the decisions, or some of them, shall be taken. Unless otherwise provided for by the contract, decisions shall be taken unanimously.

4. On the initiative of a manager or at the request of a member, the manager or managers must arrange for the members to be consulted so that the latter can take a decision.

Article 18

Each member shall be entitled to obtain information from the manager or managers concerning the grouping's business and to inspect the grouping's books and business records.

Article 19

1. A grouping shall be managed by one or more natural persons appointed in the contract for the formation of the grouping or by decision of the members.

No person may be a manager of a grouping if:

— by virtue of the law applicable to him, or

— by virtue of the internal law of the State in which the grouping has its official address, or

— following a judicial or administrative decision made or recognized in a Member State

he may not belong to the administrative or management body of a company, may not manage an undertaking or may not act as manager of a European Economic Interest Grouping.

2. A Member State may, in the case of groupings registered at their registries pursuant to Article 6, provide that legal persons may be managers on condition that such legal persons designate one or more natural persons, whose particulars shall be the subject of the filing provisions of Article 7(d) to represent them.

If a Member State exercises this option, it must provide that the representative or representatives shall be liable as if they were themselves managers of the groupings concerned.

The restrictions imposed in paragraph 1 shall also apply to those representatives.

3. The contract for the formation of a grouping or, failing that, a unanimous decision by the members shall determine the conditions for the appointment and removal of the manager or managers and shall lay down their powers.

Article 20

1. Only the manager or, where there are two or more, each of the managers shall represent a grouping in respect of dealings with third parties.

Each of the managers shall bind the grouping as regards third parties when he acts on behalf of the grouping, even where his acts do not fall within the objects of the grouping, unless the grouping proves that the third party knew or could not, under the circumstances, have been unaware that the act fell outside the objects of the grouping; publication of the particulars referred to in Article 5(c) shall not of itself be proof thereof.

No limitation on the powers of the manager or managers, whether deriving from the contract for the formation of the grouping or from a decision by the members, may be relied on as against third parties even if it is published.

2. The contract for the formation of the grouping may provide that the grouping shall be validly bound only by two or more managers acting jointly. Such a clause may be relied on as against third parties in accordance with the conditions referred to in Article 9(1) only if it is published in accordance with Article 8.

Article 21

1. The profits resulting from a grouping's activities shall be deemed to be the profits of the members and shall be apportioned among them in the proportions laid down in the contract for the formation of the grouping or, in the absence of any such provision, in equal shares.

2. The members of a grouping shall contribute to the payment of the amount by which expenditure exceeds income in the proportions laid down in the contract for the formation of the grouping or, in the absence of any such provision, in equal shares.

Article 22

1. Any member of a grouping may assign his participation in the grouping, or a proportion thereof, either to another member or to a third party; the assignment shall not take effect without the unanimous authorization of the other members.

2. A member of a grouping may use his participation in the grouping as security only after the other members have given their unanimous authorization, unless otherwise laid down in the contract for the formation of the grouping. The holder of the security may not at any time become a member of the grouping by virtue of that security.

Article 23

No grouping may invite investment by the public.

Article 24

1. The members of a grouping shall have unlimited joint and several liability for its debts and other liabilities of whatever nature. National law shall determine the consequences of such liability.

2. Creditors may not proceed against a member for payment in respect of debts and other liabilities, in accordance with the conditions laid down in paragraph 1, before the liquidation of a grouping is concluded, unless they have first requested the grouping to pay and payment has not been made within an appropriate period.

Article 25

Letters, order forms and similar documents must indicate legibly:

(a) the name of the grouping preceded or followed either by the words 'European Economic Interest Grouping' or by the initials 'EEIG', unless those words or initials already occur in the name;

(b) the location of the registry referred to in Article 6, in which the grouping is registered, together with the number of the grouping's entry at the registry;

(c) the grouping's official address;

(d) where applicable, that the managers must act jointly;

* * *

Article 26

1. A decision to admit new members shall be taken unanimously by the members of the grouping.

2. Every new member shall be liable, in accordance with the conditions laid down in Article 24, for the grouping's debts and other liabilities, including those arising out of the grouping's activities before his admission.

He may, however, be exempted by a clause in the contract for the formation of the grouping or in the instrument of admission from the payment of debts and other liabilities which originated before his admission. Such a clause may be relied on as against third parties, under the conditions referred to in Article 9(1), only if it is published in accordance with Article 8.

Article 27

1. A member of a grouping may withdraw in accordance with the conditions laid down in the contract for the formation of a grouping or, in the absence of such conditions, with the unanimous agreement of the other members.

Any member of a grouping may, in addition, withdraw on just and proper grounds.

2. Any member of a grouping may be expelled for the reasons listed in the contract for the formation of the grouping and, in any case, if he seriously fails in his obligations or if he causes or threatens to cause serious disruption in the operation of the grouping.

Such expulsion may occur only by the decision of a court to which joint application has been made by a majority of the other members, unless otherwise provided by the contract for the formation of a grouping.

Article 28

1. A member of a grouping shall cease to belong to it on death or when he no longer complies with the conditions laid down in Article 4(1).

* * *

* * *

Article 31

1. A grouping may be wound up by a decision of its members ordering its winding up. Such a decision shall be taken unanimously,

unless otherwise laid down in the contract for the formation of the grouping.

* * *

Article 35

1. The winding up of a grouping shall entail its liquidation.

2. The liquidation of a grouping and the conclusion of its liquidation shall be governed by national law.

* * *

Article 39

1. The Member States shall designate the registry or registries responsible for effecting the registration referred to in Articles 6 and 10 and shall lay down the rules governing registration. They shall prescribe the conditions under which the documents referred to in Articles 7 and 10 shall be filed. They shall ensure that the documents and particulars referred to in Article 8 are published in the appropriate official gazette of the Member State in which the grouping has its official address, and may prescribe the manner of publication of the documents and particulars referred to in Article 8(c).

The Member States shall also ensure that anyone may, at the appropriate registry pursuant to Article 6 or, where appropriate, Article 10, inspect the documents referred to in Article 7 and obtain, even by post, full or partial copies thereof.

The Member States may provide for the payment of fees in connection with the operations referred to in the preceding subparagraphs; those fees may not, however, exceed the administrative cost thereof.

* * *

Article 40

The profits or losses resulting from the activities of a grouping shall be taxable only in the hands of its members.

* * *

Article 43

This Regulation shall enter into force on the third day following its publication in the *Official Journal of the European Communities*.

It shall apply from 1 July 1989, with the exception of Articles 39, 41 and 42 which shall apply as from the entry into force of the Regulation.

This Regulation shall be binding in its entirety and directly applicable in all Member States.

21. COUNCIL DIRECTIVE 89/48/EEC

of 21 December 1988

on a general system for the recognition of higher-education diplomas awarded on completion of professional education and training of at least three years' duration

O.J. L 19/16 (Jan. 24, 1989)

THE COUNCIL OF THE EUROPEAN COMMUNITIES,

Having regard to the Treaty establishing the European Economic Community, and in particular Articles 49, 57(1) and 66 thereof,

Having regard to the proposal from the Commission,[1]

In cooperation with the European Parliament,[2]

Having regard to the opinion of the Economic and Social Committee,[3]

Whereas, pursuant to Article 3(c) of the Treaty the abolition, as between Member States, of obstacles to freedom of movement for persons and services constitutes one of the objectives of the Community; whereas, for nationals of the Member States, this means in particular the possibility of pursuing a profession, whether in a self-employed or employed capacity, in a Member State other than that in which they acquired their professional qualifications;

Whereas the provisions so far adopted by the Council, and pursuant to which Member States recognize mutually and for professional purposes higher-education diplomas issued within their territory, concern only a few professions; whereas the level and duration of the education and training governing access to those professions have been regulated in a similar fashion in all the Member States or have been the subject of the minimal harmonization needed to establish sectoral systems for the mutual recognition of diplomas;

Whereas, in order to provide a rapid response to the expectations of nationals of Community countries who hold higher-education diplomas awarded on completion of professional education and training issued in a Member State other than that in which they wish to pursue their profession, another method of recognition of such diplomas should also be put in place such as to enable those concerned to pursue all those professional activities which in a host Member State are dependent on the completion of post-secondary education and training, provided they hold such a diploma preparing them for those activities awarded on completion of a course of studies lasting at least three years and issued in another Member State;

1. OJ No C 217, 28. 8. 1985, p. 3, and OJ No C 143, 10. 6. 1986, p. 7.
2. OJ No C 345, 31. 12. 1985, p. 80, and OJ No C 309, 5. 12. 1988.
3. OJ No C 75, 3. 4. 1986, p. 5.

Whereas this objective can be achieved by the introduction of a general system for the recognition of higher-education diplomas awarded on completion of professional education and training of at least three years' duration;

Whereas, for those professions for the pursuit of which the Community has not laid down the necessary minimum level of qualification, Member States reserve the option of fixing such a level with a view to guaranteeing the quality of services provided in their territory; whereas, however, they may not, without infringing their obligations laid down in Article 5 of the Treaty, require a national of a Member State to obtain those qualifications which in general they determine only by reference to diplomas issued under their own national education systems, where the person concerned has already acquired all or part of those qualifications in another Member State; whereas, as a result, any host Member State in which a profession is regulated is required to take account of qualifications acquired in another Member State and to determine whether those qualifications correspond to the qualifications which the Member State concerned requires;

* * *

Whereas the term 'regulated professional activity' should be defined so as to take account of differing national sociological situations; whereas the term should cover not only professional activities access to which is subject, in a Member State, to the possession of a diploma, but also professional activities, access to which is unrestricted when they are practised under a professional title reserved for the holders of certain qualifications; whereas the professional associations and organizations which confer such titles on their members and are recognized by the public authorities cannot invoke their private status to avoid application of the system provided for by this Directive;

* * *

Whereas an aptitude test may also be introduced in place of the adaptation period; whereas the effect of both will be to improve the existing situation with regard to the mutual recognition of diplomas between Member States and therefore to facilitate the free movement of persons within the Community; whereas their function is to assess the ability of the migrant, who is a person who has already received his professional training in another Member State, to adapt to this new professional environment; whereas, from the migrant's point of view, an aptitude test will have the advantage of reducing the length of the practice period; whereas, in principle, the choice between the adaptation period and the aptitude test should be made by the migrant; whereas, however, the nature of certain professions is such that Member States must be allowed to prescribe, under certain conditions, either the adaptation period or the test; whereas, in particular, the differences between the legal systems of the Member States, whilst they may vary in extent from one Member State to another, warrant special provisions since, as a rule, the education or training attested by the diploma, certificate or other evidence of formal qualifications in a field of law in the Member State of origin does not cover the legal knowledge required in the host Member State with respect to the corresponding legal field;

Whereas, moreover, the general system for the recognition of higher-education diplomas is intended neither to amend the rules, including those relating to professional ethics, applicable to any person pursuing a profession in the territory of a Member State nor to exclude migrants from the application of those rules; whereas that system is confined to laying down appropriate arrangements to ensure that migrants comply with the professional rules of the host Member State;

Whereas Articles 49, 57(1) and 66 of the Treaty empower the Community to adopt provisions necessary for the introduction and operation of such a system;

Whereas the general system for the recognition of higher-education diplomas is entirely without prejudice to the application of Article 48(4) and Article 55 of the Treaty;

Whereas such a system, by strengthening the right of a Community national to use his professional skills in any Member State, supplements and reinforces his right to acquire such skills wherever he wishes;

Whereas this system should be evaluated, after being in force for a certain time, to determine how efficiently it operates and in particular how it can be improved or its field of application extended,

HAS ADOPTED THIS DIRECTIVE:

Article 1

For the purposes of this Directive the following definitions shall apply:

(a) diploma: any diploma, certificate or other evidence of formal qualifications or any set of such diplomas, certificates or other evidence:

— which has been awarded by a competent authority in a Member State, designated in accordance with its own laws, regulations or administrative provisions,

— which shows that the holder has successfully completed a post-secondary course of at least three years' duration, or of an equivalent duration part-time, at a university or establishment of higher education or another establishment of similar level and, where appropriate, that he has successfully completed the professional training required in addition to the post-secondary course; and

— which shows that the holder has the professional qualifications required for the taking up or pursuit of a regulated profession in that Member State,

provided that the education and training attested by the diploma, certificate or other evidence of formal qualifications were received mainly in the Community, or the holder thereof has three years' professional experience certified by the Member State which recognized a third-country diploma, certificate or other evidence of formal qualifications.

* * *

(b) host Member State: any Member State in which a national of a Member State applies to pursue a profession subject to regulation in that Member State, other than the State in which he obtained his diploma or first pursued the profession in question;

(c) a regulated profession: the regulated professional activity or range of activities which constitute this profession in a Member State;

(d) regulated professional activity: a professional activity, in so far as the taking up or pursuit of such activity or one of its modes of pursuit in a Member State is subject, directly or indirectly by virtue of laws, regulations or administrative provisions, to the possession of a diploma.

* * *

A non-exhaustive list of associations or organizations which, when this Directive is adopted, satisfy the conditions of the second subparagraph is contained in the Annex. Whenever a Member State grants the recognition referred to in the second subparagraph to an association or organization, it shall inform the Commission thereof, which shall publish this information in the *Official Journal of the European Communities.*

(e) professional experience: the actual and lawful pursuit of the profession concerned in a Member State;

(f) adaptation period: the pursuit of a regulated profession in the host Member State under the responsibility of a qualified member of that profession, such period of supervised practice possibly being accompanied by further training. This period of supervised practice shall be the subject of an assessment. The detailed rules governing the adaptation period and its assessment as well as the status of a migrant person under supervision shall be laid down by the competent authority in the host Member States;

(g) aptitude test: a test limited to the professional knowledge of the applicant, made by the competent authorities of the host Member State with the aim of assessing the ability of the applicant to pursue a regulated profession in that Member State.

In order to permit this test to be carried out, the competent authorities shall draw up a list of subjects which, on the basis of a comparison of the education and training required in the Member State and that received by the applicant, are not covered by the diploma or other evidence of formal qualifications possessed by the applicant.

The aptitude test must take account of the fact that the applicant is a qualified professional in the Member State of origin or the Member State from which he comes. It shall cover subjects to be selected from those on the list, knowledge of which is essential in order to be able to exercise the profession in the host Member State. The test may also include knowledge of the professional rules applicable to the activities in question in the host Member State. The detailed application of the aptitude test shall be determined by the competent authorities of that State with due regard to the rules of Community law.

The status, in the host Member State, of the applicant who wishes to prepare himself for the aptitude test in that State shall be determined by the competent authorities in that State.

Article 2

This Directive shall apply to any national of a Member State wishing to pursue a regulated profession in a host Member State in a self-employed capacity or as an employed person.

This Directive shall not apply to professions which are the subject of a separate Directive establishing arrangements for the mutual recognition of diplomas by Member States.

Article 3

Where, in a host Member State, the taking up or pursuit of a regulated profession is subject to possession of a diploma, the competent authority may not, on the grounds of inadequate qualifications, refuse to authorize a national of a Member State to take up or pursue that profession on the same conditions as apply to its own nationals:

(a) if the applicant holds the diploma required in another Member State for the taking up or pursuit of the profession in question in its territory, such diploma having been awarded in a Member State;

* * *

Article 4

1. Notwithstanding Article 3, the host Member State may also require the applicant:

(a) to provide evidence of professional experience, where the duration of the education and training adduced in support of his application, as laid down in Article 3(a) and (b), is at least one year less than that required in the host Member State. In this event, the period of professional experience required:

— may not exceed twice the shortfall in duration of education and training where the shortfall relates to post-secondary studies and/or to a period of probationary practice carried out under the control of a supervising professional person and ending with an examination,

— may not exceed the shortfall where the shortfall relates to professional practice acquired with the assistance of a qualified member of the profession.

In the case of diplomas within the meaning of the last subparagraph of Article 1(a), the duration of education and training recognized as being of an equivalent level shall be determined as for the education and training defined in the first subparagraph of Article 1(a).

When applying these provisions, account must be taken of the professional experience referred to in Article 3(b).

At all events, the professional experience required may not exceed four years;

(b) to complete an adaptation period not exceeding three years or take an aptitude test:

— where the matters covered by the education and training he has received as laid down in Article 3(a) and (b), differ substantially from those covered by the diploma required in the host Member State, or

— where, in the case referred to in Article 3(a), the profession regulated in the host Member State comprises one or more regulated professional activities which are not in the profession regulated in the Member State from which the applicant originates or comes and that difference corresponds to specific education and training required in the host Member State and covers matters which differ substantially from those covered by the diploma adduced by the applicant, or

— where, in the case referred to in Article 3(b), the profession regulated in the host Member State comprises one or more regulated professional activities which are not in the profession pursued by the applicant in the Member State from which he originates or comes, and that difference corresponds to specific education and training required in the host Member State and covers matters which differ substantially from those covered by the evidence of formal qualifications adduced by the applicant.

Should the host Member State make use of this possibility, it must give the applicant the right to choose between an adaptation period and an aptitude test. By way of derogation from this principle, for professions whose practice requires precise knowledge of national law and in respect of which the provision of advice and/or assistance concerning national law is an essential and constant aspect of the professional activity, the host Member State may stipulate either an adaptation period or an aptitude test. Where the host Member State intends to introduce derogations for other professions as regards an applicant's right to choose, the procedure laid down in Article 10 shall apply.

2. However, the host Member State may not apply the provisions of paragraph 1(a) and (b) cumulatively.

Article 5

Without prejudice to Articles 3 and 4, a host Member State may allow the applicant, with a view to improving his possibilities of adapting to the professional environment in that State, to undergo there, on the basis of equivalence, that part of his professional education and training represented by professional practice, acquired with the assistance of a qualified member of the profession, which he has not undergone in his Member State of origin or the Member State from which he has come.

Article 6

1. Where the competent authority of a host Member State requires of persons wishing to take up a regulated profession proof that they are of good character or repute or that they have not been declared bankrupt, or suspends or prohibits the pursuit of that profession in the event of serious professional misconduct or a criminal offence, that State shall accept as sufficient evidence, in respect of nationals of Member States wishing to pursue that profession in its territory, the production of documents issued by competent authorities in the Member State of origin or the Member State from which the foreign national comes showing that those requirements are met.

* * *

2. Where the competent authority of a host Member State requires of nationals of that Member State wishing to take up or pursue a regulated profession a certificate of physical or mental health, that authority shall accept as sufficient evidence in this respect the production of the document required in the Member State of origin or the Member State from which the foreign national comes.

* * *

4. Where the competent authority of a host Member State requires nationals of that Member State wishing to take up or pursue a regulated profession to take an oath or make a solemn declaration and where the form of such oath or declaration cannot be used by nationals of other Member States, that authority shall ensure that an appropriate and equivalent form of oath or declaration is offered to the person concerned.

Article 7

1. The competent authorities of host Member States shall recognize the right of nationals of Member States who fulfil the conditions for the taking up and pursuit of a regulated profession in their territory to use the professional title of the host Member State corresponding to that profession.

2. The competent authorities of host Member States shall recognize the right of nationals of Member States who fulfil the conditions for the taking up and pursuit of a regulated profession in their territory to use their lawful academic title and, where appropriate, the abbreviation thereof deriving from their Member State of origin or the Member State from which they come, in the language of that State. Host Member States may require this title to be followed by the name and location of the establishment or examining board which awarded it.

* * *

Article 8

1. The host Member State shall accept as proof that the conditions laid down in Articles 3 and 4 are satisfied the certificates and documents issued by the competent authorities in the Member States, which the person concerned shall submit in support of his application to pursue the profession concerned.

2. The procedure for examining an application to pursue a regulated profession shall be completed as soon as possible and the outcome communicated in a reasoned decision of the competent authority in the host Member State not later than four months after presentation of all the documents relating to the person concerned. A remedy shall be available against this decision, or the absence thereof, before a court or tribunal in accordance with the provisions of national law.

Article 9

1. Member States shall designate, within the period provided for in Article 12, the competent authorities empowered to receive the applications and take the decisions referred to in this Directive.

They shall communicate this information to the other Member States and to the Commission.

2. Each Member State shall designate a person responsible for coordinating the activities of the authorities referred to in paragraph 1 and shall inform the other Member States and the Commission to that effect. His role shall be to promote uniform application of this Directive to all the professions concerned. A coordinating group shall be set up under the aegis of the Commission, composed of the coordinators appointed by each Member State or their deputies and chaired by a representative of the Commission.

The task of this group shall be:

— to facilitate the implementation of this Directive,

— to collect all useful information for its application in the Member States.

The group may be consulted by the Commission on any changes to the existing system that may be contemplated.

* * *

Article 10

1. If, pursuant to the third sentence of the second subparagraph of Article 4(1)(b), a Member State proposes not to grant applicants the right to choose between an adaptation period and an aptitude test in respect of a profession within the meaning of this Directive, it shall immediately communicate to the Commission the corresponding draft provision. It shall at the same time notify the Commission of the grounds which make the enactment of such a provision necessary.

* * *

Article 11

Following the expiry of the period provided for in Article 12, Member States shall communicate to the Commission, every two years, a report on the application of the system introduced.

In addition to general remarks, this report shall contain a statistical summary of the decisions taken and a description of the main problems arising from application of the Directive.

Article 12

Member States shall take the measures necessary to comply with this Directive within two years of its notification. They shall forthwith inform the Commission thereof.

Member States shall communicate to the Commission the texts of the main provisions of national law which they adopt in the field governed by this Directive.

Article 13

Five years at the latest following the date specified in Article 12, the Commission shall report to the European Parliament and the Council on the state of application of the general system for the recognition of higher-education diplomas awarded on completion of professional education and training of at least three years' duration.

After conducting all necessary consultations, the Commission shall, on this occasion, present its conclusions as to any changes that need to be made to the system as it stands. At the same time the Commission shall, where appropriate, submit proposals for improvements in the present system in the interest of further facilitating the freedom of movement, right of establishment and freedom to provide services of the persons covered by this Directive.

Article 14

This Directive is addressed to the Member States.

22. COUNCIL RECOMMENDATION 89/49/EEC

of 21 December 1988

concerning nationals of Member States who hold a diploma conferred in a third State

O.J. L 19/24 (Jan. 24, 1989)

THE COUNCIL OF THE EUROPEAN COMMUNITIES,

Approving Council Directive 89/48/EEC of 21 December 1988 on a general system for the recognition of higher-education diplomas awarded on completion of professional education and training of at least three years' duration;

Noting that this Directive refers only to diplomas, certificates and other evidence of formal qualifications awarded in Member States to nationals of Member States;

Anxious, however, to take account of the special position of nationals of Member States who hold diplomas, certificates or other evidence of formal qualifications awarded in third States and who are thus in a position comparable to one of those described in Article 3 of the Directive,

HEREBY RECOMMENDS:

that the Governments of the Member States should allow the persons referred to above to take up and pursue regulated professions within the Community by recognizing these diplomas, certificates and other evidence of formal qualifications in their territories.

23. COUNCIL DIRECTIVE 77/249/EEC

of 22 March 1977
to facilitate the effective exercise by lawyers of freedom to provide services

O.J. L 78/17 (Mar. 26, 1977)

THE COUNCIL OF THE EUROPEAN COMMUNITIES,

Having regard to the Treaty establishing the European Economic Community, and in particular Articles 57 and 66 thereof,

Having regard to the proposal from the Commission,

Having regard to the opinion of the European Parliament,

Having regard to the opinion of the Economic and Social Committee,

Whereas, pursuant to the Treaty, any restriction on the provision of services which is based on nationality or on conditions of residence has been prohibited since the end of the transitional period;

Whereas this Directive deals only with measures to facilitate the effective pursuit of the activities of lawyers by way of provision of services; whereas more detailed measures will be necessary to facilitate the effective exercise of the right of establishment;

Whereas if lawyers are to exercise effectively the freedom to provide services host Member States must recognize as lawyers those persons practising the profession in the various Member States;

Whereas, since this Directive solely concerns provision of services and does not contain provisions on the mutual recognition of diplomas, a person to whom the Directive applies must adopt the professional title used in the Member State in which he is established, hereinafter referred to as 'the Member State from which he comes',

HAS ADOPTED THIS DIRECTIVE:

Article 1

1. This Directive shall apply, within the limits and under the conditions laid down herein, to the activities of lawyers pursued by way of provision of services.

Notwithstanding anything contained in this Directive, Member States may reserve to prescribed categories of lawyers the preparation of formal documents for obtaining title to administer estates of deceased persons, and the drafting of formal documents creating or transferring interests in land.

2. 'Lawyer' means any person entitled to pursue his professional activities under one of the following designations:

Belgium:	Avocat—Advocaat
Denmark:	Advokat
Germany:	Rechtsanwalt
France:	Avocat

Ireland:	Barrister
	Solicitor
Italy:	Avvocato
Luxembourg:	Avocat-avoué
Netherlands:	Advocaat
United Kingdom:	Advocate
	Barrister
	Solicitor.

Article 2

Each Member State shall recognize as a lawyer for the purpose of pursuing the activities specified in Article 1(1) any person listed in paragraph 2 of that Article.

Article 3

A person referred to in Article 1 shall adopt the professional title used in the Member State from which he comes, expressed in the language or one of the languages, of that State, with an indication of the professional organization by which he is authorized to practise or the court of law before which he is entitled to practise pursuant to the laws of that State.

Article 4

1. Activities relating to the representation of a client in legal proceedings or before public authorities shall be pursued in each host Member State under the conditions laid down for lawyers established in that State, with the exception of any conditions requiring residence, or registration with a professional organization, in that State.

2. A lawyer pursuing these activities shall observe the rules of professional conduct of the host Member State, without prejudice to his obligations in the Member State from which he comes.

3. When these activities are pursued in the United Kingdom, 'rules of professional conduct of the host Member State' means the rules of professional conduct applicable to solicitors, where such activities are not reserved for barristers and advocates. Otherwise the rules of professional conduct applicable to the latter shall apply. However, barristers from Ireland shall always be subject to the rules of professional conduct applicable in the United Kingdom to barristers and advocates.

When these activities are pursued in Ireland 'rules of professional conduct of the host Member State' means, in so far as they govern the oral presentation of a case in court, the rules of professional conduct applicable to barristers. In all other cases the rules of professional conduct applicable to solicitors shall apply. However, barristers and advocates from the United Kingdom shall always be subject to the rules of professional conduct applicable in Ireland to barristers.

4. A lawyer pursuing activities other than those referred to in paragraph 1 shall remain subject to the conditions and rules of professional conduct of the Member State from which he comes without prejudice to

respect for the rules, whatever their source, which govern the profession in the host Member State, especially those concerning the incompatibility of the exercise of the activities of a lawyer with the exercise of other activities in that State, professional secrecy, relations with other lawyers, the prohibition on the same lawyer acting for parties with mutually conflicting interests, and publicity. The latter rules are applicable only if they are capable of being observed by a lawyer who is not established in the host Member State and to the extent to which their observance is objectively justified to ensure, in that State, the proper exercise of a lawyer's activities, the standing of the profession and respect for the rules concerning incompatibility.

Article 5

For the pursuit of activities relating to the representation of a client in legal proceedings, a Member State may require lawyers to whom Article 1 applies:

— to be introduced, in accordance with local rules or customs, to the presiding judge and, where appropriate, to the President of the relevant Bar in the host Member State;

— to work in conjunction with a lawyer who practises before the judicial authority in question and who would, where necessary, be answerable to that authority, or with an 'avoué' or 'procuratore' practising before it.

Article 6

Any Member State may exclude lawyers who are in the salaried employment of a public or private undertaking from pursuing activities relating to the representation of that undertaking in legal proceedings in so far as lawyers established in that State are not permitted to pursue those activities.

Article 7

1. The competent authority of the host Member State may request the person providing the services to establish his qualifications as a lawyer.

2. In the event of non-compliance with the obligations referred to in Article 4 and in force in the host Member State, the competent authority of the latter shall determine in accordance with its own rules and procedures the consequences of such non-compliance, and to this end may obtain any appropriate professional information concerning the person providing services. It shall notify the competent authority of the Member State from which the person comes of any decision taken. Such exchanges shall not affect the confidential nature of the information supplied.

* * *

Article 9

This Directive is addressed to the Member States.

24. COUNCIL DIRECTIVE 88/361/EEC

of 24 June 1988
for the implementation of Article 67 of the Treaty
O.J. L 178/5 (July 8, 1988)

THE COUNCIL OF THE EUROPEAN COMMUNITIES,

Having regard to the Treaty establishing the European Economic Community, and in particular Articles 69 and 70(1) thereof,

Having regard to the proposal from the Commission, submitted following consultation with the Monetary Committee,

Having regard to the opinion of the European Parliament,

Whereas Article 8a of the Treaty stipulates that the internal market shall comprise an area without internal frontiers in which the free movement of capital is ensured, without prejudice to the other provisions of the Treaty;

* * *

Whereas advantage should be taken of the period adopted for bringing this Directive into effect in order to enable the Commission to submit proposals designed to eliminate or reduce risks of distortion, tax evasion and tax avoidance resulting from the diversity of national systems for taxation and to permit the Council to take a position on such proposals;

Whereas, in accordance with Article 70(1) of the Treaty, the Community shall endeavour to attain the highest possible degree of liberalization in respect of the movement of capital between its residents and those of third countries;

* * *

HAS ADOPTED THIS DIRECTIVE:

Article 1

1. Without prejudice to the following provisions, Member States shall abolish restrictions on movements of capital taking place between persons resident in Member States. To facilitate application of this Directive, capital movements shall be classified in accordance with the Nomenclature in Annex I.

2. Transfers in respect of capital movements shall be made on the same exchange rate conditions as those governing payments relating to current transactions.

Article 2

Member States shall notify the Committee of Governors of the Central Banks, the Monetary Committee and the Commission, by the date of their entry into force at the latest, of measures to regulate bank liquidity which have a specific impact on capital transactions carried out by credit institutions with non-residents.

Such measures shall be confined to what is necessary for the purposes of domestic monetary regulation. The Monetary Committee and the Committee of Governors of the Central Banks shall provide the Commission with opinions on this subject.

Article 3

1. Where short-term capital movements of exceptional magnitude impose severe strains on foreign-exchange markets and lead to serious disturbances in the conduct of a Member State's monetary and exchange rate policies, being reflected in particular in substantial variations in domestic liquidity, the Commission may, after consulting the Monetary Committee and the Committee of Governors of the Central Banks, authorize that Member State to take, in respect of the capital movements listed in Annex II, protective measures the conditions and details of which the Commission shall determine.

2. The Member State concerned may itself take the protective measures referred to above, on grounds of urgency, should these measures be necessary. The Commission and the other Member States shall be informed of such measures by the date of their entry into force at the latest. The Commission, after consulting the Monetary Committee and the Committee of Governors of the Central Banks, shall decide whether the Member State concerned may continue to apply these measures or whether it should amend or abolish them.

3. The decisions taken by the Commission under paragraphs 1 and 2 may be revoked or amended by the Council acting by a qualified majority.

4. The period of application of protective measures taken pursuant to this Article shall not exceed six months.

5. Before 31 December 1992, the Council shall examine, on the basis of a report from the Commission, after delivery of an opinion by the Monetary Committee and the Committee of Governors of the Central Banks, whether the provisions of this Article remain appropriate, as regards their principle and details, to the requirements which they were amended to satisfy.

Article 4

This Directive shall be without prejudice to the right of Member States to take all requisite measures to prevent infringements of their laws and regulations, *inter alia* in the field of taxation and prudential supervision of financial institutions, or to lay down procedures for the declaration of capital movements for purposes of administrative or statistical information.

Application of those measures and procedures may not have the effect of impeding capital movements carried out in accordance with Community law.

* * *

Article 6

1. Member States shall take the measures necessary to comply with this Directive no later than 1 July 1990. They shall forthwith inform the Commission thereof. They shall also make known, by the date of their entry into force at the latest, any new measure or any amendment made to the provisions governing the capital movements listed in Annex I.

2. The Kingdom of Spain and the Portuguese Republic, without prejudice for these two Member States to Articles 61 to 66 and 222 to 232 of the 1985 Act of Accession, and the Hellenic Republic and Ireland may temporarily continue to apply restrictions to the capital movements listed in Annex IV, subject to the conditions and time limits laid down in that Annex.

If, before expiry of the time limit set for the liberalization of the capital movements referred to in Lists III and IV of Annex IV, the Portuguese Republic or the Hellenic Republic considers that it is unable to proceed with liberalization, in particular because of difficulties as regards its balance of payments or because the national financial system is insufficiently adapted, the Commission, at the request of one or other of these Member States, shall in collaboration with the Monetary Committee, review the economic and financial situation of the Member State concerned. On the basis of the outcome of this review, the Commission shall propose to the Council an extension of the time limit set for liberalization of all or part of the capital movements referred to. This extension may not exceed three years. The Council shall act in accordance with the procedure laid down in Article 69 of the Treaty.

3. The Kingdom of Belgium and the Grand Duchy of Luxembourg may temporarily continue to operate the dual exchange market under the conditions and for the periods laid down in Annex V.

4. Existing national legislation regulating purchases of secondary residences may be upheld until the Council adopts further provisions in this area in accordance with Article 69 of the Treaty. This provision does not affect the applicability of other provisions of Community law.

5. The Commission shall submit to the Council, by 31 December 1988, proposals aimed at eliminating or reducing risks or distortion, tax evasion and tax avoidance linked to the diversity of national systems for the taxation of savings and for controlling the application of these systems.

The Council shall take a position on these Commission proposals by 30 June 1989. Any tax provisions of a Community nature shall, in accordance with the Treaty, be adopted unanimously.

Article 7

1. In their treatment of transfers in respect of movements of capital to or from third countries, the Member States shall endeavour to attain the same degree of liberalization as that which applies to operations with residents of other Member States, subject to the other provisions of this Directive.

The provisions of the preceding subparagraph shall not prejudice the application to third countries of domestic rules or Community law, particularly any reciprocal conditions, concerning operations involving establishment, the provisions of financial services and the admission of securities to capital markets.

2. Where large-scale short-term capital movements to or from third countries seriously disturb the domestic or external monetary or financial situation of the Member States, or of a number of them, or cause serious strains in exchange relations within the Community or between the Community and third countries, Member States shall consult with one another on any measure to be taken to counteract such difficulties. This consultation shall take place within the Committee of Governors of the Central Banks and the Monetary Committee on the initiative of the Commission or of any Member State.

Article 8

At least once a year the Monetary Committee shall examine the situation regarding free movement of capital as it results from the application of this Directive. The examination shall cover measures concerning the domestic regulation of credit and financial and monetary markets which could have a specific impact on international capital movements and on all other aspects of this Directive. The Committee shall report to the Commission on the outcome of this examination.

Article 9

The First Directive of 11 May 1960 and Directive 72/156/EEC shall be repealed with effect from 1 July 1990.

Article 10

This Directive is addressed to the Member States.

25. COUNCIL DIRECTIVE 79/279/EEC

of 5 March 1979

coordinating the conditions for the admission of securities to official stock exchange listing

O.J. L 66/21 (Mar. 16, 1979)

THE COUNCIL OF THE EUROPEAN COMMUNITIES,

Having regard to the Treaty establishing the European Economic Community, and in particular Articles 54(3)(g) and 100 thereof,

Having regard to the proposal from the Commission,

Having regard to the opinion of the European Parliament,

Having regard to the opinion of the Economic and Social Committee,

Whereas the coordination of the conditions for the admission of securities to official listing on stock exchanges situated or operating in the Member States is likely to provide equivalent protection for investors at Community level, because of the more uniform guarantees offered to investors in the various Member States; whereas it will facilitate both the admission to official stock exchange listing, in each such State, of securities from other Member States and the listing of any given security on a number of stock exchanges in the Community; whereas it will accordingly make for greater interpenetration of national securities markets and therefore contribute to the prospect of establishing a European capital market;

Whereas such coordination must therefore apply to securities, independently of the legal status of their issuers, and must therefore also apply to securities issued by non-member States or their regional or local authorities or international public bodies; whereas this Directive therefore covers entities not covered by the second paragraph of Article 58 of the Treaty and goes beyond the scope of Article 54(3)(g) while directly affecting the establishment and functioning of the common market within the meaning of Article 100;

Whereas there should be the possibility of a right to apply to the courts against decisions by the competent national authorities in respect of the application of this Directive, although such right to apply must not be allowed to restrict the discretion of these authorities;

Whereas, initially, this coordination should be sufficiently flexible to enable account to be taken of present differences in the structures of securities markets in the Member States and to enable the Member States to take account of any specific situations with which they may be confronted;

Whereas, for this reason, coordination should first be limited to the establishment of minimum conditions for the admission of securities to official listing on stock exchanges situated or operating in the Member States, without however giving issuers any right to listing;

Whereas, this partial coordination of the conditions for admission to official listing constitutes a first step towards subsequent closer alignment of the rules of Member States in this field,

HAS ADOPTED THIS DIRECTIVE:

SECTION I
GENERAL PROVISIONS

Article 1

1. This Directive concerns securities which are admitted to official listing or are the subject of an application for admission to official listing on a stock exchange situated or operating within a Member State.

2. Member States may decide not to apply this Directive to:

— units issued by collective investment undertakings other than the closed-end type,

— securities issued by a Member State or its regional or local authorities.

* * *

Article 3

Member States shall ensure that:

— securities may not be admitted to official listing on any stock exchange situated or operating within their territory unless the conditions laid down by this Directive are satisfied, and that

— issuers of securities admitted to such official listing, whether admission takes place before or after the date on which this Directive is implemented, are subject to the obligations provided for by this Directive.

Article 4

1. The admission of securities to official listing shall be subject to the conditions set out in Schedules A and B to this Directive, relating to shares and debt securities respectively.

2. The issuers of securities admitted to official listing must fulfil the obligations set out in Schedules C and D to this Directive, relating to shares and debt securities respectively.

3. Certificates representing shares may be admitted to official listing only if the issuer of the shares represented fulfils the conditions set out in I(1) to I(3) of Schedule A and the obligations set out in Schedule C and if the certificates fulfil the conditions set out in II(1) to II(6) of Schedule A.

Article 5

1. Subject to the prohibitions provided for in Article 6 and in Schedules A and B, the Member States may make the admission of securities to official listing subject to more stringent conditions than those set out in Schedules A and B or to additional conditions, provided that these more stringent and additional conditions apply generally for all issuers or for individual classes of issuers and that they have been published before application for admission of such securities is made.

2. Member States may make the issuers of securities admitted to official listing subject to more stringent obligations than those set out in Schedules C and D or to additional obligations, provided that these more stringent and additional obligations apply generally for all issuers or for individual classes of issuer.

3. Member States may, under the same conditions as those laid down in Article 7, authorize derogations from the additional or more stringent conditions and obligations referred to in paragraphs 1 and 2 hereof.

4. [Essentially replaced by Directive 82/121.]

Article 6

Member States may not make the admission to official listing of securities issued by companies or other legal persons which are nationals of another Member State subject to the condition that the securities must already have been admitted to official listing on a stock exchange situated or operating in one of the Member States.

Article 7

Any derogations from the conditions for the admission of securities to official listing which may be authorized in accordance with Schedules A and B must apply generally for all issuers where the circumstances justifying them are similar.

* * *

SECTION II
AUTHORITIES COMPETENT TO ADMIT SECURITIES TO OFFICIAL LISTING

Article 9

1. Member States shall designate the national authority or authorities competent to decide on the admission of securities to official listing on a stock exchange situated or operating within their territories and shall ensure that this Directive is applied. They shall inform the Commission accordingly, indicating, if appropriate, how duties have been allocated.

2. Member States shall ensure that the competent authorities have such powers as may be necessary for the exercise of their duties.

3. Without prejudice to the other powers conferred upon them, the competent authorities may reject an application for the admission of a security to official listing if, in their opinion, the issuer's situation is such that admission would be detrimental to investors' interests.

Article 10

By way of derogation from Article 5, Member States may, solely in the interests of protecting the investors, give the competent authorities power to make the admission of a security to official listing subject to any special condition which the competent authorities consider appropriate and of which they have explicitly informed the applicant.

Article 11

The competent authorities may refuse to admit to official listing a security already officially listed in another Member State where the issuer fails to comply with the obligations resulting from admission in that Member State.

Article 12

Without prejudice to any other action or penalties which they may contemplate in the event of failure on the part of the issuer to comply with the obligations resulting from admission to official listing, the competent authorities may make public the fact that an issuer is failing to comply with those obligations.

Article 13

1. An issuer whose securities are admitted to official listing shall provide the competent authorities with all the information which the latter consider appropriate in order to protect investors or ensure the smooth operation of the market.

2. Where protection of investors or the smooth operation of the market so requires, an issuer may be required by the competent authorities to publish such information in such a form and within such time limits as they consider appropriate. Should the issuer fail to comply with such requirement, the competent authorities may themselves publish such information after having heard the issuer.

Article 14

1. The competent authorities may decide to suspend the listing of a security where the smooth operation of the market is, or may be, temporarily jeopardized or where protection of investors so requires.

2. The competent authorities may decide that the listing of the security be discontinued where they are satisfied that, owing to special circumstances, normal regular dealings in a security are no longer possible.

Article 15

1. Member States shall ensure decisions of the competent authorities refusing the admission of a security to official listing or discontinuing such a listing shall be subject to the right to apply to the courts.

2. An applicant shall be notified of a decision regarding his application for admission to official listing within six months of receipt of the application or, should the competent authority require any further information within that period, within six months of the applicant's supplying such information.

3. Failure to give a decision within the time limit specified in paragraph 2 shall be deemed a rejection of the application. Such rejection shall give rise to the right to apply to the courts provided for in paragraph 1.

Article 16

Where an application for admission to official listing relates to certificates representing shares, the application shall be considered only if the competent authorities are of the opinion that the issuer of the certificates is offering adequate safeguards for the protection of investors.

SECTION III
PUBLICATION OF THE INFORMATION TO BE MADE AVAILABLE TO THE PUBLIC

Article 17

1. The information which issuers of a security admitted to official listing in a Member State are required to make available to the public in accordance with the requirements of Schedules C and D shall be published in one or more newspapers distributed throughout the Member State or distributed widely therein or shall be made available to the public either in writing in places indicated by announcements to be published in one or more newspapers distributed throughout the Member State or widely distributed therein or by other equivalent means approved by the competent authorities. The issuers must simultaneously send such information to the competent authorities.

2. The information referred to in paragraph 1 shall be published in the official language or languages, or in one of the official languages or in another language provided that in the Member State in question the official language or languages or such other language is or are customary in the sphere of finance and accepted by the competent authorities.

SECTION IV
COOPERATION BETWEEN MEMBER STATES

Article 18

1. The competent authorities shall cooperate wherever necessary for the purpose of carrying out their duties and shall exchange any information required for that purpose.

2. Where applications are to be made simultaneously or within short intervals of one another for admission of the same securities to official listing on stock exchanges situated or operating in more than one Member State, or where an application for admission is made in respect of a security already listed on a stock exchange in another Member State, the competent authorities shall communicate with each other and make such arrangements as may be necessary to expedite the procedure and simplify as far as possible the formalities and any additional conditions required for admission of the security concerned.

* * *

Article 19

1. Member States shall provide that all persons employed or formerly employed by the competent authorities shall be bound by professional secrecy. This means that any confidential information received in the course of their duties may not be divulged to any person or authority except by virtue of provisions laid down by law.

* * *

SECTION V
CONTACT COMMITTEE
Article 20

1. A Contact Committee (hereinafter called 'the Committee') shall be set up alongside the Commission. Its function shall be:

(a) without prejudice to Articles 169 and 170 of the EEC Treaty to facilitate the harmonized implementation of this Directive through regular consultations on any practical problems arising from its application and on which exchanges of view are deemed useful;

(b) to facilitate the establishment of a concerted attitude between the Member States on the more stringent or additional conditions and obligations which, pursuant to Article 5 of this Directive, they may lay down at national level;

(c) to advise the Commission, if necessary, on any supplements or amendments to be made to this Directive or on any adjustments to be made in accordance with Article 21.

2. It shall not be the function of the Committee to appraise the merits of decisions taken by the competent authorities in individual cases.

3. The Committee shall be composed of persons appointed by the Member States and of representatives of the Commission. The chairman shall be a representative of the Commission. Secretarial services shall be provided by the Commission.

4. Meetings of the Committee shall be convened by its chairman, either on his own initiative or at the request of one Member State delegation. The Committee shall draw up its rules of procedure.

* * *

SECTION VI
FINAL PROVISIONS

* * *

Article 23

This Directive is addressed to the Member States.

ANNEX
SCHEDULE A
CONDITIONS FOR THE ADMISSION OF SHARES TO OFFICIAL LISTING ON A STOCK EXCHANGE

I. Conditions relating to companies for the shares of which admission to official listing is sought

1. *Legal position of the company*

The legal position of the company must be in conformity with the laws and regulations to which it is subject, as regards both its formation and its operation under its statutes.

2. *Minimum size of the company*

The foreseeable market capitalization of the shares for which admission to official listing is sought or, if this cannot be assessed, the company's capital and reserves, including profit or loss, from the last financial year, must be at least one million European [currency] units.

However, Member States may provide for admission to official listing, even when this condition is not fulfilled, provided that the competent authorities are satisfied that there will be an adequate market for the shares concerned.

A higher foreseeable market capitalization or higher capital and reserves may be required by a Member State for admission to official listing only if another regulated, regularly operating, recognized open market exists in that State and the requirements for it are equal to or less than those referred to in the first paragraph.

The condition set out in the first paragraph shall not be applicable for the admission to official listing of a further block of shares of the same class as those already admitted.

* * *

3. *A company's period of existence*

A company must have published or filed its annual accounts in accordance with national law for the three financial years preceding the application for official listing. By way of exception, the competent authorities may derogate from this condition where such derogation is desirable in the interests of the company or of investors and where the competent authorities are satisfied that investors have the necessary information available to be able to arrive at an informed judgment on the company and the shares for which admission to official listing is sought.

II. Conditions relating to the shares for which admission to official listing is sought

1. *Legal position of the shares*

The legal position of the shares must be in conformity with the laws and regulations to which they are subject.

2. *Negotiability of the shares*

The shares must be freely negotiable.

* * *

3. *Public issue preceding admission to official listing*

Where public issue precedes admission to official listing, the first listing may be made only after the end of the period during which subscription applications may be submitted.

4. *Distribution of shares*

A sufficient number of shares must be distributed to the public in one or more Member States not later than the time of admission.

This condition shall not apply where shares are to be distributed to the public through the stock exchange. In that event, admission to official listing may be granted only if the competent authorities are satisfied that a sufficient number of shares will be distributed through the stock exchange within a short period.

Where admission to official listing is sought for a further block of shares of the same class, the competent authorities may assess whether a sufficient number of shares has been distributed to the public in relation to all the shares issued and not only in relation to this further block.

However, by way of derogation from the first paragraph, if the shares are admitted to official listing in one or more non-Member States, the competent authorities may provide for their admission to official listing if a sufficient number of shares is distributed to the public in the non-Member State or States where they are listed.

A sufficient number of shares shall be deemed to have been distributed either when the shares in respect of which application for admission has been made are in the hands of the public to the extent of a least 25% of the subscribed capital represented by the class of shares concerned or when, in view of the large number of shares of the same class and the extent of their distribution to the public, the market will operate properly with a lower percentage.

5. *Listing of shares of the same class*

The application for admission to official listing must cover all the shares of the same class already issued.

However, Member States may provide that this condition shall not apply to applications for admission not covering all the shares of the same class already issued where the shares of that class for which admission is not sought belong to blocks serving to maintain control of the company or are not negotiable for a certain time under agreements, provided that the public is informed of such situations and that there is no danger of such situations prejudicing the interests of the holders of the shares for which admission to official listing is sought.

6. *Physical form of shares*

For the admission to official listing of shares issued by companies which are nationals of another Member State and which shares have a physical form it is necessary and sufficient that their physical form comply with the standards laid down in that other Member State. * * *

The physical form of shares issued by companies which are nationals of a non-member State must afford sufficient safeguard for the protection of the investors.

7. *Shares issued by companies from a non-member State*

If the shares issued by a company which is a national of a non-member State are not listed in either the country of origin or in the country in which the major proportion of the shares is held, they may not be admitted to official listing unless the competent authorities are satisfied that the absence of a listing in the country of origin or in the country in which the major proportion is held is not due to the need to protect investors.

SCHEDULE B
CONDITIONS FOR THE ADMISSION OF DEBT SECURITIES TO OFFICIAL LISTING ON A STOCK EXCHANGE

A. ADMISSION TO OFFICIAL LISTING OF DEBT SECURITIES ISSUED BY AN UNDERTAKING

I. Conditions relating to undertakings for the debt securities of which admission to official listing is sought

Legal position of the undertaking

The legal position of the undertaking must be in conformity with the laws and regulations to which it is subject, as regards both its formation and its operation under its statutes.

II. Conditions relating to the debt securities for which admission to official listing is sought

1. *Legal position of the debt securities*

The legal position of the debt securities must be in conformity with the laws and regulations to which they are subject.

2. *Negotiability of the debt securities*

The debt securities must be freely negotiable.

* * *

3. *Public issue preceding admission to official listing*

Where public issue precedes admission to official listing, the first listing may be made only after the end of the period during which subscription applications may be submitted. * * *

4. *Listing of debt securities ranking* pari passu

The application for admission to official listing must cover all debt securities ranking *pari passu.*

5. *Physical form of debt securities*

For the admission to official listing of debt securities issued by undertakings which are nationals of another Member State and which debt securities have a physical form, it is necessary and sufficient that their physical form comply with the standards laid down in that other Member State. * * *

III. Other conditions

1. *Minimum amount of the loan*

The amount of the loan may not be less than 200,000 European [currency] units * * *. Member States may, however, provide for admission to official listing even when this condition is not fulfilled, where the competent authorities are satisfied that there will be a sufficient market for the debt securities concerned.

* * *

2. *Convertible or exchangeable debentures, and debentures with warrants*

Convertible or exchangeable debentures and debentures with warrants may be admitted to official listing only if the related shares are already listed on the same stock exchange or on another regulated, regularly operating, recognized open market or are so admitted simultaneously.

* * *

B. ADMISSION TO OFFICIAL LISTING OF DEBT SECURITIES ISSUED BY A STATE, ITS REGIONAL OR LOCAL AUTHORITIES OR A PUBLIC INTERNATIONAL BODY

[Essentially the same provisions as A. II (2)–(5) supra.]

SCHEDULE C
OBLIGATIONS OF COMPANIES WHOSE SHARES ARE ADMITTED TO OFFICIAL LISTING ON A STOCK EXCHANGE

1. *Listing of newly issued shares of the same class*

Without prejudice to the second paragraph of II(5) of Schedule A, in the case of a new public issue of shares of the same class as those already officially listed, the company shall be required, where the new shares are not automatically admitted, to apply for their admission to the same listing, either not more than a year after their issue or when they become freely negotiable.

2. *Treatment of shareholders*

(a) The company shall ensure equal treatment for all shareholders who are in the same position.

(b) The company must ensure, at least in each Member State in which its shares are listed, that all the necessary facilities and information are available to enable shareholders to exercise their rights. In particular, it must:

— inform shareholders of the holding of meetings and enable them to exercise their right to vote,

— publish notices or distribute circulars concerning the allocation and payment of dividends, the issue of new shares including allotment, subscription, renunciation and conversion arrangements,

— designate as its agent a financial institution through which shareholders may exercise their financial rights, unless the company itself provides financial services.

3. *Amendment of the instrument of incorporation or the statutes*

(a) A company planning an amendment to its instrument of incorporation or its statutes must communicate a draft thereof to the competent authorities of the Member States in which its shares are listed.

(b) That draft must be communicated to the competent authorities no later than the calling of the general meeting which is to decide on the proposed amendment.

4. *Annual accounts and annual report*

(a) The company must make available to the public, as soon as possible, its most recent annual accounts and its last annual report.

(b) If the company prepares both annual own and annual consolidated accounts, it must make them available to the public. * * *

(c) If the annual accounts and reports do not comply with the provisions of Council Directives concerning companies' accounts and if they do not give a true and fair view of the company's assets and liabilities, financial position and profit or loss, more detailed and/or additional information must be provided.

5. *Additional information*

(a) The company must inform the public as soon as possible of any major new developments in its sphere of activity which are not public knowledge and which may, by virtue of their effect on its assets and liabilities or financial position or on the general course of its business, lead to substantial movements in the prices of its shares. [Supplemented by Directive 82/121.]

The competent authorities may, however, exempt the company from this requirement, if the disclosure of particular information is such as to prejudice the legitimate interests of the company.

(b) The company must inform the public without delay of any changes in the rights attaching to the various classes of shares.

(c) The company must inform the public of any changes in the structure (shareholders and breakdown of holdings) of the major holdings in its capital as compared with information previously published on that subject as soon as such changes come to its notice. [Replaced by Directive 88/627.]

6. *Equivalence of information*

(a) A company whose shares are officially listed on stock exchanges situated or operating in different Member States must ensure that equivalent information is made available to the market at each of these exchanges.

(b) A company whose shares are officially listed on stock exchanges situated or operating in one or more Member States and in one or more non-member States must make available to the markets of the Member State or States in which its shares are listed information which is at least equivalent to that which it makes available to the markets of the non-member State or States in question, if such information may be of importance for the evaluation of the shares.

SCHEDULE D

OBLIGATIONS OF ISSUERS WHOSE DEBT SECURITIES ARE ADMITTED TO OFFICIAL LISTING ON A STOCK EXCHANGE

A. DEBT SECURITIES ISSUED BY AN UNDERTAKING

1. *Treatment of holders of debt securities*

(a) The undertaking must ensure that all holders of debt securities ranking *pari passu* are given equal treatment in respect of all the rights attaching to those debt securities.

* * *

(b) The undertaking must ensure that at least in each Member State where its debt securities are officially listed all the facilities and information necessary to enable holders to exercise their rights are available. In particular, it must:

— publish notices or distribute circulars concerning the holding of meetings of holders of debt securities, the payment of interest, the exercise of any conversion, exchange, subscription or renunciation rights, and repayment,

— designate as its agent a financial institution through which holders of debt securities may exercise their financial rights, unless the undertaking itself provides financial services.

2. *Amendment of the instrument of incorporation or the statutes*

(a) An undertaking planning an amendment to its instrument of incorporation or its statutes affecting the rights of holders of debt securities must forward a draft thereof to the competent authorities of the Member States in which its debt securities are listed.

(b) That draft must be communicated to the competent authorities no later than the calling of the meeting of the body which is to decide on the proposed amendment.

3. *Annual accounts and annual report*

[Identical to Schedule C.(4).]

* * *

4. *Additional information*

(a) The undertaking must inform the public as soon as possible of any major new developments in its sphere of activity which are not public knowledge and which may significantly affect its ability to meet its commitments.

The competent authorities may, however, exempt the undertaking from this obligation at its request if the disclosure of particular information would be such as to prejudice the legitimate interests of the undertaking.

(b) The undertaking must inform the public without delay of any change in the rights of holders of debt securities resulting in particular from a change in loan terms or in interest rates.

(c) The undertaking must inform the public without delay of new loan issues and in particular of any guarantee or security in respect thereof.

(d) Where the debt securities officially listed are convertible or exchangeable debentures, or debentures with warrants, the undertaking must inform the public without delay of any changes in the rights attaching to the various classes of shares to which they relate.

5. *Equivalence of information*

[Identical to Schedule C.(6).]

* * *

B. DEBT SECURITIES ISSUED BY A STATE OR ITS REGIONAL OR LOCAL AUTHORITIES OR BY A PUBLIC INTERNATIONAL BODY

[Essentially the same as A. (1) and (5) supra.]

* * *

26. COUNCIL DIRECTIVE 80/390/EEC

of 17 March 1980

coordinating the requirements for the drawing up, scrutiny and distribution of the listing particulars to be published for the admission of securities to official stock exchange listing

O.J. L 100/1 (Apr. 17, 1980)

THE COUNCIL OF THE EUROPEAN COMMUNITIES,

Having regard to the Treaty establishing the European Economic Community, and in particular Articles 54(3)(g) and 100 thereof,

Having regard to the proposal from the Commission,

Having regard to the opinion of the European Parliament,

Having regard to the opinion of the Economic and Social Committee,

Whereas the market in which undertakings operate has been enlarged to embrace the whole Community and this enlargement involves a corresponding increase in their financial requirements and extension of the capital markets on which they must call to satisfy them; whereas admission to official listing on stock exchanges of Member States of securities issued by undertakings constitutes an important means of access to these capital markets; whereas furthermore exchange restrictions on the purchase of securities traded on the stock exchanges of another Member State have been eliminated as part of the liberalization of capital movements;

Whereas safeguards for the protection of the interests of actual and potential investors are required in most Member States of undertakings offering their securities to the public, either at the time of their offer or of their admission to official stock exchange listing; whereas such safeguards require the provision of information which is sufficient and as objective as possible concerning the financial circumstances of the issuer and particulars of the securities for which admission to official listing is requested; whereas the form under which this information is required usually consists of the publication of listing particulars;

Whereas the safeguards required differ from Member State to Member State, both as regards the contents and the layout of the listing particulars and the efficacy, methods and timing of the check on the information given therein; whereas the effect of these differences is not only to make it more difficult for undertakings to obtain admission of securities to official listing on stock exchanges of several Member States but also to hinder the acquisition by investors residing in one Member State of securities listed on stock exchanges of other Member States and thus to inhibit the financing of the undertakings and investment throughout the Community;

Whereas these differences should be eliminated by coordinating the rules and regulations without necessarily making them completely uniform, in order to achieve an adequate degree of equivalence in the safeguards required in each Member State to ensure the provision of information which is sufficient and as objective as possible for actual or potential security holders; whereas at the same time, taking into account the present degree of liberalization of capital movements in the Community and the fact that a mechanism for checking at the time the securities are offered does not yet exist in all Member States, it would appear sufficient at present to limit the coordination to the admission of securities to official stock exchange listing;

Whereas such coordination must apply to securities independently of the legal status of the issuing undertaking, and accordingly, in so far as this Directive applies to entities to which no reference is made in the second paragraph of Article 58 of the Treaty and goes beyond the scope of Article 54(3)(g), it must be based also on Article 100,

HAS ADOPTED THIS DIRECTIVE:

SECTION I
GENERAL PROVISIONS

Article 1

1. This Directive shall apply to securities which are the subject of an application for admission to official listing on a stock exchange situated or operating within a Member State.

2. This Directive shall not apply to:

— units issued by collective investment undertakings other than the closed-end type,

— securities issued by a State or by its regional or local authorities.

Article 2

For purposes of applying this Directive:

* * *

(c) 'issuers' shall mean companies and other legal persons and any undertaking whose securities are the subject of an application for admission to official listing on a stock exchange;

(d) 'net turnover' shall comprise the amounts derived from the sale of products and the provision of services falling within the undertaking's ordinary activities, after deduction of sales rebates and of value added tax and other taxes directly linked to the turnover;

(e) 'credit institution' shall mean an undertaking whose business is to receive deposits or other repayable funds from the public and to grant credits for its own account;

(f) 'participating interest' shall mean rights in the capital of other undertakings, whether or not represented by certificates, which, by creating a durable link with those undertakings, are intended to contribute to the activities of the undertaking which holds these rights;

(g) 'annual accounts' shall comprise the balance sheet, the profit and loss account and the notes on the accounts. These documents shall constitute a composite whole.

Article 3

Member States shall ensure that the admission of securities to official listing on a stock exchange situated or operating within their territories is conditional upon the publication of an information sheet, hereinafter referred to as listing particulars.

Article 4

1. The listing particulars shall contain the information which, according to the particular nature of the issuer and of the securities for the admission of which application is being made, is necessary to enable investors and their investment advisers to make an informed assessment of the assets and liabilities, financial position, profits and losses, and prospects of the issuer and of the rights attaching to such securities.

2. Member States shall ensure that the obligation referred to in paragraph 1 is incumbent upon the persons responsible for the listing particulars as provided for in heading 1.1 of Schedules A and B annexed hereto.

Article 5

1. Without prejudice to the obligation referred to in Article 4, Member States shall ensure that, subject to the possibilities for exemptions provided for in Articles 6 and 7, listing particulars contain, in as easily analysable and comprehensible a form as possible, at least the items of information provided for in Schedules A, B or C, depending on whether shares, debt securities or certificates representing shares are involved.

* * *

Article 6

Member States may allow the authorities responsible for checking the listing particulars within the meaning of this Directive (hereinafter referred to as 'the competent authorities') to provide for partial or complete exemption from the obligation to publish listing particulars in the following cases:

1. where the securities for which admission to official listing is applied for are:

(a) securities which have been the subject of a public issue;

(b) securities issued in connection with a takeover offer;

(c) securities issued in connection with a merger involving the acquisition of another company or the formation of a new company, the division of a company, the transfer of all or part of an undertaking's assets and liabilities or as consideration for the transfer of assets other than cash;

where, not more than 12 months before the admission of the securities to official listing, a document, regarded by the competent authorities as containing information equivalent to that of the listing particulars provided for by this Directive, has been published in the same Member State. Particulars shall also be published of any material changes which have occurred since such document was prepared. The document must be made available to the public at the registered office of the issuer and at the offices of the financial organizations retained to act as the latter's paying agents, and any particulars of material changes shall be published in accordance with Articles 20(1) and 21(1).

2. where the securities for which admission to official listing is applied for are:

(a) shares allotted free of charge to holders of shares already listed on the same stock exchange; or

(b) shares resulting from the conversion of convertible debt securities or shares created after an exchange for exchangeable debt securities, if shares of the company whose shares are offered by way of conversion or exchange are already listed on the same stock exchange; or

(c) shares resulting from the exercise of the rights conferred by warrants, if shares of the company whose shares are offered to holders of the warrants are already listed on the same stock exchange; or

(d) shares issued in substitution for shares already listed on the same stock exchange if the issuing of such new shares does not involve any increase in the company's issued share capital;

and, where appropriate, the information provided for in Chapter 2 of Schedule A is published in accordance with Articles 20(1) and 21(1).

3. where the securities for which admission to official listing is applied for are:

(a) shares of which either the number or the estimated market value or the nominal value or, in the absence of a nominal value, the accounting par value, amounts to less than 10% of the number or of the corresponding value of shares of the same class already listed on the same stock exchange; or

(b) debt securities issued by companies and other legal persons which are nationals of a Member State and which:

— in carrying on their business, benefit from State monopolies, and

— are set up or governed by a special law or pursuant to such a law or whose borrowings are unconditionally and irrevocably guaranteed by a Member State or one of a Member State's federated States; or

(c) debt securities issued by legal persons, other than companies, which are nationals of a Member State, and

— were set up by special law, and

— whose activities are governed by that law and consist solely in:

(i) raising funds under state control through the issue of debt securities, and

(ii) financing production by means of the resources which they have raised and resources provided by a Member State, and

— the debt securities of which are, for the purposes of admission to official listing, considered by national law as debt securities issued or guaranteed by the State; or

(d) shares allotted to employees, if shares of the same class have already been admitted to official listing on the same stock exchange; shares which differ from each other solely as to the date of first entitlement to dividends shall not be considered as being of different classes; or

(e) securities already admitted to official listing on another stock exchange in the same Member State;

* * *

Article 7

The competent authorities may authorize omission from the listing particulars of certain information provided for by this Directive if they consider that:

(a) such information is of minor importance only and is not such as will influence assessment of the assets and liabilities, financial position, profits and losses and prospects of the issuer; or

(b) disclosure of such information would be contrary to the public interest or seriously detrimental to the issuer, provided that, in the latter case, such omission would not be likely to mislead the public with regard to facts and circumstances, knowledge of which is essential for the assessment of the securities in question.

SECTION II

CONTENTS OF THE LISTING PARTICULARS IN CERTAIN SPECIFIC CASES

[This section describes the modified or reduced informational requirements for various types of securities:

Article 8—shares or debt obligations convertible into shares, offered on a preemptive basis where securities of the same class are already listed;

Article 9—debt securities of an issuer which already has securities listed;

Article 10—debt securities which are normally "traded in by a limited number of investors who are particularly knowledgeable in investment matters";

Article 11—securities issued by financial institutions;

Article 12—debt securities issued by credit institutions;

Article 13—debt securities guaranteed by a financial or similar institution;

Article 14—convertible debt securities or warrants;

Article 15—securities issued in connection with a merger, asset acquisition, or takeover offer;

Article 16—certificates representing shares;

Article 17—debt securities backed by the guarantee of a Member State or regional unit.]

SECTION III
ARRANGEMENTS FOR THE SCRUTINY AND PUBLICATION OF LISTING PARTICULARS

Article 18

1. Member States shall appoint one or more competent authorities and shall notify the Commission of the appointments of such authorities, giving details of any division of powers among them. Member States shall also ensure that this Directive is applied.

2. No listing particulars may be published until they have been approved by the competent authorities.

3. The competent authorities shall approve the publication of listing particulars only if they are of the opinion that they satisfy all the requirements set out in this Directive.

Member States shall ensure that the competent authorities have the powers necessary for them to carry out their task.

4. This Directive shall not affect the competent authorities' liability, which shall continue to be governed solely by the national law.

Article 19

The competent authorities shall decide whether to accept the audit report of the official auditor provided for in heading 1.3 of Schedules A and B or, if necessary, to require an additional report.

The requirement for the additional report must be the outcome of an examination of each case on its merits. At the request of the official auditor and/or of the issuer, the competent authorities must disclose to them the reasons justifying this requirement.

Article 20

1. Listing particulars must be published either:

— by insertion in one or more newspapers circulated throughout the Member State in which the admission to official listing of securities is sought, or widely circulated therein, or

— in the form of a brochure to be made available, free of charge, to the public at the offices of the stock exchange or stock exchanges on which the securities are being admitted to official listing, at the registered office of the issuer and at the offices of the financial organizations retained to act as the latter's paying agents in the Member State in which the admission of securities to official listing is sought.

2. In addition, either the complete listing particulars or a notice stating where the listing particulars have been published and where they may be obtained by the public must be inserted in a publication designated by the Member State in which the admission of securities to official listing is sought.

Article 21

1. Listing particulars must be published within a reasonable period, to be laid down in national legislation or by the competent authorities before the date on which official listing becomes effective.

* * *

Article 23

Every significant new factor capable of affecting assessment of the securities which arises between the time when the listing particulars are adopted and the time when stock exchange dealings begin shall be covered by a supplement to the listing particulars, scrutinized in the same way as the latter and published in accordance with procedures to be laid down by the competent authorities.

SECTION IV

COOPERATION BETWEEN THE MEMBER STATES

Article 24

[N.B. Article 24 has been replaced by Directive 87/345.]

1. Where applications for admission of the same securities to official listing on stock exchanges situated or operating within several Member States are made simultaneously, or within short intervals of one another, the competent authorities shall exchange information and use their best endeavours to achieve maximum coordination of their requirements concerning listing particulars, to avoid a multiplicity of formalities and to agree to a single text requiring at the most translation, where appropriate, and the issue of supplements as necessary to meet the individual requirements of each Member State concerned.

2. Where an application for admission to official listing is made for securities which have been listed in another Member State less than six months previously, the competent authorities to whom application is made shall contact the competent authorities which have already admitted the securities to official listing and shall, as far as possible, exempt the issuer of those securities from the preparation of new listing particulars, subject to any need for updating, translation or the issue of supplements in accordance with the individual requirements of the Member State concerned.

Article 25

1. Member States shall provide that all persons employed or formerly employed by the competent authorities shall be bound by professional secrecy. This means that any confidential information received in the course of their duties may not be divulged to any person or authority except by virtue of provisions laid down by law.

* * *

SECTION V
CONTACT COMMITTEE

Article 26

1. The Contact Committee set up by Article 20 of Council Directive 79/279/EEC of 5 March 1979 coordinating the conditions for the admission of securities to official stock exchange listing shall also have as its function:

(a) without prejudice to Articles 169 and 170 of the EEC Treaty to facilitate the harmonized implementation of this Directive through regular consultations on any practical problems arising from its application on which exchanges of views are deemed useful;

(b) to facilitate consultation between the Member States on the supplements and improvements to the listing particulars which the competent authorities are entitled to require or recommend at national level;

(c) to advise the Commission, if necessary, on any additions or amendments to be made to this Directive.

2. It shall not be the function of the Contact Committee to appraise the merits of decisions taken by the competent authorities in individual cases.

SECTION VI
FINAL PROVISIONS

* * *

Article 28

This Directive is addressed to the Member States.

ANNEX
SCHEDULE A
LAYOUT FOR LISTING PARTICULARS FOR THE ADMISSION OF SHARES TO OFFICIAL STOCK EXCHANGE LISTING

CHAPTER 1. INFORMATION CONCERNING THOSE RESPONSIBLE FOR LISTING PARTICULARS AND THE AUDITING OF ACCOUNTS

1.1 Name and function of natural persons and name and registered office of legal persons responsible for the listing particulars or, as the case may be, for certain parts of them, with, in the latter case, an indication of those parts.

1.2 Declaration by those responsible referred to in heading 1.1 that, to the best of their knowledge, the information given in that part of the listing particulars for which they are responsible is in accordance with the facts and contains no omissions likely to affect the import of the listing particulars.

1.3 Names, addresses and qualifications of the official auditors who have audited the company's annual accounts for the preceding three financial years in accordance with national law.

Statement that the annual accounts have been audited. If audit reports on the annual accounts have been refused by the official auditors or if they contain qualifications, such refusal or such qualifications shall be reproduced in full and the reasons given.

Indication of other information in the listing particulars which has been audited by the auditors.

CHAPTER 2. INFORMATION CONCERNING ADMISSION TO OFFICIAL LISTING AND THE SHARES FOR THE ADMISSION OF WHICH APPLICATION IS BEING MADE

2.1 Indication that the admission applied for is admission to official listing of shares already marketed or admission to listing with a view to stock exchange marketing.

2.2 Information concerning the shares in respect of which application for official listing is being made:

2.2.0 Indication of the resolutions, authorizations and approvals by virtue of which the shares have been or will be created and/or issued.

Nature of the issue and amount thereof.

Number of shares which have been or will be created and/or issued, if predetermined.

2.2.1 In the case of shares issued in connection with a merger, the division of a company, the transfer of all or part of an undertaking's assets and liabilities, a takeover offer, or as consideration for the transfer of assets other than cash, indication of where the documents describing the terms and conditions of such operations are available for inspection by the public.

2.2.2 A concise description of the rights attaching to the shares, and in particular the extent of the voting rights, entitlement to share in the profits and to share in any surplus in the event of liquidation and any privileges.

Time limit after which dividend entitlement lapses and indication of the party in whose favour this entitlement operates.

2.2.3 Tax on the income from the shares withheld at source in the country of origin and/or the country of listing.

Indication as to whether the issuer assumes responsibility for the withholding of tax at source.

2.2.4 Arrangements for transfer of the shares and any restrictions on their free negotiability (e.g. clause establishing approval requirement).

2.2.5 Date on which entitlement to dividends arises.

2.2.6 The stock exchanges where admission to official listing is or will be sought.

2.2.7 The financial organizations which, at the time of admission of shares to official listing, are the paying agents of the issuer in the Member States where admission has taken place.

2.3 In so far as it is relevant, information concerning issue and placing, public or private, of the shares in respect of which the application for admission to official listing is made where such issue or placing has been effected within the 12 months preceding admission:

2.3.0 Indication of the exercise of the right of pre-emption of shareholders or of the restriction or withdrawal of such right.

* * *

2.3.1 The total amount of the public or private issue or placing and the number of shares offered, where applicable by category.

* * *

2.3.3 The issue price or the offer or placing price, stating the nominal value or, in its absence, the accounting par value or the amount to be capitalized; the issue premium and the amount of any expenses specifically charged to the subscriber or purchaser.

The methods of payment of the price, particularly as regards the paying-up of shares which are not fully paid.

* * *

2.3.5 Period of the opening of the issue or offer of shares, and names of the financial organizations responsible for receiving the public's subscriptions.

* * *

2.3.7 Names, addresses and descriptions of the natural or legal persons underwriting or guaranteeing the issue for the issuer. Where not all of the issue is underwritten or guaranteed, a statement of the portion not covered.

2.3.8 Indication or estimate of the overall amount and/or of the amount per share of the charges relating to the issue operation, stating the total remuneration of the financial intermediaries, including the underwriting commission or margin, guarantee commission, placing commission or selling agent's commission.

2.3.9 Net proceeds accruing to the issuer from the issue and intended application of such proceeds, e.g., to finance the investment programme or to strengthen the issuer's financial position.

2.4 Information concerning admission of shares to official listing:

2.4.0 Description of the shares for which admission to official listing is applied, and in particular the number of shares and nominal value per share, or, in the absence of nominal value, the accounting par value or the total nominal value, the exact designation or class, and coupons attached.

2.4.1 If the shares are to be marketed on the stock exchange and no such shares have previously been sold to the public, a statement of the number of shares made available to the market and of their nominal value, or, in the absence of nominal value, of their accounting par value, or a statement of the total nominal value and, where applicable, a statement of the minimum offer price.

2.4.2 If known, the dates on which the new shares will be listed and dealt in.

2.4.3 If shares of the same class are already listed on one or more stock exchanges, indication of these stock exchanges.

2.4.4 If shares of the same class have not yet been admitted to official listing but are dealt in on one or more other markets which are subject to regulation, are in regular operation and are recognized and open, indication of such markets.

2.4.5 Indication of any of the following which have occurred during the last financial year and the current financial year:

— public takeover offers by third parties in respect of the issuer's shares,

— public takeover offers by the issuer in respect of other companies' shares.

The price or exchange terms attaching to such offers and the outcome thereof are to be stated.

2.5 If, simultaneously or almost simultaneously with the creation of shares for which admission to official listing is being sought, shares of the same class are subscribed for or placed privately or if shares of other classes are created for public or private placing, details are to be given of the nature of such operations and of the number and characteristics of the shares to which they relate.

CHAPTER 3. GENERAL INFORMATION ABOUT THE ISSUER AND ITS CAPITAL

3.1 General information about the issuer:

3.1.0 Name, registered office and principal administrative establishment if different from the registered office.

3.1.1 Date of incorporation and the length of life of the issuer, except where indefinite.

3.1.2 Legislation under which the issuer operates and legal form which it has adopted under that legislation.

3.1.3　Indication of the issuer's objects and reference to the clause of the memorandum of association in which they are described.

3.1.4　Indication of the register and of the entry number therein.

3.1.5　Indication of where the documents concerning the issuer which are referred to in the listing particulars may be inspected.

3.2　General information about the capital:

3.2.0　The amount of the issued capital, the number and classes of the shares of which it is composed with details of their principal characteristics; the part of the issued capital still to be paid up, with an indication of the number, or total nominal value, and the type of the shares not yet fully paid up, broken down where applicable according to the extent to which they have been paid up.

3.2.1　Where there is authorized but unissued capital or an undertaking to increase the capital, *inter alia* in connection with convertible loans issued or subscription options granted, indication of:

— the amount of such authorized capital or capital increase and, where appropriate, the duration of the authorization,

— the categories of persons having preferential subscription rights for such additional portions of capital,

— the terms and arrangements for the share issue corresponding to such portions.

3.2.2　If there are shares not representing capital, the number and main characteristics of such shares are to be stated.

3.2.3　The amount of any convertible debt securities, exchangeable debt securities or debt securities with warrants, with an indication of the conditions governing and the procedures for conversion, exchange or subscription.

3.2.4　Conditions imposed by the memorandum and articles of association governing changes in the capital and in the respective rights of the various classes of shares, where such conditions are more stringent than is required by law.

3.2.5　Summary description of the operations during the three preceding years which have changed the amount of the issued capital and/or the number and classes of shares of which it is composed.

3.2.6　As far as they are known to the issuer, indication of the natural or legal persons who, directly or indirectly, severally or jointly, exercise or could exercise control over the issuer, and particulars of the proportion of the capital held giving a right to vote.

Joint control shall mean control exercised by more than one company or by more than one person having concluded an agreement which may lead to their adopting a common policy in respect of the issuer.

3.2.7　In so far as they are known to the issuer, indication of the shareholders who, directly or indirectly, hold a proportion of the issuer's capital which the Member States may not fix at more than 20%.

3.2.8　If the issuer belongs to a group of undertakings, a brief description of the group and of the issuer's position within it.

3.2.9 Number, book value and nominal value or, in the absence of a nominal value, the accounting par value of any of its own shares which the issuer or another company in which it has a direct or indirect holding of more than 50% has acquired and is holding, if such securities do not appear as a separate item on the balance sheet.

CHAPTER 4. INFORMATION CONCERNING THE ISSUER'S ACTIVITIES

4.1 The issuer's principal activities:

4.1.0 Description of the issuer's principal activities, stating the main categories of products sold and/or services performed.

Indication of any significant new products and/or activities.

4.1.1 Breakdown of net turnover during the past three financial years by categories of activity and into geographical markets in so far as, taking account of the manner in which the sale of products and the provision of services falling within the issuer's ordinary activities are organized, these categories and markets differ substantially from one another.

4.1.2 Location and size of the issuer's principal establishments and summary information about real estate owned. Any establishment which accounts for more than 10% of turnover or production shall be considered a principal establishment.

* * *

4.1.4 Where the information given pursuant to headings 4.1.0 to 4.1.3 has been influenced by exceptional factors, that fact should be mentioned.

4.2 Summary information regarding the extent to which the issuer is dependent, if at all, on patents or licences, industrial, commercial or financial contracts or new manufacturing processes, where such factors are of fundamental importance to the issuer's business or profitability.

4.3 Information concerning policy on the research and development of new products and processes over the past three financial years, where significant.

4.4 Information on any legal or arbitration proceedings which may have or have had a significant effect on the issuer's financial position in the recent past.

4.5 Information on any interruptions in the issuer's business which may have or have had a significant effect on the issuer's financial position in the recent past.

4.6 Average numbers employed and changes therein over the past three financial years, if such changes are material, with, if possible, a breakdown of persons employed by main categories of activity.

4.7 Investment policy:

4.7.0 Description, with figures, of the main investments made, including interests such as shares, debt securities, etc., in other undertakings over the past three financial years and the months already elapsed of the current financial year.

4.7.1 Information concerning the principal investments being made with the exception of interests being acquired in other undertakings.

Distribution of these investments geographically (home and abroad).

Method of financing (internal or external).

4.7.2 Information concerning the issuer's principal future investments, with the exception of interests to be acquired in other undertakings on which its management bodies have already made firm commitments.

CHAPTER 5. INFORMATION CONCERNING THE ISSUER'S ASSETS AND LIABILITIES, FINANCIAL POSITION AND PROFITS AND LOSSES

5.1 Accounts of the issuer:

5.1.0 The last three balance sheets and profit and loss accounts drawn up by the company set out as a comparative table. The notes on the annual accounts for the last financial year.

The draft listing particulars must be filed with the competent authorities not more than 18 months after the end of the financial year to which the last annual accounts published relate. The competent authorities may extend that period in exceptional cases.

5.1.1 If the issuer prepares consolidated annual accounts only, it shall include those accounts in the listing particulars in accordance with heading 5.1.0.

* * *

5.1.2 The profit or loss per share of the issuing company, for the financial year, arising out of the company's ordinary activities, after tax, for the last three financial years, where the company includes its own annual accounts in the listing particulars.

Where the issuer includes only consolidated annual accounts in the listing particulars, it shall indicate the consolidated profit or loss per share, for the financial year, for the last three financial years.

* * *

5.1.3 The amount of the dividend per share for the last three financial years, adjusted, if necessary, to make it comparable in accordance with the third subparagraph of heading 5.1.2.

* * *

5.1.6 A table showing the sources and application of funds over the past three financial years.

5.2 Individual details listed below relating to the undertakings in which the issuer holds a proportion of the capital likely to have a significant effect on the assessment of its own assets and liabilities, financial position or profits and losses.

* * *

5.4 When the listing particulars comprise consolidated annual accounts, disclosure:

(a) of the consolidation principles applied.

* * *

(b) of the names and registered offices of the undertakings included in the consolidation, where that information is important for the purpose of assessing the assets and liabilities, the financial position and the profits and losses of the issuer.

* * *

CHAPTER 6

INFORMATION CONCERNING ADMINISTRATION, MANAGEMENT AND SUPERVISION

6.1 Names, addresses and functions in the issuing company of the following persons and an indication of the principal activities performed by them outside that company where these are significant with respect to that company:

(a) members of the administrative, management or supervisory bodies;

(b) partners with unlimited liability, in the case of a limited partnership with a share capital;

(c) founders, if the company has been established for fewer than five years.

6.2 Interests of the members of the administrative, management and supervisory bodies in the issuing company:

6.2.0 Remuneration paid and benefits in kind granted, during the last completed financial year under any heading whatsoever, and charged to overheads or the profit appropriation account, to members of the administrative, management and supervisory bodies, these being total amounts for each category of body.

The total remuneration paid and benefits in kind granted to all members of the administrative, management and supervisory bodies of the issuer by all the dependent undertakings with which it forms a group must be indicated.

6.2.1 Total number of shares in the issuing company held by the members of its administrative, management and supervisory bodies and options granted to them on the company's shares.

6.2.2 Information about the nature and extent of the interests of members of the administrative, management and supervisory bodies in transactions effected by the issuer which are unusual in their nature or conditions (such as purchases outside normal activity, acquisition or disposal of fixed asset items) during the preceding financial year and the current financial year. Where such unusual transactions were concluded in the course of previous financial years and have not been definitively concluded, information on those transactions must also be given.

6.2.3 Total of all the outstanding loans granted by the issuer to the persons referred to in heading 6.1(a) and also of any guarantees provided by the issuer for their benefit.

6.3 Schemes for involving the staff in the capital of the issuer.

CHAPTER 7
INFORMATION CONCERNING THE RECENT DEVELOPMENT AND PROSPECTS OF THE ISSUER

7.1 Except in the event of a derogation granted by the competent authorities, general information on the trend of the issuer's business since the end of the financial year to which the last published annual accounts relate, in particular:
— the most significant recent trends in production, sales and stocks and the state of the order book, and
— recent trends in costs and selling prices.

7.2 Except in the event of a derogation granted by the competent authorities, information on the issuer's prospects for at least the current financial year.

SCHEDULE B
LAYOUT FOR LISTING PARTICULARS FOR THE ADMISSION OF DEBT SECURITIES TO OFFICIAL STOCK EXCHANGE LISTING
CHAPTER 1. INFORMATION CONCERNING THOSE RESPONSIBLE FOR LISTING PARTICULARS AND THE AUDITING OF ACCOUNTS

[Identical to Schedule A Chapter 1.]

* * *

CHAPTER 2. INFORMATION CONCERNING LOANS AND THE ADMISSION OF DEBT SECURITIES TO OFFICIAL LISTING

2.1 Conditions of the loan:

2.1.0 The nominal amount of the loan; if this amount is not fixed, a statement to this effect be made.

The nature, number and numbering of the debt securities and the denominations.

2.1.1 Except in the case of continuous issues, the issue and redemption prices and the nominal interest rate; if several interest rates are provided for, an indication of the conditions for changes in the rate.

2.1.2 Procedures for the allocation of any other advantages; the method of calculating such advantages.

2.1.3 Tax on the income from the debt securities withheld at source in the country of origin and/or the country of listing.
Indication as to whether the issuer assumes responsibility for the withholding of tax at source.

2.1.4 Arrangements for the amortization of the loan, including the repayment procedures.

2.1.5 The financial organizations which, at the time of admission to official listing are the paying agents of the issuer in the Member State of admission.

2.1.6 Currency of the loan; if the loan is denominated in units of account, the contractual status of these; currency option.

2.1.7 Time limits:
(a) period of the loan and any interim due dates;
(b) the date from which interest becomes payable and the due dates for interest;
(c) the time limit on the validity of claims to interest and repayment of principal;
(d) procedures and time limits for delivery of the debt securities, possible creation of provisional certificates.

2.1.8 Except in the case of continuous issues, an indication of yield. The method whereby that yield is calculated shall be described in summary form.

2.2 Legal information:

2.2.0 Indication of the resolutions, authorizations and approvals by virtue of which the debt securities have been or will be created and/or issued.

Type of operation and amount thereof.

Number of debt securities which have been or will be created and/or issued, if predetermined.

2.2.1 Nature and scope of the guarantees, sureties and commitments intended to ensure that the loan will be duly serviced as regards both the repayment of the debt securities and the payment of interest.

Indication of the places where the public may have access to the texts of the contracts relating to these guarantees, sureties and commitments.

2.2.2 Organization of trustees or of any other representation for the body of debt security holders.

Name and function and description and head office of the representative of the debt security holders, the main conditions of such representation and in particular the conditions under which the representative may be replaced.

Indication of where the public may have access to the contracts relating to these forms of representation.

2.2.3 Mention of clauses subordinating the loan to other debts of the issuer already contracted or to be contracted.

2.2.4 Indication of the legislation under which the debt securities have been created and of the courts competent in the event of litigation.

2.2.5 Indication as to whether the debt securities are registered or bearer.

2.2.6 Any restrictions on the free transferability of the debt securities.

2.3 Information concerning the admission of the debt securities to official listing:

2.3.0 The stock exchanges where admission to official listing is, or will be, sought.

2.3.1 Names, addresses and description of the natural or legal persons underwriting or guaranteeing the issue for the issuer. Where not all of the issue is underwritten or guaranteed, a statement of the portion not covered.

* * *

2.3.3 If debt securities of the same class are already listed on one or more stock exchanges, indication of these stock exchanges.

2.3.4 If debt securities of the same class have not yet been admitted to official listing but are dealt in one or more other markets which are subject to regulation, are in regular operation and are recognized and open, indication of such markets.

2.4 Information concerning the issue of it is concomitant with official admission or if it took place within the three months preceding such admission:

2.4.0 The procedure for the exercise of any right of pre-emption; the negotiability of subscription rights; the treatment of subscription rights not exercised.

2.4.1 Method of payment of the issue or offer price.

2.4.2 Except in the case of continuous debt security issues, period of the opening of the issue or offer and any possibilities of early closure.

2.4.3 Indication of the financial organizations responsible for receiving the public's subscriptions.

2.4.4 Reference, where necessary, to the fact that the subscriptions may be reduced.

2.4.5 Except in the case of continuous debt security issues, indication of the net proceeds of the loan.

2.4.6 Purpose of the issue and intended application of its proceeds.

[Chapters 3–7 are similar to Schedule A Chapters 3–7, although slightly less detailed.]

27. COUNCIL DIRECTIVE 87/345/EEC

of 22 June 1987
amending Directive 80/390/EEC
O.J. L 185/81 (July 4, 1987)

THE COUNCIL OF THE EUROPEAN COMMUNITIES,

Having regard to the Treaty establishing the European Economic Community, and in particular Article 54(2) thereof,

Having regard to the proposal from the Commission,

Having regard to the opinion of the European Parliament,

Having regard to the opinion of the Economic and Social Committee,

Whereas [Article 24 of Directive 80/390/EEC] does not result in the full mutual recognition of listing particulars and it is therefore appropriate to amend Directive 80/390/EEC so as to achieve that recognition;

Whereas mutual recognition represents an important step forward in the creation of the Community's internal market;

* * *

HAS ADOPTED THIS DIRECTIVE:

Article 1

Section IV of Directive 80/390/EEC is replaced by the following Sections and Sections V and VI shall become Sections VIII and IX, respectively:

SECTION IV
DETERMINATION OF THE COMPETENT AUTHORITY

Article 24

Where, for the same securities, applications for admission to official listing on stock exchanges situated or operating in two or more Member States, including the Member State in which the issuer's registered office is situated, are made simultaneously or within a short interval, listing particulars shall be drawn up in accordance with the rules laid down in this Directive in the Member State in which the issuer has its registered office and approved by the competent authorities of that State; if the issuer's registered office is not situated in one of those Member States, the issuer must choose one of those States under the legislation of which the listing particulars will be drawn up and approved.

SECTION V
MUTUAL RECOGNITION

Article 24a

1. Once approved in accordance with Article 24, listing particulars must, subject to any translation, be recognized by the other Member States in which admission to official listing has been applied

for, without its being necessary to obtain the approval of the competent authorities of those States and without their being able to require that additional information be included in the listing particulars. The competent authorities may, however, require that listing particulars include information specific to the market of the country of admission concerning in particular the income tax system, the financial organizations retained to act as paying agents for the issuer in that country, and the way in which notices to investors are published.

* * *

5. Member States may restrict the application of this Article to listing particulars of issuers having their registered office in a Member State.

Article 24b

1. Where the securities for which applications for admission to official listing on stock exchanges situated in two or more Member States have been made simultaneously or within a short interval have been the subject of a prospectus drawn up and approved in accordance with this Directive, at the time of the public offer, by the competent authorities within the meaning of Article 24 in the three months preceding the application for admission in that State, that prospectus must, subject to any translation, be recognized as listing particulars in the other Member States in which application for admission to official listing is made, without its being necessary to obtain the approval of the competent authorities of those Member States and without their being able to require that additional information be included in the listing particulars. The competent authorities may, however, require that listing particulars include information specific to the market of the country of admission concerning, in particular, the income tax system, the financial organizations retained to act as paying agents for the issuer in the country of admission and the ways in which notices to investors are published.

2. Article 24a(2), (3), (4) and (5) shall apply in the eventuality referred to in paragraph 1 of this Article.

3. Article 23 shall apply to all changes occurring between the time when the content of the prospectus referred to in paragraph 1 of this Article is adopted and the time when stock exchange dealings begin.

SECTION VI
COOPERATION

Article 24c

1. The competent authorities shall cooperate wherever necessary for the purpose of carrying out their duties and shall exchange any information required for that purpose.

2. Where an application for admission to official listing concerning securities giving a right to participate in company capital, either immediately or at the end of the maturity period, is made in one or more Member States other than that in which the registered office of the issuer of the shares to which those securities give entitlement is situated, while that issuer's shares have already been admitted to official listing in that Member State, the competent authorities of the Member State of admission may act only after having consulted the competent authorities of the Member State in which the registered office of the issuer of the shares in question is situated.

3. Where an application for admission to official listing is made for securities which have been listed in another Member State less than six months previously, the competent authorities to whom application is made shall contact the competent authorities which have already admitted the securities to official listing and shall, as far as possible, exempt the issuer of those securities from the preparation of new listing particulars, subject to any need for updating, translation or the issue of supplements in accordance with the individual requirements of the Member State concerned.

SECTION VII
NEGOTIATIONS WITH NON-MEMBER COUNTRIES

Article 25a

The Community may, by means of agreements concluded with one or more non-member countries pursuant to the Treaty, recognize listing particulars drawn up and checked, in accordance with the rules of the non-member country or countries, as meeting the requirements of this Directive, subject to reciprocity, provided that the rules concerned give investors protection equivalent to that afforded by this Directive, even if those rules differ from the provisions of this Directive.

Article 2

1. Member States shall take the measures necessary for them to comply with this Directive by 1 January 1990. They shall forthwith inform the Commission thereof. However, for the Kingdom of Spain the date 1 January 1990 shall be replaced by 1 January 1991 and for the Portuguese Republic by 1 January 1992.

* * *

Article 3

This Directive is addressed to the Member States.

28. COUNCIL DIRECTIVE 82/121/EEC

of 15 February 1982

on information to be published on a regular basis by companies the shares of which have been admitted to official stock-exchange listing

O.J. L 48/26 (Feb. 20, 1982)

THE COUNCIL OF THE EUROPEAN COMMUNITIES,

Having regard to the Treaty establishing the European Economic Community, and in particular Articles 54(3)(g) and 100 thereof,

Having regard to the proposal from the Commission,

Having regard to the opinion of the European Parliament,

Having regard to the opinion of the Economic and Social Committee,

* * *

Whereas, in the case of securities admitted to official stock-exchange listing, the protection of investors requires that the latter be supplied with appropriate regular information throughout the entire period during which the securities are listed; whereas coordination of requirements for this regular information has similar objectives to those envisaged for the listing particulars, namely to improve such protection and to make it more equivalent, to facilitate the listing of these securities on more than one stock exchange in the Community, and in so doing to contribute towards the establishment of a genuine Community capital market by permitting a fuller interpenetration of securities markets;

Whereas, under Council Directive 79/279/EEC of 5 March 1979 coordinating the conditions for the admission of securities to official stock-exchange listing, listed companies must as soon as possible make available to investors their annual accounts and report giving information on the company for the whole of the financial year; whereas the fourth Directive 78/660/EEC has coordinated the laws, regulations and administrative provisions of the Member States concerning the annual accounts of certain types of companies;

Whereas companies should also, at least once during each financial year, make available to investors reports on their activities; whereas this Directive can, consequently, be confined to coordinating the content and distribution of a single report covering the first six months of the financial year;

* * *

Whereas the half-yearly report must enable investors to make an informed appraisal of the general development of the company's activities during the period covered by the report; whereas, however, this report need contain only the essential details on the financial position and general progress of the business of the company in question;

* * *

Whereas, so as to ensure the effective protection of investors and the proper operation of stock exchanges, the rules relating to regular information to be published by companies, the shares of which are admitted to official stock-exchange listing within the Community, should apply not only to companies from Member States, but also to companies from non-member countries

HAS ADOPTED THIS DIRECTIVE:

SECTION 1
GENERAL PROVISIONS AND SCOPE

Article 1

1. This Directive shall apply to companies the shares of which are admitted to official listing on a stock exchange situated or operating in a Member State, whether the admission is of the shares themselves or of certificates representing them and whether such admission precedes or follows the date on which this Directive enters into force.

2. This Directive shall not, however, apply to investment companies other than those of the closed-end type.

* * *

Article 2

The Member States shall ensure that the companies publish half-yearly reports on their activities and profits and losses during the first six months of each financial year.

Article 3

The Member States may subject companies to obligations more stringent than those provided for by this Directive or to additional obligations, provided that they apply generally to all companies or to all companies of a given class.

SECTION II
PUBLICATION AND CONTENTS OF THE HALF-YEARLY REPORT

Article 4

1. The half-yearly report shall be published within four months of the end of the relevant six-month period.

2. In exceptional, duly substantiated cases, the competent authorities shall be permitted to extend the time limit for publication.

Article 5

1. The half-yearly report shall consist of figures and an explanatory statement relating to the company's activities and profits and losses during the relevant six-month period.

2. The figures, presented in table form shall indicate at least:
   — the net turnover, and
   — the profit or loss before or after deduction of tax.

These terms shall have the same meanings as in the Council Directives on company accounts.

3. The Member States may allow the competent authorities to authorize companies, exceptionally and on a case-by-case basis, to supply estimated figures for profits and losses, provided that the shares of each such company are listed officially in only one Member State. The use of this procedure must be indicated by the company in its report and must not mislead investors.

4. Where the company has paid or proposes to pay an interim dividend, the figures must indicate the profit or loss after tax for the six-month period and the interim dividend paid or proposed.

5. Against each figure there must be shown the figure for the corresponding period in the preceding financial year.

6. The explanatory statement must include any significant information enabling investors to make an informed assessment of the trend of the company's activities and profits or losses together with an indication of any special factor which has influenced those activities and those profits or losses during the period in question, and enable a comparison to be made with the corresponding period of the preceding financial year.

It must also, as far as possible, refer to the company's likely future development in the current financial year.

7. Where the figures provided for in paragraph 2 are unsuited to the company's activities, the competent authorities shall ensure that appropriate adjustments are made.

Article 6

Where a company publishes consolidated accounts it may publish its half-yearly report in either consolidated or unconsolidated form. However, the Member States may allow the competent authorities, where the latter consider that the form not adopted would have contained additional material information, to require the company to publish such information.

Article 7

1. The half-yearly report must be published in the Member State or Member States where the shares are admitted to official listing by insertion in one or more newspapers distributed throughout the State or widely distributed therein or in the national gazette, or shall be made available to the public either in writing in places indicated by announcement to be published in one or more newspapers distributed throughout the State or widely distributed therein, or by other equivalent means approved by the competent authorities.

* * *

3. The company shall send a copy of its half-yearly report simultaneously to the competent authorities of each Member State in which its shares are admitted to official listing. It shall do so not later than the

time when the half-yearly report is published for the first time in a Member State.

Article 8

Where the accounting information has been audited by the official auditor of the company's accounts, that auditor's report and any qualifications he may have shall be reproduced in full.

SECTION III
POWERS OF THE COMPETENT AUTHORITIES

Article 9

1. Member States shall appoint one or more competent authorities and shall notify the Commission of the appointment of such authorities, giving details of any division of powers among them. Member States shall also ensure that this Directive is applied.

2. The Member States shall ensure that the competent authorities have the necessary powers to carry out their task.

* * *

SECTION IV
COOPERATION BETWEEN MEMBER STATES

Article 10

1. The competent authorities shall cooperate whenever necessary for the purpose of carrying out their duties and shall exchange any information required for that purpose.

2. Where a half-yearly report has to be published in more than one Member State, the competent authorities of these Member States shall, by way of derogation from Article 3, use their best endeavours to accept as a single text the text which meets the requirements of the Member State in which the company's shares were admitted to official listing for the first time or the text which most closely approximates to that text.

* * *

Article 13

This Directive is addressed to the Member States.

29. COUNCIL DIRECTIVE 89/298/EEC

of 17 April 1989

coordinating the requirements for the drawing-up, scrutiny and distribution of the prospectus to be published when transferable securities are offered to the public

O.J. L 124/8 (May 5, 1989)

THE COUNCIL OF THE EUROPEAN COMMUNITIES,

Having regard to the Treaty establishing the European Economic Community, and in particular Article 54 thereof,

Having regard to the proposal from the Commission,[1]

In cooperation with the European Parliament,[2]

Having regard to the opinion of the Economic and Social Committee,[3]

Whereas investment in transferable securities, like any other form of investment, involves risks; whereas the protection of investors requires that they be put in a position to make a correct assessment of such risks so as to be able to take investment decisions in full knowledge of the facts;

Whereas the provision of full, appropriate information concerning transferable securities and the issuers of such securities promotes the protection of investors;

Whereas, moreover, such information is an effective means of increasing confidence in transferable securities and thus contributes to the proper functioning and development of transferable securities markets;

Whereas a genuine Community information policy relating to transferable securities should therefore be introduced; whereas, by virtue of the safeguards that it offers investors and its impact on the proper functioning of transferable securities markets, such an information policy is capable of promoting the interpenetration of national transferable securities markets and thus encouraging the creation of a genuine European capital market;

* * *

Whereas such an information policy also requires that when transferable securities are offered to the public for the first time in a Member State, whether by, or on behalf of the issuer or a third party, whether or not they are subsequently listed, a prospectus containing information of this nature must be made available to investors; whereas it is also necessary to coordinate the contents of that prospectus in order to achieve equivalence of the minimum safeguards afforded to investors in the various Member States;

---

1. OJ No C 226, 31. 8. 1982, p. 4.
2. OJ No C 125, 17. 5. 1982, p. 176 and OJ No C 69, 20. 3. 1989.
3. OJ No C 310, 30. 11. 1981, p. 50.

Whereas, so far, it has proved impossible to furnish a common definition of the term 'public offer' and all its constituent parts;

Whereas, in cases where a public offer is of transferable securities which are to be admitted to official listing on a stock exchange, information similar to that required by Directive 80/390/EEC, whilst being adapted to the circumstances of the public offer, must be supplied; whereas, for public offers of transferable securities that are not to be admitted to official stock exchange listing, less detailed information can be required so as not to burden small and medium-sized issuers unduly; whereas, for public offers of transferable securities that are to be admitted to official stock exchange listing, the degree of coordination achieved is such that a prospectus approved by the competent authorities of a Member State can be used for public offers of the same securities in another Member State on the basis of mutual recognition; whereas mutual recognition should also apply where public offer prospectuses comply with the basic standards laid down in Directive 80/390/EEC and are approved by the competent authorities even in the absence of a request for admission to official stock exchange listing;

Whereas in order to ensure that the purposes of this Directive will be fully realized it is necessary to include within the scope of this Directive transferable securities issued by companies or firms governed by the laws of third countries;

Whereas it is advisable to provide for the extension, by means of agreements to be concluded by the Community with third countries, of the recognition of prospectuses from those countries on a reciprocal basis:

HAS ADOPTED THIS DIRECTIVE:

SECTION 1
GENERAL PROVISIONS

Article 1

1. This Directive shall apply to transferable securities which are offered to the public for the first time in a Member State provided that these securities are not already listed on a stock exchange situated or operating in that Member State.

2. Where an offer to the public is for part only of the transferable securities from a single issue, the Member States need not require that another prospectus be published if the other part is subsequently offered to the public.

Article 2

This Directive shall not apply:

1. to the following types of offer:

   (a) where transferable securities are offered to persons in the context of their trades, professions or occupations, and/or

   (b) where transferable securities are offered to a restricted circle of persons, and/or

(c) where the selling price of all the transferable securities offered does not exceed ECU 40 000, and/or

(d) where the transferable securities offered can be acquired only for a consideration of at least ECU 40 000 per investor;

2. to transferable securities of the following types:

(a) to transferable securities offered in individual denominations of at least ECU 40 000;

(b) to units issued by collective investment undertakings other than of the closed-end type;

(c) to transferable securities issued by a State or by one of a State's regional or local authorities or by public international bodies of which one or more Member States are members;

(d) to transferable securities offered in connection with a takeover bid;

(e) to transferable securities offered in connection with a merger;

(f) to shares allotted free of charge to the holders of shares;

(g) to shares or transferable securities equivalent to shares offered in exchange for shares in the same company if the offer of such new securities does not involve any overall increase in the company's issued shares capital;

(h) to transferable securities offered by their employer or by an affiliated undertaking to or for the benefit of serving or former employees;

(i) to transferable securities resulting from the conversion of convertible debt securities or from the exercise of the rights conferred by warrants or to shares offered in exchange for exchangeable debt securities, provided that a public offer prospectus or listing particulars relating to those convertible or exchangeable debt securities or those warrants were published in the same Member State;

(j) to transferable securities issued, with a view to their obtaining the means necessary to achieve their disinterested objectives, by associations with legal status or non-profit-making bodies, recognized by the State;

(k) to shares or transferable securities equivalent to shares, ownership of which entitles the holder to avail himself of the services rendered by bodies such as 'building societies', 'Crédits populaires', 'Genossenschaftsbanken', or 'Industrial and Provident Societies', or to become a member of such a body;

(*l*) to Euro-securities which are not the subject of a generalized campaign of advertising or canvassing.

Article 3

For the purposes of this Directive:

* * *

(c) 'issuers' shall mean companies and other legal persons and any undertakings the transferable securities of which are offered to the public;

(d) 'credit institution' shall mean an undertaking the business of which is to receive deposits or other repayable funds from the public and to grant credits for its own account, including credit institutions such as referred to in Article 2 of Directive 77/780/EEC, as last amended by Directive 86/524/EEC;

(e) 'transferable securities' shall mean shares in companies and other transferable securities equivalent to shares in companies, debt securities having a maturity of at least one year and other transferable securities equivalent to debt securities, and any other transferable security giving the right to acquire any such transferable securities by subscription or exchange;

(f) 'Euro-securities' shall mean transferable securities which:

— are to be underwritten and distributed by a syndicate at least two of the members of which have their registered offices in different States, and

— are offered on a significant scale in one or more States other than that of the issuer's registered office, and

— may be subscribed for or initially acquired only through a credit institution or other financial institution.

Article 4

Member States shall ensure that any offer of transferable securities to the public within their territories is subject to the publication of a prospectus by the person making the offer.

Article 5

Member States may provide for partial or complete exemption from the obligation to publish a prospectus where the transferable securities being offered to the public are:

[issued by credit or other financial institutions, or by State monopolies, or regulated companies whose securities are guaranteed by the State.]

Article 6

If a full prospectus has been published in a Member State within the previous 12 months, the following prospectus drawn up by the same issuer in the same State, but relating to different transferable securities, may indicate only those changes likely to influence the value of the securities which have occurred since publication of the full prospectus.

However, that prospectus may be made available only accompanied by the full prospectus to which it relates or by a reference thereto.

SECTION II

CONTENTS AND ARRANGEMENTS FOR THE SCRUTINY AND DISTRIBUTION OF THE PROSPECTUS FOR TRANSFERABLE SECURITIES FOR WHICH ADMISSION TO OFFICIAL STOCK EXCHANGE LISTING IS SOUGHT

Article 7

Where a public offer relates to transferable securities which at the time of the offer are the subject of an application for admission to official listing on a stock exchange situated or operating within the same Member State, the contents of the prospectus and the procedures for scrutinizing and distributing it shall, subject to adaptations appropriate to the circumstances of a public offer, be determined in accordance with Directive 80/390/EEC.

Article 8

1. Where a public offer is made in one Member State and admission is sought to official listing on a stock exchange situated in another Member State, the person making the public offer shall have the possibility in the Member State in which the public offer is to be made of drawing up a prospectus the contents and procedures for scrutiny and distribution of which shall, subject to adaptations appropriate to the circumstances of a public offer, be determined in accordance with Directive 80/390/EEC.

2. Paragraph 1 shall apply only in those Member States which in general provide for the prior scrutiny of public offer prospectuses.

Article 9

A prospectus must be published or made available to the public not later than the time when an offer is made to the public.

Article 10

* * *

3. The prospectus must be published either:

— by insertion in one or more newspapers circulated throughout the Member State in which the public offer is made, or

— in the form of a brochure to be made available, free of charge, to the public in the Member State in which the public offer is made and at the registered office of the person making the public offer and at the offices of the financial organizations retained to act as paying agents of the latter in the Member State where the offer is made.

4. In addition, either the complete prospectus or a notice stating where the prospectus has been published and where it may be obtained by the public must be inserted in a publication designated by the Member State in which the public offer is made.

SECTION III
CONTENTS AND ARRANGEMENTS FOR THE DISTRIBUTION OF THE PROSPECTUS FOR TRANSFERABLE SECURITIES FOR WHICH ADMISSION TO OFFICIAL STOCK-EXCHANGE LISTING IS NOT SOUGHT

Article 11

1. Where a public offer relates to transferable securities other than those referred to in Articles 7 and 8, the prospectus must contain the information which, according to the particular nature of the issuer and of the transferable securities offered to the public, is necessary to enable investors to make an informed assessment of the assets and liabilities, financial position, profits and losses and prospects of the issuer and of the rights attaching to the transferable securities.

2. In order to fulfil the obligation referred to in paragraph 1, the prospectus shall, subject to the possibilities for exemption provided for in Articles 5 and 13, contain in as easily analysable and comprehensible a form as possible, at least the information listed below:

(a) those responsible for the prospectus (names, functions and declarations by them that to the best of their knowledge the information contained in the prospectus is in accordance with the facts and that the prospectus makes no omission likely to affect its import);

(b) the offer to the public and the transferable securities being offered (nature of the securities being offered, the amount and purpose of the issue, the number of securities issued and the rights attaching to them; the income tax withheld at source; the period during which the offer is open; the date on which entitlement to dividends or interest arises; the persons underwriting or guaranteeing the offer; any restrictions on the free transferability of the securities being offered and the markets on which they may be traded; the establishments serving as paying agents; if known, the price at which the securities are offered, or else, if national rules so provide, the procedure and timetable for fixing the price if it is not known when the prospectus is being drawn up; methods of payment; the procedure for the exercise of any right of pre-emption and the methods of and time-limits for delivery of the securities);

(c) the issuer (name, registered office; its date of incorporation, the legislation applicable to the issuer and the issuer's legal form, its objects, indication of the register and of the entry number therein) and its capital (amount of the subscribed capital, the number and main particulars of the securities of which the capital consists and any part of the capital still to be paid up; the amount of any convertible debt securities, exchangeable debt securities or debt securities with warrants and the procedures for conversion, exchange or subscription; where appropriate, the group of undertakings to which the issuer belongs; in the case of shares, the following additional information must be supplied: any shares not representing capital, the amount of the authorized capital and the duration of the authorization; in so far as they are known, indication of the shareholders who directly or indirectly exercise or could exercise a determining role in the management of the issuer);

(d) the issuer's principal activities (description of its principal activities, and, where appropriate, any exceptional factors which have influenced its activities; any dependence on patents, licenses or contracts if these are of fundamental importance; information regarding investments in progress where they are significant; any legal proceedings having an important effect on the issuer's financial position);

(e) the issuer's assets and liabilities, financial position and profits and losses (own accounts and, where appropriate, consolidated accounts; if the issuer prepares consolidated annual accounts only, it shall include those accounts in the prospectus; if the issuer prepares both own and consolidated accounts, it shall include both types of accounts in the prospectus; however, the issuer may include only one of the two, provided that the accounts which are not included do not provide any significant additional information); interim accounts if any have been published since the end of the previous financial year; the name of the person responsible for auditing the accounts; if that person has qualified them or refused an audit report, the fact must be stated and the reasons given;

(f) the issuer's administration, management and supervision (names, addresses, functions; in the case of an offer to the public of shares in a limited-liability company, remuneration of the members of the issuer's administrative, management and supervisory bodies);

(g) to the extent that such information would have a significant impact on any assessment that might be made of the issuer, recent developments in its business and prospects (the most significant recent trends concerning the development of the issuer's business since the end of the preceding financial year, information on the issuer's prospects for at least the current financial year).

3. Where a public offer relates to debt securities guaranteed by one or more legal persons, the information specified in paragraph 2(c) to (g) must also be given with respect to the guarantor or guarantors.

4. Where a public offer relates to convertible debt securities, exchangeable debt securities or debt securities with warrants or to the warrants themselves, information must also be given with regard to the nature of the shares or debt securities to which they confer entitlement and the conditions of and procedures for conversion, exchange or subscription. Where the issuer of the shares or debt securities is not the issuer of the debt securities or warrants the information specified in paragraph 2(c) to (g) must also be given with respect to the issuer of the shares or debt securities.

5. If the period of existence of the issuer is less than any period mentioned in paragraph 2, the information need be provided only for the period of the issuer's existence.

6. Where certain information specified in paragraph 2 is found to be inappropriate to the issuer's sphere of activity or its legal form or to the

transferable securities being offered, a prospectus giving equivalent information must be drawn up.

7. Where shares are offered on a pre-emptive basis to shareholders of the issuer on the occasion of their admission to dealing on a stock exchange market, the Member States or bodies designated by them may allow some of the information specified in paragraph 2(d), (e) and (f) to be omitted, provided that investors already possess up-to-date information about the issuer equivalent to that required by Section III as a result of stock exchange disclosure requirements.

8. Where a class of shares has been admitted to dealing on a stock exchange market, the Member States or bodies designated by them may allow a partial or complete exemption from the obligation to publish a prospectus if the number or estimated market value or the nominal value or, in the absence of a nominal value, the accounting par value of the shares offered amounts to less than 10% of the number or of the corresponding value of shares of the same class already admitted to dealing, provided that investors already possess up-to-date information about the issuer equivalent to that required by Section III as a result of stock exchange disclosure requirements.

Article 12

1. However, the Member States may provide that the person making a public offer shall have the possibility of drawing up a prospectus the contents of which shall, subject to adaptations appropriate to the circumstances of a public offer, be determined in accordance with Directive 80/390/EEC.

2. The prior scrutiny of the prospectus referred to in paragraph 1 must be carried out by the bodies designated by the Member States even in the absence of a request for admission to official stock-exchange listing.

Article 13

1. The Member States or the bodies designated by them may authorize the omission from the prospectus referred to in Article 11 of certain information prescribed by this Directive:

(a) if that information is of minor importance only and is not likely [to] influence assessment of the issuer's assets and liabilities, financial position, profits and losses and prospects; or

(b) if disclosure of that information would be contrary to the public interest or seriously detrimental to the issuer, provided that, in the latter case; omission would not be likely to mislead the public with regard to facts and circumstances essential for assessment of the transferable securities.

* * *

Article 14

A prospectus must be communicated, before its publication, to the bodies designated for that purpose in each Member State in which the transferable securities are offered to the public for the first time.

Article 15

A prospectus must be published or made available to the public in the Member State in which an offer to the public is made in accordance with the procedures laid down by that Member State.

Article 16

A prospectus must be published or made available to the public not later than the time when an offer is made to the public.

* * *

Article 18

Any significant new factor or significant inaccuracy in a prospectus capable of affecting assessment of the transferable securities which arises or is noted between the publication of the prospectus and the definitive closure of a public offer must be mentioned or rectified in a supplement to the prospectus, to be published or made available to the public in accordance with at least the same arrangements as were applied when the original prospectus was disseminated or in accordance with procedures laid down by the Member States or by the bodies designated by them.

SECTION IV
COOPERATION BETWEEN MEMBER STATES

Article 19

The Member States shall designate the bodies, which may be the same as those referred to in Article 14, which shall cooperate with each other for the purposes of the proper application of this Directive and shall use their best endeavours, within the framework of their responsibilities, to exchange all the information necessary to that end. Member States shall inform the Commission of the bodies thus designated. The Commission shall communicate that information to the other Member States.

Member States shall ensure that the bodies designated have the powers required for the accomplishment of their task.

Article 20

1. Where, for the same transferable securities, public offers are made simultaneously or within a short interval of one another in two or more Member States and where a public offer prospectus is drawn up in accordance with Article 7, 8 or 12, the authority competent for the approval of the prospectus shall be that of the Member State in which the issuer has its registered office if the public offer or any application for admission to official listing on a stock exchange is made in that Member State.

* * *

SECTION V
MUTUAL RECOGNITION

Article 21

1. If approved in accordance with Article 20, a prospectus must, subject to translation if required, be recognized as complying or be deemed

to comply with the laws of the other Member States in which the same transferable securities are offered to the public simultaneously or within a short interval of one another, without being subject to any form of approval there and without those States being able to require that additional information be included in the prospectus. Those Member States may, however, require that the prospectus include information specific to the market of the country in which the public offer is made concerning in particular the income tax system, the financial organizations retained to act as paying agents for the issuer in that country, and the way in which notices to investors are published.

* * *

SECTION VI
COOPERATION
Article 22

1. The competent authorities shall cooperate wherever necessary for the purpose of carrying out their duties and shall exchange any information required for that purpose.

* * *

Article 23

1. Member States shall provide that all persons then or previously employed by the authorities referred to in Article 20 shall be bound by the obligation of professional secrecy. This shall mean that they may not divulge any confidential information received in the course of their duties to any person or authority whatsoever, except by virtue of provisions laid down by law.

* * *

SECTION VII
NEGOTIATIONS WITH NON-MEMBER COUNTRIES
Article 24

The Community may, by means of agreements with one or more non-member countries concluded pursuant to the Treaty, recognize public offer prospectuses drawn up and scrutinized in accordance with the rules of the non-member country or countries concerned as meeting the requirements of this Directive, subject to reciprocity, provided that the rules concerned give investors protections equivalent to that afforded by this Directive, even if those rules differ from the provisions of this Directive.

SECTION VIII
CONTACT COMMITTEE
Article 25

1. The Contact Committee set up by Article 20 of Council Directive 79/279/EEC of 5 March 1979 coordinating the conditions for the admis-

sion of transferable securities to official stock-exchange listing [1], as last amended by Directive 82/148/EEC [2], shall also have as its function:

(a) to facilitate, without prejudice to Articles 169 and 170 of the Treaty, the harmonized implementation of this Directive through regular consultations on any practical problems arising from its application on which exchanges of views are deemed useful;

(b) to facilitate consultation between the Member States on the supplements and improvements to prospectuses which they are entitled to require or recommend at national level;

(c) to advise the Commission, if necessary, on any additions or amendments to be made to this Directive.

2. It shall not be the function of the Contact Committee to appraise the merits of decisions taken in individual cases.

SECTION IX
FINAL PROVISIONS
Article 26

1. Member States shall take the measures necessary for them to comply with this Directive by 17 April 1989. They shall forthwith inform the Commission thereof.

* * *

Article 27

This Directive is addressed to the Member States.

1. OJ No L 66, 16. 3. 1979, p. 1.   2. OJ No L 62, 5. 3. 1982, p. 22.

30. COUNCIL DIRECTIVE 89/592/EEC

of 13 November 1989
coordinating regulations on insider dealing
O.J. L 334/30 (Nov. 18, 1989)

THE COUNCIL OF THE EUROPEAN COMMUNITIES,

Having regard to the Treaty establishing the European Economic Community, and in particular Article 100a thereof,

Having regard to the proposal from the Commission,[1]

In cooperation with the European Parliament,[2]

Having regard to the opinion of the Economic and Social Committee,[3]

Whereas Article 100a(1) of the Treaty states that the Council shall adopt the measures for the approximation of the provisions laid down by law, regulation or administrative action in Member States which have as their object the establishment and functioning of the internal market;

Whereas the secondary market in transferable securities plays an important role in the financing of economic agents;

Whereas, for that market to be able to play its role effectively, every measure should be taken to ensure that market operates smoothly;

Whereas the smooth operation of that market depends to a large extent on the confidence it inspires in investors;

Whereas the factors on which such confidence depends include the assurance afforded to investors that they are placed on an equal footing and that they will be protected against the improper use of inside information;

Whereas, by benefiting certain investors as compared with others, insider dealing is likely to undermine that confidence and may therefore prejudice the smooth operation of the market;

Whereas the necessary measures should therefore be taken to combat insider dealing;

Whereas in some Member States there are no rules or regulations prohibiting insider dealing and whereas the rules or regulations that do exist differ considerably from one Member State to another;

Whereas it is therefore advisable to adopt coordinated rules at a Community level in this field;

Whereas such coordinated rules also have the advantage of making it possible, through cooperation by the competent authorities, to combat transfrontier insider dealing more effectively;

* * *

---

1. OJ No C 153, 11. 6. 1987, p. 8 and OJ No C 277, 27. 10. 1988, p. 13.
2. OJ No C 187, 18. 7. 1987, p. 93 and Decision of 11 October 1989 (not yet published in the Official Journal).
3. OJ No C 35, 8. 2. 1989, p. 22.

Whereas estimates developed from publicly available data cannot be regarded as inside information and whereas, therefore, any transaction carried out on the basis of such estimates does not constitute insider dealing within the meaning of this Directive;

* * *

HAS ADOPTED THIS DIRECTIVE:

Article 1

For the purposes of this Directive:

1. 'inside information' shall mean information which has not been made public of a precise nature relating to one or several issuers of transferable securities or to one or several transferable securities, which, if it were made public, would be likely to have a significant effect on the price of the transferable security or securities in question;

2. 'transferable securities' shall mean:

(a) shares and debt securities, as well as securities equivalent to shares and debt securities;

(b) contracts or rights to subscribe for, acquire or dispose of securities referred to in (a);

(c) futures contracts, options and financial futures in respect of securities referred to in (a);

(d) index contracts in respect of securities referred to in (a),

when admitted to trading on a market which is regulated and supervised by authorities recognized by public bodies, operates regularly and is accessible directly or indirectly to the public.

Article 2

1. Each Member State shall prohibit any person who:

— by virtue of his membership of the administrative, management or supervisory bodies of the issuer,

— by virtue of his holding in the capital of the issuer, or

— because he has access to such information by virtue of the exercise of his employment, profession or duties,

possesses inside information from taking advantage of that information with full knowledge of the facts by acquiring or disposing of for his own account or for the account of a third party, either directly or indirectly, transferable securities of the issuer or issuers to which that information relates.

2. Where the person referred to in paragraph 1 is a company or other type of legal person, the prohibition laid down in that paragraph shall apply to the natural persons who take part in the decision to carry out the transaction for the account of the legal person concerned.

3. The prohibition laid down in paragraph 1 shall apply to any acquisition or disposal of transferable securities effected through a professional intermediary.

Each Member State may provide that this prohibition shall not apply to acquisitions or disposals of transferable securities effected without the involvement of a professional intermediary outside a market as defined in Article 1(2) *in fine*.

4. This Directive shall not apply to transactions carried out in pursuit of monetary, exchange-rate or public debt-management policies by a sovereign State, by its central bank or any other body designated to that effect by the State, or by any person acting on their behalf. Member States may extend this exemption to their federated States or similar local authorities in respect of the management of their public debt.

Article 3

Each Member State shall prohibit any person subject to the prohibition laid down in Article 2 who possesses inside information from:

(a) disclosing that inside information to any third party unless such disclosure is made in the normal course of the exercise of his employment, profession or duties;

(b) recommending or procuring a third party, on the basis of that inside information, to acquire or dispose of transferable securities admitted to trading on its securities markets as referred to in Article 1(2) *in fine*.

Article 4

Each Member State shall also impose the prohibition provided for in Article 2 on any person other than those referred to in that Article who with full knowledge of the facts possesses inside information, the direct or indirect source of which could not be other than a person referred to in Article 2.

Article 5

Each Member State shall apply the prohibitions provided for in Articles 2, 3 and 4, at least to actions undertaken within its territory to the extent that the transferable securities concerned are admitted to trading on a market of a Member State. In any event, each Member State shall regard a transaction as carried out within its territory if it is carried out on a market, as defined in Article 1(2) *in fine*, situated or operating within that territory.

Article 6

Each Member State may adopt provisions more stringent than those laid down by this Directive or additional provisions, provided that such provisions are applied generally. In particular it may extend the scope of the prohibition laid down in Article 2 and impose on persons referred to in Article 4 the prohibitions laid down in Article 3.

Article 7

The provisions of Schedule C.5(a) of the Annex to Directive 79/279/EEC shall also apply to companies and undertakings the transferable securities of which, whatever their nature, are admitted to trading on a market as referred to in Article 1(2) *in fine* of this Directive.

Article 8

1. Each Member State shall designate the administrative authority or authorities competent, if necessary in collaboration with other authorities to ensure that the provisions adopted pursuant to this Directive are applied. It shall so inform the Commission which shall transmit that information to all Member States.

2. The competent authorities must be given all supervisory and investigatory powers that are necessary for the exercise of their functions, where appropriate in collaboration with other authorities.

Article 9

Each Member State shall provide that all persons employed or formerly employed by the competent authorities referred to in Article 8 shall be bound by professional secrecy. Information covered by professional secrecy may not be divulged to any person or authority except by virtue of provisions laid down by law.

Article 10

1. The competent authorities in the Member States shall cooperate with each other whenever necessary for the purpose of carrying out their duties, making use of the powers mentioned in Article 8(2). To this end, and notwithstanding Article 9, they shall exchange any information required for that purpose, including information relating to actions prohibited, under the options given to Member States by Article 5 and by the second sentence of Article 6, only by the Member State requesting cooperation. Information thus exchanged shall be covered by the obligation of professional secrecy to which the persons employed or formerly employed by the competent authorities receiving the information are subject.

2. The competent authorities may refuse to act on a request for information:

(a) where communication of the information might adversely affect the sovereignty, security or public policy of the State addressed;

(b) where judicial proceedings have already been initiated in respect of the same actions and against the same persons before the authorities of the State addressed or where final judgment has already been passed on such persons for the same actions by the competent authorities of the State addressed.

3. Without prejudice to the obligations to which they are subject in judicial proceedings under criminal law, the authorities which receive information pursuant to paragraph 1 may use it only for the exercise of their functions within the meaning of Article 8(1) and in the context of

administrative or judicial proceedings specifically relating to the exercise of those functions. However, where the competent authority communicating information consents thereto, the authority receiving the information may use it for other purposes or forward it to other States' competent authorities.

Article 11

The Community may, in conformity with the Treaty, conclude agreements with non-member countries on the matters governed by this Directive.

Article 12

The Contact Committee set up by Article 20 of Directive 79/279/EEC shall also have as its function:

(a) to permit regular consultation on any practical problems which arise from the application of this Directive and on which exchanges of view are deemed useful;

(b) to advise the Commission, if necessary, on any additions or amendments to be made to this Directive.

Article 13

Each Member State shall determine the penalties to be applied for infringement of the measures taken pursuant to this Directive. The penalties shall be sufficient to promote compliance with those measures.

Article 14

1. Member States shall take the measures necessary to comply with this Directive before 1 June 1992. They shall forthwith inform the Commission thereof.

2. Member States shall communicate to the Commission the provisions of national law which they adopt in the field governed by this Directive.

Article 15

This Directive is addressed to the Member States.

31. COUNCIL DIRECTIVE 88/627/EEC

of 12 December 1988
on the information to be published when a major holding in a listed company is acquired or disposed of

O.J. L 348/62 (Dec. 17, 1988)

THE COUNCIL OF THE EUROPEAN COMMUNITIES,

Having regard to the Treaty establishing the European Economic Community, and in particular Article 54 thereof,

Having regard to the proposal from the Commission,[1]

In cooperation with the European Parliament,[2]

Having regard to the opinion of the Economic and Social Committee,[3]

Whereas a policy of adequate information of investors in the field of transferable securities is likely to improve investor protection, to increase investors' confidence in securities markets and thus to ensure that securities markets function correctly;

Whereas, by making such protection more equivalent, coordination of that policy at Community level is likely to make for greater interpenetration of the Member States' transferable securities markets and therefore help to establish a true European capital market;

Whereas to that end investors should be informed of major holdings and of changes in those holdings in Community companies the shares of which are officially listed on stock exchanges situated or operating within the Community;

Whereas coordinated rules should be laid down concerning the detailed content and the procedure for applying that requirement;

Whereas companies, the shares of which are officially listed on a Community stock exchange, can inform the public of changes in major holdings only if they have been informed of such changes by the holders of those holdings;

Whereas most Member States do not subject holders to such a requirement and where such a requirement exists there are appreciable differences in the procedures for applying it; whereas coordinated rules should therefore be adopted at Community level in this field,

HAS ADOPTED THIS DIRECTIVE:

Article 1

1. Member States shall make subject to this Directive natural persons and legal entities in public or private law who acquire or dispose of, directly or through intermediaries, holdings meeting the criteria laid

---

1. OJ No C 351, 31. 12. 1985, p. 35, and OJ No C 255, 25. 9. 1987, p. 6.
2. OJ No C 125, 11. 5. 1987, p. 144, and OJ No C 309, 5. 12. 1988.
3. OJ No C 263, 20. 10. 1986, p. 1.

down in Article 4(1) which involve changes in the holdings of voting rights in companies incorporated under their law the shares of which are officially listed on a stock exchange or exchanges situated or operating within one or more Member States.

2. Where the acquisition or disposal of a major holding such as referred to in paragraph 1 is effected by means of certificates representing shares, this Directive shall apply to the bearers of those certificates, and not to the issuer.

3. This Directive shall not apply to the acquisition or disposal of major holdings in collective investment undertakings.

4. Paragraph 5(c) of Schedule C of the Annex to Council Directive 79/279/EEC of 5 March 1979 * * * is hereby replaced by the following:

'(c) The company must inform the public of any changes in the structure (shareholders and breakdowns of holdings) of the major holdings in its capital as compared with information previously published on that subject as soon as such changes come to its notice.

In particular, a company which is not subject to Council Directive 88/627/EEC of 12 December 1988 * * * must inform the public within nine calender days whenever it comes to its notice that a person or entity has acquired or disposed of a number of shares such that his or its holding exceeds or falls below one of the thresholds laid down in Article 4 of that Directive.

Article 2

For the purposes of Directive, 'acquiring a holding' shall mean not only purchasing a holding, but also acquisition by any other means whatsoever, including acquisition in one of the situations referred to in Article 7.

Article 3

Member States may subject the natural persons, legal entities and companies referred to in Article 1(1) to requirements stricter than those provided for in this Directive or to additional requirements, provided that such requirements apply generally to all those acquiring or disposing of holdings and all companies or to all those falling within a particular category acquiring or disposing of holdings or of companies.

Article 4

1. Where a natural person or legal entity referred to in Article 1(1) acquires or disposes of a holding in a company referred to in Article 1(1) and where, following that acquisition or disposal, the proportion of voting rights held by that person or legal entity reaches, exceeds or falls below one of the thresholds of 10%, 20%, ⅓, 50% and ⅔, he shall notify the company and at the same time the competent authority or authorities referred to in Article 13 within seven calender days of the proportion of voting rights he holds following that acquisition or disposal. Member States need not apply:

— the thresholds of 20% and ⅓ where they apply a single threshold of 25%,

— the threshold of ⅔ where they apply the threshold of 75%.

The period of seven calendar days shall start from the time when the owner of the major holding learns of the acquisition or disposal, or from the time when, in view of the circumstances, he should have learned of it.

Member States may further provide that a company must also be informed in respect of the proportion of capital held by a natural person or legal entity.

2. Member States shall, if necessary, establish in their national law, and determine in accordance with it, the manner in which the voting rights to be taken into account for the purposes of applying paragraph 1 are to be brought to the notice of the natural persons and legal entities referred to in Article 1(1).

Article 5

Member States shall provide that at the first annual general meeting of a company referred to in Article 1(1) to take place more than three months after this Directive has been transposed into national law, any natural person or legal entity as referred to in Article 1(1) must notify the company concerned and at the same time the competent authority or authorities where he holds 10% or more of its voting rights, specifying the proportion of voting rights actually held unless that person or entity has already made a declaration in accordance with Article 4.

Within one month of that general meeting, the public shall be informed of all holdings of 10% or more in accordance with Article 10.

Article 6

If the person or entity acquiring or disposing of a major holding as defined in Article 4 is a member of a group of undertakings required under Directive 83/349/EEC to draw up consolidated accounts, that person or entity shall be exempt from the obligation to make the declaration provided for in Article 4(1) and in Article 5 if it is made by the parent undertaking or, where the parent undertaking is itself a subsidiary undertaking, by its own parent undertaking.

Article 7

For the purposes of determining whether a natural person or legal entity as referred to in Article 1(1) is required to make a declaration as provided for in Article 4(1) and in Article 5, the following shall be regarded as voting rights held by that person or entity:

— voting rights held by other persons or entities in their own names but on behalf of that person or entity,

— voting rights held by an undertaking controlled by that person or entity;

— voting rights held by a third party with whom that person or entity has concluded a written agreement which obliges them to adopt, by concerted exercise of the voting rights they hold, a lasting common policy towards the management of the company in question.

— voting rights held by a third party under a written agreement concluded with that person or entity or with an undertaking controlled by that person or entity providing for the temporary transfer for consideration of the voting rights in question,

— voting rights attaching to shares owned by that person or entity which are lodged as security, except where the person or entity holding the security controls the voting rights and declares his intention of exercising them, in which case they shall be regarded as the latter's voting rights,

— voting rights attaching to shares of which that person or entity has the life interest,

— voting rights which that person or entity or one of the other persons or entities mentioned in the above indents is entitled to acquire, on his own initiative alone, under a formal agreement; in such cases, the notification prescribed in Article 4(1) shall be effected on the date of the agreement,

— voting rights attaching to shares deposited with that person or entity which that person or entity can exercise at its discretion in the absence of specific instructions from the holders.

By way of derogation from Article 4(1), where a person or entity may exercise voting rights referred to in the last indent of the preceding subparagraph in a company and where the totality of these voting rights together with the other voting rights held by that person or entity in that company reaches or exceeds one of the thresholds provided for in Article 4(1), Member States may lay down that the said person or entity is only obliged to inform the company concerned 21 calendar days before the general meeting of that company.

Article 8

1. For the purposes of this Directive, 'controlled undertaking' shall mean any undertaking in which a natural person or legal entity:

(a) has a majority of the shareholders' or members' voting rights; or

(b) has the right to appoint or remove a majority of the members of the administrative, management or supervisory body and is at the same time a shareholder in, or member of, the undertaking in question; or

(c) is a shareholder or member and alone controls a majority of the shareholders' or members' voting rights pursuant to an agreement entered into with other shareholders or members of the undertaking.

2. For the purposes of paragraph 1, a parent undertaking's rights as regards voting, appointment and removal shall include the rights of any other controlled undertaking and those of any person or entity acting in his own name but on behalf of the parent undertaking or of any other controlled undertaking.

Article 9

1. The competent authorities may exempt from the declaration provided for in Article 4(1) the acquisition or disposal of a major holding, as defined in Article 4, by a professional dealer in securities, in so far as that acquisition or disposal is effected in his capacity as a professional dealer in securities and in so far as the acquisition is not used by the dealer to intervene in the management of the company concerned.

* * *

Article 10

1. A company which has received a declaration referred to in the first subparagraph of Article 4(1) must in turn disclose it to the public in each of the Member States in which its shares are officially listed on a stock exchange as soon as possible but not more than nine calendar days after the receipt of that declaration.

A Member State may provide for the disclosure to the public, referred to in the first subparagraph, to be made not by the company concerned but by the competent authority, possibly in cooperation with that company.

2. The disclosure referred to in paragraph 1 must be made by publication in one or more newspapers distributed throughout or widely in the Member State or States concerned or be made available to the public either in writing in places indicated by announcements to be published in one or more newspapers distributed throughout or widely in the Member State or States concerned or by other equivalent means approved by the competent authorities.

The said disclosure must be made by publication in the official language or languages, or in one of the official languages or in another language, provided that in the Member State in question the official language or languages or such other language is or are customary in the sphere of finance and accepted by the competent authorities.

Article 11

The competent authorities may, exceptionally, exempt the companies referred to in Article 1(1) from the obligation to notify the public set out in Article 10 where those authorities consider that the disclosure of such information would be contrary to the public interest or seriously detrimental to the companies concerned, provided that, in the latter case, such omission would not be likely to mislead the public with regard to the facts and circumstances knowledge of which is essential for the assessment of the transferable securities in question.

Article 12

1. Member States shall designate the competent authority or authorities for the purposes of this Directive and shall inform the Commission accordingly, specifying, where appropriate, and division of duties between those authorities.

2. Member States shall ensure that the competent authorities have such powers as may be necessary for the performance of their duties.

3. The competent authorities in the Member States shall cooperate wherever necessary for the purpose of performing their duties and shall exchange any information useful for that purpose.

Article 13

For the purpose of this Directive, the competent authorities shall be those of the Member State the law of which governs the companies referred to in Article 1(1).

Article 14

1. Member States shall provide that every person who carries on or has carried on an activity in the employment of a competent authority shall be bound by professional secrecy. This means that no confidential information received in the course of their duties may be divulged to any person or authority except by virtue of provisions laid down by law.

2. Paragraph 1 shall not, however, preclude the competent authorities of the various Member States from exchanging information as provided for in this Directive. Information thus exchanged shall be covered by the obligation of professional secrecy to which persons employed or previously employed by the competent authorities receiving the information are subject.

3. A competent authority which receives confidential information pursuant to paragraph 2 may use it solely for the performance of its duties.

Article 15

Member States shall provide for appropriate sanctions in cases where the natural persons or legal entities and the companies referred to in Article 1(1) do not comply with the provisions of this Directive.

* * *

Article 17

1. Member States shall take the measures necessary for them to comply with this Directive before 1 January 1991. They shall forthwith inform the Commission thereof.

* * *

Article 18

This Directive is addressed to the Member States.

32. FIRST COUNCIL DIRECTIVE 77/780/EEC

of 12 December 1977

on the coordination of laws, regulations and administrative provisions relating to the taking up and pursuit of the business of credit institutions

O.J. L 322/30 (Dec. 17, 1977)

The Council of the European Communities,

Having regard to the Treaty establishing the European Economic Community, and in particular Article 57 thereof,

Having regard to the proposal from the Commission,

Having regard to the opinion of the European Parliament,

Having regard to the opinion of the Economic and Social Committee,

* * *

Whereas, in order to make it easier to take up and pursue the business of credit institutions, it is necessary to eliminate the most obstructive differences between the laws of the Member States as regards the rules to which these institutions are subject;

Whereas, however, given the extent of these differences, the conditions required for a common market for credit institutions cannot be created by means of a single Directive; whereas it is therefore necessary to proceed by successive stages; whereas the result of this process should be to provide for overall supervision of a credit institution operating in several Member States by the competent authorities in the Member State where it has its head office, in consultation, as appropriate, with the competent authorities of the other Member States concerned;

Whereas measures to coordinate credit institutions must, both in order to protect savings and to create equal conditions of competition between these institutions, apply to all of them; whereas due regard must be had, where applicable, to the objective differences in their statutes and their proper aims as laid down by national laws;

Whereas the scope of those measures should therefore be as broad as possible, covering all institutions whose business is to receive repayable funds from the public whether in the form of deposits or in other forms such as the continuing issue of bonds and other comparable securities and to grant credits for their own account; whereas exceptions must be provided for in the case of certain credit institutions to which this Directive cannot apply;

* * *

Whereas the rules governing branches of credit institutions having their head office outside the Community should be analogous in all Member States; whereas it is important at the present time to provide that such rules may not be more favourable than those for branches of institutions from another Member State; whereas it should be specified that the Community may conclude agreements with third countries providing for the application of rules which accord such branches the same treatment throughout its territory, account being taken of the principle of reciprocity;

* * *

HAS ADOPTED THIS DIRECTIVE

TITLE 1
DEFINITIONS AND SCOPE

Article 1

For the purposes of this Directive

— 'credit institution' means an undertaking whose business is to receive deposits or other repayable funds from the public and to grant credits for its own account,

— 'authorization' means an instrument issued in any form by the authorities by which the right to carry on the business of a credit institution is granted,

— 'branch' means a place of business which forms a legally dependent part of a credit institution and which conducts directly all or some of the operations inherent in the business of credit institutions; any number of branches set up in the same Member State by a credit institution having its head office in another Member State shall be regarded as a single branch, without prejudice to Article 4(1),

— 'own funds' means the credit institution's own capital, including items which may be treated as capital under national rules.

Article 2

1. This Directive shall apply to the taking up and pursuit of the business of credit institutions.

2. It shall not apply to:

— the central banks of Member States.

— post office giro institutions.

[— listed savings banks and credit unions in each of the Member States.]

TITLE II
CREDIT INSTITUTIONS HAVING THEIR HEAD OFFICE IN A MEMBER STATE AND THEIR BRANCHES IN OTHER MEMBER STATES

Article 3

[Essentially replaced by the Second Directive.]

1. Member States shall require credit institutions subject to this Directive to obtain authorization before commencing their activities. They shall lay down the requirements for such authorization subject to

paragraphs 2, 3 and 4 and notify them to both the Commission and the Advisory Committee.

2. Without prejudice to other conditions of general application laid down by national laws, the competent authorities shall grant authorization only when the following conditions are complied with:

— the credit institution must possess separate own funds,

— the credit institution must possess adequate minimum own funds,

— there shall be at least two persons who effectively direct the business of the credit institution.

Moreover, the authorities concerned shall not grant authorization if the persons referred to in the third indent of the first subparagraph are not of sufficiently good repute or lack sufficient experience to perform such duties.

3. (a) The provisions referred to in paragraphs 1 and 2 may not require the application for authorization to be examined in terms of the economic needs of the market.

* * *

4. Member States shall also require applications for authorization to be accompanied by a programme of operations setting out *inter alia* the types of business envisaged and the structural organization of the institution.

* * *

7. Every authorization shall be notified to the Commission. Each credit institution shall be entered in a list which the Commission shall publish in the *Official Journal of the European Communities* and shall keep up to date.

Article 4
[Repealed by the Second Directive.]

1. Member States may make the commencement of business in their territory by branches of credit institutions covered by this Directive which have their head office in another Member State subject to authorization according to the law and procedure applicable to credit institutions established on their territory.

2. However, authorization may not be refused to a branch of a credit institution on the sole ground that it is established in another Member State in a legal form which is not allowed in the case of a credit institution carrying out similar activities in the host country.   * * *

Article 5

For the purpose of exercising their activities, credit institutions to which this Directive applies may, notwithstanding any provisions concerning the use of the words 'bank', 'saving bank' or other banking names which may exist in the host Member State, use throughout the territory of the Community the same name as they use in the Member States in which their head office is situated. In the event of there being any danger of confusion, the host Member State may, for the purposes of clarification, require that the name be accompanied by certain explanatory particulars.

Article 6
[Replaced by Directives 89/299/EEC and 89/647/ EEC.]

1. Pending subsequent coordination, the competent authorities shall, for the purposes of observation and, if necessary, in addition to such coefficients as may be applied by them, establish ratios between the various assets and/or liabilities of credit institutions with a view to monitoring their solvency and liquidity and the other measures which may serve to ensure that savings are protected.

* * *

Article 7
[Amended by Second Directive.]

1. The competent authorities of the Member States concerned shall collaborate closely in order to supervise the activities of credit institutions operating, in particular by having established branches there, in one or more Member States other than that in which their head offices are situated. They shall supply one another with all information concerning the management and ownership of such credit institutions that is likely to facilitate their supervision and the examination of the conditions for their authorization and all information likely to facilitate the monitoring of their liquidity and solvency.

* * *

Article 8
[Modified by Second Directive.]

1. The competent authorities may withdraw the authorization issued to a credit institution subject to this Directive or to a branch authorized under Article 4 only where such an institution or branch:

(a) does not make use of the authorization within 12 months, expressly renounces the authorization or has ceased to engage in business for more than six months, if the Member State concerned has made no provision for the authorization to lapse in such cases;

(b) has obtained the authorization through false statements or any other irregular means;

(c) no longer fulfils the conditions under which authorization was granted, with the exception of those in respect of own funds;

(d) no longer possesses sufficient own funds or can no longer be relied upon to fulfil its obligations towards its creditors, and in particular no longer provides security for the assets entrusted to it;

(e) falls within one of the other cases where national law provides for withdrawal of authorization.

2. In addition, the authorization issued to a branch under Article 4 shall be withdrawn if the competent authority of the country in which the credit institution which established the branch has its head office has withdrawn authorization from that institution.

* * *

5. Reasons must be given for any withdrawal of authorization and those concerned informed thereof; such withdrawal shall be notified to the Commission.

TITLE III
BRANCHES OF CREDIT INSTITUTIONS HAVING THEIR HEAD OFFICES OUTSIDE THE COMMUNITY
Article 9

1. Member States shall not apply to branches of credit institutions having their head office outside the Community, when commencing or carrying on their business, provisions which result in more favourable treatment than that accorded to branches of credit institutions having their head office in the Community.

2. The competent authorities shall notify the Commission and the Advisory Committee of all authorizations for branches granted to credit institutions having their head office outside the Community.

3. Without prejudice to paragraph 1, the Community may, through agreements concluded in accordance with the Treaty with one or more third countries, agree to apply provisions which, on the basis of the principle of reciprocity, accord to branches of a credit institution having its head office outside the Community identical treatment throughout the territory of the Community.

TITLE IV
GENERAL AND TRANSITIONAL PROVISIONS
Article 10

1. Credit institutions subject to this Directive, which took up their business in accordance with the provisions of the Member States in which they have their head offices before the entry into force of the provisions implementing this Directive shall be deemed to be authorized. They shall be subject to the provisions of this Directive concerning the carrying on of the business of credit institutions and to the requirements set out in the first and third indents of the first subparagraph and in the second subparagraph of Article 3(2).

* * *

Article 11

1. An 'Advisory Committee of the Competent Authorities of the Member States of the European Economic Community' shall be set up alongside the Commission.

2. The tasks of the Advisory Committee shall be to assist the Commission in ensuring the proper implementation of both this Directive and Council Directive 73/183/EEC of 28 June 1973 on the abolition of restrictions on freedom of establishment and freedom to provide services in respect of self-employed activities of banks and other financial institutions in so far as it relates to credit institutions. Further it shall carry out the other tasks prescribed by this Directive and shall assist the Commission in the preparation of new proposals to the Council concerning further coordination in the sphere of credit institutions.

3. The Advisory Committee shall not concern itself with concrete problems relating to individual credit institutions.

4. The Advisory Committee shall be composed of not more than three representatives from each Member State and from the Commission. These representatives may be accompanied by advisers * * * subject to the prior agreement of the Committee. The Committee may also invite qualified persons and experts to participate in its meetings. The secretariat shall be provided by the Commission.

* * *

Article 13

Member States shall ensure that decisions taken in respect of a credit institution in pursuance of laws, regulations and administrative provisions adopted in accordance with this Directive may be subject to the right to apply to the courts. The same shall apply where no decision is taken within six months of its submission in respect of an application for authorization which contains all the information required under the provisions in force.

TITLE V
FINAL PROVISIONS

* * *

Article 15

This Directive is addressed to the Member States.

33. SECOND COUNCIL DIRECTIVE 89/646/EEC

of 15 December 1989

on the coordination of laws, regulations and administrative provisions relating to the taking up and pursuit of the business of credit institutions and amending Directive 77/780/EEC

O.J. L 386/1 (Dec. 30, 1989)

THE COUNCIL OF THE EUROPEAN COMMUNITIES,

Having regard to the Treaty establishing the European Economic Community, and in particular the first and third sentences of Article 57(2) thereof,

Having regard to the proposal from the Commission,[1]

In cooperation with the European Parliament,[2]

Having regard to the opinion of the Economic and Social Committee,[3]

Whereas this Directive is to constitute the essential instrument for the achievement of the internal market, a course determined by the Single European Act and set out in timetable form in the Commission's White Paper, from the point of view of both the freedom of establishment and the freedom to provide financial services, in the field of credit institutions;

Whereas this Directive will join the body of Community legislation already enacted, in particular the first Council Directive 77/780/EEC of 12 December 1977, Council Directive 83/350/EEC of 13 June 1983 on the supervision of credit institutions on a consolidated basis,[6] Council Directive 86/635/EEC of 8 December 1986 on the annual and consolidated accounts of banks and other financial institutions[7] and Council Directive 89/299/EEC of 17 April 1989 on the own funds of credit institutions;[8]

Whereas the Commission has adopted recommendations 87/62/EEC on large exposures of credit institutions[9] and 87/63/EEC concerning the introduction of deposit-guarantee schemes;[10]

Whereas the approach which has been adopted is to achieve only the essential harmonization necessary and sufficient to secure the mutual recognition of authorization and of prudential supervision systems, making possible the granting of a single licence recognized throughout the Community and the application of the principle of home Member State prudential supervision;

Whereas, in this context, this Directive can be implemented only simultaneously with specific Community legislation dealing with the

---

1. OJ No C 84, 31. 3. 1988, p. 1.
2. OJ No C 96, 17. 4. 1989, p. 33 and Decision of 22 November 1989 (not yet published in the Official Journal).
3. OJ No C 318, 17. 12. 1988, p. 42.
6. OJ No L 193, 18. 7. 1983, p. 18.
7. OJ No L 372, 31. 12. 1986, p. 1.
8. OJ No L 124, 5. 5. 1989, p. 16.
9. OJ No L 33, 4. 2. 1987, p. 10.
10. OJ No L 33, 4. 2. 1987, p. 16.

additional harmonization of technical matters relating to own funds and solvency ratios;

Whereas, moreover, the harmonization of the conditions relating to the reorganization and winding-up of credit institutions is also proceeding;

Whereas the arrangements necessary for the supervision of the liquidity, market, interest-rate and foreign-exchange risks run by credit institutions will also have to be harmonized;

Whereas the principles of mutual recognition and of home Member State control require the competent authorities of each Member State not to grant authorization or to withdraw it where factors such as the activities programme, the geographical distribution or the activities actually carried on make it quite clear that a credit institution has opted for the legal system of one Member State for the purpose of evading the stricter standards in force in another Member State in which it intends to carry on or carries on the greater part of its activities; whereas, for the purposes of this Directive, a credit institution shall be deemed to be situated in the Member State in which it has its registered office; whereas the Member States must require that the head office be situated in the same Member State as the registered office;

Whereas the home Member State may also establish rules stricter than those laid down in Articles 4, 5, 11, 12 and 16 for institutions authorized by its competent authorities;

Whereas responsibility for supervising the financial soundness of a credit institution, and in particular its solvency, will rest with the competent authorities of its home Member State; whereas the host Member State's competent authorities will retain responsibility for the supervision of liquidity and monetary policy; whereas the supervision of market risk must be the subject of close cooperation between the competent authorities of the home and host Member States;

Whereas the harmonization of certain financial and investment services will be effected, where the need exists, by specific Community instruments, with the intention, in particular, of protecting consumers and investors; whereas the Commission has proposed measures for the harmonization of mortgage credit in order, *inter alia,* to allow mutual recognition of the financial techniques peculiar to that sphere;

Whereas, by virtue of mutual recognition, the approach chosen permits credit institutions authorized in their home Member States to carry on, throughout the Community, any or all of the activities listed in the Annex by establishing branches or by providing services;

Whereas the carrying-on of activities not listed in the Annex shall enjoy the right of establishment and the freedom to provide services under the general provisions of the Treaty;

Whereas it is appropriate, however, to extend mutual recognition to the activities listed in the Annex when they are carried on by financial institutions which are subsidiaries of credit institutions, provided that such subsidiaries are covered by the consolidated supervision of their parent undertakings and meet certain strict conditions;

Whereas the host Member State may, in connection with the exercise of the right of establishment and the freedom to provide services, require compliance with specific provisions of its own national laws or regulations on the part of institutions not authorized as credit institutions in their home Member States and with regard to activities not listed in the Annex provided that, on the one hand, such provisions are compatible with Community law and are intended to protect the general good and that, on the other hand, such institutions or such activities are not subject to equivalent rules under the legislation or regulations of their home Member States;

Whereas the Member States must ensure that there are no obstacles to carrying on activities receiving mutual recognition in the same manner as in the home Member State, as long as the latter do not conflict with legal provisions protecting the general good in the host Member State;

Whereas the abolition of the authorization requirement with respect to the branches of Community credit institutions once the harmonization in progress has been completed necessitates the abolition of endowment capital; whereas Article 6(2) constitutes a first transitional step in this direction, but does not, however, affect the Kingdom of Spain or the Portuguese Republic, as provided for in the Act concerning the conditions of those States' accession to the Community;

Whereas there is a necessary link between the objective of this Directive and the liberalization of capital movements being brought about by other Community legislation; whereas in any case the measures regarding the liberalization of banking services must be in harmony with the measures liberalizing capital movements; whereas where the Member States may, by virtue of Council Directive 88/361/EEC of 24 June 1988 for the implementation of Article 67 of the Treaty,[1] invoke safeguard clauses in respect of capital movements, they may suspend the provision of banking services to the extent necessary for the implementation of the abovementioned safeguard clauses;

Whereas the procedures established in Directive 77/780/EEC, in particular with regard to the authorization of branches of credit institutions authorized in third countries, will continue to apply to such institutions; whereas those branches will not enjoy the freedom to provide services under the second paragraph of Article 59 of the Treaty or the freedom of establishment in Member States other than those in which they are established; whereas, however, requests for the authorization of subsidiaries or of the acquisition of holdings made by undertakings governed by the laws of third countries are subject to a procedure intended to ensure that Community credit institutions receive reciprocal treatment in the third countries in question;

1. OJ No L 178, 8. 7. 1988, p. 5.

Whereas the authorizations granted to credit institutions by the competent national authorities pursuant to this Directive will have Community-wide, and no longer merely nationwide, application, and whereas existing reciprocity clauses will henceforth have no effect; whereas a flexible procedure is therefore needed to make it possible to assess reciprocity on a Community basis; whereas the aim of this procedure is not to close the Community's financial markets but rather, as the Community intends to keep its financial markets open to the rest of the world, to improve the liberalization of the global financial markets in other third countries; whereas, to that end, this Directive provides for procedures for negotiating with third countries and, as a last resort, for the possibility of taking measures involving the suspension of new applications for authorization or the restriction of new authorizations;

Whereas the smooth operation of the internal banking market will require not only legal rules but also close and regular cooperation between the competent authorities of the Member States; whereas for the consideration of problems concerning individual credit institutions the Contact Committee set up between the banking supervisory authorities, referred to in the final recital of Directive 77/780/EEC, remains the most appropriate forum; whereas that Committee is a suitable body for the mutual exchange of information provided for in Article 7 of that Directive;

Whereas that mutual information procedure will not in any case replace the bilateral collaboration established by Article 7 of Directive 77/780/EEC; whereas the competent host Member State authorities can, without prejudice to their powers of control proper, continue either, in an emergency, on their own initiative or following the initiative of the competent home Member State authorities to verify that the activities of a credit institution established within their territories comply with the relevant laws and with the principles of sound administrative and accounting procedures and adequate internal control;

Whereas technical modifications to the detailed rules laid down in this Directive may from time to time be necessary to take account of new developments in the banking sector; whereas the Commission shall accordingly make such modifications as are necessary, after consulting the Banking Advisory Committee, within the limits of the implementing powers conferred on the Commission by the Treaty; whereas that Committee shall act as a 'Regulatory' Committee, according to the rules of procedure laid down in Article 2, procedure III, variant (b), of Council Decision 87/373/EEC of 13 July 1987 laying down the procedures for the exercise of implementing powers conferred on the Commission,[1]

HAS ADOPTED THIS DIRECTIVE:

TITLE I
DEFINITIONS AND SCOPE
Article 1

For the purpose of this Directive:

1. 'credit institution' shall mean a credit institution as defined in the first indent of Article 1 of Directive 77/780/EEC;

1. OJ No L 197, 18. 7. 1987, p. 33.

2. 'authorization' shall mean authorization as defined in the second indent of Article 1 of Directive 77/780/EEC;

3. 'branch' shall mean a place of business which forms a legally dependent part of a credit institution and which carries out directly all or some of the transactions inherent in the business of credit institutions; any number of places of business set up in the same Member State by a credit institution with headquarters in another Member State shall be regarded as a single branch;

4. 'own funds' shall mean own funds as defined in Directive 89/299/EEC;

5. 'competent authorities' shall mean competent authorities as defined in Article 1 of Directive 83/350/EEC;

6. 'financial institution' shall mean an undertaking other than a credit institution the principal activity of which is to acquire holdings or to carry on one or more of the activities listed in points 2 to 12 in the Annex;

7. 'home Member State' shall mean the Member State in which a credit institution has been authorized in accordance with Article 3 of Directive 77/780/EEC;

8. 'host Member State' shall mean the Member State in which a credit institution has a branch or in which it provides services;

9. 'control' shall mean the relationship between a parent undertaking and a subsidiary, as defined in Article 1 of Directive 83/349/EEC,[2] or a similar relationship between any natural or legal person and an undertaking;

10. 'qualifying holding' shall mean a direct or indirect holding in an undertaking which represents 10% or more of the capital or of the voting rights or which makes it possible to exercise a significant influence over the management of the undertaking in which a holding subsists.

For the purposes of this definition, in the context of Articles 5 and 11 and of the other levels of holding referred to in Article 11, the voting rights referred to in Article 7 of Directive 88/627/EEC,[3] shall be taken into consideration;

11. 'initial capital' shall mean capital as defined in Article 2(1)(1) and (2) of Directive 89/299/EEC;

12. 'parent undertaking' shall mean a parent undertaking as defined in Articles 1 and 2 of Directive 83/349/EEC;

13. 'subsidiary' shall mean a subsidiary undertaking as defined in Articles 1 and 2 of Directive 83/349/EEC; any subsidiary of a subsidiary

---

[2] OJ No L 193, 18. 7. 1983, p. 1.   [3] OJ No L 348, 17. 12. 1988, p. 62.

undertaking shall also be regarded as a subsidiary of the parent undertaking which is at the head of those undertakings;

14. 'solvency ratio' shall mean the solvency coefficient of credit institutions calculated in accordance with Directive 89/647/EEC [1].

Article 2

1. This Directive shall apply to all credit institutions.

2. It shall not apply to the institutions referred to in Article 2(2) of Directive 77/780/EEC.

* * *

Article 3

The Member States shall prohibit persons or undertakings that are not credit institutions from carrying on the business of taking deposits or other repayable funds from the public. This prohibition shall not apply to the taking of deposits or other funds repayable by a Member State or by a Member State's regional or local authorities or by public international bodies of which one or more Member States are members or to cases expressly covered by national or Community legislation, provided that those activities are subject to regulations and controls intended to protect depositors and investors and applicable to those cases.

TITLE II

HARMONIZATION OF AUTHORIZATION CONDITIONS

Article 4

1. The competent authorities shall not grant authorization in cases where initial capital is less than ECU 5 million.

2. The Member States shall, however, have the option of granting authorization to particular categories of credit institutions the initial capital of which is less than that prescribed in paragraph 1. In such cases:

(a) the initial capital shall not be less than ECU 1 million * * *.

Article 5

The competent authorities shall not grant authorization for the taking-up of the business of credit institutions before they have been informed of the identities of the shareholders or members, whether direct or indirect, natural or legal persons, that have qualifying holdings, and of the amounts of those holdings.

The competent authorities shall refuse authorization if, taking into account the need to ensure the sound and prudent management of a credit institution, they are not satisfied as to the suitability of the abovementioned shareholders or members.

1. O.J. L 386, 30. 12. 1989, p. 14.

Article 6

1. Host Member States may no longer require authorization, as provided for in Article 4 of Directive 77/780/EEC, or endowment capital for branches of credit institutions authorized in other Member States. The establishment and supervision of such branches shall be effected as prescribed in Articles 13, 19 and 21 of this Directive.

2. Until the entry into force of the provisions implementing paragraph 1, host Member States may not, as a condition of the authorization of branches of credit institutions, authorized in other Member States, require initial endowment capital exceeding 50% of the initial capital required by national rules for the authorization of credit institutions of the same nature.

3. Credit institutions shall be entitled to the free use of the funds no longer required pursuant to paragraphs 1 and 2.

Article 7

There must be prior consultation with the competent authorities of the other Member State involved on the authorization of a credit institution which is:

— a subsidiary of a credit institution authorized in another Member State, or

— a subsidiary of the parent undertaking of a credit institution authorized in another Member State, or

— controlled by the same persons, whether natural or legal, as control a credit institution authorized in another Member State.

TITLE III

RELATIONS WITH THIRD COUNTRIES

Article 8

The competent authorities of the Member States shall inform the Commission:

(a) of any authorization of a direct or indirect subsidiary one or more parent undertakings of which are governed by the laws of a third country. The Commission shall inform the Banking Advisory Committee accordingly;

(b) whenever such a parent undertaking acquires a holding in a Community credit institution such that the latter would become its subsidiary. The Commission shall inform the Banking Advisory Committee accordingly.

When authorization is granted to the direct or indirect subsidiary of one or more parent undertakings governed by the law of third countries, the structure of the group shall be specified in the notification which the competent authorities shall address to the Commission in accordance with Article 3(7) of Directive 77/780/EEC.

Article 9

1. The Member States shall inform the Commission of any general difficulties encountered by their credit institutions in establishing themselves or carrying on banking activities in a third country.

2. Initially no later than six months before the application of this Directive and thereafter periodically, the Commission shall draw up a report examining the treatment accorded to Community credit institutions in third countries, in the terms referred to in paragraphs 3 and 4, as regards establishment and the carrying-on of banking activities, and the acquisition of holdings in third-country credit institutions. The Commission shall submit those reports to the Council, together with any appropriate proposals.

3. Whenever it appears to the Commission, either on the basis of the reports referred to in paragraph 2 or on the basis of other information, that a third country is not granting Community credit institutions effective market access comparable to that granted by the Community to credit institutions from that third country, the Commission may submit proposals to the Council for the appropriate mandate for negotiation with a view to obtaining comparable competitive opportunities for Community credit institutions. The Council shall decide by a qualified majority.

4. Whenever it appears to the Commission, either on the basis of the reports referred to in paragraph 2 or on the basis of other information that Community credit institutions in a third country do not receive national treatment offering the same competitive opportunities as are available to domestic credit institutions and the conditions of effective market access are not fulfilled, the Commission may initiate negotiations in order to remedy the situation.

In the circumstances described in the first subparagraph, it may also be decided at any time, and in addition to initiating negotiations, in accordance with the procedure laid down in Article 22(2), that the competent authorities of the Member States must limit or suspend their decisions regarding requests pending at the moment of the decision or future requests for authorizations and the acquisition of holdings by direct or indirect parent undertakings governed by the laws of the third country in question. The duration of the measures referred to may not exceed three months.

Before the end of that three-month period, and in the light of the results of the negotiations, the Council may, acting on a proposal from the Commission, decide by a qualified majority whether the measures shall be continued.

Such limitations or suspension may not apply to the setting up of subsidiaries by credit institutions or their subsidiaries duly authorized in the Community, or to the acquisition of holdings in Community credit institutions by such institutions or subsidiaries.

5. Whenever it appears to the Commission that one of the situations described in paragraphs 3 and 4 obtains, the Member States shall inform it at its request:

(a) of any request for the authorization of a direct or indirect subsidiary one or more parent undertakings of which are governed by the laws of the third country in question;

(b) whenever they are informed in accordance with Article 11 that such an undertaking proposes to acquire a holding in a Community credit institution such that the latter would become its subsidiary.

This obligation to provide information shall lapse whenever an agreement is reached with the third country referred to in paragraph 3 or 4 or when the measures referred to in the second and third subparagraphs of paragraph 4 cease to apply.

6. Measures taken pursuant to this Article shall comply with the Community's obligations under any international agreements, bilateral or multilateral, governing the taking-up and pursuit of the business of credit institutions.

TITLE IV
HARMONIZATION OF THE CONDITIONS GOVERNING PURSUIT OF THE BUSINESS OF CREDIT INSTITUTIONS

Article 10

1. A credit institution's own funds may not fall below the amount of initial capital required pursuant to Article 4 at the time of its authorization.

* * *

Article 11

1. The Member States shall require any natural or legal person who proposes to acquire, directly or indirectly a qualifying holding in a credit institution first to inform the competent authorities, telling them of the size of the intended holding. Such a person must likewise inform the competent authorities if he proposes to increase his qualifying holding so that the proportion of the voting rights or of the capital held by him would reach or exceed 20%, 33% or 50% or so that the credit institution would become his subsidiary.

Without prejudice to the provisions of paragraph 2 the competent authorities shall have a maximum of three months from the date of the notification provided for in the first subparagraph to oppose such a plan if, in view of the need to ensure sound and prudent management of the credit institution, they are not satisfied as to the suitability of the person referred to in the first subparagraph. If they do not oppose the plan referred to in the first subparagraph, they may fix a maximum period for its implementation.

2. If the acquirer of the holdings referred to in paragraph 1 is a credit institution authorized in another Member State or the parent undertaking of a credit institution authorized in another Member State or a natural or legal person controlling a credit institution authorized in another Member State and if, as a result of that acquisition, the institution in which the acquirer proposes to acquire a holding would become a subsidiary or subject to the control of the acquirer, the assessment of the acquisition must be the subject of the prior consultation referred to in Article 7.

3. The Member States shall require any natural or legal person who proposes to dispose, directly or indirectly, of a qualifying holding in a credit institution first to inform the competent authorities, telling them of the size of his intended holding. Such a person must likewise inform the competent authorities if he proposes to reduce his qualifying holding so that the proportion of the voting rights or of the capital held by him would fall below 20%, 33% or 50% or so that the credit institution would cease to be his subsidiary.

4. On becoming aware of them, credit institutions shall inform the competent authorities of any acquisitions or disposals of holdings in their capital that cause holdings to exceed or fall below one of the thresholds referred to in paragraphs 1 and 3.

They shall also, at least once a year, inform them of the names of shareholders and members possessing qualifying holdings and the sizes of such holdings as shown, for example, by the information received at the annual general meetings of shareholders and members or as a result of compliance with the regulations relating to companies listed on stock exchanges.

5. The Member States shall require that, where the influence exercised by the persons referred to in paragraph 1 is likely to operate to the detriment of the prudent and sound management of the institution, the competent authorities shall take appropriate measures to put an end to that situation. Such measures may consist for example in injunctions, sanctions against directors and managers, or the suspension of the exercise of the voting rights attaching to the shares held by the shareholders or members in question.

Similar measures shall apply to natural or legal persons failing to comply with the obligation to provide prior information, as laid down in paragraph 1. If a holding is acquired despite the opposition of the competent authorities, the Member States shall, regardless of any other sanctions to be adopted, provide either for exercise of the corresponding voting rights to be suspended, or for the nullity of votes cast or for the possibility of their annulment.

Article 12

1. No credit institution may have a qualifying holding the amount of which exceeds 15% of its own funds in an undertaking which is neither a credit institution, nor a financial institution, nor an undertaking carrying

on an activity referred to in the second subparagraph of Article 43(2)(f) of Directive 86/635/EEC.

2. The total amount of a credit institution's qualifying holdings in undertakings other than credit institutions, financial institutions or undertakings carrying on activities referred to in the second subparagraph of Article 43(2)(f) of Directive 86/635/EEC may not exceed 60% of its own funds.

3. The Member States need not apply the limits laid down in paragraphs 1 and 2 to holdings in insurance companies as defined in Directive 73/239/EEC,[1] as last amended by Directive 88/357/EEC,[2] and Directive 79/267/EEC,[3] as last amended by the Act of Accession of 1985.

4. Shares held temporarily during a financial reconstruction or rescue operation or during the normal course of underwriting or in an institution's own name on behalf of others shall not be counted as qualifying holdings for the purpose of calculating the limits laid down in paragraphs 1 and 2.

* * *

7. Credit institutions which, on the date of entry into force of the provisions implementing this Directive, exceed the limits laid down in paragraphs 1 and 2 shall have a period of 10 years from that date in which to comply with them.

* * *

Article 13

1. The prudential supervision of a credit institution, including that of the activities it carries on in accordance with Article 18, shall be the responsibility of the competent authorities of the home Member State, without prejudice to those provisions of this Directive which give responsibility to the authorities of the host Member State.

2. Home Member State competent authorities shall require that every credit institution have sound administrative and accounting procedures and adequate internal control mechanisms.

3. Paragraphs 1 and 2 shall not prevent supervision on a consolidated basis pursuant to Directive 83/350/EEC.

Article 14

1. In Article 7(1) of Directive 77/780/EEC, the end of the second sentence is hereby replaced by the following: 'and all information likely to facilitate the monitoring of such institutions, in particular with regard to liquidity, solvency, deposit guarantees, the limiting of large exposures, administrative and accounting procedures and internal control mechanisms'.

---

[1] OJ No L 228, 16.8. 1973, p. 3.
[2] OJ No L 172, 4.7. 1988, p. 1.
[3] OJ No L 63, 13.3. 1979, p. 1.

2. Host Member States shall retain responsibility in cooperation with the competent authorities of the home Member State for the supervision of the liquidity of the branches of credit institutions pending further coordination. Without prejudice to the measures necessary for the reinforcement of the European Monetary System, host Member States shall retain complete responsibility for the measures resulting from the implementation of their monetary policies. Such measures may not provide for discriminatory or restrictive treatment based on the fact that a credit institution is authorized in another Member State.

3. Without prejudice to further coordination of the measures designed to supervise the risks arising out of open positions on markets, where such risks result from transactions carried out on the financial markets of other Member States, the competent authorities of the latter shall collaborate with the competent authorities of the home Member State to ensure that the institutions concerned take steps to cover those risks.

Article 15

1. Host Member States shall provide that, where a credit institution authorized in another Member State carries on its activities through a branch, the competent authorities of the home Member State may, after having first informed the competent authorities of the host Member State, carry out themselves or through the intermediary of persons they appoint for that purpose on-the-spot verification of the information referred to in Article 7(1) of Directive 77/780/EEC.

2. The competent authorities of the home Member State may also, for purposes of the verification of branches, have recourse to one of the other procedures laid down in Article 5(4) of Directive 83/350/EEC.

3. This Article shall not affect the right of the competent authorities of the host Member State to carry out, in the discharge of their responsibilities under this Directive, on-the-spot verifications of branches established within their territory.

Article 16

Article 12 of Directive 77/780/EEC is hereby replaced by the following:

Article 12

1. The Member States shall provide that all persons working or who have worked for the competent authorities, as well as auditors or experts acting on behalf of the competent authorities, shall be bound by the obligation of professional secrecy. This means that no confidential information which they may receive in the course of their duties may be divulged to any person or authority whatsoever, except in summary or collective form, such that individual institutions cannot be identified, without prejudice to cases covered by criminal law.

Nevertheless, where a credit institution has been declared bankrupt or is being compulsorily wound up, confidential information which does not concern third parties involved in attempts to rescue that credit institution may be divulged in civil or commercial proceedings.

2. Paragraph 1 shall not prevent the competent authorities of the various Member States from exchanging information in accordance with the Directives applicable to credit institutions. That information shall be subject to the conditions of professional secrecy indicated in paragraph 1.

3. Member States may conclude cooperation agreements, providing for exchanges of information, with the competent authorities of third countries only if the information disclosed is subject to guarantees of professional secrecy at least equivalent to those referred to in this Article.

* * *

Article 17

Without prejudice to the procedures for the withdrawal of authorizations and the provisions of criminal law, the Member States shall provide that their respective competent authorities may, as against credit institutions or those who effectively control the business of credit institutions which breach laws, regulations or administrative provisions concerning the supervision or pursuit of their activities, adopt or impose in respect of them penalties or measures aimed specifically at ending observed breaches or the causes of such breaches.

TITLE V

PROVISIONS RELATING TO THE FREEDOM OF ESTABLISHMENT AND THE FREEDOM TO PROVIDE SERVICES

Article 18

1. The Member States shall provide that the activities listed in the Annex may be carried on within their territories, in accordance with Articles 19 to 21, either by the establishment of a branch or by way of the provision of services, by any credit institution authorized and supervised by the competent authorities of another Member State, in accordance with this Directive, provided that such activities are covered by the authorization.

2. The Member States shall also provide that the activities listed in the Annex may be carried on within their territories, in accordance with Articles 19 to 21, either by the establishment of a branch or by way of the provision of services, by any financial institution from another Member State, whether a subsidiary of a credit institution or the jointly-owned subsidiary of two or more credit institutions, the memorandum and articles of association of which permit the carrying on of those activities and which fulfils each of the following conditions:

— the parent undertaking or undertakings must be authorized as credit institutions in the Member State by the law of which the subsidiary is governed,

— the activities in question must actually be carried on within the territory of the same Member State,

— the parent undertaking or undertakings must hold 90% or more of the voting rights attaching to shares in the capital of the subsidiary,

— the parent undertaking or undertakings must satisfy the competent authorities regarding the prudent management of the subsidiary and must have declared, with the consent of the relevant home Member State competent authorities, that they jointly and severally guarantee the commitments entered into by the subsidiary,

— the subsidiary must be effectively included, for the activities in question in particular, in the consolidated supervision of the parent undertaking, or of each of the parent undertakings, in accordance with Directive 83/350/EEC, in particular for the calculation of the solvency ratio, for the control of large exposures and for purposes of the limitation of holdings provided for in Article 12 of this Directive.

Compliance with these conditions must be verified by the competent authorities of the home Member State and the latter must supply the subsidiary with a certificate of compliance which must form part of the notification referred to in Articles 19 and 20.

* * *

Article 19

1. A credit institution wishing to establish a branch within the territory of another Member State shall notify the competent authorities of its home Member State.

2. The Member State shall require every credit institution wishing to establish a branch in another Member State to provide the following information when effecting the notification referred to in paragraph 1:

(a) the Member State within the territory of which it plans to establish a branch;

(b) a programme of operations setting out inter alia the types of business envisaged and the structural organization of the branch;

(c) the address in the host Member State from which documents may be obtained;

(d) the names of those responsible for the management of the branch.

3. Unless the competent authorities of the home Member State have reason to doubt the adequacy of the administrative structure or the financial situation of the credit institution, taking into account the activities envisaged, they shall within three months of receipt of the information referred to in paragraph 2 communicate that information to the competent authorities of the host Member State and shall inform the institution concerned accordingly.

The home Member State competent authorities shall also communicate the amount of own funds and the solvency ratio of the credit institution and, pending subsequent coordination, details of any deposit-guarantee scheme which is intended to ensure the protection of depositors in the branch.

Where the competent authorities of the home Member State refuse to communicate the information referred to in paragraph 2 to the competent authorities of the host Member State, they shall give reasons for their refusal to the institution concerned within three months of receipt of all the information. That refusal or failure to reply shall be subject to a right to apply to the courts in the home Member State.

4. Before the branch of a credit institution commences its activities the competent authorities of the host Member State shall, within two months of receiving the information mentioned in paragraph 3, prepare for the supervision of the credit institution in accordance with Article 21 and if necessary indicate the conditions under which, in the interest of the general good, those activities must be carried on in the host Member State.

5. On receipt of a communication from the competent authorities of the host Member State, or in the event of the expiry of the period provided for in paragraph 4 without receipt of any communication from the latter, the branch may be established and commence its activities.

6. In the event of a change in any of the particulars communicated pursuant to paragraph 2(b), (c) or (d) or in the deposit-guarantee scheme referred to in paragraph 3 a credit institution shall give written notice of the change in question to the competent authorities of the home and host Member States at least one month before making the change so as to enable the competent authorities of the home Member State to take a decision pursuant to paragraph 3 and the competent authorities of the host Member State to take a decision on the change pursuant to paragraph 4.

Article 20

1. Any credit institution wishing to exercise the freedom to provide services by carrying on its activities within the territory of another Member State for the first time shall notify the competent authorities of the home Member State of the activities on the list in the Annex which it intends to carry on.

2. The competent authorities of the home Member State shall, within one month of receipt of the notification mentioned in paragraph 1, send that notification to the competent authorities of the host Member State.

Article 21

1. Host Member State may, for statistical purposes, require that all credit institutions having branches within their territories shall report periodically on their activities in those host Member States to the competent authorities of those host Member States.

In discharging the responsibilities imposed on them in Article 14(2) and (3), host Member States may require that branches of credit institutions from other Member States provide the same information as they require from national credit institutions for that purpose.

2. Where the competent authorities of a host Member State ascertain that an institution having a branch or providing services within its territory is not complying with the legal provisions adopted in that State pursuant to the provisions of this Directive involving powers of the host Member State competent authorities, those authorities shall require the institution concerned to put an end to that irregular situation.

3. If the institution concerned fails to take the necessary steps, the competent authorities of the host Member State shall inform the competent authorities of the home Member State accordingly. The competent authorities of the home Member State shall, at the earliest opportunity, take all appropriate measures to ensure that the institution concerned puts an end to that irregular situation. The nature of those measures shall be communicated to the competent authorities of the host Member State.

4. If, despite the measures taken by the home Member State or because such measures prove inadequate or are not available in the Member State in question, the institution persists in violating the legal rules referred to in paragraph 2 in force in the host Member State, the latter State may, after informing the competent authorities of the home Member State, take appropriate measures to prevent or to punish further irregularities and, insofar as is necessary, to prevent that institution from initiating further transactions within its territory. The Member States shall ensure that within their territories it is possible to serve the legal documents necessary for these measures on credit institutions.

5. The foregoing provisions shall not affect the power of host Member States to take appropriate measures to prevent or to punish irregularities committed within their territories which are contrary to the legal rules they have adopted in the interest of the general good. This shall include the possibility of preventing offending institutions from initiating any further transactions within their territories.

6. Any measure adopted pursuant to paragraphs 3, 4 and 5 involving penalties or restrictions on the exercise of the freedom to provide services must be properly justified and communicated to the institution concerned. Every such measure shall be subject to a right of appeal to the courts in the Member State the authorities of which adopted it.

7. Before following the procedure provided for in paragraphs 2 to 4, the competent authorities of the host Member State may, in emergencies, take any precautionary measures necessary to protect the interests of depositors, investors and others to whom services are provided. The Commission and the competent authorities of the other Member States concerned must be informed of such measures at the earliest opportunity.

The Commission may, after consulting the competent authorities of the Member States concerned, decide that the Member State in question must amend or abolish those measures.

8. Host Member States may exercise the powers conferred on them under this Directive by taking appropriate measures to prevent or to punish irregularities committed within their territories. This shall include the possibility of preventing institutions from initiating further transactions within their territories.

9. In the event of the withdrawal of authorization the competent authorities of the host Member State shall be informed and shall take appropriate measures to prevent the institution concerned from initiating further transactions within its territory and to safeguard the interests of depositors. Every two years the Commission shall submit a report on such cases to the Banking Advisory Committee.

10. The Member States shall inform the Commission of the number and type of cases in which there has been a refusal pursuant to Article 19 or in which measures have been taken in accordance with paragraph 4. Every two years the Commission shall submit a report on such cases to the Banking Advisory Committee.

11. Nothing this Article shall prevent credit institutions with head offices in other Member States from advertising their services through all available means of communication in the host Member State, subject to any rules governing the form and the content of such advertising adopted in the interest of the general good.

TITLE VI
FINAL PROVISIONS
Article 22

1. The technical adaptations to be made to this Directive * * * shall be adopted in accordance with the procedure laid down in paragraph 2 * * *.

2. The Commission shall be assisted by a committee composed of representatives of the Member States and chaired by a representative of the Commission.

The Commission representative shall submit to the committee a draft of the measures to be taken. The committee shall deliver its opinion on the draft within a time limit which the chairman may lay down according to the urgency of the matter. The opinion shall be delivered by the majority laid down in Article 148(2) of the Treaty in the case of decisions which the Council is required to adopt on a proposal from the Commission. The votes of the representatives of the Member States in the committee shall be weighted in the manner set out in that Article. The chairman shall not vote.

The Commission shall adopt the measures envisaged if they are in accordance with the opinion of the committee.

If the measures envisaged are not in accordance with the opinion of the committee, or if no opinion is delivered, the Commission shall, without delay, submit to the Council a proposal concerning the measures to be taken. The Council shall act by a qualified majority.

If the Council does not act within three months of the referral to it the Commission shall adopt the measures proposed, unless the Council has decided against those measures by a simple majority.

Article 23

1. Branches which have commenced their activities, in accordance with the provisions in force in their host Member States, before the entry into force of the provisions adopted in implementation of this Directive shall be presumed to have been subject to the procedure laid down in Article 19(1) to (5). They shall be governed, from the date of that entry into force, by Articles 15, 18, 19(6) and 21. They shall benefit pursuant to Article 6(3).

2. Article 20 shall not affect rights acquired by credit institutions providing services before the entry into force of the provisions adopted in implementation of this Directive.

Article 24

1. Subject to paragraph 2, the Member States shall bring into force the laws, regulations and administrative provisions necessary for them to comply with this Directive by the later of the two dates laid down for the adoption of measures to comply with Directives 89/299/EEC and 89/647/EEC and at the latest by 1 January 1993. They shall forthwith inform the Commission thereof.

2. The Member States shall adopt the measures necessary for them to comply with Article 6(2) by 1 January 1990.

* * *

Article 25

This Directive is addressed to the Member States.

ANNEX

LIST OF ACTIVITIES SUBJECT TO MUTUAL RECOGNITION

1. Acceptance of deposits and other repayable funds from the public.
2. Lending [1].
3. Financial leasing.
4. Money transmission services.
5. Issuing and administering means of payment (e.g. credit cards, travellers' cheques and bankers' drafts).
6. Guarantees and commitments.
7. Trading for own account or for account of customers in:

[1]. Including *inter alia:*
— consumer credit,
— mortgage credit,
— factoring, with or without recourse,
— financing of commercial transactions (including forfeiting).

(1) money market instruments (cheques, bills, CDs, etc.);
(b) foreign exchange;
(c) financial futures and options;
(d) exchange and interest rate instruments;
(e) transferable securities.
8. Participation in share issues and the provision of services related to such issues.
9. Advice to undertakings on capital structure, industrial strategy and related questions and advice and services relating to mergers and the purchase of undertakings.
10. Money broking.
11. Portfolio management and advice.
12. Safekeeping and administration of securities.
13. Credit reference services.
14. Safe custody services.

Part III

COMPETITION POLICY

INTRODUCTION

Printed below are the most important regulations and notices regarding EC Competition law. The first document, Regulation 17, is a procedural regulation that implements Articles 85 and 86 of the Treaty. It gives the Commission the necessary powers to enforce Articles 85 and 86—the power to get information, to grant clearances and exemptions, and to impose fines and other remedies. Also it establishes the procedures for notification of agreements that fall within Article 85(1). Regulation 17 is treated at pages 631 to 632 and 698 to 718 of the Casebook.

Not included here but important in the practice of EC competition law is Regulation 27/62, O.J. 35/1118 (May 10, 1962), which specifies rules for submitting applications for negative clearance and for notification of agreements.

Document 2 is the Commission's Notice on Exclusive Agency Contracts with Commercial Agents. This notice distinguishes the principal/agent relationship from the independent trader situation; commercial agents are not separate actors from their principals and their agency contracts with their principals are not covered by Article 85 (as long as a commercial agent meets the description set forth in the notice). See also Casebook at page 765.

Document 3 is the Notice on Cooperation between Enterprises. It gives guidance regarding the application of Article 85(1). In particular, it lists agreements, such as those intended solely for joint market research or for cooperation in accounting, that are deemed by the Commission not to restrict competition and which therefore need not be notified. The notice reflects particular hospitality towards cooperation among small and medium-sized enterprises. See also Casebook at page 689.

Document 4 is the Notice on Agreements of Minor Importance. This notice describes agreements that are *de minimis* either because of the market share involved or the small aggregate turnover of the parties. These agreements are also deemed to be outside of the purview of Article 85. See also Casebook at page 689. This notice replaces a prior notice on the same subject and it complements a notice on subcontracting agreements, which may be found at O.J. C 1/2 (Jan. 3, 1979).

Documents 5 and 6 are regulations providing for block exemptions for exclusive distribution and exclusive purchasing agreements. Exclusive distribution and purchasing agreements are probably the most common kind of commercial agreements subject to scrutiny under Article 85. The regulations involved (1983/83 and 1984/83) supersede Regulation 67/67, O.J. 57/849 (March 25, 1967). Exclusive distribution and exclusive purchasing, including the block exemptions, are treated in the Casebook at page 723 et seq.

Document 7 is a regulation providing a block exemption for specialization agreements between small or medium-sized enterprises. In a typical transaction, small or medium-sized firms agree with one another to specialize in the production or distribution of complementary products. See also Casebook at 769.

Document 8 is a regulation providing a block exemption for cooperative research and development. The exemption extends to joint exploitation of the results of the R & D cooperation. See also Casebook at page 771.

Document 9 is a regulation providing for a block exemption for franchising. See also Casebook at page 758.

The final competition document is the Merger Control Regulation. This important regulation provides for advance notification of mergers that meet a size threshold and have a Community-wide dimension, gives the Community exclusive jurisdiction over covered mergers, and sets a substantive standard for illegality and prohibition. Related merger documents, which you may wish to consult but which are not printed herein, include the Commission's guidelines on ancillary restrictions accompanying mergers, O.J. C 203/5 (Aug. 14, 1990), and an interpretive notice distinguishing between concentration and cooperation (concentrative joint ventures are covered by the merger regulation; cooperative joint ventures are not), O.J. C 203/10 (Aug. 14, 1990).

There are a number of other documents that you may wish to consult. If you are doing research in the field of intellectual property, you will probably wish to examine the regulation on patent licensing, which provides for a block exemption, Reg. 2349/84, O.J. L 219/15 (July 23, 1984), corrections at O.J. C 113/34 (___, 1985), and the regulation on know how licensing, which provides for a block exemption, Reg. 556/89, O.J. L 61/1 (March 4, 1989). See also Casebook at pages 761 to 765. There is also a regulation and block exemption on motor vehicle distribution and servicing. Reg. 123/85, O.J. L 15/16 (Jan. 18, 1985). In addition, several regulations help to define the interface between competition policy and the common policies on agriculture and on transportation. See, e.g., Council Reg. 26/62, O.J. 30/62 (April 20, 1962) (agriculture); Reg. 1017/68, O.J. L 175/1 (July 23, 1968) (transport by rail, road and inland water).

Table of Contents

PART III. COMPETITION POLICY

Doc.
1. Council Regulation 17 implementing Articles 85 and 86.
2. Commission Announcement on exclusive agency contracts made with commercial agents.
3. Commission Announcement concerning agreements, decisions and concerted practices in the field of cooperation between enterprises.
4. Commission Notice on agreements of minor importance which do not fall under Article 85(1).
5. Commission Regulation 1983/83 on the application of Article 85(3) to categories or exclusive distribution agreements.
6. Commission Regulation 1984/83 on the application of Article 85(3) to categories of exclusive purchasing agreements.
7. Commission Regulation 417/85 on the application of Article 85(3) to categories of specialization agreements.
8. Commission Regulation 418/85 on the application of Article 85(3) to categories of research and development agreements.
9. Commission Regulation 4087/88 on the application of Article 85(3) to categories of franchise agreements.
10. Council Regulation 4064/89 on the control of concentrations between undertakings [Merger Regulation].

1. COUNCIL REGULATION No. 17

First Regulation implementing Articles 85 and 86 of the Treaty

O.J. English Spec. Ed., 1959–1962, at 87

THE COUNCIL OF THE EUROPEAN ECONOMIC COMMUNITY,

Having regard to the Treaty establishing the European Economic Community, and in particular Article 87 thereof;

Having regard to the proposal from the Commission;

Having regard to the Opinion of the Economic and Social Committee;

Having regard to the Opinion of the European Parliament;

Whereas, in order to establish a system ensuring that competition shall not be distorted in the common market, it is necessary to provide for balanced application of Articles 85 and 86 in a uniform manner in the Member States;

Whereas in establishing the rules for applying Article 85(3) account must be taken of the need to ensure effective supervision and to simplify administration to the greatest possible extent;

Whereas it is accordingly necessary to make it obligatory, as a general principle, for undertakings which seek application of Article 85(3) to notify to the Commission their agreements, decisions and concerted practices;

Whereas, on the one hand, such agreements, decisions and concerted practices are probably very numerous and cannot therefore all be examined at the same time and, on the other hand, some of them have special features which may make them less prejudicial to the development of the common market;

Whereas there is consequently a need to make more flexible arrangements for the time being in respect of certain categories of agreement, decision and concerted practice without prejudging their validity under Article 85;

Whereas it may be in the interest of undertakings to know whether any agreements, decisions or practices to which they are party, or propose to become party, may lead to action on the part of the Commission pursuant to Article 85(1) or Article 86;

Whereas, in order to secure uniform application of Articles 85 and 86 in the common market, rules must be made under which the Commission, acting in close and constant liaison with the competent authorities of the Member States, may take the requisite measures for applying those Articles;

Whereas for this purpose the Commission must have the co-operation of the competent authorities of the Member States and be empowered, throughout the common market, to require such information to be supplied and to undertake such investigations as are necessary to bring to light any agreement, decision or concerted practice prohibited by Article 85(1) or any abuse of a dominant position prohibited by Article 86:

Whereas, in order to carry out its duty of ensuring that the provisions of the Treaty are applied, the Commission must be empowered to address to undertakings or associations of undertakings recommendations and decisions for the purpose of bringing to an end infringements of Articles 85 and 86;

Whereas compliance with Articles 85 and 86 and the fulfilment of obligations imposed on undertakings and associations of undertakings under this Regulation must be enforceable by means of fines and periodic penalty payments;

Whereas undertakings concerned must be accorded the right to be heard by the Commission, third parties whose interests may be affected by a decision must be given the opportunity of submitting their comments beforehand, and it must be ensured that wide publicity is given to decisions taken;

Whereas all decisions taken by the Commission under this Regulation are subject to review by the Court of Justice under the conditions specified in the Treaty; whereas it is moreover desirable to confer upon the Court of Justice, pursuant to Article 172, unlimited jurisdiction in respect of decisions under which the Commission imposes fines or periodic penalty payments;

Whereas this Regulation may enter into force without prejudice to any other provisions that may hereafter be adopted pursuant to Article 87;

HAS ADOPTED THIS REGULATION:

Article 1
Basic provision

Without prejudice to Articles 6, 7 and 23 of this Regulation, agreements, decisions and concerted practices of the kind described in Article 85(1) of the Treaty and the abuse of a dominant position in the market, within the meaning of Article 86 of the Treaty, shall be prohibited, no prior decision to that effect being required.

Article 2
Negative clearance

Upon application by the undertakings or associations of undertakings concerned, the Commission may certify that, on the basis of the facts in its possession, there are no grounds under Article 85(1) or Article 86 of the Treaty for action on its part in respect of an agreement, decision or practice.

Article 3
Termination of infringements

1. Where the Commission, upon application or upon its own initiative, finds that there is infringement of Article 85 or Article 86 of the

Treaty, it may by decision require the undertakings or associations of undertakings concerned to bring such infringement to an end.

2. Those entitled to make application are:

(a) Member States;

(b) natural or legal persons who claim a legitimate interest.

3. Without prejudice to the other provisions of this Regulation, the Commission may, before taking a decision under paragraph 1, address to the undertakings or associations of undertakings concerned recommendations for termination of the infringement.

Article 4

Notification of new agreements, decisions and practices

1. Agreements, decisions and concerted practices of the kind described in Article 85(1) of the Treaty which come into existence after the entry into force of this Regulation and in respect of which the parties seek application of Article 85(3) must be notified to the Commission. Until they have been notified, no decision in application of Article 85(3) may be taken.

2. Paragraph 1 shall not apply to agreements, decisions or concerted practices where:

(1) the only parties thereto are undertakings from one Member State and the agreements, decisions or practices do not relate either to imports or to exports between Member States;

(2) not more than two undertakings are party thereto, and the agreements only:

(a) restrict the freedom of one party to the contract in determining the prices or conditions of business upon which the goods which he has obtained from the other party to the contract may be resold; or

(b) impose restrictions on the exercise of the rights of the assignee or user of industrial property rights—in particular patents, utility models, designs or trade marks—or of the person entitled under a contract to the assignment, or grant, of the right to use a method of manufacture or knowledge relating to the use and to the application of industrial processes;

(3) they have as their sole object:

(a) the development or uniform application of standards or types; or

(b) joint research for improvement of techniques, provided the results are accessible to all parties thereto and may be used by each of them.

These agreements, decisions and practices may be notified to the Commission.

Article 5
Notification of existing agreements, decisions and practices

1. Agreements, decisions and concerted practices of the kind described in Article 85(1) of the Treaty which are in existence at the date of entry into force of this Regulation and in respect of which the parties seek application of Article 85(3) shall be notified to the Commission before 1 August 1962.

2. Paragraph 1 shall not apply to agreements, decisions or concerted practices falling within Article 4(2); these may be notified to the Commission.

Article 6
Decisions pursuant to Article 85(3)

1. Whenever the Commission takes a decision pursuant to Article 85(3) of the Treaty, it shall specify therein the date from which the decision shall take effect. Such date shall not be earlier than the date of notification.

2. The second sentence of paragraph 1 shall not apply to agreements, decisions or concerted practices falling within Article 4(2) and Article 5(2), nor to those falling within Article 5(1) which have been notified within the time limit specified in Article 5(1).

Article 7
Special provisions for existing agreements, decisions and practices

1. Where agreements, decisions and concerted practices in existence at the date of entry into force of this Regulation and notified before 1 August 1962 do not satisfy the requirements of Article 85(3) of the Treaty and the undertakings or associations of undertakings concerned cease to give effect to them or modify them in such manner that they no longer fall within the prohibition contained in Article 85(1) or that they satisfy the requirements of Article 85(3), the prohibition contained in Article 85(1) shall apply only for a period fixed by the Commission. A decision by the Commission pursuant to the foregoing sentence shall not apply as against undertakings and associations of undertakings which did not expressly consent to the notification.

2. Paragraph 1 shall apply to agreements, decisions and concerted practices falling within Article 4(2) which are in existence at the date of entry into force of this Regulation if they are notified before 1 January 1964.

Article 8
Duration and revocation of decisions under Article 85(3)

1. A decision in application of Article 85(3) of the Treaty shall be issued for a specified period and conditions and obligations may be attached thereto.

2. A decision may on application be renewed if the requirements of Article 85(3) of the Treaty continue to be satisfied.

3. The Commission may revoke or amend its decision or prohibit specified acts by the parties:

(a) where there has been a change in any of the facts which were basic to the making of the decision;

(b) where the parties commit a breach of any obligation attached to the decision;

(c) where the decision is based on incorrect information or was induced by deceit;

(d) where the parties abuse the exemption from the provisions of Article 85(1) of the Treaty granted to them by the decision.

In cases to which subparagraphs (b), (c) or (d) apply, the decision may be revoked with retroactive effect.

Article 9

Powers

1. Subject to review of its decision by the Court of Justice, the Commission shall have sole power to declare Article 85(1) inapplicable pursuant to Article 85(3) of the Treaty.

2. The Commission shall have power to apply Article 85(1) and Article 86 of the Treaty; this power may be exercised notwithstanding that the time limits specified in Article 5(1) and in Article 7(2) relating to notification have not expired.

3. As long as the Commission has not initiated any procedure under Articles 2, 3 or 6, the authorities of the Member States shall remain competent to apply Article 85(1) and Article 86 in accordance with Article 88 of the Treaty; they shall remain competent in this respect notwithstanding that the time limits specified in Article 5(1) and in Article 7(2) relating to notification have not expired.

Article 10

Liaison with the authorities of the Member States

1. The Commission shall forthwith transmit to the competent authorities of the Member States a copy of the applications and notifications together with copies of the most important documents lodged with the Commission for the purpose of establishing the existence of infringements of Articles 85 or 86 of the Treaty or of obtaining negative clearance or a decision in application of Article 85(3).

2. The Commission shall carry out the procedure set out in paragraph 1 in close and constant liaison with the competent authorities of the Member States; such authorities shall have the right to express their views upon that procedure.

3. An Advisory Committee on Restrictive Practices and Monopolies shall be consulted prior to the taking of any decision following upon a procedure under paragraph 1, and of any decision concerning the renewal, amendment or revocation of a decision pursuant to Article 85(3) of the Treaty.

4. The Advisory Committee shall be composed of officials competent in the matter of restrictive practices and monopolies. Each Member State shall appoint an official to represent it who, if prevented from attending, may be replaced by another official.

5. The consultation shall take place at a joint meeting convened by the Commission; such meeting shall be held not earlier than fourteen days after dispatch of the notice convening it. The notice shall, in respect of each case to be examined, be accompanied by a summary of the case together with an indication of the most important documents, and a preliminary draft decision.

6. The Advisory Committee may deliver an opinion notwithstanding that some of its members or their alternates are not present. A report of the outcome of the consultative proceedings shall be annexed to the draft decision. It shall not be made public.

Article 11

Requests for information

1. In carrying out the duties assigned to it by Article 89 and by provisions adopted under Article 87 of the Treaty, the Commission may obtain all necessary information from the Governments and competent authorities of the Member States and from undertakings and associations of undertakings.

2. When sending a request for information to an undertaking or association of undertakings, the Commission shall at the same time forward a copy of the request to the competent authority of the Member State in whose territory the seat of the undertaking or association of undertakings is situated.

3. In its request the Commission shall state the legal basis and the purpose of the request and also the penalties provided for in Article 15(1)(b) for supplying incorrect information.

4. The owners of the undertakings or their representatives and, in the case of legal persons, companies or firms, or of associations having no legal personality, the persons authorised to represent them by law or by their constitution shall supply the information requested.

5. Where an undertaking or association of undertakings does not supply the information requested within the time limit fixed by the Commission, or supplies incomplete information, the Commission shall by decision require the information to be supplied. The decision shall specify what information is required, fix an appropriate time limit within which it is to be supplied and indicate the penalties provided for in Article 15(1)(b) and Article 16(1)(c) and the right to have the decision reviewed by the Court of Justice.

6. The Commission shall at the same time forward a copy of its decision to the competent authority of the Member State in whose territory the seat of the undertaking or association of undertakings is situated.

Article 12
Inquiry into sectors of the economy

1. If in any sector of the economy the trend of trade between Member States, price movements, inflexibility of prices or other circumstances suggest that in the economic sector concerned competition is being restricted or distorted within the common market, the Commission may decide to conduct a general inquiry into that economic sector and in the course thereof may request undertakings in the sector concerned to supply the information necessary for giving effect to the principles formulated in Articles 85 and 86 of the Treaty and for carrying out the duties entrusted to the Commission.

2. The Commission may in particular request every undertaking or association of undertakings in the economic sector concerned to communicate to it all agreements, decisions and concerted practices which are exempt from notification by virtue of Article 4(2) and Article 5(2).

3. When making inquiries pursuant to paragraph 2, the Commission shall also request undertakings or groups of undertakings whose size suggests that they occupy a dominant position within the common market or a substantial part thereof to supply to the Commission such particulars of the structure of the undertakings and of their behaviour as are requisite to an appraisal of their position in the light of Article 86 of the Treaty.

4. Article 10(3) to (6) and Articles 11, 13 and 14 shall apply correspondingly.

Article 13
Investigations by the authorities of the Member States

1. At the request of the Commission, the competent authorities of the Member States shall undertake the investigations which the Commission considers to be necessary under Article 14(1), or which it has ordered by decision pursuant to Article 14(3). The officials of the competent authorities of the Member States responsible for conducting these investigations shall exercise their powers upon production of an authorisation in writing issued by the competent authority of the Member State in whose territory the investigation is to be made. Such authorisation shall specify the subject matter and purpose of the investigation.

2. If so requested by the Commission or by the competent authority of the Member State in whose territory the investigation is to be made, the officials of the Commission may assist the officials of such authorities in carrying out their duties.

Article 14
Investigating powers of the Commission

1. In carrying out the duties assigned to it by Article 89 and by provisions adopted under Article 87 of the Treaty, the Commission may undertake all necessary investigations into undertakings and associations

of undertakings. To this end the officials authorised by the Commission are empowered:

(a) to examine the books and other business records;

(b) to take copies of or extracts from the books and business records;

(c) to ask for oral explanations on the spot;

(d) to enter any premises; land and means of transport of undertakings.

2. The officials of the Commission authorised for the purpose of these investigations shall exercise their powers upon production of an authorisation in writing specifying the subject matter and purpose of the investigation and the penalties provided for in Article 15(1)(c) in cases where production of the required books or other business records is incomplete. In good time before the investigation, the Commission shall inform the competent authority of the Member State in whose territory the same is to be made of the investigation and of the identity of the authorised officials.

3. Undertakings and associations of undertakings shall submit to investigations ordered by decision of the Commission. The decision shall specify the subject matter and purpose of the investigation, appoint the date on which it is to begin and indicate the penalties provided for in Article 15(1)(c) and Article 16(1)(d) and the right to have the decision reviewed by the Court of Justice.

4. The Commission shall take decisions referred to in paragraph 3 after consultation with the competent authority of the Member State in whose territory the investigation is to be made.

5. Officials of the competent authority of the Member State in whose territory the investigation is to be made may, at the request of such authority or of the Commission, assist the officials of the Commission in carrying out their duties.

6. Where an undertaking opposes an investigation ordered pursuant to this Article, the Member State concerned shall afford the necessary assistance to the officials authorised by the Commission to enable them to make their investigation. Member States shall, after consultation with the Commission, take the necessary measures to this end before 1 October 1962.

Article 15

Fines

1. The Commission may by decision impose on undertakings or associations of undertakings fines of from 100 to 5000 units of account where, intentionally or negligently:

(a) they supply incorrect or misleading information in an application pursuant to Article 2 or in a notification pursuant to Articles 4 or 5; or

(b) they supply incorrect information in response to a request made pursuant to Article 11(3) or (5) or to Article 12, or do not supply information within the time limit fixed by a decision taken under Article 11(5); or

(c) they produce the required books or other business records in incomplete form during investigations under Article 13 or 14, or refuse to submit to an investigation ordered by decision issued in implementation of Article 14(3).

2. The Commission may by decision impose on undertakings or associations of undertakings fines of from 1000 to 1,000,000 units of account, or a sum in excess thereof but not exceeding 10% of the turnover in the preceding business year of each of the undertakings participating in the infringement where, either intentionally or negligently:

(a) they infringe Article 85(1) or Article 86 of the Treaty; or

(b) they commit a breach of any obligation imposed pursuant to Article 8(1).

In fixing the amount of the fine, regard shall be had both to the gravity and to the duration of the infringement.

3. Article 10(3) to (6) shall apply.

4. Decisions taken pursuant to paragraphs 1 and 2 shall not be of a criminal law nature.

5. The fines provided for in paragraph 2(a) shall not be imposed in respect of acts taking place:

(a) after notification to the Commission and before its decision in application of Article 85(3) of the Treaty, provided they fall within the limits of the activity described in the notification;

(b) before notification and in the course of agreements, decisions or concerted practices in existence at the date of entry into force of this Regulation, provided that notification was effected within the time limits specified in Article 5(1) and Article 7(2).

6. Paragraph 5 shall not have effect where the Commission has informed the undertakings concerned that after preliminary examination it is of opinion that Article 85(1) of the Treaty applies and that application of Article 85(3) is not justified.

Article 16

Periodic penalty payments

1. The Commission may by decision impose on undertakings or associations of undertakings periodic penalty payments of from 50 to 1000 units of account per day, calculated from the date appointed by the decision, in order to compel them:

(a) to put an end to an infringement of Article 85 or 86 of the Treaty, in accordance with a decision taken pursuant to Article 3 of this Regulation;

(b) to refrain from any act prohibited under Article 8(3);

(c) to supply complete and correct information which it has requested by decision taken pursuant to Article 11(5);

(d) to submit to an investigation which it has ordered by decision taken pursuant to Article 14(3).

2. Where the undertakings or associations of undertakings have satisfied the obligation which it was the purpose of the periodic penalty payment to enforce, the Commission may fix the total amount of the periodic penalty payment at a lower figure than that which would arise under the original decision.

3. Article 10(3) to (6) shall apply.

Article 17

Review by the Court of Justice

The Court of Justice shall have unlimited jurisdiction within the meaning of Article 172 of the Treaty to review decisions whereby the Commission has fixed a fine or periodic penalty payment; it may cancel, reduce or increase the fine or periodic penalty payment imposed.

Article 18

Unit of account

For the purposes of applying Articles 15 to 17 the unit of account shall be that adopted in drawing up the budget of the Community in accordance with Articles 207 and 209 of the Treaty.

Article 19

Hearing of the parties and of third persons

1. Before taking decisions as provided for in Articles 2, 3, 6, 7, 8, 15 and 16, the Commission shall give the undertakings or associations of undertakings concerned the opportunity of being heard on the matters to which the Commission has taken objection.

2. If the Commission or the competent authorities of the Member States consider it necessary, they may also hear other natural or legal persons. Applications to be heard on the part of such persons shall, where they show a sufficient interest, be granted.

3. Where the Commission intends to give negative clearance pursuant to Article 2 or take a decision in application of Article 85(3) of the Treaty, it shall publish a summary of the relevant application or notification and invite all interested third parties to submit their observations within a time limit which it shall fix being not less than one month. Publication shall have regard to the legitimate interest of undertakings in the protection of their business secrets.

Article 20

Professional secrecy

1. Information acquired as a result of the application of Articles 11, 12, 13 and 14 shall be used only for the purpose of the relevant request or investigation.

2. Without prejudice to the provisions of Articles 19 and 21, the Commission and the competent authorities of the Member States, their officials and other servants shall not disclose information acquired by them as a result of the application of this Regulation and of the kind covered by the obligation of professional secrecy.

3. The provisions of paragraphs 1 and 2 shall not prevent publication of general information or surveys which do not contain information relating to particular undertakings or associations of undertakings.

Article 21
Publication of decisions

1. The Commission shall publish the decisions which it takes pursuant to Articles 2, 3, 6, 7 and 8.

2. The publication shall state the names of the parties and the main content of the decision; it shall have regard to the legitimate interest of undertakings in the protection of their business secrets.

Article 22
Special provisions

1. The Commission shall submit to the Council proposals for making certain categories of agreement, decision and concerted practice falling within Article 4(2) or Article 5(2) compulsorily notifiable under Article 4 or 5.

2. Within one year from the date of entry into force of this Regulation, the Council shall examine, on a proposal from the Commission, what special provisions might be made for exempting from the provisions of this Regulation agreements, decisions and concerted practices falling within Article 4(2) or Article 5(2).

Article 23
Transitional provisions applicable to decisions of authorities of the Member States

1. Agreements, decisions and concerted practices of the kind described in Article 85(1) of the Treaty to which, before the entry into force of this Regulation, the competent authority of a Member State has declared Article 85(1) to be inapplicable pursuant to Article 85(3) shall not be subject to compulsory notification under Article 5. The decision of the competent authority of the Member State shall be deemed to be a decision within the meaning of Article 6; it shall cease to be valid upon expiration of the period fixed by such authority but in any event not more than three years after the entry into force of this Regulation. Article 8(3) shall apply.

2. Applications for renewal of decisions of the kind described in paragraph 1 shall be decided upon by the Commission in accordance with Article 8(2).

Article 24
Implementing provisions

The Commission shall have power to adopt implementing provisions concerning the form, content and other details of applications pursuant to Articles 2 and 3 and of notifications pursuant to Articles 4 and 5, and concerning hearings pursuant to Article 19(1) and (2).

This Regulation shall be binding in its entirety and directly applicable in all Member States.

2. COMMISSION NOTICE ON EXCLUSIVE AGENCY CONTRACTS WITH COMMERCIAL AGENTS

O.J. 139/2921 (Dec. 24, 1962)

I. The Commission considers that contracts made with commercial agents in which those agents undertake, for a specified part of the territory of the Common Market,

— to negotiate transactions on behalf of an enterprise, or

— to conclude transactions in the name and on behalf of an enterprise, or

— to conclude transactions in their own name and on behalf of this enterprise,

do not fall under the prohibition in Article 85(1) of the Treaty.

It is essential in this case that the contracting party, described as a commercial agent, should, in fact, be such, by the nature of his functions, and that he should neither undertake nor engage in activities proper to an independent trader in the course of commercial operations. The Commission regards as the decisive criterion, which distinguishes the commercial agent from the independent trader, the agreement—express or implied—which deals with responsibility for the financial risks bound up with the sale or with the performance of the contract. Thus the Commission's assessment is not governed by the name used to describe the representative. Except for the usual *del credere* guarantee, a commercial agent must not by the nature of his functions assume any risk resulting from the transaction. If he does assume such risks, his function becomes economically akin to that of an independent trader and he must therefore be treated as such for the purposes of the rules of competition. In such a situation, the exclusive dealing contracts must be regarded as agreements made with independent traders.

The Commission considers that there is particular reason to assume that the function performed is that of an independent trader where the contracting party described as a commercial agent:

— is required to keep or does in fact keep, as his own property, a considerable stock of the products covered by the contract, or

— is required to organize, maintain or ensure at his own expense a substantial service to customers free of charge, or does in fact organize, maintain or ensure such a service, or

— can determine or does in fact determine prices or terms of business.

II. Unlike the contracts with commercial agents covered here, exclusive dealing contracts with independent traders may well fall within Article 85(1). In the case of such exclusive contracts the restriction of competition lies either in the limitation of supply, when the vendor undertakes to supply a given product to one purchaser only, or in the limitation of demand, when the purchaser undertakes to obtain a given product from only one vendor. Where there are reciprocal undertakings competition is being restricted by both parties. The question whether a restriction of competition of this nature may affect trade between Member States depends on the circumstances of the particular case.

On the other hand, the Commission takes the view that the test for prohibition under Article 85(1) is not met by exclusive dealing contracts with commercial agents, since these contracts have neither the object nor the effect of preventing, restricting or distorting competition within the Common Market. The commercial agent only performs an auxiliary function in the market for goods. In that market he acts on the instructions and in the interest of the enterprise on whose behalf he is operating. Unlike the independent trader, he himself is neither a purchaser nor a vendor, but seeks purchasers or vendors in the interest of the other party to the contract, who is the person doing the buying or selling. In this type of exclusive dealing contract, the selling or buying enterprise does not cease to be a competitor; it merely uses an auxiliary, i.e. the commercial agent, to distribute or acquire products on the market.

The legal status of commercial agents is determined, more or less uniformly, by statute law in most of the Member States and by case law in others. The characteristic feature which all commercial agents have in common is their function as auxiliaries in the transaction of business. The powers of commercial agents are subject to the civil law provisions of agency. Within the limits of these provisions, the other party to the contract—who is the person selling or buying—is free to decide the product and the territory in respect of which he is willing to give these powers to his agent.

In addition to the competitive situation on the markets where the commercial agent functions as an auxiliary for the other party to the contract, the particular market on which the commercial agents offer their services for the negotiation or conclusion of transactions has to be considered. The obligation assumed by the agent—to work exclusively for one principal for a certain period of time—entails a limitation of supply on that market; the obligation assumed by the other party to the contract—to appoint him sole agent for a given territory—involves a limitation of demand on the market. Nevertheless, the Commission views these restrictions as a result of the special obligation between the commercial agent and his principal to protect each other's interests and therefore considers that they involve no restriction of competition.

The object of this Notice is to give enterprises some indication of the considerations by which the Commission will be guided when interpreting Article 85(1) of the Treaty and applying it to exclusive dealing contracts with commercial agents. The situation having thus been clarified, it will as a general rule no longer be useful for enterprises to obtain negative clearance for the agreements mentioned, nor will it be necessary to have the legal position established through a Commission decision on an individual case; this also means that notification will no longer be necessary for agreements of this type. This Notice is without prejudice to any interpretation that may be given by other competent authorities and in particular by the courts.

3. COMMISSION NOTICE CONCERNING AGREEMENTS, DECISIONS AND CONCERTED PRACTICES IN THE FIELD OF COOPERATION BETWEEN ENTERPRISES

O.J. C 75/3 (July 29, 1968), corrected by O.J. C 84/14 (Aug. 28, 1968)

Questions are frequently put to the Commission of the European Communities on the attitude it intends to take up, for purposes of implementation of the competition rules contained in the Treaties of Rome and Paris, with regard to cooperation between enterprises.

In this Notice, it endeavours to provide guidance which, though it cannot be exhaustive, may prove useful to enterprises in the correct interpretation, in particular, of Article 85(1) of the EEC Treaty and Article 65(1) of the ECSC Treaty.

I. The Commission welcomes cooperation among small and medium-sized enterprises where such cooperation enables them to work more efficiently and increase their productivity and competitiveness on a larger market. While considering that its duty is to facilitate cooperation among small and medium-sized enterprises in particular, the Commission recognizes that cooperation among large enterprises, too, can be economically desirable without presenting difficulties from the angle of competition policy.

Article 85(1) of the Treaty establishing the European Economic Community (EEC Treaty) and Article 65(1) of the Treaty establishing the European Coal and Steel Community (ECSC Treaty) provide that all agreements, decisions and concerted practices (hereafter referred to as 'agreements') which have as their object or effect the prevention, restriction or distortion of competition within the Common Market (hereafter referred to as 'restraints of competition') are prohibited as incompatible with the Common Market; under Article 85(1) of the EEC Treaty this applies, however, only if such agreements may affect trade between Member States.

The Commission feels that, in the interests of the small and medium-sized enterprises in particular, it should give some indication of the considerations by which it will be guided when interpreting Article 85(1) of the EEC Treaty and Article 65(1) of the ECSC Treaty and applying them to certain cooperation arrangements between enterprises, and should indicate which of these arrangements in its opinion do not come under these provisions. This Notice applies to all enterprises, irrespective of their size.

There may also be forms of cooperation between enterprises other than those listed below which are not prohibited by Article 85(1) of the EEC Treaty or Article 65(1) of the ECSC Treaty. This applies in particular if the market position of the enterprises cooperating with each other is in the aggregate too weak for the cooperation agreement between them to lead to an appreciable restraint of competition in the Common Market and—where the agreements fall within the scope of Article 85 of the EEC Treaty—to affect trade between Member States.

It is also pointed out that other forms of cooperation between enterprises or agreements containing additional clauses, to which the rules of competition of the Treaties apply, can be exempted pursuant to Article 85(3) of the EEC Treaty or be authorized pursuant to Article 65(2) of the ECSC Treaty.

The Commission intends to clarify rapidly, by means of suitable decisions in individual cases or by general notices, the status of the various forms of cooperation in accordance with the provisions of the Treaties.

No general statement can be made at this stage on the application of Article 86 of the EEC Treaty on the abuse of dominant positions within the Common Market or in a part of it. The same applies to Article 66(7) of the ECSC Treaty.

As a result of this Notice, as a general rule, it should no longer be useful for enterprises to obtain negative clearance, as defined by Article 2 of Regulation No. 17, for the agreements listed, nor should it be necessary to have the legal position established through a Commission decision on an individual case. This also means that notification with this end in view will no longer be necessary for agreements of this type. However, if it is doubtful whether in an individual case an agreement between enterprises restricts competition or if other forms of cooperation between enterprises which, in the view of the enterprises, do not restrict competition are not listed here, the enterprises are free to apply, where the matter comes under Article 85(1) of the EEC Treaty, for negative clearance, or to file as a precautionary measure, where Article 65(1) of the ECSC Treaty is the relevant provision, an application on the basis of Article 65(2) of that Treaty.

This Notice is without prejudice to any interpretation to be given by the Court of Justice of the European Communities.

II. The Commission takes the view that the following agreements do not restrict competition.

1. *Agreements having as their sole object:*

(a) *An exchange of opinion or experience,*

(b) *Joint market research,*

(c) *The joint carrying out of comparative studies of enterprises or industries,*

(d) *The joint preparation of statistics and calculation models.*

Agreements whose sole purpose is the joint procurement of information which the various enterprises need to determine their future market behaviour freely and independently, or the use by each of the enterprises of a joint advisory body, do not have as their object or effect the restriction of competition. But if the freedom of action of the enterprises is restricted or if their market behaviour is coordinated either expressly or through concerted practices, there may be restraint of competition. This is in particular the case where concrete recommendations are made or where conclusions are given such a form that they induce at least some of the participating enterprises to behave in an identical manner on the market.

The exchange of information may take place between the enterprises themselves or through a body acting as an intermediary. It is, however, particularly difficult to distinguish between information which has no bearing on competition on the one hand and behaviour in restraint of competition on the other, if there are special bodies which have to register orders, turnover figures, investments and prices, so that it can as a rule not be automatically assumed that Article 85(1) of the EEC Treaty or Article 65(1) of the ECSC Treaty do not apply to them. A restraint of competition may occur in particular on an oligopolistic market for homogeneous products.

In the absence of more far-reaching cooperation between the participating enterprises, joint market research and comparative studies of different enterprises and industries to collect information and ascertain facts and market conditions do not in themselves affect competition. Other arrangements of this type, as for instance the joint establishment of economic and structural analyses, so obviously do not affect competition that there is no need to mention them specifically.

Calculation models containing specified rates of calculation must be regarded as recommendations that may lead to restraints of competition.

2. *Agreements having as their sole object:*

(a) *Cooperation in accounting matters,*

(b) *Joint provision of credit guarantees,*

(c) *Joint debt-collecting associations,*

(d) *Joint business or tax consultant agencies.*

In such cases, the cooperation involved covers fields that are not concerned with the supply of goods and services or the economic decisions of the enterprises taking part, and thus does not lead to restraints of competition.

Cooperation in accounting matters is neutral from the point of view of competition as it only assists in the technical handling of the accounting work. Nor is the creation of credit guarantee associations affected by the competition rules, since it does not modify the relationship between supply and demand.

Joint debt-collecting associations whose work is not confined to the collection of outstanding payments in line with the intentions and conditions of the participating enterprises, or which fix prices or exert in any other way an influence on price formation, may restrict competition. Application of uniform terms by all participating firms may constitute a concerted practice, and the making of joint price comparisons may have the same result. In this connection, no objection can be raised against the use of standardized printed forms; their use must, however, not be combined with an understanding or tacit agreement on uniform prices, rebates or conditions of sale.

3. *Agreements having as their sole object:*

(a) *The joint implementation of research and development projects,*

(b) *The joint placing of research and development contracts,*

(c) *The sharing out of research and development projects among participating enterprises.*

In the field of research, too, the mere exchange of experience and results serves for information only and does not restrict competition. It therefore need not be mentioned expressly.

Agreements on the joint execution of research work or the joint development of the results of research up to the stage of industrial application do not affect the competitive position of the parties. This also applies to the sharing of research fields and development work if the results are available to all participating enterprises.

However, if the enterprises enter into commitments which restrict their own research and development activity or the utilization of the results of joint work so that they do not have a free hand with regard to their own research and development outside the joint projects, this may constitute an infringement of the Treaties' rules of competition. Where firms do not carry out joint research work, any contractual obligations or concerted practices binding them to refrain from research work of their own either completely or in certain sectors may result in a restraint of competition.

The sharing out of sectors of research without an understanding providing for mutual access to the results is to be regarded as a case of specialization that may restrict competition.

There may also be a restraint of competition if agreements are concluded or corresponding concerted practices applied with regard to the practical exploitation of the results of research and development work carried out jointly, particularly if the participating enterprises undertake or agree to manufacture only the products or types of product developed jointly or to share out future production among themselves.

It is of the essence of joint research that the results should be exploited by the participating enterprises in proportion to their participation. If the participation of certain enterprises is confined to a specific sector of the joint research project or to the provision of only limited financial assistance, there is no restraint of competition—in so far as there has been any joint research at all—if the results of research are made available to these enterprises only in relation with the degree of their participation. There may, however, be a restraint of competition if certain participating enterprises are excluded from exploitation of the results, either entirely or to an extent not commensurate with their participation.

If the granting of licences to third parties is expressly or tacitly excluded, there may be a restraint of competition. However, the fact that research is carried out jointly warrants arrangements binding the enterprises to grant licences to third parties only by common agreement or by majority decision.

For the assessment of the compatibility of the agreement with the rules of competition, the legal status of the joint research and development work is immaterial.

4. *Agreements which have as their sole object the joint use of production facilities and storing and transport equipment.*

These forms of cooperation do not restrict competition because they are confined to organization and technical arrangements for the use of the facilities. There may be a restraint of competition if the enterprises involved do not bear the cost of utilization of the installation or equipment themselves or if agreements are concluded or concerted practices applied regarding joint production or the sharing out of production or the establishment or running of a joint enterprise.

5. *Agreements having as their sole object the setting up of consortia for the joint execution of orders, where the participating enterprises do not compete with each other as regards the work to be done or where each of them by itself is unable to execute the orders.*

Where enterprises do not compete with each other they cannot restrict competition between them by setting up consortia. This applies in particular to enterprises belonging to different industries but also to firms in the same industry to the extent that their contribution under the consortium consists only of goods or services which cannot be supplied by the other participating enterprises. It is not a question of whether the enterprises compete with each other in other sectors so much as whether in the light of the concrete circumstances of a particular case there is a possibility that in the foreseeable future they may compete with each other with regard to the products or services involved. If the absence of competition between the enterprises and the maintenance of this situation are based on agreements or concerted practices, there may be a restraint of competition.

But even in the case of consortia formed by enterprises which normally compete with each other there is no restraint of competition if the participating enterprises cannot execute a specific order by themselves. This applies in particular if, for lack of experience, specialized knowledge, capacity or financial resources, these enterprises, when working alone, have no chance of success or cannot finish the work within the required time-limit or cannot bear the financial risk.

Nor is there a restraint of competition if it is only by the setting up of a consortium that the enterprises are put in a position to make an attractive offer. There may, however, be a restraint of competition if the enterprises undertake to work solely in the framework of a consortium.

6. *Agreements having as their sole object:*

(a) *Joint selling arrangements,*

(b) *Joint after-sales and repairs service, provided the participating enterprises are not competitors with regard to the products or services covered by the agreement.*

As already explained in detail under heading 5, cooperation between enterprises cannot restrict competition if the firms are not in competition with each other.

Very often joint selling by small or medium-sized enterprises—even if they are competing with each other—does not entail an appreciable restraint of competition; it is, however, impossible to establish in this Notice any general criteria or to specify what enterprises may be deemed 'small or medium-sized'.

There is no joint after-sales and repair service if several manufacturers, without acting in concert with each other, arrange for an after-sales and repair service for their products to be provided by an enterprise which is independent of them. In such a case there is no restraint of competition even if the manufacturers are competitors.

7. *Agreements having joint advertising as their sole object:*

Joint advertising is designed to draw the buyers' attention to the products of an industry or to a common brand; as such it does not restrict competition between the participating enterprises. However, if the participating enterprises are partly or wholly prevented, by agreements or concerted practices, from themselves advertising or if they are subjected to other restriction, there may be a restraint of competition.

8. *Agreements having as their sole object the use of a common label to designate a certain quality, where the label is available to all competitors on the same conditions:*

Such associations for the joint use of a quality label do not restrict competition if other competitors, whose products objectively meet the stipulated quality requirements, can use the label on the same conditions as the members. Nor do the obligations to accept quality control of the products provided with the label, to issue uniform instructions for use, or to use the label for the products meeting the quality standards constitute restraints of competition. But there may be restraint of competition if the right to use the label is linked to obligations regarding production, marketing, price formation or obligations of any other type, as is for instance the case when the participating enterprises are obliged to manufacture or sell only products of guaranteed quality.

4. COMMISSION NOTICE ON AGREEMENTS OF MINOR IMPORTANCE WHICH DO NOT FALL UNDER ARTICLE 85(1)

O.J. C 231/2 (Sept. 12, 1986)

I

1. The Commission considers it important to facilitate cooperation between undertakings where such cooperation is economically desirable without presenting difficulties from the point of view of competition policy, which is particularly true of cooperation between small and medium-sized undertakings. To this end it published the 'Notice concerning agreements, decisions and concerted practices in the field of cooperation between undertakings' listing a number of agreements that by their nature cannot be regarded as restraints of competition. Furthermore, in the Notice concerning its assessment of certain subcontracting agreements the Commission considered that this type of contract which offers opportunities for development, in particular, to small and medium-sized undertakings is not in itself caught by the prohibition in Article 85(1). By issuing the present Notice, the Commission is taking a further step towards defining the field of application of Article 85(1), in order to facilitate cooperation between small and medium-sized undertakings.

2. In the Commission's opinion, agreements whose effects on trade between Member States or on competition are negligible do not fall under the ban on restrictive agreements contained in Article 85(1). Only those agreements are prohibited which have an appreciable impact on market conditions, in that they appreciably alter the market position, in other words the sales or supply possibilities, of third undertakings and of users.

3. In the present Notice the Commission, by setting quantitative criteria and by explaining their application, has given a sufficiently concrete meaning to the concept 'appreciable' for undertakings to be able to judge for themselves whether the agreements they have concluded with other undertakings, being of minor importance, do not fall under Article 85(1). The quantitative definition of 'appreciable' given by the Commission is, however, no absolute yardstick; in fact, in individual cases even agreements between undertakings which exceed these limits may still have only a negligible effect on trade between Member States or on competition, and are therefore not caught by Article 85(1).

4. As a result of this Notice, there should no longer be any point in undertakings obtaining negative clearance, as defined by Article 2 of Council Regulation No. 17, for the agreements covered, nor should it be necessary to have the legal position established through Commission decisions in individual cases; notification with this end in view will no longer be necessary for such agreements. However, if it is doubtful whether in an individual case an agreement appreciably affects trade between Member States or competition, the undertakings are free to apply for negative clearance or to notify the agreement.

5. In cases covered by the present Notice the Commission, as a general rule, will not open proceedings under Regulation No. 17, either upon application or upon its own initiative. Where, due to exceptional circumstances, an agreement which is covered by the present Notice nevertheless falls under Article 85(1), the Commission will not impose fines. Where undertakings have failed to notify an agreement falling under Article 85(1) because they wrongly assumed, owing to a mistake in calculating their market share or aggregate turnover, that the agreement was covered by the present Notice, the Commission will not consider imposing fines unless the mistake was due to negligence.

6. This Notice is without prejudice to the competence of national courts to apply Article 85(1) on the basis of their own jurisdiction, although it constitutes a factor which such courts may take into account when deciding a pending case. It is also without prejudice to any interpretation which may be given by the Court of Justice of the European Communities.

II

7. The Commission holds the view that agreements between undertakings engaged in the production or distribution of goods or in the provision of services generally do not fall under the prohibition of Article 81(1) if:

— the goods or services which are the subject of the agreement (hereinafter referred to as 'the contract products') together with the participation undertakings' other goods or services which are considered by users to be equivalent in view of their characteristics, price and intended use, do not represent more than 5% of the total market for such goods or services (hereinafter referred to as 'products') in the area of the common market affected by the agreement and

— the aggregate annual turnover of the participating undertakings does not exceed 200 million ECU.

8. The Commission also holds the view that the said agreements do not fall under the prohibition of Article 85(1) if the abovementioned market share or turnover is exceeded by not more than one tenth during two successive financial years.

9. For the purposes of this Notice, participating undertakings are:

(a) undertakings party to the agreement;

(b) undertakings in which a party to the agreement, directly or indirectly,

— owns more than half the capital or business assets, or

— has the power to exercise more than half the voting rights, or

— has the power to appoint more than half the members of the supervisory board, board of management or bodies legally representing the undertakings, or

— has the right to manage the affairs;

(c) undertakings which directly or indirectly have in or over a party to the agreement the rights or powers listed in (b);

(d) undertakings in or over which an undertaking referred to in (c) directly or indirectly has the rights or powers listed in (b).

Undertakings in which several undertakings as referred to in (a) to (d) jointly have, directly or indirectly, the rights or powers set out in (b) shall also be considered to be participating undertakings.

10. In order to calculate the market share, it is necessary to determine the relevant market. This implies the definition of the relevant product market and the relevant geographical market.

11. The relevant product market includes besides the contract products any other products which are identical or equivalent to them. This rule applies to the products of the participating undertakings as well as to the market for such products. The products in question must be interchangeable. Whether or not this is the case must be judged from the vantage point of the user, normally taking the characteristics, price and intended use of the goods together. In certain cases, however, products can form a separate market on the basis of their characteristics, their price or their intended use alone. This is true especially where consumer preferences have developed.

12. Where the contract products are components which are incorporated into another product by the participating undertakings, reference should be made to the market for the latter product, provided that the components represent a significant part of it. Where the contract products are components which are sold to third undertakings, reference should be made to the market for the components. In cases where both conditions apply, both markets should be considered separately.

13. The relevant geographical market is the area within the Community in which the agreement produces its effects. This area will be the whole common market where the contract products are regularly bought and sold in all Member States. Where the contract products cannot be bought and sold in a part of the common market, or are bought and sold only in limited quantities or at irregular intervals in such a part, that part should be disregarded.

14. The relevant geographical market will be narrower than the whole common market in particular where:

— the nature and characteristics of the contract product, e.g. high transport costs in relation to the value of the product, restrict its mobility; or

— movement of the contract product within the common market is hindered by barriers to entry to national markets resulting from State intervention, such as quantitative restrictions, severe taxation differentials and non-tariff barriers, e.g. type approvals or safety standard certifications. In such cases the national territory may have to be considered as the relevant geographical market. However, this will only be justified if the existing barriers to entry cannot be overcome by reasonable effort and at an acceptable cost.

15. Aggregate turnover includes the turnover in all goods and services, excluding tax, achieved during the last financial year by the participating undertaking. In cases where an undertaking has concluded similar agreements with various other undertakings in the relevant market, the turnover of all participating undertakings should be taken together. The aggregate turnover shall not include dealings between participating undertakings.

16. The present Notice shall not apply where in a relevant market competition is restricted by the cumulative effects of parallel networks of similar agreements established by several manufacturers or dealers.

17. The present Notice is likewise applicable to decisions by associations of undertakings and to concerted practices.

5. COMMISSION REGULATION 1983/83

on the application of Article 85(3) to categories of exclusive distribution agreements [Block Exemption]

O.J. L 173/1 (June 30, 1983)

THE COMMISSION OF THE EUROPEAN COMMUNITIES,

Having regard to the Treaty establishing the European Economic Community, and in particular Article 87 thereof,

Having regard to Council Regulation No. 19/65/EEC of 2 March 1965 on the application of Article 85(3) of the Treaty to certain categories of agreements and concerted practices, as last amended by the Act of Accession of Greece, and in particular Article 1 thereof,

Having published a draft of this Regulation,

Having consulted the Advisory Committee on Restrictive Practices and Dominant Positions,

(1) Whereas Regulation No. 19/65/EEC empowers the Commission to apply Article 85(3) of the Treaty by regulation to certain categories of bilateral exclusive distribution agreements and analogous concerted practices falling within Article 85(1);

(2) Whereas experience to date makes it possible to define a category of agreements and concerted practices which can be regarded as normally satisfying the conditions laid down in Article 85(3);

(3) Whereas exclusive distribution agreements of the category defined in Article 1 of this Regulation may fall within the prohibition contained in Article 85(1) of the Treaty; whereas this will apply only in exceptional cases to exclusive agreements of this kind to which only undertakings from one Member State are party and which concern the resale of goods within that Member State; whereas, however, to the extent that such agreements may affect trade between Member States and also satisfy all the requirements set out in this Regulation there is no reason to withhold from them the benefit of the exemption by category;

(4) Whereas it is not necessary expressly to exclude from the defined category those agreements which do not fulfil the conditions of Article 85(1) of the Treaty;

(5) Whereas exclusive distribution agreements lead in general to an improvement in distribution because the undertaking is able to concentrate its sales activities, does not need to maintain numerous business relations with a larger number of dealers and is able, by dealing with only one dealer, to overcome more easily distribution difficulties in international trade resulting from linguistic, legal and other differences;

(6) Whereas exclusive distribution agreements facilitate the promotion of sales of a product and lead to intensive marketing and to continuity of supplies while at the same time rationalizing distribution; whereas they stimulate competition between the products of different

manufacturers; whereas the appointment of an exclusive distributor who will take over sales promotion, customer services and carrying of stocks is often the most effective way, and sometimes indeed the only way, for the manufacturer to enter a market and compete with other manufacturers already present; whereas this is particularly so in the case of small and medium-sized undertakings; whereas it must be left to the contracting parties to decide whether and to what extent they consider it desirable to incorporate in the agreements terms providing for the promotion of sales;

(7) Whereas, as a rule, such exclusive distribution agreements also allow consumers a fair share of the resulting benefit as they gain directly from the improvement in distribution, and their economic and supply position is improved as they can obtain products manufactured in particular in other countries more quickly and more easily;

(8) Whereas this Regulation must define the obligations restricting competition which may be included in exclusive distribution agreements; whereas the other restrictions on competition allowed under this Regulation in addition to the exclusive supply obligation produce a clear division of functions between the parties and compel the exclusive distributor to concentrate his sales efforts on the contract goods and the contract territory; whereas they are, where they are agreed only for the duration of the agreement, generally necessary in order to attain the improvement in the distribution of goods sought through exclusive distribution; whereas it may be left to the contracting parties to decide which of these obligations they include in their agreements; whereas further restrictive obligations and in particular those which limit the exclusive distributor's choice of customers or his freedom to determine his prices and conditions of sale cannot be exempted under this Regulation;

(9) Whereas the exemption by category should be reserved for agreements for which it can be assumed with sufficient certainty that they satisfy the conditions of Article 85(3) of the Treaty;

(10) Whereas it is not possible, in the absence of a case-by-case examination, to consider that adequate improvements in distribution occur where a manufacturer entrusts the distribution of his goods to another manufacturer with whom he is in competition; whereas such agreements should, therefore, be excluded from the exemption by category; whereas certain derogations from this rule in favour of small and medium-sized undertakings can be allowed;

(11) Whereas consumers will be assured of a fair share of the benefits resulting from exclusive distribution only if parallel imports remain possible; whereas agreements relating to goods which the user can obtain only from the exclusive distributor should therefore be excluded from the exemption by category; whereas the parties cannot be allowed to abuse industrial property rights or other rights in order to create absolute territorial protection; whereas this does not prejudice the relationship between competition law and industrial property rights, since the sole object here is to determine the conditions for exemption by category;

(12) Whereas, since competition at the distribution stage is ensured by the possibility of parallel imports, the exclusive distribution agreements covered by this Regulation will not normally afford any possibility of eliminating competition in respect of a substantial part of the products in question; whereas this is also true of agreements that allot to the exclusive distributor a contract territory covering the whole of the common market;

(13) Whereas, in particular cases in which agreements or concerted practices satisfying the requirements of this Regulation nevertheless have effects incompatible with Article 85(3) of the Treaty, the Commission may withdraw the benefit of the exemption by category from the undertakings party to them;

(14) Whereas agreements and concerted practices which satisfy the conditions set out in this Regulation need not be notified; whereas an undertaking may nonetheless in a particular case where real doubt exists, request the Commission to declare whether its agreements comply with this Regulation;

(15) Whereas this Regulation does not affect the applicability of Commission Regulation (EEC) No. 3604/82 of 23 December 1982 on the application of Article 85(3) of the Treaty to categories of specialization agreements; whereas it does not exclude the application of Article 86 of the Treaty,

HAS ADOPTED THIS REGULATION:

Article 1

Pursuant to Article 85(3) of the Treaty and subject to the provisions of this Regulation, it is hereby declared that Article 85(1) of the Treaty shall not apply to agreements to which only two undertakings are party and whereby one party agrees with the other to supply certain goods for resale within the whole or a defined area of the common market only to that other.

Article 2

1. Apart from the obligation referred to in Article 1 no restriction on competition shall be imposed on the supplier other than the obligation not to supply the contract goods to users in the contract territory.

2. No restriction on competition shall be imposed on the exclusive distributor other than:

(a) the obligation not to manufacture or distribute goods which compete with the contract goods;

(b) the obligation to obtain the contract goods for resale only from the other party;

(c) the obligation to refrain, outside the contract territory and in relation to the contract goods, from seeking customers, from establishing any branch, and from maintaining any distribution depot.

3. Article 1 shall apply notwithstanding that the exclusive distributor undertakes all or any of the following obligations:

(a) to purchase complete ranges of goods or minimum quantities;

(b) to sell the contract goods under trademarks, or packed and presented as specified by the other party;

(c) to take measures for promotion of sales, in particular:

— to advertise,

— to maintain a sales network or stock of goods,

— to provide customer and guarantee services,

— to employ staff having specialized or technical training.

Article 3

Article 1 shall not apply where:

(a) manufacturers of identical goods or of goods which are considered by users as equivalent in view of their characteristics, price and intended use enter into reciprocal exclusive distribution agreements between themselves in respect of such goods;

(b) manufacturers of identical goods or of goods which are considered by users as equivalent in view of their characteristics, price and intended use enter into a non-reciprocal exclusive distribution agreement between themselves in respect of such goods unless at least one of them has a total annual turnover of no more than 100 million ECU;

(c) users can obtain the contract goods in the contract territory only from the exclusive distributor and have no alternative source of supply outside the contract territory;

(d) one or both of the parties makes it difficult for intermediaries or users to obtain the contract goods from other dealers inside the common market or, in so far as no alternative source of supply is available there, from outside the common market, in particular where one or both of them:

1. exercises industrial property rights so as to prevent dealers or users from obtaining outside, or from selling in, the contract territory properly marked or otherwise properly marketed contract goods;

2. exercises other rights or takes other measures so as to prevent dealers or users from obtaining outside, or from selling in, the contract territory contract goods.

Article 4

1. Article 3(a) and (b) shall also apply where the goods there referred to are manufactured by an undertaking connected with a party to the agreement.

2. Connected undertakings are:

(a) undertakings in which a party to the agreement, directly or indirectly:

— owns more than half the capital or business assets, or

— has the power to exercise more than half the voting rights, or

— has the power to appoint more than half the members of the supervisory board, board of directors or bodies legally representing the undertaking, or

— has the right to manage the affairs;

(b) undertakings which directly or indirectly have in or over a party to the agreement the rights or powers listed in (a);

(c) undertakings in which an undertaking referred to in (b) directly or indirectly has the rights or powers listed in (a).

3. Undertakings in which the parties to the agreement or undertakings connected with them jointly have the rights or powers set out in paragraph 2(a) shall be considered to be connected with each of the parties to the agreement.

Article 5

1. For the purpose of Article 3(b), the ECU is the unit of account used for drawing up the budget of the Community pursuant to Articles 207 and 209 of the Treaty.

2. Article 1 shall remain applicable where during any period of two consecutive financial years the total turnover referred to in Article 3(b) is exceeded by no more than 10%.

3. For the purpose of calculating total turnover within the meaning of Article 3(b), the turnovers achieved during the last financial year by the party to the agreement and connected undertakings in respect of all goods and services, excluding all taxes and other duties, shall be added together. For this purpose, no account shall be taken of dealings between the parties to the agreement or between these undertakings and undertakings connected with them or between the connected undertakings.

Article 6

The Commission may withdraw the benefit of this Regulation, pursuant to Article 7 of Regulation No. 19/65/EEC, when it finds in a particular case that an agreement which is exempted by this Regulation nevertheless has certain effects which are incompatible with the conditions set out in Article 85(3) of the Treaty, and in particular where:

(a) the contract goods are not subject, in the contract territory, to effective competition from identical goods or goods considered by users as equivalent in view of their characteristics, price and intended use;

(b) access by other suppliers to the different stages of distribution within the contract territory is made difficult to a significant extent;

(c) for reasons other than those referred to in Article 3(c) and (d) it is not possible for intermediaries or users to obtain supplies of the contract goods from dealers outside the contract territory on the terms there customary;

(d) the exclusive distributor:

1. without any objectively justified reason refuses to supply in the contract territory categories of purchasers who cannot obtain contract goods elsewhere on suitable terms or applies to them differing prices or conditions of sale;

2. sells the contract goods at excessively high prices.

Article 7

In the period 1 July 1983 to 31 December 1986, the prohibition in Article 85(1) of the Treaty shall not apply to agreements which were in force on 1 July 1983 or entered into force between 1 July and 31 December 1983 and which satisfy the exemption conditions of Regulation No. 67/67/EEC.

Article 8

This Regulation shall not apply to agreements entered into for the resale of drinks in premises used for the sale and consumption of beer or for the resale of petroleum products in service stations.

Article 9

This Regulation shall apply *mutatis mutandis* to concerted practices of the type defined in Article 1.

Article 10

This Regulation shall enter into force on 1 July 1983. It shall expire on 31 December 1997.

This Regulation shall be binding in its entirety and directly applicable in all Member States.

6. COMMISSION REGULATION 1984/83

on the application of Article 85(3) to categories of
exclusive purchasing agreements [Block Exemption]

O.J. L 173/5 (June 30, 1983)

THE COMMISSION OF THE EUROPEAN COMMUNITIES,

Having regard to the Treaty establishing the European Economic Community,

Having regard to Council Regulation No. 19/65/EEC of 2 March 1965 on the application of Article 85(3) of the Treaty to certain categories of agreements and concerted practices, as last amended by the Act of Accession of Greece, and in particular Article 1 thereof,

Having published a draft of this Regulation,

Having consulted the Advisory Committee on Restrictive Practices and Dominant Positions,

(1) Whereas Regulation No. 19/65/EEC empowers the Commission to apply Article 85(3) of the Treaty by regulation to certain categories of bilateral exclusive purchasing agreements entered into for the purpose of the resale of goods and corresponding concerted practices falling within Article 85;

(2) Whereas experience to date makes it possible to define three categories of agreements and concerted practices which can be regarded as normally satisfying the conditions laid down in Article 85(3); whereas the first category comprises exclusive purchasing agreements of short and medium duration in all sectors of the economy; whereas the other two categories comprise long-term exclusive purchasing agreements entered into for the resale of beer in premises used for the sale and consumption (beer supply agreements) and of petroleum products in filling stations (service-station agreements);

(3) Whereas exclusive purchasing agreements of the categories defined in this Regulation may fall within the prohibition contained in Article 85(1) of the Treaty; whereas this will often be the case with agreements concluded between undertakings from different Member States; whereas an exclusive purchasing agreement to which undertakings from only one Member State are party and which concerns the resale of goods within that Member State may also be caught by the prohibition; whereas this is in particular the case where it is one of a number of similar agreements which together may affect trade between Member States;

(4) Whereas it is not necessary expressly to exclude from the defined categories those agreements which do not fulfil the conditions of Article 85(1) of the Treaty;

(5) Whereas the exclusive purchasing agreements defined in this Regulation lead in general to an improvement in distribution; whereas they enable the supplier to plan the sales of his goods with greater

precision and for a longer period and ensure that the reseller's requirements will be met on a regular basis for the duration of the agreement; whereas this allows the parties to limit the risk to them of variations in market conditions and to lower distribution costs;

(6) Whereas such agreements also facilitate the promotion of the sales of a product and lead to intensive marketing because the supplier, in consideration for the exclusive purchasing obligation, is as a rule under an obligation to contribute to the improvement of the structure of the distribution network, the quality of the promotional effort or the sales success; whereas, at the same time, they stimulate competition between the products of different manufacturers; whereas the appointment of several resellers, who are bound to purchase exclusively from the manufacturer and who take over sales promotion, customer services and carrying of stock, is often the most effective way, and sometimes the only way, for the manufacturer to penetrate a market and compete with other manufacturers already present; whereas this is particularly so in the case of small and medium-sized undertakings; whereas it must be left to the contracting parties to decide whether and to what extent they consider it desirable to incorporate in their agreements terms concerning the promotion of sales;

(7) Whereas, as a rule, exclusive purchasing agreements between suppliers and resellers also allow consumers a fair share of the resulting benefit as they gain the advantages of regular supply and are able to obtain the contract goods more quickly and more easily;

(8) Whereas this Regulation must define the obligations restricting competition which may be included in an exclusive purchasing agreement; whereas the other restrictions of competition allowed under this Regulation in addition to the exclusive purchasing obligation lead to a clear division of functions between the parties and compel the reseller to concentrate his sales efforts on the contract goods; whereas they are, where they are agreed only for the duration of the agreement, generally necessary in order to attain the improvement in the distribution of goods sought through exclusive purchasing; whereas further restrictive obligations and in particular those which limit the reseller's choice of customers or his freedom to determine his prices and conditions of sale cannot be exempted under this Regulation;

(9) Whereas the exemption by categories should be reserved for agreements for which it can be assumed with sufficient certainty that they satisfy the conditions of Article 85(3) of the Treaty;

(10) Whereas it is not possible, in the absence of a case-by-case examination, to consider that adequate improvements in distribution occur where a manufacturer imposes an exclusive purchasing obligation with respect to his goods on a manufacturer with whom he is in competition; whereas such agreements should, therefore, be excluded from the exemption by categories; whereas certain derogations from this rule in favour of small and medium-sized undertakings can be allowed;

(11) Whereas certain conditions must be attached to the exemption by categories so that access by other undertakings to the different stages of distribution can be ensured; whereas, to this end, limits must be set to the scope and to the duration of the exclusive purchasing obligation; whereas it appears appropriate as a general rule to grant the benefit of a general exemption from the prohibition on restrictive agreements only to exclusive purchasing agreements which are concluded for a specified product or range of products and for not more than five years;

(12) Whereas, in the case of beer supply agreements and service-station agreements, different rules should be laid down which take account of the particularities of the markets in question;

(13) Whereas these agreements are generally distinguished by the fact that, on the one hand, the supplier confers on the reseller special commercial or financial advantages by contributing to his financing, granting him or obtaining for him a loan on favourable terms, equipping him with a site or premises for conducting his business, providing him with equipment or fittings, or undertaking other investments for his benefit and that, on the other hand, the reseller enters into a long-term exclusive purchasing obligation which in most cases is accompanied by a ban on dealing in competing products;

(14) Whereas beer supply and service-station agreements, like the other exclusive purchasing agreements dealt with in this Regulation, normally produce an appreciable improvement in distribution in which consumers are allowed a fair share of the resulting benefit;

(15) Whereas the commercial and financial advantages conferred by the supplier on the reseller make it significantly easier to establish, modernize, maintain and operate premises used for the sale and consumption of drinks and service stations; whereas the exclusive purchasing obligation and the ban on dealing in competing products imposed on the reseller incite the reseller to devote all the resources at his disposal to the sale of the contract goods; whereas such agreements lead to durable cooperation between the parties allowing them to improve or maintain the quality of the contract goods and of the services to the customer and sales efforts of the reseller; whereas they allow long-term planning of sales and consequently a cost effective organization of production and distribution; whereas the pressure of competition between products of different makes obliges the undertakings involved to determine the number and character of premises used for the sale and consumption of drinks and service stations, in accordance with the wishes of customers;

(16) Whereas consumers benefit from the improvements described, in particular because they are ensured supplies of goods of satisfactory quality at fair prices and conditions while being able to choose between the products of different manufacturers;

(17) Whereas the advantages produced by beer supply agreements and service-station agreements cannot otherwise be secured to the same extent and with the same degree of certainty; whereas the exclusive purchasing obligation on the reseller and the non-competition clause

imposed on him are essential components of such agreements and thus usually indispensable for the attainment of these advantages; whereas, however, this is true only as long as the reseller's obligation to purchase from the supplier is confined in the case of premises used for the sale and consumption of drinks to beers and other drinks of the types offered by the supplier, and in the case of service stations to petroleum-based fuel for motor vehicles and other petroleum-based fuels; whereas the exclusive purchasing obligation for lubricants and related petroleum-based products can be accepted only on condition that the supplier provides for the reseller or finances the procurement of specific equipment for the carrying out of lubrication work; whereas this obligation should only relate to products intended for use within the service station;

(18) Whereas, in order to maintain the reseller's commercial freedom and to ensure access to the retail level of distribution on the part of other suppliers, not only the scope but also the duration of the exclusive purchasing obligation must be limited; whereas it appears appropriate to allow drinks suppliers a choice between a medium-term exclusive purchasing agreement covering a range of drinks and a long-term exclusive purchasing agreement for beer; whereas it is necessary to provide special rules for those premises used for the sale and consumption of drinks which the supplier lets to the reseller; whereas, in this case, the reseller must have the right to obtain, under the conditions specified in this Regulation, other drinks, except beer, supplied under the agreement or of the same type but bearing a different trademark; whereas a uniform maximum duration should be provided for service-station agreements, with the exception of tenancy agreements between the supplier and the reseller, which takes account of the long-term character of the relationship between the parties;

(19) Whereas to the extent that Member States provide, by law or administrative measures, for the same upper limit of duration for the exclusive purchasing obligation upon the reseller as in service-station agreements laid down in this Regulation but provide for a permissible duration which varies in proportion to the consideration provided by the supplier or generally provide for a shorter duration than that permitted by this Regulation, such laws or measures are not contrary to the objectives of this Regulation which, in this respect, merely sets an upper limit to the duration of service-station agreements; whereas the application and enforcement of such national laws or measures must therefore be regarded as compatible with the provisions of this Regulation;

(20) Whereas the limitations and conditions provided for in this Regulation are such as to guarantee effective competition on the markets in question; whereas, therefore, the agreements to which the exemption by category applies do not normally enable the participating undertakings to eliminate competition for a substantial part of the products in question;

(21) Whereas, in particular cases in which agreements or concerted practices satisfying the conditions of this Regulation nevertheless have effects incompatible with Article 85(3) of the Treaty, the Commission may

withdraw the benefit of the exemption by category from the undertakings party thereto;

(22) Whereas agreements and concerted practices which satisfy the conditions set out in this Regulation need not be notified; whereas an undertaking may nonetheless, in a particular case where real doubt exists, request the Commission to declare whether its agreements comply with this Regulation;

(23) Whereas this Regulation does not affect the applicability of Commission Regulation (EEC) No. 3604/82 of 23 December 1982 on the application of Article 85(3) of the Treaty to categories of specialization agreements; whereas it does not exclude the application of Article 86 of the Treaty,

HAS ADOPTED THIS REGULATION:

TITLE I
GENERAL PROVISIONS

Article 1

Pursuant to Article 85(3) of the Treaty, and subject to the conditions set out in Articles 2 to 5 of this Regulation, it is hereby declared that Article 85(1) of the Treaty shall not apply to agreements to which only two undertakings are party and whereby one party, the reseller, agrees with the other, the supplier, to purchase certain goods specified in the agreement for resale only from the supplier or from a connected undertaking or from another undertaking which the supplier has entrusted with the sale of his goods.

Article 2

1. No other restriction of competition shall be imposed on the supplier than the obligation not to distribute the contract goods or goods which compete with the contract goods in the reseller's principal sales area and at the reseller's level of distribution.

2. Apart from the obligation described in Article 1, no other restriction of competition shall be imposed on the reseller than the obligation not to manufacture or distribute goods which compete with the contract goods.

3. Article 1 shall apply notwithstanding that the reseller undertakes any or all of the following obligations;

(a) to purchase complete ranges of goods;

(b) to purchase minimum quantities of goods which are subject to the exclusive purchasing obligation;

(c) to sell the contract goods under trademarks, or packed and presented as specified by the supplier;

(d) to take measures for the promotion of sales, in particular:

— to advertise,

— to maintain a sales network or stock of goods,

— to provide customer and guarantee services,

— to employ staff having specialized or technical training.

Article 3

Article 1 shall not apply where:

(a) manufacturers of identical goods or of goods which are considered by users as equivalent in view of their characteristics, price and intended use enter into reciprocal exclusive purchasing agreements between themselves in respect of such goods;

(b) manufacturers of identical goods or of goods which are considered by users as equivalent in view of their characteristics, price and intended use enter into a non-reciprocal exclusive purchasing agreement between themselves in respect of such goods, unless at least one of them has a total annual turnover of no more than 100 million ECU;

(c) the exclusive purchasing obligation is agreed for more than one type of goods where these are neither by their nature nor according to commercial usage connected to each other;

(d) the agreement is concluded for an indefinite duration or for a period of more than five years.

Article 4

1. Article 3(a) and (b) shall also apply where the goods there referred to are manufactured by an undertaking connected with a party to the agreement.

2. Connected undertakings are:

(a) undertakings in which a party to the agreement, directly or indirectly:

— owns more than half the capital or business assets, or

— has the power to exercise more than half the voting rights, or

— has the power to appoint more than half the members of the supervisory board, board of directors or bodies legally representing the undertaking, or

— has the right to manage the affairs;

(b) undertakings which directly or indirectly have in or over a party to the agreement the rights or powers listed in (a);

(c) undertakings in which an undertaking referred to in (b) directly or indirectly has the rights or powers listed in (a).

3. Undertakings in which the parties to the agreement or undertakings connected with them jointly have the rights or powers set out in paragraph 2(a) shall be considered to be connected with each of the parties to the agreement.

Article 5

1. For the purpose of Article 3(b), the ECU is the unit of account used for drawing up the budget of the Community pursuant to Articles 207 and 209 of the Treaty.

2. Article 1 shall remain applicable where during any period of two consecutive financial years the total turnover referred to in Article 3(b) is exceeded by no more than 10%.

3. For the purpose of calculating total turnover within the meaning of Article 3(b), the turnovers achieved during the last financial year by the party to the agreement and connected undertakings in respect of all goods and services, excluding all taxes and other duties, shall be added together. For this purpose, no account shall be taken of dealings between the parties to the agreement or between these undertakings and undertakings connected with them or between the connected undertakings.

TITLE II

SPECIAL PROVISIONS FOR BEER SUPPLY AGREEMENTS

Article 6

1. Pursuant to Article 85(3) of the Treaty, and subject to Articles 7 to 9 of this Regulation, it is hereby declared that Article 85(1) of the Treaty shall not apply to agreements to which only two undertakings are party and whereby one party, the reseller, agrees with the other, the supplier, in consideration for according special commercial or financial advantages, to purchase only from the supplier, an undertaking connected with the supplier or another undertaking entrusted by the supplier with the distribution of his goods, certain beers, or certain beers and certain other drinks, specified in the agreement for resale in premises used for the sale and consumption of drinks and designated in the agreement.

2. The declaration in paragraph 1 shall also apply where exclusive purchasing obligations of the kind described in paragraph 1 are imposed on the reseller in favour of the supplier by another undertaking which is itself not a supplier.

Article 7

1. Apart from the obligation referred to in Article 6, no restriction on competition shall be imposed on the reseller other than:

(a) the obligation not to sell beers and other drinks which are supplied by other undertakings and which are of the same type as the beers or other drinks supplied under the agreement in the premises designated in the agreement;

(b) the obligation, in the event that the reseller sells in the premises designated in the agreement beers which are supplied by other undertakings and which are of a different type from the beers supplied under the agreement, to sell such beers only in bottles, cans or other small packages, unless the sale of such beers in draught form is customary or is necessary to satisfy a sufficient demand from consumers;

(c) the obligation to advertise goods supplied by other undertakings within or outside the premises designated in the agreement only in proportion to the share of these goods in the total turnover realized in the premises.

2. Beers or other drinks of the same type are those which are not clearly distinguishable in view of their composition, appearance and taste.

Article 8

1. Article 6 shall not apply where:

(a) the supplier or a connected undertaking imposes on the reseller exclusive purchasing obligations for goods other than drinks or for services;

(b) the supplier restricts the freedom of the reseller to obtain from an undertaking of his choice either services or goods for which neither an exclusive purchasing obligation nor a ban on dealing in competing products may be imposed;

(c) the agreement is concluded for an indefinite duration or for a period of more than five years and the exclusive purchasing obligation relates to specified beers and other drinks;

(d) the agreement is concluded for an indefinite duration or for a period of more than 10 years and the exclusive purchasing obligation relates only to specified beers;

(e) the supplier obliges the reseller to impose the exclusive purchasing obligation on his successor for a longer period than the reseller would himself remain tied to the supplier.

2. Where the agreement relates to premises which the supplier lets to the reseller or allows the reseller to occupy on some other basis in law or in fact, the following provisions shall also apply:

(a) notwithstanding paragraphs (1)(c) and (d), the exclusive purchasing obligations and bans on dealing in competing products specified in this Title may be imposed on the reseller for the whole period for which the reseller in fact operates the premises;

(b) the agreement must provide for the reseller to have the right to obtain:

— drinks, except beer, supplied under the agreement from other undertakings where these undertakings offer them on more favourable conditions which the supplier does not meet,

— drinks, except beer, which are of the same type as those supplied under the agreement but which bear different trade marks, from other undertakings where the supplier does not offer them.

Article 9

Articles 2(1) and (3), 3(a) and (b), 4 and 5 shall apply *mutatis mutandis*.

TITLE III
SPECIAL PROVISIONS FOR SERVICE-STATION AGREEMENTS

Article 10

Pursuant to Article 85(3) of the Treaty and subject to Articles 11 to 13 of this Regulation, it is hereby declared that Article 85(1) of the Treaty shall not apply to agreements to which only two undertakings are party and whereby one party, the reseller, agrees with the other, the supplier, in consideration for the according of special commercial or financial advantages, to purchase only from the supplier, an undertaking connected with the supplier or another undertaking entrusted by the supplier with the distribution of his goods, certain petroleum-based motor-vehicle fuels or certain petroleum-based motor-vehicle and other fuels specified in the agreement for resale in a service station designated in the agreement.

Article 11

Apart from the obligation referred to in Article 10, no restriction on competition shall be imposed on the reseller other than:

(a) the obligation not to sell motor-vehicle fuel and other fuels which are supplied by other undertakings in the service station designated in the agreement;

(b) the obligation not to use lubricants or related petroleum-based products which are supplied by other undertakings within the service station designated in the agreement where the supplier or a connected undertaking has made available to the reseller, or financed, a lubrication bay or other motor-vehicle lubrication equipment;

(c) the obligation to advertise goods supplied by other undertakings within or outside the service station designated in the agreement only in proportion to the share of these goods in the total turnover realized in the service station;

(d) the obligation to have equipment owned by the supplier or a connected undertaking or financed by the supplier or a connected undertaking serviced by the supplier or an undertaking designated by him.

Article 12

1. Article 10 shall not apply where:

(a) the supplier or a connected undertaking imposes on the reseller exclusive purchasing obligations for goods other than motor-vehicle and other fuels or for services, except in the case of the obligations referred to in Article 11(b) and (d);

(b) the supplier restricts the freedom of the reseller to obtain, from an undertaking of his choice, goods or services, for which under the provisions of this Title neither an exclusive purchasing obligation nor a ban on dealing in competing products may be imposed;

(c) the agreement is concluded for an indefinite duration or for a period of more than 10 years;

(d) the supplier obliges the reseller to impose the exclusive purchasing obligation on his successor for a longer period than the reseller would himself remain tied to the supplier.

2. Where the agreement relates to a service station which the supplier lets to the reseller, or allows the reseller to occupy on some other basis, in law or in fact, exclusive purchasing obligations or prohibitions of

competition indicated in this Title may, notwithstanding paragraph 1(c), be imposed on the reseller for the whole period for which the reseller in fact operates the premises.

Article 13

Articles 2(1) and (3), 3(a) and (b), 4 and 5 of this Regulation shall apply *mutatis mutandis*.

TITLE IV
MISCELLANEOUS PROVISIONS

Article 14

The Commission may withdraw the benefit of this Regulation, pursuant to Article 7 of Regulation No 19/65/EEC, when it finds in a particular case that an agreement which is exempted by this Regulation nevertheless has certain effects which are incompatible with the conditions set out in Article 85(3) of the Treaty, and in particular where:

(a) the contract goods are not subject, in a substantial part of the common market, to effective competition from identical goods or goods considered by users as equivalent in view of their characteristics, price and intended use;

(b) access by of other suppliers to the different stages of distribution in a substantial part of the common market is made difficult to a significant extent;

(c) the supplier without any objectively justified reason:

1. refuses to supply categories of resellers who cannot obtain the contract goods elsewhere on suitable terms or applies to them differing prices or conditions of sale;

2. applies less favourable prices or conditions of sale to resellers bound by an exclusive purchasing obligation as compared with other resellers at the same level of distribution.

Article 15

1. In the period 1 July 1983 to 31 December 1986, the prohibition in Article 85(1) of the Treaty shall not apply to agreements of the kind described in Article 1 which either were in force on 1 July 1983 or entered into force between 1 July and 31 December 1983 and which satisfy the exemption conditions under Regulation No 67/67/EEC.

2. In the period 1 July 1983 to 31 December 1988, the prohibition in Article 85(1) of the Treaty shall not apply to agreements of the kinds described in Articles 6 and 10 which either were in force on 1 July 1983 or entered into force between 1 July and 31 December 1983 and which satisfy the exemption conditions of Regulation No 67/67/EEC.

3. In the case of agreements of the kinds described in Articles 6 and 10, which were in force on 1 July 1983 and which expire after 31 December 1988, the prohibition in Article 85(1) of the Treaty shall not apply in the period from 1 January 1989 to the expiry of the agreement but at the latest to the expiry of this Regulation to the extent that the

supplier releases the reseller, before 1 January 1989, from all obligations which would prevent the application of the exemption under Titles II and III.

Article 16

This Regulation shall not apply to agreements by which the supplier undertakes with the reseller to supply only to the reseller certain goods for resale, in the whole or in a defined part of the Community, and the reseller undertakes with the supplier to purchase these goods only from the supplier.

Article 17

This Regulation shall not apply where the parties or connected undertakings, for the purpose of resale in one and the same premises used for the sale and consumption of drinks or service station, enter into agreements both of the kind referred to in Title I and of a kind referred to in Title II or III.

Article 18

This Regulation shall apply *mutatis mutandis* to the categories of concerted practices defined in Articles 1, 6 and 10.

Article 19

This Regulation shall enter into force on 1 July 1983. It shall expire on 31 December 1997.

This Regulation shall be binding in its entirety and directly applicable in all Member States.

7. COMMISSION REGULATION 417/85

on the application of Article 85(3) to categories of specialization agreements [Block Exemption]
O.J. L 53/1 (Feb. 22, 1985)

THE COMMISSION OF THE EUROPEAN COMMUNITIES,

Having regard to the Treaty establishing the European Economic Community,

Having regard to Council Regulation (EEC) No. 2821/71 of 20 December 1971 on the application of Article 85(3) of the Treaty to categories of agreements, decisions and concerted practices, as last amended by the Act of Accession of Greece, and in particular Article 1 thereof,

Having published a draft of this Regulation,

Having consulted the Advisory Committee on Restrictive Practices and Dominant Positions,

Whereas:

(1) Regulation (EEC) No. 2821/71 empowers the Commission to apply Article 85(3) of the Treaty by Regulation to certain categories of agreements, decisions and concerted practices falling within the scope of Article 85(1) which relate to specialization, including agreements necessary for achieving it.

(2) Agreements on specialization in present or future production may fall within the scope of Article 85(1).

(3) Agreements on specialization in production generally contribute to improving the production or distribution of goods, because undertakings concerned can concentrate on the manufacture of certain products and thus operate more efficiently and supply the products more cheaply. It is likely that, given effective competition, consumers will receive a fair share of the resulting benefit.

(4) Such advantages can arise equally from agreements whereby each participant gives up the manufacture of certain products in favour of another participant and from agreements whereby the participants undertake to manufacture certain products or have them manufactured only jointly.

(5) The Regulation must specify what restrictions of competition may be included in specialization agreements. The restrictions of competition that are permitted in the Regulation in addition to reciprocal obligations to give up manufacture are normally essential for the making and implementation of such agreements. These restrictions are therefore, in general, indispensable for the attainment of the desired advantages for the participating undertakings and consumers. It may be left to the parties to decide which of these provisions they include in their agreements.

(6) The exemption must be limited to agreements which do not give rise to the possibility of eliminating competition in respect of a substantial

part of the products in question. The Regulation must therefore apply only as long as the market share and turnover of the participating undertakings do not exceed a certain limit.

(7) It is, however, appropriate to offer undertakings which exceed the turnover limit set in the Regulation a simplified means of obtaining the legal certainty provided by the block exemption. This must allow the Commission to exercise effective supervision as well as simplifying its administration of such agreements.

(8) In order to facilitate the conclusion of long-term specialization agreements, which can have a bearing on the structure of the participating undertakings, it is appropriate to fix the period of validity of the Regulation at 13 years. If the circumstances on the basis of which the Regulation was adopted should change significantly within this period, the Commission will make the necessary amendments.

(9) Agreements, decisions and concerted practices which are automatically exempted pursuant to this Regulation need not be notified. Undertakings may none the less in an individual case request a decision pursuant to Council Regulation No 17, as last amended by the Act of Accession of Greece,

HAS ADOPTED THIS REGULATION:

Article 1

Pursuant to Article 85(3) of the Treaty and subject to the provisions of this Regulation, it is hereby declared that Article 85(1) of the Treaty shall not apply to agreements on specialization whereby, for the duration of the agreement, undertakings accept reciprocal obligations:

(a) not to manufacture certain products or have them manufactured, but to leave it to other parties to manufacture the products or have them manufactured; or

(b) to manufacture certain products or have them manufactured only jointly.

Article 2

1. Apart from the obligations referred to in Article 1, no restrictions of competition may be imposed on the parties other than:

(a) an obligation not to conclude with third parties specialization agreements relating to identical products or to products considered by users to be equivalent in view of their characteristics, price and intended use;

(b) an obligation to procure products which are the subject of the specialization exclusively from another party, a joint undertaking or an undertaking jointly charged with their manufacture, except where they are obtainable on more favourable terms elsewhere and the other party, the joint undertaking or the undertaking charged with manufacture is not prepared to offer the same terms;

(c) an obligation to grant other parties the exclusive right to distribute products which are the subject of the specialization provided that intermediaries and users can also obtain the products from other suppliers and the parties do not render it difficult for intermediaries or users thus to obtain the products.

2. Article 1 shall also apply where the parties undertake obligations of the types referred to in paragraph 1 but with a more limited scope than is permitted by that paragraph.

3. Article 1 shall apply notwithstanding that any of the following obligations, in particular, are imposed:

(a) an obligation to supply other parties with products which are the subject of the specialization and in so doing to observe minimum standards of quality;

(b) an obligation to maintain minimum stocks of products which are the subject of the specialization and of replacement parts for them;

(c) an obligation to provide customer and guarantee services for products which are the subject of the specialization.

Article 3

1. Article 1 shall apply only if:

(a) the products which are the subject of the specialization together with the participating undertakings' other products which are considered by users to be equivalent in view of their characteristics, price and intended use do not represent more than 20% of the market for such products in the common market or a substantial part thereof;

(b) the aggregate annual turnover of all the participating undertakings does not exceed 500 million ECU.

2. Article 1 shall continue to apply if the market share referred to in paragraph 1(a) or the turnover referred to in paragraph 1(b) is exceeded during any period of two consecutive financial years by not more than one-tenth.

3. Where one of the limits laid down in paragraphs 1 and 2 is exceeded, Article 1 shall continue to apply for a period of six months following the end of the financial year during which it was exceeded.

Article 4

1. The exemption provided for in Article 1 shall also apply to agreements involving participating undertakings whose aggregate turnover exceeds the limits laid down in Article 3(1)(b) and (2), on condition that the agreements in question are notified to the Commission in accordance with the provisions of Commission Regulation No. 27, and that the Commission does not oppose such exemption within a period of six months.

2. The period of six months shall run from the date on which the notification is received by the Commission. Where, however, the notifica-

tion is made by registered post, the period shall run from the date shown on the postmark of the place of posting.

3. Paragraph 1 shall apply only if:

(a) express reference is made to this Article in the notification or in a communication accompanying it; and

(b) the information furnished with the notification is complete and in accordance with the facts.

4. The benefit of paragraph 1 may be claimed for agreements notified before the entry into force of this Regulation by submitting a communication to the Commission referring expressly to this Article and to the notification. Paragraphs 2 and 3(b) shall apply *mutatis mutandis*.

5. The Commission may oppose the exemption. It shall oppose exemption if it receives a request to do so from a Member State within three months of the forwarding to the Member State of the notification referred to in paragraph 1 or of the communication referred to in paragraph 4. This request must be justified on the basis of considerations relating to the competition rules of the Treaty.

6. The Commission may withdraw the opposition to the exemption at any time. However, where the opposition was raised at the request of a Member State and this request is maintained, it may be withdrawn only after consultation of the Advisory Committee on Restrictive Practices and Dominant Positions.

7. If the opposition is withdrawn because the undertakings concerned have shown that the conditions of Article 85(3) are fulfilled, the exemption shall apply from the date of notification.

8. If the opposition is withdrawn because the undertakings concerned have amended the agreement so that the conditions of Article 85(3) are fulfilled, the exemption shall apply from the date on which the amendments take effect.

9. If the Commission opposes exemption and the opposition is not withdrawn, the effects of the notification shall be governed by the provisions of Regulation No. 17.

Article 5

1. Information acquired pursuant to Article 4 shall be used only for the purposes of this Regulation.

2. The Commission and the authorities of the Member States, their officials and other servants shall not disclose information acquired by them pursuant to this Regulation of a kind that is covered by the obligation of professional secrecy.

3. Paragraphs 1 and 2 shall not prevent publication of general information or surveys which do not contain information relating to particular undertakings or associations of undertakings.

Article 6

For the purpose of calculating total annual turnover within the meaning of Article 3(1)(b), the turnovers achieved during the last financial year by the participating undertakings in respect of all goods and services excluding tax shall be added together. For this purpose, no account shall be taken of dealings between the participating undertakings or between these undertakings and a third undertaking jointly charged with manufacture.

Article 7

1. For the purposes of Article 3(1)(a) and (b) and Article 6, participating undertakings are:

(a) undertakings party to the agreement;

(b) undertakings in which a party to the agreement, directly or indirectly:

— owns more than half the capital or business assets,

— has the power to exercise more than half the voting rights,

— has the power to appoint at least half the members of the supervisory board, board of management or bodies legally representing the undertakings, or

— has the right to manage the affairs;

(c) undertakings which directly or indirectly have in or over a party to the agreement the rights or powers listed in (b);

(d) undertakings in or over which an undertaking referred to in (c) directly or indirectly has the rights or powers listed in (b).

2. Undertakings in which the undertakings referred to in paragraph 1(a) to (d) directly or indirectly jointly have the rights or powers set out in paragraph 1(b) shall also be considered to be participating undertakings.

Article 8

The Commission may withdraw the benefit of this Regulation, pursuant to Article 7 of Regulation (EEC) No 2821/71, where it finds in a particular case that an agreement exempted by this Regulation nevertheless has effects which are incompatible with the conditions set out in Article 85(3) of the Treaty, and in particular where:

(a) the agreement is not yielding significant results in terms of rationalization or consumers are not receiving a fair share of the resulting benefit; or

(b) the products which are the subject of the specialization are not subject in the common market or a substantial part thereof to effective competition from identical products or products considered by users to be equivalent in view of their characteristics, price and intended use.

Article 9

This Regulation shall apply *mutatis mutandis* to decisions of associations of undertakings and concerted practices.

Article 10

1. This Regulation shall enter into force on 1 March 1985. It shall apply until 31 December 1997.

2. Commission Regulation (EEC) No. 3604/82 is hereby repealed.

This Regulation shall be binding in its entirety and directly applicable in all Member States.

8. COMMISSION REGULATION 418/85

on the application of Article 85(3) to categories of research and development agreements
[Block Exemption]
O.J. L 53/5 (Feb. 22, 1985)

THE COMMISSION OF THE EUROPEAN COMMUNITIES,

Having regard to the Treaty establishing the European Economic Community,

Having regard to Council Regulation (EEC) No. 2821/71 of 20 December 1971 on the application of Article 85(3) of the Treaty to categories of agreements, decisions and concerted practices, as last amended by the Act of Accession of Greece, and in particular Article 1 thereof,

Having published a draft of this Regulation,

Having consulted the Advisory Committee on Restrictive Practices and Dominant Positions,

Whereas:

(1) Regulation (EEC) No. 2821/71 empowers the Commission to apply Article 85(3) of the Treaty by Regulation to certain categories of agreements, decisions and concerted practices falling within the scope of Article 85(1) which have as their object the research and development of products or processes up to the stage of industrial application, and exploitation of the results, including provisions regarding industrial property rights and confidential technical knowledge.

(2) As stated in the Commission's 1968 notice concerning agreements, decisions and concerted practices in the field of cooperation between enterprises, agreements on the joint execution of research work or the joint development of the results of the research, up to but not including the stage of industrial application, generally do not fall within the scope of Article 85(1) of the Treaty. In certain circumstances, however, such as where the parties agree not to carry out other research and development in the same field, thereby forgoing the opportunity of gaining competitive advantages over the other parties, such agreements may fall within Article 85(1) and should therefore not be excluded from this Regulation.

(3) Agreements providing for both joint research and development and joint exploitation of the results may fall within Article 85(1) because the parties jointly determine how the products developed are manufactured or the processes developed are applied or how related intellectual property rights or know-how are exploited.

(4) Cooperation in research and development and in the exploitation of the results generally promotes technical and economic progress by increasing the dissemination of technical knowledge between the parties and avoiding duplication of research and development work, by stimulating new advances through the exchange of complementary technical knowledge, and by rationalizing the manufacture of the products or

application of the processes arising out of the research and development. These aims can be achieved only where the research and development programme and its objectives are clearly defined and each of the parties is given the opportunity of exploiting any of the results of the programme that interest it; where universities or research institutes participate and are not interested in the industrial exploitation of the results, however, it may be agreed that they may use the said results solely for the purpose of further research.

(5) Consumers can generally be expected to benefit from the increased volume and effectiveness of research and development through the introduction of new or improved products or services or the reduction of prices brought about by new or improved processes.

(6) This Regulation must specify the restrictions of competition which may be included in the exempted agreements. The purpose of the permitted restrictions is to concentrate the research activities of the parties in order to improve their chances of success, and to facilitate the introduction of new products and services onto the market. These restrictions are generally necessary to secure the desired benefits for the parties and consumers.

(7) The joint exploitation of results can be considered as the natural consequence of joint research and development. It can take different forms ranging from manufacture to the exploitation of intellectual property rights or know-how that substantially contributes to technical or economic progress. In order to attain the benefits and objectives described above and to justify the restrictions of competition which are exempted, the joint exploitation must relate to products or processes for which the use of the results of the research and development is decisive. Joint exploitation is not therefore justified where it relates to improvements which were not made within the framework of a joint research and development programme but under an agreement having some other principal objective, such as the licensing of intellectual property rights, joint manufacture or specialization, and merely containing ancillary provisions on joint research and development.

(8) The exemption granted under the Regulation must be limited to agreements which do not afford the undertakings the possibility of eliminating competition in respect of a substantial part of the products in question. In order to guarantee that several independent poles of research can exist in the common market in any economic sector, it is necessary to exclude from the block exemption agreements between competitors whose combined share of the market for products capable of being improved or replaced by the results of the research and development exceeds a certain level at the time the agreement is entered into.

(9) In order to guarantee the maintenance of effective competition during joint exploitation of the results, it is necessary to provide that the block exemption will cease to apply if the parties' combined shares of the market for the products arising out of the joint research and development become too great. However, it should be provided that the exemption will

continue to apply, irrespective of the parties' market shares, for a certain period after the commencement of joint exploitation, so as to await stabilization of their market shares, particularly after the introduction of an entirely new product, and to guarantee a minimum period of return on the generally substantial investments involved.

(10) Agreements between undertakings which do not fulfil the market share conditions laid down in the Regulation may, in appropriate cases, be granted an exemption by individual decision, which will in particular take account of world competition and the particular circumstances prevailing in the manufacture of high technology products.

(11) It is desirable to list in the Regulation a number of obligations that are commonly found in research and development agreements but that are normally not restrictive of competition and to provide that, in the event that, because of the particular economic or legal circumstances, they should fall within Article 85(1), they also would be covered by the exemption. This list is not exhaustive.

(12) The Regulation must specify what provisions may not be included in agreements if these are to benefit from the block exemption by virtue of the fact that such provisions are restrictions falling within Article 85(1) for which there can be no general presumption that they will lead to the positive effects required by Article 85(3).

(13) Agreements which are not automatically covered by the exemption because they include provisions that are not expressly exempted by the Regulation and are not expressly excluded from exemption are none the less capable of benefiting from the general presumption of compatibility with Article 85(3) on which the block exemption is based. It will be possible for the Commission rapidly to establish whether this is the case for a particular agreement. Such an agreement should therefore be deemed to be covered by the exemption provided for in this Regulation where it is notified to the Commission and the Commission does not oppose the application of the exemption within a specified period of time.

(14) Agreements covered by this Regulation may also take advantage of provisions contained in other block exemption Regulations of the Commission, and in particular Regulation (EEC) No. 417/85 on specialization agreements, Regulation (EEC) No. 1983/83 on exclusive distribution agreements, Regulation (EEC) No. 1984/83, on exclusive purchasing agreements and Regulation (EEC) No. 2349/84 on patent licensing agreements, if they fulfil the conditions set out in these Regulations. The provisions of the aforementioned Regulations are, however, not applicable in so far as this Regulation contains specific rules.

(15) If individual agreements exempted by this Regulation nevertheless have effects which are incompatible with Article 85(3), the Commission may withdraw the benefit of the block exemption.

(16) The Regulation should apply with retroactive effect to agreements in existence when the Regulation comes into force where such agreements already fulfil its conditions or are modified to do so. The

benefit of these provisions may not be claimed in actions pending at the date of entry into force of this Regulation, nor may it be relied on as grounds for claims for damages against third parties.

(17) Since research and development cooperation agreements are often of a long-term nature, especially where the cooperation extends to the exploitation of the results, it is appropriate to fix the period of validity of the Regulation at 13 years. If the circumstances on the basis of which the Regulation was adopted should change significantly within this period, the Commission will make the necessary amendments.

(18) Agreements which are automatically exempted pursuant to this Regulation need not be notified. Undertakings may nevertheless in a particular case request a decision pursuant to Council Regulation No. 17, as last amended by the Act of Accession of Greece,

HAS ADOPTED THIS REGULATION:

Article 1

1. Pursuant to Article 85(3) of the Treaty and subject to the provisions of this Regulation, it is hereby declared that Article 85(1) of the Treaty shall not apply to agreements entered into between undertakings for the purpose of:

(a) joint research and development of products or processes and joint exploitation of the results of that research and development;

(b) joint exploitation of the results of research and development of products or processes jointly carried out pursuant to a prior agreement between the same undertakings; or

(c) joint research and development of products or processes excluding joint exploitation of the results, in so far as such agreements fall within the scope of Article 85(1).

2. For the purposes of this Regulation:

(a) *research and development of products or processes* means the acquisition of technical knowledge and the carrying out of theoretical analysis, systematic study or experimentation, including experimental production, technical testing of products or processes, the establishment of the necessary facilities and the obtaining of intellectual property rights for the results;

(b) *contract processes* means processes arising out of the research and development;

(c) *contract products* means products or services arising out of the research and development or manufactured or provided applying the contract processes;

(d) *exploitation of the results* means the manufacture of the contract products or the application of the contract processes or the assignment or licensing of intellectual property rights or the communication of know-how required for such manufacture or application;

(e) *technical knowledge* means technical knowledge which is either protected by an intellectual property right or is secret (know-how).

3. Research and development of the exploitation of the results are carried out *jointly* where:

(a) the work involved is:

— carried out by a joint team, organization or undertaking,

— jointly entrusted to a third party, or

— allocated between the parties by way of specialization in research, development or production;

(b) the parties collaborate in any way in the assignment or the licensing of intellectual property rights or the communication of know-how, within the meaning of paragraph 2(d), to third parties.

Article 2

The exemption provided for in Article 1 shall apply on condition that:

(a) the joint research and development work is carried out within the framework of a programme defining the objectives of the work and the field in which it is to be carried out;

(b) all the parties have access to the results of the work;

(c) where the agreement provides only for joint research and development, each party is free to exploit the results of the joint research and development and any pre-existing technical knowledge necessary therefor independently;

(d) the joint exploitation relates only to results which are protected by intellectual property rights or constitute know-how which substantially contributes to technical or economic progress and that the results are decisive for the manufacture of the contract products or the application of the contract processes;

(e) any joint undertaking or third party charged with manufacture of the contract products is required to supply them only to the parties;

(f) undertakings charged with manufacture by way of specialization in production are required to fulfil orders for supplies from all the parties.

Article 3

1. Where the parties are not competing manufacturers of products capable of being improved or replaced by the contract products, the exemption provided for in Article 1 shall apply for the duration of the research and development programme and, where the results are jointly exploited, for five years from the time the contract products are first put on the market within the common market.

2. Where two or more of the parties are competing manufacturers within the meaning of paragraph 1, the exemption provided for in Article 1 shall apply for the period specified in paragraph 1 only if, at the time the agreement is entered into, the parties' combined production of the products capable of being improved or replaced by the contract products

does not exceed 20% of the market for such products in the common market or a substantial part thereof.

3. After the end of the period referred to in paragraph 1, the exemption provided for in Article 1 shall continue to apply as long as the production of the contract products together with the parties' combined production of other products which are considered by users to be equivalent in view of their characteristics, price and intended use does not exceed 20% of the total market for such products in the common market or a substantial part thereof. Where contract products are components used by the parties of the manufacture of other products, reference shall be made to the markets for such of those latter products for which the components represent a significant part.

4. The exemption provided for in Article 1 shall continue to apply where the market share referred to in paragraph 3 is exceeded during any period of two consecutive financial years by not more than one-tenth.

5. Where market shares referred to in paragraphs 3 and 4 are exceeded, the exemption provided for in Article 1 shall continue to apply for a period of six months following the end of the financial year during which it was exceeded.

Article 4

1. The exemption provided for in Article 1 shall also apply to the following restrictions of competition imposed on the parties:

(a) an obligation not to carry out independently research and development in the field to which the programme relates or in a closely connected field during the execution of the programme;

(b) an obligation not to enter into agreements with third parties on research and development in the field to which the programme relates or in a closely connected field during the execution of the programme;

(c) an obligation to procure the contract products exclusively from parties, joint organizations or undertakings or third parties, jointly charged with their manufacture;

(d) an obligation not to manufacture the contract products or apply the contract processes in territories reserved for other parties;

(e) an obligation to restrict the manufacture of the contract products or application of the contract processes to one or more technical fields of application, except where two or more of the parties are competitors within the meaning of Article 3 at the time the agreement is entered into;

(f) an obligation not to pursue, for a period of five years from the time the contract products are first put on the market within the common market, an active policy of putting the products on the market in territories reserved for other parties, and in particular not to engage in advertising specifically aimed at such territories or to establish any branch or maintain any distribution depot there for the distribution of the products, provided that users and intermediaries can obtain the contract products from other suppliers and the parties do not render it difficult for intermediaries and users to thus obtain the products;

(g) an obligation on the parties to communicate to each other any experience they may gain in exploiting the results and to grant each other non-exclusive licenses for inventions relating to improvements or new applications.

2. The exemption provided for in Article 1 shall also apply where in a particular agreement the parties undertake obligations of the types referred to in paragraph 1 but with a more limited scope than is permitted by that paragraph.

Article 5

1. Article 1 shall apply notwithstanding that any of the following obligations, in particular, are imposed on the parties during the currency of the agreement:

(a) an obligation to communicate patented or non-patented technical knowledge necessary for the carrying out of the research and development programme for the exploitation of its results;

(b) an obligation not to use any know-how received from another party for purposes other than carrying out the research and development programme and the exploitation of its results;

(c) an obligation to obtain and maintain in force intellectual property rights for the contract products or processes;

(d) an obligation to preserve the confidentiality of any know-how received or jointly developed under the research and development programme; this obligation may be imposed even after the expiry of the agreement;

(e) an obligation:

(i) to inform other parties of infringements of their intellectual property rights,
(ii) to take legal action against infringers, and
(iii) to assist in any such legal action or share with the other parties in the cost thereof;

(f) an obligation to pay royalties or render services to other parties to compensate for unequal contributions to the joint research and development or unequal exploitation of its results;

(g) an obligation to share royalties received from third parties with other parties;

(h) an obligation to supply other parties with minimum quantities of contract products and to observe minimum standards of quality.

2. In the event that, because of particular circumstances, the obligations referred to in paragraph 1 fall within the scope of Article 85(1), they also shall be covered by the exemption. The exemption provided for

in this paragraph shall also apply where in a particular agreement the parties undertake obligations of the types referred to in paragraph 1 but with a more limited scope than is permitted by that paragraph.

Article 6

The exemption provided for in Article 1 shall not apply where the parties, by agreement, decision or concerted practice:

(a) are restricted in their freedom to carry out research and development independently or in cooperation with third parties in a field unconnected with that to which the programme relates or, after its completion, in the field to which the programme relates or in a connected field;

(b) are prohibited after completion of the research and development programme from challenging the validity of intellectual property rights which the parties hold in the common market and which are relevant to the programme or, after the expiry of the agreement, from challenging the validity of intellectual property rights which the parties hold in the common market and which protect the results of the research and development;

(c) are restricted as to the quantity of the contract products they may manufacture or sell or as to the number of operations employing the contract process they may carry out;

(d) are restricted in their determination of prices, components of prices or discounts when selling the contract products to third parties;

(e) are restricted as to the customers they may serve, without prejudice to Article 4(1)(e);

(f) are prohibited from putting the contract products on the market or pursuing an active sales policy for them in territories within the common market that are reserved for other parties after the end of the period referred to in Article 4(1)(f);

(g) are prohibited from allowing third parties to manufacture the contract products or apply the contract processes in the absence of joint manufacture;

(h) are required:

— to refuse without any objectively justified reason to meet demand from users or dealers established in their respective territories who would market the contract products in other territories within the common market, or

— to make it difficult for users or dealers to obtain the contract products from other dealers within the common market, and in particular to exercise intellectual property rights or take measures so as to prevent users or dealers from obtaining, or from putting on the market within the common market, products which have been lawfully put on the market within the common market by another party or with its consent.

Article 7

1. The exemption provided for in this Regulation shall also apply to agreements of the kinds described in Article 1 which fulfil the conditions laid down in Articles 2 and 3 and which contain obligations restrictive of competition which are not covered by Articles 4 and 5 and do not fall within the scope of Article 6, on condition that the agreements in question are notified to the Commission in accordance with the provisions of Commission Regulation No. 27, and that the Commission does not oppose such exemption within a period of six months.

2. The period of six months shall run from the date on which the notification is received by the Commission. Where, however, the notification is made by registered post, the period shall run from the date shown on the postmark of the place of posting.

3. Paragraph 1 shall apply only if:

(a) express reference is made to this Article in the notification or in a communication accompanying it, and

(b) the information furnished with the notification is complete and in accordance with the facts.

4. The benefit of paragraph 1 may be claimed for agreements notified before the entry into force of this Regulation by submitting a communication to the Commission referring expressly to this Article and to the notification. Paragraphs 2 and 3(b) shall apply *mutatis mutandis.*

5. The Commission may oppose the exemption. It shall oppose exemption if it receives a request to do so from a Member State within three months of the forwarding to the Member State of the notification referred to in paragraph 1 or of the communication referred to in paragraph 4. This request must be justified on the basis of considerations relating to the competition rules of the Treaty.

6. The Commission may withdraw the opposition to the exemption at any time. However, where the opposition was raised at the request of a Member State and this request is maintained, it may be withdrawn only after consultation of the Advisory Committee on Restrictive Practices and Dominant Positions.

7. If the opposition is withdrawn because the undertakings concerned have shown that the conditions of Article 85(3) are fulfilled, the exemption shall apply from the date of notification.

8. If the opposition is withdrawn because the undertakings concerned have amended the agreement so that the conditions of Article 85(3) are fulfilled, the exemption shall apply from the date on which the amendments take effect.

9. If the Commission opposes exemption and the opposition is not withdrawn, the effects of the notification shall be governed by the provisions of Regulation No. 17.

Article 8

1. Information acquired pursuant to Article 7 shall be used only for the purposes of this Regulation.

2. The Commission and the authorities of the Member States, their officials and other servants shall not disclose information acquired by them pursuant to this Regulation of a kind that is covered by the obligation of professional secrecy.

3. Paragraphs 1 and 2 shall not prevent publication of general information or surveys which do not contain information relating to particular undertakings or associations of undertakings.

Article 9

1. The provisions of this Regulation shall also apply to rights and obligations which the parties create for undertakings connected with them. The market shares held and the actions and measures taken by connected undertakings shall be treated as those of the parties themselves.

2. Connected undertakings for the purposes of this Regulation are:

(a) undertakings in which a party to the agreement, directly or indirectly:

— owns more than half the capital or business assets,

— has the power to exercise more than half the voting rights,

— has the power to appoint more than half the members of the supervisory board, board of directors or bodies legally representing the undertakings, or

— has the right to manage the affairs;

(b) undertakings which directly have in or over a party to the agreement the rights or powers listed in (a);

(c) undertakings in or over which an undertaking referred to in (b) directly or indirectly has the rights or powers listed in (a);

3. Undertakings in which the parties to the agreement or undertakings connected with them jointly have, directly or indirectly, the rights or powers set out in paragraph 2(a) shall be considered to be connected with each of the parties to the agreement.

Article 10

The Commission may withdraw the benefit of this Regulation, pursuant to Article 7 of Regulation (EEC) No. 2821/71, where it finds in a particular case that an agreement exempted by this Regulation nevertheless has certain effects which are incompatible with the conditions laid down in Article 85(3) of the Treaty, and in particular where:

(a) the existence of the agreement substantially restricts the scope for third parties to carry out research and development in the relevant field because of the limited research capacity available elsewhere;

(b) because of the particular structure of supply, the existence of the agreement substantially restricts the access of third parties to the market for the contract products;

(c) without any objectively valid reason, the parties do not exploit the results of the joint research and development;

(d) the contract products are not subject in the whole or a substantial part of the common market to effective competition from identical products or products considered by users as equivalent in view of their characteristics, price and intended use.

Article 11

1. In the case of agreements notified to the Commission before 1 March 1985, the exemption provided for in Article 1 shall have retroactive effect from the time at which the conditions for application of this Regulation were fulfilled or, where the agreement does not fall within Article 4(2)(3)(b) of Regulation No. 17, not earlier than the date of notification.

2. In the case of agreements existing on 13 March 1962 and notified to the Commission before 1 February 1963, the exemption shall have retroactive effect from the time at which the conditions for application of this Regulation were fulfilled.

3. Where agreements which were in existence on 13 March 1962 and which were notified to the Commission before 1 February 1963, or which are covered by Article 4(2)(3)(b) of Regulation No. 17 and were notified to the Commission before 1 January 1967, are amended before 1 September 1985 so as to fulfil the conditions for application of this Regulation, such amendment being communicated to the Commission before 1 October 1985, the prohibition laid down in Article 85(1) of the Treaty shall not apply in respect of the period prior to the amendment. The communication of amendments shall take effect from the date of their receipt by the Commission. Where the communication is sent by registered post, it shall take effect from the date shown on the postmark of the place of posting.

4. In the case of agreements to which Article 85 of the Treaty applies as a result of the accession of the United Kingdom, Ireland and Denmark, paragraphs 1 to 3 shall apply except that the relevant dates shall be 1 January 1973 instead of 13 March 1962 and 1 July 1973 instead of 1 February 1963 and 1 January 1967.

5. In the case of agreements to which Article 85 of the Treaty applies as a result of the accession of Greece, paragraphs 1 to 3 shall apply except that the relevant dates shall be 1 January 1981 instead of 13 March 1962 and 1 July 1981 instead of 1 February 1963 and 1 January 1967.

Article 12

This Regulation shall apply *mutatis mutandis* to decisions of associations of undertakings.

Article 13

This Regulation shall enter into force on 1 March 1985. It shall apply until 31 December 1997.

This Regulation shall be binding in its entirety and directly applicable in all Member States.

9. COMMISSION REGULATION 4087/88

on the application of Article 85(3) to categories of franchise agreements [Block Exemption]

O.J. L 359/46 (Dec. 28, 1988) *Pronuptia*

THE COMMISSION OF THE EUROPEAN COMMUNITIES,

Having regard to the Treaty establishing the European Economic Community,

Having regard to Council Regulation No. 19/65/EEC of 2 March 1965 on the application of Article 85(3) of the Treaty to certain categories of agreements and concerted practices, as last amended by the Act of Accession of Spain and Portugal, and in particular Article 1 thereof,

Having published a draft of this Regulation,

Having consulted the Advisory Committee on Restrictive Practices and Dominant Positions,

Whereas:

(1) Regulation No. 19/65/EEC empowers the Commission to apply Article 85(3) of the Treaty by Regulation to certain categories of bilateral exclusive agreements falling within the scope of Article 85(1) which either have as their object the exclusive distribution or exclusive purchase of goods, or include restrictions imposed in relation to the assignment or use of industrial property rights.

(2) Franchise agreements consist essentially of licenses of industrial or intellectual property rights relating to trade marks or signs and know-how, which can be combined with restrictions relating to supply or purchase of goods.

(3) Several types of franchise can be distinguished according to their object: industrial franchise concerns the manufacturing of goods, distribution franchise concerns the sale of goods, and service franchise concerns the supply of services.

(4) It is possible on the basis of the experience of the Commission to define categories of franchise agreements which fall under Article 85(1) but can normally be regarded as satisfying the conditions laid down in Article 85(3). This is the case for franchise agreements whereby one of the parties supplies goods or provides services to end users. On the other hand, industrial franchise agreements should not be covered by this Regulation. Such agreements, which usually govern relationships between producers, present different characteristics than the other types of franchise. They consist of manufacturing licenses based on patents and/or technical know-how, combined with trade-mark licenses. Some of them may benefit from other block exemptions if they fulfil the necessary conditions.

(5) This Regulation covers franchise agreements between two undertakings, the franchisor and the franchisee, for the retailing of goods or the provision of services to end users, or a combination of these activities,

such as the processing or adaptation of goods to fit specific needs of their customers. It also covers cases where the relationship between franchisor and franchisees is made through a third undertaking, the master franchisee. It does not cover wholesale franchise agreements because of the lack of experience of the Commission in that field.

(6) Franchise agreements as defined in this Regulation can fall under Article 85(1). They may in particular affect intra-Community trade where they are concluded between undertakings from different Member States or where they form the basis of a network which extends beyond the boundaries of a single Member State.

(7) Franchise agreements as defined in this Regulation normally improve the distribution of goods and/or the provision of services as they give franchisors the possibility of establishing a uniform network with limited investments, which may assist the entry of new competitors on the market, particularly in the case of small and medium-sized undertakings, thus increasing interbrand competition. They also allow independent traders to set up outlets more rapidly and with higher chance of success than if they had to do so without the franchisor's experience and assistance. They have therefore the possibility of competing more efficiently with large distribution undertakings.

(8) As a rule, franchise agreements also allow consumers and other end users a fair share of the resulting benefit, as they combine the advantage of a uniform network with the existence of traders personally interested in the efficient operation of their business. The homogeneity of the network and the constant cooperation between the franchisor and the franchisees ensures a constant quality of the products and services. The favourable effect of franchising on interbrand competition and the fact that consumers are free to deal with any franchisee in the network guarantees that a reasonable part of the resulting benefits will be passed on to the consumers.

(9) This Regulation must define the obligations restrictive of competition which may be included in franchise agreements. This is the case in particular for the granting of an exclusive territory to the franchisees combined with the prohibition on actively seeking customers outside that territory, which allows them to concentrate their efforts on their allotted territory. The same applies to the granting of an exclusive territory to a master franchisee combined with the obligation not to conclude franchise agreements with third parties outside that territory. Where the franchisees sell or use in the process of providing services, goods manufactured by the franchisor or according to its instructions and/or bearing its trade mark, an obligation on the franchisees not to sell, or use in the process of the provision of services, competing goods, makes it possible to establish a coherent network which is identified with the franchised goods. However, this obligation should only be accepted with respect to the goods which form the essential subject-matter of the franchise. It should notably not relate to accessories or spare parts for these goods.

(10) The obligations referred to above thus do not impose restrictions which are not necessary for the attainment of the abovementioned objectives. In particular, the limited territorial protection granted to the franchisees is indispensable to protect their investment.

(11) It is desirable to list in the Regulation a number of obligations that are commonly found in franchise agreements and are normally not restrictive of competition and to provide that if, because of the particular economic or legal circumstances, they fall under Article 85(1), they are also covered by the exemption. This list, which is not exhaustive, includes in particular clauses which are essential either to preserve the common identity and reputation of the network or to prevent the know-how made available and the assistance given by the franchisor from benefiting competitors.

(12) The Regulation must specify the conditions which must be satisfied for the exemption to apply. To guarantee that competition is not eliminated for a substantial part of the goods which are the subject of the franchise, it is necessary that parallel imports remain possible. Therefore, cross deliveries between franchisees should always be possible. Furthermore, where a franchise network is combined with another distribution system, franchisees should be free to obtain supplies from authorized distributors. To better inform consumers, thereby helping to ensure that they receive a fair share of the resulting benefits, it must be provided that the franchisee shall be obliged to indicate its status as an independent undertaking, by any appropriate means which does not jeopardize the common identity of the franchised network. Furthermore, where the franchisees have to honour guarantees for the franchisor's goods, this obligation should also apply to goods supplied by the franchisor, other franchisees or other agreed dealers.

(13) The Regulation must also specify restrictions which may not be included in franchise agreements if these are to benefit from the exemption granted by the Regulation, by virtue of the fact that such provisions are restrictions falling under Article 85(1) for which there is no general presumption that they will lead to the positive effects required by Article 85(3). This applies in particular to market sharing between competing manufacturers, to clauses unduly limiting the franchisee's choice of suppliers or customers, and to cases where the franchisee is restricted in determining its prices. However, the franchisor should be free to recommend prices to the franchisees, where it is not prohibited by national laws and to the extent that it does not lead to concerted practices for the effective application of these prices.

(14) Agreements which are not automatically covered by the exemption because they contain provisions that are not expressly exempted by the Regulation and not expressly excluded from exemption may nonetheless generally be presumed to be eligible for application of Article 85(3). It will be possible for the Commission rapidly to establish whether this is the case for a particular agreement. Such agreements should therefore be deemed to be covered by the exemption provided for in this Regulation

where they are notified to the Commission and the Commission does not oppose the application of the exemption within a specified period of time.

(15) If individual agreements exempted by this Regulation nevertheless have effects which are incompatible with Article 85(3), in particular as interpreted by the administrative practice of the Commission and the case law of the Court of Justice, the Commission may withdraw the benefit of the block exemption. This applies in particular where competition is significantly restricted because of the structure of the relevant market.

(16) Agreements which are automatically exempted pursuant to this Regulation need not be notified. Undertakings may nevertheless in a particular case request a decision pursuant to Council Regulation No. 17 as last amended by the Act of Accession of Spain and Portugal.

(17) Agreements may benefit from the provisions either of this Regulation or of another Regulation, according to their particular nature and provided that they fulfil the necessary conditions of application. They may not benefit from a combination of the provisions of this Regulation with those of another block exemption Regulation,

HAS ADOPTED THIS REGULATION:

Article 1

1. Pursuant to Article 85(3) of the Treaty and subject to the provisions of this Regulation, it is hereby declared that Article 85(1) of the Treaty shall not apply to franchise agreements to which two undertakings are party, which include one or more of the restrictions listed in Article 2.

2. The exemption provided for in paragraph 1 shall also apply to master franchise agreements to which two undertakings are party. Where applicable, the provisions of this Regulation concerning the relationship between franchisor and franchisee shall apply *mutatis mutandis* to the relationship between franchisor and master franchisee and between master franchisee and franchisee.

3. For the purposes of this Regulation:

(a) 'franchise' means a package of industrial or intellectual property rights relating to trade marks, trade names, shop signs, utility models, designs, copyrights, know-how or patents, to be exploited for the resale of goods or the provision of services to end users;

(b) 'franchise agreement' means an agreement whereby one undertaking, the franchisor, grants the other, the franchisee, in exchange for direct or indirect financial consideration, the right to exploit a franchise for the purposes of marketing specified types of goods and/or services; it includes at least obligations relating to:

— the use of a common name or shop sign and a uniform presentation of contract premises and/or means of transport,

— the communication by the franchisor to the franchisee of know-how,

— the continuing provision by the franchisor to the franchisee of commercial or technical assistance during the life of the agreement;

(c) 'master franchise agreement' means an agreement whereby one undertaking, the franchisor, grants the other, the master franchisee, in exchange of direct or indirect financial consideration, the right to exploit a franchise for the purposes of concluding franchise agreements with third parties, the franchisees;

(d) 'franchisor's goods' means goods produced by the franchisor or according to its instructions, and/or bearing the franchisor's name or trade mark;

(e) 'contract premises' means the premises used for the exploitation of the franchise or, when the franchise is exploited outside those premises, the base from which the franchisee operates the means of transport used for the exploitation of the franchise (contract means of transport);

(f) 'know-how' means a package of non-patented practical information, resulting from experience and testing by the franchisor, which is secret, substantial and identified;

(g) 'secret' means that the know-how, as a body or in the precise configuration and assembly of its components, is not generally known or easily accessible; it is not limited in the narrow sense that each individual component of the know-how should be totally unknown or unobtainable outside the franchisor's business;

(h) 'substantial' means that the know-how includes information which is of importance for the sale of goods or the provision of services to end users, and in particular for the presentation of goods for sale, the processing of goods in connection which the provision of services, methods of dealing with customers, and administration and financial management; the know-how must be useful for the franchisee by being capable, at the date of conclusion of the agreement, of improving the competitive position of the franchisee, in particular by improving the franchisee's performance or helping it to enter a new market;

(i) 'identified' means that the know-how must be described in a sufficiently comprehensive manner so as to make it possible to verify that it fulfils the criteria of secrecy and substantiality; the description of the know-how can either be set out in the franchise agreement or in a separate document or recorded in any other appropriate form.

Article 2

The exemption provided for in Article 1 shall apply to the following restrictions of competition:

(a) an obligation on the franchisor, in a defined area of the common market, the contract territory, not to:

— grant the right to exploit all or part of the franchise to third parties,

— itself exploit the franchise, or itself market the goods or services which are the subject-matter of the franchise under a similar formula.

— itself supply the franchisor's goods to third parties;

(b) an obligation on the master franchisee not to conclude franchise agreements with third parties outside its contract territory;

(c) an obligation on the franchisee to exploit the franchise only from the contract premises;

(d) an obligation on the franchisee to refrain, outside the contract territory, from seeking customers for the goods or the services which are the subject-matter of the franchise;

(e) an obligation on the franchisee not to manufacture, sell or use in the course of the provision of services, goods competing with the franchisor's goods which are the subject-matter of the franchise; where the subject-matter of the franchise is the sale or use in the course of the provision of services both certain types of goods and spare parts or accessories therefor, that obligation may not be imposed in respect of these spare parts or accessories.

Article 3

1. Article 1 shall apply notwithstanding the presence of any of the following obligations on the franchisee, in so far as they are necessary to protect the franchisor's industrial or intellectual property rights or to maintain the common identity and reputation of the franchised network:

(a) to sell, or use in the course of the provision of services, exclusively goods matching minimum objective quality specifications laid down by the franchisor;

(b) to sell, or use in the course of the provision of services, goods which are manufactured only by the franchisor or by third parties designed by it, where it is impracticable, owing to the nature of the goods which are the subject-matter of the franchise, to apply objective quality specifications;

(c) not to engage, directly or indirectly, in any similar business in a territory where it would compete with a member of the franchised network, including the franchisor; the franchisee may be held to this obligation after termination of the agreement, for a reasonable period which may not exceed one year, in the territory where it has exploited the franchise;

(d) not to acquire financial interests in the capital of a competing undertaking, which would give the franchisee the power to influence the economic conduct of such undertaking;

(e) to sell the goods which are the subject-matter of the franchise only to end users, to other franchisees and to resellers within other channels of distribution supplied by the manufacturer of these goods or with its consent;

(f) to use its best endeavours to sell the goods or provide the services that are the subject-matter of the franchise; to offer for sale a minimum range of goods, achieve a minimum turnover, plan its orders in advance, keep minimum stocks and provide customer and warranty services;

(g) to pay to the franchisor a specified proportion of its revenue for advertising and itself carry out advertising for the nature of which it shall obtain the franchisor's approval.

2. Article 1 shall apply notwithstanding the presence of any of the following obligations on the franchisee:

(a) not to disclose to third parties the know-how provided by the franchisor; the franchisee may be held to this obligation after termination of the agreement;

(b) to communicate to the franchisor any experience gained in exploiting the franchise and to grant it, and other franchisees, a non-exclusive license for the know-how resulting from that experience;

(c) to inform the franchisor of infringements of licensed industrial or intellectual property rights, to take legal action against infringers or to assist the franchisor in any legal actions against infringers;

(d) not to use know-how licensed by the franchisor for purposes other than the exploitation of the franchise; the franchisee may be held to this obligation after termination of the agreement;

(e) to attend or have its staff attend training courses arranged by the franchisor;

(f) to apply the commercial methods devised by the franchisor, including any subsequent modification thereof, and use the licensed industrial or intellectual property rights;

(g) to comply with the franchisor's standards for the equipment and presentation of the contract premises and/or means of transport;

(h) to allow the franchisor to carry out checks of the contract premises and/or means of transport, including the goods sold and the services provided, and the inventory and accounts of the franchisee;

(i) not without the franchisor's consent to change the location of the contract premises;

(j) not without the franchisor's consent to assign the rights and obligations under the franchise agreement.

3. In the event that, because of particular circumstances, obligations referred to in paragraph 2 fall within the scope of Article 85(1), they shall also be exempted even if they are not accompanied by any of the obligations exempted by Article 1.

Article 4

The exemption provided for in Article 1 shall apply on condition that:

(a) the franchisee is free to obtain the goods that are the subject-matter of the franchise from other franchisees; where such goods are also distributed through another network of authorized distributors, the franchisee must be free to obtain the goods from the latter;

(b) where the franchisor obliges the franchisee to honour guarantees for the franchisor's goods, that obligation shall apply in respect of such goods supplied by any member of the franchised network or other distributors which give a similar guarantee, in the common market;

(c) the franchisee is obliged to indicate its status as an independent undertaking; this indication shall however not interfere with the common identity of the franchised network resulting in particular from the common name or shop sign and uniform appearance of the contract premises and/or means of transport.

Article 5

The exemption granted by Article 1 shall not apply where:

(a) undertakings producing goods or providing services which are identical or are considered by users as equivalent in view of their characteristics, price and intended use, enter into franchise agreements in respect of such goods or services;

(b) without prejudice to Article 2(e) and Article 3(1)(b), the franchisee is prevented from obtaining supplies of goods of a quality equivalent to those offered by the franchisor;

(c) without prejudice to Article 2(e), the franchisee is obliged to sell, or use in the process of providing services, goods manufactured by the franchisor or third parties designated by the franchisor and the franchisor refuses, for reasons other than protecting the franchisor's industrial or intellectual property rights, or maintaining the common identity and reputation of the franchised network, to designate as authorized manufacturers third parties proposed by the franchisee;

(d) the franchisee is prevented from continuing to use the licensed know-how after termination of the agreement where the know-how has become generally known or easily accessible, other than by breach of an obligation by the franchisee;

(e) the franchisee is restricted by the franchisor, directly or indirectly, in the determination of sale prices for the goods or services which are the subject-matter of the franchise, without prejudice to the possibility for the franchisor of recommending sale prices;

(f) the franchisor prohibits the franchisee from challenging the validity of the industrial or intellectual property rights which form part of the franchise, without prejudice to the possibility for the franchisor of terminating the agreement in such a case;

(g) franchisees are obliged not to supply within the common market the goods or services which are the subject-matter of the franchise to end users because of their place of residence.

Article 6

1. The exemption provided for in Article 1 shall also apply to franchise agreements which fulfil the conditions laid down in Article 4 and include obligations restrictive of competition which are not covered by Articles 2 and 3(3) and do not fall within the scope of Article 5, on condition that the agreements in question are notified to the Commission in accordance with the provisions of Commission Regulation No. 27 and that the Commission does not oppose such exemption within a period of six months.

2. The period of six months shall run from the date on which the notification is received by the Commission. Where, however, the notification is made by registered post, the period shall run from the date shown on the postmark of the place of posting.

3. Paragraph 1 shall apply only if:

(a) express reference is made to this Article in the notification or in a communication accompanying it; and

(b) the information furnished with the notification is complete and in accordance with the facts.

4. The benefit of paragraph 1 can be claimed for agreements notified before the entry into force of this Regulation by submitting a communication to the Commission referring expressly to this Article and to the notification. Paragraphs 2 and 3(b) shall apply *mutatis mutandis*.

5. The Commission may oppose exemption. It shall oppose exemption if it receives a request to do so from a Member State within three months of the forwarding to the Member State of the notification referred to in paragraph 1 or the communication referred to in paragraph 4. This request must be justified on the basis of considerations relating to the competition rules of the Treaty.

6. The Commission may withdraw its opposition to the exemption at any time. However, where that opposition was raised at the request of a Member State, it may be withdrawn only after consultation of the advisory Committee on Restrictive Practices and Dominant Positions.

7. If the opposition is withdrawn because the undertakings concerned have shown that the conditions of Article 85(3) are fulfilled, the exemption shall apply from the date of the notification.

8. If the opposition is withdrawn because the undertakings concerned have amended the agreement so that the conditions of Article 85(3) are fulfilled, the exemption shall apply from the date on which the amendments take effect.

9. If the Commission opposes exemption and its opposition is not withdrawn, the effects of the notification shall be governed by the provisions of Regulation No. 17.

Article 7

1. Information acquired pursuant to Article 6 shall be used only for the purposes of this Regulation.

2. The Commission and the authorities of the Member States, their officials and other servants shall not disclose information acquired by them pursuant to this Regulation of a kind that is covered by the obligation of professional secrecy.

3. Paragraphs 1 and 2 shall not prevent publication of general information or surveys which do not contain information relating to particular undertakings or associations of undertakings.

Article 8

The Commission may withdraw the benefit of this Regulation, pursuant to Article 7 of Regulation No. 19/65/EEC, where it finds in a particular case that an agreement exempted by this Regulation nevertheless has certain effects which are incompatible with the conditions laid down in Article 85(3) of the EEC Treaty, and in particular where territorial protection is awarded to the franchisee and:

(a) access to the relevant market or competition therein is significantly restricted by the cumulative effect of parallel networks of similar agreements established by competing manufacturers or distributors;

(b) the goods or services which are the subject-matter of the franchise do not face, in a substantial part of the common market, effective competition from goods or services which are identical or considered by users as equivalent in view of their characteristics, price and intended use;

(c) the parties, or one of them, prevent end users, because of their place of residence, from obtaining, directly or through intermediaries, the goods or services which are the subject-matter of the franchise within the common market, or use differences in specifications concerning those goods or services in different Member States, to isolate markets;

(d) franchisees engage in concerted practices relating to the sale prices of the goods or services which are the subject-matter of the franchise;

(e) the franchisor uses its right to check the contract premises and means of transport, or refuses its agreement to requests by the franchisee to move the contract premises or assign its rights and obligations under the franchise agreement, for reasons other than protecting the franchisor's industrial or intellectual property rights, maintaining the common identity and reputation of the franchised network or verifying that the franchisee abides by its obligations under the agreement.

Article 9

This Regulation shall enter into force on 1 February 1989. It shall remain in force until 31 December 1999.

This Regulation shall be binding in its entirety and directly applicable in all Member States.

10. COUNCIL REGULATION 4064/89

on the control of concentrations between undertakings [Merger Regulation]

O.J. L 395/1 (Dec. 12, 1989), as amended O.J. L 257/15 (Sept. 21, 1990)

THE COUNCIL OF THE EUROPEAN COMMUNITIES,

Having regard to the Treaty establishing the European Economic Community, and in particular Articles 87 and 235 thereof,

Having regard to the proposal from the Commission,

Having regard to the opinion of the European Parliament,

Having regard to the opinion of the Economic and Social Committee,

(1) Whereas, for the achievement of the aims of the Treaty establishing the European Economic Community, Article 3(f) gives the Community the objective of instituting 'a system ensuring that competition in the common market is not distorted';

(2) Whereas this system is essential for the achievement of the internal market by 1992 and its further development;

(3) Whereas the dismantling of internal frontiers is resulting and will continue to result in major corporate re-organizations in the Community, particularly in the form of concentrations;

(4) Whereas such a development must be welcomed as being in line with the requirements of dynamic competition and capable of increasing the competitiveness of European industry, improving the conditions of growth and raising the standard of living in the Community;

(5) Whereas, however, it must be ensured that the process of reorganization does not result in lasting damage to competition; whereas Community law must therefore include provisions governing those concentrations which may significantly impede effective competition in the common market or in a substantial part of it;

(6) Whereas Articles 85 and 86, while applicable, according to the case-law of the Court of Justice, to certain concentrations, are not, however, sufficient to all operations which may prove to be incompatible with the system of undistorted competition envisaged in the Treaty;

(7) Whereas a new legal instrument should therefore be created in the form of a Regulation to permit effective control of all concentrations from the point of view of their effect on the structure of competition in the Community and to be the only instrument applicable to such concentrations;

(8) Whereas this Regulation should therefore be based not only on Article 87 but, principally, on Article 235 of the Treaty, under which the Community may give itself the additional powers of action necessary for the attainment of its objectives, and also with regard to concentrations on the markets for agricultural products listed in Annex II to the Treaty;

(9) Whereas the provisions to be adopted in this Regulation should apply to significant structural changes the impact of which on the market goes beyond the national borders of any one Member State;

(10) Whereas the scope of application of this Regulation should therefore be defined according to the geographical area of activity of the undertakings concerned and be limited by quantitative thresholds in order to cover those concentrations which have a Community dimension; whereas, at the end of an initial phase of the implementation of this Regulation, these thresholds should be reviewed in the light of the experience gained;

(11) Whereas a concentration with a Community dimension exists where the aggregate turnover of the undertakings concerned exceeds given levels worldwide and within the Community and where at least two of the undertakings concerned have their sole or main fields of activities in different Member States or where, although the undertakings in question act mainly in one and the same Member State, at least one of them has substantial operations in at least one other Member State; whereas that is also the case where the concentrations are effected by undertakings which do not have their principal fields of activities in the Community but which have substantial operations there;

(12) Whereas the arrangements to be introduced for the control of concentrations should, without prejudice to Article 90(2) of the Treaty, respect the principle of non-discrimination between the public and the private sectors; whereas, in the public sector, calculation of the turnover of an undertaking concerned in a concentration needs, therefore, to take account of undertakings making up an economic unit with an independent power of decision, irrespective of the way in which their capital is held or of the rules of administrative supervision applicable to them;

(13) Whereas it is necessary to establish whether concentrations with a Community dimension are compatible or not with the common market from the point of view of the need to maintain and develop effective competition in the common market; whereas, in so doing, the Commission must place its appraisal within the general framework of the achievement of the fundamental objectives referred to in Article 2 of the Treaty, including that of strengthening the Community's economic and social cohesion, referred to in Article 130a;

(14) Whereas this Regulation should establish the principle that a concentration with a Community dimension which creates or strengthens a position as a result of which effective competition in the common market or in a substantial part of it is significantly impeded is to be declared incompatible with the common market;

(15) Whereas concentrations which, by reason of the limited market share of the undertakings concerned, are not liable to impede effective competition may be presumed to be compatible with the common market; whereas, without prejudice to Articles 85 and 86 of the Treaty, an indication to this effect exists, in particular, where the market share of the undertakings concerned does not exceed 25% either in the common market or in a substantial part of it;

(16) Whereas the Commission should have the task of taking all the decisions necessary to establish whether or not concentrations with a Community dimension are compatible with the common market, as well as decisions designed to restore effective competition;

(17) Whereas to ensure effective control undertakings should be obliged to give prior notification of concentrations with a Community dimension and provision should be made for the suspension of concentrations for a limited period, and for the possibility of extending or waiving a suspension where necessary; whereas in the interests of legal certainty the validity of transactions must nevertheless be protected as much as necessary;

(18) Whereas a period within which the Commission must initiate proceedings in respect of a notified concentration and periods within which it must give a final decision on the compatibility or incompatibility with the common market of a notified concentration should be laid down;

(19) Whereas the undertakings concerned must be afforded the right to be heard by the Commission when proceedings have been initiated; whereas the members of the management and supervisory bodies and the recognized representatives of the employees of the undertakings concerned, and third parties showing a legitimate interest, must also be given the opportunity to be heard;

(20) Whereas the Commission should act in close and constant liaison with the competent authorities of the Member States from which it obtains comments and information;

(21) Whereas, for the purposes of this Regulation, and in accordance with the case-law of the Court of Justice, the Commission must be afforded the assistance of the Member States and must also be empowered to require information to be given and to carry out the necessary investigations in order to appraise concentrations;

(22) Whereas compliance with this Regulation must be enforceable by means of fines and periodic penalty payments; whereas the Court of Justice should be given unlimited jurisdiction in that regard pursuant to Article 172 of the Treaty;

(23) Whereas it is appropriate to define the concept of concentration in such a manner as to cover only operations bringing about a lasting change in the structure of the undertakings concerned; whereas it is therefore necessary to exclude from the scope of this Regulation those operations which have as their object or effect the coordination of the competitive behaviour of undertakings which remain independent, since such operations fall to be examined under the appropriate provisions of the Regulations implementing Articles 85 and 86 of the Treaty; whereas it is appropriate to make this distinction specifically in the case of the creation of joint ventures;

(24) Whereas there is no coordination of competitive behaviour within the meaning of this Regulation where two or more undertakings agree to acquire jointly control of one or more other undertakings with the object

and effect of sharing amongst themselves such undertakings or their assets;

(25) Whereas this Regulation should still apply where the undertakings concerned accept restrictions directly related and necessary to the implementation of the concentration;

(26) Whereas the Commission should be given exclusive competence to apply this Regulation, subject to review by the Court of Justice;

(27) Whereas the Member States may not apply their national legislation on competition to concentrations with a Community dimension, unless this Regulation makes provision therefor; whereas the relevant powers of national authorities should be limited to cases where, failing intervention by the Commission, effective competition is likely to be significantly impeded within the territory of a Member State and where the competition interests of that Member State cannot be sufficiently protected otherwise by this Regulation; whereas the Member States concerned must act promptly in such cases; whereas this Regulation cannot, because of the diversity of national law, fix a single deadline for the adoption of remedies;

(28) Whereas, furthermore, the exclusive application of this Regulation to concentrations with a Community dimension is without prejudice to Article 223 of the Treaty, and does not prevent the Member States from taking appropriate measures to protect legitimate interests other than those pursued by this Regulation, provided that such measures are compatible with the general principles and other provisions of Community law;

(29) Whereas concentrations not covered by this Regulation come, in principle, within the jurisdiction of the Member States; whereas, however, the Commission should have the power to act, at the request of a Member State concerned, in cases where effective competition could be significantly impeded within that Member State's territory;

(30) Whereas the conditions in which concentrations involving Community undertakings are carried out in non-member countries should be observed, and provision should be made for the possibility of the Council giving the Commission an appropriate mandate for negotiation with a view to obtaining non-discriminatory treatment for Community undertakings;

(31) Whereas this Regulation in no way detracts from the collective rights of employees as recognized in the undertakings concerned,

HAS ADOPTED THIS REGULATION:

Article 1
Scope

1. Without prejudice to Article 22 this Regulation shall apply to all concentrations with a Community dimension as defined in paragraph 2.

2. For the purposes of this Regulation, a concentration has a Community dimension where:

(a) the combined aggregate worldwide turnover of all the undertakings concerned is more than ECU 5000 million; and

(b) the aggregate Community-wide turnover of each of at least two of the undertakings concerned is more than ECU 250 million,

unless each of the undertakings concerned achieves more than two-thirds of its aggregate Community-wide turnover within one and the same Member State.

3. The thresholds laid down in paragraph 2 will be reviewed before the end of the fourth year following that of the adoption of this Regulation by the Council acting by a qualified majority on a proposal from the Commission.

Article 2
Appraisal of concentrations

1. Concentrations within the scope of this Regulation shall be appraised in accordance with the following provisions with a view to establishing whether or not they are compatible with the common market.

In making this appraisal, the Commission shall take into account:

(a) the need to maintain and develop effective competition within the common market in view of, among other things, the structure of all the markets concerned and the actual or potential competition from undertakings located either within or without the Community;

(b) the market position of the undertakings concerned and their economic and financial power, the alternatives available to suppliers and users, their access to supplies or markets, any legal or other barriers to entry, supply and demand trends for the relevant goods and services, the interests of the intermediate and ultimate consumers, and the development of technical and economic progress provided that it is to consumers' advantage and does not form an obstacle to competition.

2. A concentration which does not create or strengthen a dominant position as a result of which effective competition would be significantly impeded in the common market or in a substantial part of it shall be declared compatible with the common market.

3. A concentration which creates or strengthens a dominant position as a result of which effective competition would be significantly impeded in the common market or in a substantial part of it shall be declared incompatible with the common market.

Article 3
Definition of concentration

1. A concentration shall be deemed to arise where:

(a) two or more previously independent undertakings merge, or

(b) — one or more persons already control at least one undertaking, or

— one or more undertakings

acquire, whether by purchase of securities or assets, by contract or by any other means, direct or indirect control of the whole or parts of one or more other undertakings.

2. An operation, including the creation of a joint venture, which has as its object or effect the coordination of the competitive behaviour of undertakings which remain independent shall not constitute a concentration within the meaning of paragraph 1(b).

The creation of a joint venture performing on a lasting basis all the functions of an autonomous economic entity, which does not give rise to coordination of the competitive behaviour of the parties amongst themselves or between them and the joint venture, shall constitute a concentration within the meaning of paragraph 1(b).

3. For the purposes of this Regulation, control shall be constituted by rights, contracts or any other means which, either separately or in combination and having regard to the considerations of fact or law involved, confer the possibility of exercising decisive influence on an undertaking, in particular by:

(a) ownership or the right to use all or part of the assets of an undertaking;

(b) rights or contracts which confer decisive influence on the composition, voting or decisions of the organs of an undertaking.

4. Control is acquired by persons or undertakings which:

(a) are holders of the rights or entitled to rights under the contracts concerned; or

(b) while not being holders of such rights or entitled to rights under such contracts, have the power to exercise the rights deriving therefrom.

5. A concentration shall not be deemed to arise where:

(a) credit institutions or other financial institutions or insurance companies, the normal activities of which include transactions and dealing in securities for their own account or for the account of others, hold on a temporary basis securities which they have acquired in an undertaking with a view to reselling them, provided that they do not exercise voting rights in respect of those securities with a view to determining the competitive behaviour of that undertaking or provided that they exercise such voting rights only with a view to preparing the disposal of all or part of that undertaking or of its assets or the disposal of those securities and that any such disposal takes place within one year of the date of acquisition; that period may be extended by the Commission on request where such institutions or companies can show that the disposal was not reasonably possible within the period set;

(b) control is acquired by an office-holder according to the law of a Member State relating to liquidation, winding up, insolvency, cessation of payments, compositions or analogous proceedings;

(c) the operations referred to in paragraph 1(b) are carried out by the financial holding companies referred to in Article 5(3) of the Fourth Council Directive 78/660/EEC of 25 July 1978 on the annual accounts of certain types of companies, as last amended by Directive 84/569/EEC, provided however that the voting rights in respect of the holding are exercised, in particular in relation to the appointment of members of the management and supervisory bodies of the undertakings in which they have holdings, only to maintain the full value of those investments and not to determine directly or indirectly the competitive conduct of those undertakings.

Article 4
Prior notification of concentrations

1. Concentrations with a Community dimension defined in this Regulation shall be notified to the Commission not more than one week after the conclusion of the agreement, or the announcement of the public bid, or the acquisition of a controlling interest. That week shall begin when the first of those events occurs.

2. A concentration which consists of a merger within the meaning of Article 3(1)(a) or in the acquisition of joint control within the meaning of Article 3(1)(b) shall be notified jointly by the parties to the merger or by those acquiring joint control as the case may be. In all other cases, the notification shall be effected by the person or undertaking acquiring control of the whole or parts of one or more undertakings.

3. Where the Commission finds that a notified concentration falls within the scope of this Regulation, it shall publish the fact of the notification, at the same time indicating the names of the parties, the nature of the concentration and the economic sectors involved. The Commission shall take account of the legitimate interest of undertakings in the protection of their business secrets.

Article 5
Calculation of turnover

1. Aggregate turnover within the meaning of Article 1(2) shall comprise the amounts derived by the undertakings concerned in the preceding financial year from the sale of products and the provision of services falling within the undertakings' ordinary activities after deduction of sales rebates and of value added tax and other taxes directly related to turnover. The aggregate turnover of an undertaking concerned shall not include the sale of products or the provision of services between any of the undertakings referred to in paragraph 4.

Turnover, in the Community or in a Member State, shall comprise products sold and services provided to undertakings or consumers, in the Community or in that Member State as the case may be.

2. By way of derogation from paragraph 1, where the concentration consists in the acquisition of parts, whether or not constituted as legal entities, of one or more undertakings, only the turnover relating to the

parts which are the subject of the transaction shall be taken into account with regard to the seller or sellers.

However, two or more transactions within the meaning of the first subparagraph which take place within a two-year period between the same persons or undertakings shall be treated as one and the same concentration arising on the date of the last transaction.

3. In place of turnover the following shall be used:

(a) for credit institutions and other financial institutions, as regards Article 1(2)(a), one-tenth of their total assets.

As regards Article 1(2)(b) and the final part of Article 1(2), total Community-wide turnover shall be replaced by one-tenth of total assets multiplied by the ratio between loans and advances to credit institutions and customers in transactions with Community residents and the total sum of those loans and advances.

As regards the final part of Article 1(2), total turnover within one Member State shall be replaced by one-tenth of total assets multiplied by the ratio between loans and advances to credit institutions and customers in transactions with residents of that Member State and the total sum of those loans and advances;

(b) for insurance undertakings, the value of gross premiums written which shall comprise all amounts received and receivable in respect of insurance contracts issued by or on behalf of the insurance undertakings, including also outgoing reinsurance premiums, and after deduction of taxes and parafiscal contributions or levies charged by reference to the amounts of individual premiums or the total volume of premiums; as regards Article 1(2)(b) and the final part of Article 1(2), gross premiums received from Community residents and from residents of one Member State respectively shall be taken into account.

4. Without prejudice to paragraph 2, the aggregate turnover of an undertaking concerned within the meaning of Article 1(2) shall be calculated by adding together the respective turnovers of the following:

(a) the undertaking concerned;

(b) those undertakings in which the undertaking concerned, directly or indirectly:

— owns more than half the capital or business assets, or

— has the power to exercise more than half the voting rights, or

— has the power to appoint more than half the members of the supervisory board, the administrative board or bodies legally representing the undertakings, or

— has the right to manage the undertakings' affairs;

(c) those undertakings which have in the undertaking concerned the rights or powers listed in (b);

(d) those undertakings in which an undertaking as referred to in (c) has the rights or powers listed in (b);

(e) those undertakings in which two or more undertakings as referred to in (a) to (d) jointly have the rights or powers listed in (b).

5. Where undertakings concerned by the concentration jointly have the rights or powers listed in paragraph 4(b), in calculating the aggregate turnover of the undertakings concerned for the purposes of Article 1(2):

(a) no account shall be taken of the turnover resulting from the sale of products or the provision of services between the joint undertaking and each of the undertakings concerned or any other undertaking connected with any one of them, as set out in paragraph 4(b) to (e);

(b) account shall be taken of the turnover resulting from the sale of products and the provision of services between the joint undertaking and any third undertakings. This turnover shall be apportioned equally amongst the undertakings concerned.

Article 6
Examination of the notification and initiation of proceedings

1. The Commission shall examine the notification as soon as it is received.

(a) Where it concludes that the concentration notified does not fall within the scope of this Regulation, it shall record that finding by means of a decision.

(b) Where it finds that the concentration notified, although falling within the scope of this Regulation, does not raise serious doubts as to its compatibility with the common market, it shall decide not to oppose it and shall declare that it is compatible with the common market.

(c) If, on the other hand, it finds that the concentration notified falls within the scope of this Regulation and raises serious doubts as to its compatibility with the common market, it shall decide to initiate proceedings.

2. The Commission shall notify its decision to the undertakings concerned and the competent authorities of the Member States without delay.

Article 7
Suspension of concentrations

1. For the purposes of paragraph 2 a concentration as defined in Article 1 shall not be put into effect either before its notification or within the first three weeks following its notification.

2. Where the Commission, following a preliminary examination of the notification within the period provided for in paragraph 1, finds it necessary in order to ensure the full effectiveness of any decision taken later pursuant to Article 8(3) and (4), it may decide on its own initiative to continue the suspension of a concentration in whole or in part until it takes a final decision, or to take other interim measures to that effect.

3. Paragraphs 1 and 2 shall not prevent the implementation of a public bid which has been notified to the Commission in accordance with

Article 4(1), provided that the acquirer does not exercise the voting rights attached to the securities in question or does so only to maintain the full value of those investments and on the basis of a derogation granted by the Commission under paragraph 4.

4. The Commission may, on request, grant a derogation from the obligations imposed in paragraphs 1, 2 or 3 in order to prevent serious damage to one or more undertakings concerned by a concentration or to a third party. That derogation may be made subject to conditions and obligations in order to ensure conditions of effective competition. A derogation may be applied for and granted at any time, even before notification or after the transaction.

5. The validity of any transaction carried out in contravention of paragraph 1 or 2 shall be dependent on a decision pursuant to Article 6(1)(b) or Article 8(2) or (3) or on a presumption pursuant to Article 10(6).

This Article shall, however, have no effect on the validity of transactions in securities including those convertible into other securities admitted to trading on a market which is regulated and supervised by authorities recognized by public bodies, operates regularly and is accessible directly or indirectly to the public, unless the buyer and seller knew or ought to have known that the transaction was carried out in contravention of paragraph 1 or 2.

Article 8

Powers of decision of the Commission

1. Without prejudice to Article 9, all proceedings initiated pursuant to Article 6(1)(c) shall be closed by means of a decision as provided for in paragraphs 2 to 5.

2. Where the Commission finds that, following modification by the undertakings concerned if necessary, a notified concentration fulfils the criterion laid down in Article 2(2), it shall issue a decision declaring the concentration compatible with the common market.

It may attach to its decision conditions and obligations intended to ensure that the undertakings concerned comply with the commitments they have entered into *vis-à-vis* the Commission with a view to modifying the original concentration plan. The decision declaring the concentration compatible shall also cover restrictions directly related and necessary to the implementation of the concentration.

3. Where the Commission finds that a concentration fulfils the criterion laid down in Article 2(3), it shall issue a decision declaring that the concentration is incompatible with the common market.

4. Where a concentration has already been implemented, the Commission may, in a decision pursuant to paragraph 3 or by separate decision, require the undertakings or assets brought together to be separated or the cessation of joint control or any other action that may be appropriate in order to restore conditions of effective competition.

5. The Commission may revoke the decision it has taken pursuant to paragraph 2 where:

(a) the declaration of compatibility is based on incorrect information for which one of the undertakings is responsible or where it has been obtained by deceit; or

(b) the undertakings concerned commit a breach of an obligation attached to the decision.

6. In the cases referred to in paragraph 5, the Commission may take a decision under paragraph 3, without being bound by the deadline referred to in Article 10(3).

Article 9

Referral to the competent authorities of the Member States

1. The Commission may, by means of a decision notified without delay to the undertakings concerned and the competent authorities of the other Member States, refer a notified concentration to the competent authorities of the Member State concerned in the following circumstances.

2. Within three weeks of the date of receipt of the copy of the notification a Member State may inform the Commission, which shall inform the undertakings concerned, that a concentration threatens to create or to strengthen a dominant position as a result of which effective competition would be significantly impeded on a market, within that Member State, which presents all the characteristics of a distinct market, be it a substantial part of the common market or not.

3. If the Commission considers that, having regard to the market for the products or services in question and the geographical reference market within the meaning of paragraph 7, there is such a distinct market and that such a threat exists, either:

(a) it shall itself deal with the case in order to maintain or restore effective competition on the market concerned; or

(b) it shall refer the case to the competent authorities of the Member State concerned with a view to the application of that State's national competition law.

If, however, the Commission considers that such a distinct market or threat does not exist it shall adopt a decision to that effect which it shall address to the Member State concerned.

4. A decision to refer or not to refer pursuant to paragraph 3 shall be taken:

(a) as a general rule within the six-week period provided for in Article 10(1), second subparagraph, where the Commission, pursuant to Article 6(1)(b), has not initiated proceedings; or

(b) within three months at most of the notification of the concentration concerned where the Commission has initiated proceedings under Article 6(1)(c), without taking the preparatory steps in order to adopt the necessary measures under Article 8(2), second subparagraph, (3) or (4) to maintain or restore effective competition on the market concerned.

5. If within the three months referred to in paragraph 4(b) the Commission, despite a reminder from the Member State concerned, has not taken a decision on referral in accordance with paragraph 3 nor has taken the preparatory steps referred to in paragraph 4(b), it shall be deemed to have taken a decision to refer the case to the Member State concerned in accordance with paragraph 3(b).

6. The publication of any report or the announcement of the findings of the examination of the concentration by the competent authority of the Member State concerned shall be effected not more than four months after the Commission's referral.

7. The geographical reference market shall consist of the area in which the undertakings concerned are involved in the supply and demand of products or services, in which the conditions of competition are sufficiently homogeneous and which can be distinguished from neighboring areas because, in particular, conditions of competition are appreciably different in those areas. This assessment should take account in particular of the nature and characteristics of the products or services concerned, of the existence of entry barriers of consumer preferences, of appreciable differences of the undertakings' market shares between the area concerned and neighbouring areas or of substantial price differences.

8. In applying the provisions of this Article, the Member State concerned may take only the measures strictly necessary to safeguard or restore effective competition on the market concerned.

9. In accordance with the relevant provisions of the Treaty, any Member State may appeal to the Court of Justice, and in particular request the application of Article 186, for the purpose of applying its national competition law.

10. This Article will be reviewed before the end of the fourth year following that of the adoption of this Regulation.

Article 10
Time limits for initiating proceedings and for decisions

1. The decisions referred to in Article 6(1) must be taken within one month at most. That period shall begin on the day following that of the receipt of a notification or, if the information to be supplied with the notification is incomplete, on the day following that of the receipt of the complete information.

That period shall be increased to six weeks if the Commission receives a request from a Member State in accordance with Article 9(2).

2. Decisions taken pursuant to Article 8(2) concerning notified concentrations must be taken as soon as it appears that the serious doubts referred to in Article 6(1)(c) have been removed, particularly as a result of modifications made by the undertakings concerned, and at the latest by the deadline laid down in paragraph 3.

3. Without prejudice to Article 8(6), decisions taken pursuant to Article 8(3) concerning notified concentrations must be taken within not more than four months of the date on which proceedings are initiated.

4. The period set by paragraph 3 shall exceptionally be suspended where, owing to circumstances for which one of the undertakings involved in the concentration is responsible, the Commission has had to request information by decision pursuant to Article 11 or to order an investigation by decision pursuant to Article 13.

5. Where the Court of Justice gives a Judgement which annuls the whole or part of a Commission decision taken under this Regulation, the periods laid down in this Regulation shall start again from the date of the Judgement.

6. Where the Commission has not taken a decision in accordance with Article 6(1)(b) or (c) or Article 8(2) or (3) within the deadlines set in paragraphs 1 and 3 respectively, the concentration shall be deemed to have been declared compatible with the common market, without prejudice to Article 9.

Article 11
Requests for information

1. In carrying out the duties assigned to it by this Regulation, the Commission may obtain all necessary information from the Governments and competent authorities of the Member States, from the persons referred to in Article 3(1)(b), and from undertakings and associations of undertakings.

2. When sending a request for information to a person, an undertaking or an association of undertakings, the Commission shall at the same time send a copy of the request to the competent authority of the Member State within the territory of which the residence of the person or the seat of the undertaking or association of undertakings is situated.

3. In its request the Commission shall state the legal basis and the purpose of the request and also the penalties provided for in Article 14(1)(c) for supplying incorrect information.

4. The information requested shall be provided, in the case of undertakings, by their owners or their representatives and, in the case of legal persons, companies or firms, or of associations having no legal personality, by the persons authorized to represent them by law or by their statutes.

5. Where a person, an undertaking or an association of undertakings does not provide the information requested within the period fixed by the Commission or provides incomplete information, the Commission shall by decision require the information to be provided. The decision shall specify what information is required, fix an appropriate period within which it is to be supplied and state the penalties provided for in Articles 14(1)(c) and 15(1)(a) and the right to have the decision reviewed by the Court of Justice.

6. The Commission shall at the same time send a copy of its decision to the competent authority of the Member State within the territory of which the residence of the person or the seat of the undertaking or association of undertakings is situated.

Article 12

Investigations by the authorities of the Member States

1. At the request of the Commission, the competent authorities of the Member States shall undertake the investigations which the Commission considers to be necessary under Article 13(1), or which it has ordered by decision pursuant to Article 13(3). The officials of the competent authorities of the Member States responsible for conducting those investigations shall exercise their powers upon production of an authorization in writing issued by the competent authority of the Member State within the territory of which the investigation is to be carried out. Such authorization shall specify the subject matter and purpose of the investigation.

2. If so requested by the Commission or by the competent authority of the Member State within the territory of which the investigation is to be carried out, officials of the Commission may assist the officials of that authority in carrying out their duties.

Article 13

Investigative powers of the Commission

1. In carrying out the duties assigned to it by this Regulation, the Commission may undertake all necessary investigations into undertakings and associations of undertakings.

To that end the officials authorized by the Commission shall be empowered:

(a) to examine the books and other business records;

(b) to take or demand copies of or extracts from the books and business records;

(c) to ask for oral explanations on the spot;

(d) to enter any premises, land and means of transport of undertakings.

2. The officials of the Commission authorized to carry out the investigations shall exercise their powers on production of an authorization in writing specifying the subject matter and purpose of the investigation and the penalties provided for in Article 14(1)(d) in cases where production of the required books or other business records is incomplete. In good time before the investigation the Commission shall inform, in writing, the competent authority of the Member State within the territory of which the investigation is to be carried out of the investigation and of the identities of the authorized officials.

Undertakings and associations of undertakings shall submit to investigations ordered by decision of the Commission. The decision shall specify the subject matter and purpose of the investigation, appoint the date on which it shall begin and state the penalties provided for in Articles 14(1)(d) and 15(1)(b) and the right to have the decision reviewed by the Court of Justice.

4. The Commission shall in good time and in writing inform the competent authority of the Member State within the territory of which the investigation is to be carried out of its intention of taking a decision pursuant to paragraph 3. It shall hear the competent authority before taking its decision.

5. Officials of the competent authority of the Member State within the territory of which the investigation is to be carried out may, at the request of that authority or of the Commission, assist the officials of the Commission in carrying out their duties.

6. Where an undertaking or association of undertakings opposes an investigation ordered pursuant to this Article, the Member State concerned shall afford the necessary assistance to the officials authorized by the Commission to enable them to carry out their investigation. To this end the Member States shall, after consulting the Commission, take the necessary measures within one year of the entry into force of this Regulation.

Article 14

Fines

1. The Commission may by decision impose on the persons referred to in Article 3(1)(b), undertakings or associations of undertakings fines of from ECU 1000 to 50,000 where intentionally or negligently:

(a) they fail to notify a concentration in accordance with Article 4;

(b) they supply incorrect or misleading information in a notification pursuant to Article 4;

(c) they supply incorrect information in response to a request made pursuant to Article 11 or fail to supply information within the period fixed by a decision taken pursuant to Article 11;

(d) they produce the required books or other business records in incomplete form during investigations under Article 12 or 13, or refuse to submit to an investigation ordered by decision taken pursuant to Article 13.

2. The Commission may by decision impose fines not exceeding 10% of the aggregate turnover of the undertakings concerned within the meaning of Article 5 on the persons or undertakings concerned where, either intentionally or negligently, they:

(a) fail to comply with an obligation imposed by decision pursuant to Article 7(4) or 8(2), second subparagraph;

(b) put into effect a concentration in breach of Article 7(1) or disregard a decision taken pursuant to Article 7(2);

(c) put into effect a concentration declared incompatible with the common market by decision pursuant to Article 8(3) or do not take the measures ordered by decision pursuant to Article 8(4).

3. In setting the amount of a fine, regard shall be had to the nature and gravity of the infringement.

4. Decisions taken pursuant to paragraphs 1 and 2 shall not be of criminal law nature.

Article 15
Periodic penalty payments

1. The Commission may by decision impose on the persons referred to in Article 3(1)(b), undertakings or associations of undertakings concerned periodic penalty payments of up to ECU 25,000 for each day of delay calculated from the date set in the decision, in order to compel them:

(a) to supply complete and correct information which it has requested by decision pursuant to Article 11;

(b) to submit to an investigation which it has ordered by decision pursuant to Article 13.

2. The Commission may by decision impose on the persons referred to in Article 3(1)(b) or on undertakings periodic penalty payments of up to ECU 100,000 for each day of delay calculated from the date set in the decision, in order to compel them:

(a) to comply with an obligation imposed by decision pursuant to Article 7(4) or Article 8(2), second subparagraph, or

(b) to apply the measures ordered by decision pursuant to Article 8(4).

3. Where the persons referred to in Article 3(1)(b), undertakings or associations of undertakings have satisfied the obligation which it was the purpose of the periodic penalty payment to enforce, the Commission may set the total amount of the periodic penalty payments at a lower figure than that which would arise under the original decision.

Article 16
Review by the Court of Justice

The Court of Justice shall have unlimited jurisdiction within the meaning of Article 172 of the Treaty to review decisions whereby the Commission has fixed a fine or periodic penalty payments; it may cancel, reduce or increase the fine or periodic penalty payments imposed.

Article 17
Professional secrecy

1. Information acquired as a result of the application of Articles 11, 12, 13 and 18 shall be used only for the purposes of the relevant request, investigation or hearing.

2. Without prejudice to Articles 4(3), 18 and 20, the Commission and the competent authorities of the Member States, their officials and other

servants shall not disclose information they have acquired through the application of this Regulation of the kind covered by the obligation of professional secrecy.

3. Paragraphs 1 and 2 shall not prevent publication of general information or of surveys which do not contain information relating to particular undertakings or associations of undertakings.

Article 18

Hearing of the parties and of third persons

1. Before taking any decision provided for in Article 7(2) and (4), Article 8(2), second subparagraph, and (3) to (5) and Articles 14 and 15, the Commission shall give the persons, undertakings and associations of undertakings concerned the opportunity, at every stage of the procedure up to the consultation of the Advisory Committee, of making known their views on the objections against them.

2. By way of derogation from paragraph 1, a decision to continue the suspension of a concentration or to grant a derogation from suspension as referred to in Article 7(2) or (4) may be taken provisionally, without the persons, undertakings or associations of undertakings concerned being given the opportunity to make known their views beforehand, provided that the Commission gives them that opportunity as soon as possible after having taken its decision.

3. The Commission shall base its decision only on objections on which the parties have been able to submit their observations. The rights of the defence shall be fully respected in the proceedings. Access to the file shall be open at least to the parties directly involved, subject to the legitimate interest of undertakings in the protection of their business secrets.

4. In so far as the Commission or the competent authorities of the Member States deem it necessary, they may also hear other natural or legal persons. Natural or legal persons showing a sufficient interest and especially members of the administrative or management bodies of the undertakings concerned or the recognized representatives of their employees shall be entitled, upon application, to be heard.

Article 19

Liaison with the authorities of the Member States

1. The Commission shall transmit to the competent authorities of the Member States copies of notifications within three working days and, as soon as possible, copies of the most important documents lodged with or issued by the Commission pursuant to this Regulation.

2. The Commission shall carry out the procedures set out in this Regulation in close and constant liaison with the competent authorities of the Member States, which may express their views upon those procedures. For the purposes of Article 9 it shall obtain information from the competent authority of the Member State as referred to in paragraph 2 of that Article and give it the opportunity to make known its views at every stage

of the procedure up to the adoption of a decision pursuant to paragraph 3 of that Article; to that end it shall give it access to the file.

3. An Advisory Committee on concentrations shall be consulted before any decision is taken pursuant to Article 8(2) to (5), 14 or 15, or any provisions are adopted pursuant to Article 23.

4. The Advisory Committee shall consist of representatives of the authorities of the Member States. Each Member State shall appoint one or two representatives; if unable to attend, they may be replaced by other representatives. At least one of the representatives of a Member State shall be competent in matters of restrictive practices and dominant positions.

5. Consultation shall take place at a joint meeting convened at the invitation of and chaired by the Commission. A summary of the case, together with an indication of the most important documents and a preliminary draft of the decision to be taken for each case considered, shall be sent with the invitation. The meeting shall take place not less than 14 days after the invitation has been sent. The Commission may in exceptional cases shorten that period as appropriate in order to avoid serious harm to one or more of the undertakings concerned by a concentration.

6. The Advisory Committee shall deliver an opinion on the Commission's draft decision, if necessary by taking a vote. The Advisory Committee may deliver an opinion even if some members are absent and unrepresented. The opinion shall be delivered in writing and appended to the draft decision. The Commission shall take the utmost account of the opinion delivered by the Committee. It shall inform the Committee of the manner in which its opinion has been taken into account.

7. The Advisory Committee may recommend publication of the opinion. The Commission may carry out such publication. The decision to publish shall take due account of the legitimate interest of undertakings in the protection of their business secrets and of the interest of the undertakings concerned in such publication's taking place.

Article 20

Publication of decisions

1. The Commission shall publish the decisions which it takes pursuant to Article 8(2) to (5) in the *Official Journal of the European Communities*.

2. The publication shall state the names of the parties and the main content of the decision; it shall have regard to the legitimate interest of undertakings in the protection of their business secrets.

Article 21

Jurisdiction

1. Subject to review by the Court of Justice, the Commission shall have sole jurisdiction to take the decisions provided for in this Regulation.

2. No Member State shall apply its national legislation on competition to any consideration that has a Community dimension.

The first subparagraph shall be without prejudice to any Member State's power to carry out any enquiries necessary for the application of Article 9(2) or after referral, pursuant to Article 9(3), first subparagraph, indent (b), or (5), to take the measures strictly necessary for the application of Article 9(8).

3. Notwithstanding paragraphs 1 and 2, Member States may take appropriate measures to protect legitimate interests other than those taken into consideration by this Regulation and compatible with the general principles and other provisions of Community law.

Public security, plurality of the media and prudential rules shall be regarded as legitimate interests within the meaning of the first subparagraph.

Any other public interest must be communicated to the Commission by the Member State concerned and shall be recognized by the Commission after an assessment of its compatibility with the general principles and other provisions of Community law before the measures referred to above may be taken. The Commission shall inform the Member State concerned of its decision within one month of that communication.

Article 22

Application of the Regulation

1. This Regulation alone shall apply to concentrations as defined in Article 3.

2. Regulations No. 17, (EEC) No. 1017/68, (EEC) No. 4056/86 and (EEC) No. 3975/87 shall not apply to concentrations as defined in Article 3.

3. If the Commission finds, at the request of a Member State, that a concentration as defined in Article 3 that has no Community dimension within the meaning of Article 1 creates or strengthens a dominant position as a result of which effective competition would be significantly impeded within the territory of the Member State concerned it may, in so far as the concentration affects trade between Member States, adopt the decisions provided for in Article 8(2), second subparagraph, (3) and (4).

4. Articles 2(1)(a) and (b), 5, 6, 8 and 10 to 20 shall apply. The period within which proceedings may be initiated pursuant to Article 10(1) shall begin on the date of the receipt of the request from the Member State. The request must be made within one month at most of the date on which the concentration was made known to the Member State or effected. This period shall begin on the date of the first of those events.

5. Pursuant to paragraph 3 the Commission shall take only the measures strictly necessary to maintain or store effective competition within the territory of the Member State at the request of which it intervenes.

6. Paragraphs 3 to 5 shall continue to apply until the thresholds referred to in Article 1(2) have been reviewed.

Article 23
Implementing provisions

The Commission shall have the power to adopt implementing provisions concerning the form, content and other details of notifications pursuant to Article 4, time limits pursuant to Article 10, and hearings pursuant to Article 18.

Article 24
Relations with non-member countries

1. The Member States shall inform the Commission of any general difficulties encountered by their undertakings with concentrations as defined in Article 3 in a non-member country.

2. Initially not more than one year after the entry into force of this Regulation and thereafter periodically the Commission shall draw up a report examining the treatment accorded to Community undertakings, in the terms referred to in paragraphs 3 and 4, as regards concentrations in non-member countries. The Commission shall submit those reports to the Council, together with any recommendations.

3. Whenever it appears to the Commission, either on the basis of the reports referred to in paragraph 2 or on the basis of other information, that a non-member country does not grant Community undertakings treatment comparable to that granted by the Community to undertakings from that non-member country, the Commission may submit proposals to the Council for an appropriate mandate for negotiation with a view to obtaining comparable treatment for Community undertakings.

4. Measures taken under this Article shall comply with the obligations of the Community or of the Member States, without prejudice to Article 234 of the Treaty, under international agreements, whether bilateral or multilateral.

Article 25
Entry into force

1. This Regulation shall enter into force on 21 September 1990.

2. This Regulation shall not apply to any concentration which was the subject of an agreement or announcement or where control was acquired within the meaning of Article 4(1) before the date of this Regulation's entry into force and it shall not in any circumstances apply to any concentration in respect of which proceedings were initiated before that date by a Member State's authority with responsibility for competition.

This Regulation shall be binding in its entirety and directly applicable in all Member States.

Part IV

EXTERNAL RELATIONS AND COMMERCIAL POLICY

INTRODUCTION

We have selected only a few documents for Part IV. In the case of Chapter 26 on the external relations powers of the Community, the relevant documents are the EEC Treaty, the Single European Act and the Treaty on European Union, all of which are reproduced in the documents section for Part I.

Although there are many agreements documenting the EC's relationships with the various countries of the world, space considerations preclude including any of these agreements. Citations to the major agreements are given in Chapter 27.

With respect to customs law, the basic subject of Chapter 28, the Community adopted a Community Customs Code on October 12, 1992. Council Regulation (EEC) No. 2913/92 of October 12, 1992 establishing the Community Customs Code. O.J. L 302/1 (Oct. 19, 1992) (with effect from January 1, 1994). The Code deals comprehensively with customs law issues, except for classification and tariff rates, which will remain covered by the Taric. Since the Code was agreed upon too late for inclusion in the Documents Supplement, we have included in the Documents Supplement the current Regulation 802/68 on origin of goods and Regulation 1224/80 on customs valuation. The basic provisions in those regulations were not changed by the new customs code in any significant way.

In connection with Chapter 29, we have included two important documents. First is the Community regulation on antidumping and countervailing duties. The initial Regulation 459/68 on this subject was adopted in 1968, O.J. L 93/1 (Apr. 17, 1968), but did not cover a number of topics treated in the current regulation. Regulation 459/68 was replaced by Regulation 3017/79, O.J. L 339/1 (Dec. 31, 1979), which implemented into Community law the GATT Antidumping Code adopted in the Tokyo Round. The 1979 Regulation also significantly expanded the procedural rights of parties involved in these proceedings. Although Regulation 3017/79 was amended in certain details in the 1980s, its basic structure and provisions remain in place. We reproduce the 1988 version, Regulation 2423/88, which incorporates all amendments made since 1979.

We also include Regulation 2641/84 on illicit commercial practices. This regulation was adopted in part in response to the use by the United States of so-called Section 301 of the Trade Act of 1974 (actually now sections 301–310), 19 U.S.C. secs. 2411–2420.

We have not included any of the miscellaneous commercial policy regulations discussed in Chapter 30 in the Documents Supplement because they have not been often used. Citations to the principal miscellaneous regulations can be found in the casebook.

Table of Contents

PART IV EXTERNAL RELATIONS AND COMMERCIAL POLICY

Sec.
1. Council Regulation 1224/80 on the valuation of goods for customs purposes.
2. Council Regulation 802/68 on the common definition of the concept of the origin of goods.
3. Council Regulation 2423/88 on protection against dumped or subsidized imports from countries not members of the European Economic Community.
4. Council Regulation 2641/84 on the strengthening of the common commercial policy with regard to protection against illicit commercial practices.

1. COUNCIL REGULATION (EEC) 1224/80

of 28 May 1980
on the valuation of goods for customs purposes

OJ L 134/1 (May 31, 1980),
as amended by Regulation (EEC) 3193/80, O.J. L 333/1 (Dec. 11, 1980),
and Regulation (EEC) 1055/85, O.J. L 112/50 (Apr. 25, 1985).

[Editor's Note: The Community Customs Code (see Introduction to Part IV) deals with valuation in articles 28–36.]

* * *

TITLE 1
Article 1

1. In this Regulation:

(a) *"customs value"* means value for the purpose of applying the Common Customs Tariff;

(b) *"produced"* includes grown, manufactured and mined;

(c) *"identical goods"* means goods produced in the same country which are the same in all respects, including physical characteristics, quality and reputation. Minor differences in appearance shall not preclude goods otherwise conforming to the definition from being regarded as identical;

(d) *"similar goods"* means goods produced in the same country which, although not alike in all respects, have like characteristics and like component materials which enable them to perform the same functions and to be commercially interchangeable; the quality of the goods, their reputation and the existence of a trademark are among the factors to be considered in determining whether goods are similar;

(e) *"identical goods"* and *"similar goods"*, as the case may be, do not include goods which incorporate or reflect engineering, development, artwork, design work, and plans and sketches for which no adjustment has been made under Article 8(1)(b)(iv) because such elements were undertaken in the Community;

(f) *"goods of the same class or kind"* means goods which fall within a group or range of goods produced by a particular industry or industry sector, and includes identical or similar goods;

(g) *"the material time for valuation for customs purposes"* means:

  (i) for goods declared for direct entry into free circulation, the date of acceptance by the customs authorities of the declarant's statement of his intention that the goods should enter into free circulation,

  (ii) for goods which, after another customs procedure has been applied, enter into free circulation, the time fixed by acts of the

Council or the Commission pertaining to that customs procedure or by Member States in accordance with such acts;

(h) *"the Agreement"* means the Agreement on implementation of Article VII of the General Agreement on Tariffs and Trade concluded in the framework of the multilateral trade negotiations of 1973 to 1979.

2. For the purposes of this Regulation, persons shall be deemed to be related only if:

(a) they are officers or directors of one another's businesses;

(b) they are legally recognized partners in business;

(c) they are employer and employee;

(d) any person directly or indirectly owns, controls or holds 5% or more of the outstanding voting stock or shares of both of them;

(e) one of them directly or indirectly controls the other;

(f) both of them are directly or indirectly controlled by a third person;

(g) together they directly or indirectly control a third person; or

(h) they are members of the same family.

3. For the purpose of this Regulation, persons who are associated in business with one another in that one is the sole agent, sole distributor or sole concessionaire, however described, of the other shall be deemed to be related only if they fall within the criteria of paragraph 2.

4. For the purposes of this Regulation, the term "persons" means natural or legal persons.

Article 2

1. The customs value of imported goods is to be determined under Article 3 whenever the conditions prescribed therein are fulfilled.

2. Where such value cannot be determined under Article 3, it is to be determined by proceeding sequentially through Articles 4, 5, 6 and 7 to the first such Article under which it can be determined, subject to the proviso that the order of application of Articles 6 and 7 shall be reversed if the importer so requests; it is only when such value cannot be determined under a particular Article that the provisions of the next Article in a sequence established by virtue of this paragraph can be applied.

3. Where the customs value of imported goods cannot be determined under Article 3, 4, 5, 6 or 7, it shall be determined using reasonable means consistent with the principles and general provisions of the Agreement and of Article VII of the General Agreement on Tariffs and Trade and on the basis of data available in the Community.

4. No customs value shall be determined under paragraph 3 on the basis of:

(a) the selling price in the Community of goods produced in the Community;

(b) a system which provides for the acceptance for customs purposes of the higher of two alternative values;

(c) the price of goods on the domestic market of the country of exportation;

(d) the cost of production, other than computed values which have been determined for identical or similar goods in accordance with Article 7;

(e) prices for export to a country not comprised in the customs territory of the Community;

(f) minimum customs values; or

(g) arbitrary or fictitious values.

Article 3

1. The customs value of imported goods determined under this Article shall be the transaction value, that is, the price actually paid or payable for the goods when sold for export to the customs territory of the Community, adjusted in accordance with Article 8, provided:

(a) that there are no restrictions as to the disposition or use of the goods by the buyer, other than restrictions which:

   (i) are imposed or required by law or by the public authorities in the Community,
   (ii) limit the geographical area in which the goods may be resold, or
   (iii) do not substantially affect the value of the goods;

(b) that the sale or price is not subject to some condition or consideration for which a value cannot be determined with respect to the goods being valued;

(c) that no part of the proceeds of any subsequent resale, disposal or use of the goods by the buyer will accrue directly or indirectly to the seller, unless an appropriate adjustment can be made in accordance with Article 8; and

(d) that the buyer and seller are not related, or, where the buyer and seller are related, that the transaction value is acceptable for customs purposes under paragraph 2.

2. (a) In determining whether the transaction value is acceptable for the purposes of paragraph 1, the fact that the buyer and the seller are related within the meaning of Article 1 shall not in itself be grounds for regarding the transaction value as unacceptable. Where necessary, the circumstances surrounding the sale shall be examined and the transaction value shall be accepted provided that the relationship did not influence the price. If, in the light of information provided by the importer or otherwise, the customs administration has grounds for considering that the relationship influenced the price, it shall communicate its grounds to the importer and he shall be given a reasonable opportunity to respond.

If the importer so requests, the communication of the grounds shall be in writing.

(b) In a sale between related persons, the transaction value shall be accepted and the goods valued in accordance with paragraph 1 whenever the importer demonstrates that such value closely approximates to one of the following occurring at or about the same time:

- (i) the transaction value in sales, between buyers and sellers who are not related in any particular case, of identical or similar goods for export to the Community;
- (ii) the customs value of identical or similar goods, as determined under Article 6;
- (iii) the customs value of identical or similar goods, as determined under Article 7;

In applying the foregoing tests, due account shall be taken of demonstrated differences in commercial levels, quantity levels, the elements enumerated in Article 8 and costs incurred by the seller in sales in which he and the buyer are not related that are not incurred by the seller in sales in which he and the buyer are related.

(c) The tests set forth in paragraph 2(b) are to be used at the initiative of the importer and only for comparison purposes. Substitute values may not be established under the said paragraph 2(b).

3. (a) The price actually paid or payable is the total payment made or to be made by the buyer to or for the benefit of the seller for the imported goods and includes all payments made or to be made as a condition of sale of the imported goods by the buyer to the seller or by the buyer to a third party to satisfy an obligation of the seller. The payment need not necessarily take the form of a transfer of money. Payment may be made by way of letters of credit or negotiable instruments and may be made directly or indirectly.

(b) Activities, including marketing activities, undertaken by the buyer on his own account, other than those for which an adjustment is provided in Article 8, are not considered to be an indirect payment to the seller, even though they might be regarded as of benefit to the seller or have been undertaken by agreement with the seller, and their cost shall not be added to the price actually paid or payable in determining the customs value of imported goods.

4. The customs value of imported goods shall not include the following charges or costs, provided that they are distinguished from the price actually paid or payable for the imported goods:

(a) charges for construction, erection, assembly, maintenance or technical assistance, undertaken after importation on imported goods such as industrial plant, machinery or equipment;

(b) customs duties and other taxes payable in the Community by reason of the importation or sale of the goods.

Article 4

1. (a) The customs value of imported goods determined under this Article shall be the transaction value of identical goods sold for export to the Community and exported at or about the same time as the goods being valued.

(b) In applying this Article, the transaction value of identical goods in a sale at the same commercial level and in substantially the same quantity as the goods being valued shall be used to determine the customs value. Where no such sale is found, the transaction value of identical goods sold at a different commercial level and/or in different quantities, adjusted to take account of differences attributable to commercial level and/or to quantity, shall be used, provided that such adjustments can be made on the basis of demonstrated evidence which clearly establishes the reasonableness and accuracy of the adjustment, whether the adjustment leads to an increase or a decrease in the value.

2. Where the costs and charges referred to in Article 8(1)(e) are included in the transaction value, an adjustment shall be made to take account of significant differences in such costs and charges between the imported goods and the identical goods in question arising from differences in distances and modes of transport.

3. If, in applying this Article, more than one transaction value of identical goods is found, the lowest such value shall be used to determine the customs value of the imported goods.

4. In applying this Article, a transaction value for goods produced by a different person shall be taken into account only when no transaction value can be found under paragraph 1 for identical goods produced by the same person as the goods being valued.

5. For the purposes of this Article, the transaction value of identical imported goods means a customs value previously determined under Article 3, adjusted as provided for in paragraphs 1(b) and 2 of this Article.

Article 5

1. (a) The customs value of imported goods determined under this Article shall be the transaction value of similar goods sold for export to the Community and exported at or about the same time as the goods being valued.

(b) In applying this Article, the transaction value of similar goods in a sale at the same commercial level and in substantially the same quantity as the goods being valued shall be used to determine the customs value. Where no such sale is found, the transaction value of similar goods sold at a different commercial level and/or in different quantities, adjusted to take account of differences attributable to commercial level and/or to quantity, shall be used, provided that such adjustments can be made on the basis of demonstrated evidence which clearly establishes the reasonableness and accuracy of the adjustment, whether the adjustment leads to an increase or a decrease in the value.

[Paragraphs 2-5 of Article 5 are the same as paragraphs 2-5 of Article 4, with "similar" goods substituted for "identical" goods.]

* * *

Article 6

1. (a) If the imported goods or identical or similar imported goods are sold in the Community in the condition as imported, the customs value of imported goods, determined under this Article, shall be based on the unit price at which the imported goods or identical or similar imported goods are so sold in the greatest aggregate quantity, at or about the time of the importation of the goods being valued, to persons who are not related to the persons from whom they buy such goods, subject to deductions for the following:

(i) either the commissions usually paid or agreed to be paid or the additions usually made for profit and general expenses (including the direct and indirect costs of marketing the goods in question) in connection with sales in the Community of imported goods of the same class or kind;

(ii) the usual costs of transport and insurance and associated costs incurred within the Community; and

(iii) the customs duties and other taxes payable in the Community by reason of the importation or sale of the goods.

(b) If neither the imported goods nor identical nor similar imported goods are sold at or about the time of importation of the goods being valued, the customs value of imported goods determined under this Article shall, subject otherwise to the provisions of paragraph 1(a), be based on the unit price at which the imported goods or identical or similar imported goods are sold in the Community in the condition as imported at the earliest date after the importation of the goods being valued but before the expiration of 90 days after such importation.

2. If neither the imported goods nor identical nor similar imported goods are sold in the Community in the condition as imported, then, if the importer so requests, the customs value shall be based on the unit price at which the imported goods, after further processing, are sold in the greatest aggregate quantity to persons in the Community who are not related to the persons from whom they buy such goods, due allowance being made for the value added by such processing and the deductions provided for in paragraph 1(a).

3. In this Article, the unit price at which imported goods are sold in the greatest aggregate quantity is the price at which the greatest number of units is sold in sales to persons who are not related to the persons from whom they buy such goods at the first commercial level after importation at which such sales take place.

4. Any sale in the Community to a person who supplies directly or indirectly free of charge or at reduced cost for use in connection with the

production and sale for export of the imported goods any of the elements specified in Article 8(1)(b), should not be taken into account in establishing the unit price for the purposes of this Article.

5. For the purposes of paragraph 1(b), the "earliest date" shall be the date by which sales of the imported goods or of identical or similar imported goods are made in sufficient quantity to establish the unit price.

Article 7

1. The customs value of imported goods determined under this Article shall be based on a computed value. Computed value shall consist of the sum of:

(a) the cost or value of materials and fabrication or other processing employed in producing the imported goods;

(b) an amount for profit and general expenses equal to that usually reflected in sales of goods of the same class or kind as the goods being valued which are made by producers in the country of exportation for export to the Community;

(c) the cost or value of the items referred to in Article 8(1)(e).

2. A customs administration may not require or compel any person not resident in the Community to produce for examination, or to allow access to, any account or other record for the purposes of determining a computed value. However, information supplied by the producer of the goods for the purposes of determining the customs value under this Article may be verified in a non-Community country by the customs authorities of a Member State with the agreement of the producer and provided that such authorities give sufficient advance notice to the government of the country in question and the latter does not object to the investigation.

3. The cost of value of materials and fabrication referred to in paragraph 1(a) above shall include the cost of elements specified in Article 8(1)(a)(ii) and (iii). It shall also include the value, duly apportioned, of any element specified in Article 8(1)(b) which has been supplied directly or indirectly by the buyer for use in connection with the production of the imported goods. The value of the elements specified in Article 8(1)(b)(iv) which are undertaken in the Community shall be included only to the extent that such elements are charged to the producer.

4. Where information other than that supplied by or on behalf of the producer is used for the purposes of determining a computed value, the customs authorities shall inform the importer, if the latter so requests, of the source of such information, the data used and the calculations based on such data, subject to Article 10.

5. The "general expenses" referred to in paragraph 1(b) above, cover the direct and indirect costs of producing and selling the goods for export which are not included under paragraph 1(a).

Article 8

1. In determining the customs value under Article 3, there shall be added to the price actually paid or payable for the imported goods:

(a) the following, to the extent that they are incurred by the buyer but are not included in the price actually paid or payable for the goods:

- (i) commissions and brokerage, except buying commissions,
- (ii) the cost of containers which are treated as being one for customs purposes with the goods in question,
- (iii) the cost of packing, whether for labour or materials;

(b) the value, apportioned as appropriate, of the following goods and services where supplied directly or indirectly by the buyer free of charge or at reduced cost for use in connection with the production and sale for export of the imported goods, to the extent that such value has not been included in the price actually paid or payable:

- (i) materials, components, parts and similar items incorporated in the imported goods,
- (ii) tools, dies, moulds and similar items used in the production of the imported goods,
- (iii) materials consumed in the production of the imported goods,
- (iv) engineering, development, artwork, design work, and plans and sketches undertaken elsewhere than in the Community and necessary for the production of the imported goods;

(c) royalties and licence fees related to the goods being valued that the buyer must pay, either directly or indirectly, as a condition of sale of the goods being valued, to the extent that such royalties and fees are not included in the price actually paid or payable;

(d) the value of any part of the proceeds of any subsequent resale, disposal or use of the imported goods that accrues directly or indirectly to the seller;

(e) (i) the cost of transport and insurance of the imported goods, and
    (ii) loading and handling charges associated with the transport of the imported goods

to the place of introduction of the goods into the customs territory of the Community.

2. Additions to the price actually paid or payable shall be made under this Article only on the basis of objective and quantifiable data.

3. No additions shall be made to the price actually paid or payable in determining the customs value except as provided in this Article.

4. In this Article, the term "buying commissions" means fees paid by an importer to his agent for the service of representing him in the purchase of the goods being valued.

5. Notwithstanding paragraph 1(c) of this Article:

(a) charges for the right to reproduce the imported goods in the Community shall not be added to the price actually paid or payable for the imported goods in determining the customs value; and

(b) payments made by the buyer for the right to distribute or resell the imported goods shall not be added to the price actually paid or payable for the imported goods if such payments are not a condition of the sale for export to the Community of the goods.

Article 8a

1. Notwithstanding Articles 2 to 8, in determining the customs value of imported carrier media for use in data processing equipment and bearing data or instructions, only the cost or value of the carrier medium itself shall be taken into account. The customs value of imported carrier media bearing data or instructions shall not, therefore, include the cost or value of the data or instructions, provided that such cost or value is distinguished from the cost or value of the carrier medium in question.

2. For the purposes of this Article:

(a) the expression "carrier medium" shall not be taken to include integrated circuits, semiconductors and similar devices or articles incorporating such circuits or devices;

(b) the expression "data or instructions" shall not be taken to include sound, cinematographic or video recordings.

Article 9

1. (a) Where factors used to determine the customs value of goods are expressed in a currency other than that of the Member State where the valuation is made, the rate of exchange to be used shall be that duly published by the competent authorities of the Member State concerned.

(b) Such rate shall reflect as effectively as possible the current value of such currency in commercial transactions in terms of the currency of such Member State and shall apply during such period as may be specified by the aforementioned competent authorities.

2. (a) Until such time as a rate of exchange is published in accordance with paragraph 1, the rate of exchange to be used shall be the latest selling rate recorded on the most representative exchange market or markets of the Member State concerned at the material time for valuation for customs purposes.

(b) Where such a rate does not exist, the rate of exchange to be used shall be determined by the procedure laid down in Article 19.

* * *

Article 14

1. For the purposes of Article 8(1)(e) and Article 15, the place of introduction into the customs territory of the Community shall be:

(a) for goods carried by sea, the port of unloading, or the port of transhipment, subject to transhipment being certified by the customs authorities of that port;

(b) for goods carried by sea and then, without transhipment, by inland waterway, the first port where unloading can take place either at the mouth of the river or canal or further inland, subject to proof being furnished to the customs authorities that the freight to the port of unloading is higher than that to the first port;

(c) for goods carried by rail, inland waterway, or road, the place where the first customs office is situated;

(d) for goods carried by other means, the place where the land frontier of the customs territory of the Community is crossed.

2. For goods introduced into the customs territory of the Community and then carried to a destination in another part of that territory through the territory of a third country or by sea, after passing through a part of the customs territory of the Community, the place of introduction into the Community to be taken into consideration shall, subject to paragraph 3, be determined in accordance with the procedure laid down in Article 19.

3. For goods introduced into the customs territory of the Community and carried directly from one of the French overseas departments to another part of the Customs territory of the Community or vice versa, the place of introduction to be taken into consideration shall be the place referred to in paragraphs 1 and 2 situated in that part of the customs territory of the Community from which the goods came, if they were unloaded or transhipped there and this was certified by the customs authorities.

When those conditions are not fulfilled, the place of introduction to be taken into consideration shall be the place specified in paragraphs 1 and 2 situated in that part of the customs territory of the Community to which the goods are consigned.

Article 15

1. The customs value of imported goods shall not include the cost of transport after importation into the customs territory of the Community provided that such cost is distinguished from the price actually paid or payable for the imported goods.

2. (a) Where goods are carried by the same mode of transport to a point beyond the place of introduction into the customs territory of the Community, transport costs shall be assessed in proportion to the distance covered outside and inside the customs territory of the Community, unless evidence is produced to the customs authorities to show the costs that would have been incurred under a general compulsory schedule of freight rates for the carriage of the goods to the place of introduction into the customs territory of the Community.

The preceding subparagraph shall not apply to goods sent by post. Special provisions may be adopted for such goods in accordance with the procedure laid down in Article 19, in view of the special nature of charges in international postal services.

(b) Where goods are invoiced at a uniform free domicile price which corresponds to the price at the place of introduction, transport costs within the Community shall not be deducted from that price. However, such deduction shall be allowed if evidence is produced to the customs authorities that the free-frontier price would be lower than the uniform free domicile price.

(c) Where transport is free or provided by the buyer, transport costs to the place of introduction, calculated in accordance with the schedule of freight rates normally applied for the same modes of transport, shall be included in the customs value.

* * *

[Title II of the Regulation (Articles 17–19) establishes and provides for the operation of a Customs Valuation Committee made up of Member State representatives and chaired by the Commission.]

2. COUNCIL REGULATION (EEC) 802/68

of 27 June 1968
on the common definition of the concept of the origin of goods

O.J. English Spec.Ed.1968, at 165,
as amended by Regulation 1318/71 O.J. L 139/1 (June 26, 1971)

[Editor's Note: The Community Customs Code (see Introduction to Part IV) deals with origin in articles 22–27.]

Article 1

This Regulation defines the concept of the origin of goods for purposes of:

(a) the uniform application of the Common Customs Tariff, of quantitative restrictions, and of all other measures adopted, in relation to the importation of goods, by the Community or by Member States;

(b) the uniform application of all measures adopted, in relation to the exportation of goods, by the Community or by Member States;

(c) the preparation and issue of certificates of origin.

Article 2

This Regulation shall be without prejudice to the special rules concerning:

— trade between the Community or Member States and the countries to which the Community or Member States are bound by agreements which derogate from the most-favoured-nation clause, and in particular those establishing a customs union or a free-trade area;

— trade to which preferences granted by the Community unilaterally in derogation from the most-favoured-nation clause are applicable.

Article 4

1. Goods wholly obtained or produced in one country shall be considered as originating in that country.

2. The expression 'goods wholly obtained or produced in one country' means:

(a) mineral products extracted within its territory;

(b) vegetable products harvested therein;

(c) live animals born and raised therein;

(d) products derived from live animals raised therein;

(e) products of hunting or fishing carried on therein;

(f) products of sea-fishing and other products taken from the sea by vessels registered or recorded in that country and flying its flag;

(g) goods obtained on board factory ships from the products referred to in (f) originating in that country, if such factory ships are registered or recorded in that country and flying its flag;

(h) products taken from the sea-bed or beneath the sea-bed outside territorial waters, if that country has, for the purposes of exploitation, exclusive rights to such soil or subsoil;

(i) waste and scrap products derived from manufacturing operations and used articles, if they were collected therein and are only fit for the recovery of raw materials;

(j) goods which are produced therein exclusively from goods referred to in subparagraphs (a) to (i) or from their derivatives, at any stage of production.

Article 5

A product in the production of which two or more countries were concerned shall be regarded as originating in the country in which the last substantial process or operation that is economically justified was performed, having been carried out in an undertaking equipped for the purpose, and resulting in the manufacture of a new product or representing an important stage of manufacture.

Article 6

Any process or work in respect of which it is established, or in respect of which the facts as ascertained justify the presumption, that its sole object was to circumvent the provisions applicable in the Community or the Member States to goods from specific countries shall in no case be considered, under Article 5, as conferring on the goods thus produced the origin of the country where it is carried out.

Article 7

Accessories, spare parts or tools delivered with any piece of equipment, machine, apparatus or vehicle which form part of its standard equipment shall be deemed to have the same origin as that piece of equipment, machine, apparatus or vehicle.

The circumstances in which the presumption of origin referred to in the preceding paragraph shall also apply to essential spare parts for use with any piece of equipment, machine, apparatus or vehicle dispatched beforehand, shall be determined in accordance with the procedure laid down in Article 14.

Article 8

For purposes of application of Articles 4 to 7, the Member States shall be considered as constituting a single territorial unit.

Article 9

1. When the origin of a product has to be proved on importation by the production of a certificate of origin, that certificate shall fulfil the following conditions:

(a) It must be prepared by a reliable authority or agency duly authorised for that purpose by the country of issue;

(b) It must contain all the particulars necessary for identifying the product to which it relates, in particular

— the number of packages, their nature, and the marks and numbers they bear,

— the kind of product,

— the gross and net weight of the product; these particulars may, however, be replaced by others, such as the number or volume, when the product is subject to appreciable changes in weight during carriage or when its weight cannot be ascertained or when it is normally identified by such other particulars,

— the name of the consignor.

(c) It must certify unambiguously that the product to which it relates originated in a specific country.

2. Notwithstanding the production of a certificate of origin which fulfils the conditions prescribed by paragraph 1, the competent authorities may, if there is cause for serious doubt, demand any additional proof with the object of ensuring that the indication of origin conforms to the rules laid down in this Regulation and to the provisions adopted for its implementation.

Article 10

1. Certificates of origin for goods originating in and exported from the Community must comply with the conditions prescribed by Article 9(1)(a) and (b).

2. Such certificates of origin shall certify that the goods originated in the Community.

However, when the needs of the export trade so require, they may certify that the goods originated in a particular Member State.

If the conditions of Article 5 are fulfilled only as a result of a series of operations or processes carried out in different Member States, the goods may only be certified as being of Community origin.

3. Member States shall take the requisite steps to ensure that by the end of the transitional period at the latest the certificates of origin issued by their authorities or authorised agencies are prepared and issued in accordance with the provisions of Annex II, in so far as the needs of the export trade do not otherwise require.

Article 11

Each Member State shall inform the Commission of the steps taken by its central administration for the purposes of applying this Regulation, and of any problems which have arisen in connection with its application. The Commission shall forthwith communicate this information to the other Member States.

Article 12

1. A Committee on Origin (hereinafter called the 'Committee') shall be set up and shall consist of representatives of the Member States, with a representative of the Commission acting as Chairman.

2. The Committee shall draw up its own rules of procedure.

Article 13

The Committee may examine all questions relating to the application of this Regulation referred to it by its Chairman, either on his own initiative or at the request of a representative of a Member State.

Article 14

1. The provisions required for applying Articles 4 to 7, 9 and 10 shall be adopted in accordance with the procedure laid down in paragraphs 2 and 3 of this Article.

2. The representative of the Commission shall submit to the Committee a draft of the provisions to be adopted. The Committee shall deliver an Opinion on the draft within a time limit set by the Chairman having regard to the urgency of the matter. Decisions shall be taken by a majority of 54 votes, the votes of the Member States being weighted as provided in Article 148(2) of the Treaty. The Chairman shall not vote.

3. (a) The Commission shall adopt the envisaged provisions if they are in accordance with the Opinion of the Committee.

(b) If the envisaged provisions are not in accordance with the Opinion of the Committee, or if no Opinion is delivered, the Commission shall without delay submit to the Council a proposal with regard to the provisions to be adopted.

The Council shall act by a qualified majority.

(c) If, within three months of the proposal being submitted to it, the Council has not acted, the proposed provisions shall be adopted by the Commission.

Article 15

If the provisions in force in a Member State for the issue of certificates of origin for exports are so altered by the provisions referred to in Article 14 that an economic activity is affected, the Commission may authorise the Member State in question at the request thereof to defer the application of the provisions referred to in Article 14 in respect of a specific product for a period not exceeding one year from the entry into force of those provisions.

This Article shall remain in force for a period of five years from the date of entry into force of this Regulation.

Article 16

This Regulation shall be applicable in the French overseas departments.

Article 17

This Regulation shall enter into force on 1 July 1968.

3. COUNCIL REGULATION (EEC) 2423/88

of 11 July 1988

on protection against dumped or subsidized imports from countries not members of the European Economic Community

O.J. L 209/1 (Aug. 2, 1988)

THE COUNCIL OF THE EUROPEAN COMMUNITIES,

* * *

Having regard to the Treaty establishing the European Economic Community, and in particular Article 113 thereof.

Whereas these rules were adopted in accordance with existing international obligations, in particular those arising from Article VI of the General Agreement on Tariffs and Trade (hereinafter referred to as 'GATT'), from the Agreement on Implementation of Article VI of the GATT (1979 Anti-Dumping Code) and from the Agreement on Interpretation and Application of Articles VI, XVI and XXIII of the GATT (Code on Subsidies and Countervailing Duties);

Whereas in applying these rules it is essential, in order to maintain the balance of rights and obligations which these Agreements sought to establish, that the Community take account of their interpretation by the Community's major trading partners, as reflected in legislation or established practice;

* * *

HAS ADOPTED THIS REGULATION:

Article 1
Applicability

This Regulation lays down provisions for protection against dumped or subsidized imports from countries not members of the European Economic Community.

Article 2
Dumping

A. PRINCIPLE

1. An anti-dumping duty may be applied to any dumped product whose release for free circulation in the Community causes injury.

2. A product shall be considered to have been dumped if its export price to the Community is less than the normal value of the like product.

B. NORMAL VALUE

3. For the purposes of this Regulation, the normal value shall be:

(a) the comparable price actually paid or payable in the ordinary course of trade for the like product intended for consumption in the exporting country or country of origin. This price shall be net of all discounts and rebates directly linked to the sales under consideration provided that the exporter claims and supplies sufficient evidence that any such reduction from the gross price has actually been granted. Deferred discounts may be recognized if they are directly linked to the sales under consideration and if evidence is produced to show that these discounts were based on consistent practice in prior periods or on an undertaking to comply with the conditions required to qualify for the deferred discount.

(b) when there are no sales of the like product in the ordinary course of trade on the domestic market of the exporting country or country of origin, or when such sales do not permit a proper comparison:

(i) the comparable price of the like product when exported to any third country, which may be the highest such export price but should be a representative price; or

(ii) the constructed value, determined by adding cost of production and a reasonable margin of profit. The cost of production shall be computed on the basis of all costs, in the ordinary course of trade, both fixed and variable, in the country of origin, of materials and manufacture, plus a reasonable amount for selling, administrative and other general expenses. The amount for selling, general and administrative expenses and profit shall be calculated by reference to the expenses incurred and the profit realized by the producer or exporter on the profitable sales of like products on the domestic market. If such data is unavailable or unreliable or is not suitable for use they shall be calculated by reference to the expenses incurred and profit realized by other producers or exporters in the country of origin or export on profitable sales of the like product. If neither of these two methods can be applied the expenses incurred and the profit realized shall be calculated by reference to the sales made by the exporter or other producers or exporters in the same business sector in the country of origin or export or on any other reasonable basis.

(c) Where the exporter in the country of origin neither produces nor sells the like product in the country of origin, the normal value shall be established on the basis of prices or costs of other sellers or producers in the country of origin in the same manner as mentioned in subparagraphs (a) and (b). Normally the prices or costs of the exporter's supplier shall be used for this purpose.

4. Whenever there are reasonable grounds for believing or suspecting that the price at which a product is actually sold for consumption in the country of origin is less than the cost of production as defined in paragraph 3(b)(ii), sales at such prices may be considered as not having been made in the ordinary course of trade if they:

(a) have been made in substantial quantities during the investigation period as defined in Article 7(1)(c); and

(b) are not at prices which permit recovery, in the normal course of trade and within the period referred to in paragraph (a), of all costs reasonably allocated.

In such circumstances, the normal value may be determined on the basis of the remaining sales on the domestic market made at a price which is not less than the cost of production or on the basis of export sales to third countries or on the basis of the constructed value or by adjusting the sub-production-cost price referred to above in order to eliminate loss and provide for a reasonable profit. Such normal value calculations shall be based on available information.

5. In the case of imports from non-market economy countries and, in particular, those to which Regulations (EEC) No 1765/82 and (EEC) No 1766/82 apply, normal value shall be determined in an appropriate and not unreasonable manner on the basis of one of the following criteria:

(a) the price at which the like product of a market economy third country is actually sold:

(i) for consumption on the domestic market of that country; or

(ii) to other countries, including the Community; or

(b) the constructed value of the like product in a market economy third country;

(c) if neither price nor constructed value as established under (a) or (b) provides an adequate basis, the price actually paid or payable in the Community for the like product, duly adjusted, if necessary, to include a reasonable profit margin.

6. Where a product is not imported directly from the country of origin but is exported to the Community from an intermediate country, the normal value shall be the comparable price actually paid or payable for the like product on the domestic market of either the country of export or the country of origin. The latter basis might be appropriate *inter alia,* where the product is merely transhipped through the country of export, where such products are not produced in the country of export or where no comparable price for it exists in the country of export.

7. For the purpose of determining normal value transactions between parties which appear to be associated or to have a compensatory arrangement with each other may be considered as not being in the ordinary course of trade unless the Community authorities are satisfied that the prices and costs involved are comparable to those involved in transactions between parties which have no such link.

C. EXPORT PRICE

8. (a) The export price shall be the price actually paid or payable for the product sold for export to the Community net of all taxes, discounts and rebates actually granted and directly related to the sales under consideration. Deferred discounts shall also be taken into consideration if they are actually granted and directly related to the sales under consideration.

(b) In cases where there is no export price or where it appears that there is an association or a compensatory arrangement between the exporter and the importer or a third party, or that for other reasons the price actually paid or payable for the product sold for export to the Community is unreliable, the export price may be constructed on the basis of the price at which the imported product is first resold to an independent buyer, or if the product is not resold to an independent buyer, or not resold in the condition imported, on any reasonable basis. In such cases, allowance shall be made for all costs incurred between importation and resale and for a reasonable profit margin. These costs shall include those normally borne by an importer but paid by any party either in or outside the Community which appears to be associated or to have a compensatory arrangement with the importer or exporter.

Such allowances shall include, in particular, the following:

(i) usual transport, insurance, handling, loading and ancillary costs;

(ii) customs duties, any anti-dumping duties and other taxes payable in the importing country by reason of the importation or sale of the goods;

(iii) a reasonable margin for overheads and profit and/or any commission usually paid or agreed.

D. COMPARISON

9. (a) The normal value, as established under paragraphs 3 to 7, and the export price, as established under paragraph 8, shall be compared as nearly as possible at the same time. For the purpose of ensuring a fair comparison, due allowance in the form of adjustments shall be made in each case, on its merits, for the differences affecting price comparability, i.e. for differences in:

(i) physical characteristics;

(ii) import charges and indirect taxes;

(iii) selling expenses resulting from sales made:

— at different levels of trade, or

— in different quantities, or

— under different conditions and terms of sale.

(b) Where an interested party claims an adjustment it must prove that its claim is justified.

10. Any adjustments to take account of the differences affecting price comparability listed in paragraph 9(a) shall, where warranted, be made pursuant to the rules specified below.

(a) *Physical characteristics:*

The normal value as established under paragraphs 3 to 7 shall be adjusted by an amount corresponding to a reasonable estimate of the value of the difference in the physical characteristics of the product concerned.

(b) *Import charges and indirect taxes:*

Normal value shall be reduced by an amount corresponding to any import charges or indirect taxes, as defined in the notes to the Annex, borne by the like product and by materials physically incorporated therein, when destined for consumption in the country of origin or export and not collected or refunded in respect of the product exported to the Community.

(c) *Selling expenses* (i.e.):

(i) Transport, insurance, handling, loading and ancillary costs:

Normal value shall be reduced by the directly related costs incurred for conveying the product concerned from the premises of the exporter to the first independent buyer. The export price shall be reduced by any directly related costs incurred by the exporter for conveying the product concerned from its premises in the exporting country to its destination in the Community. In both cases these costs comprise transport, insurance, handling, loading and ancillary costs.

(ii) Packing:

Normal value and export price shall be reduced by the respective, directly related costs of the packing for the product concerned.

(iii) Credit:

Normal value and export price shall be reduced by the cost of any credit granted for the sales under consideration.

The amount of the reduction shall be calculated by reference to the normal commercial credit rate applicable in the country of origin or export in respect of the currency expressed on the invoice.

(iv) Warranties, guarantees, technical assistance and other after-sales services:

Normal value and export price shall be reduced by an amount corresponding to the direct costs of providing warranties, guarantees, technical assistance and services.

(v) Other selling expenses:

Normal value and export price shall be reduced by an amount corresponding to the commissions paid in respect of the sales under consideration. The salaries paid to salesmen, i.e. personnel wholly engaged in direct selling activities, shall also be deducted.

(d) *Amount of the adjustment*

The amount of any adjustment shall be calculated on the basis of relevant data for the investigation period or the data for the last available financial year.

(e) *Insignificant adjustments:*

Claims for adjustments which are insignificant in relation to the price or value of the affected transactions shall be disregarded. Ordinarily, individual adjustments having an *ad valorem* effect of less than 0.5% of that price or value shall be considered insignificant.

E. ALLOCATION OF COSTS

11. In general, all cost calculations shall be based on available accounting data, normally allocated, where necessary, in proportion to the turnover for each product and market under consideration.

F. LIKE PRODUCT

12. For the purposes of this Regulation, 'like product' means a product which is identical, i.e., alike in all respects, to the product under consideration, or, in the absence of such a product, another product which has characteristics closely resembling those of the product under consideration.

G. AVERAGING AND SAMPLING TECHNIQUES

13. Where prices vary:

— normal value shall normally be established on a weighted average basis,

— export prices shall normally be compared with the normal value on a transaction-by-transaction basis except where the use of weighted averages would not materially affect the results of the investigation,

— sampling techniques, e.g. the use of the most frequently occurring or representative prices may be applied to establish normal value and export prices in cases in which a significant volume of transactions is involved.

H. DUMPING MARGIN

14. (a) 'Dumping margin' means the amount by which the normal value exceeds the export price.

(b) Where dumping margins vary, weighted averages may be established.

Article 3

Subsidies

1. A countervailing duty may be imposed for the purpose of offsetting any subsidy bestowed, directly or indirectly, in the country of origin or export, upon the manufacture, production, export or transport of any product whose release for free circulation in the Community causes injury.

2. Subsidies bestowed on exports include, but are not limited to, the practices listed in the Annex.

3. The exemption of a product from import charges or indirect taxes, as defined in the notes to the Annex, effectively borne by the like product and by materials physically incorporated therein, when destined for

consumption in the country of origin or export, or the refund of such charges or taxes, shall not be considered as a subsidy for the purposes of this Regulation.

4. (a) The amount of the subsidy shall be determined per unit of the subsidized product exported to the Community.

(b) In establishing the amount of any subsidy the following elements shall be deducted from the total subsidy:

(i) any application fee, or other costs necessarily incurred in order to qualify for, or receive benefit of, the subsidy;

(ii) export taxes, duties or other charges levied on the export of the product to the Community specifically intended to offset the subsidy.

Where an interested party claims a deduction, it must prove that the claim is justified.

(c) Where the subsidy is not granted by reference to the quantities manufactured, produced, exported or transported, the amount shall be determined by allocating the value of the subsidy, as appropriate, over the level of production or exports of the products concerned during a suitable period. Normally this period shall be the accounting year of the beneficiary.

Where the subsidy is based upon the acquisition or future acquisition of fixed assets, the value of the subsidy shall be calculated by spreading the subsidy across a period which reflects the normal depreciation of such assets in the industry concerned. Where the assets are non-depreciating, the subsidy shall be valued as an interest-free loan.

(d) In the case of imports from non-market economy countries and in particular those to which Regulations (EEC) No 1765/82 and (EEC) No 1766/82 apply, the amount of any subsidy may be determined in an appropriate and not unreasonable manner, by comparing the export price as calculated in accordance with Article 2(8) with the normal value as determined in accordance with Article 2(5). Article 2(10) shall apply to such a comparison.

(e) Where the amount of subsidization varies, weighted averages may be established.

Article 4
Injury

1. A determination of injury shall be made only if the dumped or subsidized imports are, through the effects of dumping or subsidization, causing injury i.e., causing or threatening to cause material injury to an established Community industry or materially retarding the establishment of such an industry. Injuries caused by other factors, such as volume and prices of imports which are not dumped or subsidized, or contraction in demand, which, individually or in combination, also adversely affect the Community industry must not be attributed to the dumped or subsidized imports.

2. An examination of injury shall involve the following factors, no one or several of which can necessarily give decisive guidance:

(a) volume of dumped or subsidized imports, in particular whether there has been a significant increase, either in absolute terms or relative to production or consumption in the Community;

(b) the prices of dumped or subsidized imports, in particular whether there has been a significant price undercutting as compared with the price of a like product in the Community;

(c) the consequent impact on the industry concerned as indicated by actual or potential trends in the relevant economic factors such as:

— production,

— utilization of capacity,

— stocks,

— sales,

— market share,

— prices (i.e., depression of prices or prevention of price increases which otherwise would have occurred),

— profits,

— return on investment,

— cash flow,

— employment.

3. A determination of threat of injury may only be made where a particular situation is likely to develop into actual injury. In this regard account may be taken of factors such as:

(a) rate of increase of the dumped or subsidized exports to the Community;

(b) export capacity in the country of origin or export, already in existence or which will be operational in the foreseeable future, and the likelihood that the resulting exports will be to the Community;

(c) the nature of any subsidy and the trade effects likely to arise therefrom.

4. The effect of the dumped or subsidized imports shall be assessed in relation to the Community production of the like product when available data permit its separate identification. When the Community production of the like product has no separate identity, the effect of the dumped or subsidized imports shall be assessed in relation to the production of the narrowest group or range of production which includes the like product for which the necessary information can be found.

5. The term 'Community industry' shall be interpreted as referring to the Community producers as a whole of the like product or to those of them whose collective output of the products constitutes a major proportion of the total Community production of those products except that:

— when producers are related to the exporters or importers or are themselves importers of the allegedly dumped or subsidized product the term 'Community industry' may be interpreted as referring to the rest of the producers;

— in exceptional circumstances the Community may, for the production in question, be divided into two or more competitive markets and the producers within each market regarded as a Community industry if,

(a) the producers within such market sell all or almost all their production of the product in question in that market, and

(b) the demand in that market is not to any substantial degree supplied by producers of the product in question located elsewhere in the Community.

In such circumstances injury may be found to exist even where a major proportion of the total Community industry is not injured, provided there is a concentration of dumped or subsidized imports into such an isolated market and provided further that the dumped or subsidized imports are causing injury to the producers of all or almost all of the production within such market.

Article 5

Complaint

1. Any natural or legal person, or any association not having legal personality, acting on behalf of a Community industry which considers itself injured or threatened by dumped or subsidized imports may lodge a written complaint.

2. The complaint shall contain sufficient evidence of the existence of dumping or subsidization and the injury resulting therefrom.

3. The complaint may be submitted to the Commission, or a Member State, which shall forward it to the Commission. The Commission shall send Member States a copy of any complaint it receives.

4. The complaint may be withdrawn, in which case proceedings may be terminated unless such termination would not be in the interest of the Community.

5. Where it becomes apparent after consultation that the complaint does not provide sufficient evidence to justify initiating an investigation, then the complainant shall be so informed.

6. Where, in the absence of any complaint, a Member State is in possession of sufficient evidence both of dumping or subsidization and of injury resulting therefrom for a Community industry, it shall immediately communicate such evidence to the Commission.

Article 6

Consultations

1. Any consultations provided for in this Regulation shall take place within an Advisory Committee, which shall consist of representatives of each Member State, with a representative of the Commission as chairman.

Consultations shall be held immediately on request by a Member State or on the initiative of the Commission.

2. The Committee shall meet when convened by its chairman. He shall provide the Member States, as promptly as possible, with all relevant information.

3. Where necessary, consultation may be in writing only; in such case the Commission shall notify the Member States and shall specify a period within which they shall be entitled to express their opinions or to request an oral consultation.

4. Consultation shall in particular cover:

(a) the existence of dumping or of a subsidy and the methods of establishing the dumping margin or the amount of the subsidy;

(b) the existence and extent of injury;

(c) the causal link between the dumped or subsidized imports and injury;

(d) the measures which, in the circumstances, are appropriate to prevent or remedy the injury caused by dumping or the subsidy and the ways and means for putting such measures into effect.

Article 7

Initiation and subsequent investigation

1. Where, after consultation it is apparent that there is sufficient evidence to justify initiating a proceeding the Commission shall immediately:

(a) announce the initiation of a proceeding in the Official Journal of the European Communities; such announcements shall indicate the product and countries concerned, give a summary of the information received, and provide that all relevant information is to be communicated to the Commission; it shall state the period within which interested parties may make known their views in writing and may apply to be heard orally by the Commission in accordance with paragraph 5;

(b) so advise the exporters and importers known to the Commission to be concerned as well as representatives of the exporting country and the complainants;

(c) commence the investigation at Community level, acting in cooperation with the Member States; such investigation shall cover both dumping or subsidization and injury resulting therefrom and shall be carried out in accordance with paragraphs 2 to 8; the investigation of dumping or subsidization shall normally cover a period of not less than six months immediately prior to the initiation of the proceeding.

2. (a) The Commission shall seek all information it deems to be necessary and, where it considers it appropriate, examine and verify the records of importers, exporters, traders, agents, producers, trade associations and organizations.

(b) Where necessary the Commission shall carry out investigations in third countries, provided that the firms concerned give their consent and the government of the country in question has been officially notified and raises no objection. The Commission shall be assisted by officials of those Member States who so request.

3. (a) The Commission may request Member States:

— to supply information,

— to carry out all necessary checks and inspections, particularly amongst importers, traders and Community producers,

— to carry out investigations in third countries, provided the firms concerned give their consent and the government of the country in question has been officially notified and raises no objection.

(b) Member States shall take whatever steps are necessary in order to give effect to requests from the Commission. They shall send to the Commission the information requested together with the results of all inspections, checks or investigations carried out.

(c) Where this information is of general interest or where its transmission has been requested by a Member State, the Commission shall forward it to the Member States, provided it is not confidential, in which case a non-confidential summary shall be forwarded.

(d) Officials of the Commission shall be authorized, if the Commission or a Member State so requests, to assist the officials of Member States in carrying out their duties.

4. (a) The complainant and the importers and exporters known to be concerned, as well as the representatives of the exporting country, may inspect all information made available to the Commission by any party to an investigation as distinct from internal documents prepared by the authorities of the Community or its Member States, provided that it is relevant to the defence of their interests and not confidential within the meaning of Article 8 and that it is used by the Commission in the investigation. To this end, they shall address a written request to the Commission indicating the information required.

(b) Exporters and importers of the product subject to investigation and, in the case of subsidization, the representatives of the country of origin, may request to be informed of the essential facts and considerations on the basis of which it is intended to recommend the imposition of definitive duties or the definitive collection of amounts secured by way of a provisional duty.

(c)(i) requests for information pursuant to (b) shall:

(aa) be addressed to the Commission in writing,

(bb) specify the particular issues on which information is sought, (cc) be received, in cases where a provisional duty has been applied, not later than one month after publication of the imposition of that duty;

(ii) the information may be given either orally or in writing as considered appropriate by the Commission. It shall not prejudice any subsequent decision which may be taken by the Commission or the Council. Confidential information shall be treated in accordance with Article 8;

(iii) information shall normally be given no later than 15 days prior to the submission by the Commission of any proposal for final action pursuant to Article 12. Representations made after the information is given shall be taken into consideration only if received within a period to be set by the Commission in each case, which shall be at least 10 days, due consideration being given to the urgency of the matter.

5. The Commission may hear the interested parties. It shall so hear them if they have, within the period prescribed in the notice published in the *Official Journal of the European Communities,* made a written request for a hearing showing that they are an interested party likely to be affected by the result of the proceeding and that there are particular reasons why they should be heard orally.

6. Furthermore the Commission shall, on request, give the parties directly concerned an opportunity to meet, so that opposing views may be presented and any rebuttal argument put forward. In providing this opportunity the Commission shall take account of the need to preserve confidentiality and of the convenience of the parties. There shall be no obligation on any party to attend a meeting and failure to do so shall not be prejudicial to that party's case.

7. (a) This Article shall not preclude the Community authorities from reaching preliminary determinations or from applying provisional measures expeditiously.

(b) In cases in which any interested party or third country refuses access to, or otherwise does not provide, necessary information within a reasonable period, or significantly impedes the investigation, preliminary or final findings, affirmative or negative, may be made on the basis of the facts available. Where the Commission finds that any interested party or third country has supplied it with false or misleading information, it may disregard any such information and disallow any claim to which this refers.

8. Anti-dumping or countervailing proceedings shall not constitute a bar to customs clearance of the product concerned.

9. (a) An investigation shall be concluded either by its termination or by definitive action. Conclusion should normally take place within one year of the initiation of the proceeding.

(b) A proceeding shall be concluded either by the termination of the investigation without the imposition of duties and without the acceptance of undertakings or by the expiry or repeal of such duties or by the termination of undertakings in accordance with Articles 14 or 15.

Article 8
Confidentiality

1. Information received pursuant to this Regulation shall be used only for the purpose for which it was requested.

2. (a) Neither the Council, nor the Commission, nor Member States, nor the officials of any of these, shall reveal any information received pursuant to this Regulation for which confidential treatment has been requested by its supplier, without specific permission from the supplier.

(b) Each request for confidential treatment shall indicate why the information is confidential and shall be accompanied by a non-confidential summary of the information, or a statement of the reasons why the information is not susceptible of such summary.

3. Information will ordinarily be considered to be confidential if its disclosure is likely to have a significantly adverse effect upon the supplier or the source of such information.

4. However, if it appears that a request for confidentiality is not warranted and if the supplier is either unwilling to make the information public or to authorize its disclosure in generalized or summary form, the information in question may be disregarded.

The information may also be disregarded where such request is warranted and where the supplier is unwilling to submit a non-confidential summary, provided that the information is susceptible of such summary.

5. This Article shall not preclude the disclosure of general information by the Community authorities and in particular of the reasons on which decisions taken pursuant to this Regulation are based, or disclosure of the evidence relied on by the Community authorities in so far as necessary to explain those reasons in court proceedings. Such disclosure must take into account the legitimate interest of the parties concerned that their business secrets should not be divulged.

Article 9
Termination of proceedings where protective measures are unnecessary

1. If it becomes apparent after consultation that protective measures are unnecessary, then, where no objection is raised within the Advisory Committee referred to in Article 6(1), the proceeding shall be terminated. In all other cases the Commission shall submit to the Council forthwith a report on the results of the consultation, together with a proposal that the proceeding be terminated. The proceeding shall stand terminated if, within one month, the Council, acting by a qualified majority, has not decided otherwise.

2. The Commission shall inform any representatives of the country of origin or export and the parties known to be concerned and shall

announce the termination in the *Official Journal of the European Communities,* setting forth its basic conclusions and a summary of the reasons therefor.

Article 10
Undertakings

1. Where, during the course of an investigation, undertakings are offered which the Commission, after consultation, considers acceptable, the investigation may be terminated without the imposition of provisional or definitive duties.

Save in exceptional circumstances, undertakings may not be offered later than the end of the period during which representations may be made under Article 7(4)(c)(iii). The termination shall be decided in conformity with the procedure laid down in Article 9(1) and information shall be given and notice published in accordance with Article 9(2). Such termination does not preclude the definitive collection of amounts secured by way of provisional duties pursuant to Article 12(2).

2. The undertakings referred to under paragraph 1 are those under which:

(a) the subsidy is eliminated or limited, or other measures concerning its injurious effects taken, by the government of the country of origin or export; or

(b) prices are revised or exports cease to the extent that the Commission is satisfied that either the dumping margin or the amount of the subsidy, or the injurious effects thereof, are eliminated. In case of subsidization the consent of the country of origin or export shall be obtained.

3. Undertakings may be suggested by the Commission, but the fact that such undertakings are not offered or an invitation to do so is not accepted, shall not prejudice consideration of the case. However, the continuation of dumped or subsidized imports may be taken as evidence that a threat of injury is more likely to be realized.

4. If the undertakings are accepted, the investigation of injury shall nevertheless be completed if the Commission, after consultation, so decides or if request is made, in the case of dumping, by exporters representing a significant percentage of the trade involved or, in the case of subsidization, by the country of origin or export. In such a case, if the Commission, after consultation, makes a determination of no injury, the undertaking shall automatically lapse. However, where a determination of no threat of injury is due mainly to the existence of an undertaking, the Commission may require that the undertaking be maintained.

5. The Commission may require any party from whom an undertaking has been accepted to provide periodically information relevant to the fulfilment of such undertakings, and to permit verification of pertinent data. Non-compliance with such requirements shall be construed as a violation of the undertaking.

6. Where an undertaking has been withdrawn or where the Commission has reason to believe that it has been violated and where Community interests call for such intervention, it may, after consultations and after having offered the exporter concerned an opportunity to comment, apply provisional anti-dumping or countervailing duties forthwith on the basis of the facts established before the acceptance of the undertaking.

Article 11

Provisional duties

1. Where preliminary examination shows that dumping or a subsidy exists and that there is sufficient evidence of injury caused thereby and the interests of the Community call for intervention to prevent injury being caused during the proceeding, the Commission, acting at the request of a Member State or on its own initiative, shall impose a provisional anti-dumping or countervailing duty. In such cases, release of the products concerned for free circulation in the Community shall be conditional upon the provision of security for the amount of the provisional duty, definitive collection of which shall be determined by the subsequent decision of the Council under Article 12(2).

2. The Commission shall take such provisional action after consultation or, in cases of extreme urgency, after informing the Member States. In this latter case, consultations shall take place 10 days at the latest after notification to the Member States of the action taken by the Commission.

3. Where a Member State requests immediate intervention by the Commission, the Commission shall within a maximum of five working days of receipt of the request, decide whether a provisional anti-dumping or countervailing duty should be imposed.

4. The Commission shall forthwith inform the Council and the Member States of any decision taken under this Article. The Council, acting by a qualified majority, may decide differently. A decision by the Commission not to impose a provisional duty shall not preclude the imposition of such duty at a later date, either at the request of a Member State, if new factors arise, or on the initiative of the Commission.

5. Provisional duties shall have a maximum period of validity of four months. However, where exporters representing a significant percentage of the trade involved so request or, pursuant to a notice of intention from the Commission, do not object, provisional anti-dumping duties may be extended for a further period of two months.

6. Any proposal for definitive action, or for extension of provisional measures, shall be submitted to the Council by the Commission not later than one month before expiry of the period of validity of provisional duties. The Council shall act by a qualified majority.

7. After expiration of the period of validity of provisional duties, the security shall be released as promptly as possible to the extent that the Council has not decided to collect it definitively.

Article 12
Definitive action

1. Where the facts as finally established show that there is dumping or subsidization during the period under investigation and injury caused thereby, and the interests of the Community call for Community intervention, a definitive anti-dumping or countervailing duty shall be imposed by the Council, acting by qualified majority on a proposal submitted by the Commission after consultation.

2. (a) Where a provisional duty has been applied, the Council shall decide, irrespective of whether a definitive anti-dumping or countervailing duty is to be imposed, what proportion of the provisional duty is to be definitively collected. The Council shall act by a qualified majority on a proposal from the Commission.

(b) The definitive collection of such amount shall not be decided upon unless the facts as finally established show that there has been dumping or subsidization, and injury. For this purpose, 'injury' shall not include material retardation of the establishment of a Community industry, nor threat of material injury, except where it is found that this would, in the absence of provisional measures, have developed into material injury.

Article 13
General provisions on duties

1. Anti-dumping or countervailing duties, whether provisional or definitive, shall be imposed by Regulation.

2. Such Regulation shall indicate in particular the amount and type of duty imposed, the product covered, the country of origin or export, the name of the supplier, if practicable, and the reasons on which the Regulation is based.

3. The amount of such duties shall not exceed the dumping margin provisionally estimated or finally established or the amount of the subsidy provisionally estimated or finally established; it should be less if such lesser duty would be adequate to remove the injury.

4. (a) Anti-dumping and countervailing duties shall be neither imposed nor increased with retroactive effect. The obligation to pay the amount of these duties is incurred in accordance with Directive 79/623/EEC.

(b) However, where the Council determines:

(i) for dumped products:

— that there is a history of dumping which caused injury or that the importer was, or should have been, aware that the exporter practices dumping and that such dumping would cause injury, and

— that the injury is caused by sporadic dumping i.e., massive dumped imports of a product in a relatively short period, to such an extent that, in order to preclude it recurring, it appears necessary to impose an anti-dumping duty retroactively on those imports;

or

(ii) for subsidized products:

— in critical circumstances that injury which is difficult to repair is caused by massive imports in a relatively short period of a product benefiting from export subsidies paid or bestowed inconsistently with the provisions of the GATT and of the Agreement on Interpretation and Application of Articles VI, XVI and XXIII of the GATT, and

— that it is necessary, in order to preclude the recurrence of such injury, to assess countervailing duties retroactively on these imports;

or

(iii) for dumped or subsidized products:

— that an undertaking has been violated,

the definitive anti-dumping or countervailing duties may be imposed on products in relation to which the obligation to pay import duties under Directive 79/623/EEC has been or would have been incurred not more than 90 days prior to the date of application of provisional duties, except that in the case of violation of an undertaking such retroactive assessment shall not apply to imports which were released for free circulation in the Community before the violation.

5. Where a product is imported into the Community from more than one country, duty shall be levied at an appropriate amount on a non-discriminatory basis on all imports of such product found to be dumped or subsidized and causing injury, other than imports from those sources in respect of which undertakings have been accepted.

6. Where the Community industry has been interpreted as referring to the producers in a certain region; the Commission shall give exporters an opportunity to offer undertakings pursuant to Article 10 in respect of the region concerned. If an adequate undertaking is not given promptly or is not fulfilled, a provisional or definitive duty may be imposed in respect of the Community as a whole.

7. In the absence of any special provisions to the contrary adopted when a definitive or provisional anti-dumping or countervailing duty was imposed, the rules on the common definition of the concept of origin and the relevant common implementing provisions shall apply.

8. Anti-dumping or countervailing duties shall be collected by Member States in the form at the rate and according to the other criteria laid down when the duties were imposed, and independently of the customs duties, taxes and other charges normally imposed on imports.

9. No product shall be subject to both anti-dumping and countervailing duties for the purpose of dealing with one and the same situation arising from dumping or from the granting of any subsidy.

10. (a) Definitive anti-dumping duties may be imposed, by way of derogation from the second sentence of paragraph 4(a), on products that are introduced into the commerce of the Community after having been assembled or produced in the Community, provided that:

— assembly or production is carried out by a party which is related or associated to any of the manufacturers whose exports of the like product are subject to a definitive anti-dumping duty,

— the assembly or production operation was started or substantially increased after the opening of the anti-dumping investigation,

— the value of parts or materials used in the assembly or production operation and originating in the country of exportation of the product subject to the anti-dumping duty exceeds the value of all other parts or materials used by at least 50%.

In applying this provision, account shall be taken of the circumstances of each case, and, *inter alia*, of the variable costs incurred in the assembly or production operation and of the research and development carried out and the technology applied within the Community.

In that event the Council shall, at the same time, decide that parts or materials suitable for use in the assembly or production of such products and originating in the country of exportation of the product subject to the anti-dumping duty can only be considered to be in free circulation in so far as they will not be used in an assembly or production operation as specified in the first subparagraph.

(b) Products thus assembled or produced shall be declared to the competent authorities before leaving the assembly or production plant for their introduction into the commerce of the Community. For the purposes of levying an anti-dumping duty, this declaration shall be considered to be equivalent to the declaration referred to in Article 2 of Directive 79/695/EEC.

(c) The rate of the anti-dumping duty shall be that applicable to the manufacturer in the country of origin of the like product subject to an anti-dumping duty to which the party in the Community carrying out the assembly or production is related or associated. The amount of duty collected shall be proportional to that resulting from the application of the rate of the anti-dumping duty applicable to the exporter of the complete product on the cif value of the parts or materials imported; it shall not exceed that required to prevent circumvention of the anti-dumping duty.

(d) The provisions of this Regulation concerning investigation, procedure, and undertakings apply to all questions arising under this paragraph.

11. (a) Where the exporter bears the anti-dumping duty, an additional anti-dumping duty may be imposed to compensate for the amount borne by the exporter.

(b) When any party directly concerned submits sufficient evidence showing that the duty has been borne by the exporter, e.g. that the resale price to the first independent buyer of the product subject to the anti-dumping duty is not increased by an amount corresponding to the anti-dumping duty, the matter shall be investigated and the exporters and importers concerned shall be given an opportunity to comment.

Where it is found that the anti-dumping duty has been borne by the exporter, in whole or in part, either directly or indirectly and where Community interests call for intervention, an additional anti-dumping duty shall, after consultation, be imposed in accordance with the procedures laid down in Articles 11 and 12.

This duty may be applied retroactively. It may be imposed on products in relation to which the obligation to pay import duties under Directive 79/623/EEC has been incurred after the imposition of the definitive anti-dumping duty, except that such assessment shall not apply to imports which were released for free circulation in the Community before the exporter bore the anti-dumping duty.

(c) Insofar as the results of the investigation show that the absence of a price increase by an amount corresponding to the anti-dumping duty is not due to a reduction in the costs and/or profits of the importer for the product concerned then the absence of such price increase shall be considered as an indicator that the anti-dumping duty has been borne by the exporter.

(d) Article 7(7)(b) applies within the context of investigations under this paragraph.

Article 14
Review

1. Regulations imposing anti-dumping or countervailing duties and decisions to accept undertakings shall be subject to review, in whole or in part, where warranted.

Such review may be held either at the request of a Member State or on the initiative of the Commission. A review shall also be held where an interested party so requests and submits evidence of changed circumstances sufficient to justify the need for such review, provided that at least one year has elapsed since the conclusion of the investigation. Such requests shall be addressed to the Commission which shall inform the Member States.

2. Where, after consultation, it becomes apparent that review is warranted, the investigation shall be re-opened in accordance with Article 7, where the circumstances so require. Such re-opening shall not *per se* affect the measures in operation.

3. Where warranted by the review, carried out either with or without re-opening of the investigation, the measures shall be amended, repealed or annulled by the Community institution competent for their introduction. However, where measures have been taken under the transitional provisions of an Act of Accession the Commission shall itself amend, repeal or annul them and shall report this to the Council; the latter may, acting by a qualified majority, decide that different action be taken.

Article 15

1. Subject to the provisions of paragraphs 3, 4 and 5, anti-dumping or countervailing duties and undertakings shall lapse after five years from the date on which they entered into force or were last modified or confirmed.

2. The Commission shall normally, after consultation and within six months prior to the end of the five year period, publish in the *Official Journal of the European Communities* a notice of the impending expiry of the measure in question and inform the Community industry known to be concerned. This notice shall state the period within which interested parties may make known their views in writing and may apply to be heard orally by the Commission in accordance with Article 7(5).

3. Where an interested party shows that the expiry of the measure would lead again to injury or threat of injury, the Commission shall, after consultation, publish in the *Official Journal of the European Communities* a notice of its intention to carry out a review of the measure. Such notice shall be published prior to the end of the relevant five year period. The measure shall remain in force pending the outcome of this review.

However, where the initiation of the review has not been published within six months after the end of the relevant five year period the measure shall lapse at the end of that six month period.

4. Where a review of a measure under Article 14 is in progress at the end of the relevant five year period, the measure shall remain in force pending the outcome of such review. A notice to this effect shall be published in the *Official Journal of the European Communities* before the end of the relevant five year period.

5. Where anti-dumping or countervailing duties and undertakings lapse under this Article the Commission shall publish a notice to that effect in the *Official Journal of the European Communities*. Such notice shall state the date of expiry of the measure.

Article 16
Refund

1. Where an importer can show that the duty collected exceeds the actual dumping margin or the amount of the subsidy, consideration being given to any application of weighted averages, the excess amount shall be reimbursed. This amount shall be calculated in relation to the changes which have occurred in the dumping margin or the amount of the subsidy

which were established in the original investigation for the shipments to the Community of the importer's supplier. All refund calculations shall be made in accordance with the provisions of Articles 2 or 3 and shall be based, as far as possible, on the same method applied in the original investigation, in particular, with regard to any application of averaging or sampling techniques.

2. In order to request the reimbursement referred to in paragraph 1, the importer shall submit an application to the Commission. The application shall be submitted via the Member State in the territory of which the products were released for free circulation and within three months of the date on which the amount of the definitive duties to be levied was duly determined by the competent authorities or of the date on which a decision was made definitively to collect the amounts secured by way of provisional duty.

The Member State shall forward the application to the Commission as soon as possible, either with or without an opinion as to its merits.

The Commission shall inform the other Member States forthwith and give its opinion on the matter. If the Member States agree with the opinion given by the Commission or do not object to it within one month of being informed, the Commission may decide in accordance with the said opinion.

In all other cases, the Commission shall, after consultation, decide whether and to what extent the application should be granted.

Article 17
Final provisions

This Regulation shall not preclude the application of:

1. any special rules laid down in agreements concluded between the Community and third countries;

2. the Community Regulations in the agricultural sector and of Regulation (EEC) No 1059/69, (EEC) No 2730/75; and (EEC) No 2783/75; this Regulation shall operate by way of complement to those Regulations and in derogation from any provisions thereof which preclude the application of anti-dumping or countervailing duties;

3. special measures, provided that such action does not run counter to obligations under the GATT.

Article 18
Repeal of existing legislation

Regulation (EEC) No 2176/84 is hereby repealed.

References to the repealed Regulation shall be construed as references to this Regulation.

Article 19
Entry into force

This Regulation shall enter into force on the third day following its publication in the *Official Journal of the European Communities*.

It shall apply to proceedings already initiated.

This Regulation shall be binding in its entirety and directly applicable to all Member States.

ANNEX
ILLUSTRATIVE LIST OF EXPORT SUBSIDIES

(a) The provision by governments of direct subsidies to a firm or an industry contingent upon export performance.

(b) Currency retention schemes or any similar practices which involve a bonus on exports.

(c) Internal transport and freight charges on export shipments, provided or mandated by governments, on terms more favourable than for domestic shipments.

(d) The delivery by governments or their agencies of imported or domestic products or services for use in the production of exported goods, on terms or conditions more favourable than for delivery of like or directly competitive products or services for use in the production of goods for domestic consumption, if (in the case of products) such terms or conditions are more favourable than those commercially available on world markets to their exporters.

(e) The full or partial exemption, remission, or deferral specifically related to exports, of direct taxes or social welfare charges paid or payable by industrial or commercial enterprises. Notwithstanding the foregoing, deferral of taxes and charges referred to above need not amount to an export subsidy where, for example, appropriate interest charges are collected.

(f) The allowance of special deductions directly related to exports or export performance, over and above those granted in respect to production for domestic consumption, in the calculation of the base on which direct taxes are charged.

(g) The exemption or remission in respect of the production and distribution of exported products, of indirect taxes in excess of those levied in respect of the production and distribution of like products when sold for domestic consumption. The problem of the excessive remission of value added tax is exclusively covered by this paragraph.

(h) The exemption, remission or deferral or prior stage cumulative indirect taxes on goods or services used in the production of exported products in excess of the exemption, remission or deferral or like prior stage cumulative indirect taxes on goods or services used in the production of like products when sold for domestic consumption; provided, however, that prior stage cumulative indirect taxes may be exempted, remitted or deferred on exported products even when not exempted, remitted or deferred on like products when sold for domestic consumption, if the prior stage cumulative indirect taxes are levied on goods that are physically incorporated (making normal allowance for waste) in the exported product. This paragraph does not apply to value added tax systems and border tax adjustments related thereto.

(i) The remission or drawback of import charges in excess of those levied on imported goods that are physically incorporated (making normal allowance for waste) in the exported product; provided, however, that in particular cases a firm may use a quantity of home market goods equal to, and having the same quality and characteristics as, the imported good as a substitute for them in order to benefit from this provision if the import and the corresponding export operations both occur within a reasonable time period, normally not to exceed two years. This paragraph does not apply to value added tax systems and border tax adjustments related thereto.

(j) The provision by governments (or special institutions controlled by governments of export credit guarantee or insurance programmes, of insurance or guarantee programmes against increases in the costs of exported products or of exchange risk programmes, at premium rates, which are manifestly inadequate to cover the long-term operating costs and losses of the programmes.

(k) The grant by governments (or special institutions controlled by and/or acting under the authority of governments) of export credits at rates below those which they actually have to pay for the funds so employed (or would have to pay if they borrowed on international capital markets in order to obtain funds of the same maturity and denominated at the same currency as the export credit), or the payment by them of all or part of the costs incurred by exporters or financial institutions in obtaining credits, in so far as they are used to secure a material advantage in the field of export credit terms.

Provided, however, that if the country of origin or export is a party to an international undertaking on official export credits to which at least 12 original signatories to the Agreement on Interpretation and Application of Articles VI, XVI and XXIII of the GATT are parties as of 1 January 1979 (or a successor undertaking which has been adopted by those original signatories), or if in practice the country of origin or export applies the interest rate provisions of the relevant undertaking, an export credit practice which is in conformity with those provisions shall not be considered an export subsidy.

(l) Any other charge on the public account constituting an export subsidy in the sense of Article XVI of the GATT.

Notes:

For the purposes of this Annex the following definitions apply:

1. The term 'direct taxes' shall mean taxes on wages, profits, interest, rents, royalties, and all other forms of income, and taxes on the ownership of real property.

2. The term 'import charges' shall mean tariffs, duties, and other fiscal charges not elsewhere enumerated in these notes that are levied on imports.

3. The term 'indirect taxes' shall mean sales, excise, turnover, value added, franchise, stamp, transfer, inventory and equipment taxes, border taxes and all taxes other than direct taxes and import charges.

4. 'Prior stage' indirect taxes are those levied on goods or services used directly or indirectly in making the product.

5. 'Cumulative' indirect taxes are multi-staged taxes levied where there is no mechanism for subsequent crediting of the tax if the goods or services subject to tax at one stage of production are used in a succeeding stage of production.

6. 'Remission' of taxes includes the refund or rebate of taxes.

4. COUNCIL REGULATION (EEC) 2641/84

of 17 September 1984

on the strengthening of the common commercial policy with regard in particular to protection against illicit commercial practices

O.J. L 252/1 (Sept. 20, 1984)

THE COUNCIL OF THE EUROPEAN COMMUNITIES,

* * *

Whereas in the light of experience and of the conclusions of the European Council of June 1982, which considered that it was of the highest importance to defend vigorously the legitimate interests of the Community in the appropriate bodies, in particular GATT, and to make sure the Community, in managing trade policy, acts with as much speed and efficiency as its trading partners, it has become apparent that the common commercial policy needs to be strengthened, notably in the fields not covered by the rules already adopted;

* * *

Whereas the measures taken under the procedures in question should, however, be without prejudice to other measures in cases not covered by this Regulation which might be adopted directly pursuant to Article 113 of the Treaty;

Whereas the Community must act in compliance with its international obligations and, where such obligations result from agreements, maintain the balance of rights and obligations which it is the purpose of those agreements to establish;

* * *

HAS ADOPTED THIS REGULATION:

Article 1
Aims

This Regulation establishes procedures in the matter of commercial policy which, subject to compliance with existing international obligations and procedures, are aimed at:

(a) responding to any illicit commercial practice with a view to removing the injury resulting therefrom;

(b) ensuring full exercise of the Community's rights with regard to the commercial practices of third countries.

Article 2
Definitions

1. For the purposes of this Regulation, illicit commercial practices shall be any international trade practices attributable to third countries

which are incompatible with international law or with the generally accepted rules.

2. For the purposes of this Regulation, the Community's rights shall be those international trade rights of which it may avail itself either under international law or under generally accepted rules.

3. For the purposes of this Regulation, injury shall be any material injury caused or threatened to Community industry.

4. The term 'Community industry' shall be taken to mean all Community producers:

— of products identical or similar to the product which is the subject of illicit practices or of products competing directly with that product, or

— who are consumers or processors of the product which is the subject of illicit practices,

or all those producers whose combined output constitutes a major proportion of total Community production of the products in question; however:

(a) when producers are related to the exporters or importers or are themselves importers of the product alleged to be the subject of illicit practices, the term 'Community industry' may be interpreted as referring to the rest of the producers;

(b) in particular circumstances, the producers within a region of the Community may be regarded as the Community industry if their collective output constitutes the major proportion of the output of the product in question in the Member State or Member States within which the region is located provided that:

(i) where the illicit practice concerns imports into the Community, their effect is concentrated in that Member State or those Member States,

(ii) where the illicit practice concerns Community exports to a third country, a significant proportion of the output of those producers is exported to the third country concerned.

Article 3
Complaint on behalf of Community producers

1. Any natural or legal person, or any association not having legal personality, acting on behalf of a Community industry which considers that it has suffered injury as a result of illicit commercial practices may lodge a written complaint.

2. The complaint must contain sufficient evidence of the existence of illicit commercial practices and the injury resulting therefrom. Proof of injury must be given on the basis of the factors indicated in Article 8.

3. The complaint shall be submitted, to the Commission, which shall send a copy thereof to the Member States.

4. The complaint may be withdrawn, in which case the procedure may be terminated unless such termination would not be in the interests of the Community.

5. Where it becomes apparent after consultation that the complaint does not provide sufficient evidence to justify initiating an investigation, then the complainant shall be so informed.

Article 4
Referral by a Member State

1. Any Member State may ask the Commission to initiate the procedures referred to in Article 1.

2. It shall supply the Commission with the necessary evidence to support its request. Where illicit commercial practices are alleged, proof thereof and of the injury resulting therefrom must be given on the basis of the factors indicated in Article 8.

3. The Commission shall notify the other Member States of the requests without delay.

4. Where it becomes apparent after consultation that the request does not provide sufficient evidence to justify initiating an investigation, then the Member State shall be so informed.

Article 5
Consultation procedure

1. For the purpose of consultations pursuant to this Regulation, an advisory committee, hereinafter referred to as 'the Committee', is hereby set up and shall consist of representatives of each Member State, with a representative of the Commission as chairman.

2. Consultations shall be initiated at the request of a Member State or on the initiative of the Commission. The chairman of the Committee shall provide the Member States, as promptly as possible, with all relevant information in his possession.

3. The Committee shall meet when convened by its chairman.

4. Where necessary, consultations may be in writing. In such case the Commission shall notify in writing the Member States who, within a period of eight working days from such notification, shall be entitled to express their opinions in writing or to request oral consultations.

Article 6
Community examination procedure

1. Where, after consultation, it is apparent to the Commission that there is sufficient evidence to justify initiating an examination procedure and that it is necessary in the interest of the Community, the Commission shall act as follows:

(a) it shall announce the initiation of an examination procedure in the *Official Journal of the European Communities;* such announcement shall indicate the product and countries concerned, give a summary of the information received, and provide that all relevant information is to be communicated to the Commission; it shall state the period within which interested parties may make known their views in writing and may apply to be heard orally by the Commission in accordance with paragraph 5;

(b) it shall so officially notify the representatives of the country or countries which are the subject of the procedure, with whom, where appropriate, consultations may be held;

(c) it shall conduct the examination at Community level, acting in cooperation with the Member States.

2. (a) If necessary, and notably in cases of allegations of illicit commercial practices, the Commission shall seek all the information it deems necessary and attempt to check this information with the importers, traders, agents, producers, trade associations and organizations, provided that the undertakings or organizations concerned give their consent.

(b) Where necessary, the Commission shall carry out investigations in the territory of third countries, provided that the governments of the countries concerned have been officially notified and raise no objection within a reasonable period.

(c) The Commission shall be assisted in its investigation by officials of the Member State in whose territory the checks are carried out, provided that the Member State in question so requests.

3. Member States shall supply the Commission, upon request, with all information necessary for the examination, in accordance with the detailed arrangements laid down by the Commission.

4. (a) The complainants and the exporters and importers concerned, as well as the representatives of the principal exporting or importing country or countries concerned, may inspect all information made available to the Commission except for internal documents for the use of the Commission and the administrations, provided that such information is relevant to the protection of their interests and not confidential within the meaning of Article 7 and that it is used by the Commission in its examination procedure. The persons concerned shall address a reasoned request in writing to the Commission, indicating the information required.

(b) The complainants and the exporters and importers concerned and the representatives of the principal exporting or importing country or countries concerned may ask to be informed of the principal facts and considerations resulting from the examination procedure.

5. The Commission may hear the parties concerned. It shall hear them if they have, within the period prescribed in the notice published in the *Official Journal of the European Communities*, made a written request for a hearing showing that they are a party primarily concerned by the result of the procedure.

6. Furthermore, the Commission shall, on request, give the parties primarily concerned an opportunity to meet, so that opposing views may be presented and any rebuttal argument put forward. In providing this opportunity the Commission shall take account of the wishes of the parties and of the need to preserve confidentiality. There shall be no obligation on any party to attend a meeting and failure to do so shall not be prejudicial to that party's case.

7. When the information requested by the Commission is not supplied within a reasonable time or where the investigation is significantly impeded, findings may be made on the basis of the facts available.

8. The Commission shall take a decision as soon as possible on the opening of a Community examination procedure following any complaint or request made in accordance with Articles 3 and 4; the decision shall normally be taken within 45 days of referral; this period may be extended to 60 days in special circumstances.

9. When it has concluded its examination the Commission shall report to the Committee. The report should normally be presented within five months of the announcement of initiation of the procedure, unless the complexity of the examination is such that the Commission extends the period to seven months.

Article 7

Confidentiality

1. Information received pursuant to this Regulation shall be used only for the purpose for which it was requested.

2. (a) Neither the Council, nor the Commission, nor Member States, nor the officials of any of these, shall reveal any information of a confidential nature received pursuant to this Regulation, or any information provided on a confidential basis by a party to an examination procedure, without specific permission from the party submitting such information.

(b) Each request for confidential treatment shall indicate why the information is confidential and shall be accompanied by a non-confidential summary of the information or a statement of the reasons why the information is not susceptible of such summary.

3. Information will normally be considered to be confidential if its disclosure is likely to have a significantly adverse effect upon the supplier or the source of such information.

4. However, if it appears that a request for confidentiality is not warranted and if the supplier is either unwilling to make the information public or to authorize its disclosure in generalized or summary form, the information in question may be disregarded.

5. This Article shall not preclude the disclosure of general information by the Community authorities and in particular of the reasons on which decisions taken pursuant to this Regulation are based. Such disclosure must take into account the legitimate interest of the parties concerned that their business secrets should not be divulged.

Article 8

Examination of injury

1. An examination of injury shall involve in particular the following factors:

(a) the volume of Community imports or exports concerned, notably where there has been a significant increase or decrease, either in absolute terms or relative to production or consumption on the market in question;

(b) the prices of the Community producers' competitors, in particular in order to determine whether there has been, either in the Community or on third country markets, significant undercutting of the prices of Community producers;

(c) the consequent impact on Community industry as defined in Article 2(4) and as indicated by trends in certain economic factors such as:

— production,

— utilization of capacity,

— stocks,

— sales,

— market share,

— prices (that is, depression of prices or prevention of price increases which would normally have occurred),

— profits,

— return on capital,

— investment,

— employment.

2. Where a threat of injury is alleged, the Commission shall also examine whether it is clearly foreseeable that a particular situation is likely to develop into actual injury. In this regard, account may also be taken of factors such as:

(a) the rate of increase of exports to the market where the competition with Community products is taking place;

(b) export capacity in the country of origin or export, which is already in existence or will be operational in the foreseeable future, and the likelihood that the exports resulting from that capacity will be to the market referred to in point (a).

3. Injury caused by other factors which, either individually or in combination, are also adversely affecting Community industry must not be attributed to the practices under consideration.

Article 9

Termination of the procedure

1. When it is found as a result of the examination procedure that the interests of the Community do not require any action to be taken, the procedure shall be terminated in accordance with Article 12.

2. (a) When, after an examination procedure, the third country or country concerned take(s) measures which are considered satisfactory the procedure may also be terminated in accordance with the provisions of Article 11.

(b) The Commission shall supervise the application of these measures, where appropriate on the basis of information supplied at intervals, which it may request from the third countries concerned and check as necessary.

(c) Where the measures taken by the third country or countries concerned have been rescinded, suspended or improperly implemented or where the Commission has grounds for believing this to be the case or, finally, where a request for information made by the Commission as provided for by point (b) has not been granted, the Commission shall inform the Member States, and where necessary and justified by the results of the investigation and the new facts available any measures shall be taken in accordance with Article 11.

Article 10

Adoption of commercial policy measures

1. Where it is found as a result of the examination procedure that action is necessary in the interests of the Community in order to:

(a) respond to any illicit commercial practice with the aim of removing the injury resulting therefrom; or

(b) ensure full exercise of the Community's rights with regard to the commercial practices of third countries

the appropriate measures shall be determined in accordance with the procedure set out in Article 11.

2. Where the Community's international obligations require the prior discharge of an international procedure for consultation or for the settlement of disputes, the measures referred to in paragraph 3 shall only be decided on after that procedure has been terminated, and taking account of the results of the procedure.

3. Any commercial policy measures may be taken which are compatible with existing international obligations and procedures, notably:

(a) suspension or withdrawal of any concession resulting from commercial policy negotiations;

(b) the raising of existing customs duties or the introduction of any other charge on imports;

(c) the introduction of quantitative restrictions or any other measures modifying import or export conditions or otherwise affecting trade with the third country concerned.

4. The corresponding decisions shall state the reasons on which they are based and shall be published in the *Official Journal of the European Communities*. Publication shall also be deemed to constitute notification to the countries and parties primarily concerned.

Article 11

Decision-making machinery

1. The decisions referred to in Articles 9 and 10 shall be adopted in accordance with the following provisions.

2. Where a response to an illicit commercial practice within the meaning of Article 1(a) is to be made:

(a) where the Community follows formal international consultation or dispute settlement procedures, decisions relating to the initiation, conduct, or termination of such procedures shall be taken in accordance with Article 12;

(b) where the Community, after the conclusion of such an international procedure, has to take a decision on the measures of commercial policy to be adopted, the Council shall act, on the proposal from the Commission, in accordance with Article 113 of the Treaty, by a qualified majority, not later than 30 days after receiving the proposal.

3. Where the full exercise of the Community's rights within the meaning of Article 1(b) is to be ensured, the Council shall act, on the proposal from the Commission, in accordance with Article 113 of the Treaty, by a qualified majority, not later than 30 days after receiving the proposal.

Article 12

Should reference be made to the procedure provided for in this Article, the matter shall be brought before the Committee by its chairman.

The Commission representative shall submit to the Committee a draft of the decision to be taken. The Committee shall discuss the matter within a period to be fixed by the chairman, depending on the urgency of the matter.

The Commission shall adopt a decision which it shall communicate to the Member States and which shall apply after a period of 10 days if during this period no Member State has referred the matter to the Council.

The Council may, at the request of a Member State and acting by a qualified majority revise the Commission's decision.

The Commission's decision shall apply after a period of 30 days if the Council has not given a ruling within this period, calculated from the day on which the matter was referred to the Council.

Article 13

This Regulation shall not apply in cases covered by other existing rules in the common commercial policy field. It shall operate by way of complement to the:

— rules establishing the common organization of agricultural markets and their implementing provisions;

— specific rules adopted under Article 235 of the Treaty, applicable to goods processed from agricultural products.

It shall be without prejudice to other measures which may be taken pursuant to Article 113 of the Treaty.

Article 14

This Regulation shall enter into force on the third day following its publication in the *Official Journal of the European Communities.*

Part V

SPECIFIC COMMUNITY POLICIES

Introduction

Part V of the casebook examines several major Community policies and fields of action. Out of the vast number of regulations and directives adopted to implement these policies, we have selected certain key representative documents.

Although the common agricultural policy (CAP) has given rise to the greatest volume of Community legislation, the regulations are too detailed and technically complex to merit reproduction.

In the field of consumer protection, we reprinted what is undoubtedly the most important harmonization measure, Directive 85/374 on liability for defective products. This directive established the principle of strict liability for injury caused by defective products in several Member States that previously applied other rules of negligence liability, and harmonized the application of the principle in other States that already recognized it. Also discussed in Chapter 32(B) is the draft product safety directive, intended to supplement the product liability directive.

Space constraints prevented reprinting of other significant consumer rights measures. Good examples are the pharmaceutical products directives 65/65, O.J. English Spec.Ed. 1965–1966, at 20, and 75/319, O.J. L 147/1 (June 9, 1975); Directive 79/112 on labelling, presentation and advertising of foodstuffs, O.J. L 33/1 (Feb. 8, 1979); Directive 89/622 on labelling of tobacco products, O.J. L 359/1 (Dec. 8, 1989); Directive 84/450 on misleading advertising, O.J. L 250/17 (Sept. 19, 1984); and Directive 87/102 on consumer credit, O.J. L 42/48 (Feb. 12, 1987).

The environmental protection and pollution control program has also generated a substantial volume of legislation and international agreements, as described in Chapter 32(A), but the legislation tends to be technical and detailed. For representative examples, see Directive 75/440 on the quality of surface water intended for drinking water, O.J. L 194/26 (July 25, 1975); Directive 76/160 on the quality of bathing water, O.J. L 31/1 (Jan. 20, 1976); Directive 75/716 on the sulphur content of certain liquid fuels, O.J. L 307/22 (Nov. 27, 1975); and Directive 79/409 on the protection of wild birds, O.J. L 103/1 (Apr. 22, 1979). The Commission also publishes Annual Reports on the Environment, containing current useful information.

To supplement Chapter 33 on social policy, we reprinted the most famous document, the Charter of the Fundamental Social Rights of Workers. This was adopted by all of the Member States except the United Kingdom at the December 1989 European Council meeting. The Charter constitutes an enumeration and description of the various rights which the States are committed to protect in the social policy field.

Major early social directives reproduced are Directives 75/129, 77/187 and 80/987, respectively protecting economic interests of employees in the event of a collective redundancy, a transfer of an enterprise, or insolvency. To illustrate the most recent wave of Community social measures, we reprinted Directive 91/533 on employee contract terms. Chapter 33(C) describes and cites important worker health and safety measures, and 33(D) reviews several prominent draft directives, such as the proposal for the protection of pregnant women and mothers, and that for the creation of European works councils.

For Chapter 34 on equal rights for women, we have reprinted all of the important measures, namely Directive 75/117 on equal pay, Directive 76/207 on equal working conditions, Directive 79/7 on equal treatment in state social security programs, and Directive 86/378 on equal treatment in occupational (employer) social security plans. Directive 86/613 on equal treatment for the self-employed is cited and discussed in Chapter 34(C).

The essential document for understanding the details of the proposed economic and monetary union, discussed in Chapter 35(D), is the text of the Treaty on European Union, together with the relevant Protocols, reproduced in Part I of this Supplement. The most significant related material is the Delors Committee Report of April 17, 1989, outlining the initial proposal for the economic and monetary union, discussed in Chapter 35(C).

Table of Contents

PART V. SPECIFIC COMMUNITY POLICIES

Doc.
1. Council Directive 85/374 on the approximation of the law concerning liability for defective products
2. Council Directive 75/129 on the approximation of the laws relating to collective redundancies
3. Council Directive 77/187 on the approximation of the laws relating to the safeguarding of employees' rights in the event of transfers of undertakings, businesses or parts of businesses
4. Council Directive 80/987 on the approximation of the laws relating to the protection of employees in the event of the insolvency of their employer
5. Community Charter of the Fundamental Social Rights of Workers
6. Council Directive 91/533 on an employer's obligation to inform employees of the conditions applicable to the contract or employment relationship

Doc.
7. Council Directive 75/117 on the approximation of the laws relating to the principle of equal pay for men and women
8. Council Directive 76/207 on the implementation of the principle of equal treatment for men and women as regards access to employment, vocational training and promotion, and working conditions
9. Council Directive 79/7 on the progressive implementation of the principle of equal treatment for men and women in matters of social security
10. Council Directive 86/378 on the implementation of the principle of equal treatment for men and women in occupational social security schemes

1. COUNCIL DIRECTIVE 85/374/EEC

of 25 July 1985

on the approximation of the laws, regulations and administrative provisions of the Member States concerning liability for defective products

O.J. L 210/29 (Aug. 7, 1985)

THE COUNCIL OF THE EUROPEAN COMMUNITIES,

Having regard to the Treaty establishing the European Economic Community, and in particular Article 100 thereof,

Having regard to the proposal from the Commission,[1]

Having regard to the opinion of the European Parliament,[2]

Having regard to the opinion of the Economic and Social Committee,[3]

Whereas approximation of the laws of the Member States concerning the liability of the producer for damage caused by the defectiveness of his products is necessary because the existing divergences may distort competition and affect the movement of goods within the common market and entail a differing degree of protection of the consumer against damage caused by a defective product to his health or property;

Whereas liability without fault on the part of the producer is the sole means of adequately solving the problem, peculiar to our age of increasing technicality, of a fair apportionment of the risks inherent in modern technological production;

* * *

Whereas, in situations where several persons are liable for the same damage, the protection of the consumer requires that the injured person should be able to claim full compensation for the damage from any one of them;

Whereas, to protect the physical well-being and property of the consumer, the defectiveness of the product should be determined by reference not to its fitness for use but to the lack of the safety which the public at large is entitled to expect; whereas the safety is assessed by excluding any misuse of the product not reasonable under the circumstances;

Whereas a fair apportionment of risk between the injured person and the producer implies that the producer should be able to free himself from liability if he furnishes proof as to the existence of certain exonerating circumstances;

Whereas the protection of the consumer requires that the liability of the producer remains unaffected by acts or omissions of other persons having contributed to cause the damage; whereas, however, the contribu-

---

[1]. OJ No C 241, 14. 10. 1976, p. 9 and OJ No C 271, 26. 10. 1979, p. 3.
[2]. OJ No C 127, 21. 5. 1979, p. 61.
[3]. OJ No C 114, 7. 5. 1979, p. 15.

tory negligence of the injured person may be taken into account to reduce or disallow such liability;

Whereas the protection of the consumer requires compensation for death and personal injury as well as compensation for damage to property; whereas the latter should nevertheless be limited to goods for private use or consumption and be subject to a deduction of a lower threshold of a fixed amount in order to avoid litigation in an excessive number of cases; whereas this Directive should not prejudice compensation for pain and suffering and other non-material damages payable, where appropriate, under the law applicable to the case;

Whereas a uniform period of limitation for the bringing of action for compensation is in the interests both of the injured person and of the producer;

Whereas products age in the course of time, higher safety standards are developed and the state of science and technology progresses; whereas, therefore, it would not be reasonable to make the producer liable for an unlimited period for the defectiveness of his product; whereas, therefore, liability should expire after a reasonable length of time, without prejudice to claims pending at law;

Whereas, to achieve effective protection of consumers, no contractual derogation should be permitted as regards the liability of the producer in relation to the injured person;

Whereas under the legal systems of the Member States an injured party may have a claim for damages based on grounds of contractual liability or on grounds of non-contractual liability other than that provided for in this Directive; in so far as these provisions also serve to attain the objective of effective protection of consumers, they should remain unaffected by this Directive; whereas, in so far as effective protection of consumers in the sector of pharmaceutical products is already also attained in a Member State under a special liability system, claims based on this system should similarly remain possible;

Whereas, to the extent that liability for nuclear injury or damage is already covered in all Member States by adequate special rules, it has been possible to exclude damage of this type from the scope of this Directive;

Whereas, since the exclusion of primary agricultural products and game from the scope of this Directive may be felt, in certain Member States, in view of what is expected for the protection of consumers, to restrict unduly such protection, it should be possible for a Member State to extend liability to such products;

Whereas, for similar reasons, the possibility offered to a producer to free himself from liability if he proves that the state of scientific and technical knowledge at the time when he put the product into circulation was not such as to enable the existence of a defect to be discovered may be felt in certain Member States to restrict unduly the protection of the consumer; whereas it should therefore be possible for a Member State to maintain in its legislation or to provide by new legislation that this exonerating circumstance is not admitted; whereas, in the case of new legislation, making use of this derogation should, however, be subject to a Community stand-still procedure, in order to raise, if possible, the level of protection in a uniform manner throughout the Community;

Whereas, taking into account the legal traditions in most of the Member States, it is inappropriate to set any financial ceiling on the producer's liability without fault; whereas, in so far as there are, however, differing traditions, it seems possible to admit that a Member State may derogate from the principle of unlimited liability by providing a limit for the total liability of the producer for damage resulting from a death or personal injury and caused by identical items with the same defect, provided that this limit is established at a level sufficiently high to guarantee adequate protection of the consumer and the correct functioning of the common market;

Whereas the harmonization resulting from this cannot be total at the present stage, but opens the way towards greater harmonization; whereas it is therefore necessary that the Council receive at regular intervals, reports from the Commission on the application of this Directive, accompanied, as the case may be, by appropriate proposals;

Whereas it is particularly important in this respect that a re-examination be carried out of those parts of the Directive relating to the derogations open to the Member States, at the expiry of a period of sufficient length to gather practical experience on the effects of these derogations on the protection of consumers and on the functioning of the common market,

HAS ADOPTED THIS DIRECTIVE:

Article 1

The producer shall be liable for damage caused by a defect in his product.

Article 2

For the purpose of this Directive 'product' means all movables, with the exception of primary agricultural products and game, even though incorporated into another movable or into an immovable. 'Primary agricultural products' means the products of the soil, of stock-farming and of fisheries, excluding products which have undergone initial processing. 'Product' includes electricity.

Article 3

1. 'Producer' means the manufacturer of a finished product, the producer of any raw material or the manufacturer of a component part and any person who, by putting his name, trade mark or other distinguishing feature on the product presents himself as its producer.

2. Without prejudice to the liability of the producer, any person who imports into the Community a product for sale, hire, leasing or any form of distribution in the course of his business shall be deemed to be a

producer within the meaning of this Directive and shall be responsible as a producer.

3. Where the producer of the product cannot be identified, each supplier of the product shall be treated as its producer unless he informs the injured person, within a reasonable time, of the identity of the producer or of the person who supplied him with the product. The same shall apply, in the case of an imported product, if this product does not indicate the identity of the importer referred to in paragraph 2, even if the name of the producer is indicated.

Article 4

The injured person shall be required to prove the damage, the defect and the causal relationship between defect and damage.

Article 5

Where, as a result of the provisions of this Directive, two or more persons are liable for the same damage, they shall be liable jointly and severally, without prejudice to the provisions of national law concerning the rights of contribution or recourse.

Article 6

1. A product is defective when it does not provide the safety which a person is entitled to expect, taking all circumstances into account, including:

(a) the presentation of the product;

(b) the use to which it could reasonably be expected that the product would be put;

(c) the time when the product was put into circulation.

2. A product shall not be considered defective for the sole reason that a better product is subsequently put into circulation.

Article 7

The producer shall not be liable as a result of this Directive if he proves:

(a) that he did not put the product into circulation; or

(b) that, having regard to the circumstances, it is probable that the defect which caused the damage did not exist at the time when the product was put into circulation by him or that this defect came into being afterwards; or

(c) that the product was neither manufactured by him for sale or any form of distribution for economic purpose nor manufactured or distributed by him in the course of his business; or

(d) that the defect is due to compliance of the product with mandatory regulations issued by the public authorities; or

(e) that the state of scientific and technical knowledge at the time when he put the product into circulation was not such as to enable the existence of the defect to be discovered; or

(f) in the case of a manufacturer of a component, that the defect is attributable to the design of the product in which the component has been fitted or to the instructions given by the manufacturer of the product.

Article 8

1. Without prejudice to the provisions of national law concerning the right of contribution or recourse, the liability of the producer shall not be reduced when the damage is caused both by a defect in product and by the act or omission of a third party.

2. The liability of the producer may be reduced or disallowed when, having regard to all the circumstances, the damage is caused both by a defect in the product and by the fault of the injured person or any person for whom the injured person is responsible.

Article 9

For the purpose of Article 1, 'damage' means:

(a) damage caused by death or by personal injuries;

(b) damage to, or destruction of, any item of property other than the defective product itself, with a lower threshold of 500 ECU, provided that the item of property:

(i) is of a type ordinarily intended for private use or consumption, and

(ii) was used by the injured person mainly for his own private use or consumption.

This Article shall be without prejudice to national provisions relating to non-material damage.

Article 10

1. Member States shall provide in their legislation that a limitation period of three years shall apply to proceedings for the recovery of damages as provided for in this Directive. The limitation period shall begin to run from the day on which the plaintiff became aware, or should reasonably have become aware, of the damage, the defect and the identity of the producer.

2. The laws of Member States regulating suspension or interruption of the limitation period shall not be affected by this Directive.

Article 11

Member States shall provide in their legislation that the rights conferred upon the injured person pursuant to this Directive shall be extinguished upon the expiry of a period of 10 years from the date on which the producer put into circulation the actual product which caused the damage, unless the injured person has in the meantime instituted proceedings against the producer.

Article 12

The liability of the producer arising from this Directive may not, in relation to the injured person, be limited or excluded by a provision limiting his liability or exempting him from liability.

Article 13

This Directive shall not affect any rights which an injured person may have according to the rules of the law of contractual or non-contractual liability or a special liability system existing at the moment when this Directive is notified.

Article 14

This Directive shall not apply to injury or damage arising from nuclear accidents and covered by international conventions ratified by the Member States.

Article 15

1. Each Member State may:

(a) by way of derogation from Article 2, provide in its legislation that within the meaning of Article 1 of this Directive 'product' also means primary agricultural products and game;

(b) by way of derogation from Article 7(e), maintain or, subject to the procedure set out in paragraph 2 of this Article, provide in this legislation that the producer shall be liable even if he proves that the state of scientific and technical knowledge at the time when he put the product into circulation was not such as to enable the existence of a defect to be discovered.

2. A Member State wishing to introduce the measure specified in paragraph 1(b) shall communicate the text of the proposed measure to the Commission. The Commission shall inform the other Member States thereof.

The Member State concerned shall hold the proposed measure in abeyance for nine months after the Commission is informed and provided that in the meantime the Commission has not submitted to the Council a proposal amending this Directive on the relevant matter. However, if within three months of receiving the said information, the Commission does not advise the Member State concerned that it intends submitting such a proposal to the Council, the Member State may take the proposed measure immediately.

If the Commission does submit to the Council such a proposal amending this Directive within the aforementioned nine months, the Member State concerned shall hold the proposed measure in abeyance for a further period of 18 months from the date on which the proposal is submitted.

3. Ten years after the date of notification of this Directive, the Commission shall submit to the Council a report on the effect that rulings by the courts as to the application of Article 7(e) and of paragraph 1(b) of this Article have on consumer protection and the functioning of the common market. In the light of this report the Council, acting on a proposal from the Commission and pursuant to the terms of Article 100 of the Treaty, shall decide whether to repeal Article 7(e).

Article 16

1. Any Member State may provide that a producer's total liability for damage resulting from a death or personal injury and caused by identical items with the same defect shall be limited to an amount which may not be less than 70 million ECU.

2. Ten years after the date of notification of this Directive, the Commission shall submit to the Council a report on the effect on consumer protection and the functioning of the common market of the implementation of the financial limit on liability by those Member States which have used the option provided for in paragraph 1. In the light of this report the Council, acting on a proposal from the Commission and pursuant to the terms of Article 100 of the Treaty, shall decide whether to repeal paragraph 1.

Article 17

This Directive shall not apply to products put into circulation before the date on which the provisions referred to in Article 19 enter into force.

Article 18

1. For the purposes of this Directive, the ECU shall be that defined by Regulation (EEC) No 3180/78, as amended by Regulation (EEC) No 2626/84. The equivalent in national currency shall initially be calculated at the rate obtaining on the date of adoption of this Directive.

2. Every five years the Council, acting on a proposal from the Commission, shall examine and, if need be, revise the amounts in this Directive, in the light of economic and monetary trends in the Community.

Article 19

1. Member States shall bring into force, not later than three years from the date of notification of this Directive [July 30, 1985], the laws, regulations and administrative provisions necessary to comply with this Directive. They shall forthwith inform the Commission thereof.

2. The procedure set out in Article 15(2) shall apply from the date of notification of this Directive.

Article 20

Member States shall communicate to the Commission the texts of the main provisions of national law which they subsequently adopt in the field governed by this Directive.

Article 21

Every five years the Commission shall present a report to the Council on the application of this Directive and, if necessary, shall submit appropriate proposals to it.

Article 22

This Directive is addressed to the Member States.

2. COUNCIL DIRECTIVE 75/129/EEC

of 17 February 1975

on the approximation of the laws of the Member States relating to collective redundancies

O.J. L 48/29 (Feb. 22, 1975)

THE COUNCIL OF THE EUROPEAN COMMUNITIES,

Having regard to the Treaty establishing the European Economic Community, and in particular Article 100 thereof;

Having regard to the proposal from the Commission;

Having regard to the Opinion of the European Parliament;

Having regard to the Opinion of the Economic and Social Committee;

Whereas it is important that greater protection should be afforded to workers in the event of collective redundancies while taking into account the need for balanced economic and social development within the Community;

Whereas, despite increasing convergence, differences still remain between the provisions in force in the Member States of the Community concerning the practical arrangements and procedures for such redundancies and the measures designed to alleviate the consequences of redundancy for workers;

Whereas these differences can have a direct effect on the functioning of the common market;

Whereas the Council resolution of 21 January 1974 concerning a social action programme makes provision for a Directive on the approximation of Member States' legislation on collective redundancies;

Whereas this approximation must therefore be promoted while the improvement is being maintained within the meaning of Article 117 of the Treaty,

HAS ADOPTED THIS DIRECTIVE:

SECTION I

DEFINITIONS AND SCOPE

Article 1

1. For the purposes of this Directive:

(a) 'collective redundancies' means dismissals effected by an employer for one or more reasons not related to the individual workers concerned where, according to the choice of the Member States, the number of redundancies is:

— either, over a period of 30 days:

(1) at least 10 in establishments normally employing more than 20 and less than 100 workers;

(2) at least 10% of the number of workers in establishments normally employing at least 100 but less than 300 workers;

(3) at least 30 in establishments normally employing 300 workers or more;

— or, over a period of 90 days, at least 20, whatever the number of workers normally employed in the establishments in question;

(b) 'workers' representatives' means the workers' representatives provided for by the laws or practices of the Member States.

2. This Directive shall not apply to:

(a) collective redundancies affected under contracts of employment concluded for limited periods of time or for specific tasks except where such redundancies take place prior to the date of expiry or the completion of such contracts;

(b) workers employed by public administrative bodies or by establishments governed by public law (or, in Member States where this concept is unknown, by equivalent bodies);

(c) the crews of sea-going vessels;

(d) workers affected by the termination of an establishment's activities where that is the result of a judicial decision.

SECTION II
CONSULTATION PROCEDURE
Article 2

1. Where an employer is contemplating collective redundancies, he shall begin consultations with the workers' representatives with a view to reaching an agreement.

2. These consultations shall, at least, cover ways and means of avoiding collective redundancies or reducing the number of workers affected, and mitigating the consequences.

3. To enable the workers' representatives to make constructive proposals the employer shall supply them with all relevant information and shall in any event give in writing the reasons for the redundancies, the number of workers to be made redundant, the number of workers normally employed and the period over which the redundancies are to be effected.

The employer shall forward to the competent public authority a copy of all the written communications referred to in the preceding subparagraph.

SECTION III
PROCEDURE FOR COLLECTIVE REDUNDANCIES
Article 3

1. Employers shall notify the competent public authority in writing of any projected collective redundancies.

This notification shall contain all relevant information concerning the projected collective redundancies and the consultations with workers' representatives provided for in Article 2, and particularly the reasons for the redundancies, the number of workers to be made redundant, the number of workers normally employed and the period over which the redundancies are to be effected.

2. Employers shall forward to the workers' representatives a copy of the notification provided for in paragraph 1.

The workers' representatives may send any comments they may have to the competent public authority.

Article 4

1. Projected collective redundancies notified to the competent public authority shall take effect not earlier than 30 days after the notification referred to in Article 3(1) without prejudice to any provisions governing individual rights with regard to notice of dismissal.

Member States may grant the competent public authority the power to reduce the period provided for in the preceding subparagraph.

2. The period provided for in paragraph 1 shall be used by the competent public authority to seek solutions in the problems raised by the projected collective redundancies.

3. Where the initial period provided for in paragraph 1 is shorter than 60 days, Member States may grant the competent public authority the power to extend the initial period to 60 days following notification where the problems raised by the projected collective redundancies are not likely to be solved within the initial period.

Member States may grant the competent public authority wider powers of extension.

The employer must be informed of the extension and the grounds for it before expiry of the initial period provided for in paragraph 1.

SECTION IV
FINAL PROVISIONS

Article 5

This Directive shall not affect the right of Member States to apply or to introduce laws, regulations or administrative provisions which are more favorable to workers.

Article 6

1. Member States shall bring into force the laws, regulations and administrative provisions needed in order to comply with this Directive within two years following its notification and shall forthwith inform the Commission thereof.

2. Member States shall communicate to the Commission the texts of the laws, regulations and administrative provisions which they adopt in the field covered by this Directive.

Article 7

Within two years following expiry of the two year period laid down in Article 6, Member States shall forward all relevant information to the Commission to enable it to draw up a report for submission to the Council on the application of this Directive.

Article 8

This Directive is addressed to the Member States.

3. COUNCIL DIRECTIVE 77/187/EEC

of 14 February 1977

on the approximation of the laws of the Member States relating to the safeguarding of employees' rights in the event of transfers of undertakings, businesses or parts of businesses

O.J. L 61/26 (Mar. 5, 1977)

THE COUNCIL OF THE EUROPEAN COMMUNITIES,

Having regard to the Treaty establishing the European Economic Community, and in particular Article 100 thereof,

Having regard to the proposal from the Commission,

Having regard to the opinion of the European Parliament,

Having regard to the opinion of the Economic and Social Committee,

Whereas economic trends are bringing in their wake, at both national and Community level, changes in the structure of undertakings, through transfers of undertakings, businesses or parts of businesses to other employers as a result of legal transfers or mergers;

Whereas it is necessary to provide for the protection of employees in the event of a change of employer, in particular, to ensure that their rights are safeguarded;

Whereas differences still remain in the Member States as regards the extent of the protection of employees in this respect and these differences should be reduced;

Whereas these differences can have a direct effect on the functioning of the common market;

Whereas it is therefore necessary to promote the approximation of laws in this field while maintaining the improvement described in Article 117 of the Treaty,

HAS ADOPTED THIS DIRECTIVE:

SECTION I
SCOPE AND DEFINITIONS

Article 1

1. This Directive shall apply to the transfer of an undertaking, business or part of a business to another employer as a result of a legal transfer or merger.

2. This Directive shall apply where and in so far as the undertaking, business or part of the business to be transferred is situated within the territorial scope of the Treaty.

3. This Directive shall not apply to sea-going vessels.

Article 2

For the purposes of this Directive:

(a) 'transferor' means any natural or legal person who, by reason of a transfer within the meaning of Article 1(1), ceases to be the employer in respect of the undertaking, business or part of the business;

(b) 'transferee' means any natural or legal person who, by reason of a transfer within the meaning of Article 1(1), becomes the employer in respect of the undertaking, business or part of the business;

(c) 'representatives of the employees' means the representatives of the employees provided for by the laws or practice of the Member States, with the exception of members of administrative, governing or supervisory bodies of companies who represent employees on such bodies in certain Member States.

SECTION II
SAFEGUARDING OF EMPLOYEES' RIGHTS
Article 3

1. The transferor's rights and obligations arising from a contract of employment or from an employment relationship existing on the date of a transfer within the meaning of Article 1(1) shall, by reason of such transfer, be transferred to the transferee.

Member States may provide that, after the date of transfer within the meaning of Article 1(1) and in addition to the transferee, the transferor shall continue to be liable in respect of obligations which arose from a contract of employment or an employment relationship.

2. Following the transfer within the meaning of Article 1(1), the transferee shall continue to observe the terms and conditions agreed in any collective agreement on the same terms applicable to the transferor under that agreement, until the date of termination or expiry of the collective agreement or the entry into force or application of another collective agreement.

Member States may limit the period for observing such terms and conditions, with the proviso that it shall not be less than one year.

3. Paragraphs 1 and 2 shall not cover employees' rights to old-age, invalidity or survivors' benefits under supplementary company or inter-company pension schemes outside the statutory social security schemes in Member States.

Member States shall adopt the measures necessary to protect the interests of employees and of persons no longer employed in the transferor's business at the time of the transfer within the meaning of Article 1(1) in respect of rights conferring on them immediate or prospective entitlement to old-age benefits, including survivors' benefits, under supplementary schemes referred to in the first subparagraph.

Article 4

1. The transfer of an undertaking, business or part of a business shall not in itself constitute grounds for dismissal by the transferor or the transferee. This provision shall not stand in the way of dismissals that

may take place for economic, technical or organizational reasons entailing changes in the workforce.

Member States may provide that the first subparagraph shall not apply to certain specific categories of employees who are not covered by the laws or practice of the Member States in respect of protection against dismissal.

2. If the contract of employment or the employment relationship is terminated because the transfer within the meaning of Article 1(1) involves a substantial change in working conditions to the detriment of the employee, the employer shall be regarded as having been responsible for termination of the contract of employment or of the employment relationship.

Article 5

1. If the business preserves its autonomy, the status and function, as laid down by the laws, regulations or administrative provisions of the Member States, of the representatives or of the representation of the employees affected by the transfer within the meaning of Article 1(1) shall be preserved.

The first subparagraph shall not apply if, under the laws, regulations, administrative provisions or practice of the Member States, the conditions necessary for the re-appointment of the representatives of the employees or for the reconstitution of the representation of the employees are fulfilled.

2. If the term of office of the representatives of the employees affected by a transfer within the meaning of Article 1(1) expires as a result of the transfer, the representatives shall continue to enjoy the protection provided by the laws, regulations, administrative provisions or practice of the Member States.

SECTION III
INFORMATION AND CONSULTATION

Article 6

1. The transferor and the transferee shall be required to inform the representatives of their respective employees affected by a transfer within the meaning of Article 1(1) of the following:

— the reasons for the transfer,

— the legal, economic and social implications of the transfer for the employees,

— measures envisaged in relation to the employees.

The transferor must give such information to the representatives of his employees in good time before the transfer is carried out.

The transferee must give such information to the representatives of his employees in good time, and in any event before his employees are directly affected by the transfer as regards their conditions of work and employment.

2. If the transferor or the transferee envisages measures in relation to his employees, he shall consult his representatives of the employees in good time on such measures with a view to seeking agreement.

3. Member States whose laws, regulations or administrative provisions provide that representatives of the employees may have recourse to an arbitration board to obtain a decision on the measures to be taken in relation to employees may limit the obligations laid down in paragraphs 1 and 2 to cases where the transfer carried out gives rise to a change in the business likely to entail serious disadvantages for a considerable number of the employees.

The information and consultations shall cover at least the measures envisaged in relation to the employees.

The information must be provided and consultations take place in good time before the change in the business as referred to in the first subparagraph is effected.

4. Member States may limit the obligations laid down in paragraphs 1, 2 and 3 to undertakings or businesses which, in respect of the number of employees, fulfil the conditions for the election or designation of a collegiate body representing the employees.

5. Member States may provide that where there are no representatives of the employees in an undertaking or business, the employees concerned must be informed in advance when a transfer within the meaning of Article 1(1) is about to take place.

SECTION IV
FINAL PROVISIONS

Article 7

This Directive shall not affect the right of Member States to apply or introduce laws, regulations or administrative provisions which are more favorable to employees.

Article 8

1. Member States shall bring into force the laws, regulations and administrative provisions needed to comply with this Directive within two years of its notification and shall forthwith inform the Commission thereof.

2. Member States shall communicate to the Commission the texts of the laws, regulations and administrative provisions which they adopt in the field covered by this Directive.

Article 9

Within two years following expiry of the two-year period laid down in Article 8, Member States shall forward all relevant information to the Commission in order to enable it to draw up a report on the application of this Directive for submission to the Council.

Article 10

This Directive is addressed to the Member States.

4. COUNCIL DIRECTIVE 80/987/EEC

of 20 October 1980

on the approximation of the laws of the Member States relating to the protection of employees in the event of the insolvency of their employer

O.J. L 283/23 (Oct. 28, 1980)

THE COUNCIL OF THE EUROPEAN COMMUNITIES,

Having regard to the Treaty establishing the European Economic Community, and in particular Article 100 thereof,

Having regard to the proposal from the Commission,

Having regard to the opinion of the European Parliament,

Having regard to the opinion of the Economic and Social Committee,

Whereas it is necessary to provide for the protection of employees in the event of the insolvency of their employer, in particular in order to guarantee payment of their outstanding claims, while taking account of the need for balanced economic and social development in the Community;

Whereas differences still remain between the Member States as regards the extent of the protection of employees in this respect; whereas efforts should be directed towards reducing these differences, which can have a direct effect on the functioning of the common market;

Whereas the approximation of laws in this field should, therefore, be promoted while the improvement within the meaning of Article 117 of the Treaty is maintained;

* * *

HAS ADOPTED THIS DIRECTIVE:

SECTION I
SCOPE AND DEFINITIONS

Article 1

1. This Directive shall apply to employees' claims arising from contracts of employment or employment relationships and existing against employers who are in a state of insolvency within the meaning of Article 2(1).

2. Member States may, by way of exception, exclude claims by certain categories of employee from the scope of this Directive, by virtue of the special nature of the employee's contract of employment or employment relationship or of the existence of other forms of guarantee offering the employee protection equivalent to that resulting from this Directive.

The categories of employee referred to in the first subparagraph are listed in the Annex.

* * *

Article 2

1. For the purposes of this Directive, an employer shall be deemed to be in a state of insolvency:

(a) where a request has been made for the opening of proceedings involving the employer's assets, as provided for under the laws, regulations and administrative provisions of the Member State concerned, to satisfy collectively the claims of creditors and which make it possible to take into consideration the claims referred to in Article 1(1), and

(b) where the authority which is competent pursuant to the said laws, regulations and administrative provisions has:

— either decided to open the proceedings,

— or established that the employer's undertaking or business has been definitively closed down and that the available assets are insufficient to warrant the opening of the proceedings.

2. This Directive is without prejudice to national law as regards the definition of the terms 'employee', 'employer', 'pay', 'right conferring immediate entitlement' and 'right conferring prospective entitlement'.

SECTION II
PROVISIONS CONCERNING GUARANTEE INSTITUTIONS

Article 3

1. Member States shall take the measures necessary to ensure that guarantee institutions guarantee, subject to Article 4, payment of employees' outstanding claims resulting from contracts of employment or employment relationships and relating to pay for the period prior to a given date.

2. At the choice of the Member States, the date referred to in paragraph 1 shall be:

— either that of the onset of the employer's insolvency;

— or that of the notice of dismissal issued to the employee concerned on account of the employer's insolvency;

— or that of the onset of the employer's insolvency or that on which the contract of employment or the employment relationship with the employee concerned was discontinued on account of the employer's insolvency.

Article 4

1. Member States shall have the option to limit the liability of guarantee institutions, referred to in Article 3.

2. When Member States exercise the option referred to in paragraph 1, they shall:

— in the case referred to in Article 3(2), first indent, ensure the payment of outstanding claims relating to pay for the last three months of the contract of employment or employment relationship occurring within a period of six months preceding the date of the onset of the employer's insolvency;

— in the case referred to in Article 3(2), second indent, ensure the payment of outstanding claims relating to pay for the last three months of the contract of employment or employment relationship preceding the date of the notice of dismissal issued to the employee on account of the employer's insolvency;

— in the case referred to in Article 3(2), third indent, ensure the payment of outstanding claims relating to pay for the last 18 months of the contract of employment or employment relationship preceding the date of the onset of the employer's insolvency or the date on which the contract of employment or the employment relationship with the employee was discontinued on account of the employer's insolvency. In this case, Member States may limit the liability to make payment to pay corresponding to a period of eight weeks or to several shorter periods totalling eight weeks.

3. However, in order to avoid the payment of sums going beyond the social objective of this Directive, Member States may set a ceiling to the liability for employees' outstanding claims.

When Member States exercise this option, they shall inform the Commission of the methods used to set the ceiling.

Article 5

Member States shall lay down detailed rules for the organization, financing and operation of the guarantee institutions, complying with the following principles in particular:

(a) the assets of the institutions shall be independent of the employers' operating capital and be inaccessible to proceedings for insolvency;

(b) employers shall contribute to financing, unless it is fully covered by the public authorities;

(c) the institutions' liabilities shall not depend on whether or not obligations to contribute to financing have been fulfilled.

SECTION III
PROVISIONS CONCERNING SOCIAL SECURITY

Article 6

Member States may stipulate that Articles 3, 4 and 5 shall not apply to contributions due under national statutory social security schemes or under supplementary company or inter-company pension schemes outside the national statutory social security schemes.

Article 7

Member States shall take the measures necessary to ensure that non-payment of compulsory contributions due from the employer, before the onset of his insolvency, to their insurance institutions under national statutory social security schemes does not adversely affect employees' benefit entitlement in respect of these insurance institutions inasmuch as the employees' contributions were deducted at source from the remuneration paid.

Article 8

Member States shall ensure that the necessary measures are taken to protect the interests of employees and of persons having already left the employer's undertaking or business at the date of the onset of the employer's insolvency in respect of rights conferring on them immediate or prospective entitlement to old-age benefits, including survivors' benefits, under supplementary company or inter-company pension schemes outside the national statutory social security schemes.

SECTION IV
General and final provisions

Article 9

This Directive shall not affect the option of Member States to apply or introduce laws, regulations or administrative provisions which are more favourable to employees.

Article 10

This Directive shall not affect the option of Member States:

(a) to take the measures necessary to avoid abuses;

(b) to refuse or reduce the liability referred to in Article 3 or the guarantee obligation referred to in Article 7 if it appears that fulfilment of the obligation is unjustifiable because of the existence of special links between the employee and the employer and of common interests resulting in collusion between them.

Article 11

1. Member States shall bring into force the laws, regulations and administrative provisions necessary to comply with this Directive within 36 months of its notification. They shall forthwith inform the Commission thereof.

* * *

Article 12

Within 18 months of the expiry of the period of 36 months laid down in Article 11(1), Member States shall forward all relevant information to the Commission in order to enable it to draw up a report on the application of this Directive for submission to the Council.

Article 13

This Directive is addressed to the Member States.

5. COMMUNITY CHARTER OF THE FUNDAMENTAL SOCIAL RIGHTS OF WORKERS

[Adopted by all of the Member States other than the United Kingdom at a European Council meeting in Strassbourg on December 9–10, 1989.]

Whereas, under the terms of Article 117 of the EEC Treaty, the Member States have agreed on the need to promote improved living and working conditions for workers so as to make possible their harmonization while the improvement is being maintained;

Whereas following on from the conclusions of the European Councils of Hanover and Rhodes the European Council of Madrid considered that, in the context of the establishment of the single European market, the same importance must be attached to the social aspects as to the economic aspects and whereas, therefore, they must be developed in a balanced manner;

Having regard to the Resolutions of the European Parliament of 15 March 1989 and 14 September 1989 and to the Opinion of the Economic and Social Committee of 22 February 1989;

Whereas the completion of the internal market is the most effective means of creating employment and ensuring maximum well-being in the Community; whereas employment development and creation must be given first priority in the completion of the internal market; whereas it is for the Community to take up the challenges of the future with regard to economic competitiveness, taking into account, in particular, regional imbalances;

Whereas the social consensus contributes to the strengthening of the competitiveness of undertakings and of the economy as a whole and to the creation of employment; whereas in this respect it is an essential condition for ensuring sustained economic development;

Whereas the completion of the internal market must favour the approximation of improvements in living and working conditions, as well as economic and social cohesion within the European Community, while avoiding distortions of competition;

Whereas the completion of the internal market must offer improvements in the social field for workers of the European Community, especially in terms of freedom of movement, living and working conditions, health and safety at work, social protection, education and training;

Whereas, in order to ensure equal treatment, it is important to combat every form of discrimination, including discrimination on grounds of sex, colour, race, opinions and beliefs, and whereas, in a spirit of solidarity, it is important to combat social exclusion;

Whereas it is for Member States to guarantee that workers from non-member countries and members of their families who are legally resident in a Member State of the European Community are able to enjoy, as regards their living and working conditions, treatment comparable to that enjoyed by workers who are nationals of the Member State concerned;

Whereas inspiration should be drawn from the Conventions of the International Labour Organization and from the European Social Charter of the Council of Europe;

Whereas the Treaty, as amended by the Single European Act, contains provisions laying down the powers of the Community relating, inter alia, to the freedom of movement of workers (Articles 7, 48–51), to the right of establishment (Articles 52–58), to the social field under the conditions laid down in Articles 117–122—in particular as regards the improvement of health and safety in the working environment (Article 118a), the development of the dialogue between management and labour at European level (Article 118b), equal pay for men and women for equal work (Article 119)—to the general principles for implementing a common vocational training policy (Article 128), to economic and social cohesion (Article 130a to 130e) and, more generally, to the approximation of legislation (Articles 100, 100a and 235); whereas the implementation of the Charter must not entail an extension of the Community's powers as defined by the Treaties;

Whereas the aim of the present Charter is on the one hand to consolidate the progress made in the social field, through action by the Member States, the two sides of industry and the Community;

Whereas its aim is on the other hand to declare solemnly that the implementation of the Single European Act must take full account of the social dimension of the Community and that it is necessary in this context to ensure at appropriate levels the development of the social rights of workers of the European Community, especially employed workers and self-employed persons;

Whereas, in accordance with the conclusions of the Madrid European Council, the respective roles of Community rules, national legislation and collective agreements must be clearly established;

Whereas, by virtue of the principle of subsidiarity, responsibility for the initiatives to be taken with regard to the implementation of these social rights lies with the Member States or their constituent parts and, within the limits of its powers, with the European Community; whereas such implementation may take the form of laws, collective agreements or existing practices at the various appropriate levels and whereas it requires in many spheres the active involvement of the two sides of industry;

Whereas the solemn proclamation of fundamental social rights at European Community level may not, when implemented, provide grounds for any retrogression compared with the situation currently existing in each Member State,

HAVE ADOPTED THE FOLLOWING DECLARATION CONSTITUTING THE "COMMUNITY CHARTER OF THE FUNDAMENTAL SOCIAL RIGHTS OF WORKERS":

TITLE I

FUNDAMENTAL SOCIAL RIGHTS OF WORKERS

FREEDOM OF MOVEMENT

1. Every worker of the European Community shall have the right to freedom of movement throughout the territory of the Community, subject to restrictions justified on grounds of public order, public safety or public health.

2. The right to freedom of movement shall enable any worker to engage in any occupation or profession in the Community in accordance with the principles of equal treatment as regards access to employment, working conditions and social protection in the host country.

3. The right of freedom of movement shall also imply:

— harmonization of conditions of residence in all Member States, particularly those concerning family reunification;

— elimination of obstacles arising from the non-recognition of diplomas or equivalent occupational qualifications;

— improvement of the living and working conditions of frontier workers.

EMPLOYMENT AND REMUNERATION

4. Every individual shall be free to choose and engage in an occupation according to the regulations governing each occupation.

5. All employment shall be fairly remunerated.

To this effect, in accordance with arrangements applying in each country:

— workers shall be assured of an equitable wage, i.e. a wage sufficient to enable them to have a decent standard of living;

— workers subject to terms of employment other than an open-ended full time contract shall receive an equitable reference wage;

— wages may be withheld, seized or transferred only in accordance with the provisions of national law; such provisions should entail measures enabling the worker concerned to continue to enjoy the necessary means of subsistence for himself and his family.

6. Every individual must be able to have access to public placement services free of charge.

IMPROVEMENT OF LIVING AND WORKING CONDITIONS

7. The completion of the internal market must lead to an improvement in the living and working conditions of workers in the European Community. This process must result from an approximation of these conditions while the improvement is being maintained, as regards in particular the duration and organization of working time and forms of employment other than open-ended contracts, such as fixed-term contracts, part-time working, temporary work and seasonal work.

The improvement must cover, where necessary, the development of certain aspects of employment regulations such as procedures for collective redundancies and those regarding bankruptcies.

8. Every worker of the European Community shall have a right to a weekly rest period and to annual paid leave, the duration of which must be harmonized in accordance with national practices while the improvement is being maintained.

9. The conditions of employment of every worker of the European Community shall be stipulated in laws, in a collective agreement or in a contract of employment, according to arrangements applying in each country.

SOCIAL PROTECTION

According to the arrangements applying in each country:

10. Every worker of the European Community shall have a right to adequate social protection and shall, whatever his status and whatever the size of the undertaking in which he is employed, enjoy an adequate level of social security benefits.

Persons who have been unable either to enter or re-enter the labour market and have no means of subsistence must be able to receive sufficient resources and social assistance in keeping with their particular situation.

FREEDOM OF ASSOCIATION AND COLLECTIVE BARGAINING

11. Employers and workers of the European Community shall have the right of association in order to constitute professional organizations or trade unions of their choice for the defence of their economic and social interests.

Every employer and every worker shall have the freedom to join or not to join such organizations without any personal or occupational damage being thereby suffered by him.

12. Employers or employers' organizations, on the one hand, and workers' organizations, on the other, shall have the right to negotiate and conclude collective agreements under the conditions laid down by national legislation and practice.

The dialogue between the two sides of industry at European level which must be developed, may, if the parties deem it desirable, result in contractual relations, in particular at inter-occupational and sectoral level.

13. The right to resort to collective action in the event of a conflict of interests shall include the right to strike, subject to the obligations arising under national regulations and collective agreements.

In order to facilitate the settlement of industrial disputes the establishment and utilization at the appropriate levels of conciliation, mediation and arbitration procedures should be encouraged in accordance with national practice.

14. The internal legal order of the Member States shall determine under which conditions and to what extent the rights provided for in Articles 11 to 13 apply to the armed forces, the police and the civil service.

VOCATIONAL TRAINING

15. Every worker of the European Community must be able to have access to vocational training and to receive such training throughout his working life. In the conditions governing access to such training there may be no discrimination on grounds of nationality.

The competent public authorities, undertakings or the two sides of industry, each within their own sphere of competence, should set up continuing and permanent training systems enabling every person to undergo retraining more especially through leave for training purposes, to improve his skills or to acquire new skills, particularly in the light of technical developments.

EQUAL TREATMENT FOR MEN AND WOMEN

16. Equal treatment for men and women must be assured. Equal opportunities for men and women must be developed.

To this end, action should be intensified wherever necessary to ensure the implementation of the principle of equality between men and women as regards in particular access to employment, remuneration, working conditions, social protection, education, vocational training and career development.

Measures should also be developed enabling men and women to reconcile their occupational and family obligations.

INFORMATION, CONSULTATION AND PARTICIPATION FOR WORKERS

17. Information, consultation and participation for workers must be developed along appropriate lines, taking account of the practices in force in the various Member States.

This shall apply especially in companies or groups of companies having establishments or companies in several Member States of the European Community.

18. Such information, consultation and participation must be implemented in due time, particularly in the following cases:

— when technological changes which, from the point of view of working conditions and work organization, have major implications for the work force are introduced into undertakings;

— in connection with restructuring operations in undertakings or in cases of mergers having an impact on the employment of workers;

— in cases of collective redundancy procedures;

— when transfrontier workers in particular are affected by employment policies pursued by the undertaking where they are employed.

HEALTH PROTECTION AND SAFETY AT THE WORKPLACE

19. Every worker must enjoy satisfactory health and safety conditions in his working environment. Appropriate measures must be taken in order to achieve further harmonization of conditions in this area while maintaining the improvements made.

These measures shall take account, in particular, of the need for the training, information, consultation and balanced participation of workers as regards the risks incurred and the steps taken to eliminate or reduce them.

The provisions regarding implementation of the internal market shall help to ensure such protection.

PROTECTION OF CHILDREN AND ADOLESCENTS

20. Without prejudice to such rules as may be more favourable to young people, in particular those ensuring their preparation for work through vocational training, and subject to derogations limited to certain light work, the minimum employment age must not be lower than the minimum school-leaving age and, in any case, not lower than 15 years.

21. Young people who are in gainful employment must receive equitable remuneration in accordance with national practice.

22. Appropriate measures must be taken to adjust labour regulations applicable to young workers so that their specific needs regarding development, vocational training and access to employment are met.

The duration of work must, in particular, be limited—without it being possible to circumvent this limitation through recourse to overtime—and night work prohibited in the case of workers of under eighteen years of age, save in the case of certain jobs laid down in national legislation or regulations.

23. Following the end of compulsory education, young people must be entitled to receive initial vocational training of a sufficient duration to enable them to adapt to the requirements of their future working life; for young workers, such training should take place during working hours.

ELDERLY PERSONS

According to the arrangements applying in each country:

24. Every worker of the European Community must, at the time of retirement, be able to enjoy resources affording him or her a decent standard of living.

25. Every person who has reached retirement age but who is not entitled to a pension or who does not have other means of subsistence, must be entitled to sufficient resources and to medical and social assistance specifically suited to his needs.

DISABLED PERSONS

26. All disabled persons, whatever the origin and nature of their disablement, must be entitled to additional concrete measures aimed at improving their social and professional integration.

These measures must concern, in particular, according to the capacities of the beneficiaries, vocational training, ergonomics, accessibility, mobility, means of transport and housing.

TITLE II
IMPLEMENTATION OF THE CHARTER

27. It is more particularly the responsibility of the Member States, in accordance with the national practices, notably through legislative measures or collective agreements, to guarantee the fundamental social rights in this Charter and to implement the social measures indispensable to the smooth operation of the internal market as part of a strategy of economic and social cohesion.

28. The European Council invites the Commission to submit as soon as possible initiatives which fall within its powers, as provided for in the Treaties, with a view to the adoption of legal instruments for the effective implementation, as and when the internal market is completed, of those rights which come within the Community's area of competence.

29. The Commission shall establish each year, during the last three months, a report on the application of the Charter by the Member States and by the European Community.

30. The report of the Commission shall be forwarded to the European Council, the European Parliament and the Economic and Social Committee.

6. COUNCIL DIRECTIVE 91/533/EEC

of 14 October 1991

on an employer's obligation to inform employees of the conditions applicable to the contract or employment relationship

O.J. L 288/32 (Oct. 18, 1991)

THE COUNCIL OF THE EUROPEAN COMMUNITIES,

Having regard to the Treaty establishing the European Economic Community, and in particular Article 100 thereof,

Having regard to the proposal from the Commission,[1]

Having regard to the opinion of the European Parliament,[2]

Having regard to the opinion of the Economic and Social Committee,[3]

Whereas the development, in the Member States, of new forms of work has led to an increase in the number of types of employment relationship;

Whereas, faced with this development, certain Member States have considered it necessary to subject employment relationships to formal requirements; whereas these provisions are designed to provide employees with improved protection against possible infringements of their rights and to create greater transparency on the labour market;

Whereas the relevant legislation of the Member States differs considerably on such fundamental points as the requirement to inform employees in writing of the main terms of the contract or employment relationship;

Whereas differences in the legislation of Member States may have a direct effect on the operation of the common market;

Whereas Article 117 of the Treaty provides for the Member States to agree upon the need to promote improved working conditions and an improved standard of living for workers, so as to make possible their harmonization while the improvement is being maintained;

Whereas point 9 of the Community Charter of Fundamental Social Rights for Workers, adopted at the Strasbourg European Council on 9 December 1989 by the Heads of State and Government of 11 Member States, states:

'The conditions of employment of every worker of the European Community shall be stipulated in laws, a collective agreement or a contract of employment, according to arrangements applying in each country.';

Whereas it is necessary to establish at Community level the general requirement that every employee must be provided with a document

1. OJ No C 24, 31. 1. 1991, p. 3.
2. OJ No C 240, 16. 9. 1991, p. 21.
3. OJ No C 159, 17. 6. 1991, p. 32.

containing information on the essential elements of his contract or employment relationship;

Whereas, in view of the need to maintain a certain degree of flexibility in employment relationships, Member States should be able to exclude certain limited cases of employment relationship from this Directive's scope of application;

* * *

Whereas, in order to protect the interests of employees with regard to obtaining a document, any change in the main terms of the contract or employment relationship must be communicated to them in writing;

* * *

HAS ADOPTED THIS DIRECTIVE:

Article 1
Scope

1. This Directive shall apply to every paid employee having a contract or employment relationship defined by the law in force in a Member State and/or governed by the law in force in a Member State.

2. Member States may provide that this Directive shall not apply to employees having a contract or employment relationship:

(a) — with a total duration not exceeding one month, and/or

— with a working week not exceeding eight hours; or

(b) of a casual and/or specific nature provided, in these cases, that its non-application is justified by objective considerations.

Article 2
Obligation to provide information

1. An employer shall be obliged to notify an employee to whom this Directive applies, hereinafter referred to as 'the employee', of the essential aspects of the contract or employment relationship.

2. The information referred to in paragraph 1 shall cover at least the following:

(a) the identities of the parties;

(b) the place of work; where there is no fixed or main place of work, the principle that the employee is employed at various places and the registered place of business or, where appropriate, the domicile of the employer;

(c)(i) the title, grade, nature or category of the work for which the employee is employed; or

(ii) a brief specification or description of the work;

(d) the date of commencement of the contract or employment relationship;

(e) in the case of a temporary contract or employment relationship, the expected duration thereof;

(f) the amount of paid leave to which the employee is entitled or, where this cannot be indicated when the information is given, the procedures for allocating and determining such leave;

(g) the length of the periods of notice to be observed by the employer and the employee should their contract or employment relationship be terminated or, where this cannot be indicated when the information is given, the method for determining such periods of notice;

(h) the initial basic amount, the other component elements and the frequency of payment of the remuneration to which the employee is entitled;

(i) the length of the employee's normal working day or week;

(j) where appropriate;

   (i) the collective agreements governing the employee's conditions of work;

   or

   (ii) in the case of collective agreements concluded outside the business by special joint bodies or institutions, the name of the competent body or joint institution within which the agreements were concluded.

3. The information referred to in paragraph 2(f), (g), (h) and (i) may, where appropriate, be given in the form of a reference to the laws, regulations and administrative or statutory provisions or collective agreements governing those particular points.

Article 3
Means of information

1. The information referred to in Article 2(2) may be given to the employee, not later than two months after the commencement of employment, in the form of:

(a) a written contract of employment; and/or

(b) a letter of engagement; and/or

(c) one or more other written documents, where one of these documents contains at least all the information referred to in Article 2(2)(a), (b), (c), (d), (h) and (i).

2. Where none of the documents referred to in paragraph 1 is handed over to the employee within the prescribed period, the employer shall be obliged to give the employee, not later than two months after the commencement of employment, a written declaration signed by the employer and containing at least the information referred to in Article 2(2).

Where the document(s) referred to in paragraph 1 contain only part of the information required, the written declaration provided for in the first subparagraph of this paragraph shall cover the remaining information.

3. Where the contract or employment relationship comes to an end before expiry of a period of two months as from the date of the start of work, the information provided for in Article 2 and in this Article must be made available to the employee by the end of this period at the latest.

Article 4
Expatriate employees

1. Where an employee is required to work in a country or countries other than the Member State whose law and/or practice governs the contract or employment relationship, the document(s) referred to in Article 3 must be in his/her possession before his/her departure and must include at least the following additional information:

(a) the duration of the employment abroad;

(b) the currency to be used for the payment of remuneration;

(c) where appropriate, the benefits in cash or kind attendant on the employment abroad;

(d) where appropriate, the conditions governing the employee's repatriation.

2. The information referred to in paragraph 1(b) and (c) may, where appropriate, be given in the form of a reference to the laws, regulations and administrative or statutory provisions or collective agreements governing those particular points.

3. Paragraphs 1 and 2 shall not apply if the duration of the employment outside the country whose law and/or practice governs the contract or employment relationship is one month or less.

Article 5
Modification of aspects of the contract or employment relationship

1. Any change in the details referred to in Articles 2(2) and 4(1) must be the subject of a written document to be given by the employer to the employee at the earliest opportunity and not later than one month after the date of entry into effect of the change in question.

2. The written document referred to in paragraph 1 shall not be compulsory in the event of a change in the laws, regulations and administrative or statutory provisions or collective agreements cited in the documents referred to in Article 3, supplemented, where appropriate, pursuant to Article 4(1).

Article 6
Form and proof of the existence of a contract or employment relationship and procedural rules

This Directive shall be without prejudice to national law and practice concerning:

— the form of the contract or employment relationship,

— proof as regards the existence and content of a contract or employment relationship,

— the relevant procedural rules.

Article 7
More favourable provisions

This Directive shall not affect Member States' prerogative to apply or to introduce laws, regulations or administrative provisions which are more favourable to employees or to encourage or permit the application of agreements which are more favourable to employees.

Article 8
Defence of rights

1. Member States shall introduce into their national legal systems such measures as are necessary to enable all employees who consider themselves wronged by failure to comply with the obligations arising from this Directive to pursue their claims by judicial process after possible recourse to other competent authorities.

2. Member States may provide that access to the means of redress referred to in paragraph 1 are subject to the notification of the employer by the employee and the failure by the employer to reply within 15 days of notification.

However, the formality of prior notification may in no case be required in the cases referred to in Article 4, neither for workers with a temporary contract or employment relationship, nor for employees not covered by a collective agreement or by collective agreements relating to the employment relationship.

Article 9
Final provisions

1. Member States shall adopt the laws, regulations and administrative provisions necessary to comply with this Directive no later than 30 June 1993 or shall ensure by that date that the employers' and workers' representatives introduce the required provisions by way of agreement, the Member States being obliged to take the necessary steps enabling them at all times to guarantee the results imposed by this Directive.

They shall forthwith inform the Commission thereof.

2. Member States shall take the necessary measures to ensure that, in the case of employment relationships in existence upon entry into force of the provisions that they adopt, the employer gives the employee, on request, within two months of receiving that request, any of the documents referred to in Article 3, supplemented, where appropriate, pursuant to Article 4(1).

3. When Member States adopt the measures referred to in paragraph 1, such measures shall contain a reference to this Directive or shall be accompanied by such reference on the occasion of their official publication. The methods of making such a reference shall be laid down by the Member States.

4. Member States shall forthwith inform the Commission of the measures they take to implement this Directive.

Article 10

This Directive is addressed to the Member States.

7. COUNCIL DIRECTIVE 75/117/EEC

of 10 February 1975

on the approximation of the laws of the Member States relating to the application of the principle of equal pay for men and women

O.J. L 45/19 (Feb. 19, 1975)

THE COUNCIL OF THE EUROPEAN COMMUNITIES,

Having regard to the Treaty establishing the European Economic Community, and in particular Article 100 thereof;

Having regard to the proposal from the Commission;

Having regard to the Opinion of the European Parliament;

Having regard to the Opinion of the Economic and Social Committee;

Whereas implementation of the principle that men and women should receive equal pay contained in Article 119 of the Treaty is an integral part of the establishment and functioning of the common market;

Whereas it is primarily the responsibility of the Member States to ensure the application of this principle by means of appropriate laws, regulations and administrative provisions;

Whereas the Council resolution of 21 January 1974 concerning a social action programme, aimed at making it possible to harmonize living and working conditions while the improvement is being maintained and at achieving a balanced social and economic development of the Community, recognized that priority should be given to action taken on behalf of women as regards access to employment and vocational training and advancement, and as regards working conditions, including pay;

Whereas it is desirable to reinforce the basic laws by standards aimed at facilitating the practical application of the principle of equality in such a way that all employees in the Community can be protected in these matters;

Whereas differences continue to exist in the various Member States despite the efforts made to apply the resolution of the conference of the Member States of 30 December 1961 on equal pay for men and women and whereas, therefore, the national provisions should be approximated as regards application of the principle of equal pay,

HAS ADOPTED THIS DIRECTIVE:

Article 1

The principle of equal pay for men and women outlined in Article 119 of the Treaty, hereinafter called 'principle of equal pay', means, for the same work or for work to which equal value is attributed, the elimination of all discrimination on grounds of sex with regard to all aspects and conditions of remuneration.

In particular, where a job classification system is used for determining pay, it must be based on the same criteria for both men and women and so drawn up as to exclude any discrimination on grounds of sex.

Article 2

Member States shall introduce into their national legal systems such measures as are necessary to enable all employees who consider themselves wronged by failure to apply the principle of equal pay to pursue their claims by judicial process after possible recourse to other competent authorities.

Article 3

Member States shall abolish all discrimination between men and women arising from laws, regulations or administrative provisions which is contrary to the principle of equal pay.

Article 4

Member States shall take the necessary measures to ensure that provisions appearing in collective agreements, wage scales, wage agreements or individual contracts of employment which are contrary to the principle of equal pay shall be, or may be declared, null and void or may be amended.

Article 5

Member States shall take the necessary measures to protect employees against dismissal by the employer as a reaction to a complaint within the undertaking or to any legal proceedings aimed at enforcing compliance with the principle of equal pay.

Article 6

Member States shall, in accordance with their national circumstances and legal systems, take the measures necessary to ensure that the principle of equal pay is applied. They shall see that effective means are available to take care that this principle is observed.

Article 7

Member States shall take care that the provisions adopted pursuant to this Directive, together with the relevant provisions already in force, are brought to the attention of employees by all appropriate means, for example at their place of employment.

Article 8

1. Member States shall put into force the laws, regulations and administrative provisions necessary in order to comply with this Directive within one year of its notification and shall immediately inform the Commission thereof.

2. Member States shall communicate to the Commission the texts of the laws, regulations and administrative provisions which they adopt in the field covered by this Directive.

Article 9

Within two years of the expiry of the one-year period referred to in Article 8, Member States shall forward all necessary information to the Commission to enable it to draw up a report on the application of the Directive for submission to the Council.

Article 10

This Directive is addressed to the Member States.

8. COUNCIL DIRECTIVE 76/207/EEC

of 9 February 1976

on the implementation of the principle of equal treatment for men and women as regards access to employment, vocational training and promotion, and working conditions

O.J. L 39/40 (Feb. 14, 1976)

THE COUNCIL OF THE EUROPEAN COMMUNITIES,

Having regard to the Treaty establishing the European Economic Community, and in particular Article 235 thereof,

Having regard to the proposal from the Commission,

Having regard to the opinion of the European Parliament,

Having regard to the opinion of the Economic and Social Committee,

Whereas the Council, in its resolution of 21 January 1974 concerning a social action programme, included among the priorities action for the purpose of achieving equality between men and women as regards access to employment and vocational training and promotion and as regards working conditions, including pay;

* * *

Whereas Community action to achieve the principle of equal treatment for men and women in respect of access to employment and vocational training and promotion and in respect of other working conditions also appears to be necessary; whereas, equal treatment for male and female workers constitutes one of the objectives of the Community, in so far as the harmonization of living and working conditions while maintaining their improvement are inter alia to be furthered; whereas the Treaty does not confer the necessary specific powers for this purpose;

Whereas the definition and progressive implementation of the principle of equal treatment in matters of social security should be ensured by means of subsequent instruments,

HAS ADOPTED THIS DIRECTIVE:

Article 1

1. The purpose of this Directive is to put into effect in the Member States the principle of equal treatment for men and women as regards access to employment, including promotion, and to vocational training and as regards working conditions and, on the conditions referred to in paragraph 2, social security. This principle is hereinafter referred to as 'the principle of equal treatment.'

2. With a view to ensuring the progressive implementation of the principle of equal treatment in matters of social security, the Council, acting on a proposal from the Commission, will adopt provisions defining its substance, its scope and the arrangements for its application.

Article 2

1. For the purposes of the following provisions, the principle of equal treatment shall mean that there shall be no discrimination whatsoever on grounds of sex either directly or indirectly by reference in particular to marital or family status.

2. This Directive shall be without prejudice to the right of Member States to exclude from its field of application those occupational activities and, where appropriate, the training leading thereto, for which, by reason of their nature or the context in which they are carried out, the sex of the worker constitutes a determining factor.

3. This Directive shall be without prejudice to provisions concerning the protection of women, particularly as regards pregnancy and maternity.

4. This Directive shall be without prejudice to measures to promote equal opportunity for men and women, in particular by removing existing inequalities which affect women's opportunities in the areas referred to in Article 1(1).

Article 3

1. Application of the principle of equal treatment means that there shall be no discrimination whatsoever on grounds of sex in the conditions, including selection criteria, for access to all jobs or posts, whatever the sector or branch of activity, and to all levels of the occupational hierarchy.

2. To this end, Member States shall take the measures necessary to ensure that:

(a) any laws, regulations and administrative provisions contrary to the principle of equal treatment shall be abolished;

(b) any provisions contrary to the principle of equal treatment which are included in collective agreements, individual contracts of employment, internal rules of undertakings or in rules governing the independent occupations and professions shall be, or may be declared, null and void or may be amended;

(c) those laws, regulations and administrative provisions contrary to the principle of equal treatment when the concern for protection which originally inspired them is no longer well founded shall be revised; and that where similar provisions are included in collective agreements labour and management shall be requested to undertake the desired revision.

Article 4

Application of the principle of equal treatment with regard to access to all types and to all levels, of vocational guidance, vocational training, advanced vocational training and retraining, means that Member States shall take all necessary measures to ensure that:

(a) any laws, regulations and administrative provisions contrary to the principle of equal treatment shall be abolished;

(b) any provisions contrary to the principle of equal treatment which are included in collective agreements, individual contracts of employment, internal rules of undertakings or in rules governing the independent occupations and professions shall be, or may be declared, null and void or may be amended;

(c) without prejudice to the freedom granted in certain Member States to certain private training establishments, vocational guidance, vocational training, advanced vocational training and retraining shall be accessible on the basis of the same criteria and at the same levels without any discrimination on grounds of sex.

Article 5

1. Application of the principle of equal treatment with regard to working conditions, including the conditions governing dismissal, means that men and women shall be guaranteed the same conditions without discrimination on grounds of sex.

2. To this end, Member States shall take the measures necessary to ensure that:

(a) any laws, regulations and administrative provisions contrary to the principle of equal treatment shall be abolished;

(b) any provisions contrary to the principle of equal treatment which are included in collective agreements, individual contracts of employment, internal rules of undertakings or in rules governing the independent occupations and professions shall be, or may be declared, null and void or may be amended;

(c) those laws, regulations and administrative provisions contrary to the principle of equal treatment when the concern for protection which originally inspired them is no longer well founded shall be revised; and that where similar provisions are included in collective agreements labour and management shall be requested to undertake the desired revision.

Article 6

Member States shall introduce into their national legal systems such measures as are necessary to enable all persons who consider themselves wronged by failure to apply to them the principle of equal treatment within the meaning of Articles 3, 4 and 5 to pursue their claims by judicial process after possible recourse to other competent authorities.

Article 7

Member States shall take the necessary measures to protect employees against dismissal by the employer as a reaction to a complaint within the undertaking or to any legal proceedings aimed at enforcing compliance with the principle of equal treatment.

Article 8

Member States shall take care that the provisions adopted pursuant to this Directive, together with the relevant provisions already in force, are brought to the attention of employees by all appropriate means, for example at their place of employment.

Article 9

1. Member States shall put into force the laws, regulations and administrative provisions necessary in order to comply with this Directive within 30 months of its notification and shall immediately inform the Commission thereof.

However, as regards the first part of Article 3(2)(c) and the first part of Article 5(2)(c), Member States shall carry out a first examination and if necessary a first revision of the laws, regulations and administrative provisions referred to therein within four years of notification of this Directive.

2. Member States shall periodically assess the occupational activities referred to in Article 2(2) in order to decide, in the light of social developments, whether there is justification for maintaining the exclusions concerned. They shall notify the Commission of the results of this assessment.

3. Member States shall also communicate to the Commission the texts of laws, regulations and administrative provisions which they adopt in the field covered by this Directive.

Article 10

Within two years following expiry of the 30-month period laid down in the first subparagraph of Article 9(1), Member States shall forward all necessary information to the Commission to enable it to draw up a report on the application of this Directive for submission to the Council.

Article 11

This Directive is addressed to the Member States.

9. COUNCIL DIRECTIVE 79/7/EEC

of 19 December 1978
on the progressive implementation of the principle of equal treatment for men and women in matters of social security

O.J. L 6/24 (Jan. 10, 1979)

THE COUNCIL OF THE EUROPEAN COMMUNITIES,

Having regard to the Treaty establishing the European Economic Community, and in particular Article 235 thereof,

Having regard to the proposal from the Commission,

Having regard to the opinion of the European Parliament,

Having regard to the opinion of the Economic and Social Committee,

Whereas Article 1(2) of Council Directive 76/207/EEC of 9 February 1976 on the implementation of the principle of equal treatment for men and women as regards access to employment, vocational training and promotion, and working conditions provides that, with a view to ensuring the progressive implementation of the principle of equal treatment in matters of social security, the Council, acting on a proposal from the Commission, will adopt provisions defining its substance, its scope and the arrangements for its application; whereas the Treaty does not confer the specific powers required for this purpose;

Whereas the principle of equal treatment in matters of social security should be implemented in the first place in the statutory schemes which provide protection against the risks of sickness, invalidity, old age, accidents at work, occupational diseases and unemployment, and in social assistance in so far as it is intended to supplement or replace the abovementioned schemes;

Whereas the implementation of the principle of equal treatment in matters of social security does not prejudice the provisions relating to the protection of women on the ground of maternity; whereas, in this respect, Member States may adopt specific provisions for women to remove existing instances of unequal treatment,

HAS ADOPTED THIS DIRECTIVE:

Article 1

The purpose of this Directive is the progressive implementation, in the field of social security and other elements of social protection provided for in Article 3, of the principle of equal treatment for men and women in matters of social security, hereinafter referred to as 'the principle of equal treatment'.

Article 2

This Directive shall apply to the working population—including self-employed persons, workers and self-employed persons whose activity is interrupted by illness, accident or involuntary unemployment and persons seeking employment—and to retired or invalided workers and self-employed persons.

Article 3

1. This Directive shall apply to:

(a) statutory schemes which provide protection against the following risks:

— sickness,

— invalidity,

— old age,

— accidents at work and occupational diseases,

— unemployment;

(b) social assistance, in so far as it is intended to supplement or replace the schemes referred to in (a).

2. This Directive shall not apply to the provisions concerning survivors' benefits nor to those concerning family benefits, except in the case of family benefits granted by way of increases of benefits due in respect of the risks referred to in paragraph 1(a).

3. With a view to ensuring implementation of the principle of equal treatment in occupational schemes, the Council, acting on a proposal from the Commission, will adopt provisions defining its substance, its scope and the arrangements for its application.

Article 4

1. The principle of equal treatment means that there shall be no discrimination whatsoever on ground of sex either directly, or indirectly by reference in particular to marital or family status, in particular as concerns:

— the scope of the schemes and the conditions of access thereto,

— the obligation to contribute and the calculation of contributions,

— the calculation of benefits including increases due in respect of a spouse and for dependents and the conditions governing the duration and retention of entitlement to benefits.

2. The principle of equal treatment shall be without prejudice to the provisions relating to the protection of women on the grounds of maternity.

Article 5

Member States shall take the measures necessary to ensure that any laws, regulations and administrative provisions contrary to the principle of equal treatment are abolished.

Article 6

Member States shall introduce into their national legal systems such measures as are necessary to enable all persons who consider themselves wronged by failure to apply the principle of equal treatment to pursue their claims by judicial process, possibly after recourse to other competent authorities.

Article 7

1. This Directive shall be without prejudice to the right of Member States to exclude from its scope:

(a) the determination of pensionable age for the purposes of granting old-age and retirement pensions and the possible consequences thereof for other benefits;

(b) advantages in respect of old-age pension schemes granted to persons who have brought up children; the acquisition of benefit entitlements following periods of interruption of employment due to the bringing up of children;

(c) the granting of old-age or invalidity benefit entitlements by virtue of the derived entitlements of a wife;

(d) the granting of increases of long-term invalidity, old-age, accidents at work and occupational disease benefits for a dependent wife;

(e) the consequences of the exercise, before the adoption of this Directive, of a right of option not to acquire rights or incur obligations under a statutory scheme.

2. Member States shall periodically examine matters excluded under paragraph 1 in order to ascertain, in the light of social developments in the matter concerned, whether there is justification for maintaining the exclusions concerned.

Article 8

1. Member States shall bring into force the laws, regulations and administrative provisions necessary to comply with this Directive within six years of its notification. They shall immediately inform the Commission thereof.

2. Member States shall communicate to the Commission the text of laws, regulations and administrative provisions which they adopt in the field covered by this Directive, including measures adopted pursuant to Article 7(2).

They shall inform the Commission of their reasons for maintaining any existing provisions on the matters referred to in Article 7(1) and of the possibilities for reviewing them at a later date.

Article 9

Within seven years of notification of this Directive, Member States shall forward all information necessary to the Commission to enable it to draw up a report on the application of this Directive for submission to the Council and to propose such further measures as may be required for the implementation of the principle of equal treatment.

Article 10

This Directive is addressed to the Member States.

10. COUNCIL DIRECTIVE 86/378/EEC

of 24 July 1986
on the implementation of the principle of equal treatment for men and women in occupational social security schemes

O.J. L 225/40 (Aug. 12, 1986)

THE COUNCIL OF THE EUROPEAN COMMUNITIES,

Having regard to the Treaty establishing the European Economic Community, and in particular Articles 100 and 235 thereof,

Having regard to the proposal from the Commission,

Having regard to the opinion of the European Parliament,

Having regard to the opinion of the Economic and Social Committee,

Whereas the Treaty provides that each Member State shall ensure the application of the principle that men and women should receive equal pay for equal work; whereas 'pay' should be taken to mean the ordinary basic or minimum wage or salary and any other consideration, whether in cash or in kind, which the worker receives, directly or indirectly, from his employer in respect of his employment;

Whereas, although the principle of equal pay does indeed apply directly in cases where discrimination can be determined solely on the basis of the criteria of equal treatment and equal pay, there are also situations in which implementation of this principle implies the adoption of additional measures which more clearly define its scope;

* * *

Whereas the principle of equal treatment should be implemented in occupational social security schemes which provide protection against the risks specified in Article 3(1) of Directive 79/7/EEC as well as those which provide employees with any other consideration in cash or in kind within the meaning of the Treaty;

Whereas implementation of the principle of equal treatment does not prejudice the provisions relating to the protection of women by reason of maternity,

HAS ADOPTED THIS DIRECTIVE:

Article 1

The object of this Directive is to implement, in occupational social security schemes, the principle of equal treatment for men and women, hereinafter referred to as 'the principle of equal treatment'.

Article 2

1. 'Occupational social security schemes' means schemes not governed by Directive 79/7/EEC whose purpose is to provide workers, whether employees or self-employed, in an undertaking or group of undertakings, area of economic activity or occupational sector or group of such

sectors with benefits intended to supplement the benefits provided by statutory social security schemes or to replace them, whether membership of such schemes is compulsory or optional.

2. This Directive does not apply to:

(a) individual contracts,

(b) schemes having only one member,

(c) in the case of salaried workers, insurance schemes offered to participants individually to guarantee them:

— either additional benefits, or

— a choice of date on which the normal benefits will start, or a choice between several benefits.

Article 3

This Directive shall apply to members of the working population including self-employed persons, persons whose activity is interrupted by illness, maternity, accident or involuntary unemployment and persons seeking employment, and to retired and disabled workers.

Article 4

This Directive shall apply to:

(a) occupational schemes which provide protection against the following risks:

— sickness,

— invalidity,

— old age, including early retirement,

— industrial accidents and occupational diseases,

— unemployment;

(b) occupational schemes which provide for other social benefits, in cash or in kind, and in particular survivors' benefits and family allowances, if such benefits are accorded to employed persons and thus constitute a consideration paid by the employer to the worker by reason of the latter's employment.

Article 5

1. Under the conditions laid down in the following provisions, the principle of equal treatment implies that there shall be no discrimination on the basis of sex, either directly or indirectly, by reference in particular to marital or family status, especially as regards:

— the scope of the schemes and the conditions of access to them;

— the obligation to contribute and the calculation of contributions;

— the calculation of benefits, including supplementary benefits due in respect of a spouse or dependents, and the conditions governing the duration and retention of entitlement to benefits.

2. The principle of equal treatment shall not prejudice the provisions relating to the protection of women by reason of maternity.

Article 6

1. Provisions contrary to the principle of equal treatment shall include those based on sex, either directly or indirectly, in particular by reference to marital or family for:

(a) determining the persons who may participate in an occupational scheme;

(b) fixing the compulsory or optional nature of participation in an occupational scheme;

(c) laying down different rules as regards the age of entry into the scheme or the minimum period of employment or membership of the scheme required to obtain the benefits thereof;

(d) laying down different rules, except as provided for in subparagraphs (h) and (i), for the reimbursement of contributions where a worker leaves a scheme without having fulfilled the conditions guaranteeing him a deferred right to long-term benefits;

(e) setting different conditions for the granting of benefits or restricting such benefits to workers of one or other of the sexes;

(f) fixing different retirement ages;

(g) suspending the retention or acquisition of rights during periods of maternity leave or leave for family reasons which are granted by law or agreement and are paid by the employer;

(h) setting different levels of benefit, except insofar as may be necessary to take account of actuarial calculation factors which differ according to sex in the case of benefits designated as contribution-defined;

(i) setting different levels of worker contribution;

setting different levels of employer contribution in the case of benefits designated as contribution-defined, except with a view to making the amount of those benefits more nearly equal;

(j) laying down different standards or standards applicable only to workers of a specified sex, except as provided for in subparagraphs (h) and (i), as regards the guarantee or retention of entitlement to deferred benefits when a worker leaves a scheme.

2. Where the granting of benefits within the scope of this Directive is left to the discretion of the scheme's management bodies, the latter must take account of the principle of equal treatment.

Article 7

Member States shall take all necessary steps to ensure that:

(a) provisions contrary to the principle of equal treatment in legally compulsory collective agreements, staff rules of undertakings or any other arrangements relating to occupational schemes are null and void, or may be declared null and void or amended;

(b) schemes containing such provisions may not be approved or extended by administrative measures.

Article 8

1. Member States shall take all necessary steps to ensure that the provisions of occupational schemes contrary to the principle of equal treatment are revised by 1 January 1993.

2. This Directive shall not preclude rights and obligations relating to a period of membership of an occupational scheme prior to revision of that scheme from remaining subject to the provisions of the scheme in force during that period.

Article 9

Member States may defer compulsory application of the principle of equal treatment with regard to:

(a) determination of pensionable age for the purposes of granting old-age or retirement pensions, and the possible implications for other benefits:

— either until the date on which such equality is achieved in statutory schemes,

— or, at the latest, until such equality is required by a directive.

(b) survivors' pensions until a directive requires the principle of equal treatment in statutory social security schemes in that regard;

(c) the application of the first subparagraph of Article 6(1)(i) to take account of the different actuarial calculation factors, at the latest until the expiry of a thirteen-year period as from the notification of this Directive.

Article 10

Member States shall introduce into their national legal systems such measures as are necessary to enable all persons who consider themselves injured by failure to apply the principle of equal treatment to pursue their claims before the courts, possibly after bringing the matters before other competent authorities.

Article 11

Member States shall take all the necessary steps to protect worker against dismissal where this constitutes a response on the part of the employer to a complaint made at undertaking level or to the institution of legal proceedings aimed at enforcing compliance with the principle of equal treatment.

Article 12

1. Member States shall bring into force such laws, regulations and administrative provisions as are necessary in order to comply with this Directive at the latest three years after [July 30, 1986]. They shall immediately inform the Commission thereof.

2. Member States shall communicate to the Commission at the latest five years after notification of this Directive all information necessary to enable the Commission to draw up a report on the application of this Directive for submission to the Council.

Article 13

This Directive is addressed to the Member States.

†